HOLLYWOOD REMEMBERED

HOLLYWOOD REMEMBERED

An Oral History of Its Golden Age

PAUL ZOLLO

Cooper Square Press

First Cooper Square Press edition 2002

This Cooper Square Press cloth edition of *Hollywood Remembered* is an original
publication. It is published by arrangement with the author.

Published by Cooper Square Press
A Member of the Rowman & Littlefield Publishing Group
200 Park Avenue South, Suite 1109
New York, New York 10003-1503
www.coopersquarepress.com

Distributed by National Book Network

Composition and design: Barbara Werden Design

Library of Congress Cataloging-in-Publication Data

Zollo, Paul, 1958–
    Hollywood remembered : an oral history of its golden age / Paul Zollo.—1st
Cooper Square ed.
        p.   cm.
    Includes bibliographical references and index.
    ISBN 0-8154-1239-8 (alk. paper)
    1. Motion picture industry—California—Los Angeles—History. 2. Motion
    pictures—California—Los Angeles—Biography. I. Title.

PN1993.5.U65 Z65 2002
384'.8'0979494—dc21

                                                            2002005847

Manufactured in the United States of America.

Dedicated to Leslie
and Joshua,
who make Hollywood
the happiest place in the world
every day.

Hollywood is wonderful.
Anyone who doesn't like it is either crazy or sober.

RAYMOND CHANDLER, 1941

CONTENTS

Preface   xi

Acknowledgments   xvii

PART ONE
A HISTORY OF HOLLYWOOD   1

PART TWO
THE MEMOIRS   53

Frederica Sagor Maas   55

Lothrop Worth   64

David Raksin   69

Karl Malden   74

Lloyd Rigler   85

Jules Fox   95

Robert Cornthwaite   102

Zelda Aronson   108

A.C. Lyles   112

Tom Jones   118

Hank Sievers   122

Evelyn Keyes   127

Walter Bernstein   139

Hal Riddle   144

Johnny Grant   150

Don Farquhar   155

Jerry Maren   160

Else Blangstead   169

Lois Sidney   175

Steve Allen   180

Tommy Farrell   185

Totty Ames   191

Bob Board   198

Marie Windsor   211

Leatrice Joy Gilbert Fountain   215

Ken Paradise   226

Jonathan Winters   228

Charles Champlin   245

Bill Welsh   251

Lee Bolman   253

Aaron Epstein   258

Geraldine Holt   264

Roberta Murray   272

Pippa Scott   279

Burl Smith   286

Manny Felix   290

Bill Heyward   293

PART THREE
A TOUR OF HOLLYWOOD   303

Bibliography   362

Index   363

PREFACE

Hollywood's like Egypt. Full of crumbling
pyramids. It'll never come back. It'll just keep
crumbling until finally the wind blows the last
studio prop across the sands.
  —DAVID SELZNICK, 1949

Hollywood really is an imaginary city that exists in
the mind of anyone who has, in his mind, lived
there. My Hollywood is different from your
Hollywood.
  —OTTO FREIDRICH, from
  City of Nets, 1979

Hollywood.
  I've always felt a powerful yet melancholy connection for this famous town
under the big sign; melancholy because a
part of me still seems to recall what it was
like here long before the freeway was constructed, back when Hollywood was still
an enchanted town of grand movie studios, fantastic homes, great restaurants,
hotels, and theaters. Now a different world
has been overlaid upon the matrix of
streets and buildings that was old Hollywood. But when I look at Hollywood, I
still tend to see it as it was.
  The first time I came to Hollywood was
in 1980. Ronald Reagan, a genuine Hollywood movie star, had recently been elected
president of the United States, sparking the
surreal season of my arrival. I remember
standing on Hollywood Boulevard on a
typically sun-drenched, dusty Angeleno
afternoon, looking north up the steep
avenues of Cherokee and Whitley toward
the old neighborhood at the top of the
hill, and concluding that it was up there that
the stars must live. And I wasn't right, but I
wasn't entirely wrong. As I later learned, at
the top of that hill is Whitley Heights, a

melange of mansions where the stars did
live, many lifetimes ago, in the dawning
decades of the twentieth century. Though
I'd yet to learn anything about Hollywood
or its history, I already felt that melancholy
longing I've felt ever since, for the days
when Whitley Heights was still Whitley
Heights, and when Hollywood was still
Hollywood.
  Hollywood.
  My first home here was a little guest
house on Franklin Avenue directly below
Whitley Heights, a house like so many
others that was subsequently decimated
and replaced by a soulless looking stucco
apartment building. But a small patch of
wilderness once flourished behind my
little home, a haven for cats, squirrels, and,
sometimes very late at night, an old
coyote. I used to hike straight through this
little woodland to Whitley Avenue and up
that steepest of Hollywood inclines into
the old circular neighborhood of Whitley
Heights to take in the neighborhood. Rare
was the day when I'd encounter other
humans up there; although these houses
were occupied, Whitley Heights always
had a haunted quality, as if peopled much
more by ghosts of its past than by any current occupants, who were evidently away
at work or perhaps on extended vacations.
  At the summit of the Heights I discovered an abandoned lot in which were
strewn the stone ruins of a once grand
estate; a long, winding driveway
remained, as did a regal circle of twenty
royal palms, which miraculously avoided
the decimation that laid the mansion to
waste. It was a mystery to me—admittedly
an appealingly Hollywood noir type of
mystery—why a palatial estate would be

erected here on this highest hill only to be demolished and left in ruins, its majestic grounds left undeveloped and overgrown.

It was but one of the many mysteries Hollywood would render, and these ruins were the ideal if obvious cinematic symbol of it all: the forsaken Hollywood mansion, once elegant and majestic, abandoned and neglected for decades like the once great city that sprawls south from these foothills.

I used to spend a lot of time at this summit of ruins, looking out, looking down on Hollywood, and contemplating its many mysteries. Why, I wondered, would something so beautiful and grand be built, only to be abandoned and left to decay?

After all, this was *Hollywood*. This was a town that the whole world talked about. They *thought* about Hollywood. Their dreams were painted here. The silents and the talkies, the epics and odysseys, the human and heroic, the mortal and divine. All of the mythical histories, mysteries, romances, and musicals, the electric illusions of motion and emotion, the indelible iconic images of Charlie Chaplin, Marilyn Monroe, Humphrey Bogart, Groucho Marx, James Dean, Clark Gable, wrapped up in radiant Technicolor brilliance and black-and-white streams of shadow and substance; all of it emanated from the studios and soundstages that sprung up throughout the flatlands of this little town.

Hollywood.

I remember walking west on Hollywood Boulevard one morning in 1984. I was with my dear friend Miriam Corrier, who must have been eighty then although she neither looked or admitted it, and who often regaled me with stories both romantic and fantastic of old Hollywood as she remembered it. Like many others I've spoken to since, she spoke of Hollywood as if it were another world. As we walked past homeless men huddled in doorways, and past a sad succession of tawdry souvenir stores, I asked her the question that had been on my mind since the day I arrived. *What happened to Hollywood?*

Her answer was immediate and concise. "The sixties," she said. But like most answers about Hollywood, as I would come to discover, it was the truth, but not the whole truth. And attaining anything even approximating the whole truth about Hollywood, as I would come to find, was going to take some time.

Like F. Scott Fitzgerald, who once said he came to Hollywood with the resignation of a ghost assigned to a haunted house, I became resigned to haunt Hollywood myself, in hope of unraveling some of its mysteries. Over the next years I embarked on an ongoing quest to peel back the layers of old Hollywood in order to reveal its mysteries, and to gain some insight into how it felt to live a real life in this surreal city. What was *real* Hollywood all about? *Was* there ever a real Hollywood? And if so, what happened to it?

With the optimistic intent of exploring and maybe even answering this question, I posted small, signal-orange flyers on community bulletin boards, lampposts, telephone poles, and elsewhere around Hollywood. Each posed a question I felt couldn't have been more direct (although I was later informed by many that they took it metaphorically): "DO YOU REMEMBER HOLLYWOOD?" It was followed by the predictable clincher, "And, if so, are you willing to talk about it?" Also included was my name, telephone number, and stated mission in life: "Author, working on a book of Hollywood history."

Responses I received were vast and diverse; I met with everyone who called, some who still lived in Hollywood, some who didn't, but each of whom harbored individual theories about its glory and decline. Many expressed a deep and lasting love for Hollywood; others regarded it as little more than an old frame for a painting that faded decades ago. Many of them led me to others, forming this chain of shared remembrances you now hold. I spoke to people who worked inside and outside of the studios, people who became stars, people who hoped to become stars, people who worked for stars, people who lived in awe of stars, and people singularly unimpressed by stardom. I spoke to actors, extras, producers, editors, writers, composers, carpenters and publicists, as well as broadcasters, comedians, secretaries, songwriters, bartenders, journalists, shopclerks, models, and more. As I searched for some overall, absolute truth about Hollywood, I found instead a kind of collective truth, and one that probably comes closer to reflecting the fullness of what Hollywood once really was. As each of these witnesses affirmed, Hollywood holds as many facets of the truth as there are edges to a diamond. I like to think of this collection of history and remembrances, *Hollywood Remembered*, as that diamond.

The abandoned lot at the top of Whitley Heights, I was to discover, was the site of Topside, the mansion of one of the greatest silent movie stars, Francis X. Bushman. Bushman, who was an extremely handsome matinee idol in his day, was known to be driven down Hollywood Boulevard in his limo illuminated by a hidden light, designed to give him a rosy incandescence. His house, which legend says was used in the late thirties as a "celebrity bordello," was knocked down in 1957 to clear the way for condos. The neighbors organized in protest again the development, and succeeded in saving the land but were too late to save the house. The lot remained in ruins for decades until the late 1990s, at which time developers overcame their opposition, acquiring the lamentable authorization to build a complex of six houses on this single plot of land. The twenty royal palms still stand high on this hill above Hollywood, but Topside itself, the memories of Topside, and memories of the ruins of Topside, all belong to the ages now. This book is an attempt to savor those memories, and to celebrate the unique history that belongs only to this little hamlet

within Los Angeles known as Hollywood. *Hollywood.*

It might all have become Figwood had Harvey Henderson Wilcox gotten his way. Needing a name for the new ranch he purchased in 1881 several miles northwest of his Los Angeles home, it seemed only fitting for him to honor the predominant fruit of his new orchards: figs.

Yet Harvey's wife Daieda had something else in mind. It was a name she heard spoken by a stranger on a train. It's a motif that reoccurs many times in Hollywood history—the stranger on a train. This one was an affluent woman from Illinois who spoke with so much love and passion about her country home near Chicago that Daeida was entranced. And the name of that woman's home stuck with her from the instant she heard it: *Hollywood.*

It had a certain ring to it, a measure of bygone grace she suspected might be welcome in the new century around the corner. She prevailed upon her husband to agree, which he evidently did, and despite the general absence of any actual *holly* in the area, he personally painted the name "Hollywood" in bold white on a wooden sign, which he nailed to the front gate.

A humble and pious man of honor, Harvey Wilcox sought to justify the use of this fanciful name by importing two expensive English holly bushes, which he planted prominently on the grounds of his new property. Within weeks, both bushes withered and died. Holly, as Harvey discovered, to his dismay, simply doesn't thrive in the dry, temperate climate of Hollywood. Yet it was a historic endeavor nonetheless, the first-ever attempt to match the *ideal*—the original abstraction of Hollywood, the inaugural illusion—with something authentic. And it failed.

Still the name survived, and flourished in ways that the Wilcoxes never could have imagined. What the Wilcoxes had in mind was something else altogether, the establishment of Hollywood as a peaceful and sacred oasis where devout Methodists like themselves could practice abstinence and other virtues. It wasn't to be.

What was to be was something entirely different. Hollywood, as we know, soon became the luminous national nucleus of a newfangled technology which arose from what was a modest storefront novelty, and evolved into such a beloved and integral component of modern life that moviemakers by the hundreds arrived, lured by the promise of perpetual sunshine, orange-blossom sweetness, and warm weather. And they built their dream factories right in the heart of Harvey and Daeida's former fields of figs, placing Hollywood forever on the map of the world and the human psyche.

To this day the distance between Hollywood as it exists and Hollywood as it's imagined remains a considerable one. People arrive daily in search of the ideal only to be confronted and confused by the actuality. Hollywood persists in existing as both an actual place and as a metaphor for the entertainment industry that extends far beyond its physical borders. It's no small wonder why present-day Hollywood should seem perplexing to those searching for any trace of its fabled shimmer, and why the physical past of this singularly surreal city is obscured by a confusing mix of myth and misinformation.

But none of this is new. As I discovered, this disparity between an abstract and authentic Hollywood has been prevalent since as early as the 1920s, when C. Clayton Hutton, an Englishman reporting for the *New York Times*, came to Hollywood expecting to find a modern Sodom and Gomorrah. What he found surprised him. "Forget Hollywood as a bacchanalian forest where ill-concealed orgies of its people find credence among all peoples," Hutton wrote, "and begin all over again with your mental picture of this famous place if you really prefer to be grounded on the subject."

It's a fair request. Hollywood, as it is remembered, is a different place for

everyone. It's a place where the past and the present coincide with the real and imagined, where memory and metaphor beckon abstractions and ideals, where dreams and aspirations merge with faith and resignation. It's a living, changing continent, both physical and imagined. *Hollywood Remembered* is in many ways as much about the nature of memory—how we remember our lives—as it is about Hollywood itself. People file and organize their remembrances in diverse ways, linking them to locations, to people, to events, and to aspirations. One of the few constants here in these memories is food; there are evidently few aspects of the speakable memory more prominent than the remembrance of great meals past. The other most common links in these memoirs is a sad sense of regret over the plight of present-day Hollywood, and a kind of astonishment—sometimes bemused, sometimes regretful—over the lightning-swift speed at which the decades have flown by.

Yet by no means is this a collection of weepy, mournful elegies for something lost forever. More than anything these memoirs affirm that the spirit of early Hollywood is deeply ingrained in this place, and that the cliché of a "Lost Hollywood,"—a city in ruins with no remaining links to its glory days—really isn't true. It's been a revelation for me to have discovered over the years that the list of historic structures that still stand in Hollywood is actually a much longer one than the sad lexicon of landmarks missing. Far from being lost, the bold, expansive spirit of historic Hollywood can still be found within its scores of legendary structures, its old studios, hotels, restaurants, and theaters. And it's there in the fantastic stylistic farrago of Moorish, Spanish, Colonial, Italian, and Victorian houses that still stand in the hills, and in the impossibly steep and winding tapestry of hillside streets that would never be allowed under modern construction codes, but which still breathe with the brash,

XIV

unbound essence of early Hollywood.

None of which should imply that Hollywood is or has ever been static. Since its inception as a city, it's always been in a constant state of flux, perpetually building new buildings on the bones of old ones, and then knocking those down to build newer ones. As of this writing, the autumn of 2001, physical Hollywood is poised on the precipice of an immense, inexorable transition. Gargantuan new building projects are being developed throughout its old streets and thoroughfares. Despite David Selznick's prediction that Hollywood will never come back, forces have been vying to bring it back for years.

Presently the "Hollywood-Highland" project, an immense development constructed on the site of the bank building that was constructed on the site of the Hollywood Hotel, is the most conspicuous of these efforts. Spanning a full city block and adjoining Grauman's Chinese Theater, it houses the Kodak Theater, the new home of the Academy Awards, as well as a bevy of nightclubs, restaurants, movie theaters, cafes, and a new hotel. And it is only one of the many new developments rising around Hollywood; the intersections of Hollywood & Vine, Yucca & Vine, Sunset & Vine, Sunset & Ivar, and many more are all undergoing massive reconstruction.

How positive the effect of this new building boom will be remains to be seen. Hollywood's entire history has been marked by alternating interludes of prosperity and disheartenment. Back in 1937, when Edwin Palmer was writing the conclusion to his *History of Hollywood*, he looked toward its immediate future and saw the advent of a new technology on the horizon. "All this new construction is planned with television in view," he wrote with marked uncertainty. Hollywood then, as it is today, was undergoing vast physical and technological changes, of which the outcome was equally unpredictable. Palmer's ultimate conclusion, however, was one of optimism. "Whatever the future status of this disorganized terrestrial heap," he wrote, "Hollywood is destined to be at the top of it."

Although more than sixty years have passed since those words were written, I still tend to share Dr. Palmer's optimism. And however Hollywood's future status is shaped, I'm hopeful that its past will at last be preserved with a focus equal to its immense historic significance. By virtue of the valiant efforts of neighborhood preservationists, such as those who founded the Hollywood Heritage organization, existent links to historic Hollywood have been renovated and revitalized, while developers determined to build Hollywood's future by destroying its past have been defied. This book is written in the honor of all of those who have worked throughout the years to honor and preserve Hollywood's history.

It's also written in the honor of the thirty-six rememberers whose memoirs are preserved here. These witnesses to Hollywood's past graciously allowed me entrance into their remembered Hollywoods, and joined me in journey to an empire that eventually outgrew and abandoned its hometown. Yet the unique past of that beloved hometown, that little city under the big sign, remains resoundingly fluid and dynamic, and is kept forever alive in the hearts and minds of those who care to remember. This book is for them. And it's for you.

XV

PAUL ZOLLO
Hollywood, California
December 2001

ACKNOWLEDGMENTS

This book was many years in the making, and I am deeply grateful to all of those who have helped and encouraged me during these years, with special thanks extended: To all the rememberers whose memoirs are preserved herein, thank you for sharing your personal Hollywood histories, and for introducing me to others who also remember; to Else Blangstead, for sharing your shimmer and the details of your astounding life with me, and for generously introducing me to a legion of other great rememberers for this book, who all love you with good reason; to Van Dyke Parks, for introducing me to Else Blangstead; to Sean Heaney, for your great breadth of knowledge about the movies, and for your excitement about this project over a pizza at Davio's in Boston; to Judy Moll Mafia Close, for easing me through the L.A. Library system, and for combing through countless historic books on behalf of this project; to my father, Burt Zollo, for your enthusiasm and support, and for being the first person to ever walk through Whitley Heights with me to sing the praises of Beulah Bondi, Marie Dressler, and others who once lived there; to my mother, Lois Zollo, for going to great lengths to determine the proper English spelling of such Yiddish words as *Geshray* that were spoken in these memoirs; to Lorin Hart for introducing me to your mother, Leatrice Fountain; to Mandi Martin for introducing me to your father-in-law Jules Fox; to Hal Riddle, for your kindness in introducing me to many of your friends at the Motion Pictures Country Home; to Jay Winters, for arranging my interview with your father, the great Jonathan Winters; to Eddie Muller, for your great books about Film Noir, and for introducing me to Evelyn Keyes; to Janet Heaney, whose love of Hollywood and the movies is what first drew me to this town; to Jean Stawarz, for being such a great writer and friend; to *The Hollywood Independent*; to all members and supporters of Hollywood Heritage, for your valiant persistence in fighting for the preservation of Hollywood's unique heritage; to Marc Wanamaker, for providing much valuable information about Hollywood history; to Patt Morrison, for your rare inclination to report on the present by remembering the past; to Leslie, as always, for all the things you are, including a fine editor; to Michael Dorr, Ginger Strader, and everyone at Cooper Square Press for your ongoing support of this book and ongoing patience; to Barbara Werden for your great design of this book; to Peter Sherman for your wonderful photography; and to Peter Zollo, Peggy Miller, Mark Salerno, Neil Jano, Carl Kraines, Andrew and Anne Kurtzman, Howard Diller, Nancy Robbins, Sharon Pearsall, Jeff Gold, Holly Goldsmith, Tomas Ulrich, Mark Dubrow, Daniel Woodington, Jill Freeman, Sandy Ross, Stuart Walzer, Kerry Slattery and Skylight Books, Hollywood Farmer's Market, Book City, Lucy's El Adobe, Book Soup, Victor's Deli, Joseph's Café, Christie Daniels, David Mack, Amelia Monsour, Dan Kirkpatrick, James Coberly Smith, Jane Atwater, Gussie DeSouza, Joe Frisco, and Purlie Olloz; and to everyone who loves Hollywood as much as I do.

PART ONE
A HISTORY OF HOLLYWOOD

W HAT FOLLOWS is a condensed chronology of physical Hollywood, an overview of the unprecedented evolution of this singular American town, intended to function as a foundation for the collective remembrances that comprise the body of this book. This chapter is exposition, intended to set the stage for what's to come.

It spans from the dawn of man and progresses through various periods of light and darkness, through the momentous events and actions of remarkable people that shaped the physical landscape of Hollywood and sparked its evolution; through times of turmoil and times of triumph. Beginning with an epoch of seemingly infinite, unspoiled tranquility, it advances through the successive incursions of Spanish missionaries, religious zealots, farmers, businessmen, filmmakers, and others, all of which resulted in its phenomenally swift expansion and subsequent decline. It concludes in modern times following twin periods of darkness, the initiation of the Hollywood Blacklist, and the construction of the Hollywood Freeway, both of which cast dark and enduring shadows over the spiritual and physical landscape of Hollywood.

This history was compiled from a variety of sources, each of which have varying degrees of accuracy. I'm indebted to the historian Paul Soifer, who shared his personal knowledge and also located many extremely rare, historic documents from the files of the Department of Water & Power concerning William Mulholland and his controversial construction of the Mulholland Dam above Hollywood. I'm

also indebted to the archives of the *New York Times* and the *Los Angeles Times*, as well as to a trio of Hollywood historians: Laurence Hill, who wrote *La Reina*, a 1929 history of L.A., Bruce Torrence, the author of *Hollywood: The First 100 Years*, and Dr. Edwin Obadiah Palmer, who wrote the unrivaled *History of Hollywood* in 1937.

The words and research of all of these men are woven through this narrative, but Palmer is the primary source, since in addition to being a fine writer and historian, he had firsthand, intimate knowledge of Hollywood's earliest days. He moved to Hollywood from New York in 1900 and was one of the first doctors ever to practice in Hollywood, and also a civic leader who both supported and opposed various developments that shaped physical Hollywood, such as the construction of a public library, club, and bank, which he supported, and the construction of the Mulholland Dam, which he opposed.

Palmer knew Mrs. Wilcox, who founded Hollywood, as well as Hollywood's first cast of characters, which included Paul DeLongpre, H.J. Whitley, Philo Beveridge, Christine Weatherill Stevenson, C.M. Pierce, and others. He is a rare historian in that he includes himself in his history, even offering this profile of himself in the third person: "Dr. Palmer was a thin, pale young man whose principal assets were a Columbia College degree in medicine, a New York certificate to practice, an intern's certificate from Lebanon Hospital of New York, a square, dark beard, and about $500 in cash; his principal liability an occasional pulmonary hemorrhage." My gratitude goes to the kind doctor for his thoughtful, comprehensive work, and for his evident love of Hollywood and its unique history, which I share.

Early Origins

For many millennia, this vicinity of the world designated today as Hollywood, California, has been a temperate and pacific portion of the Southwest, ruled by the elemental, intrinsic laws of nature. Prehistoric geologic evolution transpired in such a way as to ensure this region a sunny, pleasant climate that has endured throughout the span of human existence on this earth.

"Hollywood is no exception to the rule that great cities have developed on sites blessed with great natural advantages," wrote Dr. Palmer. "The 34th parallel on which she stands passes through some of the most repellent desert in America and Asia but wherever it meets the sea we find the most charming and comfortable climate."

Such is the source of the steadfastly comfortable climes of this California basin, shielded as it is by the presence of great winding ribbons of foothills and mountain ranges. Hollywood's location in the Cahuenga Valley makes it the lucky beneficiary of some of the planet's most agreeable geographical combinations; its mountain ranges are ideally situated to provide access to cool ocean breezes while concurrently shielding the city from the brutal, oppressive desert heat, which transforms the San Fernando Valley each summer into a scorched and dusty desert.

Yet the Cahuenga Valley is not entirely cut off from the San Fernando Valley. While the continents were still in the fluid midst of their prehistoric formation, the earth folded back upon herself in such a way as to form a providential passageway through the hills, a portal that connects the twin valleys to this day. "As this 1,100-foot-high windbreak was reared at a point where the rock was less resistant," Palmer wrote, "a canyon from the north met a

canyon from the south." The result was the Cahuenga Pass, named El Portozuelo by the Spaniards, nature's monumental ancient gateway into Hollywood.

The Native People

Historians and archeologists alike estimate that it was in approximately 7,200 B.C. that the Chumash people first ventured south to California, establishing small coastal villages along the Pacific shore from northern to southern California. Taking advantage of the ample amount of natural tar that bubbled up then as it still does today in various pits throughout the region, they built boats of wooden planks sealed with this tar, and sailed regularly to Catalina and the Channel Islands.

Untouched by war, disease, or urban blight, these natives lived for successive eons in harmonious accord prior to the arrival of eighteenth-century Spaniards. The years between 7,200 B.C. or so until A.D. 1781 were years of tranquility, except for the occasional natural interventions of active earthquakes and aftershocks.

The Chumash were skilled hunters, stone-carvers and basket-weavers. They had about thirty villages scattered all over what would become Los Angeles County. Their capital village, known as Yang-na, was located in what is now downtown Los Angeles, near the present-day intersection of Commercial & Alameda. Present-day Hollywood was known as Co-Yang-Na, which referred to its landscape of little hills and deep canyons. At the north end of Western Boulevard at what is now the Fern Dell section of Griffith Park was the site of sacred traditional council grounds known as Moco-Yang-Na. The area of present Outpost Drive at the north tip of Sycamore Avenue was a settlement known as Ca-Oug-Na. And to the north on the other side of the hills, the vast, verdant canyon we now know as the San Fernando Valley was called Pa-Seg-Na.

The natives lived off the land, eating the acorns of white oaks and wild plums, both of which were dried and pummeled into a powdery paste used to make cakes. They considered all the beasts of the region to be fair game, with the exception of three: old coyotes, which were felt to possess spiritual wisdom; bears, which were considered to be connected to divinity; and rattlesnakes, which were shunned with respect for the manifest power of their venom.

But this still left a veritable smorgasbord of wild game in the hills and canyons: deer, badgers, rabbits, young coyotes, squirrels, rats, gophers, raccoons, wildcats, crows, blackbirds and hawks. Locusts and grasshoppers were considered delicacies, and only consumed during sacred ritual banquets.

Many tribes of Shoshone newly moved into California circa 6,000 B.C., settling in different places throughout what is today the counties of Los Angeles and San Bernardino. They became known as the Tongva people, and together with the Chumash, the Tatavium, Miwok, and Ipi-Tapai tribes, created a unified and compassionate community that coexisted for centuries.

Yet the epoch of harmony known by these native people was brought to an abrupt and awful end. The ways of the Shoshone, the Chumash and the ancient villages of Yang-Na were all vanquished in less than fifty years, destroyed by the invasion of Spanish missionaries a single century prior to the founding of Hollywood.

In this respect, Hollywood signifies all of America, in that the indigenous people of this area were considered savages, and like the entirety of natives who populated this nation, were wiped out by exile, disease and slaughter. Although they had existed for successive centuries in peace and had mastered the delicate art of living off the land without destroying it, they were branded as ignorant pagans by the

missionaries. In the 1964 edition of *The California Missions*, its editors reflect the unenlightened, arcane view of Native Americans that was indoctrinated into American children for generations: "The Indians whom the padres encountered may well have seemed the most unpromising of prospects for conversion. Short of stature, swarthy and unkempt, they were still living in the Stone Age, some 15,000 years before the Spaniards."[1]

Throughout the fifteenth and sixteenth centuries, Spain ruled the New World. After eventually depleting the wealth and natural resources of its dominion, they continued to expand their empire, and moved into Central America, the Caribbean, about half of South America, much of what is now the United States, and Mexico, where they established the capital of New Spain in Mexico City. It was an empire expanded over the centuries via a force that combined both military and religious power. When natives attempted to oppose their incursion, military might was introduced first in order to conquer the natives. Once subdued, religion was then introduced to save their souls while simultaneously seizing their lands. Mexico, for example, had to be taken by force. But it was agreed that the natives up north in Alta California were a mild, malleable people, and that their conversion would require the power only of the clergy, without the aggression of a military invasion.

And so it was toward the end of the eighteenth century Spain turned to not to an army but to two men, Governor Gaspar de Portola and Father Junipero Serra, to establish in the honor of the cross and the crown a northwest frontier in California. Serra was a teacher and missionary who was born in Mallorca, Spain in 1713 and who served as the head of the missions in Baja California (in Mexico, south of San

[1] Originally published by Sunset Books in 1964, this passage of *The California Missions* was significantly rewritten in a 1979 edition of the book, diminishing much, but not all, of its original anti-aboriginal language.

Diego). Portola was an aristocratic soldier born in Catalan, who served in the Spanish army in Italy and Portugal before appointed the governor of Baja from 1768–1770. But with little of Baja for him to govern, he was happy with his assignment to join Serra in this northern expansion of the Spanish empire. Ironically, this man responsible for the foundation of a long chain of missions up the California coast was also responsible for ousting every Jesuit in Baja from the fourteen missions that they'd established over their seventy-two-year span. Their missions were consequently occupied, first by the Franciscans and later by the Dominicans.

4

In the hot July of 1769, Serra and Portola led Spain in a significant expansion of its empire by invading Alta California, and founding the first of twenty-one missions along the West Coast, the Mission San Diego de Alcala.

Two days prior to the dedication of the new mission, Portola headed north with one servant, twenty-seven soldiers, and an arsenal of assorted weapons. They arrived in Yang-Na on the second day of August 1769, and forever displaced the spiritual dynamics of these peaceful people. Oblivious to the sacred dimensions of this land, the Spaniards erected crude camps along a waterway the natives knew to be holy, the Los Angeles River.

These missionaries were immediately alerted to the totally unexpected and frequently terrifying aspects of their new Angeleno existence on their first night in the area. Two severe earthquakes struck the L.A. region within a few minutes of each other, followed by a succession of aftershocks. Since they had never experienced anything even remotely like this, the Spaniards feared it might be the wrath of God. They hiked in terror for hours through acres of wild grapes and rosebushes, ultimately concluding that the nearby mountain ranges had to harbor several active volcanoes. It was the force of their repeated eruptions, they reasoned, that had caused the awful trembling of the earth. They renamed the river "Rio de los Temblores," or "The River of the Temblors."

Moving west along what is today Wilshire Boulevard, they came upon the La Brea Tarpits—which still exist in the Mid-Wilshire district of L.A., scant miles south of Hollywood. Viewing the dark pools of bubbling, oozing tar, they surmised that it was the aggregate residue of lava flowing down from the nearby volcanoes.

Rather than head due north, which would have led them directly into the heart of Hollywood, they ventured west through what is today Westwood and the campus of UCLA, persisting westward till they reached the ocean. From the shore they were discouraged by the mountain ranges they saw to the north, a section of the Santa Monica mountains that looms over modern-day Malibu. They reversed their direction once again and headed northeast, through the Sepulveda Canyon into the San Fernando Valley. Friar Juan Crespi, the designated diarist for the expedition, named this valley for its prominent groves of oaks, or *encinos*, calling it *Santa Catalina de Bononia de los Encinos*, which means, "St. Catherine of Bologna's Valley of the Live Oaks." Years later, after the establishment of the San Fernando mission, the Valley was renamed in its honor the San Fernando Valley.

The Spaniards continued north from the valley until they reached Point Reyes, north of San Francisco. Starving by this point and suffering from scurvy, they turned south again and headed back to San Diego. Evidently, they were not as superior to the natives as they assumed. Even arcane histories such as *The California Missions* recognize that the natives had much natural wisdom that the Spaniards did not possess. "The California Indian has often been criticized because he lived a life of slothfulness, not stirring himself to raise crops, herd flocks, or practice other disciplined forms of food production. . . . Over the centuries, the natives had evolved a sensible pact with nature. . . . Ironically, the civilized Spaniards who looked down upon the childlike Indian suffered famines after they first settled in the same environment when their imported foodstuffs failed to arrive on time."

It was on January 16, 1770, that the Spaniards passed south through the Cahuenga Pass, then a rugged trail covered in nopal cacti, and for the first time entered what today is Hollywood. They made their camp at the southern edge of the Pass, which is the present site of the Hollywood Bowl, and dubbed this region *La Nopalera*, which translates, "The land covered with cactus." They then proceeded to clear away most of the cactus, and used the remaining land for the grazing of their sheep and cattle; because of a scarcity of water, it could be used for little else. The native name for Hollywood, *Co-Yang-na*, evolved through Spanish usage into its present form, *Cahuenga*.

The Spaniards returned to San Diego by the same route that they had first forged. Toward the end of April of that same year, a new camp arrived in better health and with more provisions. On June 3, 1770, the second of the California Missions was founded by Junipero Serra. It was then that the people of Cahuenga became considered the "property of Spain." The fourth and largest of the missions was San Gabriel, founded in 1771. Its domain included the present site of Hollywood, and its name was used to extend to all natives of this region, who were forever classified as a single tribe, known as *Gabrielino*.

All of what is present-day Hollywood was divided into two by the Spaniards, who named all of the area to the west of the Cahuenga Pass, Rancho La Brea, and all of the area to the east Rancho Los Feliz.

When L.A. was established by Spain as a pueblo in 1781, the Cahuenga Pass became an official link of the established Spanish trail up the Californian coast known as El Camino Real de Rey. A rugged trail covered with nopal cacti, the Pass was used to move cattle and sheep from the Cahuenga Valley to San Fernando. In time it became a more established wagon road and eventually a paved highway. In 1947, it was transformed into one of the first segments of the Hollywood Freeway.

In 1828, a German immigrant John Grogignan bought all the land on which the sacred village of Yang-na had stood for eons. With aid from the Mexican authorities, all the remaining natives were evicted. By 1835, the many thousands of natives that had lived in the region for centuries had been reduced to 600. In time those who did not die from new diseases introduced to their homeland by the Spaniards were either expelled to the various missions dotting the California coast or slaughtered.

It needs to be noted that the aim of the Spanish missionaries was an essentially humanistic one, convinced as they were that the natives would suffer both in heaven and on earth without the requisite salvation that the Spaniards offered. Yet this imposed redemption saved few, and in reality resulted in genocide. "Critics of the mission system charge that it was a thinly disguised form of slavery, masquerading under a pious front," wrote Paul Johnson in *The California Missions*. "The culture that it forced upon the natives was alien to their traditions, and no attempts were made by the padres to retain any of the rich heritage of the past. . . . [T]he Indians trained in the mission life were ill-adapted to live under any other system and could never again return to their old ways. . . . The introduction of the system brought with it diseases that destroyed thousands of the natives because they had no immunity against white man's ailments."

But in what many have seen as karmic justice, the Spaniards would suffer at the hands of the American government much as they had caused the natives to suffer. California officially joined the Union in 1850; in the following year, the U.S. Congress passed a law that required all Spanish and Mexican land grants to be newly confirmed by American authorities. Because many of the landowners didn't understand English, they neglected to seek the official confirmation required under law, and the government took over their land, and sold it. Farmers from all over America flocked to the Cahuenga Valley to buy acres of farmland at reasonable prices, and despite inadequate sources of water, an agricultural community spread throughout the area. Barley, hay, and grain were the most common crops, but experiments with the subtropical climate proved that fruits such as bananas and pineapples could also flourish here. By 1875, Cahuenga Valley farmers managed to irrigate their fields with precious water pumped up from the ground by windmills into large wooden tanks supported by stilts.

But a severe drought in 1879 made it impossible to maintain the herds, and several thousand starving cattle were rounded up and forced to stampede west to the ocean, and over the palisades into the sea. It was then that farmers began experimenting with a new crop, oranges and lemons, and gradually began planting citrus groves.

The Dawn of Hollywood

Harvey Henderson Wilcox and his wife Daeida Hartell Wilcox were pious abolitionists from Topeka, Kansas who moved to the thriving Western metropolis of Los Angeles in 1883. Their first home was an ornate Hill Street mansion in downtown L.A., which was later the site of the Los Angeles Pacific's Hill Street Station. Tragedy and fortune always seemed to come hand in hand for the Wilcoxes; Harvey made a substantial fortune in the real estate business, buying up parcels of lands throughout the city, subdividing them, and selling them for enormous profit. But he also lost the use of both legs due to a severe bout of typhoid fever. And even more tragically, the Wilcoxes' only child, a daughter, died while she was only nineteen months old.

So perhaps it was as a diversion from this pervasive darkness that Harvey and Daeida would regularly take leisurely drives in their carriage, drawn by two prized Pinto horses named Duke and Royal, through the lovely Cahuenga Valley, northwest of their downtown home. Their favorite spot to stop and savor was a lush orchard of figs and apricots, which they decided would be an ideal location for a country home. They ultimately purchased 160 acres of the valley, which they renamed "Hollywood" at Daeida's insistence. As discussed in the Preface, it was a name she first heard spoken by a stranger on a train, an affluent woman who talked lovingly of her own Hollywood home near Chicago. Harvey and Daeida's Hollywood would be in California. Its main thoroughfare would ultimately become the world-famous Hollywood Boulevard. But in Harvey and Daeida's day it was known by its original name, Prospect Avenue.

The completion of the Santa Fe Railroad in 1885 resulted in a tremendous land boom, and Harvey Wilcox wisely cashed in on it. He sold the majority of his downtown holdings, including his Hill Street home, and moved with Daeida to live permanently in a small, renovated farmhouse on their newly christened Hollywood ranch.

Harvey and Daeida were devout Methodists who were dedicated to temperance, abstaining from any temptations that could dilute the purity of the spirit. Chief among these, of course, was that demon alcohol. The Wilcoxes established Hollywood with the ironic aspiration of creating a kind of Christian Utopia, a place where like-minded people could unite to live good, clean Christian lives.

Their vision was of a "genteel, Bible-quoting suburb," according to historian Sam Hall Kaplan, "for those wanting to escape the hard-drinking, decadent lifestyle of downtown L.A." Hollywood was founded as a dry community, one that prohibited the sale and consumption of all alcoholic beverages several years prior to the national Prohibition of the 1920s, which made alcohol illegal throughout all of America.

Harvey Wilcox subdivided his 160 acres of Hollywood into a grid of streets and avenues with Franklin Avenue at its northern perimeter, Sunset Boulevard to the south, Gower Street to the west and Hudson Avenue to the east. Wilcox landscaped his new town with rows of pepper trees that he personally planted along the incipient thoroughfares. He filed a streetmap of his new community with the L.A. City Recorder on February 1, 1887, which was the first formal registration of Hollywood as a community within Los Angeles.

Within a few years of Hollywood's inception, Prospect Avenue became a preferential address among affluent Angelenos, who swiftly moved into Hollywood and erected a succession of spacious Queen Anne Victorian and Mission Revival–style manors. A beautiful and peaceful neighborhood arose. Daeida Wilcox persuaded many of her new neighbors and other assorted Angelenos to follow her lead in making substantial donations to finance construction of churches, schools and a city library. Now feeling her fledgling community was prepared to be a true city, she pushed for a vote on incorporation, and on November 14, 1903, it was decided by a slim vote of its citizens (with 88 for and 77 against incorporation) that this little farming community should officially be incorporated as the new City of Hollywood.

Immediately south of Hollywood was the 500-acre ranch of Cornelius Cole, a former Washington senator and lawyer, who moved to Los Angeles in 1881. He was awarded this valuable real estate as the settlement of a long-standing legal fee, and named it in honor of his wife, Olive Colegrove. To this day, streets named for him and his family remain in Hollywood, including Cole Avenue as well as Willoughby Street and Seward Street, for his sons Willoughby and Seward.

Dr. Palmer remembered Cole as a "large, dignified man with heavy white chin whiskers and mustache, a black service hat, string tie, and Prince Albert coat. . . . His secret sin was verse, which he published anonymously." Cole continued to practice law in downtown L.A. along with his son, Willoughby. He died in 1924 at the age of 102 at his home in Colegrove.

The promise of Hollywood's prosperity, however, began to wither and die on the proverbial vine; severe droughts throughout the Southwest delivered a season of scorched devastation to the thirsty farms and orchards of Hollywood. The Wilcox's prayers for rain remained evidently unanswered as each of their newly burrowed wells ran dry. Desperately seeking a way to save his pepper trees, Wilcox broke open dozens of watermelons and saturated the roots of his trees with the juice.

Through powers of persistent persuasion, Harvey Wilcox succeeded in convincing the proprietors of the Cahuenga Valley Railroad to extend their existing route north on Western Avenue so that it would go all the way through to Prospect (now Hollywood) Boulevard, and from there to turn left to head west down the boulevard to Wilcox Avenue, one block beyond Cahuenga.

It was at this same time that a wealthy Colorado miner named E.C. Hurd purchased a plentiful plot of land that stretched west of Hollywood & Wilcox, and built a large home at the its northwest corner. Hurd sold seven acres of this land to a friend from Colorado, E.L. Baker, and together Baker and Hurd planted the first lemon orchard in Hollywood, a vast grove that stretched between Sunset & Yucca and Wilcox & Whitley. Hurd spent a small fortune on water by having wells drilled on his own land and also at Sunset & Hudson. He also financed the construction of a reservoir for water and a tunnel in Brush Canyon, at the north end of Bronson, near what is today the Bronson Caves.

Hurd then bought out the Cahuenga

7

Valley Railroad, and wasted no time in extending its routes ever westward, all the way down Prospect to where it meets Laurel Canyon. This access by rail made Hollywood increasingly accessible to tourists and other potential landowners. But times remained tough in this little town, and both Hurd and Wilcox were frustrated by their failure to sell much of their Hollywood land.

8

Harvey Wilcox died in 1891.[2] Three years later, E.C. Hurd was also gone. Daeida Wilcox took over control of all of her husband's property holdings, carefully maintaining their investments while also generously donating ample parcels of land to the city to be used for a myriad of municipal structures.

Dr. Palmer remembered Daeida well, and with great fondness. "She was a woman of great personal charm," he wrote, "a genial companion, the best and truest of friends, and a worthy opponent. Her word was as good as her oath and she spared no pains to accomplish her undertakings. In benevolence she was outstanding."

It was on yet another train ride east in 1893 that Mrs. Wilcox fell into conversation with yet another stranger on a train. His name was Philo Beveridge, the son of Illinois Governor John Beveridge. Born in 1850 in Tennessee, he attended college at Northwestern University near Chicago in Evanston, Illinois. Separated from his own wife, Beveridge was charmed by Mrs. Wilcox, and accepted her offer to visit Hollywood. Like many, once he came, he never left. Philo married Daeida the following year, and they had four children together. Dr. Palmer remembered him as a "genial, jovial, athletic-appearing man."

In 1889, Rene Blondeau, a native of Normandie, France, came to Hollywood with his young wife Marie by way of New Orleans, and purchased from Wilcox six acres of land at the northwest corner of Sunset & Gower, where they built a home. In time they built additions onto the house, and opened a saloon, Blondeau's Tavern, where they served food as well as wine and assorted liquors.

Their timing couldn't have been more ideal for Paul DeLongpre, a world-famous French artist who moved into Hollywood only months after his countrymates, the Blondeaus, opened their tavern for business. Paul DeLongpre was born in 1855, and was renowned for his beautifully colorful oil and watercolor paintings of flowers. He moved with his wife and children from New York to Los Angeles in 1889 in order to have an ample and varied supply of floral subjects to paint. His chosen means of transport was a bicycle, and it was on one of his regular bike rides that he discovered Hollywood, which he felt was one of Los Angeles' most appealing locations. When he stumbled upon the fine French food being served at the Blondeau's Tavern, he knew he was in heaven, and he began to dine there nearly every day.

It was at a local exhibition of his paintings that he first met Mrs. Wilcox Beveridge, who admired his work. When he spoke of his desire to build a grand estate with extensive gardens, Mrs. Beveridge offered him a large parcel of her ranch, as long as he would establish his studio there. He agreed, and took over three connecting lots north of her corner lot at Hollywood & Cahuenga. But he still felt the area was too small for the kind of grand garden he envisioned, so Mrs. Beveridge offered him the corner lot as well, on which she lived, in exchange for three of his paintings. She had her own home moved to the northwest corner of Cahuenga & Yucca street, so that

---

[2] Initially buried beside the grave of his mother and sister in the Rosedale Cemetery, Wilcox was later reinterred in 1937 to a new crypt at the Hollywood Memorial Cemetery (see page 336) next to the crypt of his wife, Daeida, where both still rest to this day.

DeLongpre could build his own home.

The house he built was a masterpiece, an expansive Moorish mansion surrounded by the natural splendor of sumptuous flower gardens. His house and garden quickly became Hollywood's first tourist attraction; sightseers would breakfast downtown, and then ride a horse-drawn carriage along the Sunset Trail—now Sunset Boulevard—to make it to Hollywood in time for lunch, and a good viewing of the DeLongpre estate.

In 1901 the newly incorporated Los Angeles Pacific Boulevard and Development Company, funded by the investments of such notables as L.A.Times editor Harrison Gray Otis, and businessmen H.J. Whitley and George Hoover, purchased an expansive plot of Hollywood property, the entire realm north of Prospect (Hollywood Boulevard) between Cahuenga and La Brea. This they laid out into a fairly orderly grid of graded streets with sidewalks, curbs and sewers, and called it the Hollywood Ocean View Tract. Though the bulk of it was planned to be an entirely residential street, a portion of Highland Avenue, north of Prospect, was designated as a business zone. Hoover took over the northwest corner of Prospect & Highland, where he constructed the Hollywood Hotel. Across the street on the northeast corner was slotted as the site of the Bank of Hollywood.

Hollywood's first general store was established by Horace Sackett, who came to Hollywood in 1887. Sackett, who was from one of the eight British families who founded Cambridge, Massachusetts, was a "short, spare busy man with a brief beard," Dr. Palmer remembers. "He was cheerful and kindly but firm in his convictions." Sackett moved west from Connecticut with his wife and children, and bought a large acreage of land from Harvey Wilcox at the southwest corner of Hollywood & Cahuenga. On this lot he built his home and also established one of Hollywood's first hotels, a three story building with the general store at its corner that provided the populace of Hollywood with all sorts of necessary provisions, as Dr. Palmer recalled: "Here butter and eggs bought crackers and cheese, overalls, jumpers, boots and shoes, ribbons and yardage, and the canned goods then becoming popular."

The Glen Holly Hotel also opened in Hollywood this same year, built by M.J. Warneke at the southeast corner of Franklin & Ivar. A quiet, nicely furnished small hotel that would figure into Hollywood's incipient tourist trade, it was encircled by bounteous rose gardens.

Another man whose name remains prominent on Hollywood street signs and maps is H.J. Whitley, who was born in 1859 in Toronto, Canada, and made his fortune establishing small towns and small-town banks along the route of the Northern Pacific Railroad throughout Kansas, Minnesota and Oklahoma. He came to California in 1893 and established the largest jewelry store then in all of Los Angeles, the H.J. Whitley Jewelry Store. Seven years later he bought a large acreage of land owned by E.C. Hurd south of Yucca between Wilcox and Whitley, and subdivided it into what became known as the Whitley Home Tract.

"He stood well over six feet in height, rather more rangy than athletic in build," remembered Dr. Palmer. "He was a serious, persuasive, dominating, indefatigable personality who expected cooperation from his associates and industry, efficiency and loyalty from his employees, and got it."

Not everyone would succumb to Whitley's wishes, however. When he made a formal business proposal to Mrs. Beveridge suggesting he be given free reign to control development of her ranch, she turned him down.

Nearly two decades later, in 1918, Whitley acquired the hillside land north of Franklin and east of Highland, and transformed it into the elegant and star-studded hillside community of Whitley Heights.[3] Rudolph Valentino was one of the first, and maybe the greatest, of all the stars who lived in Whitley Heights. He bought an eight-room estate at 6776 Wedgewood Place and lived there with his wife, Natacha Rambova, setting the standards for the style and manner in which movie stars should live. As would be the prevalent pattern in coming years, the Valentinos erected both a large wall and a metal fence to encompass the perimeter of their property.

By the late 1890s, daily existence within Hollywood suffered from the ongoing scarcity of water. Untold numbers of farms were ruined due to drought. Though the windmill pumps used in the 1870s had been supplanted by new gasoline-powered pumps that siphoned the water up from deep wells, the demand created by the irrigation of so many new farms and orchards exceeded the supply, and all the wells ran dry.

Despite this, a tourist trade continued to thrive in Hollywood, access to which was simplified by the advent of the electric street-cars which ran from downtown Los Angeles through Hollywood and on to the city of Santa Monica and the sea. Beginning their journey in downtown L.A., tourists could travel directly to Hollywood and disembark at the Hollywood depot, which was at Prospect & Cahuenga. Waiting there to greet them was C.M. Pierce, a young entrepreneur who would spirit them along in his horse-drawn tallyho to see the shimmering sites of the Cahuenga Valley, including the DeLongpre studio and gardens and a chicken dinner at the Glen Holly hotel, all for the modest price of seventy-five cents.

Pierce had moved from Oregon to Hollywood in hopes of finding a healthy home to overcome illnesses from which he'd long suffered. When he learned that the world-famous artist DeLongpre had settled into Hollywood and established his studio there, he saw an easy opportunity to exploit, and established his tallyho service. It proved so successful that Pierce enlarged his operation and began using electric streetcars to shuttle his tourists to the studio and hotel. He later extended his route all the way to the beach at Playa Del Rey, where his guests dined by the sea, before taking a train back direct to downtown L.A. This extension created a full-day excursion that roughly formed the shape of a balloon when diagrammed—from downtown to Hollywood to Playa Del Rey to downtown—and thus became known as the Balloon Route Excursion. Many of the sightseers who were first entranced with Hollywood during one of these excursions decided to move there permanently, triggering the establishment of many residential subdivisions throughout the city.

Up at the north end of Bronson, north of Franklin, the already picturesque Brush Canyon was being carved into a location that would ultimately serve as one of Hollywood's most frequently used outdoor sets. In 1903 the Union Rock Company carved a quarry here that created caves in the foothills; the resultant crushed rock was used as railroad ballast and for street surfaces. Transported initially by trucks that would roll up Bronson Avenue early in the morning and late at night, disturbing the neighbors as it tore up the newly paved streets, this rock was later moved in trains, thanks in part to the efforts of Dr. Palmer, who secured a forty-year franchise for an extension of the Cahuenga Valley Railroad. At his suggestion, they ran a route from up Western Boulevard from Santa Monica to Franklin, and from there west to Bronson and up to the quarry. This allowed the gravel to be moved easily out of the caves, saving wear and tear on the roads, but still caused an infernal racket of which the nearby nuns were none too glad. "The Mother Superior never forgave the doctor," wrote Palmer,

---

[3] See "A Tour of Hollywood," page 357.

"as there was never found a cure for the squeak of the cars as they turned the corner of Franklin & Western in front of the convent."

In the late 1920s, the quarry ceased operation, but the mysterious caverns created there remain, and have been utilized as a great outdoor set for movies and television ever since, most famously as the "Batcave" in both the TV and film versions of *Batman*. Nestled as it is within the folds of foothills in Brush Canyon, it's ideal both as a set for Westerns, but has also served as an extraterrestrial landscape on innumerable occasions.[4]

In 1904, Dr. Palmer met often with Mrs. Wilcox Beveridge to discuss all things Hollywood. One of their chief concerns was competing with the new businesses opening along Highland—especially the new bank at Hollywood & Highland. They worried that people would be drawn away from their part of town, which was only a few blocks east at Cahuenga. Their aim was to establish Cahuenga as a viable commercial corridor, and to enable this endeavor the doctor suggested that they build a bank of their own at the corner of Hollywood & Cahuenga. He promised to secure the bank if Mrs. Beveridge would finance the construction of the building. And while they were at it, he thought, why not also build a town clubhouse of sorts above the bank?

But Mrs. Beveridge wasn't so sure a small town like Hollywood could support more than one bank, and to help her decide she turned to her attorney for advice. He informed her in no uncertain terms that a second bank in Hollywood was nonsensical, and shouldn't be considered. Yet she was a woman of her word, and felt she and the doctor already had an agreement on which she wouldn't renege.

"The Wilcox Building was at once erected," wrote Dr. Palmer. "Above was a large dance floor with rostrum, a billiard and card room, and office, with soft drinks and cigars on sale, while below on the corner was a spacious banking room. . . . The billiard and card rooms were well attended. Mr. Paul DeLongpre was the first president. . . . Here the weary business man stopped in for a game before dinner and the orchardist played a string of pool after depositing his lemon check. Many old Hollywood residents feel that these were her best days."

The Movies

Though Hollywood became in time the movie capital of the world, the movies were not invented here, nor were the first films shot within Hollywood confines. It's Thomas Edison, working out of his East Orange, New Jersey lab, who is officially credited with the invention of the movies. But his work was built on the foundation of centuries of invention and experimentation, dating back to the ancient magic lantern, a device that would project various spectral shapes and colors.

Movies create the illusion of motion by projecting a succession of still photos in rapid succession. Many men experimented along these lines, including the photographer Eadweard Muybridge, working in Palo Alto, California, who in 1872 studied the motion of humans, horses and other animals by rigging up an arsenal of still cameras to capture the split-second progression of action on film.

In 1895, two brothers in Lyon, France, Louis and Auguste Lumière, invented a camera that shot a swift series of photos, and which many consider the first true movie camera, the Cinematograph. Newspaper advertisements of 1897 boast of its unprecedented, magical properties: "The Cinematograph presents a series of realistic Motion Pictures taken in various parts of America, England, Spain, Italy, Germany and Africa, and presented to view exactly as though you were there looking at the scene actually occurring. . . . People walking about the Streets, Street Cars run-

11

---

[4] For more on the Bronson Caves, see "A Tour of Hollywood," page 303.

ning, Soldiers marching, the Ocean Waves, People Bathing, Cavalry Charges, Comic Incidents, etc., outrivalling any entertainment in interest and novelty ever presented . . . "

But it was Edison who got there first. With his assistant William Dickson, he developed in 1890 the two chief components of moviemaking, a camera and a projector. The Kinetograph was the camera, and the Kinetoscope the projector, which ran a continuous fifty-foot loop of 35-millimeter film with a revolving shutter that flashed each image so quickly—originally eighteeen frames to every second—that the human eye computed it as uninterrupted motion. Edison's first film was more significant for its achievement than its subject, which was his assistant Fred Ott sneezing. Since Edison was the first to file a patent for his inventions, he is forever recognized as the official and sole inventor of the movies.

Edison's Kinetoscope was one of the star attractions at the 1893 Chicago's World Fair. In April of 1894, having shot a few films of vaudeville acts, circus shows and rodeos, Edison opened a parlor to exhibit his invention on Broadway in New York City, a prototype of the first movie theaters.

In 1903 came a new concept in movies from a cameraman named Edwin Porter, who worked for Edison. Porter came up with the idea of not simply filming an event, but contriving an event to be filmed. The first one was *The Life of an American Fireman*, which showed a woman and child being heroically saved from a burning building. Next came *The Great Train Robbery*. These films were shown in storefronts projected on bed-sheets hung in the back. Thousands shelled out nickels to see these "photo-plays," and an American tradition was born. By 1911, when the first film company came to Hollywood, 5,000 movie theaters already existed throughout America. Hollywood, however, didn't have one. As Laurence Hill wrote, "It wasn't that kind of town."

12

Paul DeLongpre passed away in 1911, and his beautiful estate and gardens were quickly torn down, forever closing a chapter of Hollywood history. "The steamroller of progress obliterated the home and the flowers," wrote Hill. "Few now living in Hollywood know that DeLongpre used to pluck his choicest roses where now stands the Warner Brothers Theater."

Ironically, it was only a handful of weeks following DeLongpre's death that the movies first arrived in Hollywood. Perhaps the timing of his departure was perfectly planned, for the serene beauty that he achieved at his estate, connected as it was to the era of the Wilcox's vision of Hollywood as a peaceful paradise, would be entirely erased by the melee and sprawl sparked by the arrival of movie companies. Only days after establishing a studio in Hollywood, the Nestor Company was already disturbing the perennial serenity of Hollywood by staging small battles in the streets: "The natives . . . were actually frightened," wrote Hill, "when they saw heavily armed cowboys galloping up Beachwood Drive to 'fight' Indians in what is now Hollywoodland."

Bad weather in Chicago was the primary reason the movies first turned toward the West, and eventually migrated to Hollywood. It's the same reason that so many of the men who would shape Hollywood's history, such as L. Frank Baum, Edgar Rice Burroughs, and others, all came: to escape the ongoing struggle with the volatile ever-shifting elements that is life on Lake Michigan and its environs.

And so it was that Colonel William Selig, who ran the Selig Polyscope Company in Chicago, sent a film crew to California in 1907 to shoot *The Count of Monte Cristo*. They filmed first in downtown L.A. and seaside Santa Monica before moving onto Colorado. But when the climate of Colorado proved to be nearly as temperamental as Chicago's, the Selig troupe returned to L.A. to stay. Renting a building that had previously housed a Chinese laundry, they set up offices, dressing rooms, and a soundstage, and got to work. The first film they shot was *The Heart of a Race Tout*, which was the first film completed completely in California. It would be, of course, the first of many.

In 1909 The Bison Company came to Los Angeles from New York and set up shop in what was then Edendale—east of Hollywood, what is now the serene suburb of Glendale. Charlie Chaplin called it "an anomalous-looking place that could not make up its mind whether to be a humble residential district or a semi-industrial one."

Bison began churning out several Westerns each week. The director D.W. Griffith arrived with the Biograph movie company from New York in 1910, including a troupe of actors that included future stars Mary Pickford and Florence Lawrence. That same year two other companies arrived: Essanay, which set up shop in nearby Niles, and the Kalem Company, which also settled near Edendale.

In 1910, the rows of pepper trees planted by Harvey Wilcox along Hollywood's main thoroughfare still flourished. It was an year in which the Angeleno's favorite horse and buggy took them to Hollywood to saunter slowly along Melrose Avenue. Now a fashionable street of outdoor cafes and chic boutiques, it was originally named for E.A. Melrose, whose ranch ran from Western Avenue east to Wilton Boulevard and from Melrose north to Santa Monica Boulevard.

Obtaining an adequate water supply for Hollywood has been an ongoing obstacle since its conception. Though some underground pools of water were discovered and drilled at various locations throughout Hollywood—at the corners of Las Palmas & Franklin, Selma & Hudson, Santa Monica & Kings Road, and Sunset & Western—by 1906, most of these wells had already been tapped out.

Enter William Mulholland. Born in Dublin, Ireland, Mulholland moved to California in 1877 and, without the benefit of any formal education, learned the ropes of civil engineering while working as a ditchdigger for the city. He studied the infrastructure of the city diligently, and worked his way up eventually to be appointed chief engineer of the Bureau of Waterworks and Supply for Los Angeles, which merged in 1925 with the Bureau of Power and Light, to become the Department of Water and Power (DWP). He was responsible for shaping much of what is modern Hollywood. It was his idea to pave the crest of the Santa Monica mountain range that runs from Hollywood to the sea, with a long, winding skyline highway that bears his name—Mulholland Drive.

Mulholland had a scheme he felt could save Los Angeles. Launching a career that would comprise both tremendous glory and ruin, he devised a plan by which a profusion of water could be channeled into the San Fernando Reservoir across the desert plains and over mountain ranges from Owens Lake, which was some 250 miles away in Inyo County. It was a process that would result in devastation to the thousands of acres of farmland which had flourished there, transforming the Owens Valley into "a dust bowl before the Dust Bowl," as the columnist Patt Morrison wrote in the *L.A. Times*. Still Mulholland won civic support for the construction of this, the longest aqueduct in the Western Hemisphere at that time. It was 338 miles long, and worked entirely on gravity.

"In some places, the aqueduct had to climb mountains that topped 1,000 feet," wrote Dave Hogan in *The Rise and Fall of William Mulholland*. "Ingeniously, in these cases Mulholland utilized gigantic siphons. As the pipeline approached the mountain, the bore of the pipe became narrower and narrower which increased the pressure and speed of the water in the pipe. Thus, the water was pushed up the mountain and upon reaching the top, the pipeline opened up wide again, creating a suction that would continue to pull the water along on its path."

13

Completed on November 5, 1913, it was a project launched with two simple declamatory sentences spoken by Mulholland as the water gushed for the first time ever to L.A. via the new Los Angeles Aqueduct. "There it is," he said. "Take it."

It was an ingenious civic solution that changed Los Angeles forever, yet one that many considered to be preposterous and even criminal. "It was as if Boston had decided to draw its water from the St. Lawrence," wrote the historian Kevin Starr, "or St. Louis was reaching across the state of Illinois to Lake Michigan." The humorist Will Rogers painted the proceedings in even more graphic terms, writing later that "the federal government . . . held Owens Valley while Los Angeles raped it."

14

As with Mulholland's later controversial decision to build a giant dam high in the Hollywood Hills, there were ulterior motives at play. It just so happens that one of the members of the L.A. Board of Water Commissioners, Moses Sherman, was part of a land syndicate that was headed by the publisher of the *L.A. Times*, Harrison Gray Otis, and Harry Chandler, Gray's son-in-law. Though it's never been proven absolutely, all signs point to the fact that Sherman used his insider information to purchase much of the San Fernando Valley at low rates prior to the construction of the aqueduct. Once this previously parched land became possible to irrigate with the water from the Owens River, its value skyrocketed, and the syndicate was able to sell it off at enormous profit.

Ironically, in the year 2001, a new process was started to divert water from the aqueduct back into the dry Owens Lake, where the profusion of dust had become toxic in recent years, carrying poisonous arsenic and cadmium. Though the water now being channeled back to the lake bed will never be sufficient to bring back the lake itself, it will serve to dampen the dangerous dust into stable mud.

The promise of a new and enduring water supply appealed to the citizens and civic leaders of Hollywood, as did access to the citywide sewer system, and the need for annexation—reconnecting Hollywood to Los Angeles—was recognized. Though it would result in relinquishing Hollywood's identity as an individual city to become instead a community within L.A., many of its residents and civic leaders felt that this was the only reasonable course of action.

Hollywood's reputation in 1910 was already well established as a desirable residential community that offered all the traditional trappings of modern American life—good schools, churches, clubs, effective police and fire departments (in fact, the first fire department in all of Los Angeles to replace their horse-drawn fire carriages with a full fleet of modern, motorized fire trucks), and an active, ethical city government—all before becoming the movie capital of the world. But it had outgrown its own primitive infrastructure. "Hollywood's population had grown too dense to depend any longer on cesspools," recalled Dr. Palmer, "surrounding areas were too valuable for sewer farms or septic tanks, and the distance to the sea was too great to consider the cost of an outfall sewer. Annexation assured drainage through the city's outfall sewer and water from the Owens river basin."

When Hollywood's annexation to the City of L.A. was initially considered, there arose considerable opposition to the idea from members of the waterworks board, who were apprehensive about their ongoing ability to provide sufficient water for those who already lived and worked within the existing city boundaries. But when Mulholland devised his plan to bring water to the city, their fears were alleviated. In February of 1910, Los Angeles voted on the annexation of Hollywood. "Election day brought no contest," Dr. Palmer remembered. "The few straggling negative votes were inconsequential. . . .

Annexation was a fact." But though officially annexed, Hollywood, as the doctor and others were happy to discover, easily maintained its own unique identity, which has endured throughout the decades.

It was a tall Texan by the name of C.E. Toberman whose influence on the shape of physical Hollywood was among the most profound of all. Born Charles Edward Toberman in 1880, he tried his hand at a variety of vocations before settling on a mix of real estate and insurance, and opened an office to do both on Hollywood Boulevard in 1907. He was a "six-foot, square-shouldered, meticulously attired, smooth-faced, talented gentleman," according to Dr. Palmer, who also became Hollywood city treasurer for $1,000 a year. Incorporating his business as the C.E. Toberman Company in 1910, he built a four-story building six years later on the southeast corner of Hollywood & Highland, which served as his office. In later years, for reasons that remain a mystery, the uppermost three stories of this building were removed. Today it's the Guinness Book of World Records Museum.

Toberman became one of Hollywood's most vital and significant developers, constructing twenty-six commercial buildings within Hollywood, plus one movie studio—the Hollywood Center Studios on Las Palmas, south of Santa Monica Boulevard, which became Zoetrope decades later when purchased by Francis Ford Coppola. His Hollywood buildings also include the four-story Hollywood Storage Company on Highland, The Kress Department Store (now Frederick's of Hollywood), the El Capitan Theater and adjoining office building, the Egyptian Theater and the Chinese Theater, all of which are on Hollywood Boulevard.

The Krotona Colony

Krotona is a religious organization that grew out of The Theosophical Society, which was founded in 1875 in New York City. It was based primarily on the work of Helena Petrovna Blavatsky, who delivered and published numerous lectures on her unique union of spiritualism, Eastern religion, Masonic lore, and scientific thought. She wrote three books detailing her philosophies: *Isis Unveiled* of 1877, *The Secret Doctrine*, 1888, and *The Key to Theosophy* in 1889.

A Virginian attorney named Albert Warrington was so inspired and empowered by her teachings, that within two years of joining the society in 1896, he decided to devote his life to it. His mission became the construction of a physical colony that would house the study and worship of the Theosophical school of thought, called Krotona. This mission remained unfulfilled for several years, until the death of his wife in 1908, at which time he abandoned his law career to found a Krotona society.

He originally planned its construction in his home state of Virginia, but for reasons unknown he abandoned that concept. From the winter of 1910 through the spring of 1911, he traveled around America to find the ideal location for his new society. Texas, Oklahoma, and New Mexico were all considered and ultimately rejected in favor of Southern California.

Still the search needed to be narrowed down, and Warrington contemplated cities such as Alhambra and Pasadena before finally finding the perfect location: the Hollywood Hills. In December of 1911, he purchased acreage on the south slope of the hill between Argyle and Gower. Known forever since as Krotona Hill, he said that he chose it because he felt these hills were "magnetically impregnated," and that "a spiritual urge seems to be peculiar to all this area."

Like the Wilcoxes, Warrington was convinced that this peaceful and temperate region would be ideal for the establishment of a spiritual haven. He invited all followers of Krotona, many of whom lived in Chicago, to relocate to his new society in its existing ranch houses as well as in new homes he would build. Many

15

families of followers accepted, and old houses were renovated as new ones were built. In addition, a residential building called the Krotona Inn was constructed, as was a temple, a library, a science building, and a walkway built into the upward slope of the hills called Krotona Flight, where the faithful could ascend physically as well as spiritually. Most of these structures, including the temple, inn and flight, still exist to this day, though modified for modern residential usage. Construction of the Krotona Colony occurred over a span of seven years, from the autumn of 1912 to the spring of 1919.[5]

The residents of the Krotona Colony never sought to isolate themselves from Hollywood. In fact, quite the opposite was true: Once open, they welcomed the community into their realm by offering public lectures each Sunday afternoon, and a full roster of courses throughout the week. Not unlike the "adult extension courses" known today, these courses covered subjects such as theosophy, astrology, philosophy, psychology, and were designed to bridge the modern discoveries of science with the enduring truths of the spirit.

Hollywood also became famous at this time for the grandeur of other hillside homes erected within its realm. At the northeast corner of Franklin & Argyle, now a strip mall shadowed by an overpass of the Hollywood Freeway, the phenomenal Glengarry Castle was built in 1909 by Alfred Guido Randolph Schloesser. A retired surgeon from Chicago who made his fortune in mining, he uprooted the lemon grove that was there and erected a giant castle with leaded glass windows, a ten-story tower, and a fortune of antique treasures, including tapestries, armor and marble statues.

Three years later he built another castle directly across the street, at the Northwest corner of Franklin & Argyle, which he also filled with art. Both homes became tourist attractions. When intense anti-German

sentiment began to spread during World War I, he attempted to mask his Germanic heritage by exchanging his name with that of his house, becoming Randolph Castles and renaming the castle Schloesser Terrace. Both castles were destroyed in 1929, and on the spot of the second one a new castle was erected, an apartment building called the Castle Argyle, which is now a senior-citizen residence on the eclipse of the freeway.

Just a couple miles west of Schloesser's twin castles two other remarkable mansions were built, both of which still remain. At the hillside corner of Orange & Franklin the Holly Chateau was constructed—a three-story, seventeen-room Victorian house owned by Rollin Lane and his wife, who both lived out their lives in the home. Today it is the Magic Castle, a private club for magicians.[6]

And up the hill from the Holly Chateau an extraordinary mansion was built in 1914 by two Jewish brothers, Adolph and Eugene Bernheimer, who bought the seven acres behind the Lanes' home and transformed it into an Asian paradise. Among the foremost American importers of Japanese artifacts, the Bernheimers built a magnificent Japanese manor called Yamashiro, which means "mountain palace" in Japanese. Following the death of Eugene Bernheimer in 1923, the house was sold. Today Yamashiro still stands. Now a fine Japanese restaurant, it's been used as a Japanese backdrop in countless movies, and still affords a breathtaking view of Hollywood below.

The year 1910 was also when the Wizard arrived in Hollywood. L. Frank Baum, the author of the *Wizard of Oz* series of books, settled with his family in a little Hollywood kingdom he christened *Ozcot*, just north of Hollywood Boulevard on Cherokee Avenue. Baum was among the first of millions of native Chicagoans to escape those icy blackhawk winds off of Lake Michigan in the winter to enjoy the

[5] See "A Tour of Hollywood," page 341.

[6] See "A Tour of Hollywood," page 346.

peaceful sunshine of Southern California. He wrote almost all of the Oz books in this home, which he proudly surrounded with lush, award-winning gardens.

"A spacious, tastefully furnished upper-middle-class house," wrote Kevin Starr of Ozcot. "There was a great fireplace in the parlor which Baum kept crackling on chilly days, and an equally spacious sun porch. Baum's library study was snug with books, Morris chairs, a desk lamp of his own design, and his file cabinets, including the drawer labeled O–Z which had first inspired the name of his fairyland. Measuring 100 by 183 feet, Baum's lot left plenty of room for a spacious backyard. . . . Baum built a small open-air cottage on one end, where he wrote on summer days, and put in a large gold fish pond and aviary housing over forty birds. Enclosing his backyard with a six-foot-high fence, Baum made of it a *hortus conclusus*, an Oz within Ozcot, where he would repair each morning to tend the dahlias and chrysanthemums that soon won him twenty-one prize cups and a regionwide reputation among horticulturists."

To the children of all ages who were enthralled with Oz back in Baum's day, and ever since, the author wrote this:

> If Dorothy keeps her word and I am permitted to write another Oz book, you will probably discover how all these characters came together in the famous Emerald City. Meantime, I want to tell all my little friends—whose numbers are increasing by many thousands every year—that I am very grateful for the favor they have shown my books and for the delightful little letters I am constantly receiving. I am almost sure that I have as many friends among the children of America as any story writer alive; and this, of course, makes me very proud and happy.
>
> Signed, L. Frank Baum.

Baum died here at Ozcot on May 6, 1919; his last words, spoken to his wife, were, "Now is the time to cross the shifting sands."

Though Ozcot sadly belongs now only to the ages, one of its nearest neighboring houses built in the same era still stands. A unique home constructed by H.J. Whitley at 6541 Hollywood Boulevard, it was purchased by Herman Janes to live in with his wife and children. A Combination of a Queen Anne Victorian and Dutch Colonial Revival home, it was accented by archaic turrets and shingled gables. Starting in 1911, Herman's wife Mary and their trio of daughters ran a school in the house called The Misses Janes School of Hollywood, which began as a kindergarten, and over the years expanded to offer classes from first grade through high school. With the exception of inclement days during the rainy season, classes were held outside under the trees planted all around the grounds. In time, many prominent Hollywood businessmen and movie stars sent their children to school here, including Chaplin, DeMille, Jesse Lasky, Thomas Ince, Noah Beery, Carl Laemmle and others.

Hollywood proper began to be extended farther to the north in 1911, when Albert Beach acquired the land north of Franklin and east of Argyle. He paved the street that cuts straight up this hill to what is now Beachwood Village, and named it Beachwood Drive in his own honor (not *Beechwood*, which is the prevailing British spelling still found in books and magazines to this day).

The placid, residential Hollywood that Baum, Beach, Janes and others chose as their new home was about to undergo a transformation of epic proportions. Though it already had an active tourist industry, that industry was about to expand exponentially as Hollywood's attractions and its promise of potential employment developed. As Laurence Hill wrote, "DeLongpre's paintings had attracted hundreds. DeMille's pictures were to attract thousands—tens of thousands. A fame based on water colors, frostless citrus groves and winter vegetables was to be overshadowed and entirely

17

replaced by one based on studios, styles and stars."

The First Films

It was in October of 1911 that the first film company to officially set up shop within Hollywood arrived. The Nestor Company, owned by two brothers, William and David Horsley, came to California with a staff of forty employees. Upon arrival, with the advantageous advice of yet another stranger on a train, a man named Murray Steele, they set their sites on the Blondeau Tavern at the northwest corner of Sunset & Gower, which had recently been forced to close due to the Wilcox's ban on alcohol. In addition to its main tavern building, it also had an adjoining corral for horses, a barn, a bungalow, and several small structures.

Horsley met with Mrs. Blondeau, who agreed to lease the property to him for thirty-five dollars. It became the first movie studio in Hollywood. *Her Indian Hero*, starring Dorothy Davenport, Victoria Ford and Jack Conway was Hollywood's first movie, and was soon the first of many: Only three months later, fifteen other companies moved into Hollywood to make movies. These included the Pat Powers Company, the Eclair Company, and the Lux Company, all of which settled south of Sunset on Gordon Street.

As movies quickly gained popularity throughout America, Thomas Edison grew more concerned with protecting what he felt were the fruits of his labor, and began suing independent movie producers for patent infringement. In the hope of establishing a conglomerate powerful enough to crush all competition, he licensed the use of his patent to a cabal of companies that came to be called The Trust. These included Edison's own company, Vitagraph, as well as Selig, Essanay, Kalem, Pathe, Melies and Lubin. Those companies who were excluded from The Trust fled the East Coast, some as far as Cuba, to escape Edison's reach. It's another reason California became the movie capital of the world. After many independent companies set down their roots in Southern California and refused to yield, the power structure shifted and in time The Trust was dust.

Although Edison was unquestionably interested in turning a profit and has been characterized as capitalizing to a great extent on the work of other men, he was cognizant that the profound potential of the movies was a tool that should never be taken lightly. In a 1924 speech before the moguls of the movie industry, he warned them to be careful with this extraordinary tool. "I believe, as I have always believed," he said, "that you control the most powerful instrument in the world for good or evil. Remember that you are servants of the public and never let a desire for money or power prevent you from giving to the public the best work of which you are capable. It is not the quantity of riches that count; it is the quality that produces happiness, where that is possible. I wish you a prosperous, useful, and honourable future."

In 1912, Carl Laemmle folded the I.M.P. Movie Company into his newly formed Universal Film Manufacturing Company, and took over the Nestor Company, including their studio at Sunset & Gower. He also bought adjoining property to the south. The following year the studio burnt to the ground, and a larger, more modern studio was constructed to replace it. (Of Laemmle's predilection toward nepotism, the poet Ogden Nash wrote a famous couplet years later: "Uncle Carl Laemmle/Has a very large faemmle.")

In 1915, Laemmle leased 250 acres of the Taylor Ranch on the other side of the Cahuenga Pass in the San Fernando Valley, and moved his operations there to what is now Universal City. The Sunset-Gower studio was then used by the Quality Pictures Company for a year, before it was taken over by the Christie Brothers, who remained there till the thirties, making their "Christie Comedies."

In 1913 Jesse Lasky, Samuel Goldfish,

Arthur Friend and Cecil B. DeMille formed a new film company in New York called the Jesse L. Lasky Feature Play Company. They succeeded in luring a major Broadway star—Dustin Farnum—to join their enterprise, and DeMille and Farnum, along with a small group of actors and crew, headed west to find a suitably western location for their first project, a film version of Farnum's hit Broadway play, *The Squaw Man*. They headed initially to Flagstaff, Arizona, where the presence of warring cattlemen and sheep ranchers there taking potshots at each other was deemed too realistic for their needs, and far too dangerous.

"The quick decision was made," wrote DeMille in his autobiography. "When the train puffed out of the Flagstaff station, we were back on it. . . . The Company was on the move . . . to a quiet village of orange groves and pepper trees, out there to the northwest of Los Angeles, 'Hollywood' was about to be born."

This newest birth of Hollywood was not to occur in any hospital or even studio, but more humbly, in a barn. There on the southeast corner of Selma & Vine in Hollywood, on the edge of an orange grove, was the foundation of a Hollywood movie empire. "Turning off the sparsely settled main thoroughfare, grandly called Hollywood Boulevard, we drove down a broad, shady avenue more appropriately named Vine Street," DeMille recalled, "and there it was. It was a barn. Unmistakably, it was a barn. That did not bother me. I was not unfamiliar with stables. . . . Besides, I expected to be working like a horse: what did it matter being housed like one?"

Jacob Stern, the owner of this barn, was a German immigrant who purchased the land in 1904, at which time it was already being used as a lemon grove. He added a large grove of orange trees to the northern half of his lot, and also invested in Hollywood in other ways. He joined a coalition of businessmen in the area to commercially develop the intersection of Hollywood & Vine, where he financed the

construction of the nine-story Plaza Hotel, which still stands to this day. He also leased a parcel of his land on Vine just south of Hollywood Boulevard to enable the construction of a legitimate venue for live theater in Hollywood, the Vine Street Theater.

But it is for the use of his barn that Jacob Stern is best remembered in the annals of Hollywood history. It's there that the Lasky company made their inaugural film, the first full-length motion picture to be shot entirely within Hollywood, *The Squaw Man*. At first Stern reserved the right to share the barn with them, continuing to house his horses and his carriage there, an arrangement DeMille found to be reasonable. "After all," he said, "they *were* there first." However, when Stern would water his horses, the water would run down throughout the office, forcing DeMille to start wearing galoshes while working there. Eventually the fledgling film company took over the entire barn, and also expanded into many acres of land around the barn. On that land Lasky built his empire.

Almost as soon as the filmmakers arrived, the residue of their moviemaking began to contaminate the streets and sewers of their new town. At the time, all of their film was processed in a large tank of fixing fluid, or "hypo," as it was called. Each afternoon they would take the tank of hypo and dispose of it by dumping it down the sewers. When the city authorities caught on to this practice, they fined the company, who paid the fines but persisted in dumping the fluid in the sewers. When the authorities threatened to jail the filmmakers for this crime, DeMille decided to comply, and hired a man with a truck to haul away the refuse. This guy did well—not only did he get paid a few dollars for each truckful, he also began to amass a small fortune by extracting silver from the fluid, which he then sold at a healthy profit. DeMille was envious but impressed by the guy's ingenuity. "Evidently the city fathers had been as ignorant as I," he wrote. "Otherwise they could have advertised that in Hollywood the very gutters ran with silver."

DeMille settled with his family in a little cottage in the Cahuenga Pass, and made his daily commute up Cahuenga to his studio by the most preferential means of transport at that time, a horse. "It was possible to drive a car (if one had a car in 1914), over the bumpy, pitted, dirt road which was then Cahuenga Boulevard," he wrote, "but a horse was a much more practical means of transportation between my home and the barn-studio. . . . It was a pleasant ride in the freshness of the morning and the cool of the evening on horseback past the vineyards and between the trees and brush which then grew wild in the pass through which thousands of cars now boil hourly on the Hollywood freeway. It was also a lonely ride. Houses were few and far between."

Nineteen-thirteen was also the year that an English vaudeville comedian named Charlie Chaplin received an offer from Charles Kessel, one of the owners of the Keystone Company, to leave the traveling Karno troupe and come to California to make movies. "I had often played with the idea of working in films," Chaplin wrote in his autobiography, before going on to explain his proposed strategy of making some big bucks fast in silent films before returning to what mattered most, the stage. Keystone offered him $150 a week, which was twice what he was earning with Karno, and he accepted.

His estimation of Keystone comedies prior to his profound influence upon them, was fairly negative, revealing the values he felt were necessary to bring to his own movies: "I thought [Keystone comedies] were a crude melange of rough-and-tumble. However, a pretty dark-eyed girl named Mabel Normand, who was quite charming, weaved in and out of them and justified their existence." At Keystone Chaplin developed one of filmdom's most beloved and timeless characters, The Little Tramp, which was

embraced in time by the world at large. Within two years, he was the most famous man in the world, and also one of the richest, earning $10,000 a week.

In 1915, D.W. Griffith, the man who would become known as the "father of the movies" formed The Triangle Film Corporation with Thomas Ince and Mack Sennett, and took over the Majestic Reliance Studios at 4500 Sunset, renaming it the Fine Arts Studio. That same year he started filming *The Birth of a Nation*, the first movie ever to use many thousands of extras. The news of this remarkable undertaking astounded Los Angeles, and also outraged many who were less than thrilled by the thought of a movie celebrating the Ku Klux Klan.

When it opened in February 1915, police were stationed at the theater prepared for a potential riot. No such skirmish ensued, however, and the premiere proceeded as planned with the radiant appearance of many stars of the silent screen, including Mae Marsh and Lillian Gish, who starred in the film. It went on to become one of that decade's most popular and profitable films, generating more than $15 million in ticket sales, and thus establishing the business of movies as a vital and very real new business on the American landscape, a rapidly expanding industry that California and the rest of the world could no longer ignore. And Hollywood was the heart of it.

In 1916, Griffith began work on *Intolerance*, for which he constructed the most immense set ever built in Hollywood up to that moment, a full-scale re-creation of ancient Babylon replete with colossal columns on which sat gargantuan white elephants. This set was never destroyed following the completion of filming, and stood strangely for many years—the first real symbol of Hollywood's disregard for its landmarks—looming over the intersection of Hollywood & Sunset Boulevards until it ultimately deteriorated. Its presence was felt for years, and had an undeniable symbolic and concrete influence on the whimsical melange of Angeleno architecture styles that developed in its wake. ". . . [T]he *Intolerance* set not only provided Hollywood and Los Angeles with ones of its most important metaphors, the Babylonian ziggurat atop Los Angeles City Hall," wrote Kevin Starr, "it also introduced an element of theatricality into Los Angeles/Hollywood architecture itself. . . . The more sets Hollywood created . . . the more expressively scenic became the popular architecture of the Southland." Ironically, the Babylonian court of *Intolerance* has been erected once again, replete with immense white elephants perched upon towering columns, as the main design of the new Hollywood-Highland project on Hollywood Boulevard, which was under construction during the writing of this book.

The Vitagraph movie company, after spending five years in Santa Monica, also moved into east Hollywood, and erected a sprawling studio on twenty-five acres of previously undeveloped property at Prospect & Talmadge Avenue. In 1925, this lot was sold to Warner Brothers and renamed the Warner Brothers-Vitagraph Studios. Many of their most famous films were created on this lot. Today it is the Hollywood home of ABC Television.

The Lubin Company built a studio at the corner of Sunset & Hoover in 1912, which was subsequently bought and sold by a series of companies, including Essanay, Kalem, Monogram and others. Since 1970 it's been the home of Los Angeles' public television station, KCET.

The Clune Studios—now known as The Raleigh Studios—still stands in Hollywood at 650 Bronson at Melrose, just east of Paramount. Built in 1914, it's been owned by many companies through the years. For decades it was the California Studio, the home of the *Hopalong Cassidy* movies. Many famous films have been made here, including *The Mark of Zorro, The Three Musketeers, In the Heat of the Night*, with Rod Steiger and Sidney Poitier (which won the Oscar for Best Picture of 1967),

The Best Years of Our Lives (Best Picture of 1946), *What Ever Happened to Baby Jane?* (1962, with Bette Davis and Joan Crawford) and the original *A Star Is Born* (1937). In the sixties, this became The Producer's Studio, and many famous TV shows were made here, including "Gunsmoke" and "Superman," as well as "Death Valley Days," which featured Ronald Reagan. In 1980, it became the Raleigh Studios.

This advent of the movies in Hollywood generated a kind of an overnight Gold Rush—an unparalleled upsurge in the population from about 500 residents in 1900 to nearly 8,000 by 1913. Along Hollywood Boulevard and its sidestreets a score of fashionable clothing shops and boutiques appeared, as did restaurants, cafes, taverns and hotels. The business of tourism began to flourish as it never had in DeLongpre's day—now hundreds came to Hollywood's gates night and day to stroll along the grand promenade that was Hollywood Boulevard to see some of the "perpetual vaudeville," as the constant public filming of the silent movies became known.

And it was quite a show. Spilling out from the assorted studios were teams of filmmakers, who used the real streets and structures of physical Hollywood to its greatest advantage, as they still do today. As Dr. Palmer recalled, once the movies moved in, they exploited every element of Hollywood available to them, and their presence was dramatic and pervasive: "Private homes were gratuitously used for elopments and domestic dramas. Banks were utilized on holidays, Saturday afternoons, and Sundays for hold-up scenes. Drug stores and other places of business were regularly robbed before the camera. Citizens were halted on the streets to augment mob scenes. Streets were roped off for automobile accidents, often hosed down to make autos skid and turn over—a characteristic stunt for Wally Reid. An army of almost any nation or age marching down Hollywood Boulevard behind a camera on the rear of a car, with one over the hood of the car following, was a common sight. . . . Christies' Bathing Beauties in costumes many years in advance of the time would rush down the street to their favorite restaurant for a between-acts lunch. Face paint and lipstick were introduced to the rural maiden as the conventional thing."

Within a few short years and for reasons somewhat random, Hollywood became known throughout the entire world as the shimmering heart of this radically new, dreamlike discovery known as the movies. "From 1914 into the 1920s, Hollywood grew from a handful of wooden bungalows in an orchard realm into a village where elaborate mansions reared themselves above streets of box-shaped stucco dwellings," wrote Jesse Lasky Jr. "Hilltops sported bogus Spanish haciendas where the stars, directors, and producers were grandly housed above the hovels of the technicians and extras who fed the growing factories."

Even the existent Angeleno suburbs that adjoined Hollywood wanted to capture some of this newfangled shimmer for their own, and so renamed their communities to get in on the action. The twin towns of Toluca and Lankershim, both of which were tiny residential farm communities just north of Hollywood in the San Fernando Valley, merged into a single, new town dubbed "North Hollywood." The city of Sherman, which extended immediately west of Hollywood to Beverly Hills, changed its name to "West Hollywood." And to the south, all of what was once Colegrove, the former ranch of Senator Cole, was newly named "South Hollywood."

As the population of Hollywood swiftly expanded, so did its cultural composition. The arrival of movie companies to Hollywood resulted in a mass influx of Jewish New Yorkers and Chicagoans into this once primarily Christian community, a multicultural shift that didn't thrill many of Hollywood's original inhabitants. "As New York City was steadily moving in,"

Dr. Palmer remembered, "the local merchants were quick to obtain the merchandise familiar to their new customers. Jewish proprietors soon took the place of Gentiles, kosher restaurants appeared on the boulevard, and the first synagogue, Beth-El, opened on Wilton Place, north of Hollywood Boulevard."

With this shift also came elevated esteem for motion pictures. The previous perception of the movies as a mere entertainment novelty, a somewhat crude form of automatic vaudeville worth no more than its nickel admission, gradually became supplanted by the incipient understanding that here was a medium capable of capturing the beautiful mystery of our very dreams, and of aspiring to the realm of serious art. Evidence of this evolution is found in a 1916 issue of *Harper's Weekly*, in which the inherent artistry of Chaplin's Little Tramp is recognized: "The slapstick star of the slum nickelodeons of 1913 has begun to be classic," wrote Minnie Madden Fiske, "and a pet of the philosophizing literati."

The allure of Hollywood began then, as it has ever since, to lure thousands of young hopefuls each week from all parts east to Hollywood Boulevard, which quickly became known as a boulevard of dreams and, as was inevitable, of broken dreams. As early as 1915, this former farm town was flooded with an abundance of young, pretty girls, who would arrive with a dream only a handful could ever attain. "Hollywood boasted a few beautiful girls in 1910," recalled Dr. Palmer, "but by 1915 all the nation's fond mothers brought or sent the daughters they thought beautiful or talented. Many of them have become famous. Many fell short in one way or another and joined the extras waiting for a call, while other hopefuls became waitresses in the boulevard restaurants."

In 1916, aware of this abundance of young women flocking into Hollywood, a librarian named Eleanor Jones persuaded the Young Women's Christian Association

(YWCA) to sponsor the construction of a building that could provide these girls with safe and reasonable room and board. A small clubhouse for this purpose was rented on Carlos Avenue, and a decade later the majestic Studio Club was constructed on Lodi Place. Designed by the architect Julia Morgan, who designed much of William Randolph Hearst's San Simeon, it became the first Hollywood home for thousands of hopeful women, many of whom ultimately did succeed in becoming starlets, including Marilyn Monroe, Marie Windsor and Evelyn Keyes.[7]

High Culture Comes to Hollywood

Nineteen-sixteen was also the year that high culture came to Hollywood in the form of public theater. A presentation of Shakespeare's *Julius Caesar* was performed in the natural amphitheater at the heart of Beachwood Canyon, now the site of Beachwood Village, with its market and cafe. Featuring numerous superstars of the silent screen such as Tyrone Power and Douglas Fairbanks, the producers of this extravaganza appropriated Hollywood magic with magnificent sets reproducing the ruins and battlefields of Ancient Rome. Though nearly $20,000 was spent to create the lavish sets for this one-night-only performance, the show still managed to generate a profit and earned some $15,000, which was donated to the Actor's Fund of America.

The success of *Caesar* inspired a member of the Krotona Colony, Christine Wetherill Stevenson, to establish an alliance of her neighbors with the aim of building a permanent outdoor amphitheater somewhere within the untamed expanse that was then still Hollywood. Mrs. Stevenson, a former Philadelphian, suggested the summit of the Krotona Colony itself, Krotona Hill. This location

was given an audition of sorts when a thirty-five-night-run dramatization of a long poem, *The Light of Asia*, was staged there. Starring the silent star Ruth St. Denis, like *Caesar*, it was a rousing and inspiring success. "Thousands found solace and diversion from the sorrow and strain of the War," wrote Hill, "by attending this sacred drama."

The Alliance determined then that a better location was the Daisy Dell, a wilderness of cactus and sage just north of the Cahuenga Pass, which formed an immense, natural bowl in the foothills. Along with Mrs. Chauncey Clarke, Stevenson purchased all fifty acres of this property from Myra Hershey. Adjoining acreage there was purchased from a man named Lacy who owned a carpet cleaning business, and from a woman named Teele, who owned a little chicken ranch at the Highland Avenue entrance to the Bowl. For a total of $47,500, she acquired all the land and agreed to grant the Alliance an option to buy it for $42,000. It's on this ground that the world-famous Hollywood Bowl was ultimately erected.

Before she started building a theater, however, Mrs. Stevenson wrote a play to be presented there. A narrative detailing the life of Christ, she called it *The Pilgrimage Play*, and staged it on a hillside not far from the current site of the Hollywood Bowl. *The Pilgrimage Play* became a Hollywood tradition.

The alliance, however, felt that Mrs. Stevenson's plans for the development of the Daisy Dell were too expensive, especially her proposal to bring in the notable San Francisco architect Louis Mullgardt to design the theater. They also disagreed with her vision of the theater as a venue only for religious dramas, feeling it could be better suited for outdoor musical presentations. So although Mrs. Stevenson was responsible for finding the location and raising the money to purchase it, her proposal for its usage was rejected. Some

23

---

[7] See "A Tour of Hollywood," page 301; Evelyn Keyes, page 127; and Marie Windsor, page 211.

suggested selling the property instead of developing it, but C.E. Toberman insisted the site be saved for civic performances.

Mrs. Stevenson was not to be dissuaded from her vision, however, and elected to stage her *Pilgrimage Play* elsewhere. She amassed the necessary funds to erect a rudimentary structure capable of containing her presentation of the life of Christ. For accuracy, she traveled to Jerusalem to obtain authentic props for her show. Starring Henry Herbert as Jesus, the *Pilgrimage Play* was presented each summer at Mrs. Stevenson's Pilgrimage Play Theater until 1929, when it was destroyed by fire. A new, more substantial theater was built in ancient Judean style to replace the original, and presentations of the play continued there each summer for many decades. That theater still stands across the street from the Hollywood Bowl, and is now known as the John Anson Ford Theater.

The *New York Times* took note of *The Pilgrimage Play* when their forementioned roving reporter, C. Clayton Hutton, came to California in 1928 searching for the "sins of Hollywood," only to discover, somewhat to his disappointment, sobriety and sanctity. "We found the *Pilgrimage Play* telling its story of Golgotha, Calvary and the Cross, Hollywood's Oberammergau; an institution of divine uplift, telling the story of the divine Nazarene in the eternal hills beneath blinking stars," he wrote. "We who had set out to find the lair of Hollywood's sin listened to the Sermon on the Mount given in sublime voice by the Christus of Christine Weatherill Stevenson's great play."

Sadly, Mrs. Stevenson didn't live long enough to see the new theater built for which she was responsible. Her death in 1922 was deeply felt by the community, who responded by erecting in her honor a forty-foot-tall cross covered with thousands of light bulbs on the hill across from the theater. Decades later in 1965, this cross was replaced by the county by a steel cross covered by fluorescent bulbs, which

still stands above Hollywood to this day on Pilgrimage Hill, now separated from the Bowl by the overpasses of the Hollywood Freeway.

The Alliance proceeded with their plans of building a bowl in the Daisy Dell for musical events. But even prior to any building there, they began to present classical music performances in the still-wild dell, with audiences hiking through the thickets to get near the music, which they would take in by watching through the weeds and tall grass. In time all the brush was cleared away, and rows of long wooden benches were installed.

In 1922, the first Easter sunrise service was held in the bowl, starting an annual tradition which was enriched by a performance by the L.A. Philharmonic. This led in turn to a summer tradition of the Philharmonic at the Hollywood Bowl. Led by the efforts of Mrs. Artie Mason Carter, the Alliance instituted a "Symphony under the Stars" series, as well as the production of several operas, including *Carmen* and *Aida*. The beauty of the outdoor setting and the great natural acoustics of the bowl combined to form a classic outdoor venue even before the structure of the Bowl was in place.

The people of Hollywood built the bowl itself, donating the lumber and manpower to construct seats and a stage, under the volunteer direction of local architect Charles Richmond. Students from Hollywood High School presented a one-night performance of Shakespeare's *Twelfth Night*, and donated all the proceeds to the Bowl in order to purchase electrical equipment to power the lights. Soon audiences of 15,000 people would pour into the Bowl to hear symphonies conducted by great conductors such as Fritz Reiner, Sir Henry Wood, Rudolph Ganz, and others. Decades later the Bowl began to be used for the presentation of popular music concerts in addition to classical; most of the greatest artists of each generation have performed at the Bowl, including Frank Sinatra, the Beatles, Bob Dylan, Paul

24

Simon, the Beach Boys, Elton John, and Prince.

Lake Hollywood and the Mulholland Dam

In 1922, it was decided by William Mulholland that a large reservoir of water contained by a dam was needed in Hollywood, and Weid Canyon was selected as its ideal location. Situated high in the foothills beneath Mt. Lee, where the Hollywoodland sign would soon be erected, this deep dell once occupied by Ivar Weid and his sister Selma would soon be submerged beneath many thousand tons of water.

Not everyone felt it was such a wise, if even necessary, idea. Dr. Palmer opposed it for a number of reasons, not the least of which was that Weid Canyon provided an excellent secondary passageway between Hollywood and the San Fernando Valley, for which there was already a pressing need. "It was early in 1922 that the traffic in Cahuenga Pass became intolerable," he wrote. Familiar with Weid Canyon, the doctor suggested to the City Planning Commission that a road to the Valley through Weid Canyon was a natural choice. But he was informed Mulholland had already planned for a dam to be built there, making any throughway impossible.

Palmer then turned to the Hollywood Chamber of Commerce, persuading them to appoint a dam committee to explore the implications of building a dam in the Hollywood Hills. The committee called upon the members of the waterworks board. "Each stated that Mr. Mulholland had selected it for a dam," Dr. Palmer recalled, "and they deferred to his judgment."

But not one member of the board even bothered to look at this parcel of land before approving its usage as an immense reservoir. Palmer managed to persuade one board member, A.G. Bartlett, to view the site before giving his consent. Bartlett saw that a dam built on this site high above the flatlands of Hollywood would result in a flood of massive proportions if it gave way, and admitted its construction would pose a threat to Hollywood. Yet he still acceded to the judgment of Mulholland, whose prominence was so great at the time that few men chose to defy him.

The doctor was not easily dissuaded, however, putting up $1,000 of his own money, as well as collecting smaller contributions from his bank and other local businessmen, to hire a team of lawyers who could oppose the dam construction. His lawyers investigated the situation and informed him that the waterworks board had absolute power, which the DWP retains today; there existed no legal means by which to stop them.

Palmer also enlisted a consulting engineer, who reported that such a dam simply wasn't necessary as there were already existing dams that could hold sufficient amounts of water. Armed with this report and the support of both the San Fernando Valley and Hollywood Chambers of Commerce, Palmer arranged for a meeting between his dam committee, Mulholland and the waterworks board. None of the board members bothered to attend, much to the doctor's dismay, but the meeting ensued nonetheless. Palmer delivered his findings and expected some reasonable defense of the dam from Mulholland. None was forthcoming. Like New York City planner Robert Moses' ability to create massive urban structures untouched by intense public opposition, Mulholland's power was too prodigious to be challenged. "His only argument was that he had decided to build the dam there," Palmer recalled.

By 1923, L.A. was in the midst of securing a steady water supply by buying out most of the remaining farms in the Owens Valley and abandoning them, so as to increase the water available to rush down into the aqueduct. This severely ravaged the populations of several small towns, such as Bishop, and left shops and businesses there without any customers to keep them afloat. To fight this, many Owens Valley farmers resorted to attempts to destroy the aqueduct that had decimated their lives. "Farmers, feeling hoodwinked and going belly-up, dynamited dams and ditches, and their children danced with joy at the manmade thunder," wrote Patt Morrison. "Once, near Lone Pine, farmers shut down the aqueduct, and for four days, L.A. went thirsty." Though it was never totally put out of commission, the aqueduct was dynamited on several occasions between 1924 and 1927.

According to historian Dr. Paul Soifer, part of Mulholland's insistence on building a dam in Hollywood came from a reaction to these attacks on the aqueduct. "He wanted reservoirs within city limits," Soifer said, "that would guarantee a year's water supply if the aqueduct was put permanently out of commission. That was the thinking behind the Mulholland Dam and the St. Francis Dam."

When Mulholland was later pressed by his own bureau to provide the reasons behind his choice of the Weid Canyon location, he answered that its high elevation in the hills would allow gravity to greatly increase existing water pressure to the homes below, as well as provide improved fire protection throughout the foothill district. He also added, with unexpected religiosity, "Engineers recognize that reservoir sites are only made by God and must be used by men where they are found."

There was no real reason, at this point in time, to doubt his wisdom and ability. As the water board noted in their review of this project prior to construction, "Chief Engineer Mulholland, recognized as one of America's greatest engineers, has constructed more than a dozen dams along the Aqueduct line alone, none of which have ever failed."

Mulholland, as was his way, expressed nothing but steely confidence in his ability to circumvent nature with the power of technology. "If the proposed Weid Canyon dam should ever break or weaken in the slightest detail," he wrote in 1923, "it would establish a world's record, since there has never been a recorded instance of that mighty type failing in any degree."

In spite of such speculation, Hollywood residents continued to be concerned by the prospect of a reservoir looming over their heads. As articles printed in the local *Hollywood News* noted as early as 1921, the ramifications of constructing this dam included risks that were not only physical, but also financial and psychological. "Any dam, however safe, would have such a psychological effect as to depreciate the value of the property lying in the (path) of the water . . . from the Hollywood-Cahuenga District . . . for two miles toward the sea . . . should the dam ever go out. This depression (of values) would approximate 10 percent. . . . If a severe earthquake shock should come the reservoir MAY break and Hollywood should not be asked to take that chance."

Regardless of these admonitions, Mulholland was given free reign to build the dam to his own specifications. The only deviation from his design was a substantial reduction in the overall capacity of the dam, from 7,500 acre feet to 4,250 acre feet of water.

Construction of a mammoth, curved concrete embankment commenced in August of 1923 and continued until December of 1924. At a height of 200 feet, it rose to a height taller than any other structure then standing in all of Los Angeles. Its crest was appointed with curved arches separated by a succession of stone busts depicting the California brown bear, which is featured on the state flag. Officially called Mulholland Dam by the city, Mulholland preferred for it to be known by a name that called attention not to the structure itself, but to the blue bayou that he had created in the canyon, Lake Hollywood.

Ironically, that aspect of the dam that many recognized as its most severe liability, its hillside position above Hollywood, was heralded as a distinctive accomplishment in the water bureau's press releases of the day: "What is said to be the most unique feature in connection with the dam is that it is situated in the midst of a great metropolitan area and serves to store water in a reservoir which stands at an elevation much higher than the surrounding city. The high altitude of the Hollywood reservoir makes it possible for the water bureau to serve practically the entire Hollywood foothill area by gravity flow."

St. Patrick's Day of 1925 was declared a day of celebration in honor of Mulholland's monumental contribution to Hollywood. At a ceremony on the sloping bridge of the dam, Mulholland extended great gratitude to his chief engineer and co-designer, H.L. Jacques, and expressed his belief that this was his most beautiful creation to date. He spoke of colleagues who complained that his other dams had all the design appeal of "an old woman's apron—an object of utility, but not of beauty." But Mulholland felt the sweeping curve of the Hollywood dam achieved a grandeur none of his previous dams possessed. "In this job," he said, "I think I may take a little pardonable pride."

In 1924, prior to the completion of his Hollywood dam, Mulholland began construction of his largest project, the St. Francis Dam in San Francisquito canyon, north of L.A in what is today the community of Valencia. It was designed as a twin to the new Mulholland Dam being built above Hollywood.

The St. Francis Dam was completed on March 12, 1926. Exactly two years after the day of its completion it was filled to total capacity. For reasons then unknown, this caused a catastrophe of horrendous proportions, the incessant, total collapse of the dam. A torrential deluge was unleashed across the Santa Clara Valley in Ventura County. Twelve billion gallons of water came cascading out, creating a tidal wall of water nearly a hundred feet high which roared from the reservoir, destroying towns and farmlands as it surged unstoppable for some six hours, eventually covering fifty-five miles of land.

The waters met the Santa Clara River at Castaic Junction and headed west toward the Pacific, leveling the towns of Piru, Fillmore, Santa Paula, Saticoy, and much of Ventura before finally merging into the sea. More than 400 people lost their lives, many of whom were never found. The devastation was vast and terrible, as thousands of animals, buildings, cars and people all were swept up by the dreadful force of the water. Mulholland's eerily ironic prediction that such a failure would result in a "world record" was accurate: It was the most severe civil engineering failure in American history.

Experts were unable to determine the cause of the dam's collapse. Mulholland, who was then seventy-two years old, publicly took full blame for the failure, but privately suspected some kind of sabotage as its source, most likely the work of displaced Owens Valley farmers.

This catastrophe caused much understandable consternation among Hollywood residents fearing that the Mulholland Dam would also go the way of the St. Francis. Groups formed that urged the city to empty the lake at once, and immediately discontinue the use of the dam. Hundreds of homeowners in the neighborhood of Holly Drive, which lies directly below the dam, abandoned their homes and put them up for sale, even though the value of their property had plummeted since the St. Francis disaster. "The many beautiful homes that have been abandoned on Holly Drive," wrote David Horsley in a letter to the Board of Education, "and the hundred for sale signs that are on the property in the streets immediately under the dam will convince you that the fear of a disaster is universal amongst those whose lives and property would be the first to get the flood."

Many prominent members of the

Hollywood community sought various avenues of activism in order to oppose the continued use of the dam. The aforementioned David Horsley, who with his brother William started the Nestor film company, brought a lawsuit against the city demanding that the water be removed from the dam. To garner public support for this movement, he began publishing a weekly newspaper called the *Hollywood Dam News* that accused the water bureau of placing all of Hollywood at immense, unnecessary risk. He also advanced the contention that there were obvious and ulterior motives at play that influenced Mulholland's choice of this location for the dam. "Among the many subdivisions of 1924 was one called Hollywoodland, which didn't click," Horsley wrote, "and some bright mind got the idea that if it had a lake for the hillside suckers to look at, it might be put over. So the brilliant scheme was hatched of getting the water department to buy part of the land for $800,000 and build a dam (out of your money and mine), at a cost of $1,200,000."

This contention—that the location of the lake was in part chosen at the desire of Hollywoodland's developers—is not outlandish. One of the chief developers of the Hollywoodland development—Harry Chandler—was also an integral part of the land syndicate that bought out much of the San Fernando Valley at low rates prior to the construction of the aqueduct. As previously mentioned, Chandler's partner Moses Sherman was an influential member of the L.A. Board of Water Commissioners.

David Horsley would occasionally publish humorous anecdotes that also succeeded in expressing his ongoing opposition to the dam, such as the account of a Scottish businessman who came to Hollywood precisely because the most important American branch of his business had its headquarters in Hollywood, in the direct line of the flood which would ensue if the dam failed. He

stayed at the Hollywood Athletic Club on Sunset, where his room on the seventh floor faced north toward the Hollywood hills. In those days the stone-white dam was visually prominent in the hills, as it had yet to be covered by the grove of trees that obscures its view today. The Scotsman was terrified by the prospect of doom that would be his if the dam broke during this visit. His associates tried and failed to reassure him by telling him the dam would never break, unless, of course, there was an earthquake.

Then, on September 11, 1928, Hollywood was hit hard by a severe earthquake. "He was in the bathroom enjoying his morning's bath," wrote Horsley of his Scottish friend, "when without warning there came a violent swaying from east to west, with a vicious slap at each end of the swing that nearly snapped his head off. ... He rushed half clad to the telephone and demanded . . . accommodations on the first train for points east, without daring to cast a look over his shivering shoulder at that terrible Mulholland Dam."

Unsure how to assuage the fears of the public without totally forsaking the use of the dam, the water bureau brought in a team of consulting engineers and geologists to examine its structure and foundation, and offer reports on how best to proceed. They also ordered an urgent reduction in its water level, a decision that some experts said probably saved it from eventual failure.

Internal department records preserved from this time reveal that the panels of experts arrived at no unanimity of opinion about the dam's safety. Some pointed to numerous inherent problems with its structure, including "insufficient base width; no allowance made in the design for uplift or earthquake stresses; inferior concrete and foundation rock . . . no inspection galleries; no contraction joints; foundation not properly terraced and stepped to provide against sliding of the dam on its foundation," and more.

Others felt that the dam was in no danger whatsoever. "From the geological point of view, with full consideration of the possibility of future fault-movements and earthquakes," wrote Dr. F.L. Ransome, "it is concluded that the Mulholland Dam occupies an excellent site."

Still others, such as the team of Hill, McDonnell & Hill, filed the alarming opinion that a significant earthquake would topple the dam, but it wouldn't really matter: "Any seismic disturbance which would seriously affect the dam would be of such intensity as to *destroy Hollywood completely* and render the failure of the dam of little consequence."

In order to alleviate the perceived risk of the dam, a decision was made to hide it from the public, who were expected to forget about the peril of if they didn't face it each day. A plan was proposed and adopted to cover the entire front facade of the dam with many tons of soil, on which ascending terraces of trees and shrubs would be planted.

Evidently, the driving reasons for this procedure was much more for the psychological well-being of residents near the dam than for any practical benefits. "The Department felt, to an extent, that it was a P.R. gesture to cover the facade," said Dr. Paul Soifer. "They felt that the dam was safe, that they really didn't have to do anything, but there was so much public concern, and they were getting so much bad press from St. Francis and the Owens Valley all coming together, that it was easier to do that, to cover it with an earthen blanket."

According to a report submitted to the DWP in 1930 by State Engineer Edward Hyatt, although such an earthen covering would have some practical benefits, it could also create further problems. "You will note that the stresses at the upstream . . . are slightly increased by the blanket. . . . You will also note that the vertical pressures, or the pressures on the rock of the foundation, at the downstream too . . . are likewise slightly increased by the building of the blanket."

Chief Engineer Van Norman, who was Mulholland's successor, wrote to the water board stating that he had reviewed the report of the state engineer and other experts and arrived at the conclusion that although the foundation rock on which the dam is built "is affected by small fault slips, its physical condition is otherwise good." He also wrote that "filling the canyon below the dam and planting shrubs and trees would change the apparent menace to a pleasing view carrying no suggestion of a dam. . . . The proposed embankment of mixed rock and earth, sufficiently drained, placed against the downstream face of the Hollywood Dam to elevation 715 feet will increase the safety of the dam."

The Mulholland Dam was completely closed down between 1932 and 1934, at which time 300,000 cubic yards of earth was used to cover the facade of the dam, which was also substantially fortified and retrofitted. An additional reservoir of smaller size was subsequently built at the north section of Lake Hollywood to provide additional reservoir capacity.

In a June 1934 edition of *Intake*, the in-house newspaper published by the DWP, is a photo of the previously imperial facade covered nearly to its crest with five immense terraces of barren earth buttressed in giant steps against the dam like an ancient pyramid. The caption of the photo notably omits any mention of Mulholland, and advances the party line that such a precaution, though helpful, was unnecessary: "Hollywood Dam as it appears with the completed earth fill blanketing its face . . . The fill was made to allay unfounded fears of Hollywood residents. Repeated investigations by leading consulting engineers of the nation have testified to the dam's stability."

Covering the immense dam with the earthen blanket took a full year, after which came the planting of a forest of trees and shrubs there. According to internal records from the DWP dated

1933, this new landscape included deodars and Arizona cypress on the upper terrace, Arizona cypress on the second terrace, evergreens on the third, hemlocks and pines on the fourth, and arbor vita on the lowest terrace. Heavy pines and oaks were planted at the base of the dam.

Rogers and other experts expressed a certainty that had the St. Francis Dam disaster never occurred, there would have been no need to retrofit the Hollywood reservoir, and it probably would have failed eventually. If any good could possibly have emerged from this tragedy, this is it. Alterations to the original design and capacity have rescued the Mulholland Dam thus far from any problems. The dam has withstood many earthquakes since that date, including the powerful Northridge quake of 1994 which wrought much damage throughout Hollywood and all of Los Angeles. As this author and other Hollywood residents who live near the lake recall, the dam was immediately scrutinized by an assembly of police helicopters just minutes following that quake, as it is following any earthquake or aftershock in the region.

The St. Francis Dam disaster and ensuing controversy ruined Mulholland. He was tried for murder, and although acquitted, his once-great reputation was toppled. He'd been publicly crucified for this disaster by a fervent prosecutor, and shunned by those who once revered him. He retired in 1928 and died only a few years later, after a dark passage of grief and isolation.

Although Mulholland's colleagues did not consider him to blame for the St. Francis collapse, he remained such a public relations liability that subsequent group photos of DWP managers were doctored before being printed in *Intake* so that Mulholland's image was eliminated.

Only in recent years, due to the work of the engineer J. David Rogers, has it been determined that the St. Francis failed because its left abutment was built directly over an active fault in the earth—a Paleolithic landslide—which was triggered by the full weight of the dam when it was filled to capacity. But this was information impossible for Mulholland to have attained with the technology of the times. The standard procedure of conducting an intensive geologic survey of the area prior to construction simply wasn't protocol in Mulholland's day as it is today.

As one might guess, Lake Hollywood and the dam have been used in countless TV shows and movies, including the classic film about the history of the Los Angeles waterworks, *Chinatown*, directed by Roman Polanski and starring Jack Nicholson, which deals with many of the myths of L.A's water wars and well as perpetuating some new ones of its own. There's also *Earthquake*, starring Charlton Heston and Ava Gardner, which features the dam more prominently than any other film, and in which the memorable lines are uttered, *"If this dam breaks, there won't be nothing between here and Wilshire Boulevard left to burn,"* only minutes before the unthinkable does occur, and Hollywood is flooded when the Mulholland Dam fails.

In real life, the Mulholland Dam, despite its potential dangers, has given birth to a beautiful, wooded oasis in the Hollywood hills, just over three miles in diameter around the eternally sparkling blue lake. It's become somewhat of a wilderness refuge over the years, where one can regularly see deer, coyotes, hawks and even turtles. To this day, it remains one of the loveliest and most peaceful places in all of Hollywood.[8]

---

[8] It also offers open access to one of L.A.'s main reservoirs, the potential target of terrorists attempting to affect the water or harm the dam. Since the terrorist attacks of September 11, 2001 on the World Trade Center in New York and the Pentagon in Washington, D.C., extra security efforts in Los Angeles resulted in a closure of Lake Hollywood to the public for several months.

The Origins of the Studios

Throughout the teens and into the twenties, a bevy of small, independent movie companies set up shop in Hollywood, building a veritable shantytown of tiny studios around the nexus of Sunset & Gower. Producing mostly short comedies and westerns, few of these companies were able to stay financially solvent, which is the reason this region became known as Poverty Row. Since these and other studios needed a constant influx of experienced cowboys for their Westerns, these cowboys would congregate near the site of the former Blondeau Tavern at the corner of Sunset & Gower. Their perpetual presence at that intersection inspired the locals to dub it the Gower Gulch, a name that extends to the small mall which stands there today.

Paulis, Waldorf, Quality, Loftus, Sterling, L-ko, Century, Wilnat, Wade, Bischoff, Snub-Pollard, Chadwick. These are but some of the companies on the long list of Poverty Row studios that set up shop only to fold it up shortly thereafter, lasting little longer than the span of one of their own one-reel movies.

United Artists, Columbia, Paramount, Warner Brothers, 20th Century Fox, RKO. These are companies that were more fortunate and succeeded in creating popular movies that scored with the public. They ultimately evolved into industry giants that reigned supreme for successive decades.

United Artists

United Artists was formed in 1919 by the union of Charlie Chaplin, Douglas Fairbanks, Mary Pickford, and the director D.W. Griffith. Their concept was to create a company that could finance and distribute each of their independent productions. Along these lines, they built their own

independent kingdoms. Mary Pickford and Douglas Fairbanks took over the Jesse D. Hampton studio on the north side of Santa Monica Boulevard just west of La Brea, and renamed it the Pickford-Fairbanks studio. Many of Fairbanks most famous roles were created here in films such as Robin Hood, The Thief of Baghdad, and others.[9]

Chaplin had already erected a studio for himself at La Brea & Sunset, where it still stands to this day.[10] He bought a five-acre orchard for $35,000, and designed his studio there to resemble a row of English country homes. Many of his masterpieces were created here, including Modern Times, City Lights, A Dog's Life (1918), Shoulder Arms (1918), Pay Day (1922), The Pilgrim (1923), The Circus (1928), and one of his final films, Limelight (1953), the only movie in which Chaplin and Buster Keaton appeared together.

"At the end of the Mutual Contract I was anxious to get started with First National, but we had no studio," Chaplin wrote in his autobiography. "I decided to buy land in Hollywood and build one. The site was the corner of Sunset and La Brea and had a very fine ten-room house and five acres of lemon, orange and peach trees. We built a perfect unit, complete with developing plant, cutting room and offices."

31

Columbia

Columbia rose to prominence when two brothers, Harry and Jack Cohn, teamed up with Joe Brandt to form their own company. At first it was the CBC Film Sales Corporation, but when it was pointed out that CBC stands for corned beef and cabbage, a shorter and more refined sounding name was adopted. They purchased what was then the California

[9] This studio eventually became known as the Samuel Goldwyn studios when Goldwyn, who began by renting space here in 1924 from Mary Pickford, gradually took over the entire studio, even entering into a legal skirmish with Pickford to officially rename it in honor of himself.

[10] For more on Chaplin's studio, see "A Tour of Hollywood," page 306; and David Raksin, page 69.

Movie Company lot at Sunset & Gower, and from there began to slowly expand, gradually acquiring most of the nearby Poverty Row studios.

Columbia went on to produce both classics and B-movies throughout the years, from the Three Stooges movies to It Happened One Night in 1939 to Lawrence of Arabia in 1962. Other Columbia classics include Born Yesterday (1950), From Here to Eternity (1953), On the Waterfront (1954), The Caine Mutiny (1954, 1962), Bye Bye Birdie (1963), Dr. Strangelove, Fail Safe (1964), Guess Who's Coming to Dinner (1967), and Funny Girl (1968). Columbia didn't contract stars in the way the other studios did, but essentially borrowed various stars from all the studios. Though Clark Gable was an MGM actor, for example, Columbia used him for It Happened One Night, which was the film that launched his stardom. Other stars who appeared in the movies of Columbia include Marlon Brando, Claudette Colbert, Jimmy Stewart, Judy Holiday, William Holden, Peter O'Toole, Omar Sharif, Henry Fonda, Sidney Poitier, Spencer Tracy, Katharine Hepburn, and Barbra Streisand.

20th Century Fox

20th Century Fox was created when William Fox, who made his first film Life's Shop Window in 1914 in Staten Island, New York, migrated to California in late 1915, and settled at first into the former Selig Studio in Edendale. The success of his comedies quickly created a need for a larger studio, and in 1916, Fox acquired the Thomas Dixon Studio on the northwest corner of Sunset & Western. They soon required even more space, and so constructed additional studios on acreage purchased on the other side of Sunset.

Fox pioneered the famous Movietone Newsreels that preceded the movies, presenting news of the day in a newly visual style, which had a profound influence on the look of TV newscasts to come. In 1928 Fox opened their studios in Century City on 250 acres of ranch land formerly

owned by the Western movie star Tom Mix. In 1935, Fox merged with Darryl Zanuck's Twentieth Century Pictures to become 20th Century Fox.

Many time-honored films emerged from Fox, including The Grapes of Wrath (1940), Rebecca (1940), Song of Bernadette (1943), Laura (1944), State Fair (1945), the original Miracle on 34th Street (1947), All about Eve (1950), Cleopatra (1963), The Sound of Music (1965), Hello Dolly (1969), Patton (1970), M*A*S*H (1970), and The French Connection (1971). They also released some of the most popular films of recent times, including Star Wars (1977), The Empire Strikes Back (1980), and Titanic (1998). Fox also produced the Sherlock Holmes serial starring Basil Rathbone, the original Planet of the Apes series, and the motion picture debut of Elvis Presley, Love Me Tender (1956).

The stars of Fox films include Tyrone Power, Shirley Temple, Elizabeth Taylor, Henry Fonda, Marilyn Monroe, Jane Russell, Richard Burton, Natalie Wood, Betty Grable, Jean Harlow, Sonja Henie, Gregory Peck, Don Ameche, Barbra Streisand, and many others. Today, on the former backlots of their West L.A. studio stands the towers and office buildings of Century City.

Warner Brothers

The origins of the Warner Brothers company trace back to 1918, when the four brothers Warner—Harry, Jack, Sam and Albert—made their first feature, a popular success entitled My Four Years in Germany. The brothers then built a massive studio with immense sound stages, all situated respectably at 5858 Sunset Boulevard behind a formal Colonial facade that resembled a Southern plantation manor more than a movie studio.

When the popularity of their films resulted in a need for more space, they bought the old Vitagraph studio on Prospect in east Hollywood. Much of the Warners' greatest accomplishments, most notably the transition from silents into sound, occurred at their first studio on Sunset. It's there that their first official

32

talking picture, or "talkie," was created. In 1926 they pioneered the use of synchronized sound in film, effectively linking music and sound effects to the action on the screen in the movie *Don Juan*. Less than a year later in 1927 they released the first film that also incorporated synchronized dialogue, *The Jazz Singer*. Starring the beloved singer Al Jolson, it quickly became an enormous success.

In 1928, recognizing the need for larger studios spacious enough for the new equipment of talkies, Warner Brothers took over the former studios of First National on Barham Boulevard in nearby Burbank, which remains the center of their empire to this day.

Through the years Warner Brothers provided a contrast to the bright Technicolor films of other studios by creating countless film noir gems, and other classic films in beautiful black-and-white, such as *Casablanca*, *The Maltese Falcon*, and *The Big Sleep*, all starring Humphrey Bogart, as well as *The Public Enemy* with Jimmy Cagney, shot in 1921, *The Story of Louis Pasteur* (1936), *The Life of Emile Zola* (1937), and *The Treasure of Sierra Madre* (1948).

The stars of Warner Brothers, in addition to Bogart and Cagney, included Ingrid Bergman, Errol Flynn, John Barrymore, Edward G. Robinson, Bette Davis, Barbara Stanwyck, Dick Powell, George Raft, Loretta Young, Douglas Fairbanks Jr., Joan Crawford, Burt Lancaster, Paul Muni, Carole Lombard, Gary Cooper, Dennis Morgan, Peter Lorre, Cary Grant, Henry Fonda, Doris Day, and Rin Tin Tin. Ronald Reagan made his first film, *Love in the Air*, in 1937 at Warners.

Paramount

Paramount, which began its life as the Famous Players–Lasky Corporation, also outgrew their original studio space adjoining the old barn on Vine. Electing to remain within Hollywood, they purchased the massive United Studios at Marathon & Van Ness, just north of Melrose. Their former studio was completely

laid to waste, with the fortunate exception of the barn itself, which was saved and moved to their new lot, where it was used over the years for a variety of purposes, including a stint as the studio gymnasium. Within a few years of the move their name was changed to Paramount–Famous Lasky and later to Paramount Publix.

By 1930, the name became simply Paramount Pictures, as it has remained ever since. Many of Hollywood's most celebrated movies and movie stars emanated from Paramount: Valentino in *The Sheik* in 1921, and the first film to win the Academy Award for Best Picture, *Wings*, in 1927.

Paramount was the home of directors such as Cecil B. DeMille and D.W. Griffith, and stars that have included Mary Pickford, Clara Bow, Gary Cooper, and Marlene Dietrich. Countless classics have been made here, including Billy Wilder's *Sunset Boulevard* (1950), starring William Holden and Gloria Swanson, *White Christmas* (1954), *True Grit* (1969), *The Godfather* (1972) and *Chinatown* (1974). It's here that the Marx Brothers filmed *Duck Soup* and *Coconuts*, Alfred Hitchcock filmed *Rear Window* (1954) and *Vertigo* (1958), and Bob Hope and Bing Crosby shot their road movies, Jerry Lewis and Dean Martin made all seventeen of their films here, and Elvis Presley made both *Blue Hawaii* and *Girls, Girls, Girls*.

"Paramount was like a delightful country club at the time," said screenwriter Richard Maibaum of his stint there in the late forties. "It was the days of Brackett and Wilder and *Sunset Boulevard* and all the other wonderful pictures and good writers. The atmosphere around the place was so good, and of course, the motion picture business was so easy. There was no such thing as the terrible phenomenon called television. Which really didn't have any impact until 1949, when it hit us like a ton of bricks."

For many, Paramount endures as the essential Hollywood studio, the one that still best represents that great juncture of

33

romance, glamour and illusion that typi-
fied the legendary studios of the past. As
the famed director Ernst Lubitsch once
said, "I've been to Paris, France and I've
been to Paris, Paramount. Paris, Paramount is better."

RKO

The origins of RKO date back to 1925,
when Joseph Kennedy, the father of U.S.
President John Kennedy, bought a British
film company called FBO for $1 million.
He teamed up with RCA president David
Sarnoff, who merged his company with
Kennedy's in the hope of cashing in on the
developing craze of talking pictures. RKO
was created by this merger, and their first
release was a talkie called Syncopation. In the
thirties RKO merged with Pathe Pictures
and began distributing the films of other
companies, most prominently the animated movies of the Disney company, Snow
White and Fantasia. In 1941, RKO released
Citizen Kane.

In 1948, Howard Hughes purchased
929,000 shares of RKO stock and thus
took control of this major company. He
immediately instituted layoffs of more
than two-thirds of all RKO employees, and
also started selling the rights to many of
the most famous RKO films. He fired
another 1,000 RKO employees in 1952
whom he suspected of being communists.
Three years later, after essentially decimating a once great studio, Hughes sold
RKO to General Teleradio, Inc., a subsidiary of General Tire and Rubber.

The RKO lot was sold to Desilu Productions in 1957 for television production
of "I Love Lucy," which was a far better
fate for it than the other considered alternative, turning it into a tire manufacturing
plant. In 1958, Paramount extended their
own studio by taking over the former RKO
property. Though they initially painted
over the trademark RKO globe which juts
out from the studio at the intersection of
Gower & Melrose, in later years it was
repainted back to its original colors, as it
remains today.

In its heyday, RKO was one of Holly-
wood's greatest studios, a home to many
of the world's greatest directors, such as
John Ford, Alfred Hitchcock and Orson
Welles, who made his classic Citizen Kane,
considered by many to be the greatest
American film ever, at RKO. Stars of RKO
movies included Katharine Hepburn, Cary
Grant, Ingrid Bergman, Robert Mitchum,
Bette Davis and Lucille Ball.

Other classic RKO films include It's a
Wonderful Life, starring Jimmy Stewart, as
well as King Kong, The Hunchback of Notre Dame,
The Bells of St. Mary's, The Best Years of Our Lives,
and a series of musicals starring Fred
Astaire and Ginger Rogers.

"Although RKO was a major studio
with a host of stars, compared to MGM it
was a minor major studio," said the
screenwriter Allan Scott (father of Pippa
Scott, see page 279) in an interview with
Pat McGilligan. "[RKO] did not make
huge, plush pictures like MGM or gangster
melodramas like Warner Brothers, but it
was known for its 'classy pictures.' My first
office at RKO was in the newly erected
building called 'The New Writers'
Building'—very pleasant, large paneled
woodwork offices with a room for one's
secretary. Between assignments you'd
come in, gossip, have lunch, wander
around the lot, talk with other writers—a
nice life. . . . We laughed together, lunched
together, and met together at night."

RKO, as Scott said, specialized in no
singular genre but created classics across
the board, including the musical Top Hat,
the western She Wore a Yellow Ribbon, romantic
comedies such as Bringing Up Baby, the film
noir Murder, My Sweet, and horror films such
as Invasion of the Body Snatchers.

The Building Boom

The blossoming of these film companies within Hollywood changed the look
and feel of this little town forever. "Studios
of unbelievable magnitude, erected at
expenditures that stagger the imagination,
are now far-flung in a circle that recognizes Hollywood as its center," wrote Lau-

rence Hill in 1929. "Throughout the world, wherever the film flickers, the name of Hollywood is a household word."

A new building boom of office buildings, theaters, hotels and apartment houses ensued between 1921 to 1931, forever altering the landscape of physical Hollywood. Significant office buildings that have defined the look of Hollywood Boulevard for decades were built at this time, including the Taft Building near Hollywood & Vine, the Security First National Bank Building at Hollywood & Highland, the Security Trust and Savings Building at Hollywood & Cahuenga, and the Guaranty Bank building at Hollywood & Ivar. Hollywood Boulevard, once a serene, residential row of old Victorians, was transformed into the thriving center of a new metropolis.

Many of Hollywood's most enduring hotels and apartments also arose during these years, including the Garden Court Apartments, the Garden of Allah, The Christie Hotel, the Knickerbocker, the Plaza, the Roosevelt, and the Chateau Elysee.

The Christie Hotel was built in 1922 to provide a luxurious inn for the new royalty of Hollywood, movie folk. Owned by the same Christies who owned the Nestor movie studios, it was the very first hotel in the community to offer rooms that each came with a private bath, an innovation that was a tremendous luxury at the time. Designed in a distinctive Georgian style by the architect Arthur B. Kelley, it's an entirely unique building on the boulevard, and its distinction remains to this day, though it's no longer used as a hotel.

The Garden of Allah[11] was the creation of Alla Nazimova, a Russian-born actress from Yalta who first came to Hollywood in 1918 to star in silent films. In 1920, for $50,000, she purchased a Spanish Revival house on Sunset Boulevard surrounded by orange groves, vineyards, and a field of ferns, bamboo, banana, poplar and cedar

trees. She received a loan to finance the construction of a series of twenty-five separate two-story, stucco bungalows, each containing two apartments, all arranged around one of the most famous swimming pools in all of Hollywood; shaped like a figure eight, it was designed to resemble the Black Sea of her childhood.

The Garden opened as a hotel on January 9, 1927, launched by a wild, eighteen hour party that featured such stars as Clara Bow, John Barrymore, Francis X. Bushman, Marlene Deitrich, and Jack Dempsey, the boxer.[12] Until the late forties, it was one of Hollywood's most beloved hotels, the chosen residence of authors such as Scott Fitzgerald, Robert Benchley and Dorothy Parker.

The Chateau Elysee was constructed between 1928 and 1929 on Franklin at Bronson, where the director Thomas Ince had previously lived in a modest bungalow. Long considered one of Hollywood's grandest and most beautiful estates, the Chateau was built by Randolph Hearst for Ince's widow, after Ince was mysteriously murdered aboard Hearst's yacht, a crime that remains unsolved. It was the first resident hotel in Hollywood, and the temporary home of many movie stars, including Carole Lombard, Cary Grant, George Burns and Gracie Allen, Douglas Fairbanks Jr., Ginger Rogers, as well as the creator of *Tarzan*, Edgar Rice Burroughs. Burroughs ultimately bought a large parcel of land out in the valley, which he named his Tarzana ranch, a name that still applies to the modern suburb that was developed there.

The Knickerbocker Hotel was built in 1925 soon after the population of Hollywood exploded. On Ivar Avenue just north of Hollywood Boulevard, it was designed by the architect E.M. Frasier in 1923 in the luxurious Renaissance Revival/Beaux Arts style, and was a glamorous hotel that was popular with celebrities from both coasts.

35

---

[11] For more information on *The Garden of Allah*, see "A Tour of Hollywood," pages 315.
[12] Starr, *Material Dreams*.

Rudy Vallee, Gloria Swanson, Dick Powell, Bette Davis, and Errol Flynn all lived here, and both Frank Sinatra and Elvis Presley stayed here many times. Harry Houdini also stayed here when he came to Hollywood, and his widow held a seance for him here on the roof in 1936. The Knickerbocker was also the sad home of D.W. Griffith, who lived his last years here, mostly forgotten by the general public.

Constructed in 1927, The Roosevelt Hotel was designed by C.E. Toberman, and was owned originally by silent stars Mary Pickford and Douglas Fairbanks and the director Louis B. Mayer. The very first Academy Awards banquet was held here in the hotel's Blossom Room in 1929. Countless legends stayed here over the years, including Marilyn Monroe, who posed for her first-ever commercial photo shoot by the pool, as well as Clark Gable, Montgomery Clift, Carole Lombard and others.

The hotel's night club, the Cinegrill, continues to present top music acts to this day, and provided a showcase for such stars as Mary Martin. Other celebrities were frequently found at the bar and in the audience of the Cinegrill, including Frank Capra, Dick Powell, W.C. Fields, Errol Flynn, and Ronald Reagan.

The twenties was also the decade in which several classic movie palaces now known the world over were erected on Hollywood Boulevard. Two of the most significant are the Egyptian and the Chinese Theaters, both of which were created by Sid Grauman. Grauman was an Indiana native who first made a living by selling newspapers to Alaskan miners during the Klondike gold rush of 1896. He was a man of distinct style and vision, and a great lover of practical jokes. He had an elfin charm, with wild, frizzy hair parted down the middle. He'd go to great lengths to perfect a practical joke, once even to the extent of hiring actors to pose as pilots on a plane, run down the aisle and parachute out, all to get a rise out of the director Ernst Lubitsch, who was already terrified to fly. It worked better than intended;

Lubitsch was so frightened he had a minor heart attack.

On another occasion, Grauman phoned Charlie Chaplin in a panic to say that he'd discovered a dead woman in his hotel room. Chaplin rushed over to Grauman's room, where a female corpse was clearly visible beneath bloody sheets. Chaplin insisted they do the honorable thing and call the police instantly. But Grauman resisted, crying that he didn't want a scandal. The increasingly frantic Chaplin finally relented when Sid showed him that the dead woman was really just a dummy covered in ketchup. Evidently, there was no gag too elaborate for Sid.

Grauman had a vision of creating movie palaces as magical as the movies themselves. The initial embodiment of this vision in Los Angeles was not in Hollywood but downtown L.A., where Grauman spent an unprecedented $1 million to construct the grand Metropolitan Theater.

But Grauman had his eye on Hollywood Boulevard, which would forever be changed by his vision. His next creation was the Egyptian Theater. Designed by C.E. Toberman in 1922 in the time of the popular craze caused by the discovery of the ancient Egyptian tomb of King Tutankhamen, it featured stationed guards attired in ancient Egyptian outfits, hieroglyphic murals, a sunburst ceiling and a giant scarab above the stage. It was here that Grauman invented not only a palatial theater, but also a historic concept: the Hollywood premiere, designed to be as flashy and glamorous as the movies were magical, and providing that rare opportunity for the public to see movie stars in the flesh. His inaugural premiere was for the film *Robin Hood* starring Douglas Fairbanks. Fairbanks' entrance, as Grauman knew, was as dramatic as anything on the screen itself. Here suddenly was a man— Grauman—who could make a bridge between those magic people on the screen, and those "marvelous people in the dark," as the character of Norma

Desmond calls them in *Sunset Boulevard*. In 1923, Cecil B. DeMille premiered *The Ten Commandments* at the Egyptian.

Extending his new tradition of celebrating the modern American spectacle of the movies with the ancient spectacles of foreign lands, Grauman soon opened another movie palace on Hollywood Boulevard just a few blocks west of the Egyptian. Also designed by Toberman, the Chinese Theater quickly became Grauman's most lasting and cherished contribution to the mythic fabric of Hollywood life, and may be the most famous movie theater in the world. Originally envisioned as a museum of Chinese history and art as well as a movie theater, it became more theater than museum. But it was a remarkable shrine of a theater, ornamented with beautifully rendered Oriental murals, a carved ceiling and detailed columns, a large pagoda with a red roof, punctuated by giant dragons. Flanking the main entrance to the theater were two immense Ming dynasty "heaven dogs," as Grauman called them, which were identified by a plaque that read:

> *Half lion and half dog these sacred sentinels stood guard for many centuries at a Ming tomb in China. These massive monsters surnamed the dogs of Foo or Buddha combined leonine ferocity with dog-like devotion and served to terrify the transgressors and inspire the righteous.*

Construction of the Chinese Theater commenced on Armistice Day, November 11, 1925, when the actress Anna Mae Wong drove the first rivet into its steel girders. It opened on May 18, 1927. The first film to be shown on its screen was Cecil B. DeMille's religious extravaganza, *King of Kings*.

But even more famous than the films shown there is the fabled forecourt of the Chinese Theater, into which countless movie stars through the decades have placed their footprints, handprints and autographs in segments of wet cement. The origin of this tradition is the subject of much debate, and a great example of the mix of myth and misinformation at the heart of Hollywood history.

Perhaps the most famous and least-reliable of these accounts is that which Grauman personally perpetuated, that the movie star Norma Talmadge accidentally sparked the tradition by stepping out of a car directly into the forecourt's newly laid wet cement. The same exact scenario has also been suggested but substitutes Mary Pickford for Norma Talmadge. Pickford's husband Charles "Buddy" Rogers claimed it all started not at the Chinese Theater, but at their home, when Mary spotted their pet poodle trotting onto the newly laid pavement of their driveway, leaving his little paw prints there for posterity.

A more likely scenario has Grauman himself admonished by the theater's main mason for foolishly walking straight through a portion of wet cement, which gave him the unlikely idea of inviting three stars, Pickford, Douglas Fairbanks, and Norma Talmadge, to do the same. The stars complied, but when the cement dried, their original effort was too indistinct, and Grauman cajoled all three to return and try again. Fairbanks and Pickford came first, and a few days later Norma Talmadge arrived to memorialize herself once more.

Although this honor was eventually extended to a bevy of movie stars, according to Fairbanks' son, Douglas Fairbanks Jr., it was only originally conceived to honor a chosen few. "The gimmick had originally been thought up by Sid Grauman himself, but only for Mary [Pickford], Dad [Douglas Fairbanks Sr.], Chaplin, and [John] Barrymore," he wrote. "Later he was pressured by the studios to do the same thing for their Big Names."

Since this was still the era in which movie companies could legally own and operate theaters to show their own films, Warner Brothers wanted a Hollywood Boulevard theater of their own, and the northwest corner of Hollywood & Wilcox was chosen as its location. Designed to project the same kind of elegant formality that was instilled into their expansive Sunset Boulevard studio, the Warner Brothers Theater was the largest movie theater in Hollywood, with a capacity of 2,700 people. It also housed a mammoth Marr & Colton pipe organ to provide intense, dimensional soundscapes for the silent films shown there. The theater opened on April 26, 1928, with a star-studded premiere of *Glorious Betsy*, starring the radiant Dolores Costello.

Only two years following the opening of the Warner Brothers Theater, an even more expansive movie palace was constructed on Hollywood Boulevard. The Pantages Theater, just east of Vine, was designed by B. Marcus Priteca and financed by the entrepreneur Alexander Pantages. Envisioned as Hollywood's grandest movie palace, its grandeur was apparent even before one entered the auditorium itself. The elegant 18-foot-high marble and bronze entrance from Hollywood Boulevard was extraordinary, as was the red-carpeted pathway brilliantly illuminated by thousands of light-bulbs that led into an exalted vaulted lobby with beautiful chandeliers, and vast gold staircases on either end. The inner auditorium was similarly stunning, containing one of the largest stages of any theater in Los Angeles.

The Pantages opened officially on June 4, 1930, with the premiere of *Floradora Girl*, starring Marion Davies. Purchased by RKO in 1949, the Pantages became the home of the Academy Awards for many years. Today it's still one of Hollywood's grandest theaters, and is now a showcase for live theatrical productions such as live concerts and Broadway shows.

Other grand palaces that were originally designed to be legitimate theaters for stage shows were also constructed at this time, such as the glorious El Capitan theater, on Hollywood Boulevard across from the Chinese Theater. It opened with a revue starring Beatrice Lilly and Gertrude

Lawrence, and continued as a live theater until 1942, when it was converted into a movie house and renamed the Paramount Theater. Years later in the 1980s, it was acquired by Disney, who renovated it to its prior glory, and gave it back its original name, El Capitan.

Other theaters designed for live performances included the Vine Street Theater on Vine, south of Hollywood Boulevard. It later became a theater for live radio presentations and was renamed the Lux Theater, and later the CBS Playhouse Theater. By 1954, it became a theater for stage shows once again, changing its name to the Huntington Hartford, and by the 1980s, it was the Doolittle Theater.

The Hollywood Palace was built on Vine in 1927 north of Hollywood Boulevard, across the street from what is today the Capitol Records tower. In the forties it became the home for one of the stage's most popular revues, *Ken Murray's Blackouts*. By the late fifties and into the sixties it became an ideal place to shoot TV shows, and several were produced here each week.

Despite the commercial development of Hollywood Boulevard and its offshoots, the actual urbanization of Hollywood wouldn't set in for decades. By the end of the twenties, Hollywood still retained much of the pastoral splendor it possessed when the Wilcoxes first arrived. "From terraced hillsides that somehow recall places in the Scottish Highlands and again mountain shoulders that brings spots in Ireland to mind," wrote C. Clayton Hutton in the *New York Times*, "Hollywood looks across a sea of homes by day and a constellation of brilliant lights by night. Miles of smoothly paved streets radiate from the towering buildings of downtown Hollywood into sections of charming homes, set in a year-around garden; palms and roses and pepper trees, brilliant bougainvilleas, bright variegations of lantana hedges, graceful lilies, tall, clustering bamboos, waving plumes of pampas grass—every shape, every color and tint to delight the eye, and every fruit to delight the palate. "

Hollywoodland and the Big Sign

Hollywoodland was a 1924 real estate development on 500 acres of hillside land at the north end of Beachwood Canyon. Financed by L.A.Times owner Harry Chandler and his partners, the same guys who were integral in buying up most of the San Fernando Valley just prior to its tranformation by aqueduct, Hollywoodland was envisioned as a little storybook community "above the traffic congestion, smoke, fog, and poisonous gas fumes of the Lowlands," as newspaper advertisements promised at the time.

To promote Hollywoodland to the those who lived and worked in those very lowlands, Chandler came upon the unique notion of erecting an immense billboard of sorts in the hills above the tract. At a cost of $21,000, thirteen gargantuan letters that spelled out HOLLYWOODLAND were constructed high on the chapparal-covered south side of Mt. Lee, held in place by a ramshackle scaffold of pipes, wires and telephone poles. Each letter was thirty feet wide, fifty feet tall and made of sheet-metal panels painted flat white. Four thousand 20-watt bulbs ran around each letter, illuminating each syllable of the name in sequence: HOLLY . . . WOOD . . . LAND.

To punctuate the big sign, a giant white circle was also set into the hillside a few hundred feet below the sign. Made of matching white sheet-metal, it was thirty-five feet in diameter, and studded also with light bulbs.

Though the sign certainly won the attention of Angelenos and in time became one of L.A.'s most famous landmarks, Hollywoodland itself failed to become as popular as its investors had hoped and many of its parcels of land remained unsold. It's the reason previously proposed by David Horsley for the construction of Lake Hollywood in the

dell beneath Hollywoodland, to lure those "hillside suckers" to build their homes on these vacant hillside lots, which suddenly offered stunning views of the crystal blue lake below.

The total conception of Hollywoodland was never completed, due to the stock market crash of 1929, which drained the coffers of the investors and literally halted the development in its tracks. To this day, one can see where the process of paving the road abruptly was discontinued at the top of Hollywoodland. A dirt road cut into the canyon remains, which would have been the continuance and completion of the development.

C.E. Toberman also developed his own Hollywood real estate tract. Located just northeast of Franklin & La Brea in what was the ancient village of Ca-Oug-Na, he created a well-to-do community of upscale homes with fire-safe plastered walls and tile roofs, and called it Outpost Estates.

Radio

Nineteen-twenty-two marked the year that radio officially arrived in Hollywood. Three separate radio stations were established: KNX, KHJ, and KFI. KNX broadcasted from a Studebaker auto dealership at 6116 Hollywood Boulevard. It was launched mainly to promote the Los Angeles Express newspaper, the brainchild of promotion manager Guy Earl who concocted a savvy publicity event—he gave away one thousand crystal-set radios in a circulation drive that both sold newspapers and introduced Angelenos to a new medium. In 1938, CBS erected a new multimillion-dollar building at Sunset & Gower and made KNX the West Coast outpost of their network.

KFI was instigated by a car salesman, Earle Anthony, who sold Packards. Concluding that his potential customers were the kinds of cultured, affluent folk who would appreciate the classics, he instigated a classical music format, broadcasting live concerts by symphonic orchestras as well

63

as operas. In 1927, KFI became part of the NBC Red radio network. NBC built a beautiful art deco studio for radio production in the heart of Hollywood near the Northwest corner of Sunset & Vine. Like the new CBS structure, it housed expansive new broadcast studios set up like live theaters to hold hundreds of audience members, as well as high-tech studio control rooms. Although the majority of network radio shows continued at first to emanate from New York City, L.A. gradually became a major player in terms of creating and broadcasting original programming. In time, Hollywood became synonymous with radio glamour, as when gossip-columnist Louella Parsons would put the old boulevard on the national map by announcing each week, "This is Louella Parsons, broadcasting from the Hollywood Hotel."

KHJ was owned by Harry Chandler of the *L.A.Times*, and established a format of educational and public affairs shows and programming for children. In 1927, KHJ joined the CBS Radio Network and in 1936 merged with the Mutual Network.

Legendary Restaurants and Clubs

With good hotels, radio, and theater came fine restaurants to Hollywood, such as Musso & Frank's Grill, the Brown Derby, and the Montmartre Café. Of these, the greatest and most enduring of them all is Musso & Frank's Grill, known throughout the world simply as Musso's. It was founded in 1919 by John Musso and Frank Goulet at 6669 Hollywood Boulevard, serving fine food from the start. It instantly became popular with merchants and businessmen in the area, as well as with movie stars, such as Charlie Chaplin, who began to lunch there daily.[13] Musso's was sold six years after its opening to Joseph Carissimi and his partner, whose name, remarkably, was John Mosso. Caris-

simi and Mosso expanded Musso's in 1936 into 6667 Hollywood Boulevard, where it has endured at that location ever since, attracting a loyal clientele through the decades that has included the legion of legendary authors who came to Hollywood to write for the movies, including William Faulkner, F. Scott Fitzgerald, Dorothy Parker, Nathanael West, Raymond Chandler, and Dashiell Hammett. Musso's exists to this day as the oldest restaurant in Hollywood.

The Brown Derby on Vine opened for business on Valentine's Day of 1929 by Herbert Somborn, whose main assistant Robert Cobb took over ownership after Somborn's death in 1934. Cobb invented the world-famous Cobb salad here at the Derby, a delightful chopped confederacy of lettuce, tomato, avocado, bacon, and chicken all abounding with fresh bleu cheese dressing. It was but one of the highlights of the fine cuisine offered by the Derby, a level of quality that kept the stars coming, as did added amenities, such as the advent of bringing telephones to the tables. The walls of the Derby were filled with the framed caricatures of comic and dramatic stars of the day, and the tables were often filled by those very stars, and by bit players and extras, all of whom would dash into the Derby in full makeup and costume from nearby studio sets, and dash back to shoot another scene after lunch was over. Because of this steady stream of stars, the Derby was beloved by the public, who were hungry to see these spectral titans in the flesh.

Another place to see the stars wastThe Montmartre Cafe at 6757 Hollywood Boulevard. Opened in 1923 by Eddie Brandstatter, it was a favorite meeting place of many of the movies' most famous stars, such that fans would line up for hours in hopes of getting an autograph. In 1929, to afford the stars some relief, Brandstatter broke through the wall of the

40

---

[13] For more about Chaplin at Musso's and about Musso's in general, see Manny Felix, page 290, see David Raksin, page 69.

Montmartre into the adjoining building to establish an even more exclusive and elite retreat called the Embassy Club.

Appearing in movies required actors to stay fit, and so to provide a club in which they could "take some daily exercise," as the saying went, the Hollywood Athletic Club was built in 1923 on Sunset at Hudson. With a swimming pool, gymnasium, barbershop and guest rooms, it became an ultra-exclusive men's club. Both Rudolph Valentino and Charlie Chaplin became members almost immediately, and could frequently be found swimming laps, working out, or spending the night at the club. Decades later, the legend goes, John Wayne would hurl billiard balls from its roof at passing cars.

In 1928, the Russian makeup mogul Max Factor bought the building at the Southeast corner of Hollywood & Highland, diagonally across the street from the Hollywood Hotel. After massive renovations, the building was opened on November 17, 1928, as his headquarters, and soon became a Hollywood institution. In 1934, he hired the famed art deco architect S. Charles Lee to give the building a fresh look. Lee designed an entirely new, formal marble facade for the building, with Westfieldian marble and fluted pilasters. This new version of the old building opened with a giant "premiere" of a party, replete with kleig lights, and attended by scores of Hollywood luminaries, including Sid Grauman, Claudette Colbert, Rita Hayworth, Marlene Dietrich and a 13-year-old Judy Garland. So impressive was the new building that the party-goers were said to be speechless, according to a New York Times account of the event: "They stood in open-mouthed awe until they were rudely awakened by their cigarettes burning their fingers. They then hastily dropped them on the burgundy carpet and ground them in."

The life of Colonel Griffith J. Griffith was marked by a distinctive mix of madness and munificence. Griffith was a serious drinker and a paranoiac, yet he donated a parcel of Hollywood land so expansive that it enabled the creation of the largest city park in the world, Griffith Park. In 1903, Griffith, however, became convinced that his wife was plotting with the pope to poison him and take over the country. To stop this, he tried to kill her by shooting her in the eye. Though she miraculously survived, he was tried for attempted murder, and served one year of a two-year sentence at San Quentin. He later bequeathed 3,000 acres of Hollywood northeast of Franklin & Western to the city for used as a magnificent city park that would encompass an outdoor amphitheater called the Greek Theater and an Observatory and Hall of Science for investigation of the heavens. But because of his infamous reputation, the city was slow in fulfilling his intentions. It wasn't until 1930, more than a decade after his death, that L.A. accepted a grant from his estate to finance the construction of the proposed buildings. The Greek Theater was completed first, in September of 1930, providing a verdant venue where an audience of 4,500 can hear music under the stars.

41

That same year the construction of the majestic Griffith Observatory began. Sadly, it was marred by tragedy when a fire started in the dry hillside brush at the lower end of the canyon and quickly began to spread. Workers at the observatory saw the smoke and fire below and began to climb down the hill in hopes of putting it out. But the wind shifted suddenly, and the fire swept up the slope, taking the lives of twenty-seven men.

It took five years to complete construction of the iconic Observatory, which is now famous to film-lovers for its usage in the classic Rebel without a Cause starring James Dean, as well as many other films. Though it was Griffith's intention that access to the observatory be provided by a funicular from the flatlands, similar to that which ascended Angel's Flight in downtown, by 1930 it was evident Angelenos would prefer to drive their own cars, and so the observatory was constructed on a lower ridge of Mt. Hollywood than the one designated by the colonel. Easily accessible in a car via a winding route up the hillside, the new location provided ample space for parking.

Plans were set into motion in 2001 to radically rebuild, renovate and expand the observatory, which will be closed for several years during this operation.

A historic Hollywood debut occurred on October 29, 1936, when one of the world's first and most distinctive shopping malls, The Crossroads of the World, first opened for business. Located on the north side of Sunset east of Las Palmas, it was designed by Robert Derrah as a ship sailing to the many corners of the globe; to achieve this effect he blended together the grove of existing trees with an amalgam of architectural approaches from around the world. The result is a quaint village that is at once Spanish, French, Mexican and Moorish, all connected by a narrow Cape Cod lane. Like a ship at sea with its big bow on Sunset, its nautical motif is accentuated by a sixty-foot crow's nest crested with a revolving globe, eight feet in diameter. Through the years, the Crossroads has held a variety of stores and businesses, from travel agencies to recording studios to hair stylists. To this day, it still sails behind its glorious globe on Sunset.

The Sunset Strip

Throughout the thirties, the former horse trail to the sea called Sunset was transformed, between Fairfax and Doheny, into the world-famous Sunset Strip, and several significant nightclubs opened there. These were the decades prior to the development of Las Vegas, and so the world's greatest entertainers were in need of fine nightclubs on the West Coast in which to perform. The Trocadero was one of the first. Opened in 1934 by the publisher of the *Hollywood Reporter*, W.R. Wilkerson, it was a place where one could dance and dine among the stars, and enjoy

performances by many of the great performers of the day, such as Judy Garland, Mary Martin and Deanna Durbin. Although it burned to the ground in 1936, the Troc was rebuilt and back in operation within a year; until 1946 it persisted as one of Hollywood's premiere clubs.

The Mocambo opened in 1938 at 8588 Sunset, where it remained open until 1958, the year that its owner, Charles Morrison, died. During its short life it was one of the hottest nightspots in Hollywood, attracting an audience of movie stars who came to hear some of the world's greatest musical stars perform, including Edith Piaf and Lena Horne.

Wilkerson was also responsible for establishing another of the Strip's most notable, and even notorious, nightclubs. Ciro's, at 8433 Sunset Boulevard, was not an immediate success, but after a few years and a shift of management, it soon became the choice venue of several classic entertainers. Eartha Kitt debuted at Ciro's, and Jerry Lewis, Dean Martin, Liberace, Sammy Davis Jr., and many other greats all performed on its stage. Also beloved by mob bosses such as Bugsy Siegel, Ciro's closed its doors toward the conclusion of the fifties, at which time it was purchased by Mitzi Shore, who reopened it as The Comedy Store.

It was also in 1938 that Earl Carroll opened the famous theater he named after himself at Sunset & Argyle, launching a new revue based on his infamous "Vanities," which he produced in New York, and which was considered so racy in its time, due to the presence of beautiful women in scanty costumes, that it was continually raided by police. Presuming Hollywood was a more suitable community for this kind of attraction, Carroll moved across the country to launch his new night club with an opening gala as glamorous as the Academy Awards. A procession of Hollywood's royalty passed through its new portals as hundreds of onlookers crowded around for a glimpse of the stars. Marlene Deitrich, Tyrone

Power, Dolores Del Rio, Clark Gable, Errol Flynn, Carole Lombard and more were all in attendance, a turnout that secured Earl Carroll's Theater a reputation from the start as one of the places to see and be seen. It was also a place to see beautiful women; its slogan was spelled out in neon letters in front of the theater: "Through these portals pass the most beautiful girls in the world." The theater was immense, with a capacity of 1,160 people, and was illuminated by a brilliant amalgamation of 10,000 separate neon tubes.

Carroll's life was cut short in 1948 when he died in a plane crash in Pennsylvania. Other owners took over Earl Carroll's, and in 1953 Frank Sennes bought it, extensively remodeled it, and reopened it as the Moulin Rouge. He followed Carroll's lead and presented a show replete with 100 beautiful women in revealing costumes, followed by leading musical entertainers of the day, such as Peggy Lee, Ella Fitzgerald, Frankie Laine, Johnnie Ray and Liberace. In 1955, the Moulin Rouge also became a theater for television broadcasts, providing the venue for the show "Queen for a Day," hosted by Jack Bailey.

On Halloween, 1940, the Palladium was born. Built by L.A. Times publisher Norman Chandler for $1,600,000 on a full block of Sunset at Argyle, it quickly became the place to dance and to hear the big bands of the day. Its initiation was star-studded, as Lana Turner broke ground with a silver shovel in a ceremony launching the construction.

"In the forties, after the war, the Palladium was like New Year's Eve every night with all the servicemen in town," said the late Les Brown, leader of His Band of Renown, who played countless shows at the Palladium from the forties all the way into the 1990s, when he played his final show there, "Swing Alive," which also featured Tex Benneke and Bob Hope. All the greatest entertainers of the day performed through the years on the stage of the Palladium, including Judy Garland, Doris Day, Glenn Miller, Harry James and even Marilyn Monroe. Five U.S. presidents have also appeared at the Palladium: Truman, Eisenhower, Kennedy, Johnson and Nixon.

In the late thirties and throughout the forties, many of America's greatest authors came to Hollywood, lured by the studios offering them decent money to write for the movies. F. Scott Fitzgerald, William Faulkner, Nathanael West, Lillian Hellman, Dashiell Hammett, Raymond Chandler, Aldous Huxley and others all arrived. When not working, many of them would gather at Musso's, and also at two great bookstores that had opened on the boulevard, Pickwick's and Stanley Rose's. Pickwick's opened in 1938, and was owned and operated by Louis Epstein.[14] Stanley Rose's was owned by Rose himself, and both shops became landmarks on the boulevard.

43

World War II

On December 7, 1941, the day that the Japanese bombed Pearl Harbor, Orson Welles' *Citizen Kane* and Chaplin's *The Great Dictator* were playing on Hollywood Boulevard. But Hollywood was never the same after that day, after America entered what became World War II. All Japanese employees of all the studios were removed to "relocation camps," while thousands of studio technicians, drivers, actors and more immediately enlisted in the armed services. Within months, 70 percent of all Hollywood families had members in the military, including many movie stars who sacrificed their careers to serve as soldiers, including Clark Gable, Jimmy Stewart, Robert Taylor, Robert Montgomery, and Victor Mature. Scores of other stars aided the war effort by performing for the USO, and by working and performing at the Hollywood Canteen.

[14] For more on Pickwick's, see Aaron Epstein, page 258.

During the war, thousands of soldiers on leave came through Hollywood. Because of their sheer numbers, many of them would be found sleeping on benches in the parks or other public places. Various canteens run by the USO and Red Cross offered servicemen a place to relax and have a drink, but none of them offered a room for the night. Anne "Mom" Lehr changed all that by transforming the big house she lived in at 1284 Crescent Heights—the former mansion of The Squaw Man star, Dustin Farnum—into a haven for military men on leave.

44

On May 15, 1942, she opened it as Hollywood Guild and Canteen, soon the most popular place for soldiers to stay in all of Hollywood. It's estimated that from 800 to 1,200 soldiers stayed there each night, eating and drinking all that they wanted. Soon other structures were built as add-ons to the original house so as to make room for additional beds, and though Lehr remained in charge, various stars such as Myrna Loy, Mary Pickford and Janet Gaynor governed over its business.

The Hollywood Guild and Canteen run by Lehr, however, should not be confused with the Hollywood Canteen founded by John Garfield and Bette Davis. Run out of a former stable just south of Sunset on Cahuenga, this Canteen opened on October 3, 1942, with a glorious gala show emceed by Eddie Cantor that featured four fabulous big bands, including the Duke Ellington Orchestra, and comic interludes provided by Abbott and Costello. From that night on the Canteen was usually packed with about 2,000 servicemen; the only admission required was the wearing of an American military uniform.

Hollywood's greatest stars volunteered their time at the Canteen; Fred MacMurray, Basil Rathbone, John Garfield and other male stars worked as busboys, while starlets such as Marlene Deitrich, Betty Grable, Greer Garson, and Olivia de Havilland would serve snacks, slice cakes, and take turns dancing with the servicemen, who were understandably enthused by this tradition.

When President Truman made his historic announcement on August 14, 1945 that the war was over, Hollywood, like the rest of America, exploded with excitement. More than 3,000 soldiers flooded into the Hollywood Canteen and spilled out into the streets of Hollywood, which became an enormous public celebration. Spontaneous parades started up of their own accord and marched from end to end of Hollywood Boulevard, which was transformed into a giant dance floor where thousands danced for hours. The singer Carmen Miranda and her band set up on a bandstand in front of the Roosevelt Hotel on the boulevard, and for a shining moment the promise of peacetime in America resulted in one of the most amazing street parties ever given.

The Hollywood Canteen hosted approximately 100,000 servicemen a month during the war. Soon after the war ended its doors were closed; its farewell performance was on the night of November 22, 1945, and starred Bob Hope, Jack Benny and Jerry Colonna.

Wallich's Music City and Capitol Records

Glenn Wallich opened a radio store on Ivar, south of Hollywood, to cash in on the new radio craze sweeping the country. Quickly growing in popularity, it expanded to a new site at the northwest corner of Sunset & Vine and was called Wallich's Music City. Within a couple of years, records as well as radios began to be sold, and before long were its principal commodity. Music City became the first record store in the nation to allow customers to sample new records in listening booths before making any buying decisions, a tradition that spread throughout the industry.

In 1942, Wallich teamed up with the songwriter Johnny Mercer and the producer Buddy DeSylva to launch their own record company, which they called Liberty, and later changed to Capitol Records. At first they operated their fledgling organization out of the music store until 1949, when Wallich decided to devote all his time to Capitol, and sold his financial interest in Music City to his brother, Clyde Wallich. Under Clyde's leadership, Music City continued to expand and flourish, adding a huge selection of musical instruments, sheet music and phonograph equipment, and thus becoming one of the most expansive music stores in the world.

Capitol Records, meanwhile, blossomed from the little company run out of the back room of a music store into a giant of the music industry. They were the first company to send promo copies of their records to radio DJs, a now common practice in the music business.

Between 1954 and 1956, Capitol built its own office building to serve as its international headquarters. A thirteen-story circular tower was erected on Vine Street, north of Hollywood Boulevard, across the street from the Palace.[15] Though people assumed for years that its design was intended to resemble a stack of record albums, in fact its circular architecture was adopted so that all outer offices would have windows. With its famous recording studio in the basement, Capitol quickly developed into a music empire; countless legendary recording artists recorded there. Frank Sinatra would have all-night sessions to which all Capitol employees were invited to attend, and many other legends, including Nat "King" Cole, Peggy Lee, and the Beatles, all famously recorded there.

Television

As early as 1928, the technology of television was in the works. As with the advent of sound pictures, the potential of television initially struck the film industry as just another trendy novelty, a trifle that would soon go the way of all trends. And as with talkies, they couldn't have been more wrong, as they soon came to discover.

How TV would affect Hollywood and the world was an unknown factor for years. Dr. Palmer saw it in 1937 connecting links in a chain that had previously been severed. "The silent film brought those who could act regardless of voice or diction. The speaking film discarded the artists who could not speak acceptably. The radio absorbed those with acceptable voice and diction regardless of their appearance or ability to act. Television has arrived and will soon require those such as are now alone acceptable on the screen, who can both act and speak."

Hollywood's first television station actually began broadcasting in 1931, but since no one had a TV set, few people knew about it for years to come. TV station W6XAO, owned by Don Lee, went on the air the week of Christmas 1931, utilizing a television broadcast system devised by Harry Lubcke.

In 1942, Lee purchased the crest of Mt. Lee, above the Hollywoodland sign, and it's there that he created his first TV studio and broadcast tower. It was subsequently bought by CBS in the fifties, who broadcast their first show from there.

In the forties, although there were only about 300 operational televisions in all of Los Angeles, the potential of television began to dawn on people throughout the entertainment industry. Soon other TV stations were established. The ABC Radio Network purchased their TV station from a Packard dealer named Earle Anthony, who had established KECA. In 1948, ABC moved their TV operations to the former Warners Studio at Prospect & Talmadge, changed its call letters to KABC, and began broadcasting from that lot, where they have remained ever since 1949.

NBC expanded and converted portions of their grand Radio building at Sunset &

[15] For more on Capitol Records, see Roberta Murray, page 272.

Vine for television usage, and they went on the air in 1949 as KNBH, which evolved into KRCA and eventually to KNBC.

Paramount also recognized the need to get in on the bottom floor of this new technology, and hired the engineer Klaus Landsberg to come to Hollywood and establish a TV station under their ownership. W6XYZ, as it was first known, broadcast out of a small studio on the Paramount lot. In 1949 it became KTLA, the first commercial station in all of the western United States. Their first show was hosted by Bob Hope, and also featured Cecil B. DeMille, William Demarest, Dorothy Lamour and others. In 1955, Paramount took over the old Warners Studio at 5858 Sunset and made it the new home of KTLA.

As with the advent of talkies, which required larger lots and resulted in companies such as Warners moving out of Hollywood, so did the advent of TV result in additional companies leaving Hollywood to build more spacious studios in outlying areas. NBC abandoned their landmark building at Sunset & Vine and enlarged their West Coast TV facilities by moving to Burbank, where they built the big lot which has housed "The Tonight Show" and other famous NBC network shows for many years.

Similarly in need of more TV space, CBS left Hollywood to take over the site of the old Gilmore baseball field at Beverly & Fairfax, where they constructed their own TV empire, CBS Television City.

An exception to this pattern was the Public Broadcasting System, which has always been an anomaly among television networks by striving to edify and educate rather than profit from their broadcasts. In the sixties they reversed the prevalent trend and moved into Hollywood, where they established KCET, Public Television for Southern California. Their first studio

stood at 1313 Vine, and in 1970 they moved to what was by then already a historic Hollywood landmark, the old Lubin studio at Sunset & Hoover, built back in 1912.

HUAC and the Blacklist

After the real war came the Cold War, which led to an era called "scoundrel times " by Lillian Hellman, who was but one of a multitude of writers whose careers were obstructed and derailed by the notorious "blacklist."[16] For these were the times of the hearings held by HUAC— the House Committee on Un-American Activities, an organization initiated in 1938 to root out potential communists assumed to be active in America's undoing, lurking among the elite and working classes of the United States.

Hollywood was scourged by the HUAC allegations. Hundreds of writers, actors, directors and producers were blacklisted, and condemned to unemployment, obscurity and worse. Those who had so much as attended a meeting of the Young Communist League in their school days were branded "Un-American," as if they were actively working against the interests of their country, when in fact they were actively working in the employment of the movie industry, a collection of companies that annually pumped millions into the American economy, and concurrently provided an obligatory, essential cinematic escape from the mundane reality of everyday life. Yet for reasons that had more to do with empowering the political profiles of Joe McCarthy, Richard Nixon and others who spearheaded this campaign, the McCarthy "witch-hunts," as they came to be known, were allowed to ensue.

In the autumn of 1947, a rash of subpoenas were sent out to prominent Hollywood executives, actors, producers, and directors, calling for them to testify before

46

---

[16] For more about HUAC and the blacklist, see Walter Bernstein, page 139; Pippa Scott, page 279; and Evelyn Keyes, page 127.

the committee. A procession of "friendly witnesses" appeared first, who willingly shared hearsay and cast aspersions on the characters of their colleagues. Given total immunity, they demonstrated what some considered true patriotism and others regarded as categorical cowardice; they pointed fingers at their peers, their employees, their families and friends, branding them as communists, and offering "evidence" of their transgressions.

Warner Brothers' own Jack Warner offered an abundance of evidence. He suggested that John Garfield, who had starred in a string of classic films made by Warners, attempted to sneak subtle but subversive messages into various movies by changing certain lines in the script.

In stark contrast, however, to those witnesses friendly to the cause of the committee, there came before the panel ten men in succession. In a pattern of action unanticipated by the committee, each declined to entertain any questions from what they considered an unconstitutional tribunal. These men were all ultimately convicted of "Contempt of Congress," given substantial fines to pay, and sentenced to jail terms. They became known as the "Hollywood Ten." They were:

Alvah Bessie, the author of *Men in Battle*, a novel, and the screenwriter of several films including *Northern Pursuit* and *Hotel Berlin*.

Herbert Biberman, the writer and director of *The Master Race*, and the writer and producer of *New Orleans*.

Lester Cole, the writer of more than forty movies, including *None Shall Escape*, *Blood on the Sun*, and *The Romance of Rosy Ridge*.

Edward Dmytryk, the director whose many films include *Crossfire*, *Cornered*, *Murder My Sweet*, and *Hitler's Children*.

Ring Lardner Jr., the writer who won an Oscar for writing *Woman of the Year*, and also wrote such movies as *The Cross of Larraine* and *Tomorrow the World*.

John Howard Lawson, the author of *Blockade*, *Sahara*, and *Action in the North Atlantic*.

Albert Maltz, who wrote the novel *The Cross and the Arrow* and the screenplays of *Destination Tokyo* and *Naked City*.

Samuel Ornitz, the novelist who wrote *Haunch Paunch and Jowl* and the movie *China's Little Devils*.

Adrian Scott, the screenwriter of *Miss Suzie Slagle* and producer of *Crossfire*, *Cornered*, *Deadline at Dawn*, and *Murder My Sweet*.

Dalton Trumbo, novelist who wrote *Johnny Got His Gun* and writer of several movies, including *Kitty Foyle*, *Thirty Seconds over Tokyo*, and *A Guy Named Joe*.

47

Of all the movie moguls, Samuel Goldwyn was the only one to speak against HUAC, questioning the entire premise on which it was based. "The entire hearing is a flop, and I think the whole thing is a disgraceful performance," he said. . . . "What do they want us to do, make anti-Communist pictures? Is that the way to bring about peace?"

After the suspension of the hearings at the end of October 1947, Goldwyn spoke again. "The most un-American activity which I have observed," he said, "has been the activity of the committee itself." But despite his statements and profuse public sentiment in opposition to HUAC's attack on Hollywood, the appalling blacklist was officially put into effect. Days before Thanksgiving of 1947, the president of the Motion Picture Association (called the "Czar of Hollywood" by insiders), issued an official condemnation of the Hollywood Ten:

"We will forthwith discharge or suspend without compensation," it said, "and we will not re-employ, any of the ten until such time as he is acquitted, or has purged himself of contempt, and declared under oath that he is not a Communist."

In addition to the Hollywood Ten, hundreds of other creative people found themselves named in a notorious book called "Red Channels" which circulated throughout the industry, listing all those to be blacklisted. Countless careers were destroyed, and Hollywood was changed.

Remarkably, the movie industry survived scoundrel times as it has survived other significant setbacks. As the blacklist gradually faded and McCarthy's influence waned, those who had been forsaken by the industry were welcomed back into the fold. Many returned as heroes for refusing to buckle under to the greatest of pressures. But return they did, to an industry that had expelled them, by directing the bulk of the blame for the blacklist not to the studio bosses of Hollywood, but to the money men of New York who financed the studios and called all the shots.

48

San Fernando Valley and Construction of the Hollywood Freeway

Upon returning from the war, thousands of servicemen entranced during the war by the multitude of charms that was Hollywood returned in massive numbers to Los Angeles in order to start new lives. Since the majority of apartment houses within Hollywood were built prior to the advent of the automobile and had no garages or outdoor parking space, and since single homes in Hollywood, especially those in the hills, were either unaffordable or unavailable, thousands settled instead in the rapidly expanding San Fernando Valley.

They were armed with the newly instituted GI Bill, which provided low-interest mortgages to veterans, and led to a postwar housing boom and expansion of suburbs throughout America. Nearly 20 percent of all single-family homes built from 1945 to 1965 in America were completely or partially financed by the GI Bill's loan guarantee program. In Los Angeles this sparked the suburban sprawl known today simply as "The Valley."

Newly hatched divisions of brand-new houses sprung up over the untold acres of bygone orange and lemon groves, and were quickly purchased by veterans from small towns and big cities throughout America. They moved into the Valley to live in the proximity of Hollywood's fabled shimmer, while keeping sufficient distance to raise their families in safe, salubrious communities.

Much of this new mass of Valley citizenry found employment in downtown L.A., to which there existed only two means of access: There was the Red Car streetcar line, which still ran then along its course through the Cahuenga Pass and east through the streets of Hollywood, Silverlake and Echo Park to downtown. The other alternative was simply to pilot one's own automobile every day. But the drive from the Valley through the surface streets of Hollywood to get downtown was a long and indirect commute. So with the primary aim of providing a fast and direct auto route between the Valley and downtown, it was determined that a freeway which cut clear across Hollywood was the only reasonable remedy. In 1947, the State of California designated $55 million in building funds for the construction of the Hollywood Freeway.

Its design cut straight through the Cahuenga Pass into Hollywood, slicing through old neighborhoods like Whitley Heights and decimating scores of historic houses there, while marring other neighborhoods with its colossal tunnels and overpasses.

It also resulted in the destruction of the Red Car streetcar line. Like Mulholland's controversial solution of siphoning water from the Owens Valley, for years it has been accepted as gospel that the death sentence imposed on the Red Car system was engineered as a conspiracy between the big gas, auto and tire companies, who compelled the freeway construction so as to forsake public transport and force Angelenos for generations to come to drive their own cars.

Seven years of construction, destruction and extended desolation ensued. Though much of it was complete by 1949, it took several years before the freeway's final leg, which cut through the Pass, could be effectively completed. Causes for this delay were diverse: The scale of fabricating a freeway of such immense proportions through the mammoth slope of the Pass was entirely unprecedented. Engineers at the time were unschooled in attempting construction of this immensity, which cut directly through the heart of healthy, long-abiding communities.

Various debates and protests about the appropriate design of the freeway understandably abounded. State engineers and regional L.A. honchos clashed fervently over which would be wiser: for Franklin Avenue to be enclosed in a tunnel over which the freeway could flow, which was the wish of state engineers, or for Franklin to remain unwrapped, with the freeway flowing above it via a series of bridges and overpasses, which was the cause championed by local merchants and residents. The latter solution was ultimately implemented.

In 1952, the world's first "four-level interchange" was constructed just northwest of downtown to connect the eastern end of the Hollywood Freeway (the 101), with the Harbor and Pasadena freeways (the 110). In 1954, the Hollywood Freeway was finally complete, forever bringing to a close a chapter of Hollywood history that can never be recovered. The serenity of Hollywood prior to the freeway exists only in the hearts and minds of those who remember it, and who still cherish the days before the roar of freeway traffic became relentless and unremitting. The total loss of hundreds of Hollywood homes, as well as the surfeit of old neighborhoods divided or darkened by the giant tunnels and overpasses, is a profound wound from which Hollywood has never healed.

There were those who believed the freeway would have a beneficial, healing effect on Hollywood, allowing more people than ever to come to Hollywood and enjoy its restaurants, theaters and stores. In many ways it actually had the opposite effect, making it more possible to work in Hollywood and then leave to eat and entertain elsewhere in the L.A. area. "The phenomena that caused Hollywood's rapid decline in the postwar era intensified during the sixties," wrote Bruce Torrence. "The San Fernando Valley continued to boom, and as regional shopping malls and suburban movie theaters sprang up, Valley residents no longer needed to drive over the hill for goods, services, or entertainment."

"Urbanization" was the solution the business owners in Hollywood chose to inject new vitality into their city, transforming Hollywood into a city of office-buildings. Now people who lived downtown or in the Valley could easily take the freeway into Hollywood, where they would work during the day, but eat, entertain and shop elsewhere at nights and on the weekends. In this way the intimate connection and pride felt by those who both lived and worked in Hollywood was severed.

Throughout the fifties and sixties, nondescript, faceless office buildings were erected throughout Hollywood, often by destroying the graceful and beautiful buildings that existed. At the same time, hundreds of new apartment buildings were constructed on streets that once held single-family dwellings, profoundly shifting the residential tone of the old neighborhoods. Attempts at "modernization" of many of Hollywood's most classic existing buildings involved crassly covering their former facades so as to hide any sign of the past, stylistically retrofitting them for modern times by obscuring the genuine, if old-fashioned, beauty that was there. It all had to do with the same concept that blighted countless other American cities during this era: that newness, by its own virtue, was always preferable to anything belonging to previous generations. It's a belief system that has fortunately shifted in recent years to encompass an understanding and appreciation for the beauty and grace instilled

49

into American architecture through the early decades of the twentieth century.

The Walk of Fame

Now the leaders of Hollywood had a dilemma of their own making. Having demolished many of the existent links to its glamorous past, and having masked the former grandeur of many of the boulevard's classic buildings, they had created a Hollywood Boulevard devoid of any connection to that which gave it cache, its former promenade of stars. And so a symbolic connection to the stars was created, a physical reminder that this old boulevard was not simply another busy business thoroughfare in Anytown, USA, but the Street of Dreams itself, the very street where the world's greatest stars once walked.

And so the Walk of Fame was conceived; a series of brass stars set in the sidewalk to honor the past and present human stars of Hollywood. Replacing the old concrete sidewalk, they installed a series of shiny charcoal terrazzo squares that framed coral terrazzo stars. Each star was inscribed in brass with the name of a star, along with an icon to designate their field of endeavor, be it movies, radio, TV or records. It is an honor that has always been somewhat questionable, since certain legends, such as Lon Chaney, David Selznick, and Steve McQueen were never awarded stars, while others received multiple stars for their work in different media, such as W.C. Fields, Groucho Marx, Bing Crosby, and Bob Hope.

To fund this project, an organization called The Hollywood Assessment District was created, which raised the requisite $1,250,000 for this project by requiring property owners all along the boulevard to pay a sizable fee. Though these owners were told that the development of the Walk of Fame would result in a great upsurge in all of their businesses, many of them were understandably underwhelmed

50

by the prospect of shelling out significant amounts of money to put stars in the sidewalk.

The first eight stars of the Walk of Fame were dedicated at the northwest corner of Hollywood & Highland, the former site of the Hollywood Hotel, in September of 1958. Though the rest of the Walk of Fame would not be complete for two more years, these first stars were installed as to already be in place in time for the completion of the new Pacific Savings building being constructed there, which was subsequently demolished in 1999 to make way for the aforementioned Hollywood-Highland project currently under construction as of this writing.

The initial eight stars installed in the new Walk of Fame reflect the odd amalgam of obscure and legendary names that has characterized this expansive sidewalk shrine since the start. They were:

> Joanne Woodward
> Preston Foster
> Ernest Torrence
> Olive Borden
> Edward Sedgwick
> Louise Fazenda
> Ronald Coleman
> Burt Lancaster

The Walk of Fame was officially completed and dedicated in February of 1960, at which time about a thousand stars were put into place. Since then, many new stars have been dedicated throughout the years. The honor is traditionally bestowed in a late-morning star ceremony which is always emceed by the man known as "Mr. Hollywood," Johnny Grant.[17]

Throughout the sixties and seventies, much of America's most moving music was created here. Many first-class recording studios, such as Gold Star, Wally Heider's, Paramount, A&M, The Bijou, Baby-O and others abounded in Hollywood. Much of the American popular

---

[17] See Johnny Grant, page 150.

music that served as the soundtrack of the sixties, seventies, and on emanated directly from Hollywood, and many of America's most beloved bands of the sixties, such as the Doors, the Byrds, and the Beach Boys all recorded their classic albums in Hollywood recording studios.

Yet physical Hollywood suffered through the sixties. Masses of people angry at America for persisting in fighting the Vietnam War came as far west as they could come, and then landed in Hollywood; regard for Hollywood's historical eminence seemed frivolous in the context of the nation's ongoing struggles. Hollywood became a home for the homeless, a place where those opposing the perceived precepts of the day would escape. They slept in the streets and in abandoned, boarded-up, formerly grand old buildings, such as the Garden Court Hotel.

Various venues catering to the new underground opened along Hollywood Boulevard, selling black-light posters, records, and drug paraphernalia in-between tourist traps, T-shirt shops and fast food joints. Hollywood was distanced ever further from its glory days, as more movie companies left, and many of those who lived in Hollywood and remembered its magic felt dispossessed and discarded along with the city they loved. In 1972, Columbia abandoned its lot at Sunset & Gower to move to Burbank, which left Paramount as the only existing movie studio still in Hollywood.

Years would pass before substantial efforts to heal the spirit and renovate the landmarks of this unique city were implemented. Throughout the eighties and nineties, Hollywood underwent several serious setbacks, each of which profoundly injured the streets and spirit of Hollywood. In April of 1992 came the L.A. riots, in which several stores and buildings on the boulevard were burnt and looted. The massive Northridge earthquake

rocked Hollywood severely in January of 1994, destroying and damaging countless buildings. Many of these were rebuilt and renovated, but many others were hit so harshly that they had to be entirely demolished. To this day, several significant structures along the boulevard have yet to recover from this quake.

And in what seemed like it could be the final blow to this old community, the construction of a subway system beneath the streets of Hollywood commenced in 1996, which wrought as much harm and heartbreak to Hollywood's historic structures as did the recent earthquake. Innumerable buildings were severely damaged by the force of the underground detonation and drilling of subways tunnels, while many others were forced to close because of the massive upheaval caused by above-ground construction crews, which ravaged and barricaded much of the old boulevard for many months at a time.

But as with European cities reduced to ruins during World War II that ultimately arose from ashes and wreckage with a new and shining spirit, Hollywood has survived its successive calamities, and was emerging in the year 2001 with more power and promise than it has possessed in ages. The construction of the massive Hollywood-Highland project on the site of the original Hollywood Hotel has the capacity to bring a new level of vitality and prosperity to Hollywood Boulevard and beyond. And for the first time in decades, many of Hollywood's cherished landmarks, such as the El Capitan, the Chinese Theater, the Egyptian and Pantages, are all shining with a more substantial glimmer than they have in ages. It seems inevitable, as Dr. Palmer recognized back in the thirties, that despite the outcome of the entire human experiment that unfolds endlessly across America and beyond, the distinctive shimmer of Hollywood will exist forever.

51

PART TWO
THE MEMOIRS

Frederica Sagor Maas

BORN JULY 6, 1900
NEW YORK, NEW YORK
SCREENWRITER

"It's the story that matters," she says more than once. "The story." Her own story starts literally at the turn of the twentieth century, and entails her success and struggles as a screenwriter for both the silent movies and the talkies. With her husband Ernest Maas and on her own, she was one of the first female screenwriters, and one of the best. From her typewriter came such classics as Flesh and the Devil, starring John Gilbert and Greta Garbo, and The Plastic Age, which starred Clara Bow, and many others. She discovered then, as did all writers for movies, that regardless of the necessity for good scripts, the writers of these scripts were often exploited, overworked and undercredited, if credited at all. It was not unusual for a script to be rewritten and reworked to such an extent that the original writer's name was omitted from the final film, something that happened to her more than once. But though she was often downhearted, she was never defeated, and to this day expresses a knowing defiance of the powers-that-were. "A writer is never surprised by anything that happens," she says with authority. Though she had the looks to be a star and was offered ample opportunities to act in the movies, she had no interest either in acting or stardom. All that mattered to her was the story, the material, the word. Today she is in La Mesa, California, in a senior residential community not far from San Diego, and kindly submits—with the gentle urging of her niece Phoebe—to a gentle interrogation about a writer's life in Hollywood. "I must tell you," she says almost apologetically, "it all really seems like a thousand years ago to me now."

When I first came to Hollywood, it was nothing but a great big open space where they occasionally made movies. It was not glamorous. It had a variety of stores. Good stores at the beginning. Hollywood was a location. It was a name. Motion pictures were being made there, but they were being made everywhere, wherever the location demanded they be made. As always, the story, the basic story, the book, the play, the original story, was the organ around which everything was developed. Hollywood just happened to be the place where most of the studios were located. It was an ideal place for the movies. You were safe from inclement weather. You always knew you would be able to shoot. That's what drew the film exodus to Hollywood. It was the climate.

I lived at The Halifax when I first got to Hollywood. It was an apartment-hotel. Rent was fifty dollars a month and it came with a fully equipped kitchen and a Murphy Bed in the wall. I couldn't use the Murphy Bed. I didn't know how to use it. Every time I tried to use it, it would fall on my head! I was scared to death of the damn thing. Very often I slept in a chair. [Laughs] I wasn't interested in mechanics. I just wanted to write.

I remember it was very hot in there. No air conditioning, of course, and my room faced east so that the sun blazed in each morning. Out the window were empty lots all around and I could look up into the Hollywood hills. They still hadn't put up that Hollywood sign yet. I remember looking up at the hills. I didn't find them beautiful. They were barren.

I remember the neighborhood around the Halifax then well. It was very quiet. It was a serious neighborhood, as I remember. There were hardly any cars, because there weren't many automobiles then at all. You only had an automobile if you were a personality. We used to walk to Hollywood Boulevard then. Some of the stores and business changed on Hollywood Boulevard, but the face of Hollywood Boulevard never changed.

The last time I was in Hollywood I looked into the Halifax and it was filled with every single nationality you could possibly name. I just heard every language. I smelled every kind of cooking there. When I stayed there, there were very few other buildings around it. We were alone. It was somewhat barren. This was before they put up the Hollywoodland sign. I don't remember it as being particularly beautiful. It was very dead.

It was a nice neighborhood then. Now it's so closely built up, with buildings next to every building. Back then it was not that way at all. It was a quiet neighborhood and respectable. There were some other apartment buildings around; none taller than four stories. All of them were fully furnished. That was the way it was then.

The Villa Carlotta was our favorite place to stay. That was such a long time ago. All those things are so far away. I remember Adolphe Menjou had an apartment on the first floor. I could never stand Menjou. He was a terrible person. He was an awful, dirty man. And a little high-sexed. He was nothing to be celebrated. I never considered him to be handsome. But I was never interested in men like him, and I wasn't interested in the sex life of Hollywood. I was a writer. I worked on the periphery. And the things that were going on around me, they didn't touch me, so I didn't bother with them. I more or less expected that that would be the way it would be in an industry like the motion-picture business.

I stayed at the Chateau Elysee once when we couldn't get into the Villa

Carlotta, across the street. It was a nice place. It wasn't fancy. It was kind of elegant, as I recall. It was an interesting place. At the time there weren't many other buildings. I later moved to an apartment just off of Beachwood Avenue, which I shared. We had a maid when we were in Beachwood. Siska. She could play Debussy on the piano, so I would tell her to play, and I could do the dishes as she played Debussy. I *love* Debussy. I remember she would play "Clair De Lune."

I remember seeing movies as a child. I think it was a cowboy-and-Indian thing. I do remember seeing it; my father had me on his shoulders and we were in the back of a movie house. And I do remember faintly just the whole idea of seeing something on the screen, and how *wondrous* it was.

I was a journalism student at Columbia. I suppose my goal was to write for newspapers, but I'm not really sure. I got a job working for the *New York Globe*. It was while I was working there I read the novel *The Plastic Age* and I knew it could be a good picture. I brought the book to Carl Laemmle at Universal and he rejected it. Said he didn't want to do a "doity picture" like that. You know, that seems like a *thousand* years ago now. Then I brought it to Preferred Pictures and then made it with Clara Bow. And it made her a star.

I was not terribly impressed with Clara Bow. She was just a stupid little girl who was fortunate enough to be picked out to have an outstanding position in motion pictures. She didn't know what it was all about. She didn't know anything about material. She wasn't even a stage actress. She had little experience. She was just thrown into the arena. And she followed suit. She did what she had to do. She was brought up on doing anything she needed to do to get ahead, and that was her excitement, I guess. But I'm sure exaggerations about her were made. I did not think she was particularly good on film. She was no actress.

I understand Clara Bow had a very unhappy end. Lonely and deserted. You don't make friends in the motion picture business. You had a lot of acquaintances but really very few friends.

When I started working in movies, they were a very new medium. But at the time I didn't think of movies as being new, because I had seen them since I was a child.

I started with Universal in New York. I was a story editor, working on other people's scripts. I started reading manuscripts. And that's how I made my entrance in the business. Then, as I recall, I wanted to go to Hollywood, where the pictures were made. And I somehow maneuvered it. Whatever I wanted, I somehow maneuvered. Right or wrong.

My interest always was in the material itself. I viewed everything from that point of view. I was in the story department, developing material. Where they unloaded all the crap. We had readings, and various things were recommended. And we had to choose the good from the bad.

Though we were writing silent movies, we wrote *dialogue*. We wrote both the title-cards and the dialogue. Everything had to be *said*, whether there was sound or not. That was the storyline. In films, that's what you saw. It was not that different from writing a play. We followed Broadway and the plays. That was our school. We wrote our dialogue just as you would write dialogue for the stage. And the actors and actresses would speak the dialogue, but since there was no sound then, you wouldn't hear what they said, but there would be written titles on the screen as to what it was all about.

They used to have fine musicians playing music while shooting the silent movies, to create a mood, an atmosphere, for the movie. They had many little combos, and some very good musicians, who played in the orchestras. They would double. They'd play in these little string quartets and also in the Philharmonic. We had some good music.

Norma Shearer was a very lucky girl. She fell into the right hands. And her mother was smart enough to keep her hands off her, and her career just developed naturally. She had some ability. She wasn't a great actress, but she learned as she went along. Things were very simple in those days.

Very few Broadway stars became stars in silent movies. They found it very hard to adapt to the silent medium. It was not their cup of tea. They were used to getting out onstage and emoting. Dialogue was very important on the stage. Motion pictures, don't forget, they were *silent!* All you had were titles.

I was a *writer*. I didn't give a *damn* about actors or actresses. That was another field and it was far away from the way we thought and the way we had to operate. I was a writer and I was interested in the word, and what was going to go down on paper.

A good script takes a good story, good character, and a good plot. No actor or actress ever made an outstanding film. It was the material that made the movie alive. It was good material.

Chaplin wrote his own material. He knew his forte and he knew what he could do, and he was very brilliant. Very clever man. I met Chaplin. He was a pretty damn serious man. He liked good literature. He was serious about films. He had a pretty good idea which way the movies were headed—this is before sound. Chaplin was an outstanding person, and he was an innovator. Chaplin was unique. He was a genius. He was very outstanding, and he did a great deal for the medium of motion pictures.

I loved to eat at Musso's. I still love to eat at Musso's. It was very important in my life. I didn't run around a lot. Always had good food. And you met everybody you had to meet there, so you didn't have to do a lot of running around. Everybody came to Musso's so you met them there. Certainly all the writers would go to Musso's.

I met my husband Ernest [Maas] there. He came in and came over to talk to John Brownell, who was having dinner with me. He didn't pay any attention to me at all. He was very businesslike with John. I found him very attractive. So I looked him up and found out where he worked, and decided to go meet him. I was walking toward his office, telling myself, "Frederica, don't bother him. He might not like it. Don't interfere with what he's doing. He might not like you at all. Wait, wait, be more patient." "Oh no, I've got to meet that guy!" So I went to his office and knocked on the door. He didn't answer, so I opened the door and walked in. There he was with his feet up on his desk, totally engrossed in reading something. I introduced myself. And he didn't have a chance. [Laughter] He was a very nice man.

59

I also loved the Montmartre. A very important part of my life, the Montmartre was. *Everybody* ate there. You met everybody that was important. You did a lot of business there. It was very important, the Montmartre. It was run by Eddie Brandstatter, who was left hanging dry. Eddie was not very talkative, not very intelligent. He had an ordinary mind. But he knew the restaurant business. He was interested in good food and could supply it. He knew a lot about food. Everybody went there. When the Trocadero became the new hot spot, everybody abandoned Eddie. And he died. He committed suicide, more or less. He died of a broken heart. I remember, oh, how pitiful it was. The tiny eatery he finally opened after the Montmartre. It was such a drab little place. And even that was not successful.

I remember Irving Thalberg. He was a very lucky fellow at the time. At the time that he was advancing in motion pictures, most of the pictures were growing and becoming more serious and he just played along. I don't think he was an innovator. I think he was unique in that he understood good material when it was offered to him or he had a chance to use it, and he was clever enough to take advantage of it. I think he was just someone who had a good appreciation of literature and sensing motion picture material when it was hidden in books and stories, what made good pictures.

I remember when talkies came in. I remember shaking in my boots wondering if Ernest and I could write dialogue. We wrote dialogue for the silent movies, but this was different. That was just to get a general feeling of what was going on. It wasn't heard on the screen. This was dialogue that would be *heard*. But Ernest had originally started with writing plays in Greenwich Village, so he was very adept at writing dialogue. And I learned from the experience of working with him. But I did find it difficult at first. Dialogue did not come easy to me.

Naturally, the talkies did have a profound effect on Hollywood and the music business. It changed the whole thing. Before, things had little meaning. You could give it any interpretation you wanted. But when sound came in, you had actual dialogue. It had to have definition. And it had to *mean* something. And you could no longer fake it. So it did make a big difference. It changed the medium completely. From the start, I knew it was an advance, not just a novelty. My husband Ernest had been a producer, and he was involved in sound pictures, even before the big studios developed them. He produced many shorts, and he also developed a game called "You Spot It" for people to play in the theaters during the Depression.

Sound was definitely an improvement. Silent pictures was a static phase of motion pictures. It was only when sound came in that motion pictures came *alive*. Instead of trying to read lips, you had real people saying dialogue. Like on the stage, it has some finish and purpose to it.

I remember wanting very much to meet June Mathis. She was also a writer, and was famous for writing *Four Horsemen of the Apocalpyse* for Valentino. It was his big break. I met her at the Montmarte. I thought she was very stupid. I was very disappointed. I thought I would meet somebody brilliant, who I could glean something from. But I met her and found her so banal.

Hollywood Boulevard then was what it should be today: Glamorous. It had good stores like I. Magnin. The best of everything was there. I think we had a feeling that it was very special. If you bought anything good, you went there. People would walk on the boulevard from Vine to La Brea every night. I loved it, and I loved going to films at the Egyptian Theater.

I remember Hollywood changed because there was a huge earthquake which tumbled a lot of the houses in the thirties. And then after the Depression, new housing developments went up in the Hollywood area where there had been orchards and gardens. The scenery of Hollywood changed a lot then.

I wrote *Flesh and the Devil* starring Garbo and John Gilbert. But I received no credit on that film. There were several films I worked very hard on that I never got my credit. We wrote that film based on the title; it's a title that had been floating around the studio, and we just picked it up and started to work on it. It was a good title.

I don't think John Gilbert was terribly important to our calculations. He just happened to be a leading man, and he fell into it. I was never interested in actors or actresses. As a writer, you had no influence on that whatsoever.

We worked in separate departments. We had separate interests. An actor or an actress could not turn out their own material, and when they do, it's usually awful. They are very important in interpreting material. They could make or break a movie. Gilbert wasn't very profound. He was just a very ordinary intellect. Garbo was a great exception. She was a *great* exception.

I met Valentino a couple of times. He had a reputation for being a great lady's man. But it think he had more of a reputation than he deserved. But I never was interested in that part of Hollywood. It just never meant anything to me. I met actors by the dozen but I never thought actors were important.

I remember Joan Crawford very well. I knew her before she was a star, when she was still Lucille LeSeur. I did not think she was very talented. I thought she was very ambitious, very clever. She went after everything that would make her stand out as a good actress. She was a gum-chewing tart from New York. But she had an opportunity, and she seized it. And she worked on it. She became a star out of pure drive. She took the opportunity and seized on it with both hands, and she made something of it. She took time to go to school, to study. She started to dress differently. She changed her whole lifestyle. I didn't have that much contact with her to get to know her well. You know, writers and stars, they are from different worlds in a motion-picture studio. They don't have much contact with each other.

Many great authors came to Hollywood to write movies. But they didn't understand the medium. They were interested in the printed word and writing. And they didn't know much about stagework either. The main thing was that they would write the material, and the people who were more suited to screenwriting took their material and made it work for the screen. Writing for the screen and writing words to be read in a book are entirely different, and require a different kind of talent and know-how.

I remember the St. Francis Dam disaster. Hundreds of people were killed. I saw it in the newspaper. It was terrible. But disasters happen. My understanding is that it broke because it was poorly built. And Mulholland built an identical dam—right in the hills above Hollywood, under the sign.

I was invited to the Hearst Castle. The thing I remember about it were the meals. There would be about thirty, forty people sitting at long tables. And we'd have these *exquisite* meals there at the castle. That still lingers in my mind. Mostly it was actors and actresses there. They have their own ideas of happiness. If they have a good role, they're happy. If they play in something where they don't have enough opportunity, they're not happy. They're not people of real mental capacity. If they are, they're not good actors. Everybody came to Hearst Castle in those days. But it was mostly, as I remember it, a place for actors and actresses.

Ben Schulberg told me I could be a star. Like Theda Bara. God forbid. [Laughs] I told them, I have too much intelligence to be an actress. I'm a writer. It didn't appeal to me at all to be a star. I was told I had the face to be a star. But I don't know how photogenic I really was. I never really posed for the camera. And I never had the opportunity to act before the camera. I might have been a perfect dud. [Laughs]

62

I never regretted not becoming an actor. I never had much respect for actors. Actors never interested me. They were superficial. Actors came from the stage, and the motion picture was a new medium for them. Most of them were floundering and didn't have their niche yet. They hadn't found a picture that would put them forward in the business, and they were all more or less looking for that big chance.

Acting did not appeal to me at all. It was the written word. That's what I cared about. I never dwelled on the background of the motion picture business. I was a writer and I was interested in what came out the end of my pen. Now I'm an old woman who bites her nails.

I met Irving Berlin on many occasions. Personally, Berlin and the other songwriters were always very annoying to me. They were childlike and so involved with their music. They weren't interested in the word. I was a writer. I was interested in what was written on paper. Popular songs had value, sure, but only as popular songs. Irving Berlin's personal dilemma was that he needed always to be pushing and pitching. He played his songs all the time, but he wasn't much of a piano player, really. He played with only two or three fingers. I liked his music but I heard it so much, I wanted to hear *any-thing* but that.

I wrote a movie with my husband Ernest Maas called *Miss Pilgrim's Progress*. It was based on a play about how the invention of the typewriter really changed the work lives of thousands of women. We wanted to make a serious movie about this, almost like a docudrama. We wrote it, and it got put aside during World War II, and when they finally made the film, it got turned into a musical starring Betty Grable called *The Shocking Miss Pilgrim*. A totally frivolous movie. But I wasn't surprised. A writer is never surprised by the sacrilegious treatment of their material. We're *never* pleased. It's never done the way we see it or want it to be done. It's always emasculated. Nearly always.

When they came to me for a script, I wrote the script. What they did to it after that, a writer had no influence. No participation in the development of the actual film. So anything could happen to our material and did.

At the start of movies, there were many more women writers than men. Pictures became more physical, and men went into it, and women subsequently declined. They had the money. At the beginning, I had no problem being a woman writer. Most men were attached to the physical making of the movie, and they couldn't care less about the writing. But the climate changed.

I wrote a movie called *The Waning Sex*. It was a title I was given and we wrote the title around it. I got into a lot of fights with the co-writer on the film, Hugh Herbert. It was rough. I would work so hard on some of the scripts, and the minute I'd turn it in, someone else would take credit for it. It was *awful*. But there was absolutely nothing I could do about it. You'd be ticketed as a troublemaker. Unless you wanted to quit the business, you just kept your mouth shut.

When the Depression came, there was no work. We lost $10,000 when the stock market crashed. We went back to New York.

The blacklist in Hollywood was an awful period. It was terrible. You'd be accused of things you were absolutely innocent of, and knew very little about, and suddenly you'd be ticketed and ostracized. It was a very, very, very difficult time for writers. I was not surprised that it happened. I saw it coming. Those things are always in the air and developing, and suddenly they mature. And then the bad things start happening. I had to get a job in an insurance agency. I couldn't get a job writing. My husband and I were interrogated by the FBI. In our house in Hollywood. They wanted to know what my affiliations were. But I was clean. They wanted me to name the names of people I knew to be communists, which I didn't do. First of all, because I didn't know of any. But I wouldn't have named anyone if I did. Oh, that was a *miserable* time. Everybody was suspicious of everybody else. You didn't know who your friends were.

But it was always great to see one of my films on the screen. Even if I didn't get screen credit. Writers were accustomed to that. But you had spent hours conceiving the film, and it was your baby, and it could be a thrill to see them as finished films on the screen.

Hollywood is a different place now. And attitudes have changed. Hollywood's history hasn't been preserved well. But every history is worth saving. It was a very poignant, interesting time.

I never was interested in the background of my work. I was interested in my work. I was interested in writing. I wasn't interested in the politics around me. And they were always around me. The Red Scare. Most of my so-called friends were labeled as communists and I didn't know whether they were or they weren't, and I didn't really care. And so I just quit motion pictures, and I worked on the outside, in whatever jobs I could get.

Movies will always be with us. They are part of the entertainment medium. In the theater. Because in the theater, on the big screen, movies are alive, and they are different. Movies are serious art. *Original* movies.

I'm thrilled if people still want to see my films. I don't see them around myself these days. But I'd like to get a peek at one of them.

I'm 101 years old now. But I have no real secret to longevity. I have good genes. And I never drank too much, although I do like liquor. I try to stay active. I walk. And I can sleep *anytime* I want to. I sleep more now than I used to, but if I want to stay alive, I need to sleep.

64

The brain is the most incredible computer in the world. It's important to take your memories and tell them to somebody you love. My husband Ernest and I would come up with a memory of the past that we would talk about and enjoy and share. And after we had talked about it, we would *delete* it from our memory banks so that there would be enough room for something new. Because the only way to stay alive and kicking and intellectual is to learn something new every day. The brain survives if you keep it alive and kicking.

Lothrop Worth

BORN JULY 11, 1903
MELROSE, MASSACHUSETTS
CAMERAMAN

An extremely tall man, even in his nineties he seemed too large for the small surroundings of his cottage at the Motion Picture Country Home. "Talk to Lothrop," his friend Hal Riddle said. "If you want to know about Hollywood, he should be first on the list. Lothrop Worth. Famous cinematographer. Worked with Griffith, DeMille. Talk to him. Talk to him today." Riddle was right. A pioneer of the movies, Lothrop was a cameraman who began near the very beginning of movies. Hard of hearing, he had trouble understanding some of the questions posed to him, but it didn't matter; he seemed happy to relate once again the remarkable details of his life in Hollywood. He was clearly world-weary, and ready to shed the mortal coils that still kept him here when so many of those he'd worked with were long gone. Less than two weeks after our meeting, he was gone, too.

My family came to Hollywood when I was seven years old in 1910. My father was a prosperous banker and broker. And the crash of 1907 completely ruined the family financially. So it was "Go west, young man," and he came west. He got his first job at a shooting gallery [laughs] in the summer. He came here to be a streetcar motorman. And then he sent for us.

My mother fell on the ice and fractured her spine in Massachusetts. This was about 1875. They had surgery. They offered her opium but she refused to take it. They thought that she was going to die. But then she met a Doctor Brett. From whom I got my crazy middle name. It's Lothrop Brett Worth. He did a laying on of hands for her. Some people have an electricity in them, and he had this. He touched her solar plexus and she said she found some kind of relief, some kind of release. She had been in bed for three years at that point, and he got her up. He put her in a cast, with a steel belt around her and crutches. Then she seemed to get stronger. Eventually she was able to take it off and she was able to walk. But if she put the wrong stress on her spine, she would pass out just like that.

When we moved out here to Hollywood, she applied for a job at the finest beauty parlor in Hollywood. She had done much beauty work in the east, so when she went to them with her credentials they hired her immediately. She introduced hot oil treatments for hair out here. It was the latest thing in the east. And she got for clientele all the richest people, including Mrs. DeMille. C.B. was just getting started then.

We lived on a little street on the edge of Griffith Park, overlooking the Valley, which was all truck farms then. There was a little subdivision of houses and a little tiny one-room school. These houses there were little gray prefabricated houses, and there was a song popular then, "My Little Gray House in the West." There was a pumpkin patch out in the back. When the pumpkins were ripe, we used to go out there and steal them, bring them home and eat them.

We used to ride the big red streetcars all over the city. We used to walk up and down these stairs that they carved into the hill, because it was so steep. And when it rained, we would have a heck of a time getting up and down those stairs.

My father died suddenly when I was completing my first year at USC and I needed a job. What was I going to do? Constance—Mrs. DeMille—was at the house and she offered me a job in the movies with her husband C.B. Well, I was a smart young jerk. I got up on my hind-legs and said, "Thank you very much, Mrs. DeMille. I'll get my own job." She was very sweet about it. She said, [slowly] "As you wish, Lothrop." So I got a job running the record department at Bullock's downtown. I could have made more money if I were out selling papers on 7th & Broadway.

So I changed my mind and went back to Mrs. DeMille. She told me I could have a job and I should go to Paramount. Well, what I didn't know was that it was summer and they were in between shooting pictures. So there was no work. I went there every day for a week but no work, so I stopped going. Months went by and Mrs. DeMille asked my mother how it was working out for me, and my mother told her there was no work for me.

Mrs. DeMille told her to tell me to go back, which I did, and sure enough there was a job waiting for me. As a cameraman.

The studios were like a bunch of shacks. They would do only exteriors. There was no sign of high-powered lights or that kind of thing. In the beginning they used Ortho film, which had a gray scale between three and four. That's between white and black. The main thing was that people had their faces *so* white, they all looked like clowns running around.

Of course, in those days, they would *never* move the camera. They worked in the frame. And the second camera, that was originally set side by side with the first camera, and that was for foreign release. And all the second cameraman did was look through the viewfinder and make sure the actors didn't go out of the frame.

The whole development of movies is very interesting. Billy Bitzer was Griffith's cameraman, and I met him and I saw that his career was almost over when we met, though Griffith would still use him for some films. The whole development of the matchbox in front of the camera was practically *all* Billy. Because you'd see those early cameras, they were just boxes with a lens. There's no shade at all. They could only shoot things with front light— if the light shone back at you, it got in the lens.

So Billy extended the shooting day by holding his hat over the lens. But you couldn't see through the film back then, there was no way, so sometimes he got the hat in the frame. Griffith told him to stop fooling around with the hat. But he finally got the idea and took a soup can, cut out the end, put it on there, and that made a shade. But he couldn't tell when it was cutting in on the corners. It looked like a portrait setup, with the corners shadowed. The cameramen went to that, and I think the directors did too. But that got refined.

By the time I came into the business, they used to make burnouts. The photography went from one extreme to another, in terms of what they thought was desirable. I didn't come in until the early twenties. By that time they were still doing a lot of fancy fading. Today we do it all with the lamps. You can control what is called a barn door.

By the time I got to be a cameraman, there was camera movement but very little. On one of my first pictures with DeMille, I was supposed to slowly pan the camera over. And I did it perfectly the first three times but on the fourth take I got lost, and I went up instead of over. [Laughs] C.B. said to print that take, so I told him we needed to do another.

"Why do we need to do another?" he asked.

I told him, "Too much headroom."

He said, "How much was it?"

I said, "Too much, it's not worth printing."

He said, "Okay. But on my pictures, we only do three or four takes, no more."

I said, "You can print the first three, they're all good for me." That kind of stopped him. And he said, "Okay, I'll give you another one." And he did. But he printed that bad one anyway.

So we made another take. And three days later we're in the rushes, and he's at the panel of controls with his editor. And this scene comes on and I thought, "Here we go. The boom will be lowered now." And everything was fine and all of a sudden the camera goes up. And it was much worse than I even thought. C.B. turned to his editor and said, "You know, he told me that was no good. I should have listened to him." And from that day on I never had any problem with him. And I worked at Paramount for twenty years. And I worked everywhere else for another twenty years.

67

The thing that set me off in camera really was one thing. I got interested in 3-D, and that became my baby, and that really set me up in Hollywood. Then I did *Gog*, a 3-D science-fiction movie with Herbert Marshall. It's as good of a picture as any you will on the screen today. Every once in a while they will show it on TV on *Movie Classics*, but they only run one of the eyes, the left or the right eye. They both are perfectly good flat pictures.

I worked on some of the pictures that were produced at Paramount by A.C. Lyles. Hell of a nice guy. There was an amusing thing I remember about him. I had been at Paramount for some years and I heard I was going to work on some films there produced by a man named A.C. Lyles, and I heard he had been a messenger boy when I was first there. So I wracked my brain trying to figure out which one of the kids delivering the mail was Lyles. So I was called in to have a conference with him about the picture. And when I walked in, he said, "Oh, it's you!" And I said the same thing to him: "Oh, it's you!" [Laughs] He was trying to figure out who I was, too. He is a very nice man. I understand he's still there.

In those days people had steady jobs. Not anymore. In those days the stars didn't have enough brains to save money when they were making it, so they'd be destitute. That's why they made this place. In the early days we used to have a lot of stars here. Not so many anymore.

I used to do a lot of the screen tests for people who became big stars. Victor Mature came out of the Pasadena Playhouse, like so many, and I shot his first test. I remember that a lot of them would be all wired up to do their first take perfect. And then when the director would ask for another take, the museum sort of collapsed and they figured they were a failure right there.

And even when I was just an assistant I would try to help them. I'd say, "You know, Von Sternberg made fifty-two takes of a scene with Deitrich just the other day." So I'd put them at ease, you know.

The funniest one of all who I could never understand was Buster Crabbe. Buster Crabbe had been an Olympic champion, terrific physique and all. So they decided to make him a Johnny Weismuller type of thing. [Laughs] I can't illustrate how poorly he read. He had *no idea at all* of acting in any way, shape or form. And he had his little scene written up for him. I can't exaggerate how badly he did. He was supposed to be like Tarzan in the jungle, and every time he would come into the jungle, he would say, "A-hem?" Now where the hell is that? I never heard of it. So they would cut and try it again and again, but he could *never* get it. He finally got be a pretty decent actor. But this was the most extreme case. *Hilarious.*

When the silent era started ending and sound came in, I went into sound. I had been in sound for years. I learned the whole principle of how things were done. What happened was that the first original sound crew came out from the phone company—three men with a recorder. They had *carte blanche.* They could get anything they asked for. They asked for the top salary that cameramen were making then, which was $250 a week. And that's what they got. So everybody wanted to get into working with sound. I didn't make any move at all to do it. I got to know these fellas, and I talked to them. When the new recorder came out, one of these men came to me and asked if I wanted to join his crew. I thought that this was opportunity really knocking on my door. So I agreed to it and I worked in sound and learned how to handle a recorder.

But then when new people were needed, the guys brought in other people they knew from the phone company. And when layoffs came, why, they laid me off first. So I stormed into the front office and I got reinstated. But then they laid me off again in a week. So I said, the *hell* with this, and I went over to Paramount to work in camera. No sooner did I get there, I was on the porch of the camera department, and here comes Eddie Gooley. We had done the return of Gloria Swanson, *Salome.* She was signed by [Joseph] Kennedy, you know. And he signed her for more than acting. [Laughs] And Eddie Gooley wrote it and directed it. Eddie was quite a talented man, and that was the first show that Gregg Toland operated on. *Salome* was quite a big success. I was on the sound crew.

So Eddie Gooley, he saw me at Paramount, and asked me to mix the sound for his next movie. Well, Paramount had a whole different system that I had never used. And I had already gotten my throat cut working in sound. So I had made a decision to stay in camera. But he told me to come to his office. So I went up there and he gave me a script and sat me down in the outer office, and there was Ina Clair reading a script over there. [Laughs] And I turned him down. I stayed in camera. And I never regretted it for a minute.

David Raksin

BORN AUGUST 4, 1912

PHILADELPHIA, PENNSYLVANIA

FILM COMPOSER

69

He's busy at work writing his own memoirs, and like everything he's done in his long life, he approaches this project with much diligence, and makes considerable progress on the manuscript every morning and afternoon. Still, a man must eat, and so he allots an hour at midday to make the quick trip to Froman's Deli, just a short drive from his Encino home, and it's there he's willing to reflect, over a brisket sandwich and chicken soup, on his own personal past. Hoping for but never receiving an acceptable pickle, he speaks intimately of legendary figures such as George Gershwin, Charlie Chaplin and Johnny Mercer in a matter-of-fact tone, as if discussing college chums. Unruffled even in his twenties by working with world-famous men, he remains decidedly indifferent to fame now in his nineties. What does impress him is the work, especially the work that has endured through all these years, such as the music of Gershwin, or the classic film Modern Times, *on which he took on the challenging task of translating Chaplin's musical ideas into a score. Like others who attempted to play this role before him, he was summarily fired when he expressed too many opposing opinions. But unlike the others, he was rehired—at the insistence of Alfred Newman—and the rest truly is history.*

My father, Isadore Raksin, was a wonderful musician, and quite a good conductor. He conducted for silent films, and sometimes played with the Philadelphia Orchestra. My mother played piano. I had two brothers, both of whom were musicians.

Philadelphia had a huge theater called the Metropolitan, and my father was the conductor there for silent films. He had an orchestra of thirty to forty musicians. In those days, scores for movies were assembled from different sources. A guy would say he needed three minutes of this, three minutes of that. My father would go down to his library and find the right pieces of music, and sometimes write a little bit. That's they way it was done in those days. It was not an easy job—you had to conduct while keeping your eyes on the screen. But they got to be pretty slick. He did all kinds of films.

On Saturdays, when I'd been a good boy, I'd be allowed to go and sit next to him as he conducted. He had a baton with a battery in the handle with a little light on the end. The lights were off in the pit except for the lights on the music. They would run the picture and he'd stand there and conduct.

I took piano lessons when I was a kid since I was quite small. I was a lousy student. I'd look at the guys out in front playing ball and I'd be in the house, practicing. My father finally got disgusted with me and gave me a saxophone. An alto. I took to that right away and got very good at it. It was easier than the violin. I liked the saxophone. I played the pop tunes of the day. A lot of jazz. I was going to be a musician no matter what. I thought my father was a pretty smart guy. He realized that the life of a musician was very chancy, and he didn't want me to be one.

I started composing from the very beginning. It annoyed the hell out of my piano teachers, because I would come in with my lessons unpracticed but I would have a new piece. By the time I was twelve I was writing music down. Taught myself. I had my own band. I played sax first and then my father gave me a clarinet, which I played that night with my band. I'm not so sure how good I sounded, but I played it.

I had several bands. The corniest name for one was the Four Bars of Harmony, though there were actually five of us. I learned how to write my own arrangements, and we also used stock arrangements. By the time I was sixteen I was doing arrangements for a lot of bands, and did an arrangement of "I Got Rhythm" by Gershwin. I made it for a big band. It started for a small band, but then I converted it to this huge arrangement for Jay Savitt's big band, which had strings in it. And it became kind of famous.

Oscar Levant, the composer, heard this arrangement and was so amazed by it, he told George [Gershwin] about it. George heard it, and he recommended me to Harms, a music publishing company. I was nineteen. I came out here and met George. It was 1935. He was a wonderful man. He lived then on Roxbury Drive in Beverly Hills. In the same house with his brother Ira. I was a guest at his house from time to time and I got to know him well.

George did not make me nervous at all. He recognized that I was a colleague who knew what he was doing. I met a lot of great musicians that way—Stravinsky, Schoenberg. I never had to be obsequious to any of them. I never would have done that. I studied with Schoenberg, and I worked with Stravinksy. I orchestrated the only one of his pieces which he didn't orchestrate himself, which was the Circus Polka.

George was always eager to play his new songs. He played them for everybody. He played me many songs. Songs from Goldwyn Follies, like "Love Walked Right In." I don't remember him singing. He just played the piano. He was a very good player. I think he was very happy living out here.

Harms Music invited me to work with Charlie Chaplin on the score of

Modern Times. The first time I met him was at his studio at La Brea & Sunset. There used to be a house at Sunset, next to it. Charlie's brother Sydney lived in that house. It was a *very* nice part of town then.

My first impression of Chaplin was that he was a very, very marvelously dressed little guy. A wonderful suit, and shoes that had tops like spats. Really a *dandy.* I had never seen him as himself in photos, only as the Little Tramp. He seemed like a different person at first from the Tramp, but then you could see it in him, you know. I'd be sitting there with him in the studio and there he was, he'd also be on the screen in character.

71

He was sometimes funny offscreen, but not a lot. We worked at the studio. We plunged right in working the first time we met. He was still editing the film a little bit when we started. He showed me the film first. I thought it was *wonderful.*

He had little notions for the music. He'd play them. Sometimes he'd play these little three-fingered chords. Sometimes just the melody. We'd discuss them, I would take notes, I'd sometimes make suggestions, and I would tell him what I thought.

After a week and a half of that he fired me. He didn't like to have some twenty-three-year-old kid telling the great man in Hollywood what to do with his own picture. He was a *total* autocrat. And he wasn't used to having anybody, saying, "Wait a minute, Charlie, we can do better than that."

But Alfred Newman saw the sketches I had been making of Charlie's little tunes. He spoke to Chaplin and said, "You'd be *crazy* to fire this guy."

So they asked me to come back. But I told them that I couldn't come back without some understanding with Charlie. I said I had to have a session with Charlie in private. Because what I had to say to him, if I said it in front of his employees, it would have jeopardized his standing.

So we met and I told him, "Charlie, look—if you want a musical secretary, that is not me. If you want another stooge, you don't need one. You're already up to your ears with them—nobody *ever* dares say no to you, or make any change in what you're doing. But if you want somebody who is willing to risk his job every day of the week to make sure this score is what it should be, I'm willing to do that." And he liked that.

We would work at the piano together. He would play with two fingers at the piano. He had nice ideas, but he didn't know how to extend or develop them. That was my job. He knew a lot of music, he had records. But he wasn't a musician. He had no concept of key or anything. He wasn't in C major or *any* other major, he'd just play, "ding, ding, ding," like that. And then I would figure it out. He'd play something and I would say, "You mean like this?" Then we would talk about where it goes from there.

He learned to accept my suggestions, and he was very grateful for them, and I am really the co-author of that score. I came there as an arranger, and so I would naturally defer to him. But he wasn't really up to being a composer. When he had a sequence like the factory sequence, he had just an idea for three notes. So he had those, and I would write some, and then he wrote some, and that's how we wrote the score. We talked about orchestration. He was like a magpie. He learned everything, and he understood the orchestra and had some pretty good ideas about the orchestration.

The song "Smile" came from that film. He retained credit for writing the music to it, but we wrote it together. He had the beginning, and played those opening notes [sings the first two measures: "Smile, though your heart is breaking..."] and I said [sings next two measures: "smile, even though it's aching..."] and we talked about it all the way through, and that's how it got written. The guys that made the song out of it were very clever guys and really knew what the hell they were doing. The theme in the picture is somewhat different from that. The song is not in the picture, and the lyrics were written later. I didn't get credit on the song but there was no point in making anything of it, because that's how things were done in those days. I was credited as arranger and orchestrater, though I did all the sketches. I didn't mind. When you were an arranger, you were sometimes asked to compose. That was what the arranger did.

We worked on the score for four and a half months. Which is not that long for a movie that is 100 percent music. Mostly it was working with him. There was no point in ever making a complete sketch with all the counterlines and correct harmonies and the correct bass part. So I always shorthanded it down when I was with him. Then when he was away doing studio business, then I'd fill in the sketch. Or I'd work at night. Or I'd come in early before he was there, and that's how I did it. I'd take it home with me and work at night.

We had regular working hours. He would get in around ten and leave around four. We would have lunch together five days a week. We used to go to Musso & Frank's every day for lunch. Everybody recognized him; everybody knew who he was. He liked that, but it wasn't so important to him. He'd been idolized since he was a boy. He was the number-one guy. One of the first worldwide stars ever, along with Mary Pickford and Douglas Fairbanks. Fans rarely came up to him.

The room where Charlie and I used to eat there no longer exists. It's now part of the Vogue Theater next door. They closed that part of it, and moved over to that big room, which is now over on the right. They took that big room over from a store. We had songs we used to sing there. To the tune of "When Irish Eyes Are Smiling," we'd sing, "An Irish stew with vegetables…" [Laughter] Or there was a tune, "I Want a Girlie," and we would sing, "I want a curry, a nicey spicey curry, with a dish of chutney on the side…." Chaplin never drank alcohol at lunch.

We recorded the score at United Artists. Alfred Newman conducted it. He was *some* conductor. Chaplin was very much involved in the recording. He listened, and he was very impressed with what he heard, because these little tunes were suddenly being played by a symphonic orchestra. That worked very well until the very end when their nerves all got shot to hell, and he had a big quarrel with Newman, and insulted him in some way, and Al walked off the stage and refused to conduct anymore.

A few nights before then I had gotten sick from working so much. I was so exhausted, Newman looked at me and told me to stay home the next day. I was as tall as I am now, and I weigh over 170 pounds; at that time I weighed 135. So I stayed away and got some sleep, came in the next morning to find out about this fight Charlie had with Newman. And Charlie, who had depended on me and who loved me dearly—I was like a son to him—was angry at me for not being there. We later made up. So I didn't go to the premiere because Charlie was still mad at me at this time. We saw each other after that, but we weren't on very good terms because he was angry at me because he felt I had chosen to side with Al. But eventually we became very good friends again and I went to see him when he was living in Switzerland.

He made *so* few films. When he made the next film after *Modern Times*, *The Great Dictator*, he asked me to do some things for it. So I helped him out with some things on it, but when it came time to do the score, I wasn't a new kid in town anymore, and I was busy. But I was my own man by then, so he got Meredith Wilson, who later wrote *The Music Man*, to work with him on that.

Modern Times is a great film. It's a very good movie. But I like *City Lights* more, for its depth of feeling.

I met Paulette Goddard many times during my work at the studio. She was just as beautiful offscreen as on. She was an absolute knockout.

I went then to United Artists to work for Alfred Newman, and then went to Europe for a while, and then worked for Universal. I was always working somewhere. Except a few times I wasn't working at all, which was tough.

I wrote the song "Laura" with Johnny Mercer. The music came first; it was from the score of the film. I gave Mercer a record of the music and he went home and wrote the lyric. He wrote it very quickly. He came over and showed it to me. He was a very highly skilled professional. I made two changes in the lyric. There were two places in the lyric where he wasn't sure which word to use, and I helped him decide. I told somebody I was making suggestions on how to write a lyric to Johnny Mercer of all people and they thought I was crazy. But it's true.

Karl Malden
BORN MARCH 22, 1912
CHICAGO, ILLINOIS
ACTOR

"I talked a lot, didn't I?" he asks with a hearty laugh. "I thought you would come in here and ask me some questions and I would say, 'Yes, no, yeah . . .' Instead you asked me one question and I kept talking from then on!" He sits in a big chair in the sunny living room of his West L.A. home, a baby grand piano to his right bedecked with framed photos of his family, his children and his children's children. It's a nice house, and a fairly large one. But it's not a mansion—it could be the house of any successful family man, but it's not what one might think of as a movie star's house. There are no walls around it or even a high fence, and there are no awards in sight, though he is the recipient of an Oscar, an Emmy and more. It's but one of the many dichotomies in the life and career of this famous man. Though he's been a major star of stage and screen for more than fifty years, he never made what he considered to be "the big money" until he starred on television and did TV commercials. Though he's portrayed countless tough and even contemptible people, in real life he's far from gruff, a man known in and beyond Hollywood circles for a genuine generosity of spirit. Though his reputation as a serious, dedicated actor is entrenched within many years now of cinema history, he's the essence of apologetic modesty. There have been few like him in Hollywood, and Hollywood is lucky to have him; a trained actor who worked nonstop for two full decades on Broadway, he brought to the movies an authenticity of character that few other actors of his generation, with the notable exception of his friend and colleague Marlon Brando, of whom he speaks at length, ever achieved.

I first came to Hollywood in 1940 in the play *Key Largo*, with Paul Muni and Tom Ewell. We were at the Biltmore Theater downtown for two weeks. We did shows at night and two matinees, on Saturdays and Wednesdays. A guy came backstage and asked Tom and I if we wanted to do a movie. We said, "How can we do it? We're in this play here."

He said, "It's small parts; do the play at night, we'll shoot during the day, you'll get about six weeks work, and Wednesdays we won't shoot you."

So Tom and I looked at each other and said, "Let's do it." And we did it, and that guy was Garson Kanin. We played two small parts, but we made some money. That was in 1940, and I didn't make another movie until 1948.

I remember Hollywood clearly from then. Orange groves, lemon groves, a lot of groves. [Laughter] It was a lot different than it is today. Every city changes, but Hollywood has changed more. It's because it's a facade; they just build the front, the hell with the back. [Laughter]

It was different. I didn't have a car. When the play closed, we still had about a week to go working on the movie. So Tom and I got a little courtyard apartment on Beachwood Drive, just a couple of blocks north of Franklin. And we walked to Paramount each day. It was a nice walk. I couldn't do it today, but I could do it then.

Our favorite place to eat then—if somebody took us—was Musso & Frank's. We were there a lot. Other than that, we'd eat at some hamburger joint.

75

We walked everywhere then, no problem. It was safe. Hollywood Boulevard was very glamorous then; all those movie theaters were really sparkling and shining. There weren't as many cheesy, crimey stores, chintzy shops. There were nice stores around. At the corner of Hollywood & Vine, the Broadway, a great big department store. The Brown Derby was there, if you remember. It had class then, a lot of class.

I was born in Chicago on Fullerton & Clybourn. Then we moved immediately just two blocks from Riverview Park. I have always had a secret hunch that Disney as a young man went to Riverview Park a lot, and then when he did Disneyland, it's Riverview Park, but with just a fancy glow on it. It's the same rides, same kind of thing. Everything's the same.

My real name is Mladen Sekulvich. We moved to Gary, Indiana, when I was four years old. My father went to work in the steel mills there. I have early memories of the movies from then. Gary, Indiana had a theater called the Family Theater. I think they charged ten cents. It was nothing but a store with benches. And I think they could only seat 150 people. A store with a screen on the end and a guy on a platform in the back projecting pictures.

The first picture I remember seeing was Charlie Chaplin in *Three O'Clock in the Morning*. In that one he was all dressed in tails, and came home and couldn't find his key, so he couldn't get in the door. So he climbs in a window. The set was nothing but a stairway going up with a platform and a stairway coming down. And in the middle of the platform up above is a great, big grandfather clock with a pendulum swinging back and forth. It's obvious what he did: the *whole* routine, five minutes or ten minutes, he would drunkenly come up the steps. He'd have a hard time getting up, but finally he'd get up the steps and go across on that platform, and *boom*, the clock would hit him back down again. And then he'd come up the steps again, and *boom*, it hit him back down again. So this time he's being clever, and he went up and he stepped aside, and it missed him at first and then *boom*, it hit him down the other side. That's the *whole* routine [laughs], how he played with a clock. That's the first one that I remember.

Getting back to Gary, there was the Grand Theater. And then they went big in the twenties. They built a place called the Palace Theater. It had a sky with twinkling lights—remember that period?—a big stage, where you could put an orchestra if you wanted it. That was the big theater; they charged, I think, twenty-five cents to get in. It showed Tom Mix, all the old timers, Clara Bow, Douglas Fairbanks, those were all the stars, Mary Pickford, Lillian Gish. Every once in a while they would have a stage show—a movie and a stage show. They had an organ player who would play between movies.

Now that was a good Saturday or Sunday for me when I was a kid. I'd go with a friend, and we'd each have fifty cents. I remember right next door to the movie theater was a Walgreen's drugstore, and for twenty cents you'd go in there and get a good malted milk, and if you knew the person behind the counter, he'd let you have two. So we'd each have a malted milk for twenty cents, and that would be a good day.

I worked in the steel mills in Gary for three years. And I knew I had to get out of that some way. I didn't want to spend my whole life there. And the Goodman Theater [in Chicago] used to admit one person every year in Gary, for the winner of a one-act play contest.

And that's how I got into acting. I really thought I was going to go there and be a stagehand. I had some connections in Chicago, so if I learned how to build scenery, work on lights, and stuff of that sort, I might be able to get a job. That's what I was looking for. Anything to get out of Gary, to get out of the mills.

I went down there and saw the head of the Goodman Theater. He said, "You know, it costs money to come to this school, we don't give scholarships."

I said, "I don't have much money; how much does it cost?"

He said, "Nine hundred dollars."

I said, "I don't have $900."

He said, "How much do you have?" I said I had $300, which I had saved up working in the mills.

He said, "Are you a gambler?"

I said, "No, I don't gamble."

He said, "Would you gamble on yourself?"

I said, "How?"

He said, "Well, I'll let you stay here for three months for $300. After that time I'll let you know if you belong here. And if you do belong here, I'll give you a full scholarship."

I said, "That's a gamble. I'll try it." And I stayed for three years.

That was a big turning point in my life. To do that, and to graduate after three years from the Art Institute—the Goodman was part of the Art Institute.

Then I had to decide if I wanted to go to Hollywood, or I wanted to go to New York. And I decided to go to New York. I spent twenty years in New York. I wanted to be onstage. That's what I *really* studied for. I did a lot of plays, a lot of failures. As a matter of fact, I did twenty-four plays in twenty years in New York. I had about five that were hits. I had at least nineteen plays that were failures. My theory was that the only way to learn was to keep working. Maybe other people could learn from books or classes, but I had to get up there to do it. I also felt that in order to hit a home run, you had to get up to bat. And I just wanted to get up to bat.

I don't audition well. I think I auditioned twice, and I didn't make it. I'm not a sight-reader, I can't do it. It takes me a while to figure it out. And also for me, as an actor, what matters more is who I'm acting with. His reaction to what I'm saying, my reaction to him. Can I stimulate him, can he stimulate me? If I may say so, I think that's why Marlon [Brando] and I got along so well together. We could *really* go at each other. You'd do things that you never did before, and he would come back to you and you would come back to him, and it kept yourself really *thinking* and *busy*.

I did *A Streetcar Named Desire* in 1947 on Broadway. I met Tennessee Williams then. My memories of him are not too brilliant, but that was my own fault. I was so awed of this great writer that I couldn't talk much around him, because I fell in love with *A Glass Menagerie*. Personally, I think that's a greater play than *Streetcar*. [Elia] Kazan was directing *Streetcar*, and he told Tennessee to go away during the rehearsals after the first week because when he was there, he would laugh hysterically at his lines. He *loved* Marlon's part, and would laugh hysterically at what Marlon would do. He just thought it was the greatest thing he'd ever seen. So Kazan told him to go away and come back in a couple of weeks. And he came back in a week, and I think he was pleased with the play.

At the few little parties we'd have, I sat, with twelve or so other people around, talking to him. But I didn't put myself out. It was my fault, because I was so in awe of this great writer. And he is a great writer. His plays are like poetry. He puts words together just like Shakespeare. You can't ad lib Tennessee Williams. He gets everything just right.

In *Streetcar*, there was no ad libbing. It might have seemed like Marlon was ad libbing, but he wasn't. Marlon changed the style of acting in America. He was so natural. I had worked with a lot of good actors. But Marlon was the first one to make it sound with every line as if it were happening for the first time. Other great actors were great. But after a while it got to be like they

77

were doing it, and doing it as good as you can professionally. With Marlon, it was happening right here for the first time. And that's after two years. He just had that knack. It's something I wish I had but I don't. I don't think I was at his level. I've always said, when you work with a genius, you know you can't be as great as a genius, but you certainly are going to try to push him around. [Laughs]

I was doing the play of *All My Sons*, written by Arthur Miller. It was running. I did *Boomerang* for Kazan before *All My Sons*. Zanuck liked what I did in *Boomerang*. So he had a guy call me to hire me to do *Kiss of Death*. So I got this call, "Zanuck wants you. I got to hire you."

I said, "Fine, but I'm in a play. I got Wednesday matinees and Saturday matinees."

He said, "Well, we don't work on Saturday but for the Wednesday matinees, we'll work around you."

I said, "Fine," and I signed the contract.

They called me on a Tuesday to go to work. I went and I did the day's work. They said, "All right, Wednesday, be here at 8:30."

I said, "Wednesday's my matinee day, I can't be here."

They went, "What do you mean you can't be here? Jesus Christ!" In other words, I was stopping production. "I don't care what you have to do, just let the understudy go on."

So I called Kazan and told him, "I'm in a pickle here."

He said, "Your first commitment is with the play. *Screw* them. Let them worry about it." So I did one day's work for four week's salary. [Laughs] They never called me back. That was it. They took my lines and gave them to somebody else. That's how they do pictures. The technique of acting in movies is different than the technique of acting in theater. The difference is that the closer the camera gets to you, the less you do. So that when you come to a close-up, you act with only your face. That's all you use. This is important. The thinking process is different. As the camera gets farther away, you can begin to expand, and become more theatrical in what you're doing. I've always worked on that premise.

Then the equipment [of movies] and the lenses they used became *so* fine that after a while, if the camera was half a block away, I always had to look at the operator to see if it was a close-up. Because they didn't have to come close to get a close-up anymore. They could change a lens and be right up to your face. So you have to know that. I wasn't embarrassed just to ask.

I don't know if I would have been a different kind of actor if I had never worked with Marlon. You must remember that I did two plays with him in New York, and I saw the way he acted. If you're competitive, you can't fool around. You've got to get in there and work. You can't just sit back and let him do it. Cause he can take it, hook, line and sinker, the whole goddamn thing. So I knew that you had to be alert. And with Marlon, my whole approach would be to stimulate him. So that he in turn will stimulate me. And he will stimulate me, I knew that. But it was up to me—I knew I couldn't be better than he was, but by God, I was gonna give him a run for his money. That was my whole thing with him.

We did Streetcar both as a movie and a play, with the same director. And what has never happened ever is that the entire cast of the play was brought to play the movie, except for Jessica Tandy. Marlon at that time was nobody; he'd made one movie then and it wasn't too big, so he wasn't a big star. Streetcar made him a big star. So he couldn't carry anybody. But Vivien Leigh [who played Tandy's part in the film] could carry all of us. She was the biggest star in town. Gone with the Wind. She hadn't done a movie in ten years and now she was coming back to do another movie. She was the biggest thing. If Jessica had played it, Kim Hunter and I wouldn't have been in the picture. They would have had two big stars. Which is what they did with The Glass Menagerie. The four leads were played by four stars and they fell right on their fanny.

79

I enjoyed making the movie very much. Because the stuff that we talked about onstage, you could see. The big scene with me is when I take her out. We went dancing. We couldn't do that in the theater. We went on the waterfront, if you remember. And she's telling me all about the boy. In the theater, that was done in the living room. So it opened it up for me. It let it breathe a little bit. Onstage it was one set.

I won an Oscar for my role in Streetcar. Which might have helped from a reputation standpoint. But from a monetary standpoint, it didn't make much difference. After that, Warner Brothers wanted me to sign a contract. I thought it over carefully, with the help of a lot of other people helping me, I signed the contract, a regular two-pictures-a-year deal. But all the while I was making those two pictures a year here, I was in New York. I did two plays in New York. When they say it can't be done, I say it can be done because I did it. But I thought, to hell with them if they want to fire me. I'm living in New York. They kept saying, "Why don't you move here? Your work is here." And I kept saying, "You just send me the script. I'll be there when it's time to shoot, ready to go." And that's the way it was.

I was under contract to Warners for nine years. I never hired my own press agent, and I never had a manager. I had an agent because you need an agent in this town. But Warners publicized me. I was their property. They made money off of me. They loaned me out and made more money than I made. They paid me so much and they made double that money when they loaned me out. So the Oscar had a purpose because people got to know me. And they got to know me as a serious actor.

I worked with Marlon both as a director and as a fellow actor. He directed *One-Eyed Jacks*, the only film he ever directed. And I will tell you, as a director he would have been as great as he was as an actor. He's a *genius*. I'm sorry they didn't let him do more. He could have been one of the top directors in town if they'd just have given him another picture. But they didn't. It didn't happen. I think the film industry missed a lot when he didn't go on as a director.

One-Eyed Jacks was supposed to be done for a certain figure, and it went *way* over budget. It was supposed to have been shot in eight weeks and it took six months. That's a lot of money. The film business is a *business*. And he didn't listen. And I don't blame him. I don't think I could have done it, because I don't have the guts. But he wouldn't shoot a scene unless it was right. If he sat down to do a scene on a Tuesday, then that's the scene we're going to do, and we're going to wait for the weather to change. And we waited. That's the way everyone used to shoot. The way Chaplin used to make a movie. The only difference is that it was much cheaper then, and he owned the picture. [Laughs]

I think of *One-Eyed Jacks* as a classic. It's the only Western with an ocean background. No other Western's had that. That was his idea. Usually you go up to Arizona, the mountains, Utah, all that, that's [John] Ford country. All those big rocks, that's Western country. [Brando] did just the opposite. [Laughs]

There are rules that he knew and that I knew. Since we both learned from one of the *best* directors in town, Elia Kazan. Anything is worthwhile, as long as you get it. *Anything goes*. Because you only have to do it once. And he did a lot of things that a lot of people think was crazy. But he *got* it. In *One-Eyed Jacks*, he had the cowboys in there—Slim Pickens, all those guys. Those guys were *nobody*. They were cowboys. But, boy, some of the guys, the best job they've ever done was working with him. He got it out of them. Pina Pelisier, who played the little girl, never did anything but one little play in Mexico. And he saw her somewhere and sat down and talked to her. He did things to her to make her cry. Some terrible things he had to do with her, but he made her cry. [Laughs] It was his movie, he wanted to do it as well as he could do it. See, I'm comparing myself with him and I shouldn't. But I'm not in his class.

I directed a movie called *Time Limit*. For Richard Widmark, my dear friend. About the Korean War. Kazan was always trying to get me to direct. So I decided to direct. But there's one thing a director has to have, and which Kazan said, "You don't have, but you're gonna get it if you work on it." You've got to be *mean*. You've got to make people do what you would never do yourself. I can't do that. And if I can't do it, I don't want anybody else to do it. I don't want to take the chance. If someone's afraid of water, and there's a scene in the water, and the girl is really nervous, and the director tells her, "Don't worry, the water's only up to there, don't worry about a thing, we got a guy standing right here beside the camera and if anything goes wrong, he's there in a minute." And she gets out there in the water and that guy's not there. But the director gets what he wants. [Laughs] You have to be a little ruthless.

When I signed with Warner Brothers, within a year's time, Cagney left, Humphrey Bogart left, all these guys that were the Warner Brothers company, left. So I never had the joy of working with all these old-timers. I got to know Cagney. I used to kid Humphrey Bogart. We rode bicycles on the lot, and Bogart always said, "Hey! You didn't put out your hand when you made that right turn. Put out your hand!" [Laughs] That kind of stuff. I would say, "I can only drive with two hands!" The old-timers to me were Gable, Tracy, Katie Hepburn, Tyrone Power. I wasn't here when the real glamour of Hollywood was here. Though people like Michael Douglas say to me that I did films like Streetcar and Babydoll. To him, that's the glamour part of Hollywood. It wasn't to me.

Babydoll was done—Kazan is a brilliant director—Eli Wallach's first movie, Carrol Baker's first movie. Kazan had a theory, and I didn't know it till I saw the movie. It was what the Italians call Commedia dell'arte, in which street players would come out on the street and play the plays, and say, [in Italian accent], "What do you like us to play today? Would you like comedy? Tragedy? What would you like?" It's just like Second City in Chicago. You have an opening, a middle and an end. So you can do anything that you want in between, and you know where you're going. You know you're going to have to do this to get off. And that's exactly what we were doing. I said to Kazan, "You're doing Commedia dell'arte!"

And he said, "Yeah, but it works." [Laughs]

You watch that sometime, and you'll see Commedia dell'arte like you never saw. Uh God! Eli and I especially. We fell for it hook, line and sinker cause we loved doing it. [Laughter] See, Eli's smaller than I am, and I was making it tough for him. I got right up to him nose to nose. And then I got higher and higher, and I got up on my toes and was looking down at him. He said, "Jesus, what are you doing?" [Laughs] That was the kind of thing we did with one another. It was a fun picture, a good picture.

I could never tell, while filming, if a movie was going to be good. The only one I was sure of was Streetcar. I didn't know On the Waterfront was going to be that big of a hit. There were too many heartaches in Waterfront. It was so hard to make. So *cold*. You see in *Waterfront* what we call salamanders, those great wood-burning things on the dock, with guys feeding wood into those. They put those there cause it was cold. *Freezing* cold. You couldn't put enough clothes on.

There's a film that nobody sees, it was one of my contract films for Warners. And it's one of my favorites. It's called *Hotel*. It's a hotel in New Orleans and the things that happen in this hotel. They gave me a part of a young guy who comes in to buy the hotel from the old owner, played by Melvyn Douglas. I read the script, and told them that I wasn't refusing to do the movie, but that there was a different part I knew that I could do something with, the hotel thief. They said, "Look, Carl, there's no dialogue. He has nothing to say."

82

I said, "That's what makes it fascinating for me. I think with nothing to say I could do something."

They said, "You're *crazy*, but if that's what you want, okay, do it."

So I did it, and I had a great time. Not one word of dialogue, except one line. He goes around raiding the rooms, comes into his room, opens a briefcase, and there's nothing in it. And I say, "Damn those credit cards." It gets a tremendous laugh because I was doing American Express commercials at that time. All the time he's in the lobby, watching people, seeing people come in. Or he's in a train station, watching people. A guy throws his key away cause he forgets to give it back. So he goes and gets the key and puts it in his suitcase. And you see there's five keys in there, all stolen. I learned a lot from that picture. It was written where he'd raid a room, come in and see what he got. Then he'd raid another room.

I was introduced to a pro, who said, "It's not done that way."

I said, "Well, how's it done?"

He said, "We sign in for a room, and we stay there for a week. And we start to look at people who we think have money. We find out where their rooms are. And then all in one night we do it, many rooms, and *out*." And that's the way we did it. And it was fun.

Cagney was a wonderful person, a very giving man. He gave an awful lot. He helped a lot of people. He was grateful that he got as far as he did with what talent he had. He'd say, "I'm nothing but a vaudeville hoofer, that's what I am."

Working on TV in "The Streets of San Francisco" is the *hardest* work I ever did. We filmed the whole show there. I lived in San Francisco for eight months out of the year, every year. I was old. I was in my middle Sixties. Running up those hills and up the steps and jumping fences and all that kind of stuff that we did. And I *enjoyed* it, but the minimum of time we worked was twelve hours a day. And many times, we worked eighteen, eighteen and a half hours, to finish that episode, because it had to be done. And then you go to work on the next one, and work twelve hours. So it was hard work. But I had a wonderful partner, Michael [Douglas]. We were like family.

Kirk [Douglas] and I are very close. I started in summer stock with him. And I never met Michael. But the producer of the show, Quinn Martin, called me and said, "I've got a guy here who might be pretty good with you as your partner. Why don't you come down here to see him?" So I got in the car and drove down there and saw him.

The minute I walked in I said, "He'll do, Quinn."

He said, "How can you tell? You haven't even spoken to the guy."

But I saw that cleft in his chin. I said, "Are you a Douglas?"

He said, "Yeah, I'm Michael Douglas."

I said, "He'll do!" And that's how we got together. Kirk had told him, "Listen, if anybody can teach you to act, listen to him." And I did teach him. I didn't go out of my way to say, "This is how you got to do it." But just the things that you do, and how you do it. He was great. He deserves everything he's getting. And he's taking a gamble. He's doing little character parts. He's not a leading man anymore. He's starting to do character things. It's good.

Everything we did on "Streets of San Francisco" was location. Everything. We shot it documentary style. We had to shoot it quick, and we had no sets. There were always advance men ahead of the show finding out where you could shoot the scene. They'd rent a house for $200 or a stairway or an alley. We always had two motorcycle cops with us always. To stop traffic when we needed it fast. It was fun. It was a great point in my career.

For the first time in my life, I made some money. In all those movies, I never made big money. As I told you, I just had to get up to bat. I just kept working. I made better than I could make in a clothing store. But if I hadn't gotten "Streets of San Francisco," and if I hadn't gotten the American Express commercials, I would still have to be working. But after thirty years of doing what I did here, I could say to myself, if I want to quit, I can quit. And that show did it for me, because I own part of "Streets of San Francisco." Quinn Martin was a great producer. I am very grateful to Quinn Martin. Fifty percent of the show went to ABC and we split the other 50 percent. He didn't have to do that but he did. He said, "I want you in this, because you've never been in a TV show, and I think you can do it." And I said, "I'll do it."

When TV came, the studios were really worried that it would kill the movies. I was under contract to Warners at the time, and I had a clause in my contract that said I was not allowed to do television. Then when Warners got hot in TV, they wanted me to do them, and I said, "Read the contract. I can't do TV."

They said, "No, we'll cut it out."

I said, "No. That's in the contract. I can't do TV." And I didn't. [Laughter] If anybody can make money on it, they thought they should. But I wouldn't do it.

It's not possible to pinpoint exactly why Hollywood changed so much. I can give you one reason it changed. I didn't think I would ever see the day when I missed Jack Warner. And Darryl Zanuck, Louie B. Mayer, Harry Cohn. All these people who ran the business. They were competitive. Plus, they *loved* what they were doing. And even if they did four or five *miserable* movies, they always had to have one or two films with *class*. Because it was a business; they had to fill the theaters with *something*. But there was always a moment when they said, "We're going to spend an extra million on *this*, we're going to get every movie star we *can*, the best director. . . ." In other words, they were *proud* of their name "Warner Brothers." They were *proud* of their name "20th Century Fox." And this was their pride. MGM was *proud* of the musicals that they were able to do with Astaire and Gene Kelly. That was their *pride*. Each studio had their pride.

They don't have that today. There is no studio today. It's all independent productions. Everything's independent. There are no Warner Brothers anymore. It's just a studio you can *rent*. It's, "I'm gonna make a big pile of money now, the hell with tomorrow. It's great *now*." Not *then*. Jack Warner was a *bastard*, but when he made a deal, you didn't have to shake hands, *that* was your deal. Today you can make a deal and tomorrow they'll say, "*Forget* it, there's no deal." It's a different business.

It takes a while to learn how to watch your own films. First time I see them, I walk away saying, "Oh, Jesus." And after I watch it two or three times, I begin to relax. But I'm too hard a critic on everybody and especially on myself. Because I *love* this business. I started with *nothing* in this business, and it's been good to me, and I *respect* this business. And I respect the two or three people who took me under their wing and did what they did for me.

I want to continue holding on to that part of the business that I idolize. But I see the business going down the drain. I see bad pictures being made, and I see people who don't show up on time or come to work unprepared. They don't care. It's just the glamour that counts. Believe me, with Spencer Tracy and Clark Gable and Jimmy Cagney and Humphrey Bogart, it wasn't glamour, it was a *job*. You were the *pro* in this job, and boy, you *stayed* a pro. Now it's all different. It's a different world.

84

Lloyd Rigler

BORN MAY 3, 1915

LEHR, NORTH DAKOTA

ENTREPRENEUR

Wearing a white jacket over a red shirt, he speaks while sitting at a long, white table in the conference room of the foundation he runs, The Ledler Foundation, which is housed in a series of offices above Franklin Avenue. Though a rare rain is breaking outside these windows overlooking Sunset Boulevard and beyond to the south, in here there's that old-fashioned comfort of a warm library on a cold day. We're surrounded with bookshelves that stretch from floor to ceiling, overflowing with books on the subjects about which he's most passionate: Hollywood, the movies, and classical music. His name is well-known in Hollywood and will remain so due to a sizable donation he made to American Cinematheque for their renovation of the historic Egyptian Theater on Hollywood Boulevard, where the main theater is now called The Lloyd Rigler Theater. The preservation and celebration of Hollywood is something that matters deeply to him, for it's in Hollywood that he made his fortune, along with his partner Laurence Deutsch, through a series of fairly ingenious maneuvers, all of which are related in the following memoir. Although his is a story that encompasses all of America, it's a "Hollywood story," as he says, "because it all started here."

I was born in Lehr and raised in a little town called Wishek, North Dakota. We had a movie theater in Wishek, and when I was about ten years old I became an usher at the movie theater. It was just a long, flat theater. All the seats were on the same level.

I worked there from about 1925 to 1932. I was at the movie theater every week. I remember the silents and when talkies came in. I *loved* the movies. I liked the Gish girls in the silents, and I loved Charlie Chaplin.

There were very few Jewish families in our town, I remember. I remember Hyman Rappoport used to come and take me to the movies. I remember seeing *The Evil Eye*. And he used to read me what it said, because I couldn't read the title cards. The silents were slower. You'd see the action and then you'd read what they said. They never put the words on the screen at the same time as the action.

Sound came in about '27. I was twelve years old. I remember *The Jazz Singer*. It seems strange that we accepted talkies so easily; we accepted change. You'd read that it was going to happen, and there it was.

In 1933, I got a ride to Chicago for the World's Fair. And I stayed with relatives and stayed down there. Got a job working for the Edison company, selling electric irons from house to house. I worked at that for some time until the Jewish holidays, when I got a job at a shoestore, cause all the other Jewish salesmen took off for the holidays and they needed someone, so I got a chance to learn. I ultimately ended up working at the Cutler Shoe Company in the Palmer House. Shoes were $6.77 a pair, I remember. Then I finally got a job at Marshall Field's, and by 1935 I had saved enough money to go to the University of Illinois. Spent four years there. Every holiday I would work on a train selling food. In 1939 I went to New York. Got a job at the World's Fair for RCA. We introduced television there in 1940 at the *Century of Progress*. I worked for RCA for a few years, and then I took a vacation and came out to Los Angeles.

I spent my first night here in Hollywood at the Padre Hotel on Cahuenga Boulevard. It's still there. I walked over to Cherokee, and just below Franklin was the Commodore Hotel. I found a studio apartment at the back of the first floor, and I rented that. And I tried to get the RCA company to transfer me out here. But they wouldn't, so I got a job working as a city salesman for Decca Records, near Melrose & Gower. I worked there and hit all the record stores in the greater L.A. area. All of the record stores were run by women then.

This was 1941, the period of Bing Crosby, and we also had a lot of blues records, like Big Joe Turner. I remember going to meet Big Joe Turner at a hotel in Hollywood. Went up to his room and he was in bed with a woman, and he just slapped her on the behind and said, "Don't worry, baby, he's a friend of mine." [Laughs]

Even then, although there were no freeways, you needed a car to get around. I bought a secondhand car; I called it the Yellow Peril. It was a Ford sports car with a canvas top. An orange-yellow two-seater convertible, much like a Model T, but made two years later. It wasn't difficult driving around then. There was never a traffic jam.

The thing that was most exciting were the evenings on Hollywood Boulevard. It was active and lit up; every store had lights on, as the Sunset Strip is now. Everybody walked on the boulevard and everybody met on the boulevard. The corner of Cherokee & Hollywood Boulevard was Bradley's Five & Ten Bar. You'd get a beer for ten cents. The Pickwick Bookstore was open, I remember it well. The Broadway department store was open. Hollywood & Vine was very active. The Brown Derby was on Vine Street. The boulevard was very safe then. People parked and walked there.

I went into the navy in 1941. I enlisted at the American Legion Center on Highland. I've always had a lazy left eye, and I never learned how to use it. But I lied about it, so I could get into the navy. They sent me to San Diego and Arizona and then Long Beach. We would practice shooting rifles, and I injured the nerve endings in my ears and lost my hearing. So I got into the navy by lying about my eyesight. And my life was saved in Long Beach, when they did more sophisticated tests on us, and they tested my eyesight and I couldn't read with my left eye, so they wouldn't let me go overseas with my crew. And my crew never came back. My life was saved.

So I fought the battle of San Pedro, and lived in Hollywood, and hitch-hiked from Hollywood to San Pedro every day to work in a warehouse there with surplus and supplies. I spent the entire war here in Hollywood. Even though I was in the navy, my life was still centered at night on Hollywood Boulevard. I would go out, and go to the Chinese Theater, and the Vogue, and the Egyptian. And I often ate at Musso's, even then. Look at this. [*From his wallet he removes an old credit card, inscribed with the Musso & Frank's logo.*] Look at the number. It's Number Eight. I got it in 1941, and I've kept it all these years. I just go there, sign my name, and they bill me. It's still very good there.

After the war, there was a tremendous increase in population here, and a movement west. And Hollywood Boulevard changed, and it wasn't safe any-more. The stores began to close, because the boulevard wasn't fun anymore and people wouldn't go there at night. And there was little enough business during the day. And nobody took interest in seeing any of it preserved. So the Broadway closed. People moved west, and business went down.

The war ended in 1945. I started working for an independent record company then, and for awhile I lived in San Francisco. In '46 I came back here and became an agent for a motion-picture company. I discovered William Holden. I had him first and then I lost him. One of my jobs was to go to little theaters and see if I could find potential clients. Once they got a motion picture, then they'd be picked up by a larger agency. William Holden was a wonderful guy. A really wonderful person.

Our office was on Sunset Boulevard, two blocks west of Doheny. A little small office. It's gone now.

Claudette [Colbert] was our lead client. She was very bright. She married Jules Pressman. He was an EE&T man and took care of her throat, so she could talk. She never lost her voice. She never ate studio food. She always carried her own lunch wherever she went. She never bought food out. She was a very gracious lady. She really was a very great lady. You know, the family spoke French, they never learned English. She lived in the east for a long time, after that.

A production of *Othello* came to the Biltmore Theater from New York. Edith King played Desdemona's mistress. She was a *wonderful* actress. So I went backstage and said, "I'd like to represent you for movies. Would you be interested?" And she was interested, so I picked her up in my Yellow Peril, and took her out to meet Charles Farrow—Mia Farrow's father—at Para-mount. And he was doing a movie with Alan Ladd in which they needed to have a woman in the Far East who was a fence for stolen jewelry who smoked cigars. And I got Edith the job; I'll never forget it. At $1,500 a week.

She was always grateful to me. It was the only movie she ever made, I think. That was one of the highlights while I was an agent. But even then, I was only making $50 a week. I never got a commission on my clients, because that went to the office.

So I answered an ad in the *Hollywood Citizen News*. It was a blind ad for a quarter-million-dollars-worth of war surplus at 10 percent commission, if you could sell it. They didn't even say what the surplus was. Their office was in the Security Pacific Bank building at Hollywood & Highland.

It turned out to be "Her Secret Brassiere" company. They had a quarter-million dollars worth of pink and blue nylon satin, black French lace, and a lot of English net. So I went to the library, did my research, and found out that the quality of English net had to do with the hole-size and how fine it is. So I made up a whole lot of samples of this stuff, and I had a friend who was also in the agenting business. His father was a food broker in Michigan. They had contacts in Hong Kong. So he said, "I'll give you the contact, but you have to give me part of the commission if you sell it."

So we sent out samples to Hong Kong, and a letter came back that said, "The weather's cold. We can't use these fabrics to make clothing." As if I wouldn't know that. But they gave me a whole list of things they *did* want, such as pens and pencils. So I found out where to get these things, and I sent them samples. And they must have sold the samples, because I never got an order. So I finally wrote back and said, "Tell me what it is that every man, woman and child uses every day in Hong Kong, and send me a sample." I thought maybe I could find out what they used there, and make it cheaper here. So they sent me a rice bowl and wrote, "Everybody carries one of these. And children carry the adult size, but they only get half a bowl."

Styrene had just been discovered. Flexible plastic. In color. So I went to a mold manufacturer I found in Pasadena. I asked them if they could make a mold of the rice bowl, only half the size. And if so, how much would the mold cost and how much would you charge per gross to make them for me? And if I could get an order with a letter of credit, would you finance the making of the mold and the pressing of the bowls, and then collect your money from the bank when it goes on the ship? That's how it works. The money is sent in advance. He said yes.

I priced out the bowls so I would know how many I'd have to sell to pay him back and make some money for myself. And I put this all in a letter and asked for 150 gross—twelve dozen to a gross. I had a nice price attached to it. But it was so unique; nothing like that had ever been there. And so I knew I could make some money on it, and it *worked*. I got the order, and the letter of credit, and I shipped the rice bowls. And I had a few orders of that go through, where I was shipping rice bowls to China.

I knew that it wouldn't last. So my friend John said he had a contact with the Michigan Mushroom Company. And they packed Dawn-fresh mushrooms. That was the trademark: Dawn-fresh. And they also packed three kinds of soup. And they were not represented in Los Angeles. So, he said, "Why don't you become a broker for them and represent them?"

I had another friend by the name of Marshall Edison. He lived with Neil Vanderbilt, who was Gloria's brother. He was a gossip columnist for the *Herald Examiner*. They lived up above the Sunset Strip. Marshall was living with Neil rent-free, because he would introduce Neil to starlets, who were trying to get somewhere. He knew a lot of young girls in Hollywood, coming here to make movies. One of whom was Shelley Winters.

89

So Marshall got Shelley Winters and John Ireland to do *The Taming of The Shrew* at The Biltmore. He produced it. He got a Hungarian director from New York. This director knew he needed a man-Friday, cause he was new out here, and needed someone to assist him. This was '47. And that guy was Larry Deutsch. He came out here from Chicago where he was working; his mother lived here already, in the Wilshire District.

Marshall, in order to keep working as a producer, needed an office. So he found a twenty-five-foot storefront on Santa Monica Boulevard in Hollywood. The corner was occupied by a used-car dealer by the name of Jack 100 one hundred feet long. But all they needed was the first twenty-five feet [laughs]. They had all this extra space, so they decided to use it as a cleaning store. He wanted to open this cleaners so he could have an office for Marshall Edison productions. And he wanted to have something that would pay the rent. So that you'd bring in your shirts to be cleaned for a dollar, and they sent it out, and made forty cents on every dollar. He did this while *The Shrew* was going on. So the telephone on the wall was in the name of Marshall Edison Productions, but it was the Zippy Cleaners.

Jack gave him a station wagon to use, to deliver the cleaning. And in return for renting this storefront and paying the rent, he got to meet the girls. The stable.

In the meantime, I had gotten the Michigan Mushroom Company to appoint me their broker for Dawn-fresh mushrooms. And I knew that I needed a place to store them, because if I put them in a warehouse, it would be too much in-and-out handling. I needed a space where I could have access myself to them. and I knew that the Zippy Cleaners had all this room behind it. So it was to my advantage to be able to get Marshall and his friend Larry to let me have that space behind there.

The *Herald Examiner* told Neil Vanderbilt, "Your column is getting stale. We're gonna have to move you to another city." So Neil said to Marshall, "In order to help you out, I'm going to give a party for your birthday, which is

September the third. And I'll invite everyone in Hollywood that I know so that you can meet them."

Marshall was a friend of mine, so I was invited to this party as well. Chaplin came. I remember meeting him. He was very different from how you remember him in the movies. He was a very soft-spoken British gentleman, quite polite.

There were a whole number of stars who came. I went to this party primarily to meet Larry, which I did over champagne, which he didn't know how to drink. I remember one of the older character actors took Larry's mother out to his car and tried to make out with her. [Laughs] She went by the name of Bobbie Dale, and she was an attractive woman. At any rate, Larry and I became good friends, and I got to move my mushrooms in behind the Zippy.

So there was the Zippy, and there was Larry, so Larry started to work with me. He wrote out export letters. We paid him twenty-five cents a letter to type our letters and answer our phone for us. I got the mushroom company to give me a white hat and a white coat and a two-burner electric plate and some kettles, and I went out and sold soup. They had three types of soup.

At that time, most of the supermarkets in Los Angeles belonged to a group called Certified Grocers, so that they could compete in the purchasing power of Safeway and A&P. Those were the two chains then. In order for me to get my mushrooms on the floor of Certified, they wanted 25 percent of their membership to have it on the shelf. Then I could get it on the floor, and it would be in their book that they ordered from each month. In order for me to get it into the store, I would go to stores and demonstrate the soup on a weekend, if they would put a case of the mushrooms on the shelf. I began serving soup every weekend in grocery stores.

By this time I'd sold the Yellow Peril and got a two-door Chevrolet. And I moved out of the Commodore and I got a house on Pinehurst Road. It's behind the First Methodist Church on Franklin & Highland. Fifty steps up was a little one-bedroom bungalow. Didn't have a view because it was in the canyon. The woman who had the house at the very end of the cul-de-sac was Carrie Jacobs-Bond, who wrote "I Love You Truly." She was my neighbor, and she played the piano, and I remember singing with her all the time.

I moved into this little house, and my sister moved in with me, because she came out to go to UCLA. I was living in that house, and I was doing the mushroom thing, and I met Larry, and we became good friends, and he kept typing the letters, and I kept selling the soup and mushrooms. The commission was, I don't know, 8 percent. I began to make money. And in one month I had $1,200! My friend John, who owned half of the business and helped me get the Michigan Mushroom Company, didn't do any work. He just wanted to collect the commission.

I said to him, "Let's not pay Larry twenty-five cents a letter. Let's give him a share of the business." So we both gave up 12 percent to give Larry 25 percent of the business. That gave Larry and me control. So that once we had control, when the check came in, we said to John, "We don't think we should give you any of this commission. What about splitting up? We'll give you the export business—you can sell the rice bowls—and we'll take the brokerage business."

So we got rid of John. And we got rid of Marshall by going further up Santa Monica Boulevard, near Ogden, and found a storefront near a liquor store with a garage in the back. So we could store the mushrooms in the garage.

So we moved all the mushrooms, and we opened up Dawn Fresh Valet Service—to sell the mushrooms and to take in cleaning and deliver it. I delivered the clothes and sold the mushrooms, and Larry ran the cleaning store and wrote the letters. And we became Rigler & Deutsch food brokers. I was getting more and more distribution. I finally got my mushrooms on the floor at Certified, and I was still doing demonstrations. Imagine: Cream of Mushroom, Barley Mushroom, and Potato Mushroom. Barley and Potato were not known then. Campbell's didn't make it. They're very good soups.

One day I was out at Certified Grocer's, and waiting to see my buyer. They had a waiting room. A man comes along and sits beside me and asks, "How do you introduce a new product to Certified?"

I said, "What's the product?"

He reaches into his case and he brings out a bottle of Adolph's Meat Tenderizer. I told him I cooked myself and I would be interested in trying it, would he give me a sample? He said sure.

I said, "You're going to have to put this into 25 percent of the stores before they'll let you put it on the shelf. It won't be easy."

So I left him there, and a couple of weeks later I was demonstrating soup in East Hollywood, in a store there, and he comes by and sees me and remembers me. So I said, "So what happened?"

He said, "I took the product back to Adolph and told him to forget it."

I said, "Where's Adolph?"

He said Adolph had a restaurant in Santa Barbara. He said he makes it in his kitchen, and puts it in a bottle and sells it out of his restaurant.

So, I said to Larry, "We're gonna drive to Santa Barbara." We drove to Santa Barbara to meet Adolph. And I said to him, "I'd like to represent you on this product."

He said, "Well, I've had so many salesmen that come in to eat at the restaurant and they want to represent me, and nobody has ever done anything with it."

I said, "Well, you might at least just let me try it."

I set up a demonstration of Adolph's at the May Company downtown. They had a very large food department. I said, "You come down and we'll do it together." Adolph came down, and we were a tremendous success. Adolph said, "Well, you guys could probably do something with this that nobody else can. Why don't you take it over?"

So I started to demonstrate it at stores. But it was difficult, because of having to fry the meat and all. So I waited for the Home Show. Every year they had a Home Show at the Pan Pacific. We had decided we would demonstrate Adolph's Meat Tenderizer there. And let people taste the steak, and have a list of stores where they could buy it. And every morning I'd go out and find another store to put it in. On consignment.

And while we were at the show, KTLA came. Imagine: This is 1948. Television had only been introduced in 1940 at the World's Fair. This was eight years later and still nobody had television. Television was expensive, and were very large cabinets, and were sold in stores around Los Angeles where they would have a receiver in the window, and a speaker outside, and you could stand in front of the window at night when the store was closed, and watch the television and hear what they were saying. And that's the way television was perceived in Los Angeles then. Excepting for those few people who could afford to pay several thousand dollars for a set.

KTLA, which was one of the first local stations here, wanted to televise it. They wanted me to buy commercial time. But they wanted fifty dollars for five minutes. I told them to forget it, because we were putting all of our money into meat, and I didn't have any more to spend. Besides, what could I do with a commercial? There was hardly anywhere people could buy the product. They said, "You have a big bottle up there on the shelf."

I said, "That's enough for 200 pounds of meat. It's restaurant size."

They said, "Well, could you sell it for a dollar?"

I said, "Well, we wouldn't make much money on it. But nevertheless, we would make something."

They said, "Well, could we sell it on television? You say that people can call a number, you give an address, and say they can buy a bottle for a dollar. We'll give you the airtime for twenty dollars, as long as you don't tell anybody."

I decided to risk the twenty dollars. They were going to come with their cameras to our booth at 10:00 at night, and we would be able to demonstrate our product on television. But I had lost my voice by talking so much, and I couldn't talk, so I told Larry that he would have to do it.

On the night that this happened, I went to the Dawn Fresh Cleaners on Santa Monica to answer the phone, because Larry was going on the air at ten. We had two lines. And nothing happened. At five after ten, nothing, ten after ten, *nothing*. Twenty bucks shot down to hell.

About ten-fifteen, both lines rang. They said they just saw us on television and they wanted to know where to send the money.

Well, it *never stopped*. About a quarter of eleven, Larry walked in and said, "Why didn't you come and pick me up?" I told him I couldn't get off the phone. We answered for a while more and finally we just said, "To hell with it," and we just went home and went to bed. We were tired. And the next day it began again.

93

We got $3,800 worth of orders. Well, we didn't have 3,800 bottles filled. We had to fill them. So we had a party and got our friends to help fill them. We mixed it in a cement mixer by hand in the garage behind the cleaning store. My father was in town, so he came and started working for us and mixing it, and my sister came with her friends from college, and we all helped label it and fill it.

So I had this $3,800 when it all came in, and I found an advertising company that specialized in introducing new products. They said we had to test this in a market that had only one newspaper. And we chose Santa Ana.

We went to Santa Ana and told them that we wanted to place a small, one-column, six-inch ad. Once a week, *every* week. And they *love* that kind of business. We said there was only one condition. We said we didn't want the ad to run until their food editor writes a story about this product.

They said, "We don't even have a food editor."

I said, "Well, you do now. I'll be the food editor."

So I wrote a story about what the product was about and I got my sister to pose for a picture using the product, and we offered a small sample. Like the size of a Sweet & Low package. It was good for two pounds of meat. And we said you can write in for a sample, or you can buy it at your local market. And I went to every supermarket in Santa Ana and I put ten cases in and I told them I would take back every case that was unopened. We were packing four dozen to the case. It was unheard of.

Well. It was a Thursday that it ran, and on the following Friday they called and said, "We're getting mail like we've never ever had in the history of the newspaper." They got something like 10,000 letters. Which they didn't know how to handle. From people who wanted samples. The stores sold out. So we obviously had a model.

So we moved to Long Beach. And they had a food editor. And when she saw what we had done in Santa Ana, she gave us an eight-column spread. So she got 20,000 letters. That was the beginning of our success. We did *every city* on the West Coast the *same way*. *Every* newspaper.

Well, this is getting far from Hollywood but this is a Hollywood story because it all happened here. We were living in Hollywood, on Pinehurst Road, and then Larry moved in with me. He started living with me instead of his mother. And then when the business began to grow, we had to find offices on Melrose Avenue, near Gardner. We had offices upstairs. This is how it started. This was 1947, 1948. By 1950, we had done eleven western states. And Chicago and New York.

94

I went to the *Reader's Digest* and told them I thought I had a story for them. They told me it needed a woman's angle, and sent me to a roving reporter in New York by the name of Lois Miller. I went to visit her with a steak under my arm, and I cooked it for her, and she said she would put the research department on it. They researched us with the AMA, who had also endorsed us because we were promoting high protein. Low cost, high protein. That was the idea.

At the end of '52 I received a letter from *Reader's Digest* stating that they planned to do a story in February of '53, but I would have to have the product in every marketing area in America to do it, because they had a circulation of 78 million. I said, "If you give me a letter, telling me it's going to run and when, I can deliver."

In November of '52 I bought a Dacron suit and Dacron underwear, and I embarked on a tour of sixty-three cities in sixty days. I had the advertising agency set up meetings with food brokers in every city to meet me and to have prospective food brokers come to talk to me about representing me. I said, "You can't tell them what the product is. Just say it's an unusual food product, and I want to make the decision who's gonna do it after I interview them." So they interviewed me and they never knew what the product was. Then when I decided which one, and I showed them the letter from *Reader's Digest*, it was like a Christmas present for them.

And so that changed our lives. When the story broke in February of '53, I had eight employees. We had already closed the cleaning store, and we built a building in Burbank in 1954. We bought a house in East Hollywood on Holly Vista. We looked right down on Hollywood Boulevard. We drove around the Hollywood Hills and when we got up to Outpost Drive, we found a property up above Mulholland. Four and a half acres, and it was for sale. So we bought this property in 1954. I'm building a new house up there right now. So I'm still living in Hollywood, but a little bit higher.

I did my tombstone already in Hollywood. It's at the Egyptian Theater. That's my Hollywood tombstone. I always felt that it was such a terrible thing that a world-known area with a name such as Hollywood—and I look at the Hollywood sign every day, wherever I live, I see it—that it should have been allowed to deteriorate, and that the industry hadn't been concerned about preserving a landmark that could be the Disneyland of America. So I've always been very anxious to be part of the reconstruction of Hollywood Boulevard, but I don't know if it will ever happen. Of course, I'd like to see a department store on the corner of Vine, but I don't know if it will ever happen.

I'd like to see Hollywood revived. It's as important as London or Rome or Moscow or Beijing. There isn't a place you can go in the world that doesn't know the name Hollywood.

Jules Fox

BORN DECEMBER 27, 1916
COVINGTON, KENTUCKY
SONGWRITER/PUBLICIST

He's sitting outside in front of his house on a sunny day, waiting on a wooden porch swing with a large Irish setter stretched out in the sun beside him. He smiles with sad eyes, and walks through the house, stopping in his piano room to play a demo of his latest song, which is upbeat and country-tinged. A songwriter since he was a kid, he's best known for co-writing "The Woody Woodpecker Song." He was also a publicist, and it was as one-half of a mighty P.R. duo with his late wife Jo that he made his living over the years. Tears swell up in his eyes as he talks of her and the remarkable life they shared, a life filled with music performed by many of the greatest jazz musicians of modern times. He moves through his den, stopping to show assorted souvenirs, articles and awards celebrating the work he did with his wife over the years. "It's nice out here," he says, and walks outside into the backyard to sit at a yellow metal table under giant trees. His shimmering blue pool sparkles through the foliage, as suburban squirrels scurry in the overhead branches. He talks of the legendary late-night jam sessions that once took place in this yard, at this very table. "They'd all sit right here," he says, "and they'd play and sing all night. All of them. Ella. Sarah. Hamp. Right here. They'd play till one, two in the morning. And the neighbors? The neighbors used to love it. Wouldn't you?"

I was born in Covington, Kentucky, and grew up in Cincinnati at two orphanages. I survived both of them [Laughs]. I grew up until I was about sixteen or so in Cincinnati. There was a piano in the orphanage. I wrote music and I wrote lyrics and songs, and a publisher in downtown Cincinnati saw some of my stuff and he said I had a lot of possibilities. And then when I had a chance to come with a friend out to California, I was scared. I thought I would drop off the earth [laughing], you know. I was never out of Cincinnati. So he said, "You go ahead, you go. Don't look back."

I was inspired then by music I would hear on the radio. Always ballads. Ballads all the time. But you learn to write novelty stuff as the years went by cause that was the stuff that would sell. So I started writing some specialty material for some different shows that were being put on in Cincinnati. I got into it more and more and more after I got out of the orphanages. Words and music, from the beginning.

There was a sailor who wanted a friend and myself to help drive to California. And my friend drove right off the road right away, so this tough sailor threw us both in the back seat [laughs] and drove all the way through himself.

So I came out here and I lived with some people who were luckily very close to the musical director at MGM. And I got an appointment with a fellow at MGM, Wolfie Gilbert, who wrote "Robert E. Lee." I brought some material I had with me and he sat way across the plush room and I sat over there scared to *death*. He just read it and sang it. It took a long time, scared the hell out of me, really. Finally he said, "Come on over here." He says, "Keep this up, you have a wonderful flair."

So I kept on writing and got a few breaks with Republic Studios. I wrote some country-western stuff. For a short while. I got a break through them and gradually I got to meet other people, and when I did, I submitted my stuff to them; they said, "Great stuff, good stuff, good lyrics," and that kept me writing. I wrote some stuff for MGM for some of the movies, and I wrote for Republic.

I wrote most of the stuff for Spade Coolie, a singing cowboy who was the number-one country-and-western man at that time, before Roy Rogers and the rest of them. He was the first fellow in L.A. to ever appear on television. I wrote cowboy songs, but I still liked good music and sensible lyrics and things, which was very hard to sell at that time.

I lived with a family in Hollywood on Taft Avenue. They lived there and they knew people at the studios. It was north of Franklin just a few houses. They had six sons, and I felt like I was adopted by them. They were very close to a lot of the studio people and so I got lucky that way. I remember the neighborhood well; it was mostly family homes. There were a couple of drug stores around and it was strictly residential. We would walk down to Hollywood Boulevard all the time to meet people. I got closer and closer to a lot of studio people and that's how I got my break. Mostly through writing country songs, which I didn't like very much. A lot of times you didn't write what you liked, you wrote what they wanted. I wrote a lot of country things at that time and I didn't like it. I also did a lot of jingles for commercials. [Sings] "Have a bottle of Squirt for a tasty drink . . . Squirt!"

After that I got my own place and had a little old piano up in Hollywood.

I was in an apartment first; then a house. I wrote a lot of stuff for the army and for the air force, too. It was a living. At that time, if you'd make two-hundred and fifty bucks doing a job, that wasn't bad then. I did an awful lot of commercials for a lot of the big companies.

Hollywood Boulevard was fun then. It was fun to walk down because all the places were very nice, the shops were nice. You could walk down at twelve o'clock midnight just for fun and not think a thing about it. No trouble, nothing bad happened then. People shopped and made a good living on Hollywood Boulevard, and if you were on Hollywood Boulevard, you were in heaven. People thought Hollywood was heaven then, and people would come out and do whatever they thought they could do and it was fine. But, of course, it changed through the years.

97

My wife and myself got married in 1939. I met her up on Sunset Boulevard, and we saw each other and she looked at me going away through the window and I looked back at her and we got together after that. Jo, she was known as Jo Brooks, she was a famous writer. She wrote for the big magazines and did a lot of wonderful stuff. She had more talent in her little finger than just about anyone I've ever met. A *wonderful* woman. She wrote slogans for people. She wrote for some very big agencies. What a great gal. She was with a magazine, one of the top magazines of the country, up on Sunset Boulevard and she advanced one step at a time to another until she became quite big in this country.

So we finally married and I had to go off in the air corps and we stayed together. When I came back, we had a little boy. I kept up with my writing and I admired Johnny Mercer, Francis Webster and some of those guys that wrote some great things and they were my idols. Always. Johnny Mercer, to me, was the greatest writer on earth, yeah, because he could write *everything*. Great music. Well, I was in good company all the time, with good writers. I liked good stuff, but I wrote a lot of cruddy stuff, too, to make a living. I wrote a lot of the commercials; Rit Dye was one.

I was one of the writers of the "Woody Woodpecker" song. I wrote it with Daryl Caulker, who wrote for a lot of B movies. He had me write the lyrics for the music then, and he liked it. So I wrote with him. One day he came up to me and said, "Jules, you wanna write a thing for Woody Wood-pecker thing with me?" He'd always have me write words with him. He'd say, "Hey, I got a good song, Jules, you wanna do the lyric on it?" I'd say, "Sure." So I wrote a lot of stuff with him. But I never realized what the hell was gonna happen with the Woody Woodpecker [laughing], you know. [Sings] *"Ha ha ha ha ha, ha ha ha ha ha, that's the Woody Woodpecker song, ha ha ha ha ha, ha ha ha ha ha, keep peckin' it all day long . . . he pecked a few holes and he . . ."* I know the lyrics but I forget them. I never thought it was going to be a big deal. *Never!*

No way in the world! [Laughter] But I can show you my checks! They just keep coming in from Oshkosh, from Hoboken, from over in Europe.

Jo and I met Billy Eckstine, who was one of the true greats of jazz. We handled his public relations and he was number one in the nation. One thing led to another and all of a sudden he called Sarah Vaughan back in New York and said, "I got two of the greatest people in the world. You gotta have them when you come out here." Always good people. So from Sarah, we got Ella Fitzgerald and Billie Holiday and one after another jumped on the bandwagon. All of our big names came from other names, but Billy was the start of everybody. Then we got Lionel Hampton. We handled Lionel Hampton for fourteen years. Yeah, we were his family, Hamp. He liked Jo, so Jo would kind of handle him, and I would handle other people like Billy Eckstine. Everybody would choose the favorite that they liked, they'd choose Jo or myself. It wound up being not only a wonderful business, but friendly. We became family to most of the big stars.

So we became publicists, but I never stopped writing songs. I would never stop that. A songwriter never stops writing, you know. I got a number of pictures to write and one thing led to another and I wrote some pretty good stuff.

A couple of jazz clubs opened up, and then another one and another one and first thing you know there are a lot of jazz clubs all over L.A. They all made money, and the booking agencies would book their artists into these clubs for $250 a week. They put a door charge on a night club, which was not to be done, you never put a door charge on a night club ever. But these guys started it, and they would have a guy at the door who'd collect the two dollars and fifty cents and come in and see all the great names, big names. That started here, and then New York started to do it, and then all over the country and San Francisco especially. Everyone you could think of would play the small night clubs. It was cheap enough then, just a couple of bucks.

Jo and I became two of the top PR people anywhere. Our main strategy was radio. We'd take our clients on fifty, maybe eighty different shows! I remember KPH on Vermont Avenue; many times we would take Sarah Vaughn or people like that at midnight after they had finished their gig. KPH was national then. So all the artists would go, because radio was king then. Radio controlled everything then, and there were a lot of radio stations. And they loved to have these great artists come on. Magazines and the print press were also very important, but most of our artists liked to go on radio and talk. They liked to yak it up.

The jazz people we worked with were wonderful. It was easy to do P R with them because they had big names, and you know how *great* some of them were. *Legends*, yeah. They're all gone. All my people are gone. Jo, Billie Holiday, Ella, Sarah, Billy Eckstine, Diana Washington. But I've got memories of them all.

Billy Eckstine. We called him B. He was a strong personality from the beginning. He'd go out there and he'd be dressed in a white suit, and he'd say, "You bastards are gonna *love* me." You know, that was his attitude all the time. He was confident, and he would really show it in the way he dressed and the way he sang, and that was B. all the time.

99

Billie Holiday. The one way I remember Billie Holiday is that she had these damn Chihuahuas that would bite me to pieces. She'd go to talk to somebody and say, "Hold 'em." And I'd hold them and they were *mean*, mean little dogs, you know, Chihuahuas. And she'd always have me take her places for interviews and she'd say, "Hold them," and I'd hold them and they were *mean*, they'd bite me and I'd say, "Billie, take them back, take them back!" You know. She was a funny gal. She was a nice gal. Billie loved what she was doing, she loved her singing. And she was all right in interviews, but she didn't like it too much. She could be fine, though, if you got her started. You had to get Billie started, because she was very shy.

In the later years, Billie could be unstable. She was a funny gal. Hard to handle, but she cooperated all the way through. Sometimes she wouldn't show up where she was supposed to be, you know. We'd say, "We got an appointment." She'd say, "I'll get there, don't worry." You know, she'd have a chauffeur, but she wouldn't show up.

Sarah Vaughan. Sarah was always scared. She'd sing but she was scared with stage fright. But she was so good she just sang and everything would come out, people would love her and pretty soon she'd be into it. She was Number One. Sarah Vaughan could hit notes you couldn't *believe*. You know, way up *there*, and way down *there*. And she was sweet. Sarah Vaughn was sweet all the time and quiet, always quiet.

Sarah was the sweetest, she was the sweetest of all of them.

Ella Fitzgerald. Ella could be a little difficult to get along with, but she was a wonderful, generous, kind woman. And I know when I got her up in San Francisco she was at a dingy little night club, and she started crying, and said, "Jules, why did they book me here?" And she was a pretty good name then and she was crying right there on my shoulder, but she played the place, packed it and went on with what she had to do. I'll never forget that, Ella. Sarah Vaughn was the sweetest of all but Ella was kind and generous. She cried on my shoulder a number of times and we were close. I can remember things about these people.

One time Ella, I'll never forget, she sent me Christmas shopping when we were at the night club on Hollywood Boulevard. She didn't have time to shop but she wanted to get gifts for everyone. So I did her shopping for her.

Ella didn't care much for doing interviews. Ella would kind of balk. I'd have her up in San Francisco and book her on different shows and she didn't like it much. I'll never forget, one time we were in a hotel where she was performing, and a woman said, "I have all your albums, Ella, could you sign this for me?" and Ella had just come off the stage and she was angry; it had been a disturbing gig for her, because people were talking, and that used to really upset her. So she didn't sign it, and she went upstairs to her room. I went up to her room with her, and she said, "Jules, go find that lady downstairs, tell her to come back with the album and I'll sign it." She was good at heart.

100

Dinah Washington. She was evil [Laughs], but Jo liked her. She could be a mean son-of-a-gun. But a *talent*. We handled her right for fourteen years. She'd send me away! I'd be over at her house, and she'd say, "Jules Fox, *go home*. Jo Brooks and me are going to cook up some chitlins." So, I'd go home and Jo would stay there. She would beat up on people, throw things. . . . Oh, she beat up on all of her husbands. She had five of them. She'd always get into a fight with somebody at the bar. She was mean, but a great talent. Great singer.

Lionel Hampton. Hamp was Jo's fellow. They'd go fishing together and wherever Hamp had to go, mostly Jo would take him. He loved Jo, *loved* her, and thought she was the greatest thing on earth. He did a couple of my songs, Hamp did. But I didn't usually bring my music to our clients. Back then you kept things separate. I wasn't smart enough to know better!

Johnny Mathis. A friend of ours was handling Johnny Mathis back when he was starting out, before he had a record deal. She said, "Jules, do me a favor and go up and catch him." I went up to the club in San Francisco—the Blackhawk—and I went to see him and I thought he sang sharp and flat and everything. I turned him down like he was *nothing* [Laughs]. That was my *biggest* mistake ever. [Laughter] My biggest mistake in life was to turn down Johnny Mathis. Can you imagine that?

[In a whisper] I *was* right, though. I was right, yeah, he was off a lot, but he got better. Though even when he sang a lot of his later stuff, you can hear, if you had an ear, even on his recordings, a *lot* of stuff was sharp. But he became the hit of the country, and I turned him down. That was my biggest mistake ever. Yeah, that was a *biggie*.

Sammy Davis Jr. We did some work for Sammy at Ciro's on Sunset. He was a great guy. Wonderful talent, wonderful talent. We got the owner of Ciro's, who was a good friend, to come down to the Oasis Night Club—down on Western—to hear this guy, Sammy. We said, "You have got to hear this guy." So he came down there one night, paid his two bucks to get in, and we sat with him. And when he was walking out, we said, "So what did you think of him?" And all he did was shake his head. He seemed *stunned*.

Next thing you know, three weeks later, Sammy was in Ciro's. And that was really the start of Sammy Davis Jr. He launched him then. Singing. Dancing. Impressions. He did *everything*, Sammy was a *talent*.

Oh, I had all the great ones, though, and Jo and I loved them all. It was a pleasure to work for all of them because they were all so nice. It was easy to do a good job on singers like that.

Jo and I lived in Hollywood first and then we moved here [to North Hollywood]. So I've been here a long time, a *long, long* time. Fifty years. Before the freeway was built. It was not easy driving to Hollywood then, over Laurel Canyon Boulevard or Coldwater Canyon. You drove over those to get to Hollywood and back.

There's no explanation for what happened to Hollywood, except that I think it grew in population. People, more and more, got places to live up in Hollywood and some of them were characters. One time Jo and I were walking with our little daughter late at night on Hollywood Boulevard. We see this little guy walking toward us with two pretty blondes, one on each arm. Then these two big fellows came up to him and tried to butt in on him and these blonde girls. And this little guy turned around and hit one of the big guys, and he went down *so* hard, I thought he was dead! Then the little guy knocked the other fellow straight through a *window*. And who was he? A boxer! [Laughs] Turned out he was a bantam weight champion! Little did they know what they were messing with! He had these two blonde girls on his arms, and they fooled around with him and he turned around and punched one of him and knocked him out—I didn't think he was going to ever get up. The other one he knocked through a window. I'll never forget that. That happened on Hollywood Boulevard, but other than that, it was always presentable and nice.

I don't believe Hollywood will ever be like it was. *Never* again. Maybe a little bit up toward the Chinese Theater. People have said that maybe Hollywood Boulevard could develop again, but it hasn't so far and I don't think it ever will. I remember the days when it was nice. . . . I guess the memories are still all there.

Robert Cornthwaite
BORN APRIL 28, 1917
ST. HELEN, OREGON
RADIO ANNOUNCER/ACTOR

With his neatly trimmed silver beard and regal bearing, he beams with a relaxed elegance, and expounds on theories of acting in movies, television and the theater. In movie circles, he's most famous for his appearances in science-fiction films, most famously The War of The Worlds. *But to TV aficionados he will always be foremost in their thoughts in his role as Windish on* "Get Smart," *or as the evil attorney Alan O. Dale on* "Batman." *Although he is not an Englishman, his speaking voice bears faint remnants of the many British roles he played, as he discusses his place in American pop culture with the rich eloquence of a Shakespearean. He is formal but at ease in a canary yellow sweater, sitting at a desk in his bungalow at the Motion Picture Country Home, smiling a sagacious, professorial smile.*

102

If you go back far enough, about 1,200 years, about A.D. 800, The Danes came into the north and west of England, and all the -thwaite names are descended from those Danish Viking people who came in and took over. They got all of England except the little kingdom of Wessex, where Alfred the Great was. All the rest was Denmark's. In Hamlet, remember the King of England has to do what the King of Denmark tells him.

I never wanted to act as a kid. My brother was in a play and he hated it, so I always avoided it. But I was eventually forced to be in a play. It was the Thanksgiving play about the first Thanksgiving, and I played Governor Bradford. I was all of thirteen. My voice was changing then and I discovered I had this new voice I could throw off the back of the auditorium. I was hooked from then on, and in high school I was in every play I had time for.

My parents moved to Hollywood in 1935. It was the depths of the Depression. My father had an older brother who worked as an extra in films here, and behind the camera. Then he made the mistake of marrying his boss' fiancee, Dolores, and that pretty much ended his career at Warner Brothers. They were living in Long Beach, and my father had what they used to call asthma. He actually had TB but nobody knew it—nobody tested him for it. He felt better here, so we moved here, and we had a little store, what you call a mom & pop market. I was the meatcutter.

I remember the first time I ever saw Hollywood Boulevard. We had just driven in from Oregon, and we came in at dawn. My brother and I had driven all through the night. And came down through the Cahuenga Pass—there was no freeway in those days. And came to Hollywood Boulevard. And I couldn't believe it. It was flashy, it was sleazy, it was unlike anything I had ever seen. There was Grauman's Chinese Theater and the Egyptian Theater. Musso & Frank's Grill, the Brown Derby.

I loved the movies. But I never thought of myself as a film actor and I never intended for that to happen. I never thought there would be anything for me in movies. I wanted to be a theater actor. I started working in radio in Hollywood. And after the war, I came back. I would have liked very much to strike out and be a theater actor, but there was no money. And my mother was completely dependent on me. And I was lucky enough to get my old job back on radio as an announcer. I also did "fee shows," as it was known—you would get an extra fee, naturally, for doing those.

103

My regular radio job was a forty-two-hour across-the-board job. You did anything that happened in your shift: newscast, which I loved, disc jockeying, which I hated because most popular music is just terrible. As time went on, I began to rewrite my newscasts when I had time. Other times I would take them off the United Press teletype. And sometimes you would read them cold; you'd never read them before. I remember reading ball scores, and it would garble. And I would make up a score.

The teletype machine was nowhere near the announcer booth, because when there were urgent stories, bells would go off from it. So the announcer's job involved going through the hall and down the corridor to the machine to get the news. Years after doing radio, I would have a nightmare about doing radio, being in the booth, finishing up a show, and realizing I don't have my news. And I don't have any time to go and get it. I've had this many times, and boom, I always wake up right before I have to go back on the air. That was my nightmare for years.

I did a lot of radio drama in Hollywood. At KFI, which was the NBC station, and KNX, the CBS station. I used a half-dozen different names, because the radio station where I was employed as an announcer wanted my exclusive services. So I would use another name. My favorite was Alexander Vanderzant. [Laughs] Simply because it sounded like a bucket falling down stairs, I guess.

NBC was at Sunset & Vine, and CBS was at Sunset & Gower. Hollywood was a strange place then. I met Mary Pickford when I interviewed her on the radio about her work on the Wendell Wilkie campaign [for president]. Roosevelt was running for his third term, which was unprecedented, so all the Republican stars worked for Wilkie.

[Mary Pickford] wanted people to know she had been in pictures since she was five, and that she had struggled. She was a highly intelligent woman. She was married at that time to Buddy Rogers, who had been her leading man in her last silent picture. He was younger than she was.

I remember she was wearing a fur coat over a black dress with a lot of fringe on it, and she had bangles and bracelets all up and down her arms. And she was struggling to get out of her coat and Buddy Rogers, her husband, just left her to struggle and went and took his seat on the sidelines. And our soundman, Creek Moore [laughs], everyone called him "Creeky," said, "Can I help you, Mary?" And she looked over her shoulder at him startled that he would call her Mary.

She said, "Do I *know* you?" Which was the standard response. Because she wanted to know what footing are we speaking on?

He said, "Well, yes, Mary, I doubled you in *Joanna Goes to War* in 1915."

She said, "Oh," and looked over at Buddy Rogers to make sure he didn't hear. But he must have known she started in pictures in 1905 or something. [Laughs] She was a *character*. She made a big impression on me.

Hollywood was an unusual town just by the nature of it, that everybody in town works in or lives off, in a sense, the motion picture industry. That was *the* industry in town. It was a real company town. I guess the only thing like it would be a steel town in Pennsylvania, something like that. People had a feeling it was all glamour and parties and clubs. But the truth was it was a lot of work. Especially in those days, before the unions were strong, or even before there were unions, you would work *ungodly* hours. It still is true, but you get paid overtime. In television you can work fourteen, sixteen hours a day on the last day of shooting. I worked once *twenty-four hours straight* on location in Hollywood. That was on a feature. *God*, you'd get so tired you couldn't hit the floor with your hat. I had a dressing room out on the street. And I was on call so I didn't have time to go way out there, so I could just lie down and go to sleep on the cables on the floor. You could only sleep for a few minutes at a whack, but you would just get *groggy*.

When I was working at CBS radio, there was a little diner near there where we would go for lunch. And it was the first time I ever saw Lucille Ball. I was with some friends who were also in radio, and we were having coffee and Lucille Ball came in through the kitchen of this place. My friend pointed her out and said, "That's Lucille Ball. She's looking for Desi." [Laughs] She was checking out the kitchen!

I never played myself in films. I always played characters. But if you have an attractive enough personality, you can do very well playing yourself. Robert Mitchum did that, and he could, because he was Robert Mitchum. He was a highly intelligent guy. I knew and worked with him onstage in 1940 before either of us were in pictures. He got a day's work in a Western while we were working on that play.

I was in the air force and spent a lot of time with the RAF. Maybe some of their accent rubbed off on me, even though I was a Yank always to them. But I have been accused of having an accent, and people have sometimes thought I was British. I also spoke some Italian and could speak and read French and some German. So people assumed I could speak many other languages, too, which I couldn't. I remember being cast as a Mexican once, which was embarrassing to me, because I can't speak Spanish. I had to learn lines phonetically, which annoyed the actors who could really speak Spanish well. But when they cast me, my agent said I did speak Spanish. Agents lied a lot in Hollywood, you know. [Laughs]

105

I think in general it was a kinder society then. It was a smaller game, and there were fewer people here. I never enjoyed movie work as much as theater. Movies are not made by actors, they are made by actors, directors, cameramen and editors. They are the makers of the films. The creators. They shape it. Actors really have little to do with it. But onstage that's not true. Once the curtain goes up before an audience, you are in charge. And you had better behave yourself, of course. If you don't have discipline, you're not a very good actor. But the bit is in your teeth. That's the best way I can express it. And you know you're on. And you're getting response from an audience that you do not get in film. Now and then in film, a director can be your audience. Sometimes you can tell, if the crew is paying attention, you've grabbed them. But frequently crews couldn't be less interested in anything that an actor is doing. But if you grab them, then you've got your audience.

The first sizable sequence I did in a picture was with Victor Mature. It was a one-day job but I had a lot to do in this one day. They cast me because they thought I spoke any number of foreign languages, which I do not. But this guy was supposed to be a Pole, I think, but he was speaking Italian to Italian immigrants on Ellis Island. Because I was a one-day actor they didn't provide me with a dressing room. If you are an actor of some stature, you get a dressing room on the soundstage. When Mature found that out, he said, "Hey! Come in with me." He was a very [laughs] decisive kind of guy. I liked him very much because he was very good to me. He was resentful—he was on loan-out from Fox, and this was being filmed at RKO—at Melrose and Gower, which was run by Howard Hughes then.

Terry Moore was in the film too, who was Hughes' girlfriend at the time. The script had been totally tailored for Terry Moore. Hughes was very specific about what he wanted, and what he wanted was for Terry Moore's bosom to be featured on camera.

This infuriated Mature. He had a lot of grievances. I remember him throwing the script out of the dressing room door out onto the floor. That's the way he felt about it. But he was great. He knew how to handle himself on camera. And he taught me a lot. We did many scenes together shot in close-up, and as it wound up the cutter gave most of the footage to me. I remember the producer talking to the editor saying, "Mature isn't going to like this." But Mature had no problem with it at all. He understood the scene belonged to my character.

The most famous film I ever worked on was The Thing, directed by Howard Hawks. It was the only science-fiction film he ever made. I knew it would be a good film—cause he knew movies. He was a great director but also a great writer. He had an ability to strip dialogue down not only to the fewest possible words, but syllables. It's rarely found among directors to have the high sensitivity that he had toward dialogue. And he was a complete master of how to shoot a scene, place a camera, all the things that were important to a film director. And he was an absolute autocrat. He liked to only work with the best, and he had the best crew in town—great cameramen and gaffers and cutters. I was in very good company there.

Hawks saw my screen test for the film, and he liked it but wanted me in a beard. Every bit of my wardrobe was his decision, too. The pants I wore were Donald O'Connor's. [Laughs] I wore a paste-on beard for almost the whole movie. But then we were laid off before doing the end of the film, where they discover the flying saucer out on the ice. They were planning to shoot that in Montana, and then in North Dakota, because they wanted real snow. But it didn't snow that winter, and we ended up shooting that scene in Encino. [Laughs] By that time, I had been laid off so long that I had time to grow a real beard, so that is my real beard in the final scene of the picture.

When I read the script of The Thing, though, I wasn't convinced it would be very good. I thought it was routine. And a lot of good people had worked on that script. But that's not Hawks' method. He rewrites on the set, and he rewrote most of that. So you had to be a quick study to learn the new stuff. We had a big set, and within it there were all these rooms and corridors and generators. He always kept on the soundstage a big table. We would walk through a scene so that it could be lit, and keylights and all could be adjusted. There were no close-ups on The Thing. The second team would step in for us, and go through the blocking of the scene for the camera crew. At which time Hawks would have the cast sitting around the table, and Hawks' secretary would take everything down in shorthand. Hawks would say, "Let's not pay any attention to the script. If this were to happen, what would you say?" And you could make suggestions. But you had to be careful with your suggestions, because most of the things would be rejected. [Laughs]

Sometimes he would take what you said and modify it. And that is the way the dialogue for each scene was written, sitting at that table. And you would learn the lines while sitting there, and you played it three or four times, go into the set, shoot the master shot of what you have just rehearsed, and in the meantime the secretary is typing it all up, and turning out the copies. And then we shoot the second shots that fit into the master, and the script would have your lines. But you had already said these lines on film but you hadn't seen it on the page yet. [Laughs] And that's how it came together. It was very unusual, but I enjoyed it.

I got cast in *The War of the Worlds* because of the success of *The Thing*. We made it eleven months after *The Thing* in March of '51. That was not nearly as much fun. It was very cut and dry. Also, it was baffling and boring, because none of the effects had yet to be designed. Only George Pal, the producer, knew. But it was a secret he kept from us. He would just say, "There's something out here about twenty feet away and it's about twelve feet tall...." You don't know *what* you are looking at and you have to react to stuff that doesn't *exist* yet! It's a hell of a way to make a picture.

They did a lot of location work on *War of the Worlds*—they used the church on Franklin & Highland in Hollywood, but I was not in that scene. I did all my scenes on the lot. I have worked in that church since then, however, on the television series "Picket Fences."

TV acting is the same as movie acting, you just do it faster. And they don't cover, as they say, with as many camera angles. I did the *Batman* TV show twice. That was fun, and it was absolutely ruined by the director. They thought it was the best script they'd had. So they opened the second season with that. But the director they chose was deadly. He had the gift of killing *dead* whatever was in the script. He was an acting coach too. A nice guy, but just *deadly*.

I loved the script, though. I played Alan O'Dale, an attorney. And the writer told me how to do the speech for the character. [In a pretentious, upper-crust, effeminate Eastern accent] "He's Ivy league, and he talks through his teeth." [Laughs] I had one line that the crew picked up, and it was all over the lot, everyone was saying this one line I had: "Oh, I like that cape, Batman. *Wash and wear?*"

I did three episodes of "Twilight Zone." I got to work with Dana Andrews on one, which was nice. One was about shooting a TV series. And I played the director. Which I enjoyed very much, because at one point the director, in just *sheer* frustration—he can't get anything out of his actors—starts to cry. [Laughs] I have seen directors practically on the edge of breakdowns, they just *weep* with frustration.

I did the first few episodes of "Get Smart!" I played Windish, an inventor who invented things for Agent 86—Don Adams—to use, and 86 was a screw-up, and he could never do anything right. Mel Brooks was one of the producers, and he kept writing me into it because he thought my role was funny. Don Adams asked me, after we had done two or three of them, "Do you think Windish gets exasperated with 86?"

And I said, "Yeah, I think he gets exasperated, but he gets over it because 86 is the only means he has of trying out his inventions."

Don didn't agree. He didn't think anyone should *ever* get mad at him. And I think that's what ended my time with that show. I did that one and one more, and that was it, it was already in the works. I was replaced, amazingly, by Frank DeVol, who was an orchestra leader and composer.

108

It's funny being an actor because I've done so many things. This thing [motions to television] is going, and something catches your eye—this has happened to me many times—and they'll cut to a close-up, and I'll suddenly realize, "I'm *in* that!" And I don't remember that at all. It's very strange. It's happened to me several times.

I played Napoleon in a couple of films. Once I was in a department store and they had about twenty televisions all tuned to the same thing. They were showing a Napoleonic film. And they cut to a close-up, and it's *me!* And the floorwalker comes up and says, "Can I help you?" And I said, pointing at the TV, "No, I was just looking at me." And he turns and sees Napoleon [laughter] and he had this panicked look in his eyes and I knew he was thinking, "Oh *God,* I've got a nut on my hands!" [Laughter] There was no use trying to explain.

Zelda Aronson
BORN OCTOBER 11, 1917
BROOKLYN, NEW YORK
SECRETARY/OFFICE MANAGER

"I spend my whole life in bed," she says in a raspy voice that betrays successive decades of dedicated cigarette smoking. "I started smoking when I was a kid," she says. "Everybody smoked then. It was the thing to do." Though she hasn't lived in New York since Herbert Hoover was president, she still retains her native Brooklyn accent as she relates stories of running Irving Berlin's West Coast office throughout his amazingly prolific and long career. To explain what she sees as the tragedy of Hollywood Boulevard's evolution, she evokes voices of her personal past by using Yiddish, but checks first to see if she'd be understood. "Are you Jewish?" she asks. "You are? Good. Then you know what 'dreck' is. That's the best word I can use to describe what it looks like now. Dreck."[1]

---

[1] Yiddish for cheap, junky stuff.

Yes, I was born in 1917. You can see that I'm a young kid. I was sixteen when I first visited Los Angeles. I came with my mother and sister from New York on a boat. Through the canal. We stayed in Hollywood for about a month. We stayed initially at the Knickerbocker Hotel on Ivar. It was very nice at the time. We stayed there for a few days and then moved to an apartment on Cherokee & Yucca—the Canterbury. God knows what it is like now. We had a nice apartment and Mama cooked, of course. Though we usually had dinner out.

My mother's brother was a musician and we knew all of his friends. And all musicians are crazy. Mama cooked primarily for the guys because they had never gotten a home meal since leaving New York. And in-between we would eat at Musso & Frank's. Because it was close by. It's still there. It's about the only place still left. I used to love the flannel cakes there. Their chicken pie is good there, too. Everything is good there, even the martinis.

People used to walk on Hollywood Boulevard in the evenings and look in all the nice windows of the pretty shops. The boulevard then was pretty and clean. It was one of the main reasons we came here, because it was so clean here.

I moved here permanently on my own in 1943. Before the war was over. I was twenty-six. I didn't know what to do. I had no profession. I didn't know how to do anything. But the war was on, so you didn't have to know anything; if you could maybe read or write or stand up, you could get a job. And I got a job in the music business. My friend Lois Sidney got me my first job in the music business. She picked me up and drove me to Hollywood Boulevard for a job interview.

I got the job because it was the worst job in town. The boss was Armenian and didn't know what he was doing. He used to chase me around the desk. Of course he chased me because I wouldn't stay put. He knew nothing about music publishing and, of course, neither did I. He was in his late forties with a wife who was much older. To me she looked to be about 102 but maybe that was from living with him, I don't know. But she was rich, so he decided he wanted to become a music publisher.

When he dictated to me, he would say, "Take a letter to so and so at Ruthross & Ryan." I didn't know Ruthross & Ryan was an advertising agency. To me it sounds like three different words. But it isn't, it's two. I had to learn all that. They didn't really know what the hell they were doing, any of them, when I was offered a job to work for the Irving Berlin Music Company. The man who worked for Berlin came down to my office and said he wanted me

109

to work for him. I don't know how he knew I wasn't happy. So I went to work for the Irving Berlin company. All the guys in the music business had come from New York and Chicago. And this guy checked out all the girls in the business and was warned not to hire most of them, because they were considered spies for New York. They guys spent their lives trying to get performances on the songs of their publishers. They'd stay out all night with Freddy Martin, or whoever, at the Grove. Mostly with the guys who had air-time.

The Grove used to have a radio show and it was the radio performances we were after. So if the guys were out all night till two in the morning they couldn't be in the office at nine the next morning. They needed the protection of the girls who were in the office at ten. We all opened at ten. My boss would come in at eleven, or later, depending on how late he'd been out all night. They liked me because they knew I wasn't going to tell New York anything against him. I had that job with the Berlin company for forty-four years.

My boss was wonderful. Ben Gilbert. He was my boss for forty-four years. I loved him, really. I mean, no romance. Nothing. We published only the songs of Irving Berlin. And Berlin lived in New York, so we rarely saw him. He would come out to Hollywood when he did pictures. He did the Fred Astaire–Ginger Rogers stuff, and a whole slew of other movies. And when he was here, he was mostly at the studio.

Berlin called once from 20th Century Fox. He wanted to talk to my boss. Who was probably home sleeping. So Berlin said to me, "Take a letter." My hand was shaking. I took the letter and I typed it up and I put it on my boss' desk. When he came in he said, "What's this?"

I said, "Read it."

He said, "Where did you get it?"

I said, "Over the phone!" It's *crazy*.

But Berlin never gave us any trouble. We never had any complaints from New York. But Berlin was really an egomaniac. Rightfully so. He was the most successful American songwriter ever. But it didn't last long enough. It all ended when Elvis came in during the end of the fifties and then the Beatles. To me that's *not* music. My derogatory remarks about what is called pop music now should be easily understandable. Because as far as I'm concerned, this stuff that you hear these days, if you accidentally turn the dial wrong, it's not fit for human consumption unless you're *twelve*. The music used to be so great and the lyrics were so great. And they were so romantic, and the pictures they painted were so lovely.

Irving Berlin was truly great. I was impressed. I learned the catalogue. You ask somebody now who wrote "God Bless America," they say Kate Smith.

They don't know "White Christmas" wasn't written by Bing Crosby. And some of the songs that didn't become standards were great musically and lyrically. And some of the show tunes—we had five songs from *Annie Get Your Gun* on the "Hit Parade" at the same time.

Our first office was in the Warner Theater building, at Hollywood & Wilcox. Then we moved to 1537 Vine, and then to the RCA building at Sunset & Ivar. Then we moved to 6430 Sunset, at Sunset & Cahuenga.

I made $35 a week. I couldn't afford to eat at Musso's like when we first came to town. We used to go to a joint called Tip's, on the east side of Vine just north of Hollywood. It had a little wooden menu. They had hamburgers and sandwiches. That disappeared and became Dupar's. We also ate at a Chinese restaurant on Cahuenga. In the same building at 6430 Sunset downstairs on the main floor was the Jolly Roger, which lasted for a long time.

111

Hollywood Boulevard used to have an I. Magnin on it, at Hollywood & Ivar. There was a beautiful ladies shop called Harry Cooper's. Beautiful. Beautiful store and beautiful merchandise. All the shops were nice. People used to walk on the boulevard and window shop; the stores were closed at night, but it was pretty. Now they have all these shops with 4,800 things in the window. That alone would scare me away. The whole thing is a nightmare. Compared to what is was. It was lovely. There was a Sardi's on Hollywood Boulevard, just west of Vine. There was the Gotham Deli, which was *wonderful*. It had the *greatest* sandwiches in the world. They had great pastrami and cold cuts, and *delicious* rye bread.

I loved going to Grauman's Chinese Theater. I liked the Egyptian too. Sometimes you would see stars walking on the boulevard. I saw a film at the Warner Theater one time with Robert Taylor and Barbara Stanwyck sitting behind me. The stars were around more than they are now. People behaved differently then. Nobody would bother anybody. People were well mannered to a much greater extent than they are now.

At Sunset near Gardner there was a little movie house called the Oriental Theater. We used to walk down there at night. We would go walk down and go to the movies, and walk home in the dark. It never occurred to anybody that you might not be safe.

There were no high-rises anywhere in Los Angeles then. The tallest building in the whole city was City Hall. So it just seemed more . . . *livable*. The traffic was nothing like it is now, and there were no freeways. Everything was prettier.

I live on Hollywood Boulevard now, west of La Brea, which is all residential. On Hollywood Boulevard between Camino Palmero and Fuller there were just two houses. Two mansions, one on each end. That's what most of

Hollywood Boulevard was. There were no tall buildings, and all the buildings had empty lots in between them. Sometimes people would buy these lots next to their houses and have a lawn.

The whole thing was beautiful. And it was kind of heavenly when I first came. It was magical. Especially to people who came from the east. Even the climate was better then. The smog wasn't here yet. The canyons of tall buildings weren't built. And there weren't five billion cars. And they didn't know that the gasoline was causing the fog. It was a whole different world, and it was really blissful to live here.

112

What happened to Hollywood is that is just got too crowded. This happened after the war. A lot of people passed through Hollywood during the war and decided they wanted to settle here. Television became important here, and that is one of the reasons for the growth. I doubt it will ever be nice again like it was. They keep talking about it. They're building the theater for the Oscars on the boulevard. I don't know if it will help. First they have to get rid of the dreck. I won't live long enough to see the changes. But you will. I wish you luck.

A.C. Lyles
BORN MAY 17, 1918
JACKSONVILLE, FLORIDA
PRODUCER

Paramount Pictures, Hollywood's oldest existent studio. He's worked here on this old lot for more than sixty years. The only time he wasn't here for any real duration was while his best friend "Ronnie" Reagan was president, and invited him to the White House to offer advice and guidance on the business of America, as he had for years on the business of movies in Hollywood. Known as the "Ambassador of Goodwill" for Paramount, in this role he frequently edifies college audiences and TV crews with his firsthand knowledge of movie history, but will also take the time in the middle of his always busy days to sit with solo writers who make the trek to Paramount with a multitude of questions. He sits in the office that's been his on the Paramount lot for multiple decades, wearing an immaculate black suit with a crisp white shirt, platinum cufflinks and a black and silver striped tie. His large desk is dark wood, and holds the framed photos of many famous friends, including the former president and first lady. Almost every inch of the ocher walls are filled with more framed photos. There he's beaming a brilliant smile beside stars from Gary Cooper to John Travolta, all framed in black with chocolate-brown mats, and illuminated by the dusty sunlight that filters through silver venetian blinds. After a spoken tour of his past, he instructs his secretary to dim the lights, close the blinds, and lower a little movie screen. Suddenly a movie is being projected, narrated by Ronald Reagan and featuring cameos by John Wayne,

Charlton Heston, Jimmy Stewart and other stars, all affirming the enduring eminence of a remarkable Hollywood career.

When I was ten I wanted to make movies. I never wanted to be in movies or be an actor. Which is probably fortunate for me, because I probably would have failed at that. I just wanted to make movies, even though I didn't know what constituted making movies. I didn't know the difference between a producer or a director. I just knew somebody wrote it, somebody photographed it, somebody was in them, and I wanted to be a part of it.

I had seen a picture called *Wings*—the first and only silent picture to win the Academy Award—with Clara Bow and Richard Arlen and Charles Buddy Rogers and a new fella named Gary Cooper. I went and just fell in love with that picture. It was a Paramount picture playing at the Paramount Theater in Jacksonville. I had seen that it said *Adolph Zukor Presents*, so I was in awe of Adolph Zukor. I spoke to the manager of the theater that day if he would give me a job. And he gave me a job handing out leaflets on pictures coming up. And then made me a pageboy with a uniform.

After four years in this job I eventually met Adolph Zukor, who was head of Paramount, when he came to Jacksonville. I asked him to let me come to Hollywood to work with him. He said, "Well, you're just a kid, but you've been working for Paramount now for four years at the theater. So you finish high school, keep in touch, and I'll hire you when you get out of high school."

Now that was extremely kind of him. He probably had people every day saying, "Take me to Hollywood," but when he said to keep in touch and finish high school, my main object then was to finish high school. But the most important thing was writing him a letter every Sunday. He didn't tell me to write him every Sunday, he just told me to keep in touch. So I wrote him every Sunday for four years. He didn't write back—I didn't hear from him but it didn't matter. I never lost confidence or lost courage. I just knew he was looking forward to my letter each week as much as I was looking forward to writing to him.

One day Gary Cooper came to my hometown. I was writing movie news for the hometown paper. I saw Mr. Cooper and I told him I would be out here in Hollywood to work at Paramount as soon as I got out of high school. This was his home-lot. And there again, for some reason, he took a quick liking to me. I told him about my letters to Zukor every Sunday and he asked me what I would be writing about this week, and I said, "Oh, about meeting you, Mr. Cooper."

So he said, "Give me a piece of paper." So he took a piece of paper and wrote a note to Adolph Zukor saying, "I'm looking forward to seeing this kid on the lot." So I wrote to Mr. Zukor telling him I had met Gary Cooper and enclosed the note to him.

Then I heard from Mr. Zukor indirectly. A woman named Sidney Brecker, who was his secretary, wrote to me and said, "Mr. Zukor has been receiving your letters. But he feels that you don't have to write every week. If you wrote once every three or four or five months, that would be enough." Well, that didn't discourage me at all. I continued to write to Mr. Zukor every Sunday. But I also had a new pigeon, Sidney Brecker, his secretary. So I wrote her every Sunday too. My whole main objective all week was what I was going to write to Mr. Zukor. Then I had to write another original letter to Sidney Brecker. Sidney later became a very dear friend of mine.

114

I also wrote Clara Bow and Gary Cooper and Richard Arlen and Charles Buddy Roger a letter after *Wings*. I told them I had seen this picture and I was going to come out and work in the movies. And I got an autographed picture of Clara Bow and one from Richard Arlen and Gary Cooper. And Charles Buddy Rogers wrote a little note to me. He said, "When you come out, why don't you try acting? Because if I can do it, anybody can do it."

Oddly enough, they all became friends of mine. I just gave the eulogy for Charles Buddy Rogers eight weeks ago. I gave the eulogy for Richard Arlen. When I became a producer, as long as Richard Arlen lived, I never made a picture without him. I got to know Gary Cooper very well and got to know Clara very well. I participated in her funeral. She asked me if I would try out her son, Tony Rex Bell Jr., to see if he could be an actor, and I used him in a couple of pictures.

I wrote [Zukor] a letter every Sunday for four years, keeping in touch. The day after I got out of highschool, I was in a day coach headed for Holly-wood, where you sit up—probably four days and four nights. I had $48 in cash that I had saved up, and two loaves of bread, and two jars of peanut butter and a sack of apples, and I headed for Hollywood. Got off the train downtown, took the streetcar straight to Paramount, and told them at the gate to tell Mr. Zukor I was here. And I've been here ever since.

I had no conception of what Hollywood would be like before I moved here. I never thought what it would be like, nor did I know what a studio would be like. I had seen several movies depicting Hollywood, but most of those were comedies and farces. I just knew there was a big entrance to the studio and I could see the soundstages. But I didn't have any conception about the technology of making movies. But I wanted to find out.

I lived with a family from my hometown when I first moved here. My salary was $15 a week. When I saved enough, I sent for my mother. She was the only family I had. We got a little apartment close to the studio that was $29 a month. My salary was $60 a month, so that left us $31. That was a dollar to day to live on, and we did quite well by it. We lived on Melrose; the building is no longer there. One of the buildings we moved to, [peers out window] I can see the top of it from here. It was the same rent but it was a little better. It was a furnished one-bedroom apartment. My mother slept in the bedroom and in the living room there was a Murphy bed in the wall that I slept on.

My first impression of Hollywood was the Paramount gate. It was my first sign of anything Hollywood, the original Paramount gates—the Marathon gates—which I still pass and see every day. It's the gate made famous in *Sunset Boulevard*, with Billy Wilder directing and Gloria Swanson in the lead and Erich Von Stroheim as the chauffeur, and she comes up to the Paramount gate in a very fancy car to see Cecil B. DeMille. That gate is one of the most famous landmarks in town.

115

The studio used to be at 5451 Marathon. About fifteen years ago Earl Letts came on as president of facilities. He bought five blocks of property on Melrose, and tore down all the buildings there and pushed the studio out to Melrose. What was the front of the studio is now a block inside of the studio. And the big famous main gate is inside the studio. The new entrance [looks out window], the two archways which I am looking at now from the four story office here is the new building.

When I was a kid I fell in love with that famous Paramount logo with the mountain and the sky and the twenty-two stars around it. It says Paramount and it says Adolph Zukor Presents. That is the closest thing that I ever had to Hollywood when I was back in my hometown, that Paramount logo, and wanting to be part of that Paramount logo. I wanted to be part of that mountain, part of those stars. Not as a star or as an actor but just making pictures.

I didn't know what a grip was, what an electrician was or any of the terminology. I knew there were credits on the screen that said "Directed by Cecil B. DeMille" and produced by someone. But at ten I didn't know what kind of unit it took to make a movie. When I got here and became an office boy, an errand boy, a mail boy, mostly assigned to Adolph Zukor, it didn't take me too long because of my association with Adolph Zukor, even though I was only an office boy. People associated me with him because I was always bringing messages to them from Mr. Zukor. Or going out to get a message for Mr. Zukor from them—the writers, directors, other executives, and stars. It didn't take me long to know almost everybody on the lot. That was just Paramount.

Some years ago we bought RKO, which was then owned by Desilu—Lucille Ball and Desi Arnaz. We bought that and expanded, doubled the size of the lot. All the way to Gower and from Gower over to Van Ness. When I came here we were making fifty-five features a year. That's an awful lot. We had a lot of activity on the lot. There were always four or five big features shooting in the lot every day, and we had 125–130 actors under contract, from big-name stars down the feature players. We probably had fifty directors and producers on the lot, and a large number of writers.

We had so much production that we had a fifty-piece orchestra which reported every morning and worked every day, scoring a picture or prerecording songs. We had a school here for children. We had a principal and two teachers, and all the kids under contract went there every day. Shirley Temple went there at one time, before she went to Fox. Jackie Cooper and a lot of other well-known young actors went there. It was great for those kids because they grew up around the studio. I grew up around the studio. I was seventeen. They put me over in the publicity department working with a lot of the young stars. They had a lot of people under contract around my age. And I worked with them in publicity.

Before long I was very fortunate in that I loved this business so much and for whatever reason gravitated to almost everybody on the lot, and they were very generous with their time, and very generous in their efforts to see that I had a good start, and that I learned the business. That was everybody from Adolph Zukor and Cecil B. DeMille to the biggest stars we had on the lot. I got to know them all: Bob Hope and Bing Crosby, Dorothy Lamour, Joel MacRae, Claudette Colbert. And more important, they got to know me. It was a wonderful learning period for me at that time.

Being in publicity put me in close daily touch with everybody on the lot who was making a movie. Then I became an assistant producer, and then a producer, and I started making pictures for my own little company, A.C. Lyles Productions, in association with Paramount. There was a whole series of Westerns I made under those auspices.

Adolph Zukor was one of the true giants of the movie business. We had giants like Jack Warner, Louie B. Mayer, Sam Goldwyn, Jesse Lasky, and Carl Laemmle out at Universal. Those people were really giants in this business. Even today the studios are greatly inclined to follow those men and remember those men. Those people contributed so much, not only to their own studios, but to the industry as a whole.

Zukor was a rather small in stature man. He had this accent. He had one little cauliflower ear from trying to be a boxer. He was very energetic and the most optimistic man I've ever known. He had great optimism and a great love for this business. He also had the wonderful ability to recognize talent. He saw Mae West come out and do one small part in a picture, and [snaps fingers] he made her a star. Gary Cooper had a small minute and a half scene in *Wings* and he saw that and made him a star. Bob Hope came out and did a picture—sixth billing—and Zukor saw that talent and put him on a series of pictures. He had that magic touch, I always felt. He could also be a very tough businessman.

He saw the great talent of a young girl from Canada when she was fifteen years old, Mary Pickford, put her under contract and she became the first big star we had. He saw a picture called Four Horsemen of the Apocalypse and recognized the great talent of Rudolph Valentino, put him under contract, and those stars became the biggest stars we had.

The whole time Mr. Zukor was at Paramount he was finding talent—executives, writers, directors, producers, actors, actresses. He was a really inspiring man. I spent a lot of time with him, with his family. I have a letter that I treasure very much from his son Eugene, who was a producer on the lot. It said, "My father couldn't have loved you more had you been his son. And I couldn't have loved you more had you been my brother." That was a very touching letter for me.

117

Mr. Zukor lived to be 103. I used to have a birthday party for him each year. There's a picture of me, once his office boy and now a producer on the lot, cutting the cake for his ninety-eighth birthday. He was at ninety-eight the most energetic, enthusiastic, crafty man, it was incredible. And he knew what pictures would do well, what talent would do well. He had that inborn ability to project and anticipate. I have never met anybody quite like Adolph Zukor. I was so fortunate to have been somehow brought together with him and have my presence brought to his attention [laughs], I guess, through my drive.

Clara Bow was at one time a very, very popular actress. When sound came in, there was some feeling that her voice wasn't right. She was from Brooklyn and she had a Brooklyn accent. Then some personal circumstances came about and it damaged her career some. They called Clara "The Flapper," and she was well known as the "It" girl. A women writer named Eleanor Glyn named her that and wrote a picture for her called It. Clara Bow left the business at a young age, and after the death of her husband Rex Bell, she moved to Santa Monica. I was in touch with her till she died.

I remember Cecil B. DeMille vividly. I can, in between words, hear his voice. And I can see his presence and I can see his face so easily. I can see the way he walked. DeMille was a very knowledgeable man who knew how to make movies. He had his own brand of movies. His name was one of the first to be above the title: It was Cecil B. DeMille's Ten Commandments, Cecil B. DeMille's Greatest Show on Earth, Cecil B. DeMille's Sign of the Cross, Cecil B. DeMille's Cleopatra. And that's the way it was.

He was the king. He was a very exacting person. If you went to him for something, he would want to know exactly what the subject was and wanted to know exactly the answers when he asked you what they were. And you couldn't con him. He knew the business. He made the business. I always found him to be very friendly, cordial, very open to suggestions, very willing to help people who wanted to be helped. And he was so helpful with me. I was around him a lot when I was Zukor's office boy and later. When I went through the different ranks of publicity, he was so nice to me.

When I became a producer, he was exceedingly helpful to me. I don't remember ever calling him when he didn't come right to the phone. I don't remember ever going on his set when he didn't call to Carl, the prop man, to get A.C. a chair. And if he was shooting and I hadn't been out there yet to the set, it was not uncommon for him to call me and say, "You haven't been out here. Where are you? Come on out." Or in the commissary if he had guests, he would always send a waitress over to my table to tell me he wanted me to meet his guests.

118

In real estate there are three words: *location, location, location.* And in this business there are three words: *obsession, obsession, obsession.* I think you have to be obsessed to be in this business. You can't say, "I think I'll try it and see how I like it." You have to say, "I have to be in this business." I really can't tell you *how* to get in this business. I can't tell you how to *stay* in this business. But I've been in this business since I was ten years old and with one studio almost seventy-one years. There are hundreds of thousands of people all over the world trying to get here. This is a mecca for motion picture business and television. And people all over the world are wanting to walk through those gates that I am looking at outside of my window. And come here and be a part of this studio, or be a part of the motion picture industry.

It's not just Hollywood. Hollywood is the banner, the mecca, the place. But actually Hollywood is all over the world. Pictures are made all over the world. Hollywood is much better known around the world than Los Angeles. Hollywood has a whole different appeal to people than Los Angeles. Someone once said Hollywood is a state of mind. I think that is true.

Tom Jones

BORN JANUARY 31, 1919
CHICAGO, ILLINOIS
STUDIO CARPENTER

He's a gentleman. It's an admittedly old-fashioned distinction, but one that applies, especially to the manner in which he discusses legendary men for whom he worked, such as Walt Disney and Charlie Chaplin. Though both were known as notoriously difficult employers, he has only kind words to say about them. "Walt was a real nice, gracious kind of man," he says of Disney, for whom he worked for thirty years. "In fact he called me up one day and gave me this ring." It's a gold ring engraved with the face of Mickey Mouse and the year 1955. Of Chaplin, he says, "Charlie was a genius, and probably the funniest man who ever lived." He shows off an autographed photo of Chaplin from The Pilgrim *that he keeps in a small frame on a small table* with his telephone. His job was to build, and he built everything from sets for the early talkies to the Tea-Cups Ride at Disneyland. He grew up in Hollywoodland, and remembers the night back in 1927 that the big sign up in the hills was lit up for the first time. A tall man with long arms and big hands, he projects a buoyant pride about his work as well as astonishment over all the decades that have flown so swiftly past. "I'm older than the pope now," he says with the slightest of smiles. "I didn't think that would ever happen."

I remember the night in 1927 when they first lit the Hollywoodland sign. It used to have lightbulbs all over it. It would light up in sequence: Holly—wood—land. And then the whole thing would light up. We watched from our porch, looking up the hill.

We lived in the Hollywoodland development. We moved there in 1922. There weren't many other houses at the time. It was *beautiful*. It's all built up now. At that time, Bela Lugosi lived up in the house above us. He was making *Dracula*. He was a very nice gentleman. Then after a while he got into the dope and all, but that was much later. He wasn't scary at all at first. He was a great actor. But after I saw *Dracula*, then I was scared. [Laughs] Knowing he lived right up the hill. [Laughter] I was just a kid then.

My dad was a millinery salesman, sold lady's hats, a traveling salesman, traveled all around the country by train. He was on the road for about sixty years. He knew Eddie Mannix, who was a big boy at MGM at the time. And he knew about Hollywood from him. As a child I had asthma, and they figured that this territory out here in California was better for people with asthma. At that time. It's all changed now. So that's the reason we came out here.

When I first went to Hollywood Boulevard there were orange trees on the boulevard. The only thing left down there now that was from then is Musso & Frank's.

After a while my folks moved down to the Montecito down there on Franklin. I went to Blessed Sacrament School [at Sunset & Cherokee] and Hollywood High. At that time the people that were in the same class as mine were Jason Robards and Alexis Smith. And Joel MacRae. And Mickey [Rooney] and Judy [Garland] were there at first, but then they took off and transferred to the Motion Picture school. Now they have big iron fences all around Hollywood High. But it wasn't like that then. It was nice.

I was at Hollywood High during the days of the Big Bands. They had jitterbug contests at the old Hollywood Legion Stadium on El Centro. It was a fight stadium. This was about 1937. One night we went to the old Palomar, a dance hall on Vermont. I was double dating with Mickey Rooney and two girls. And at that time Charlie Barnett and his band were playing there. At eleven that night we went out to a hot dog stand, which was good, because that place burned down that night. There were about 200 people in there, but they all got out okay.

There's a myth that Lana Turner was discovered at Schwab's. But it is just a myth. Because I was there the day she was discovered. We went across the street from Hollywood High to Curry's Ice Cream, on the southeast corner of Sunset & Highland. *That's* where she was discovered.

120

My father took me to the first ever Academy Awards, which were in the Blossom Room of the Hollywood Roosevelt Hotel in 1927. I remember that Emil Jannings and Janet Gaynor won their Oscars. And the movie *Wings* won for Best Picture. I was just a kid, but I enjoyed it. They had a big dinner.

You used to see stars out in the streets making movies. I remember seeing Laurel & Hardy making a movie out on the corner of Hollywood & Cherokee, and also on Hollywood & Las Palmas, just north of the boulevard. They were very funny, but when the camera went off they were very serious. Laurel & Hardy seemed like friends, but they would go their separate ways when they weren't together on camera. Stan Laurel, who was English, seemed like the brains. He guided the films more than Hardy did. Which you wouldn't have guessed from seeing their movies.

I remember seeing a lot of Westerns getting shot all around Hollywood. In the streets, and up in Bronson Canyon, by the rocks and the caves. They shot a lot of movies there, and I used to love going there to play in the cave and to watch.

Peter the Hermit used to live up in a little shack by the Hollywoodland sign. He would walk up and down Hollywood Boulevard. He had a long white beard and a cane. He would walk all up and down the boulevard saying hello to all the people. I remember seeing Mae West walking down there on the boulevard. I remember the first Christmas Parade on Hollywood Boulevard. Joe E. Brown was the grand marshal. It was a little parade then, from La Brea to Vine Street.

They used to have big double-decker buses on Sunset. And the big red cars on Hollywood Boulevard. *Those* were the days. It was a nice ride. You'd go through the Gardner Junction there. You could go all the way to *Newport Beach* for a *dime!* But Standard Oil and Atlantic Richfield put a stop to that. They wanted us to buy their gas. So they stopped that.

During the war I was in the navy. When I first got out of the service I got a job at the Fogcutters, a bar on Hollywood & La Brea. I worked there for about a year and a half. Johnny Carson was a bartender at one of those bars on Las Palmas. Eventually I got a job at Monogram Studios as a carpenter's assistant. Monogram was at Santa Monica & Vermont. I worked there for a while. They used to have one-day calls, so you would work when you could.

They made China's Little Devils when I was there with Harry Carey Sr. They made little B pictures there then. talkies. This was in the early forties.

Then I worked at Universal Studios for about two years, and then the strike came along. I went to the Palladium. My future wife, June Bennett, was a band singer who was singing with Charlie Barnett then. Sure enough we got into a conversation, and we got married, and we were married for forty-five years. She was wonderful.

I worked at Charlie Chaplin's studio for about a year and a half. It was a nice studio. I worked building sets. Hard work. I did meet Chaplin a couple of times when he came in. He was with Oona O'Neill at the time. He was a nice guy, very polite. I loved his movies. Charlie Chaplin was a great actor, as far as I was concerned. And one of the funniest of them all.

121

Then I got a one-day call to Walt Disney Studios, and it lasted thirty years. I fooled them a long time. I worked on the Mickey Mouse Club, The Shaggy Dog, and Mary Poppins. Disney started in Hollywood but then moved to Burbank. In fact, Walt, when he was living, he wanted to have Disneyland in Burbank and Toluca Lake. He wanted to buy all that land and put Disneyland there.

I worked on quite a few of the rides for Disneyland, like the Tea-Cups and other things. We built that Mark Twain boat—it took a year and a half to do it and I was there from day one to the end—we built it on Stage Three and they put it in three sections, and trucked it down to Disneyland. The hull of the boat they made near Ports O'Call, and then put it all together at Disneyland.

I had no idea what Disneyland was going to be. We just knew it was going to be a big amusement park. [Laughs] I was there the first day it opened. All Disney employees were there that first day. It was hotter than hell that day. Ronald Reagan was there then, he was the governor. And Art Linkletter. Being with Disney so long, I got a lifetime silver pass to Disneyland. So I can take people anytime I want to.

Walt Disney was a lovely guy, wonderful to work for. Oh, he could be exacting. He was the boss, there was no question about that. But if you got on the good side of him, it was just dandy. And I was on the good side. I fooled him for a long time. And then I retired there before this new regime came in. When I started there at Walt Disney Studios there were only about 600 people. Now there are 600,000 or so. And they own everything. And like a damn fool, I never took any stock.

But things turned out good for me in the movie industry. Because I did last so long. The money kept coming in, which was grand. It was hard work, though, believe me. Long days. The longest stretch that I worked was at Charlie Chaplin studios. Went in one morning at seven and didn't get off until eight the next morning. They needed to finish a picture. Of course, they had coffee breaks and all. And in those days you got about a dollar an hour. [Laughs] Maybe two dollars an hour. But that was big stuff then.

Hank Sievers
BORN APRIL 13, 1919
HAMBURG, GERMANY
BARTENDER

122

"All I know is old people," he says. "I like young people. My best friend Eddie, he makes commercials. He's thirty-three years old and we run around together." Though he's been retired now for years, he's still a bartender at heart, and retains the habit of standing when talking; he walks around, sorts and shows multiple sets of photos, and keeps his hands busy, as if he was still tending bar back at Victor's, or the Saratoga, or any of the other joints where he used to tend bar. Photos are shown immediately, most of which were taken at or near a big bar: a young Hank with an also young, beaming, muscular Robert Mitchum; Hank with "Ronnie" and Nancy Reagan; Hank with Shelley Winters. All are scattered on a white wood coffee table, along with a couple of scraps of paper on which he's written the lexicon of his life: the places he lived and the years he lived there, as well as all the hotspots he remembers with great fondness: Ciro's, Mocambo, Larue, Victor's, Players, Cock 'n' Bull, Perrino's, Villanova, Scandia, Dominic's, Musso & Frank's, Saratoga, Marquee, Formosa, Melody Room, Coach, Chasen's. Showing a recent photo of himself, sitting with a young woman in a car, he says, "This is two weeks ago. I'm in the car. This broad is from Phoenix and she's got her arm around me and I said, 'Let's take a picture.'" He laughs and adds, "I'm old but I ain't dead."

I should write a book called *Eighty Years behind Bars*. Because I've spent my entire life behind bars. I worked for years at Victor's, up on Sunset Boulevard & Hayworth, where the car wash is. How do you like this guy? [Shows photo of himself standing with a young Robert Mitchum.] He was my best friend from 1943 until he died. But the other guy [pointing to his own image] is a handsome guy, too, isn't he? Here's Shelley Winters. You know this girl? [Shows a candid photo of Marilyn Monroe.] Marilyn. She wasn't really a blonde. And she never wore any panties, I'm sorry. They were interviewing her and they got a shot like that.

I was born in Hamburg in 1919. I was eight when we came here in '27. My father had been here in L.A. in 1910, and he went back to Germany and got stuck in the German army as a cook, like I was in our army. Did you know that in World War II I killed about forty Americans? You know why? I was a cook. [Laughter]

Incidentally, would you like to shake hands? Now you just shook hands with a guy that shook hands with Lindbergh. In 1927, in Omaha, Nebraska.

I didn't speak any English, and they put me in kindergarten at about eight years old with all these little kids because I couldn't speak one word of English. So my dad says, "We're going to a parade."

I said, "What parade?"

He says, "I don't know, it's downtown."

So here comes this big touring car, there's this guy sitting there. He gives me a kick in the ass and says, "Go and shake hands with Lindy!" I thought, "Who the hell is Lindy?" I walked up and shook hands with Lindbergh. Today you wouldn't get very far but in those days it was different. Everything was different in the old days.

123

My dad was a German chef. What a schmuck he was. Don't ever have a German chef for a father. We never had a home, we were always moving. This is the only place I have ever had my home. I been here forty-six years in this dump, do you believe that? I lived in Hamburg from 1919 until 1927. Then Omaha, Hollywood, then Chicago in 1935. Then San Diego, Beverly Hills, Coronado, Santa Monica, and Hollywood.

I got me a job in Chicago as an elevator boy at the Sherman Hotel. I got fired. I got fresh with some movie actress [laughter]. It was in the old days, you know. Toby Wing. She just died about two weeks ago. She complained about me being fresh. So guess what they did? They made me a bar boy. Was that so terrible? In the Panther Room. [Laughs] I had to work with Harry James and Frank Sinatra. Isn't that awful? I was twenty. I used to give Frank [Sinatra] free drinks. He was a terrific guy.

When you are in the entertainment business you have to work with all those gangsters from Chicago. I worked for Ralph Capone, Al's brother. He owned every bar in the Loop, as we call it in Chicago. I never met Al. He owned all the bars downtown. When I went to get my check it says "Ames Incorporated" or something. Some phony name. This was after Prohibition, after the war. I was down in San Diego and went back to Chicago to get my mother and brought them out here in '45. That's when they went to work for Chaplin.

Charlie Chaplin. When we moved out here [to Hollywood], Chaplin had Japanese help. Until the war, you know, when they had to get rid of them. They said to my father, "You want to go to work for Charlie Chaplin?" He said, "Okay, but my wife has to go, too." My dad was very selfish, and he didn't want to work the lawn, so he became the chef and she became the maid. Chaplin had apartments over the garage. I lived there, too, but not too long. Until I got married. You know, you don't want to live with your mother and father. He also had a tennis court.

My dad called me up and said, "I want you to do me a favor." I said,

"What do you want?" He said, "Well, Charlie just called and he forgot his jacket. So, can you bring it to the studio?" I got the thing and drove to the studio, and the guards there said, "You can't come in here."

I said "What do you mean I can't come in here? I've gotta see Mr. Chaplin."

He says, "Everybody wants to see Mr. Chaplin." You know how those guys are in the guard shack. [Laughter]

124

I said, "Well, this is his coat and he wants it." [Laughter]

So he let me in, and I gave it to Charlie. He looked a lot different than in his movies. He had gray hair; he dyed his hair dark for the movies. He put on a fake mustache for movies, too. My dad said he was very nice, but then something happened again, I don't know why, but he quit. He never got fired in his life, he always quit [laughter].

When Chaplin and his wife Oona went to Europe, they wouldn't let Charlie back in [the States]. So [Oona] came, being an American citizen, [Eugene] O'Neill's daughter. She came and she left the Bank of America with three suitcases full of money. [Laughter] Then she went back to Switzerland and had a couple more kids.

Charlie's son Charlie Jr. and I used to drink together. You wouldn't believe that I'm eighty-two years old and I used to drink a quart of vodka a day, man. No, not anymore, no. Charlie Jr. was *crazy*. He thought I was Mr. Peepers from television because I had that kind of glasses then [laughter]. He was a nice guy but he was *crazy*.

Sidney and Charlie were brothers from when Chaplin was married to Lita Grey, who was sixteen when they got married. He liked young girls, Chaplin did. Nothing wrong with a dirty old man that a young girl can't straighten out. [Laughs]

I was in the marine corps down in San Diego and I was off on weekends. Saturday and Sunday I'd come up here and tend bar one night, and be a soda jerk another night, drive-in another night, wash dishes, you name it. Twenty-six dollars a month, pal. They pay you *cash*.

Then I came back to Hollywood in 1941. Hollywood Boulevard back then was *great*. In those days, right after the war, they used to have the Christmas parade every night for about a month before Christmas. Now they only have it once.

Used to spend a lot of time at a bar called Dominic's. It was a great joint. He was a character, this Dominic. He was his own bartender and his wife Peggy was the chef and he had one of them old registers, a red one, and a little piano.

I remember waiting to sit down one night with my girlfriend and Billy

Wilder comes in, and a table opens up, and Billy Wilder asked if he could have it. And they say, "No, it's Hank's!" I was so embarrassed. But that's how they were. They didn't give famous people any more attention than the regulars. And then Billy Wilder and I are talking, yakata yakata, in German. I speak German, Yiddish, Spanish. Everybody from Europe speaks other languages. And Billy Wilder and I, we had a ball. He's a very nice man. And very, very funny.

I worked a couple of other Mickey Mouse jobs but then I went to Victor's and got hired. At Hayworth & Sunset. Later it was called the Saratoga. You know who owned it later? Johnny Stompanato. The one that got killed by Lana Turner's daughter.

125

I worked at the Marquee for a while. That was across the street from The Players. A friend of mine owned it. He's dead now. Everybody's dead. [Laughs] But that was a great joint. It had a round bar and everybody would come in there. Bugsy Siegel, George Raft. George was a good friend of mine. Mickey Cohen was the local bookie. A gangster supposedly. The only thing they got him on was income tax, and then he got killed in jail. Nice guy, never had a drink. I had to go in the back and make him ice cream and grenadine, or make him a malted and bring it. And [slaps table] twenty dollars.

Right after lunch one day a big tall man with a big nose, dressed to the nines, comes in and sits down. He was an old guy, about seventy-something. I made him a drink and he looked around at the people, and nobody spoke to him. Then he says, "How soon they forget." It was D.W. Griffith. He died about three months later. A handsome big guy. Looked good, too. He was sad, because he said, "How soon they forget." I will never forget that he said that. This is a Hollywood quote.

Bobby [Robert] Blake used to be our parking lot attendant. He got fired because he was on drugs. Got fired and went across the street where the Screen Director's Guild is now, there was a gas station and he was pumping gas over there. He did a lot of "Tonight Shows" because Johnny Carson loved him.

One night I was working at the Saratoga—Hayworth & Sunset. Opened the bar and a guy comes in. I say, "What do you want?"

He says "Give me a screwdriver."

I say, "No, all we got is Vodka and orange juice." [Laughs] Kidding. I said, "For Christ's sake sit down, will ya, don't be so nervous. Wait a minute, you should be nervous. I just saw your television show. It's pretty bad. It's called 'Johnny's Cellar.'" It was Johnny Carson. [Laughter] He liked the way I talked to him. Then when he moved to New York, every time he came out here he'd come into the bar to say hello, him and Ed [McMahon] They were both big drinkers in those days.

One night Shelley [Winters] was in Victor's with Johnny Ireland, an actor who just died a few years ago. And they are sitting at the bar, and she says, "What is this stuff supposed to do to you when you're smoking it?" [Laughter] They were smoking a joint. Johnny's like, "Sssshhh." [Laughter]

I still see her around. She teaches acting. She lived with Marilyn Monroe up on Hollywood, right up about over there. Marilyn used to come in all the time and sit at the piano bar. She'd say, "Somebody ought to buy me a drink, don't you think?"

126

I'd say, "What for?" This was before she was a star. She was pretty, but when you put makeup on ladies they look a lot better than they do at other times. The thing about Marilyn is: [in a whisper] Some broads got tits, and some broads have an ass, but she had *both* tits and ass. She really *did*!

Let me tell you who the biggest drinkers are. You'll *never* guess. *Pilots*. Airline pilots. They don't drink when they are flying, don't get me wrong, but *boy*, when they aren't flying, they *drank*. They had a lot of time off in those days and I had ten of them. They lived up on top of the hill there where Yamashiro is now. They'd close *my* joint and then we'd go up there and drink. Oh *Jesus*, they had a big coffee table inlaid with a control panel just like an airplane.

I said, "If one of you guys crash…"—which is no problem talking to those guys like that—"I want that table."

They said, "No, no, if I crash first, *he* gets it." That's they way they talk, you know. We're up there at four o'clock in the morning hitting golf balls [laughing] on to Hollywood Boulevard.

Most actors are very cheap. And they want a lot of attention and they want it their way and this and that. I had a lot of problems, Tony Quinn used to give me a lot of problems. That's when he was married to [Cecil B. DeMille's daughter] Katherine DeMille. [Laughs] You gotta know how to handle it.

Bogie was a big drinker and a big smoker. Same as John Wayne. I've been with rich people all my life, cause my dad worked for rich people. My wife married a rich guy, my daughter married a rich guy [laughing], you know what I mean? I ain't got *nothing*. Zilch. [Laughs]

I met my wife at Hollywood & Vine at the Melody Lane Restaurant. Guess what my daughter's name is? Melody! My wife was working at *Ken Murray's Blackouts* on Vine. She was a usherette. Then she turned into an ice skater, she played with Sonje Henning and with the Ice Capades. Then she got her Guild card and took pictures with Bob Hope. When I met her she was living in an apartment at Sunset & Hayworth, right by the bar. She was living with a girl there and then we got rid of the girl [laughs] and I said, "Come on, let's go to Vegas and get married." So we went to the El Rancho in Vegas and got married. She was eighteen, I was twenty-six. [Laughs] April 8, 1946.

Then we came back, and they threw out us of the building because she was already [pregnant]. You know when you first get married, that wasn't okay. We moved to Van Ness & Melrose. My mother and father lived across the court, forty dollars a month—big money [laughs]. Jackie Coogan's brother lived right next door. He was six foot five and weighed about three hundred pounds.

127

There was an old guy across the street, and every day he's out there mowing the lawn with no shirt and his bare chest showing. And I said, "Jesus Christ! Doesn't that guy *ever* get tired of mowing the lawn, that old bastard?"

She said, "Don't you know who that is? That's Elmo Lincoln, the first Tarzan."

I said, "Holy Jesus, no wonder!" He was *very* hairy, you know. (laughing) Elmo Lincoln. I didn't know. [Laughter]

My son was born on the Paramount lot at Van Ness & Melrose.

Evelyn Keyes

BORN NOVEMBER 20, 1919
PORT ARTHUR, TEXAS
ACTRESS/MOVIE STAR

A handmade Spanish guitar in an antique case. Diamond and emerald rings. An immense glass table constructed on an ancient tree trunk. Several vivid paintings of bullfighters fighting bloody bulls in the ring framed in silver. A big comfortable couch covered with needlepointed pillows. Overflowing bookshelves filled with thousands of books. A new edition of her former husband John Huston's autobiography open on the table, from which she reads aloud. Fresh flowers. Framed photographs. Framed posters from movies she's acted in: The Man behind the Mask, Here Comes Mr. Jordan, Union Pacific, A Thousand and One Nights, The Seven Year Itch, Around the World in 80 Days. *All of this and more compose the living room of her present home, an apartment some five floors over Doheny in West Hollywood. "You can tell that table wasn't made for this room," she says, explaining that this room holds the treasures of many houses and many marriages—a house in Spain with second husband Huston, homes in Paris and Connecticut with third husband Artie Shaw, and more. She opens her eyes wide as she speaks, and beams with remembrances of an enchanted life, a life within and around the movies, including that one film she points to as* THE *movie,* Gone with the Wind, *in which she played the role of the eternally jilted little sister of Scarlet O'Hara, Suellen. It's a life as magical as those lives she portrayed on the silver screen, and she remembers it like a dream, with colorful characters, ongoing romance, and a marvelous compression of time. She was, remarkably, one of the only stars to ever* be signed directly to Cecil DeMille, as he affirmed in his autobiography: ". . . A lovely young Georgia girl who is one of the stars I can truly claim to have discovered, Evelyn Keyes. . . . Her beauty and talent made her one of the very few players to whom I have given a personal contract."

She speaks of rising every day to jog at exactly 5:03 A.M., armed with pepper spray to glide slowly through the dark streets, this tiny woman in her eighth decade who says in the flirtatious tone of a heartbreaker, "You got my number, don't you? Call me anytime," before catching herself falling into this old familiar role, and laughing delightedly. She speaks with an admittedly affected voice, the result of an active effort to lose her Southern accent upon DeMille's insistence, as well as some years spent living abroad. "It would be too false to go totally British," she says. "But just a flavor of it I felt was all right."

128

I was born in Port Arthur, Texas, and taken away at eighteen months, when my father died. I grew up in Atlanta. My mother had four other children. Three were in their teens, and the other was eleven when I was born. So it was like I was an only child with all these parents. Father didn't leave them a lot of money. So they all had to go to work, and my grandmother was stuck with me. She paid little attention to me, but she taught me to read when I was two. I remember that the books seemed enormous. I guess when you're two, any book would.

I remember The Arabian Nights. I loved that book. I remember I wanted to go to the desert and ride a camel. I remember that being my first desire in life. There were such marvelous lives in the books I was reading. And I was also taken to the movies. I realized how you could live the magic life of the books: Be an actor. Because I had seen the same actors in different roles, as time went by. And so that was my first, early ambition and I never had another one. I realized that was the way you could live all those lives. By being an actor.

By the time I finished high school, one of my sisters was living out here in Hollywood. I was going to go to UCLA and get into movies, that was my plan. My mother let me move here when I was seventeen.

I met and married my first husband, Barton Bainbridge, in Hollywood. He had an apartment in the Hollywood Hills, up Gower, north of Franklin. He had a death wish. He would keep the gas burners on all night with the windows all closed. I didn't know what to think, I was just a teenager. He must have been crazy. He acted mentally disturbed in many ways. But I must tell you, he had a most marvelous voice. It was a deep, marvelous, beautiful voice. He was very blonde and British.

Did you know he held a gun to my head? He didn't want me to have anything to do with pictures. I told him, you know, that's what I came here for. And I remember I was sitting in bed, and suddenly he pushed me back, and he held the gun right here. [Points between her eyes.] And his face is right *over* me. And the *gun*.

Now I knew nothing of guns, but I had sense enough not to move. I didn't talk, I didn't do *anything*. And all of a sudden, he *burst* into tears. *This* is the kind of man he was. He said, "I can't do it." And I don't think until he said that and burst into tears did I really understand what could have happened.

I'm lucky to be here. Because the man went out, and I packed when he wasn't there and moved to the Studio Club. And he came by to say good-bye. And he swapped cars. We had two cars, and he took my car, a white Pontiac, deliberately. To go out and kill himself. He drove down Ventura Boulevard into the Valley and parked there on the street, and then he shot himself. They found him with blood splattered all over the interior of my white car. No doubt he chose my car on purpose to punish me.

The next day it was the headline of the newspaper, I can still remember it: "Estranged Husband of Actress Kills Self." It was big stuff.

And what does Harry Cohn say to me? Years later, when we met. "So— what did *you* do to kill a man?"

Living at the Studio Club was nice. A respectable place—no men allowed, ten dollars per week for room and board. There were all newcomers there like me. Young actresses. I shared a room there. It was a place where you were protected, and it was reasonable. They weren't trying to make money. They were trying to make a haven for young girls. God, I guess there still are so many of them coming to Hollywood.

I was sitting with a sister at a little diner in Hollywood one day. An elderly man—he must have been all of thirty—came over to the table, and said, "Young lady, you ought to be in pictures."

I replied with my Southern accent, "Thay-at's *whah* ahm *he*-uh."

He said, "Perhaps I can help you. I'm an agent."

I said, "What's an agent?" I knew *nothing*.

He took me to see God. Cecil B. DeMille. So that's how that came about. It's as simple as that.

It took me some time to get over it. I had so many people supporting me that it made it much easier. I had Cecil B. DeMille. And I had a whole studio taking care of me and keeping me busy. I went right from one picture to another. I was new, I had everything to learn, and I hadn't ever even acted before. I was taking acting lessons and speech lessons.

DeMille had his own separate gate at Paramount, and his own bungalow, with grass around it. He really was King of the Walk at that time. I remember seeing him for the first time. He was bigger than life. He was the MC of the

Lux Radio Theater of the air. And all of the country sat down on Monday night to hear that. So I already knew his voice. He had a wonderful voice. One of the first things he said to me was, "Yes, I believe I would like to do something with you. But that accent *has* to go. You don't want to play Southern girls your whole life, do you?"

"N-n-n-n-no, sir. M-m-m-m-Mr. D-d-d-d-d-DeMille." [Laughs]

So that's why my Southern accent left me. He put me under contract, and I was sent to an acting coach they had on the lot, and a speech coach to improve on my voice. Years later I realized why. [DeMille] was voice-conscious, and accent-conscious. I was lucky to get mine to where he felt it was acceptable.

130

And so having been the baby of the family, I was called "Baby" around the office. Because I was the *only* one under *personal contract* to DeMille on the Paramount lot. You can't start better than that.

My family was *floored* when they heard the news. They thought it was magic. It was beyond them. It was bigger than anybody thought. Everybody knew his name. He was bigger than a star, you see? Because of the Lux Radio Theater. Because that was front-page news.

The studio days were *the* days. They had a stage there and you would do *scenes*. To learn how to project, if you needed to. It's where I met Anthony Quinn. We dated a few times, but we made love only once. He was just too big, in every way. There was just too much of everything. All the parts. When we were together, the earth stood perfectly still. [Laughter] Of course, back then I didn't really know who was a good lover or not. I didn't have that much experience.

DeMille didn't like Quinn at all. He actually told me to "Stay away from that half-breed." And he got his, because Quinn ended up marrying DeMille's daughter, Katherine. And his grandchildren were quarter-breeds. [Laughs] I did admire Quinn as an actor. *Tremendously.*

I was put in a DeMille film, *The Buccaneers*, in 1938 with Frederic March. It was the first set I was ever on, and I remember well, because there were also 200 extras. And DeMille, he didn't go to New Orleans, the bayous. He *made* the bayous right there at Paramount. With the water going through. And the trees. And the moss hanging down. The whole works of a bayou on a soundstage. And birds in there. And I had, like, *a* line. That's all. I was taught slowly.

So the makeup and hair people would come up and fix me, and everybody's fixing me, right? And DeMille was up on a boom, way up there. And the makeup person said, "You need some lipstick," and started putting some on me. And then through a microphone, in front of 200 extras, from way up on high, DeMille said, [Loudly] "You *need* to think about your *acting, not* the way you *look.* You'll *never* get *anywhere* that way."

I just shrunk. And Frederic March patted my hand and said, "Don't worry, he does that to *everybody*." And then another actor sidled up to me and said, "Oh, it's your turn, that's all." They all were gathering around, because they knew DeMille. And that's how I got to know about movies. From being there.

I was put into one movie and I think I had a line, to begin with. And then in the next movie I had a little more. You learned your craft. On the movie set, you know? It's the way to go, isn't it? And then, as I said, they had a theater there and you would do scenes, and so the directors and the producers on the lot could come and see what the new talent was, too. While you were learning.

131

I was never scared of DeMille. I just learned to pay attention to him, that's all. [Laughs] I knew that was the thing to do. I was busy learning, and I learned that was the way to behave. He didn't take any nonsense. So if you were around him—certainly in my position—you paid attention. And waited for him to speak.

My contract had to be sent back to my mother. I wasn't old enough to sign it legally. So you can imagine the terror I was in when it was going to her and coming back. That he'd change his mind, or that my mother would have forgotten how to write her name. [Laughs]

Studios? Today? They call them studios but you just rent the *space*. You don't have a Harry Cohn or an L.B. Mayer or a Zanuck. They *knew* movies. When I would go to Harry Cohn's house for dinner, there would be a long table. And most of the people at that table would be writers. He knew that the story mattered most—the play's the thing. I believe Shakespeare said that. He knew. They all knew. See, the people in charge don't even know that. They just know about money.

Think about the faces and the way stars used to look. You know the faces. Each looked different. You didn't mix up Garbo with Joan Crawford, know what I mean? Or the men. Gary Cooper didn't look like Humphrey Bogart. Clark Gable didn't look like Cary Grant. The men all looked different. Because you had a whole studio seeing that that was so. From top to bottom. The sound of you, the look of you. All of you. Somebody was in charge. Clothes, hair, face. Everything. *Experts*.

I had an occasion to see one of my pictures at USC recently; they wanted me to speak to a class. I hadn't seen this film in about fifty years. And I was *amazed* when I saw all that hair I had. Because I have *baby* hair; it's very fine, it never grew up. But the head of the hairdressing department would give me all this marvelous hair. She devised a way of curling it so it would go away from my head and up, and also she put pieces on in the right places. Not really a wig, just pieces. So when I would go on a picture, mostly, the hairdresser she had trained to do my hair would be with me. *That* one. If that one was busy on a picture, she'd train another one. So it would be done *right*. And *all* of you would be done that way. The clothes. The shoes. *Everything*. *That's* why they looked the way they did. I'm talking about men and women. Well, there's nobody to do that anymore. Back then it was a family. Now the *space* is still there. But it used to be a place where you *belonged*. Where *everybody* belonged, and that included the makeup and the hair people, the prop people and the cameramen. *Everybody*. Everybody who worked on a movie. Writers under contract. Producers.

My relationship with DeMille was strictly professional. He never even had me over to dinner. I can remember lunches in the cafeteria, but I don't believe he ever invited me to his house. You must understand that at the time I didn't think of that one way or the other. I was so awed by even being in Hollywood. I felt that *whatever* DeMille did was what people did. I was just so happy to be under contract to *Cecil B. DeMille*. It was just unbelievable all the whole time.

[DeMille] often did wear riding britches and he carried a whip frequently. It is true that he always had an assistant carry a chair for him. And it was his *son-in-law* who had to carry it. It seemed to me it was a high chair. DeMille wouldn't even bother to look around, he was so sure that that *chair* was going to be there. And it *was* there. His son-in-law was there every day with the chair. Anytime DeMille backed up, it was there. Think about doing that to your son-in-law. That's *rotten* mean, isn't it?

I did *The Buccaneers* with Frederic March. He invited me into his trailer. Mr. March. He was in a costume, a period piece, with tight white pants. We were sitting on a little couch together. And we were talking, and [softly] he took my hand and placed it right on his *cock*. Because since the pants were tight, it was *very* prominent. And I was so *stunned*, I just left it there. Well, he saw he had made a mistake. [Laughs]

So he took my hand and gave it back to me. I never had much to do with him after that. He lost my respect. And I don't even have any now. That's a *lousy* thing to do to a young girl who has just come to town and really doesn't know her way around any place. I *really* didn't. I hadn't traveled *anywhere*. We had *no* money. And he *had* to know that. I think he was taking advantage of me. But he was the *only* one who did anything like that. Everyone else I met was lovely; very good and helpful.

I did go to UCLA for a little while, between pictures. But what did DeMille do? Came over and took pictures of me on campus. [Laughter] It didn't work out, trying to be a movie star and a student at the same time.

In 1938, DeMille lent me out to Selznick to audition for *Gone with the Wind*.

I had to do it, because DeMille said to me, "You'd *better* get the part, otherwise I will have to shoot you at sunrise." [Laughs] So I had no choice but to get the part of Scarlet O'Hara's younger sister.

Nothing since then has been anything like the way it was when they were casting *Gone with theWind*. Has there ever been any other book like that which has been read by everyone in the country? It was extraordinary. The casting was front-page news. *Every* star in *every* studio was going out to see if they could do this part or that part. It was a big *do*.

DeMille never thought I could be Scarlet. I was a little too young, and my acting wasn't really up to that then. And *all* the big stars wanted that role, even Bette Davis. In front of Selznick studios, there were people in period costumes all the time showing that they could do it. It was an *extraordinary* happening. DeMille would send me out there. All the studios were sending actors and actresses all the time. Nothing has been like that.

123

First time I went to Selznick's office I met George Cukor. I think they decided then when they met me. I told them that I lost my accent. But [with Southern accent] "Ah . . . can get it back *anytime*."

Selznick was disheveled. He was a little shaggy. Cigarette ashes on his sleeves. Taking Benzedrine like it was candy. He chased me around his desk a few times. And to be honest, I don't think his heart was really into it. It was almost a formality. It didn't offend me at all. It was part of the business. That's what you are supposed to do if some young actress is in your office. To make her feel good.

I got to know him better when he was married to Jennifer Jones, who was my maid of honor at one of my weddings, I can't remember which. She was a nice, gentle person. Nothing flamboyant, not a great conversationalist, just a nice person.

When I found out that they were considering me for *Gone with theWind*, I thought they were joking. Because they fooled around with everybody. And I know they must have been seeing people like me every day for *weeks*.

It was ironic that I would be cast in *Gone with theWind*. I had read the book on the train coming from Atlanta to Hollywood. It was already out. I had hoped to get into pictures, but I never dreamed I would get into *that* picture. But God spoke on my behalf—DeMille—and he must have felt if I was in the picture it would be good publicity for him. And they did use it. And you certainly can remember in Atlanta when I was cast, it was front-page news. *Dead* center.

I met Gable, of course. But I was just a teenager then, and he was in his late thirties. Which to me was like an elderly man, really. I never got to know him as a person. I was around when he was working, but I didn't have any scenes with him. Rhett Butler came to Tara. I'd be there on the set, and I'd watch him. He was the greatest looking man I ever met in my life. He had the *perfect* physique. The *height*. He was what manly *was*, what it's supposed to be. Maybe six-foot-three and the *shoulders* were just right, and the *hips*, and the legs on the long side. And he had a *marvelous* voice and that good face. He *had* it. Whatever *it* is. He was effective on the screen, he certainly was.

I didn't get to know Vivien Leigh very well. *Stars* did not associate with bit players like myself. And the reason is clear: Vivien had *reams* of new scenes to learn every day that were being rewritten. She had all this to learn, and I would just have a line or two. I mean, it's another world from being a bit player and being a star. The star has the whole burden. You think since both are acting, you have something in common. But not at *all*. Really it's a *wide* gap. Including the *money* you're making.

134

I really learned how to act on a set by watching Vivien Leigh. She would take these *long*, new pages of dialogue. And it seemed to me she learned them *as* she read them. And then she would *become* Scarlet O'Hara *instantly* from Vivien Leigh. She was an *incredible* actress. When I saw her, I learned how to act. To not fiddle around, like some people did. I'm *still* impressed.

In the movie, Scarlet is pissed off at Suellen the whole time. She *whacked* me. She *really* did. And she didn't pull her punch. She punched me *hard*. Which *is* the only way to do it. Otherwise, it wouldn't look right. But it hurt.

I am a Southern girl and Vivien was British, of course. But she could do a Southern accent much better than most Americans. Most Americans have hard 'R's. But Southerners have no 'R's at all. Vivien Leigh was a step ahead because she had no 'R's either, being British. So all she had to do was spread out the vowels. See, I learned what a Southern accent was by thoroughly unlearning it. The vowels are spread out. And she had a very good ear, and could do it well.

Vivien Leigh was one of the best actresses ever. And the fact that she was mentally disturbed might have *helped* her be good. Oh, for heaven's sake, I have never connected that before. But Scarlet O'Hara, you can see her emotions. She got the part right at the perfect time in her life. She was the right age and the right look. And it was before her own emotions got further out of whack. But it was *there*, the disturbance. You can see it in her eyes. That's why that worked so well.

The filming of *Gone with the Wind* was like a party on the set that Selznick was giving each day. Especially since the dialogue was always being handed to us at the last minute as if he was thinking of some charade to play.

Soon after that, DeMille let me go. I was taken by my agent to Columbia. And the casting director there said, "We're about to do a picture. I think you'd be just right for it. I want you to meet the director." And that's how I met Charles Vidor. Who walked in, said, "How do you do?" And then he said [in Hungarian accent], "She vill do," and walked out. I noticed he had an accent and I asked what it was. Hungarian. You know I married him, don't you? He had an office there; he was under contract to the studio.

I was at Columbia for eleven years with Harry Cohn. He wanted to *marry* me. He was ready to go get married. Isn't it a shame I didn't do it? You know what I'd own now? [Laughter] *Columbia*. How about *that*? But I *couldn't* have really married him. Isn't it a shame that I'm me and not somebody else who could do it? [Laughs] Some people can. I could not be intimate with him; I simply could not have sexual intercourse with somebody I didn't care for, and I didn't care for him. I can't do that. I couldn't. I know some women can. And men can. But how? You would have to pretend. In the sack. And I couldn't do that.

I didn't care for Harry Cohn. As a lover. I did admire him, though. He knew what movies were. He looked at *every single inch* of footage *every single day*. And he *knew*. He knew about story. He knew about writers, who were always at his house. There is no doubt that he knew about this business. And I admired him for that. I just didn't want him for a lover.

But I did love working at Columbia. It was similar to being at Paramount, though the lot was a little smaller. You couldn't drive on to the lot like you did at Paramount. But the soundstages there were quite large. And I always *loved* soundstages. I loved those big, thick, windowless, soundproof walls where you could go *anywhere*, and be *anything*. The rest of the world *vanished* outside. It just vanished. It was lit to be day or night, and there you were. There was no other world. I don't think you can do it and think of anything else. You step into this world.

Hollywood was a nice town. But I didn't spend much time in Hollywood itself. I was in the studio. I just went from one picture to the next, and I worked from very early morning till late at night often. They kept you busy. You belonged to them. If you weren't on a film, you'd be doing stills, or you'd be taking some kind of lessons.

Harry Cohn put me in some good films and many that were not so good. But I think that's par for the course. They're paying you and they want to get their money's worth.

I did 1001 *Nights* there. It was my favorite part, playing the Genie. I just loved doing that. I have a picture of me from it sitting on an elephant. In the elephant's trunk! As the Genie, I snapped my fingers and created an entourage for Aladdin who was going to marry the princess. I was buzzing around being jealous. You know at the end how I got Aladdin? I snapped my fingers and made another Aladdin for myself. It was a cute idea.

I did *The Jolson Story* then, too. That was a good film. Al Jolson recorded the singing himself for Larry Parks. It was Jolson's voice. When he was recording on the soundstage, I sneaked in. I will *never* forget it, because it was a thrilling experience. There was a full orchestra, and there was Jolson, singing his *heart* out. I hid over in the corner so I wouldn't get thrown out. It was one of the highlights of my life. His concentration on himself was amazing. He believed, and he sent out these vibrations that were tremendous. He was really *something* as an entertainer. He was an amazing singer. I guess he *loved* singing. It showed. I remember looking at the expression on his face, and he was *in* it. *Totally.* And it was only on a soundstage.

136

Larry Parks did a wonderful job at portraying him. He must have watched him, too, because he did it very well. Larry really did it *beautifully*. He's gone, too.

Jolson wanted to play Jolson. He was pissed off that he couldn't. He had the *biggest* ego. There's a scene in which I am at a party, and we had all just seen Jolson, and I'm up there imitating Jolson. We did several takes, and they took it from many angles. And the extras are all dressed as party guests, and they were to clap after my little performance. And after a few takes, I guess they were bored, and their applause was not very loud. They were tired. And Jolson—the real Jolson—came in and saw this. And he *balled* them out. He gave them *hell*. He said to them, "You *applaud!*" [Laughs] And it was just *me* doing him. He wanted his work applauded, see?

I met Rita Hayworth at Columbia. I can remember. It was seven in the morning and we were both sleepy, getting our makeup on, and our hair was wet and all in tangles, and even so she looked *beautiful*. She was a *star*.

Rita. I don't know that she was terribly bright. She didn't ever talk much about anything. I have a feeling she never read. She was just this lovely thing. She obviously took direction well, and was good on the screen. But in person she didn't have a vivid personality when you met her.

I remember going to the Players Club with Vidor quite a few times. I remember seeing Marlene Deitrich with Charles Boyer. Can you imagine seeing *those* two? *Charles Boyer!* Suddenly sitting right over *there*.

I had a brief romance with Kirk Douglas. I liked him. He was a good person. But Harry Cohn didn't like him for some reason, and he made it *so* difficult for us to be together. But Kirk was the *hottest* thing in town at the time. I had lunch with him one day and asked him to go on the set with me. I didn't have a hard scene to do or anything. And the guard at the entrance said to me, "Mr. Cohn wants to see you *immediately*. And Mr. Douglas can't come in." Can you imagine a movie studio—Columbia—turned down Kirk

Douglas—the hottest thing in town? They wouldn't let him come in! [Laughs]

Cohn gave me hell. The son of a bitch. He said to me, "What are you doing? Don't you know he *fucks* everybody in sight?" Saying things like that. "Just *stop* it." Cohn was extremely possessive of me. I belonged to him.

I did the movie *Face behind the Mask* with Peter Lorre. I played a blind woman in that one. Lorre was very good. It was fun acting with him. He was a hell of an actor. A serious actor. He really knew his stuff. Talk about distinctive presences on the screen. He really *had* it.

137

I remember going to a party then at the house of "Big Boy" Williams way out near Malibu. Everybody was sitting around an enormous bonfire. And Errol Flynn was there, and Lupe Velez. And Flynn encouraged her to do her dance. And she danced in front of the fire, and somehow she was able to make her breasts rotate. All on their own. [Laughs] Isn't that *strange*?

I first met John Huston at a party given by Charles Mendl. He sat me between Huston and Errol Flynn. And I knew which one I wanted. Yeah. I chose Huston. There was just something about him. Of course, Flynn was very handsome. But Huston was *fascinating*. That tall body of his, that posture. And that *voice*.

This is the way that John Huston remembers our meeting. This is from his autobiography: [Takes book and reads]

I met a pretty girl at a dinner party.... I met her again on a weekend cruise.... She had played Scarlet O'Hara's younger sister.... She was young and vivacious and amiable. As an antidote to my depression, I took her out for dinner a few times. One night at Romanov's, she leaned across the table and said, out of the blue, "John, why don't we get married?" I'd had cocktails before dinner, wine with dinner, and I was now into the brandy.

"Hell, Evelyn, we hardly know each other!"

She said, "Do you know a better way for us to get to know each other?"

She had a point there. I said, "All right, why not? When?"

"Right now. Tonight. Let's go to LasVegas."

I had another drink and suddenly heard myself say, "Okay, let's do it!"

It's true! At 4 A.M. that night we were in Vegas getting married. We flew back to Los Angeles. I tell young women nowadays to stop dressing up so that their whole body is showing so that some man will choose them. As Artie [Shaw] said, "We didn't have *marriages*. We had legalized love affairs." Which is really what they were. The idea of marriage that people go by now is so honest and serious. The wedding, they get all dressed up, the bride all dressed in white.

During the blacklist, I went east with John. This was a *terrible* chapter of our history. *So* many great careers were *destroyed*. Dalton Trumbo, the writer, and so many. Those *bastards*. That *gavel*. During the hearings, anytime anyone tried to speak out, they would bang that gavel. I will never forget it in my life. They were blocking out freedom of speech in America. I kept saying, "*Everybody* must know about it. So that it will never happen again." Even the name of it—the House Un-American Activities Committee. How *dare* they even call it that? It's hard to conceive.

138

Jack Warner had given them a name, and John balled him out for that. Jack said, "I guess I made a mistake," but John wouldn't take that so lightly. The studio heads were afraid that they were going to lose the whole studios. So you can't blame them. This was the government of the whole United States doing this. And they might have shut down the studios. I guess we did blame them somewhat, but we understood. And then they came around, and they stopped the blacklist.

I got to know [Humphrey] Bogart because he was good friends with John. Bogart in real life acted a lot like Bogart in the movies. He was a gentle guy. He was a very good actor. Distinctive on the screen. In person, he wasn't very tall, just about my height. But he had this *marvelous* voice. He was *good* on the screen. He did it. He *knew*. He had a quality that worked. They have that phrase that the camera loves a person. And the camera does. Some faces just work on camera. His did. And then you have to have the voice and the ability to go with it. And he had all of it.

Bogie and John were a great team. I went along with them when they did *The African Queen*. Bogie wanted to get back home to his boat. And he kept bugging John, "John, I need to get back. You're taking too much time." I was there, sitting at lunch between the two of them. And he complained again to John, saying, "*Jesus*, John, do you have to . . . ?" And John just reached over, took him by the nose, and *twisted* it. *All* the way around. And I don't mean just a little tweak. He *twisted* it. Bogie was *stunned*. But he shut up. And he didn't talk about it anymore. [Laughs] John was going to make a good picture, a proper picture. And you don't rush it just because your star wants to go on a boat. I remember that the only two Spanish words that Bogie ever felt were worth learning were Dos Equis. [Laughs]

I remember going to a party in the Hollywood Hills once. I parked my car, and it started to pour, and I didn't have a hat or a raincoat or anything. I was getting *drenched* and all I wanted was to get out of the rain, and I was on this mountain and it was slippery, and getting scary. And I saw these steps up to a house, so I walked up this long stairway though I wasn't even sure I was at the right house.

When I got to the door, it was only a screen there and the door was open. Because we are in California. There was a fire in the fireplace going. And *Katherine Hepburn* was sitting there. I didn't know *where* the hell I was. The party was many houses down the street. But she was very kind to me, and offered me a towel and invited me to sit by the fire with her to dry off. And she gave me a raincoat to borrow. I never did give it back. Isn't that awful? Every so often I feel absolutely guilty. Now I'm feeling guilty about it again. [Laughs] I'll admit I would sometimes open the closet to show it off, and say, "Look at Katherine Hepburn's coat!"

139

I was thinking just the other day that everything in my career came too easily. I got signed by DeMille when I was so young I didn't even know what it *meant*. And I think that because of this it never taught me to *fight* for something. I just kind of fell into everything. I've only realized that later. Though I never really got *the* part. The part that takes you to the Oscars. The way Vivien Leigh got *the* part of Scarlet O'Hara. I was in *the* movie, but I didn't get *the* part.

I'm happy that people are appreciating movies again. Somebody is catching on that there was a time when movies were *movies*. And not just TV affairs. A time when movie stars were really movie *stars*. The so-called stars of today come into your living room. It's a *big* difference. Real stars don't do that. [Laughs] Stars are those distant creatures who—[breathlessly] if you ever come across them at *all*—your breath stops. The world stops. Everything *stops*.

Walter Bernstein
BORN AUGUST 20, 1919
BROOKLYN, NEW YORK
WRITER

He was born in New York, and in New York he remains, although his life has been fundamentally altered by his time working as a screenwriter—and his time being forbidden to work—in Hollywood. His most famous movie is The Front, *about the blacklist that forced him and others to hire fronts—people who posed as writers for those who were blacklisted. Starring Woody Allen, the movie is a humorous account of one of Hollywood's darkest chapters. A collaboration between himself and others who were blacklisted, including its director Martin Ritt, it also stars Zero Mostel, who delivers a performance both hilarious and heartbreaking.*

Today Walter's in his Manhattan home, reflecting on his Hollywood years from a great distance of both time and space. With sounds of sirens and garbage trucks just outside his window, he admits to harboring some bitterness over the industry's treatment of him and other artists during the blacklist. But more than anything, his sentiments surrounding Hollywood are happy ones, and his love for the movies, both watching and writing them, endures.

I was *always* a movie fan, since the time I was five years old and I went to my first movie. I was *stuck* on it. I even remember my first movie. It was a picture with Richard Barthlemess. Another film that made a big impression on me with Barthlemess was one called *The Patent Leather Kid*. And I saw *He Who Gets Slapped*, with Lon Chaney. I remember seeing *The Ten Commandments* and *Ben-Hur* and *The Big Parade*.

I started writing as soon as I could write. I always loved movies, but when I was growing up, writing for movies was thought of as a second-rate thing. Movies meant Hollywood, and that was not considered serious. If you wanted to be a serious writer, you became a novelist or a poet or a playwright. I began writing short stories. The first one I wrote I sold to the *New Yorker*. I wrote a lot for them, short fiction, and also a lot of nonfiction "Reporter at Large" pieces. I wrote a lot for them while I was in college at Dartmouth. And very shortly after graduating, I went into the army. I was a soldier, and part of the time I was in the infantry, and for the last two or three years, I was on staff of *Yank*, the official army weekly magazine.

After the war, I had a book published, mostly a collection of pieces I wrote for the *New Yorker* about the war. And on the basis of that, I got a contract to go to Hollywood in 1947.

I went out to work for a writer-producer named Robert Rossen, who was working on a movie called *All the King's Men*. I had a ten-week deal with him for Columbia Pictures. My agent was a man named Harold Hecht, and he had just started a production company for another one of his clients, Burt Lancaster. And they had just bought the rights to a book called *Kiss The Blood off My Hands*, an English thriller. They wanted me to work on the script, and they offered me more money than what Rossen was paying, so I went to work with them on that script. And that was the first credit I had. It starred Lancaster and Joan Fontaine.

First place I lived was an apartment I shared on Wilcox in Hollywood. That part of Hollywood hasn't really changed a lot since I lived there. Hollywood was *great*. The weather was wonderful. There was not as much traffic or smog. They still had those wonderful trolley cars, the Red Car. I remember when I was first working at Universal, the freeway wasn't built then, and I would take the Red Car. I liked traveling on them, they were wonderful. And then after a while I bought a secondhand car. Hollywood was very nice then. It was much lower key, much pleasanter, than it is now.

I also worked at Columbia. I had an office at their studios at Sunset & Gower. I *loved* working at the studios. I loved movies, and I always wanted to be part of them. I remember the first time I went into the studio and walked onto a stage and walked around a lot, I thought, "My God, they're *paying* me for this!" I *loved* it. I loved the commissary, I loved everything about it. Still do.

I only came out to Hollywood at first for ten weeks, and then I ended up staying six months. But my home was always here in New York, and I was married and we had a son. And when I finished *Kiss the Blood*, I had to come back to New York. My marriage was breaking up. But there was no movie work here in New York. Television was just starting. So I went to work in television, and that's when I got blacklisted. 1950. The blacklist went from '50 to '58 in movies, and another couple, two or three more years in television.

141

I was working on a show that Sidney Lumet was directing. It was called "Danger," a half-hour melodrama show. And our producer said to me one day, "They tell me I can't use you anymore. You're on some kind of list." And that's when it happened. I knew this book had come out called *Red Channels*, and my name was in it, and I knew something was going to happen. *Probably*. *Red Channels* had about eight listings for me. I had always been on the Left. I supported the loyalists in the Spanish civil war, Russian war relief. I had written for Communist magazines. It's all true.

But when the blacklist first started, I didn't understand how serious it was going to be. Nobody did when it first started. We didn't know McCarthyism was coming. You know, it happened very rapidly. To a lot of people.

There was a subpoena out for me. When I heard about it, I went on the lam. I hid out till they had the hearing. It was the last hearing they had here in New York. And then they never came after me after that. I never testified.

The only way I could make a living during those eight years of the blacklist was by using fronts. That's the only way I could exist. Like a lot of other people. We would get people we knew to put their names on our scripts, and pose as the writers of the scripts. There were a number of fronts over a period of time. People did it for different reasons. It never lasted too long. It was a difficult thing to do. There were questions of ego, there were questions of money, there were people who wanted their own careers. There were lots of reasons. People got scared. Some people we asked to be fronts were already writers. We tried to pick people who could legitimately be in the business. I mean, he might have another day job, but he ought to be able to handle himself in story conferences, if necessary.

We'd pay the fronts differently depending on who they were. Some people I gave 20 percent. Some people wouldn't take any money at all. They thought it was a lousy thing that was happening, and they wanted to help.

I was never surprised at all that Hollywood and the studios gave in to this pressure to support the blacklist. The government was putting the squeeze on them, and they were not going to stand up for a bunch of lefty writers. Or actors, or whatever. No, they capitulated right away. And I wasn't surprised at all by that. They did have a choice. But they had no morality, or anything like that. Most of them were right-wing people like the Warner Brothers or Louie B. Mayer. Some of them like Darryl Zanuck didn't like it— he tried to keep people on as long as possible. But the power was here in New York. With the banks and with the boards of the studios. And they just told them, "You gotta do it," and that's all.

142

The ones I really can't forgive, though, are the ones who were called to testify and named names. I *hated* them. Where I came from, the *worst* possible thing you could be was a stool pigeon. And that's what they were. Then there were those who only named names of people who were already named. That was a big rationale. They would say, "Well, I didn't hurt anybody, because they'd already been named already and blacklisted." But the truth of that was that if you were named, you couldn't work in the business. You had to get work elsewhere. I had a friend, just like Woody's character [in *The Front*] who was a cashier somewhere, and the FBI came around. And said to his boss, "You know who you got working here?" And he got fired. It was because he was named again, he was in the papers. So that's an easy out, but it doesn't really hold water. And also the fact is, they *had* all the names. They didn't need any other names. They wanted *your* name. That's the point I make in *The Front*. The friend says to Woody, "They want you." They want to say. "This person is on our side." That's what they want. That's what you're giving them. By naming somebody who has already been named, you are saying, "I will be an informant for you."

The blacklist ended for me in about 1958. And around that time it was breaking up. The cold war was taking another turn, and they had run out of *communists*. They blacklisted everybody they *could*. McCarthy was discredited and it kind of slithered away. And I started working again.

I got a job then working for Sophia Loren. Her husband, Carlo Ponti, was the producer. I did a movie for them after being blacklisted that Sidney Lumet directed. I moved out to Hollywood. I got a great little poolhouse on top of Coldwater & Mulholland. It wasn't tough at all to come back to this industry. There were some people it was a little *awkward* with. Producers who wouldn't hire me. But, you know, most people you met during the blacklist didn't like it. Most producers didn't like it, they didn't want it. They were *scared*. But most people were not venal. So coming back was *great*. I mean, it was kind of a vindication, really, in a way.

My next project was to write *The Magnificent Seven*. I wrote the first draft of it. Originally, Yul Brynner was supposed to direct it. Martin Ritt was going to produce it. I wrote one draft. And then Tyrone Power died. He was doing a movie, I think *Solomon and Sheba,* in Spain. They offered Yul a humongous amount of money to replace him. So Yul said good-bye to directing. And then I left the project. And so the movie now has little, if anything, to do with my script. It's a good movie. Mine had followed the line of the original, *The Seven Samurai,* much more closely. As a matter of fact, the lead character who Yul wanted for it was Spencer Tracy. It would have been totally different.

I kept doing the same kind of projects I was doing before the blacklist. There's a kind of social movie that I've always been interested in. I've written other things, but most of what I wrote was that. I took the jobs I thought I could do.

143

Martin Ritt is a close friend who also was blacklisted. Once we got cleared, we always wanted to do a movie about the blacklist. We wanted to just tell a straight story about somebody who was blacklisted, why he's blacklisted, what happens to him, the rest of it. And we could never get anybody interested in it. It wasn't until we came up with the idea of coming at it sideways, doing it as kind of a black comedy about a front, that we got a studio interested—Columbia—and they paid for the script. And when we brought them the script they liked it and said, "Fine. We like it. We'll do the movie if you get a star." And by a star they meant Robert Redford, Paul Newman, Warren Beatty. You know, *those* people. That wasn't who we wanted. And it wasn't until we came up with the idea of Woody [Allen], and sent it to him, and he said he would do it, that it got made. Once Woody said he would do it, that made it a go.

I think it is the best acting he's ever done. He's playing a real character. He's not really that much like any of the real people we used. I mean, he's just so much *Woody.* But he made it work.

People ask me if I had something to do with the writing of Woody's film *Annie Hall.* The only thing I had to do with *Annie Hall* is that I was in the last shot of the movie. There's a shot from across the street of four people talking in front of a movie theater. And it's Woody and Diane Keaton and Sigourney Weaver and me. That's my contribution to *Annie Hall.* I still get a SAG check for $7.50.

I've been lucky that most of my movies came out pretty well. I've been lucky to work with directors who didn't want to be writers. I liked doing *Semi-Tough* with Michael Ritchie. And the two films I did with Marty Ritt, *The Front* and *The Molly McGuires,* those were both very happy experiences. Those are my two favorite films I've done, and I think both are still underestimated and underrated. Working with Sidney Lumet on *Fail-Safe* was good. So, as I say, I've been lucky. And *Yanks,* with John Schlesinger, was also one I liked.

I think people will always want to have movies in their lives. Of course, with big corporations owning the movie studios now, you get an erosion of quality. Just by the nature of who owns it. Occasionally stuff will slip through and there will be good movies. But most commercial movies are pretty weak.

God knows what's going to happen. You'll be able to get movies on your computer. But there's something about the experience of going in to that dark movie theater and seeing that big screen that has always been special. Television hasn't killed it. There may very well be different ways of showing movies. And also movies are going to be increasingly easier to make. Because of digital. Cheaper and all. So I don't know, maybe it's just wishful thinking on my part that people will still want to go into a theater and see a movie on a big screen.

144

Hal Riddle

BORN DECEMBER 11, 1919
CALHOUN, KENTUCKY
CHARACTER ACTOR

"I came out to Hollywood to be a movie star," he says. "I admit it. I wanted to be the next Clark Gable. And you know what? With the exception of going to the same barber, Gable and I had only one thing in common. Our ears. Both of us have big ears." He's a dapper and cordial man, with neatly trimmed white hair, stylish silver glasses, an elegant charcoal cardigan over a crisp white button-down shirt, gray tailored slacks and, black leather loafers. Though he's been retired from acting now for many years, he's readied himself for this interview like he might have in his heyday for an audition, groomed and buffed to the hilt, looking and feeling his best. His smile is warm and gracious, as he resides affably over his small bungalow at the Motion Picture Country Home. He's a happy man, though none too thrilled about a recent L.A. Times article about he and his friends there, all Hollywood veterans, which portrayed them as pitiable old folks, sadly clinging to a bygone era. "They made it seem as if our New Year's party was some boring, quiet little tea party. Truth is, after we all got a few cocktails in us, things started to get pretty wild!" He genially expounds on a life focused on the movies and the stars before speaking tenderly and with great reverence about his friendship with a luminous legend of the silent screen, Billie Dove.

My mother told me that before I was born, while she was carrying me, she would take me to the movies to see the early comedies of people like Charlie Chaplin and Harold Lloyd. It's why she named me Harold, after Harold Lloyd.

I saw my first movie when I was eight in about 1927. My father took my brother and I to see *The Life of Jesse James*, because he wanted to show his young sons what not to grow up to be. It was a silent picture. There was a piano player who would play along with the whole thing. When the action would get real strong, the piano player would play very fast, and when it got sad, he would play a slow, sad melody.

I remember looking at that screen and being just *entranced*. And I remember hearing the word "Hollywood," and hearing that these pictures came from a place called *Hollywood*.

Every Saturday we kids got to go see the Saturday movies. And we'd see the Saturday serials, often cowboy pictures. But our father took us to a lot of movies, too, like the silent version of *Ben-Hur*, and *The Big Parade* with John Gilbert. These were all silents. Even then I was getting hooked on film, and Hollywood was becoming more and more important to me.

145

From that age on I wanted to move to Hollywood to become a movie star. At that time we had moved to Fulton, Kentucky, and no one in Fulton ever thought of going to Hollywood. They would laugh at me, and I became ashamed of it. After that, I just started buying movie magazines and learning about Hollywood, but I didn't tell anyone about it anymore.

In 1931 I skipped off from school to see a picture called *Adoration* with Billie Dove, a very famous beautiful star. Oh, my *goodness*, I came home and told my mother I had fallen in love. She thought I had fallen in love with some little schoolgirl.

She said, "With whom?"

I said, "Billie Dove," and she said, "Oh?" Of course, she knew who Billie Dove was.

I said, "I saw her this afternoon in the movies—" and of course right away I knew I had given myself away. But she didn't chide me. She suggested I write her a letter.

I knew I could find the address of her studio in *Fotoplay*, and I wrote her, and sure enough, within a few weeks I received a beautiful five-by-seven of her sent by the studio. There it is. [Points to framed photo on the wall.] I was just in *hog-heaven*. So from that time on Billie Dove was one of my all-time favorites. It's funny how you can become a part of Hollywood even when you're a young kid back in some little town in Kentucky. So many of us learned about Hollywood from what we read about Hollywood. Those magazines painted a pretty beautiful picture of Hollywood, but even as a kid you could read between the lines.

Billie Dove's career started about in 1918, and in 1927 she was one of the biggest stars in the world. In 1927 she received the most fan mail of any star in Hollywood: 27,000 letters in July 1927 alone! She became the girlfriend of Howard Hughes. They had a torrid romance, and she loved him very much but he was a womanizer, so they broke up.

She took a role in the movie *Blondie of the Follies* with Marion Davies. Now she had always starred alone in movies, so she wasn't sure she wanted to do this role. And at that time William Randolph Hearst controlled the career of Marion Davies. But she got pressured into doing this picture. So she did it, and when Hearst saw a rough cut of the film, he said, "Well, it's a good Billie Dove picture." Which was a death knell for Billie to hear. Because he took the picture back and had it recut and rewritten to make Billie the heavy, so that Marion would come out on top. When that happened and when Billie saw that, she said, "That's it. I'm through." And she quit Hollywood with that picture. In 1933.

146

By that time I had already fallen in love with Jean Harlow, and also my biggest idol in terms of acting was Clark Gable. They came along in 1931 and 1932. I heard Billie had left pictures to get married, had a beautiful house out on Amalfi near the ocean. And I lost touch with her then.

I went into naval intelligence during World War II, and when I got out I went to New York City, hoping to work as an actor. I did some summer stock, and eventually landed some roles on Broadway. My first role on Broadway was in *Mister Roberts* with Henry Fonda in 1951. I also started to do a lot of live TV right there in New York. And I toured with *Mister Roberts* for more than a year.

I got my first film in the summer of '57 in New York City called *The Copier*, starring Robert Loggia. Norman Turlog was doing a film out here called *Onionhead* with Andy Griffith and Walter Matthau, and he invited me to come out here to do it. It was a very good film. That was my first film in Hollywood. I moved here in 1957 to do my first film. And I thought about Billie Dove and wanted to track her down but I didn't want to bother her. I didn't want her to think I was a *stalker* or something.

When I got here, I knew *exactly* where I wanted to go and who I wanted to see because I already knew all about Hollywood and who the stars were. But by 1957, TV was getting big, and already the studios were making the big shift toward television. And most of the stars were already gone from the studios by then. My friend James Dean was already gone—he died in '55. I knew him in New York, when we were both struggling on Broadway. We would see each other when we were on our rounds of producers. Jimmy and I both auditioned to be on the *Beat the Clock* TV show. You had to do outrageous things to beat the clock in sixty seconds. They needed actors to test out these things to see how long they would take. I will always remember what Dean had to do: They told him we will give you this fully inflated balloon and you have to stick two straight pins in it, and you have to walk from A to B without the balloon bursting. Well, his concentration then was just so intense, even then. He had scraggy clothes but he had an *aura* about him, just like Brando. And he stuck those pins in there so carefully, and he didn't take his eyes off that balloon, and he started to walk. He did it perfectly, and that balloon didn't burst, and everyone was just *amazed*. And that was the first time I met James Dean.

James Dean used to love Googies. It was a little sandwich shop right down Sunset from Schwab's, where the Director's Guild is now. After he became a star he used to go there a lot. When he became really big, he had an office in the back of the Villa Capri restaurant. It was owned by a man named D'Amato. He was very fond of Jimmy because Jimmy would come in there late at night and do his shtick. So he gave Jimmy a little office back there with a phone, and he used to make his phone calls. Frank Sinatra and his Rat Pack would come in there too. But everyone was in awe of Jimmy. Even Bogart. Bogart said Jimmy was the *best*, right before he died. He stopped by at the Villa Capri the night that he died, before he headed out of town.

147

I first lived in Hollywood at the Montecito. A friend of mine told me I had to go to the Chateau Marmont. At the time there was a great exodus of actors out of New York coming to Hollywood, such as myself. And the Chateau Marmont was all booked. So they suggested the Montecito, and I stayed for several weeks there. I found the Montecito delightful. I had a little nice apartment up there. It was delightful because it was total Hollywood. You'd go down to the pool and meet all the other actors down there and talk about work. Someone would say that they just got a six-week deal and that would be a big deal, back then, a six-week deal!

There's no two ways about it: It had an *aura*. Even to this day, now that Hollywood is pretty trashy, it still has an aura.

I would walk right down the hill to Hollywood Boulevard, which I loved. I'd have my breakfast down there. It had all these marvelous little coffee shops. I just loved it. I was breathing the air of Lotus Land. It was what I had dreamed of. It was everything I dreamed of, except that so many of the stars were gone from the studio. There were very few high-rises then. No graffiti. When I got here, I knew I was home. That is why I never went back to do any more plays. I had worked so hard and so long to get here that I was never interested in going back. Once I got out here in Hollywood, which was my *mecca*, it was so delightful, still in 1957, I couldn't ever leave. I remember lying awake there at night and hearing the roar of sports cars down Hollywood Boulevard. I remember thinking that the feeling was so different from the Lamb's Club, where I had lived in Times Square in New York City.

There was an ambiance out here that was so exciting that the very air was just intoxicating for me. Hollywood was glamorous then. And I knew where everything was, and where to go. Right off the bat I went to Musso & Frank's, because I had read about that from year one. And I went to the Cinegrill, which I loved. I would eat at the Roosevelt. And I would go to Grauman's Chinese Theater, of course, and see the footprints there. And C.C. Brown's! I had read about it for years and it was just like I had expected: There were the same booths that all the stars had been sitting in for years and years. The same decorations on the ceiling. And the same good hot fudge chocolate sundaes. I remember going to Ciro's. It felt like I had arrived.

148

After I had been at the Montecito for a couple of weeks, I got a car and I wanted to get an apartment near there. I found a little place at 910 North Serrano. Right off of Western, one block east. I thought, "How Hollywood can you get?" It was right down there in Hollywood. It was a beautiful cottage right behind a little hacienda. It was a perfect place for an actor just getting started in Hollywood. It originally was a guest house, and it had a little courtyard. I lived there till I finished Onionhead. It was very nice then. There was no theft or crime. You couldn't ask for a more Hollywood place to start out your Hollywood life.

One of my friends was Stuart Hamblin who was a songwriter who lived in the house that used to belong to Errol Flynn up on Mulholland. He took me around and showed me the peep holes [laughs] that Flynn had drilled in the bathroom so he could stand there and watch people take baths. He had peepholes up in the attic above the beds so he could look down. He was a voyeur.

I grew up with the idea of the golden era of Hollywood and movies. But when I got here that was all in dispersion. The big studios were letting their stars go, and TV was taking over. And I never really liked TV. I came out here to be a movie actor. But I realized if I wanted to live I had to take TV work. Onionhead gave me about eight weeks of work, but then it was over. So I made one of the first color TV series ever, Northwest Passage, based on the movie, which was shot at MGM. That was '58. And I did many commercials. For about five years I was on the soap opera Days of Our Lives, and also General Hospital. I played an FBI agent on The FBI Story for six or seven years.

I started seeing some of my friends, like Jack Lemmon, becoming big stars. I would go out for lunch with Jack, and he wouldn't have any privacy. Maybe that's one of the reasons I lost that drive to become a movie star. I didn't have what the Jewish people called chutzpah. I didn't push. I got very active in church work, along with Roy Rogers and Dale Evans, at the Hollywood Presbyterian church at Franklin & Highland. People told me to buy a Cadillac, even though I couldn't afford one, and go to parties. But it just wasn't my bag. But that was many times where you got jobs. But I never could badger anybody for a job. I couldn't put on that whole act that ingratiates you to people that most actors have. I never had that. I would just go in and audition to the best of my abilities. And that isn't enough in this town.

I had small parts in a number of films. I did *Career* with Tony Franciosa and Dean Martin. I did *Marooned* with Gregory Peck. I did *Don't Give Up the Ship*, with Jerry Lewis. With Elvis Presley I did *Live a Little, Love a Little* and another called *Speedway*. There was one where I was playing cards with Elvis all night. I got to meet and know him pretty well, because he and I were from the same part of the country. He was still playing little Coca-Cola games with his Memphis Mafia friends, where they would shake it up and squirt Coca-Cola on each other. He was a nice kid. We would joke. I know he was King to some people, but in terms of music, Sinatra was my boy. And Clark Gable is the only King I'll admit to in Hollywood. I liked Elvis, sure enough, but I would *never* call him the King. No, I would call Clark Gable the King. *He's* the King of Hollywood.

149

Hollywood shifted in the mid-sixties. All the studios divested themselves of the stars. And this changed the whole structure of the old Hollywood as we knew it when stars were built up into stars. That's why we have such a mortality rate for stars these days. In the past they would sign someone like Lana Turner, who was just a frumpy little girl with marvelous *bazooms*. MGM took her and turned her into the most beautiful sex goddess you had ever seen. They were able to hold onto her career and turn her into a star. And when she got into trouble, they protected her and no one knew about it. Stars had a better chance of holding on in those days.

I retired and moved here [to the Motion Picture Country Home] in 1995. First week I was here I was sitting with some ladies and talking about my first love, Billie Dove. One of the ladies said to me, "Did you know she's here?" Well, my knees turned to jelly.

I said, "Oh no!"

She said, "Yes. She has just been here a short while. Would you like to meet her?" So I got to meet her.

Of course, when you meet a star of this magnitude, they often keep their distance. But she was so sweet. She was in a wheelchair. There's the picture over there of the two of us. [Shows photo of he and Billie smiling together.] I told her all about myself and about the picture I got. And she said, "Oh, I remember that picture very well. I remember that beret." So we talked for a while, and she said, "Will you come back to see me?"

And I said, "May I?"

She said, "Oh, please do." She was rather standoffish to many people around her, but she pulled me right in and we got very close. I would go see her every day. Her nurses told me she would fix her makeup before I would come. She was so darling.

Over that year we spoke all about her life in Hollywood, about Howard Hughes. She was very reclusive. Many people wanted to do books on her but she didn't want to talk to anyone, and she didn't want people to see her in the wheelchair. I took care of her fan mail, and she was still getting an extraordinary amount of fan mail. From all over the world. People everywhere knew of the Billie Dove. She said, "You wouldn't mind taking care of my fan mail?" She had stacks of it.

I said, "Of course I wouldn't mind. Remember, I was the little boy who wrote you and somebody took care of mine, even though it wasn't personal."

It was so beautiful and delightful how things worked out. The Italians have a phrase, "The world has a long tail." For me to have met this person I adored from so far away and long ago as a child. I had been with her on New Year's Eve that year, and then I left to go to a party we had here. When I came back, that's when she passed away. Before I left she said to me, "Now you will come back, won't you?"

I wanted to be a movie star like Elvis and I wanted everything he had, the leading roles and the cars and the girls. But I didn't get that. But what I did get is all this. I ended up being in a business I really loved for forty years.

Johnny Grant
BORN MAY 9, 1923
LA GRANGE, NORTH CAROLINA
ACTOR/"HONORARY MAYOR OF HOLLYWOOD"

———————

Hollywood Boulevard. The lobby of the Roosevelt Hotel. On a high stool at a small table he is perched, smiling warmly to various admirers who pass by. A bronze full-size statue of Charlie Chaplin sits peacefully with cane and derby hat on a bench near his table. A tall glass of Coca-Cola on ice appears even before he asks for one. He's treated like royalty here because he is royalty here, the designated "Honorary Mayor of Hollywood," who lives for free at the Roosevelt in their penthouse high above Hollywood Boulevard, and who presides not unlike the Wizard of Oz over all important Hollywood rituals: the annual Christmas parade, the Walk of Fame ceremonies, and the very rare occasions when a movie star is memorialized with a footprint ceremony in the forecourt of the Chinese Theater. He's small, roundish, and bespectacled, quite like his friend Mickey Rooney in countenance and stature. A veteran of radio, stage, movies, and many overseas tours for the troops with Bob Hope, his most famous appearance was in White Christmas. While some in the community consider him an adversary in the goal of preserving the past, there's no mistaking that few men have done more to remind the world that Hollywood matters today.

———————————

I grew up in North Carolina, and the movie theater was our window to the world. You know, we didn't have much down there. There was no television, and you didn't get to travel much. So that was where we built our dreams, in the movie theaters, in newsreels and travelogues. That's how I got interested in Hollywood.

I loved all movies. I appreciated the silent movies. I thought it was *marvelous* that they could tell stories without words. We might be better off today if they were still silent. Because you had to be a *real* talent in those days to perform in the movies.

151

Chaplin was a genius. In everything but his political life. But that was his right to do that. That's *real* talent. And who was that old sad-faced comedian? Buster Keaton. A *genius*. No question. All those people. But I'm not an aficionado of the movies. I'm more interested in what makes things happen in the *community* of Hollywood here.

I first came to Hollywood during the war in the forties. I came back in early '47 and I've been here ever since. I knew before I went into the service that I wanted to live here. I fought like hell to get to be the NCO in charge of a troop parade so I could get a trip out here. Then I came back in the nose of B-25 bomber, and did a lot of things for celebrities and all while I was stationed in New York. I knew quite a few people out here when I got here.

During World War II, Hollywood was a very hospitable place. If someone saw a soldier walking on the street, they would pull over their cars and say, "Hi soldier, where you going?" and give him a ride. Or they would take him on the streetcar and make sure he got on the right one. Probably Hollywood and St. Louis, Missouri, were the two most hospitable cities in the country.

When I came here after the war, it was a practically all-white community. It was what you would call a "company town." People were either involved in the business or on the periphery, servicing the business. If you went to a gas station, they would probably have told you, "That's Gene Autry's car on the grease rack," or if you went to the stationery store, they might tell you that Ann Sheridan or Bette Davis had just left.

Everybody was a part of it. It was good people having a good time about being good neighbors. There was no pressure like today. It was a very clean community. No graffiti and that kind of stuff. And safe. You could walk the streets at night with no worry.

I used to live at the Knickerbocker Hotel after the war. They had a good restaurant there, and the best cinnamon buns in town. I was there when Elvis was there, with Colonel Parker. And D.W. Griffith was still living there then, and I met him. I went up to him and introduced myself. I was born in

La Grange, North Carolina, and he was from La Grange, Kentucky. I had a little talk with him. He was not a happy man then. He was pretty much forgotten in his later years. And that is still going on. I can tell you that there is ageism in Hollywood. There was then and there still is now.

The downfall of Hollywood and Hollywood Boulevard happened during the Vietnam War when the young people became disenchanted with their parents, with their country, with the war and everything, and they rebelled. And where do you think they are going to go? They're going to Hollywood. What's the first thing they did? They went to the army surplus store and they bought army fatigues. And then tore the knees out of them and did their thing.

152

Right across the street from where we are was the Garden Court Apartments. One of the most elegant buildings in Hollywood. And they started living in there after it became abandoned, and they were also living, you know, in garbage dumpsters, and all kinds of stuff. And they were all high on marijuana or more, and started walking up and down the street, and people were *afraid*, and they just left.

Why the history of the movies in Hollywood wasn't preserved better from the very start is a good question. I'd like to know. Maybe the preservationists then were a pain in the ass, like they are today. Today I can't repair the Walk of Fame because one person thinks the pink terrazzo should be declared historic. It was put in there so we could repair it. We knew it was going to crack. It's forty-some years old now. So we're fighting with that. There's a lot of that going on. I am not pleased at all with the way Hollywood history has been preserved.

Hollywood never was glamorous. It was what *happened* here that was glamorous. It was the premieres. It was the events that happened here, the showmanship. Sid Grauman. I *knew* Sid Grauman. I was one of the last who knew him. I used to drive him home. He and Charlie Chaplin were both great practical jokers, and they'd play practical jokes on each other. As a matter of fact, once Sid Grauman had a Charlie Chaplin look-alike contest. And Chaplin found about it, and he went down, and entered into the contest. And placed *second*. [Laughter] Yeah. Somebody else, they figured, looked more like Charlie Chaplin than he did. Oh, they did *outrageous* things.

Somehow Chaplin's slab with his handprints and footprints has been removed. I don't know why. I know Sid Grauman would not have done that.

The original two to put their footprints in at the Chinese Theater were Mary Pickford and Douglas Fairbanks. I know how that started. It started when Mary Pickford came home one day. They were putting in a new driveway at [her home] Pickfair in cement, and her little dog Zorro jumped out of the car and ran through the wet cement, with the workmen chasing him with the shovels, yelling, trying to kill him, and Mary's yelling, "No, no, no! We'll have little Zorro with us *forever!*" Then when she got in the house, the phone was ringing. It was Sid Grauman. And she *told* him about it. And Sid, with his showmanship computer mind, he put the thing together and called them back the next day and asked if they would come down to the Chinese Theater and do theirs. It is not true that they were just putting the cement in at that time, because if you look at the pictures of that day, all the cement is in and they just dig out that one place. And that was told to me by Buddy Rogers, who later married Mary Pickford, who happened to be at the house when the phone call was made. He was visiting Doug Jr. So I know where that story came from.

I've done 550 star ceremonies. All the stars are similar; all actors are somewhat insecure. But some are more than others. Walter Matthau arrived at his ceremony about an hour and a half early and sat in the back of a store there on the boulevard, and had me go look out, at least ten times, to see if anyone was out there. He wasn't convinced he was going to draw a crowd. I said, "*Walter, Walter,* you're going to have a *huge* crowd." And he did.

Tom Cruise, he even said, when we gave him his star, "I thought only Mr. Grant and my girlfriend were going to be here." [Laughs] Actors are very insecure people. I'm lucky with stars, though. I get them when they're on their best behavior. I'm representing somebody who is giving them something. Most of them have been very gracious, and are good people. There's a few, if I never saw them again it wouldn't matter, but I'm not going to tell names. But who knows what happened before they left their house that morning?

There are a lot of names on a lot of the stars on Hollywood Boulevard that people don't remember. A lot of people want us to dig those ones up. I tell them, "There wouldn't be a Hollywood if those people hadn't been here." But I'd never dig them up, as long as I'm chairman. They never will be dug up. We have a lot of space. There are still many blank stars, and I've started double. You know, stars have the opportunity to ask for a specific spot if there is a blank star there. We've had several who wanted to be in front of Musso & Frank's, because Musso & Frank's fed them or let them run a tab. And then when they got big, they wanted to do something for them. Aaron Spelling was one of them.

I've been doing the Walk of Fame for twenty-two years. "Honorary Mayor of Hollywood" is a title given to you by the Chamber of Commerce. Since Hollywood is not its own city, they can have an honorary mayor. I've gotten along with all the other mayors of L.A. When they dedicated that building over there, the Johnny Grant Building, they had all three living mayors of L.A. there. The only time in history. They had never been together. And that was Yorty, Bradley and Riordan.

Hollywood is more famous than Paris or London or New York. It's the most famous trademark in the whole world. I can tell you that when I travel around the world, my identification with Hollywood is a passport to the whole world. Thanks to CNN and those people, people around the world *see* the Walk of Fame ceremonies, and all that stuff over there. So a lot of them recognize me. And because I am associated with Hollywood, it opens the doors.

154

There are several Hollywoods. Especially two: the entertainment industry and this physical place. I think people come to Hollywood to see stars. I've never had anybody in all the years I've been here say, "Hey, where can I see television stars?" Every person—*thousands* of them—says, "Where can I see the movie stars?" So Hollywood is identified as a movie capital. And they come in here with emotion for a name on a star.

The Hollywood Sign, there's no emotion to that. We wanted to get it rebuilt, and we all worked to get it done. Because we knew it was a great trademark. We knew that it started out as an advertisement for a real estate development, and all of that. So you won't find a lot of people who come here just to see the Hollywood *sign*. But planeloads of people come here just to see one individual star. There's a group that comes here every year, and they only thing they're interested in is Bing Crosby. There's another group that is only interested in Frankie Laine. And you have fan clubs for all the stars. I've seen them come in here year after year. That Walk of Fame brings a lot of people here.

There's no longer any question about if Hollywood could ever come back. Hollywood is coming back. We have a lot of new people coming in here. New developers. I don't know if they have the kind of passion for Hollywood that I have.

Remember, I was on that boulevard by myself for a lot of years. And not getting a lot of help. And my friends would tell me, on Saturday nights over in Beverly Hills and Westwood, that they were all laughing at me, saying, "What is he doing? Why is he out there? He's beating that dead horse to death." But I'm not beating something. I'm *resuscitating*. And it was the Walk of Fame, and a lot of the events, the Christmas Parade, the hand and footprint ceremonies, that kept us in the news.

Then all the people said, "We'd better get in on this," and they're in here now. I don't know many of the new people. I have had some strong conversations with some of them, trying to encourage them not to just come in looking for the money, but to be a part of the community. You have to give something back. And that includes all of them. I don't see a lot of giving right now. But we'll win this.

Television runs the world now, whether you like it or not. Television has the impact now. But it hasn't surpassed movies yet. Movies, and Hollywood, influences the world. Soon movies won't even be on film anymore, they'll come in on the satellite dish. I think they'll start doing things again like Sid Grauman used to do. When they had a major boxing match, they didn't show a movie that day, they showed the boxing event on a big screen there. It was a venue where Sinatra used to go. Sinatra was the greatest little guy you could ever meet.

As far as an attraction, there was no star greater than Gable. I talked to him just a few days before he died. I'll tell you what day it was. It was the last day he shot with Marilyn Monroe on *The Misfits*, his final film. He was waiting for her. And he had a long wait. They were doing the blue screen at Paramount.

So we went over to Oblath's, which was right across the street, and I remember we had about forty-five minutes before they came to get him because she had arrived. He thought *The Misfits* was the best movie he'd ever done. Best performance he'd ever given. He said he thought he had one more in him.

And that's all I'm gonna give you!

Don Farquhar
BORN SEPTEMBER 11, 1922
HOLLYWOOD, CALIFORNIA
OWNER, HOLLYWOOD TIRE COMPANY

Early morning at the Hollywood Tire Company on Las Palmas, just south of the old boulevard. An old office with a big iron desk. Yellowed, wrinkled maps of old Hollywood in black frames. A poster with a diagram depicting the "Five Finger Plan" in which streets were extended in central Hollywood. Miniatures of antique autos. Displays of car tires from the Teens through the fifties. Yellowish light filtering through ancient venetian blinds. It's a company started by his grandfather in 1915, and this office, except for its computer and modern telephone, could easily belong to that era. He's one of the rare ones, a genuine Hollywood native, and can remember back to when the streets were laid out in different patterns before being extended and connected to contain all the cars, for which his family supplied tires. He's a big man with a booming voice who sits back in his big chair, focusing through black-framed bifocals. In addition to his tire business, he's active in the community, and happily fields several phone calls as he delves into his personal past.

I was born in Hollywood in 1922, and raised here. My folks lived down on Gardner, near what was then called The Gardner Junction. Years ago we had streetcars. And the streetcars ran down Hollywood Boulevard and one ran down Santa Monica Boulevard. It would go west down Hollywood Boulevard to La Brea, and then it cut across at an angle. And Gardner Junction was where Gardner crossed Sunset Boulevard.

My family had a tire business in Hollywood. My grandfather started the tire business in 1915. It was one of the early ones. He was up here at Hollywood & Hudson. People would drive there, and they'd service the cars right out on the street because this was before anyone had garages—they didn't come inside to a stall or anything, they would just change tires on the street.

Then my dad moved from there in 1924 to Sunset Boulevard, at the corner of Sunset & Wilcox for forty years, until 1964. Wilcox didn't go through [south of Sunset] then. They extended it many years later in what was called the "Five Finger Plan." They extended Wilcox through, and they also extended Cahuenga through, and they put in the Hollywood fire station then, and redid the whole area.

I can remember as a kid riding our bikes in the neighborhood on a Thanksgiving afternoon and Johnny Weismuller came around the corner in a convertible Packard doing that Tarzan yell of his. We'd run into that kind of thing. My mother was shopping at Robertson's one time and Lupe Velez was there with a Rolls Royce. In the tire business, Wallace Beery was a customer of ours, Charlie Chaplin was a customer. I knew Harold Lloyd, who was a customer up until he died.

In 1924, my dad built a house out on King's Road, off of Santa Monica. Everyone asked him, "Vernon, why are you going out so far?" Nothing was built much beyond that. My dad went to Hollywood High School in 1916. He had an L.A. Times route and he carried all of the Times west from La Brea, if you can imagine, on a bicycle.

My dad was born in Chicago but he grew up here. My grandfather was a real entrepreneur. In 1929, he owned the Taft Building at Hollywood & Vine. In 1930 he lost it. He had a big ranch in the Valley up till 1930, and after that he had a little teeny apartment on Avocado off of Los Feliz. He lost it all.

Hollywood was a marvelous town to grow up in. Actually there were really two Hollywoods, there was my Hollywood, which was the guys who run the tire shop and run the newspapers and run the banks. Like they do in any town in the country. And superimposed on top of this was this magical

Hollywood of the entertainment industry. And there was not always a lot of interaction between the two worlds. We'd sell tires to them and sometimes see them at church. I did know Judy Garland in school—she was a semester ahead of me at Bancroft. And at Fairfax, Mickey Rooney was there, and Ricardo Montalban was in everybody's senior play for as long as he was at Fairfax. He was about a year behind me in school. He was in our senior play and in the next year's senior play.

When I was a kid I carried newspapers for the *Hollywood Citizen*. And they'd have a pier party every once in awhile if you got so many subscriptions. And they'd run the streetcar and it would go down Santa Monica Boulevard and it would stop at each corner and pick up kids, and we'd ride down to Santa Monica. There was a line that ran across parallel to the beach and we'd end up at Venice or Ocean Park, the pier down there, and we'd be there all night and we'd have tickets to go on rides, get back on the streetcar, and come home and drop us off along the way.

157

My route for the *Citizen* was from La Cienega to Larrabee, and from Santa Monica to Sunset. Where Holloway Drive goes up, I had all of that. On the north side of Holloway Drive there was nothing but poinsettia fields in those days. During high school I carried a free throw-away, the *Valley Shopping News*, on Wednesday to Saturday. I used to make seventy-five cents a route, and sometimes you would carry double, and get $1.50. We'd sometimes do department stores on Friday, so I'd get seventy-five cents for that.

I was the district manager for my little area, and got jobs for all my friends in the area, and I got ten cents a week for taking care of those guys. And I could make $4.50 to $5.00 a week. And that's all you needed! It would give you enough money to take your girl to the show, or buy her a gardenia and go to a dance.

There were a lot of school dances back then with Fairfax and Hollywood and Hamilton and University and Dorsey. Gosh, we used to go to country clubs, or the Hollywood's Woman's Club on La Brea, we used to go there. And it would cost $2 and go to the dance without girls. And you could do that back then on two and a half dollars.

When I was growing up, there were only two main places to shop in the L.A. area. One was downtown. And the other place to shop was Hollywood Boulevard. We had the Broadway, Robertson's, Innis Shoe Company, Barker Brothers, I. Magnin's. There were a number of high quality men's stores where you could really buy quality clothes. Now all you can really get is a T-shirt.

The Brown Derby was there and Mike Liman's right across the street, which was a men's grill, a steakhouse, and Musso's, of course, and the Tick-Tock on Cahuenga, and Alan's Tearoom over on Ivar above the boulevard. There was another good tearoom right at Las Palmas & Yucca where we used to go after church and have lunch on Sunday. There was the Pig & Whistle, which was a soda fountain, really, right next to the Egyptian Theater. And we had C.C. Brown's for the best hot fudge sundaes anywhere. And the Roosevelt Hotel had a good restaurant. Still does.

My grandfather had a house on Gardner—the third house on the street. Mr. Gardner had the first. Across the street from where the Gardner Library is.

NBC was down here at Sunset & Vine, Wallich's had the Music City on the other side of the street, and Sy Devore had a *really* nice shop. All the big actors at NBC would walk over and hang out at the barber shop, or at Sy Devore's.

I was married in 1947 and had a baby born in 1948. We moved to one of those little 1920 wooden houses on DeLongpre, just a block down from the police station. We had another baby, another little girl, and on a Saturday night my wife and I put the two kids in a stroller, and we'd walk up Wilcox to the boulevard and we'd walk down to Vine Street, cross the street, go down to Highland, cross the street, and come back and walk back down Wilcox and home. And you never had a problem; you never even *expected* a problem. You could walk anywhere in those days.

I had an aunt who was a schoolteacher in North Hollywood. And when my wife and I were married in 1947, housing was very short. You couldn't find a place to live. My aunt lived at the Halifax Apartments, at the corner of Cahuenga & Yucca. She had a one-room apartment with a Murphy bed. My mother's folks had a ranch in Garden Grove, so my aunt would go there for the summer and give us her apartment. When we were married we lived there till we could find a place to live for about four months.

I think two or three things happened to Hollywood. Prior to the war we had good public transportation and people didn't live way out. My grandfather was building houses in the Valley in the thirties. But the other side of Laurel Canyon was all farm. Van Nuys was there, but it was just a little dot. Chatsworth was way out there. Woodland Hills was all walnut orchards. So the Valley was all farms. I had an aunt that had an orange grove on Ventura Boulevard in Encino.

I think the downfall of Hollywood was due to the car and the freeways, and the end of good public transit. We had a streetcar on Hollywood Boulevard and we had a streetcar on Santa Monica. We had a bus on Melrose and a bus on Sunset and a bus on Franklin that went up into the Hollywoodland area. So there was lot of transportation here. But the people moved out. If you look around, there was no place to park a car. At the Halifax where my aunt lived, she had a nice apartment but no parking. And they were *all* built that way. All the old buildings north of the boulevard don't have any parking.

So people began to buy automobiles. My aunt never did; she was getting to be pretty old and she was a schoolteacher, and she rode the streetcars. On Friday when she was done with school, she'd catch the streetcar and ride down to the terminal, walk down to 5th & Main, and then get on the big Red Car, where her folks were. Someone would drive down and meet her. So you could get anywhere. But as the more affluent guys came in and had cars, there were no places to park them, so they moved out, and the people that followed were low-income people primarily, and the low-income people couldn't support the good stores on the boulevard. So little by little the good stores moved out to Beverly Hills or the San Fernando Valley or down to Wilshire.

159

I think that's basically what happened. It caused an exodus of people out of town. My generation, all of my friends, lived in town, in Hollywood. When the war came we all went to war, we all came home, we all lived with our folks till we got married, and then everyone all moved to the Valley or to the beach or somewhere else. The second generation all moved out. And that just left the old people here. Out in the Valley there were young people and bigger yards and new neighborhoods.

I served in the Korean War, and after that we wanted to move into the Valley. My wife said, "You can't go any farther than twenty minutes from Sunset & Wilcox." So we ended up in Burbank, buying a lot and building our own home. Houses now around there sell for $250,000 to $320,000. In 1952 and 1953 they were selling for $14,500 to $17,500. Nobody had any money either so it didn't make that much difference.

In 1955 there was only one guy importing the Mercedes automobile, and he was out of New York. He was going to bring the Mercedes to Los Angeles. He said, "Where do I go to attract my kind of buyer? My kind of buyer is going to live in Beverly Hills, Brentwood, Hancock Park, the Hollywood Hills, Pasadena or Encino. Where is the area that is the most conducive to all of those people? And it's Hollywood. We're central. I don't know how Century City ever got going. It was just the old Fox studio and a golf course. It's so crowded it's hard to get there. It's easy to get here from anywhere.

I've heard that story that Standard Oil and Firestone were behind getting the Red Cars off of the street, but I don't know if that's true. That's political. But you know, streetcars were also a pain in the neck because the pavement was always rough around the tracks, the road would get so bumpy along the rail, and there were safety zones you had to drive around. The streets were much nicer after they got rid of the tracks. But we used to have a good, good system here. You could go anywhere.

It was a nice world then. And Hollywood was a really nice town to grow up in.

Jerry Maren
BORN JANUARY 24, 1920
BOSTON, MASSACHUSETTS
ACTOR

160

Dark hair, a big mustache, and warm friendly eyes form his famous face, a face first seen in the first movie he ever did, and the one for which he will always be best known, The Wizard of Oz, in which he played a munchkin. But not just any munchkin—he was the middle Lollipop kid, the one in green plaid who presents a lollipop to Dorothy after singing his famous song: "We represent the Lollipop Guild / And we welcome you to Munchkin Land." These days he lives with his gregarious wife Elizabeth, also a little person like him, yet both have such generous and expansive spirits that any lack of stature is pretty well unnoticeable after a few moments in their presence. They live in a small, cozy house on the top of a hill in Hollywood. It's an unseasonably cold and rainy day, yet in their home all is warm and welcome. She serves tea and cookies as he shows photos and other memorabilia of a lifetime in the movies, including the famous lollipop. Laughter remains constant throughout, especially when he tells of his time working as a stand-in for Charlie McCarthy, Edgar Bergen's dummy, in the movies. "When you saw Charlie in the distance walking, that would be me," he explains, "and then for close-ups they would bring in the real dummy." To which Elizabeth chimes in with the impeccable timing of a seasoned comic: "And how would they know the difference, dear?"

I've done so many things in show business, but people say, "You were in *The Wizard of Oz?*" It takes people's breath away. But then I realized, geez, it must have been a hell of a picture, everybody remembers it everywhere I go. It must have been a good picture. It became a national event around Thanksgiving. That movie has made me feel good for sixty years because it's such a great movie. And you're not afraid to tell anyone you were in it, because when you tell them, they get so excited. So I don't even tell them anymore because they get so excited.

There were 124 munchkins and there are only fourteen still living today. And my wife insists I'm going to be the last one.

Hollywood was a little town when I came here in 1938. I expected it to be a big town. I remember that at night we would see lights in the sky and that meant there was going to be a premiere that night. And I would go up and see the premiere if I could, but I could never see because I'm so small, you know. But it was a wonderful place. Just a little town, and everybody was friendly.

There were friends of my dancing teacher in Boston, the Farmers, who let me stay with them in Hollywood. They had a little home on DeLongpre Avenue, right by the fire station. Hollywood wasn't exciting at all when I first saw it. It was just a little town. It was fine. We used to walk up on Cahuenga Boulevard, Hollywood Boulevard, walk past the Palladium.

Hollywood Boulevard was nice in those days. Back then, not the real big stars but the character actors, would all stroll along Hollywood Boulevard. I would walk down the boulevard and stop to see this little guy I knew who sold papers at the corner of Wilcox & Hollywood Boulevard, Angelo Rossito. Right near the Warner Brothers theater. He was smaller than me so I liked to be with him, I could look down at him. [*Laughs*]

He introduced me to a friend of his, Bobby Watson, a famous Broadway star who was in *No No Nanette*. In the meantime he was playing Hitler in a picture. He was the best Hitler they ever had in pictures. I couldn't believe he could play Hitler, but his makeup was so good, he was terrific.

I asked him, "Where do you live?" He said a friend of his had a lot behind Hollywood Boulevard, and he lived there in a trailer. Which surprised me, this big movie star living in a trailer. But he was alone and that's where he liked it.

He introduced me to another guy named Charlie Catlin. They were all members of the Masquers Club, which was up on Sycamore, so they used to come out of there and walk. We used to walk together and see other character actors: Hello there! It was fun, nothing like it is today. Now you're afraid to walk. But we had a good time walking. It was strolling.

There were great restaurants there. Musso & Frank's was right there. I used to go to the Pig & Whistle restaurant, next to the Egyptian Theater. That was good—I used to go in there and have hot chocolate, which was delicious. They always had an organist playing there, which was terrific. The organist was on the second floor, I believe. It was real atmosphere. That was Hollywood.

Then right down the street was the Palladium, which had just opened and it was terrific. They used to have a big band there every week.

We would keep walking down to Vine Street and back. That's a long walk for a little guy like me. I'd meet another little guy there, Billy Curtis. Billy Curtis was a big shot, talking to everyone. He was the Lord High Mayor in Munchkin Land, the guy who came out with the big tall hat and said, "Welcome to Munchkin Land!" That was him. He worked as the page boy at the

Plaza Hotel on Vine Street. That was the hotel in Hollywood at the time. He was a bookie on the side too. He used to give me the dirt on everybody. Buddy Rich, the drummer, used to fight with Frank Sinatra. I'd hear all the scuttlebutt.

We used to eat at that restaurant in the first floor of the Plaza. Billy knew all the gangsters and the detectives and everything. At night we'd go in and have a snack. I used to have those wonderful Monte Cristo sandwiches with the ham and the bacon and the turkey and the cheese. It was deep-fried. It was terrific. I'm a little guy so for me that was like having a big dinner. We'd talk about horses and fights and football. I learned all about the horses and gambling. And smoking. It was exciting, you know, growing up. I mean maturing. But I never gambled much.

162

Both of these Billys were from Massachusetts like me: Billy Curtis was from Springfield, Mass. And Billy Rhodes was from Lynn, Massachusetts. And Holy Toledo, he was the star of the movie *Terror of Tiny Town*, Billy Curtis. Billy Rhodes was the villain and Billy Curtis was the hero. I met the villain and the hero of the same movie. Billy Rhodes was very nice. He was a very explosive little man. He didn't hold back anything. Whatever was on his mind he said. It didn't matter how little or how tall you were. He was *honest*. He smoked cigars and I was amazed at the cigar he smoked. I got to know him better. He taught me how to play the racehorses. We used to go to Simon's, a big drive-in at the corner of Sunset & Highland. It was nice. Good food.

Hollywood was so nice then. Now you're afraid to go out of the house. You don't know who is going to hit you over the head. But dope wasn't big then. Now it's a big thing. People who take dope act erratic. They have to do bad things to stay alive and get dope. But Hollywood was *beautiful* then. *Beautiful*.

I grew up near Boston. When I was a kid, my sister used to go to dancing school every week and my mother told me, "Go to dancing school with your sister. You might like it." So I went with my sister and I kind of liked it. I liked the theatrical part of it. Twice a year we had recitals at certain theaters. I was in both those shows, which was nice. The teachers liked me, they thought I was cute, and I could sing and dance. So they asked me if I wanted to join them to do an act around New England for the summer. I asked my parents, and they felt as long as I was within 200 miles, they could come and get me in case something went wrong.

So we were playing the Bond Hotel in Hartford, Connecticut, 1938. After a show a gentleman came backstage and said, "We're going to make a movie in Los Angeles called *The Wizard of Oz* and we need quite a few little people like you. We need about four or five who can sing and dance, and I've seen your act and I know what you can do. We'd love to have you in our picture." I said, "I'd love to," and he said he'd get in touch with me within three months or so. I was seventeen at the time. Three months exactly I got a telegram, and it said I would have six weeks guaranteed, plus transportation and the best of everything—food, hotel. My parents thought that was all right. They said, "Go ahead and do it." I had just graduated high school so I did. That's how I got into pictures.

I had never heard of The Wizard of Oz or L. Frank Baum. All I knew was that it was going to be a big motion picture. It looked like a typical musical when I got there and saw all the sets and the music and the direction and the choreography. They went to a lot of expense. I said, "Man, look at all the people behind the camera!"

163

We stayed at the Culver City Hotel. Three guys to a room, and we all slept in the same bed but there was plenty of room, you know? [Laughs] They were about my size. That first morning I woke up to the sound of music, looked out the window and saw a big band playing! I woke up the other guys and said, "Hey, look—they got a parade out there for us! We must be important!" They got up and looked out the window, and after closer observation we realized it was Armistice Day! It was November 11. I was fooled again. And that was my beginning.

They didn't tell us anything about the movie, who was in it or anything. It was none of our business. We were there about eight weeks but it took two weeks of makeup preparation. They used those skullcaps then, and wardrobe had to be made for us.

When they did the makeup, they started with the skullcap, which makes everyone look bald, and then they did the rest from there, they put the hair on top of the skullcap. It was a pain in the a-s-s. I'm telling you. Every morning you had to look forward to that, oh Jesus. They used to have five or six barber chairs down below street level on one of the stages, and that's where we had to go every morning. It took at least forty-five minutes every morning to put it on. We'd go from chair to chair—one guy was a specialist with wigs, one guy was a specialist with prosthetics—fake cheeks, noses, chins. It was not fun. I was not used to it. I didn't know what makeup was.

Then we had to learn how to dance the routines and the singing of the songs. It took a lot of preparation, and then shooting took two or three weeks. That was all for one sequence, the Munchkin Land sequence, and that was ours.

I remember when I first saw the sets and all of us. I thought, "Geez, look at that. Boy, they went to a lot of pain to get all these little people from all over the world. This must be important." The set was monstrous and it was beautiful. They had a beautiful pond and the Yellow Brick Road and all the flowers. And I noticed that they had about ten guys who just took care of all the flowers and the trees. They were called greenmen. I didn't know who a greenman was but I figured it out. Usually a movie might have one of them—we had about ten. That shows you how big this picture was. Ten of them, just to take care of the flowers and the trees. My imagination went wild because I had seen all the people behind the cameras. It was exciting to see so many.

I learned quite a bit about special effects. Like where the Good Witch, Billie Burke, first shows up. They told us to look up, that she would be in a bubble. So we had to listen to what they said and we were supposed to imagine what they said because we didn't know what the hell was going on. They said, "Wave good-bye," and I was thinking, "What the hell are we waving to?" They had this guy with a broom waving a white towel, and we had to believe that that was Glinda the Good Witch going away. Same thing when Dorothy was going away up the Yellow Brick Road. Toward this old, dirty, musty stage at the end, you know. They said, "Say good-bye!" So you learned a lot about point of view, and it was exciting, different for me. I said, "My goodness, these motion pictures are *incredible*."

They told us a little bit about the scene. They said, "When Dorothy landed in Munchkin Land, she surprised you. All you know is the Good Witch and the Bad Witch." When she landed, she landed on the witch, and one of the Bad Witches was dead. If you remember, her feet were sticking out from under the house. I was one of the three Lollipop guys who met her. So I sang my song. Would you like to hear it? [Sings] "We represent the Lollipop Guild, the Lollipop Guild, the Lollipop Guild. And in the name of the Lollipop Guild, we wish to welcome you to Munchkin Land!"

That was my introduction to Judy Garland. She was a lovely gal. She always waved at us and said, "Hi kids, hi gang!" She was a typical teenager. She loved us as much as we loved her. In the morning she'd say, "Hi kids, how you feeling? Did you get a good night's rest?" And all that stuff. We used to say that she was a regular gal, she's pretty nice. So we fell in love with her and more so when she got personal with us. But we couldn't get too personal with her because she didn't have time. She had to go to school on the set—three hours of school, four hours of work, and one hour of recreation. That was the rules for the kids.

I didn't know if it would be a hit, but I knew it would be a typical Metro-Goldwyn-Mayer musical. I thought, "Holy Toledo, they sure go to a lot of trouble." Then they spent a lot of time with us three little tough guys. They said they were going to feature us, which was good. I thought I would be part of a big production. Then they had the three little lovely ladies doing the dance which they called "The Lullaby League." Then when I sang the song about the Lollipop Guild, I thought, "What the hell is that?" I had never heard of the word "guild" before because I was never in a union.

My impression later was that the songwriters were having a lot of fun writing this—E.Y. Harburg and Harold Arlen—this was when the Screen Actor's Guild first came together. So they made us members of the guild. And the girls were members of the Lullaby League, because at the time in Hollywood they had the Hollywood Women's League. So they had fun with the conditions of the time.

165

So we learned the lyrics and a few steps. And I added this: [gestures triumphant hand clasping over his head]. They said, "That's good—leave that in." That was a big part of it, but I didn't realize it at the time. But it needed a finish. We had fun with it. I was the one in the middle. The others were much older than me. They passed away about twenty-five years ago. I was one of the youngest munchkins—there were about three or four ladies that were younger than I was. A couple of the gals are still living. One lives in Arizona now—Margaret Pelligrini. She was from Alabama.

All those stories about the munchkins having wild parties every night was a lot of B.S. There might have been one or two. But that was expected, because there were a couple of Irish kids. Even when I was a kid in Boston, I knew they were all drunks. When I found out their name was Kelly, I thought, what do you expect, it's in their blood. That's what they do. Other than that, there was nothing.

We made a movie fifteen years ago called *Under the Rainbow*, and I was in it. And they tried to duplicate that phoniness. Even the producers of that film came to me and said, "Jerry—did this really happen?" I said, "Hell, no, it's a lot of B.S." They wanted to exploit the idea that everybody got drunk, because I think Judy Garland had said that on the Jack Paar show. But it wasn't true, that's all.

First of all, it couldn't be that way because we had to work from six in the morning to eight at night, six days a week. Fifty dollars a week. Which we, of course, thought was good money at the time because we didn't know better. I was making more than my father, which I thought was doing pretty good. He was making $25 a week and I was making $50.

There wasn't time to mess around, even if you wanted to. You were tired. And the weather was miserable—it was November, and it was cold and rainy and dampish. A lot of rain that year. We had to get home and rest. We got up early in the morning to get that awful makeup on.

All the music was prerecorded—"Ding, Dong, the Witch Is Dead" and "Follow the Yellow Brick Road." But we had to sing it anyway, to be in sync with the recording.

There were a lot of rumors about The Wizard of Oz. There was one that said that somebody killed themselves on the Munchkin Land set. People still come up to me and ask about it. It wasn't true. Never happened. That is one of the rumors that I wanted to squelch, which is why I'm telling you now that it's a lot of B.S.

Margaret Hamilton was so effective as the witch. And she was a lovely gal, too. She got hurt one time. That was bad. There's one sequence where the witch makes her big entrance in Munchkin Land. All the munchkins were frightened because we feared her more than anything.

One time she made an entrance on her broomstick and screamed and scared the hell out of all the little people. We ducked down to hide. And then when she disappears, she hits a certain mark, which is the elevator. And she goes down, you know. She did so many takes of that, and during one take she got burnt. Because special effects had to be fire, smoke, and the elevator. Everything had to be perfect. The broom caught on fire and it burnt part of her face and her hand, and they had to rush her to the hospital. Fortunately, it wasn't serious. She got well fast and came back. She was a lovely gal. I think she was a kindergarten teacher. We met her after the picture at festivals and special events and she was so nice.

I was ecstatic when I first got to see the film. It was so good. I was at the premiere at the Grauman's Chinese Theater but I wasn't invited to go inside the theater. I was invited to ballyhoo the picture on the outside of the theater. They had four or five of us little guys—I was dressed as the mayor of Munchkin Land. We were in front of the theater, you know. To hype the movie, you know. So I didn't actually see the movie then, but I heard it. And I heard my lines and I said, "Good, they kept it in, they kept it in!" Because people told me how they cut out every goddamn thing. So I was thrilled.

Then when I finally went to see the movie myself, I was thrilled. Geez, that was amazing. I mean, all I remember was our sequence. Which was probably ten of the greatest minutes of motion picture history. I'm not bragging—from beginning to the end, it's so entertaining. It never stopped. Not just that I was in it. I was looking at it and thinking, "These choreographers knew what they were doing, the music people knew what they were doing." No wonder it was so good, because they all were so good. When it goes from black and white to color, and everyone said, "Aaahhhh." And then the rest of the movie—the Lion! The Strawman! The Tin Man! They all went through their routines and they were terrific: Ray Bolger, Jack Haley, and Bert Lahr, he was so damn funny as the Lion—I was laughing like hell when he was the Lion.

I thought, man this is quite a buildup, isn't it, and we were at the beginning. Everything was a big scene—the field of poppies. I couldn't believe how they did it and I was there and I couldn't believe it.

Victor Fleming directed it. He just got finished doing *Gone with the Wind*. I think they had two other directors, too, but I don't know, they don't tell us anything.

After working on *The Wizard of Oz*, I was all ready to leave Hollywood and go back home. And I got a call from a guy at MGM telling me that they wanted me for the "Our Gang" comedies. There was one called *Tiny Troubles* in which a midget was one of the stars. So I said I would be delighted to stay, and my departure was delayed about two weeks.

167

I did that picture and I played a character called Light-Fingered Lester. I would sit in my mother's lap—she used to sell papers—so as people came by to pay for their papers I would steal their wallets or watch-fobs, or whatever we could get, while they were reading the headlines. The cop finally caught us and we had to disperse. She ran one way and I ran the other way and hid under a tree. In the meantime, Spanky McFarland and Alfalfa Sweitzer, they were walking with a baby in the park. And their baby was screaming and they saw me under the tree and said, "Let's take that baby home instead." So they put that kid under the tree and took me for their baby. Put me in the carriage. And when I got to their house it was the comedy bit—I raided the refrigerator and drank beer and smoked cigars.

When I was smoking a cigar, they said they needed more smoke coming out of my mouth. I didn't smoke and I didn't know how to smoke. So they put a tube from the side of my face all the way down, under the chair, and the special effects man was under there blowing smoke up through the tube. George Sidney was the director.

After doing the "Our Gang" movie I was ready to go home and they said, "We have one more thing for you. The Marx Brothers want to see you." They wanted to interview me for a movie they were doing called *At the Circus*. It was a good part—a feature, so it made me feel good. And I got the part, the part of Professor Atom. I was a member of the circus. I had a little automobile of my own, it was right on the train. And they had my house on the train. And the Marx Brothers come to see me. They were terrific. They were so funny. They made me laugh all the time. The director would say, "Stop laughing, this is serious." I said I was sorry, but with Groucho Marx there making jokes, it makes you laugh. So I had to watch my language—I couldn't say "cahn't" with my Boston accent, I had to say "can't."

Groucho was absolutely the funniest. Chico was always on the phone, talking to his bookie, making bets. Groucho was very nice. In fact, he invited me to his home for dinner. I got so excited and so nervous. I said, "Geez, I'm going to a movie star's house for dinner! I wonder why." He probably thought I was an old performer that never had a good meal while I was in Hollywood, like let's give the kid a break.

So he invited me and I went there and had a wonderful time. It was so good. There was a Swedish chef and we had chicken and dumplings—I'll always remember that. His son came home while we were eating, carrying a tennis racket—Arthur Marx: "Hello Dad!" It was just like in the movies in the drawing room comedies, somebody always comes in with a tennis racket. "Hello Dad!" And here comes the rich kid with the tennis racket.

Groucho showed me all around his house, showed me his bedroom, on the big staircase he had pictures on the wall which he showed me. Harpo was very quiet and very nice. But Groucho was the smart one—the other two played along with whatever he said.

It was exciting being in that picture. It was fun. I told everyone that I was in a Groucho Marx picture and they said, "Oh yeah!" It was a big deal.

I loved the movies my whole life. I used to work at a little movie theater in Boston growing up called the Madison. And I got passes—I always used to put a lot in my pockets. I used to go every week, see every show. They used to change the shows twice a week. It was the time they were making movies galore.

When I was walking around MGM while working in The Wizard of Oz, it was loaded with people! It was like walking in downtown Times Square. That's how busy it was. You'd see different wardrobes—you'd see African junglemen from the Tarzan pictures and a couple of guys in togas working in some Roman period picture. There was so much going on even when we were shooting The Wizard of Oz. They were shooting twenty-seven movies at the same time! Twenty-seven movies! Back then MGM owned their own theaters, so it was like a factory, turning out so many pictures. But then the anti-trust laws changed all that.

I learned that when I worked for Oscar Meyer. I was the "World's Smallest Chef, Little Oscar." Oscar Meyer made the world's best sausages, but they couldn't own ranches, they couldn't own cattle. I also played Buster Brown for Buster Brown Shoes. "My dog Ty lives in a shoe. I'm Buster Brown, look for me in there, too." That was on national television for five years, and national radio.

I got residuals. I had money in the bank. Every day there was more money in the mailbox. It was a blessing. It helped secure my future. I bought property here in Agoura and Los Angeles. I'm not well-to-do, but I'm not hurting. I get checks from all three unions: AFTRA, the Screen Actor's Guild—I did that and I made quite a reputation as a stand-in, photo double, stunt man. The producers loved us. We could stand in for the kid when the kid had to be in school. So whenever they rehearsed the lights or whatever, we would stand in. And in long shots, we could be photo doubles. And doing stunts was very lucrative, too, if it wasn't too dangerous.

I did a little radio. I was on the Edgar Bergen program. I played Gopherpuss, the intellectual friend of Charlie McCarthy in school. It was recorded at NBC studios at Vine & Sunset. I was scared of radio a little bit. I wasn't sure of myself. I wasn't competent. I didn't know what was funny or anything. And they had an audience.

My first line on coast-to-coast television was, "Due to the phrenological development of the occipital bone." That was my line on Edgar Bergen's TV show. It means pointed head, I think. But I didn't know what any of those words meant. I was lucky I could pronounce it. I appeared on the show four or five times. I was slimmer then, about three-foot-five, sixty pounds—skinny and small. And Edgar Bergen said I would be good for his movies. RKO called me and said they wanted me to be Charlie McCarthy in a couple of scenes and Mortimer Snerd. They made me up to look like Charlie McCarthy. I was in the movie *Here We Go Again*. At the beginning of every scene when he would walk in, sit down and whatever, that was me, and then for the close-ups they would bring the real dummy in.

Else Blangstead
BORN MAY 22, 1920
WERTSBURG, GERMANY
MUSIC EDITOR

A path of red and yellow roses leads to her front door, where she waits with a warm smile in a long robe. Though it's an unseasonably rainwashed day in North Hollywood, in her home it seems the sun is shining. She sits back on her big couch before a long table; beneath its glass is an immense mosaic of photographs. They're her family, friends, children of friends, lovers, all surrounded by tall bookshelves overflowing with books. At eighty she's spirited and funny, and beams with a beauty that seems to stem from a keen understanding of herself and her fellow humans. She's a person who knows and is known by scores of famous people, yet she's singularly unimpressed with fame. "I'm a talent groupie," she says with a smile. "Talent, to me, is far more impressive than celebrity." When speaking of Chaplin, for instance, her comments have less to do with his greatness, and much more to do with his egotism and lack of compassion.

Her life has been punctuated by passages of both triumph and tragedy, and though she modestly insists that living through it all hasn't resulted in any surplus of wisdom, she does admit that, if anything, she maintained a healthy sense of humor through it all. After the New Yorker magazine printed a forty-page narrative in 1988 detailing the remarkable series of events that is her life, from growing up in a Jewish family during the early days of Nazi Germany, getting pregnant out of wedlock as a teen, attempting suicide, giving birth to a daughter she was told was dead, leaving Germany as a girl to come to work in Hollywood as a nanny for Mervyn LeRoy before getting work in the studios, appearing in DeMille's Samson and Delilah, and eventually becoming one of Hollywood's best and most accomplished sound editors, through love affairs and marriages, through the death of her husband, to meeting again the daughter she thought she had lost long ago, and much more—her main response to it all is regret: "It all seems pretty grim," she says. "They left out all the humor."

170

I was born in 1920. I am happy to tell you that. I am very pleased to be alive at eighty. I am. I left Germany in 1935 to have a child. An illegitimate child. Which I was told was born dead. She *wasn't*. It's another story for another time. I went back to Germany in '37, worked in a house in Munich with children who simply had been abandoned by the Nazis, who took the parents away to be killed. They ranged from six months to sixteen years. It was a terrifying thing to talk about in detail, but it was good for me because I had lost this child. In my head. I am Jewish. *Very*. I like it. You undergo things. I did that from March to September and they shipped me off to go to America. I was seventeen.

So I came to Los Angeles, I went into service as a maid at $20 a month. I knew school English because I had shared a room with girls from Wales, Cardiff. So I spoke it a little strange, but I spoke it. I don't know how many people understood what I said [laughs] but I spoke it.

I worked for Mervyn LeRoy as a maid and took care of his son. When the boy went away to school, Harry Warner, who was the father-in-law, put me in the wardrobe department at Warners. I sewed there for a while. This was '38, '39, '40. I married the father of the baby who I thought was dead. I watched the people on the lot. I knew I wasn't going to be a director or a producer. So I watched the editors—they took the longest lunches, which really appealed to me.

I said, "Show me how to do this." And they did. And then eight years later, after a long struggle, you decide which part you choose. You do an apprenticeship as an assistant. They don't do it anymore, but in those days they did. And you determine if you want to be sound effect cutter, a music cutter, or a picture cutter. I liked music. There was a nice man who was a sound effect cutter and I told him to show me how to do it. He said, "You don't want to do this for a living. This is hard, this is boring. Go to the music department." My only music training is that I played piano as a girl, which every European child who had a piano in the house did. But I had to stop playing, because my father had a stroke and it irritated him.

I had a small part in *Samson and Delilah* with Cecil B. DeMille. He was a very strange man. You can see me in the movie—I am standing behind Hedy

Lamar and they put this wig on me with blonde curls that made me look like a cocker spaniel. There were 300 extras in this scene, who had to start running when Samson pulled down the walls of the temple. I asked DeMille if we could have a rehearsal, because there were all these extras running by and I didn't want to be trampled. But he refused, and did the scene, and—as you know, anytime you fear anything, that is when it will happen—I did get trampled. And I got hurt. It was terrible. And I never came back again, and that was the finish of my acting career.

DeMille was a strange man. He *was* Hollywood. He was a *concept*. He was an ugly, bald man in riding britches with a whip. He wanted *terror*, he wanted *confusion*, and when he got what he wanted he would get an erection. Such that everyone could see; there was no missing it. I did not like him.

So I start in a place called the Primrose Company. It was started by a little fellow who claimed to play clarinet for Paul Whiteman. He didn't but he always said he did. He and another crook at Columbia got together, and they charged Columbia $1,000 per reel. I was getting a lot of money, like $300 a week. They were getting rich.

I married Formar Blangstead, who was a film editor. He was sixteen years older than I was. I didn't want to be an editor, because they really get squeezed between the director and the producer. The director wants art, and the producer wants to save money. And the editor is in the middle. My husband, who I had not yet married at the time, was finishing *A Star Is Born*, with George Cukor directing. It was a wonderful movie, and they made him cut out, I think, six or seven songs. He suffered from that. He *loved* Cukor, he *loved* the film, and they butchered it.

I did a lot of television. Lots of television. The *worst*. *Hazel. Dennis the Menace*. And on and on, I don't remember them all, but they were God-awful. But I learned to cut music.

Many actors today believe in drugs. Just as those people in the olden days believed in glamour. They believed that there was *another* world. [Very slowly, pausing after each word.] There . . . is . . . no . . . other . . . world. But the one you live in. And you'd better make it as comfortable and as nourishing for yourself as you can. I'm saying that to *you*. And to everyone else who wants to listen.

I never went into that glamour world. I was working all the time. I did not go to premieres. I went only once to the Oscars. I went because my husband was up for an Academy Award for editing *Summer of '42*. He was in Rome at the time and couldn't go, so I went. That's boring. Now let me tell you. You sit there and then commercials come on and everything stops. When you see it on television, it's wonderful. I *never* miss it. Even if it's to belittle everybody. I *never* miss it.

Back then I was very nervous. For him. And the body is such an amazing instrument—they were getting to the editor category. "And the winner is . . . " And I couldn't hear it. I was *so* keyed up. It wasn't him that won. [Laughs] It was *French Connection*. But by that time when I realized he hadn't won, I was so glad to be back in the world. I *can't* describe it. It happened to him. He was nominated for *A Star Is Born*. And he was already in the aisle. And he didn't get it. This husband—Formar Blangstead. Look him up. Very good editor. I was a very good music editor. Basically, we loved drama. And it's an interpretation. He *loved* this business. He was a little Danish boy parking cars. And one day Zukor, who ran Paramount, Formar parked his car. Formar, this little Danish man, said, "I want to be in show business." Zukor gave him an appointment, and said, "Talk to C.B. DeMille." And DeMille said to him, "How much money do you have in the bank?" And Formar told him, and DeMille said, "That's not enough. Because even if I hired you, they'll be so much time you will not work, and you will not eat. So when you get some money in the bank, come back." He gave him a job in packing film, I think, is how he started. You see how prosaic this is?

172

So now he works, he works himself up to directing. He married Frank Capra's sister, and Capra decided one year to go to Europe. And there was a marquee: A Frank Capra Film. It was some cockamamie movie that Capra had nothing to do with. They were selling it in Europe as a Capra film. Capra sued Harry Cohn for a million dollars, which is like a *billion* dollars now. And Capra retired and Formar was blacklisted as a director, because he was Capra's son-in-law. And then he got a job as an editor at Warner Brothers for a very nice man who pretended to be sick. The movie was *Rhapsody in Blue*, and he said, "I'm not really feeling that well, let Formar finish it." And Formar did it, and that was his first feature, and he worked there for forty years.

Now comes the catch. He's retired, reluctantly, but retired. And he writes an autobiography. It was called *The Not So Sad Dane*. And he—remembering—*glorified* these people. These *villains*. Because he *needed* to do that. He needed them to be as great as he obviously always thought they were. And I *swear* to you, I think the disappointment killed him. Something happened. He was hired to do *Man of La Mancha*, and they came back with a very bad movie. Everybody was drunk, everybody was fucking each other, it was just a *mess*. And United Artists, who this picture was made for, confronted the director and said, "You're *fired*. We spent millions on this." He said, "Don't fire me. I will give you a picture." And that was the end of my husband's career. And he became ill. And he imagined this illness, and when he imagined it, it became true. And the heart . . . and the prostate . . . and he *died*.

This love affair, and I am the one who got away, so you have to really talk to people who believe it. There are many more. They need to. But it wasn't glamorous. I was working in my cubicle. And before I could work, I had to wash the walls down, because they were so filthy.

When Formar became ill, which was probably '76, I couldn't leave him alone, and I built myself a studio on top of the garage. And I worked from there. And did well. Liked it. It was unusual then to have a home studio. In fact, it was against the law. Cops kept coming up. Didn't bother me much, though. Yes, I did that, and then it became easier and easier. And I would do a movie like *The Color Purple*, and I would hire people. I became a company. I was the spearhead. And the pictures got better. I could choose who I worked with. Mostly Dave [Grusin]. Really mostly Dave. Quincy [Jones] didn't want to do any more films then, he just wanted to do records. That was the beauty. Because the people I chose or who chose me, they did well. There was something about the chemistry. Patrick Williams. Johnny Mandel. Mandel is a great melodian. And give me a melody, and I am happy.

173

We were hired to do a film for Stanley Kramer, who I loved. Nice man. Played it tough on the outside, butterball on the inside. It was called *Bless the Beasts and the Children*. It wasn't very good. Stanley wasn't a good director. He was a good producer, but not a good director, though he didn't want to know it. And Perry and some guy named Barry DeVorzon did the music. And DeVorzon did *diddly-winks*. But he was the front man. Perry was the worker. Good man. Nice man. So there's talking and we're spotting, and the choir is *singing*, the trumpets are *blowing*, and the violins are *sawing*, in every-body's imagination. And we got through about seven, and I said, "Are you guys free for dinner?" And we went to the Nickodell on Melrose. We went frequently to the Nickodell because it was next door to Paramount, and everybody at Paramount went there.

And I said, "Now, let's forget the trumpets, let's forget the choir, let's forget it all, and remember only one thing. It's a lullaby for abused children. It's a *lullaby*. And they wrote this *stunner* of a song. Which became a hit because a little acrobat [Nadia Comenici] used it as her theme in the Olympics—They called it "Nadia's Theme," but it was "Bless the Beasts and the Chil-dren." So I did that and I did that well because I am verbal. And musicians are not.

Hollywood was a nice town back then. It's not now. It wasn't ever Beverly Hills, even then. But I once saw Ava Gardner on Hollywood Boulevard. And I was *knocked out*. It was the prettiest human I ever saw. *Beautiful* girl. I knew I recognized her from a movie. So, yes, *Hollywood* was nice then, because there was Paramount, there was Columbia and that drugstore on Sunset & Gower around the corner.

Lee J. Cobb, the actor, was a dear friend of mine. Sinatra saved his life. Lee had a series of heart attacks and couldn't recuperate. It was a bad time, after the Un-American thing. He was doing *Death of a Salesman* and they would be in front of his door at the hotel every night and ask him the same question. And he finally became ill. Frank Sinatra, who had done a film with him, gave him an apartment when he got out of the hospital. Sent him a key. A gorgeous apartment with a houseboy on Fountain Avenue in Hollywood.

174

Lee then met my best friend, Mary. He was by then doing *The Brothers Karamazov*, and they got married. And Lee said to me, "You're good with words. Write me a letter to send to Frank and tell him how he saved my life." So I did.

Yearrrrrrs go by. I am reunited with my David [Wayne]. And Mary, my friend, is very ill. And very poor, because Lee was a gambler. *Big* time. I told David the story of how Sinatra did this for Lee. David, who did a film and was friends with Sinatra, called him. And Sinatra sent $5000 to Mary.

So when my David was dying, I was here with him. He was dying of lung cancer. I wrote *another* letter to Sinatra. It was funny, now. I told him we had become best pen-pals! I wrote him, "Our David is dying. I want you to write to him to make him feel that all the wonderful things he ever thought about you his whole life were true."

[Softly] And he *did*. Makes me cry. It was a *wonderful* letter. [Affecting Sinatra-like tone] "Hey Buddy. Wilbur is still going strong," Wilbur, probably the name for the genitals, "and I'm glad you're going well, and glad that you got Else back." You know, *stuff*. And I never met him. *Never* met him. But I know he did terrible things, but he did wonderful things, too. This is *certifiable*. I still have that letter.

Then Elmer Bernstein, who is still my friend, hired me to work on *Walk on the Wild Side*. He did a wonderful blues score for it. I did that and I got my taste for feature. Big difference. *Big* difference. Television, they just mostly want to get it fast. I worked with Elmer a lot, I liked him. They tell me he's a womanizer, but I don't care. I never had this problem with any of them. It never went below the belt.

Yes, I met Chaplin. There was no awe meeting Chaplin. Charlie Chaplin was a human. He was the most egomaniacal guy I have ever met. I went to a party. You may wonder how all these parties happened. I don't really know, but I think that what that crowd found attractive in me is that there was no fear or adoration; there was an equality. How that happened I don't know. I'm an Oppenheimer by birth and we're naturally arrogant people. [Laughs]

Tim Durant had a few people for dinner, and Charlie and Oona [O'Neill

Chaplin] were there, and Oona was already very pregnant. And Charlie was telling story after story, and wonderfully acting them out. And Oona kept saying, "Charlie, I really have to go home." She looked like she was going to faint. He'd say, "Yes, honey," and then right back into a story: "Now, let me tell you. . . ." I felt very sorry for Oona. More sorry than I was entertained by Chaplin's stories.

I am a talent groupie, you might as well know that. Not a Hollywood groupie but a talent groupie.

I lived near Charlie and Oona in Switzerland, in Lake Geneva. Their house was very beautiful—but not as beautiful as mine. He lived there with his family and his servants. He was God there. On the lake there's a wonderful, wonderful statue of him. He was really God there. I think he lived a good life. Many children. At peace.

I am divorced from my first husband and the rent was $42 a month on Curson. So I took two girls to share the rent. And one of them was in love with Sydney Chaplin. She came from San Francisco, where her parents were Communist Party members. Now Charlie had the reputation of being, if not a Communist, certainly very socially to the left. And they were in love and Charlie said to Sydney, "If you marry this girl, I will disown you." She married Huntington Hartford instead. [Laughs] This is Hollywood. At least it was my Hollywood. Huntington Hartford was good looking, but he didn't have a brain in his head. I met him and I didn't want any part of him but I told him I had a really pretty girl with a broken heart who shares my house, they met, he fell in love with her, she married him, she stayed drunk on champagne for seven years. [Laughs] They never had children. She left him without alimony. Just left. Married a poor actor in New York somewhere. So I'm trying to give you the human side of what is headlines.

Lois Sidney
BORN APRIL 4, 1921
HOLLYWOOD, CALIFORNIA
SECRETARY / MOTHER / WIFE

She lives in a nice house in West Hollywood, on a street called Norma, named in honor of the actress Norma Talmadge, who once lived on the corner. A happy, pretty woman, she projects an air of calm contentment, and gets rattled only once and only slightly, when she receives a phone call from her daughter regarding finances. Eager to share her memories of old Hollywood, which she had outlined prior to my arrival, she tapes the interview herself for her own records. She sets out a tray of bagels, cream cheese, jelly and coffee, and sits at her dining room table in the center of her sunny home. A Hollywood native, her first memories are of sneaking into movie studios back in the silent era to watch while films were being made.

There was a movie studio on the southeast corner of Irving & Melrose in the mid-twenties when I was a kid. It was called Tec-Art. I can remember that we kids used to crawl over the back fence of that studio. And we would watch them shooting movies. You know, you could do that then. I do remember watching Noah Berry—Wallace Berry's brother—and Gertrude Olmstead, a silent star—shooting a film there.

We lived on Norton & Windsor in the twenties when I was growing up. I went to a motion picture theater on Larchmont. It was there for many years, just south of Beverly Boulevard on the west side of the street. Admission was ten cents. I remember that I liked to go alone because when I came home, I could rehearse all the dialogue in my head and figure out how I would have done it. They would show a feature and there were also lots of short subjects and serials. Serials were a big thing then.

I remember one about Stoneface, a man whose face would never change. It was very scary. There was another short subject where you would sing along with the bouncing ball—the words were on the screen, and the ball would bounce from word to word and everybody would sing along. Those were the days of features with people like Ramon Navarro. I remember somehow my mother got a dime every Saturday and sent me off to the movies.

In the thirties, we lived near KHJ, the radio station. We kids would walk up to listen to them recording radio dramas. We went because they had a warmup before the recorded performances and Morey Amsterdam was the warmup comedian and they passed out doughnuts. Well, we kids were always there for the doughnuts.

There was a restaurant just to the west of there. A lot of the comics went there. I remember I dated this comic for a long time, Louie Quinn. His claim to fame was that he was Roscoe in "77 Sunset Strip." I remember Louie used to take me up there and all the comedians would hang out. It was fun.

There used to be a restaurant right off Marathon, behind the Paramount lot, called Oblath's. Oblath's was there for years and years and years and all the studio guys used to hang out there and get tanked. It was an institution.

On Van Ness, just south of Melrose, for many years, was a big indoor ice-skating rink. It was a very popular place because you could go for a quarter and skate. I worked in Beverly Hills. I was a TV writer's agent then. I would leave the door unlocked.

In 1942, my husband enlisted in the army because he was so scared of being drafted. He was in the first motion picture unit. That was where

Ronald Reagan said he was killing all the Nazis. The first motion picture unit was at the old Selznick studios in Culver City. It was set up to make training films, which they did.

Since my husband was stationed in Culver City, he came home every night. We lived on Doheny in our first apartment then. He lived at home, and then went to the studio every day, where he was supposed to put music to training films. And I will tell you, parenthetically, that he told me one day that a friend of his from the Motion Picture Unit would be coming over to pick up something. The doorbell rang, and I opened the door, and I swear to God, I thought I would faint. There stood the most beautiful man I have *ever* seen. His name was Frances X. Shields. He had been a tennis champ and had had several marriages, including one to an Italian contessa. He was the most handsome man I had ever seen, and he was Brook Shields' grandfather. And she looks just like him. He was very tall, and a Wimbledon player. He's in all the books.

All of the guys in the Motion Picture Unit were *so* hilarious. Because they were all show-biz people. What used to happen was that the writers would go to the fence—there was a fence around the first Motion Picture Unit—and their agents would come up to the fence and they would negotiate deals through the fence. And they'd go home at night and write.

They used to do drills in the parking lot of the Cotton Club in Culver City. The parking lot was huge, so that all these Hollywood clowns could use it and pretend that they were real soldiers. One particular day the guy in charge said, "We're going to have a volunteer who is going to drill us today." So there was a kid there from Wisconsin who volunteered to lead the drill. He stood up there and the guys were ready for him, all lined up, and the kid says, "Forward march!" So they march, but there was an automobile parked in the parking lot in their way. So the men march up the car, over the top of the car, down the other side, and this kid is watching them with such horror that he can't remember what to say. So he says, "To the rear, march!" So the guys turn around, walk up, over the car, and down again. I mean they were such clowns.

When I was growing up, nobody had any money. I mainly wore hand-me-downs from my mother's friends. And my father who had a factory would send me fabric and I would make clothes. The main place to shop in Hollywood was the big department store that became the Broadway, but it was the H.B. Guyes Company then. And then there were some well-known specialty shops, like Mandell Shoes. But shopping was not a big deal, because after World War II, nobody had any money. So shopping was limited to the essentials.

Because my husband lived at home and made $52 a month, obviously I had to go to work. A friend of ours ran Consolidated Film Industries, on Hudson in Hollywood. Still there. It's where all the film is developed for studios who don't have their own labs. So Sid Solow, who ran it for forty years or so, hired me. I worked there and learned all about how film is developed. I printed *The Outlaw* on the automatic printer.

In the fifties I went to work for a man who was a writer's agent. He was the first person to hire blacklisted writers during the Hollywood blacklist of the fifties. The House Un-American Activities Committee ruined more lives than I could possibly go into here. This agent was one of the nicest people in the whole world. He would get them work, but they would have to write under pseudonyms. It was all the best talent in Hollywood.

I can tell you that around 1940 on Santa Monica Boulevard an ice cream parlor opened up called Will Wright's. It was *fan-tastic*. Susan Heyward was one of the owners. I only met her once. There was also a restaurant on Sunset & Doheny called the Nu Burger that made traditional hamburgers, but with chopped peanut butter on it. It was the most delicious, most *fabulous* thing you would ever want to eat.

On the corner of Crescent Heights & Sunset was Schwab's. In 1939 I dated a guy who was the cook there. His name was Chuck Jones. He was an American Indian. I remember one night he got so drunk that he said to me, "I don't think I should drive you home. You'd better drive." I said, "That's great. Except I don't know how to drive." You know, not everybody had cars in those days. It was a big deal to have a car. We rode the public transportation.

Also on the southwest corner of Crescent Heights & Sunset was the Garden of Allah, which was a fabulous hotel with little bungalows. Very famous because F. Scott Fitzgerald wrote there. I dated a musician, a very good-looking Jewish guy, and I would go there while he played his set. It was a favorite hangout for many stars, but it was very discreet.

My husband worked with Harold Lloyd. Now when Harold Lloyd decided to put music to some of his films, my husband was the editor, and he went to Europe to record music because it was cheaper, and Harold Lloyd was very cheap. But Harold Lloyd was very fond of him. Everyone liked him.

I remember driving to Santa Barbara to a preview of one of his films, *The Freshman*. And somehow I ended up in the limo with Harold Lloyd. And all I remember about that trip is that he talked a lot about the fact that he would buy a two-pound box of chocolates and put it in his entry hall, and all of these freeloading friends from his silent days would come and eat all the chocolates.

Harold Lloyd was probably the richest man in Hollywood. He owned all his own films. He owned a lot of land—he had a thick notebook, and each page represented another parcel of land that he owned in the city of Los Angeles. He was *enormously* rich. At the house he had a famous Christmas tree with a world-famous collection of imported Christmas tree ornaments. It would go up in the entry hall. It was huge and would stay there for a couple of months. He also had a room in the house devoted to his photography. He was a skillful still photographer and he liked to photograph nudes. He had some guy who found locations, and he would go out to the desert and shoot all these artistic nude shots. He had a whole room devoted to this.

He had a granddaughter that he doted on. He left her in charge of the estate when he died. She was the *dumbest* little girl imaginable. [*Whispers*] He was very tight. And he was very rich. What happened to his money, I don't know.

I can remember when Sunset Boulevard had a horseback path down the middle. Sunset Boulevard used to be divided from just west of Doheny to about Walden. Maybe further than that. There was a path in the center of the street with hedges on the side, right down the middle, where people rode horses.

A friend of mine was secretary to the Marx Brothers, and I helped Groucho's second wife decorate her house. He was also very tight. Like a lot of people, he was extremely careful with the small amount of money. Groucho would not pay to park. He would circle the block endlessly until he found a parking place. But he was very generous with large amounts. I remember once that my friend said to me that one year Groucho got a $25,000 refund check from the IRS. This was back when $25,000 was a lot of money. Groucho said to my friend, "Send it to Betty." Betty was his first wife, the mother of Arthur Marx. He said, "Send it to Betty, because I know she needs it."

There is a street in the Hollywood Hills called Magnetic Terrace. It is north of Sunset and east of Doheny. I remember as a kid, during one of my father's infrequent visits to either us kids or Los Angeles—I don't know *where* the hell he was—he drove an air-cooled Franklin. And he took us up to this very steep street, and put the car in neutral. And it rolled uphill. This street still exists. The explanation either was that it was an optical illusion—which I find hard to believe, because the car rolled right up and I was sure my father was going to go over the edge because it was so close—or that this hill was on a larger hill, and the magnetic force of the larger hill was greater than the magnetism in the earth of the smaller hill, and created this effect. He wasn't stepping on the gas, I know it. I had forgotten about Magnetic Terrace till now.

The decline of Hollywood saddens me greatly. And it's just a perfect example of how the ability to manage complicated urban society is simply beyond the grasp of the bureaucrats who are in charge. They don't know what to do. They spent all that money on those dumb stars on the Walk of Fame.

I remember that Hollywood Boulevard was an inviting and vibrant and wonderful place to visit in those days. The Pig & Whistle was a wonderful restaurant. And I loved C.C. Brown's—they had the absolute best ice-cream sundaes. And the Garden Court Hotel. I learned to play tennis at the Poinsettia playground court. This tennis pro used to hang around there and watch us—he was a pedophile. But there were some champion players who came out of Poinsettia.

190

Also the Gotham Deli, just west of Highland, was a very good deli. And when you hit La Brea, that's where the Red Cars went diagonally through what is now an alley—it's why those houses are all shaped that way, because of the Red Car track that were there.

The Red Cars rode on electricity from overhead wires. People said they were dirty, and that they caused damage to the streets. Totally untrue. They didn't do a damn thing. We just woke up one morning in 1947 and General Motors and Standard Oil had ripped up all the tracks, and they were gone. They wanted to put buses in. I know for a fact it was them; General Motors sold the buses, and Standard Oil put the gas in them, and smog was born. Smog was unheard of when I was growing up. Unheard of.

But what happens now, because the memory of Hollywood & Vine still lingers, you take people up there and they're horrified. It is all in a state of decay. And it needn't have been that way. Because it used to be special. It used to be beautiful.

Steve Allen

BORN DECEMBER 16, 1921
NEW YORK, NEW YORK
COMEDIAN/TV HOST/SONGWRITER/AUTHOR

The summit of a long stairway adorned with many hundred framed magazine covers, each of which bears his famous name and equally famous face, almost iconic now behind his black glasses. He sits at the same desk he's sat at for more than fifty years, here in the Van Nuys office that seems to appear much as it did when he first moved in, back in the fifties. At the top of this stairway are the twin office suites of Meadowlane, the company he founded with his beloved wife Jayne Meadows. His suite contains a busy staff of people, each working on the multiple facets of his remarkable career. There are new songs to be transcribed, new books coming out, a new musical he's completed, new versions of his PBS historical talk-show series "Meeting of the Minds" coming out on video, and more. Yet despite this whirlwind of ongoing activity, he takes out the time in his schedule on more than one occasion to answer questions about his days in Hollywood, days which began when he was a child and continued into stardom. A writer himself, he appreciates the focus of the questions, and unlike others who veer continuously into many tangents, he never strays once from the subject.

Most of the world knew he was tremendously funny, inventive and productive. What they might not have known, but probably could sense, was that he was also a tremendously nice guy. Up to his eightieth year, the man never stopped creating, yet he always took substantial time out, and with much joy, to spend with his wife and children. People that knew him well knew that the only thing more important to him than his work was his family. He died in October 2000, at a place known to be among his happiest, the home of his son.

181

I first came to Hollywood when I was four years old—I remember because I have seen a photograph of me here. But my first memories of Hollywood are when I was six, and I came to Hollywood to live with my aunt. I lived at the home of a then-director of films, Ben Holmes, who was married to my mother's vaudeville partner, Flossie Everett. So I have a very clear recollection of that time. To this day when I go into Hollywood off of the 101 at Highland, I often find myself looking up the hillside at the old house, which was on Camrose. It was a very pleasant experience and therefore it leads to very pleasant recollections. The house is still there. In that day there was no freeway, of course, and little traffic. That was in the late twenties.

So I can remember living up there with another little boy who lived in the neighborhood. His name was Peter and my mother told me he was the son of some well-known actor or writer. Anyway, here we were, just two little six-year-old kids, sitting on what seemed to us like a high mountain. It was just two blocks up the hill, but when you're little everything seems so big. And I remember seeing the little red streetcars going up Cahuenga. They're not there anymore. They looked like toys wandering around the green hills and the green trees. So all of Hollywood to me, coming from Chicago, seemed like a park. I thought people here live in a park! Cause in Chicago they also had places where they had trees and grass—but only in the park. Other than that, in the poorer neighborhoods where I came from, there was just broken glass and garbage, like in any big city.

My memories of Hollywood from then are just little snapshot memories, most memories of childhood are. You remember a twelve-second scene from my fourth birthday but what-the-hell else was going on I have no recollection. One of the things I remember with pleasure was that Ben Holmes had a car with a rumble seat. And I can still remember it as if it was right there.

I remember ice being delivered. I can still smell the wet wood in the back of the trucks. It was wet because ice would melt during the day as they delivered it. I can remember what an important figure the iceman was, especially to kids. It was pretty important to adults too, because there was no refrigeration in those days. Either you got ice or your fish turned rotten in about twenty minutes. The milk soured. They were big strong guys—they had to be bruisers because they carried hundred-pound blocks of ice three or four stories, with tongs over their shoulders, wearing a big leather thing to protect their clothing. There were always chips of ice because sometimes they would chop the ice and split it for people. So as soon as they left the trucks, about nine kids—of which I was one—would jump up on the back step and stick our hands under the canvas cover and grab little pieces of ice and on a hot day begin to chew on them to alleviate the suffering from the heat. That must have gone on in all big cities.

182

I had a very disorganized childhood, as you may have already assumed. There was always some question of who the hell's gonna take care of him between now and Tuesday. I would be given to uncles and strangers and the people upstairs and so forth. I thought that was life, so I didn't complain. It was because my folks were in show business. And also because my mother's family was a little nutty. Today the key word is "dysfunctional."

At one point I was put in the care of my Uncle Bill. His profession was meatpacker. He was a bachelor, and he had to go to work. He would show up about six at night. I remember coming in off the street one day from school and he wasn't there. And I was *hungry*. So I looked in the icebox, but there was no food I could eat there, no sausage or butter or bread. *Nothing*. So I looked in the cupboard and I found a supply of Carnation condensed milk. So I made myself some cocoa and to show my Uncle Bill that he was a schmuck and to make him feel guilty, I made it with six cans of condensed milk and piled them up in a big pyramid so he could see it when he walked in.

We were on the second floor and I used to spend a lot of time looking out the window. There wasn't much to see inside the window. In those days milk was delivered to the house. And I suddenly saw this milk wagon, which was pulled by two white horses, and the horses were in *runaway* mode. They were running like hell, like horses in a Western movie. There was enormous commotion, and the wagon was getting pulled from side to side over the cable car tracks, and you could hear the glass breaking inside as all the bottles broke. It must have been a *hell* of a mess. When you're six years old, you remember a sight like that.

The next time I was in Hollywood after that period is when I was sixteen, and I hitchhiked there from Chicago. I remember from that time being impressed by the glamour of the fact that I was in the town where motion pictures came from. About once a week I would go to the movies alone. In those days, during the Depression, they used to give away sets of dishes at the movies. If you went to twelve movies, you could have a complete set of cups and saucers and dishes.

I was there one night. I had no interest in the dishes. The movie stopped and a guy went up to make some announcements. Now in the movie I had seen there were probably fifty-seven actors, and one of them had one line, a bit player. Then the announcer said, "By the way, we have with us tonight Harvey Krellman—or whatever his name was—who played the part of the doctor in the movie you just saw." And I was about as thrilled as you would be today if Elvis really *was* alive and he suddenly stood up right here in front of you. A person off the *screen*, and I had just *seen* him! He passed about an inch from me, and I was *really* impressed.

183

I've never forgotten that early conditioning to fame or celebrity or glamour, so that to this day if somebody interprets me in that way—simply because I'm on television—I'm kinder to them than I might otherwise be. It's not that I'm such a nice guy, but I was once the guy standing there with his mouth open staring at some actor. So I understand how people feel about that.

In 1944 I got my first job in Hollywood in radio, after working in radio in Phoenix. I got a crummy one-room place in this crummy rooming house on Cahuenga, just north of Franklin, where the road now goes under the freeway. There was an old Raymond Chandler–like hotel there across the street, I think it was called the St. Francis.

At night I would go down to the Mayflower donut shop on Hollywood Boulevard and buy a bag of six chocolate-covered doughnuts—I didn't know much about nutrition then—and I'd buy a quart of milk, and that would be my evening meal, because money was getting low and I had to pay the rent. I would eat two or three of those just to disguise the hunger enough so I could fall asleep, and then when I awakened in the morning I would eat a couple more doughnuts.

I used to keep the bag by the bed so that I would have enough strength to get out of bed. I'd finish the milk, get dressed, and go down to the drugstore. I remember they had the worst-tasting orange juice ever. I didn't know orange juice could be bad. But the reason it was bad is because these were the reject oranges. All the good oranges went to the military. If you were in the army, you had all the orange juice you wanted because it served the nation's interest to keep you in good shape. But I remember the guy used to cut them in half and squeeze them with the hand squeezer. It was terrible, but the only reason I used to drink it was because it was better than no juice at all.

Hollywood Boulevard then had a very great restaurant—Musso & Frank's—but I couldn't afford to eat there. But I knew about it because of my mother, Flossie, who was an entertainer, told me that it was a very glamorous place. Hollywood Boulevard also had the memorabilia shops, where you could get eight-by-tens of Greta Garbo or Clark Gable. And it had some good bookstores, which they still do.

In later years, after I was working in radio, I used to go to the Brown Derby fairly often because it was right in the heart of Hollywood. It was one of those touches of glamour which lasted for a long time. It was a good restaurant, prices were fair, good food and very good service. It was a large space. All of us who were in the business would frequently find ourselves there. It was more of a radio hangout than a movie hangout because radio was all centered just a few blocks from there.

184

NBC was at the corner of Sunset & Vine. Right across from a then-famous music store, Wallich's Music City. It was in the window of that store that I sat once for a week, in fact, and wrote 350 songs in one week, that had to be publicly demonstrated.

Hollywood's decline had to do with economic factors. The studios needed more space. And most of what people now think of as Hollywood moved out into the Valley—like Warner Brothers and Universal.

Hollywood had the great system of red street cars, and it's a true scandal why we no longer have those. The real answer was offered by Carey McWilliam in his magazine *The Nation*. It was actually a plot by the people who were in the rubber tire business. They realized that nobody would need their tires if these streetcars were so inexpensive and could take you every place you want to go. It was a great system. Cars were big and serviceable, they were electric, there was no pollution, so they were great. So the tire people and the oil and fuel people—the Standard Oil types—conspired together. They bought up the transportation system and they junked it, to force people to use cars. That's an abuse of the free enterprise system.

To this day occasionally if time factors are not important, I deliberately get off the freeway and drive surface streets just because I like to see people and trees and stores and dogs and life. Whereas on the freeway all you see are other cars and concrete, and maybe mountains, if there are any in the area. Hollywood was more like a city that was organic then. Hollywood was more *hamishe*—so to speak—in the old days.

Tommy Farrell
BORN OCTOBER 7, 1921
HOLLYWOOD, CALIFORNIA
ACTOR/COMEDIAN

Friendly, warm smiling eyes. Lots of large photos. Photos of him on a horse in cowboy duds; photos of him in Singing in the Rain, photos of his children and his wife and his famous, beloved mother, the actress Glenda Farrell; photos of famous friends such as Lucille Ball and Gene Kelly. Within this little bungalow he shares with his wife at the Motion Picture Country Home, it feels more like a rural Connecticut home than a California cabana. He's survived three separate cancers to not only talk but joke about them: "They took out the entire first floor and most of the wine cellar," he says, evoking abundant laughter from all lucky enough to be within earshot. Later he mentions that the one good thing about testicular cancer is that his pants fit better now. His is a narrow, elfish face framed by large silver aviator glasses and a profusion of wavy silver hair. With his wife listening and occasionally tossing in her own comments, he speaks happily and jokes frequently about a life that has been totally shaped by Hollywood and the movies.

I was born in what was then the Hollywood Hospital. My mother was not well-off then, and she used to make my diapers out of rags she'd sew together. My mother started on the stage when she was fourteen. Doing *Rebecca of Sunnybrook Farm*. In the twenties my mother was in New York. She was on the stage, she did one play right after another. She was in a show in New York called *Life Begins*, and Warner Brothers bought the show. Mervyn LeRoy was doing the picture. They brought her out to Hollywood to do that picture. But instead she did *Little Caesar*. That was the first one that came out. Then she did *I'm a Fugitive from a Chain-Gang* with Paul Muni, and then she did *Life Begins*.

My mother was a delight to be with. A wonderful person. She always put me first. I didn't know the other mothers, but mine was a beauty. She loved people, and she had a great sense of humor. Oh, she loved to laugh. She was the best audience, the best laugh ever. She was also very serious about her work, and a very professional actress. A fast study, she'd always learn her lines very quickly.

During the twenties, when she was in New York, my grandpa and grandma took care of me. They lived on Crenshaw, just south of Wilshire. In 1931, we lived at the Hillview Hotel on Hollywood Boulevard. Now that's about as much into Hollywood as you can get. The Hillview was a small hotel that is still there at Hollywood & Wilcox, right next to the Janes' House. Back then it was an actor's hotel. The five Blondells lived there: Joan and her father, Bobby, and Gloria. The whole *meshpuchah* lived there. Pat and

Eloise O'Brien. Jack LaRue. Jack LaRue used to make spaghetti once a week. For *everybody*. The way he would tell if it was done [laughs] is that he'd throw it up against the kitchen wall. And if it stuck, it was done.

Then we moved to the Montecito, which was another actor's hotel. When Mom was signed at Warner Brothers, she had two pictures out by that time and she got a raise, so we moved to the Sunset Towers. Which is still there. (Now called *The Argyle*.) Then she bought a house in Studio City and she liked it, so she bought three more. And moved her whole family out there from Oklahoma.

186

Hollywood Boulevard in the thirties was *delightful*. Strolling the boulevard was a very popular pastime. And you'd see everybody there, walking up and down the boulevard. There was no crime, nothing to worry about. It was very pleasant. It was a nice place to live.

There were a million great places on the boulevard. We would love to go to Musso & Frank's, especially for their flannel cakes. That was a very special place to go. Pig & Whistle, next to the Egyptian Theater. I remember their cream of tomato soup was their specialty. It was *sensational*. C.C. Brown's for hot fudge sundaes. Which was great up until it closed. The hot fudge sundae was 35 cents then. [Laughs]

It was a whole different world then. The Red Car ran down Hollywood Boulevard. There were no traffic jams ever. You never knew such a thing existed then. And you could get on the Red Car and ride all the way to Santa Monica. And go to the beach. And get on the Red Carr and ride all the way back. [Laughs]

And Sunset Boulevard had a bridal path running right down the middle of it. You'd see people riding horses.

My mother sent me to St. John's boarding school, which was near downtown. But I would come home on the weekends. My mother was dating Lyle Talbot for a while, and he took me to my first movie. It was Joe E. Brown in *Top Speed*. At the Warners Theater right there on Hollywood Boulevard at Wilcox.

My mother bought a 1937 Ford, which was a very fancy car at the time. And we had a wonderful colored man who was the houseman and also the chauffeur. So if I wanted to go somewhere, he would take me in the Ford. We would drive through the Valley—which was different then. All citrus fruit—oranges, grapefruit, lemons, tangerines—as far as the eye could see. Driving out to the Valley then from Hollywood was different, because there was no freeway. The Cahuenga Pass then was just a little road, with two lanes on each side, and cars got stuck going up the hill. The Model A made it, but the Model T didn't like it. That was the only way to get from Hollywood into the Valley. You could go over Laurel Canyon then—but only if you had a good horse. [Laughs]

When Mom started working at Warners it was Warners-First National. It was at 5858 Sunset, which is now a TV station KTLA-TV. That's where they made *Life Begins* and *Little Caesar* and *Fugitive*—those movies were all done there.

The thing I remember best about that studio was the big cars. The Duesenbergs and the Packards and the great big Cadillacs, V-12s and V-16s. They were enormous, these things, and *beautiful*. If an actor wanted to buy a car, he had his secretary call the car company and say so-and-so was interested in a car, and the company would bring a car that day out to the studio. And if you liked it, you would say, "Can I get it in brown and yellow?" And they would say yes and deliver your car to the studio.

I watched my mom work in the movies and I figured it was a good thing to do. I loved the people. But movie work interfered with what I *really* wanted to be—a *cowboy*. [Shows photo of himself at about age eight riding a horse on Crenshaw.]

I must have been fifteen before I realized that "That-sonofabitch-Jack-Warner" was not one word. [Laughs] He was never liked. Nobody that was under contract to the studio really liked him. Just when you were about to get a raise, he'd fire you. Unless you were making a lot of money for the studio, and then he'd give you half of what you should get. Or if somebody was ready to retire [laughs], he'd let them go so that he wouldn't have to pay retirement. My mom finally left [Warners] in 1939. Because they wanted her to make eight pictures a year, which was too many. Some years she'd have to do two or three pictures at the same time.

I met Paul Muni many times. A wonderful actor, and a nice man. My mom used to come home raving about the scenes they were in together. They did a picture together called *High Nelly*. And she said, "Oh, it's such a pleasure to work with that man."

Joan Blondell was my godmother. Funny, wonderful—another good laugher. Full of life, full of energy. She'd say, "Let's go—what are we doing now?"

I remember visiting my mom when she was making *The Mystery of the Wax Museum* with Lionel Atwell. Scared the living hell out of me. Oh boy, I let out a *geshray* that you could hear in Cleveland. [Laughs] He had the mask on. In the studio there's a double-door going into the set. He came through that door with that terrible mask on and whoa! It scared the hell out of me. He was doubled up laughing. He said, "Tommy, it's me—Mr. Atwell." And I said, "But what happened to you?" And he said, "This is for the picture," and I said, "Oh boy!" But he was very nice. They almost all were nice—that includes Errol Flynn and Humphrey Bogart and Jimmy Cagney.

Bogart couldn't have been nicer. He was different offscreen than on. He was never that serious—that I remember. He laughed all the time and he always talked about his boat. The big love in his life was his boat. And he was down there all the time whenever he had a chance. He showed me pictures of his boat. Everybody had boats then.

My first movie was *At War with the Army*, with Martin and Lewis. It was their first picture, too. Jerry Lewis ran the show. Dean Martin was the most easygoing guy in the world. And Jerry had this great hyperkinetic energy. Dean would say, "Can't we go and play golf now?" [Laughs]

I started on Broadway. In 1941 I did a show called *Strip for Action*. Then the war came and I enlisted in the air force. After the war I did a show for George Abbott and then I went into nightclubs. And I did nightclubs from 1946 to 1950. I did an act with Peter Marshall, who went on to fame as the host of "Hollywood Squares." I was a song and dance man. [Shows photo of "Marshall & Farrell" in action.] Peter sang, and we did some patter songs together. He was the straight-man and I was the comic. And we did a *helluva* good act. We played the Waldorf in New York. We were in the last days of vaudeville; the theaters were closing behind us. We played the Olympian in Miami, the Chicago Theater and the Palmer House in Chicago, the Paramount, the Palace in New York, we opened the Fountainebleu in Miami, Ciro's in Hollywood and the Biltmore downtown. We did a benefit show one day here in L.A., and they had added a couple of acts to fill out the bill. Opening for us was a young magician, and he was very funny doing his stuff. His name was Johnny Carson. He started out doing a magic act.

Peter Marshall and I were both offered TV shows. He was offered one called "Shorty" with Buddy Hackett for Columbia. About sailors. I was offered a show at Desilu called "This is Alice." A story about a little girl, and I was the father. There was a whole plethora of dumb father shows, which featured the children. "Hi, honey, I'm home!" One of *those* kind of characters.

Desilu had two studios then—one in Culver City and one in Hollywood. We were in Hollywood. Lucy [Lucille Ball] would come by at least once a week and stick her head in the dressing room, and say, "How are you doing, darling? You need anything? You need anything, you know where to find me." She ran the studio. Oh boy. Every part of it. People thought Desi [Arnaz] was the businessman. [Laughs] Desi was either at the track or on his boat. Or traveling between the two. Lucy ran it. Desi just liked to play around. Lucy was the brains. *Oh, was she smart.* The ultimate professional, that lady. I did eleven of the "Here's Lucy" shows with her. She liked me. ["Lucy liked *professionals*," Tommy's wife injected. "Tommy's a very fast study."]

If you knew your lines and came on and did what you were supposed to do, Lucy was behind you 150 percent. But if you came on and you didn't know your lines, you'd get hollered at. [Pause] She was wonderful with me.

We did those in front of a live audience. Three cameras. She'd have all the big storyboards up on the wall, and you could read your dialogue from the boards. If you didn't know it. But I always knew it. She liked that.

189

I liked doing movies more than doing TV. Because there was more pressure on TV. You shoot a picture and it depends—a good one you shoot for months. That TV show's gotta be done in a week. My favorite of all was vaudeville. I wasn't crazy about nightclubs. Except for a very few places. Vaudeville, they came in to see you. And they're not drinking, they're sitting there listening. And you don't have to do an hour an a half, or forty-five minutes. You take your best fifteen, eighteen minutes and walk out there and knock 'em dead.

In the movies, there's no audience, but you get used to it. When I started doing these old B Westerns, we did them in a week. You're either on a horse or you're fighting somebody. I loved it. In those days, there were only two parts for a young fella. You were either the girl's brother, or the young deputy. And I was a lot of young deputies, and a lot of girls' brother. [Laughs]

I was good at riding horses, which is how I got a lot of roles in Westerns. The day of shooting I did on a Western, I was riding a bucking horse. I said, "Oh, how bad does this horse buck?" They said, "Well, they said you were a pretty good rider." I said, "I am a pretty good rider, and if he doesn't buck back I have no qualms about getting on him." They said, "Don't worry—he bucks just a little bit." Well, he bucked for way over eight seconds, I'll tell you that. But I stayed on. [Laughs] And I said, "Do we have to do that again?" They laughed and said, "No, we think we got it."

When I did the movie *Strip for Action* on Broadway, Gene Kelly was doing *Pal Joey*. So we used to meet at a little saloon after work. Everybody on Broadway knows everybody. So we were friends, and I was hoofing a little bit then. So my agent called me and said that MGM was doing a musical and Stanley Donen wanted to see me. So I went out, I went into the office, and Donen was sitting there at the desk. I said I was Tommy Farrell and I heard a voice behind me say, "Take off your hat." The voice said, "*Sonofabitch*—you grew out your hair." It was Kelly! [Laughs] He said, "I'm not sure exactly

what we're going to use you for. There are several parts that you could play."
Donen says, "Can he dance?" And Kelly says, "Of course he can dance!" So I
got the part. And the movie was *Singing in the Rain*.

I didn't know it would be the classic that it's become, but I knew that
with Gene Kelly and Donald O'Connor dancing together, how can it be bad?
And Cyd Charisse, too. I remember the dance Kelly did with Donald—
"Moses Supposes"—and it was just *great*. Gene was a perfectionist. Everything just had to be just *so*. He would do many takes of a dance scene, and he
could have printed the first take. It was good enough. But it had to be better.
It had to be perfect. It was just wonderful being around. That was Debbie
Reynolds' first picture—she was only eighteen. And Rita Moreno, that was
her first picture, too.

190

I did a number of pictures with my mother. The first one was *Girls in the
Night* at Universal. And the next time we worked together was *Kissing Cousins*.
We did an episode of "Rawhide" on TV together, and that was funny because
they said I wasn't the right type to play my mother's son. Frankie Avalon
played my mother's son. I played her secretary. [Laughs] Frankie Avalon
doesn't look like my mom, I'll tell you that much.

I loved working with Elvis. He was a hardworking man. He *always* knew
his lines. He worked very hard at his craft. He was very conscientious about
everything he did. He knew he was new in the film business, but he was a
master at handling an audience. He wanted to be good, so he was. I
remember meeting Priscilla [Presley] when she came on the set. She looked
like a teenager. Cause she was—she was just a highs chool girl.

The big change in Hollywood is when they broke up the theaters. The
studios could no longer run their own theaters. That was the beginning of
the big change. Before that, the studios were like schools; when Hugh
O'Brien and Tony Curtis and those guys went to Universal, they taught them
how to ride horses, they taught them how to fence, they taught them how
to do everything. They taught actors their craft. They don't do that anymore.
They told you where to work and how to work and when.

Hollywood changed because people in Sandusky, Ohio, would go the
movies, and they'd be sitting there in fourteen inches of snow and look at
the palm trees and say, "What are we doing *here?*" So *thousands* of people
moved here.

In those days, you could get to the desert from Hollywood Boulevard in
twenty minutes. And there was nothing out there but desert. It was a lizard
ranch. If you wanted to be in the forest, you had Arrowhead, Big Bear, just
two hours. The Valley had horses. So the stars moved away from Hollywood.
A lot of them had ranches, like Gable, out in the Valley, and they lived on
their ranches.

Now they are trying hard to bring back the old Hollywood. They're building a new complex on Hollywood Boulevard for the Academy Awards. That should help a lot.

Hollywood used to be the center of the movie business. Everything was there. Warners, Paramount, United Artists, the Goldwyn studios. That was when Hollywood was *Hollywood*. NBC, CBS and ABC were all in Hollywood— their radio stations. The industry was still there.

I remember the Vine Street bowling alley right there near Sunset. The lounge of the bowling alley had music, and I remember hearing Nat "King" Cole and his trio there. First time I saw him.

191

At Hollywood & Highland was the Hollywood Hotel. And in 1938, my mother was in the movie *Hollywood Hotel*. That was a very nice hotel. The grounds had palm trees, and there was a fountain and fish in a pond. Kind of Victorian, in a way. The Roosevelt and the Knickerbocker were both very nice hotels, too.

I remember going to premieres of movies on Hollywood Boulevard with my mother. They were very glamorous. All the searchlights in the sky, and the big cars, the Rolls Royces.

I remember the Christmas parades on Hollywood Boulevard. I was in quite a few of those. What were they like? They were cold! *Freezing!* You'd be so full of sweaters and scarves, only a little bit of your face would stick out. We used to have big crowds. It was a big event.

People thought TV would kill the movies and it didn't. Then they thought video would kill the movies but it didn't. Movies will always live on. People like to go out. Young people. Old people, not so much. ["And there were so many places to go out to back then," says his wife. "That was the place to be seen. They just don't have that anymore."]

Right. The Trocadero, Ciro's. I was happy then. But I'm happy now. I'm very happy to be wherever I am. It's a wonderful place to be.

Totty Ames
BORN NOVEMBER 3, 1922
WILLOW, OKLAHOMA
THEATER CASHIER/LINGERIE MODEL/FILM AND TV EXTRA/SINGER

Still radiant even after all these years since she posed for racy photographs in the forties and appeared as the first-ever lingerie model for a fledgling Frederick's of Hollywood, she sits at the dining room table of her small West Hollywood home with photos of her remarkable life spread out before her. She projects a sense of genuine joy, and of gratitude for a life that she lived by her own design without regret or apology, savoring each moment of it, from taking tickets on Holly-wood Boulevard during World War II to working as a model and a beauty queen to becoming an

extra in movies and from there Neil Diamond's personal assistant while falling in love with soldiers and producers and one extremely gifted chef, to becoming a singer at long last, a dream she
harbored her whole life. She shows old photos of herself in provocative bathing suits and lingerie—photos that reveal she was as beautiful and shapely as a movie star, somewhat of a cross
between Ava Gardner and Paulette Goddard. But she never had any interest herself in being a
movie star. "I just wanted to have fun," she says. "And I did."

Totty was my grandmother's last name, so I'm the only one. Ames sounded
good with Totty. I was born in Willow, Oklahoma, not far from Granite. We
moved to Oklahoma City when I was about three years old. I lived there
until I was twenty-onewhen I got on a train and came to California.

I was a total movie fan as a child. My mother worked and so I would go
downtown where she worked and the movies would babysit me. I would
just go from one to the other waiting for her to get off work. I thought Mae
West was the greatest thing, and then later, Ginger Rogers and Fred Astaire,
Dolores Del Rio, and, of course, Clark Gable and Cary Grant.

I took the train here, during the war, to Los Angeles. I have never had any
interest in New York City, never have, have none, nope. The films, the movies,
the glamour . . . I just wanted to be around them.

I got here in 1943. The first place I lived was with a family, a mother and
daughter, on Third Street, not too far from here. The woman's husband had
gone to war. He was in the service and so mother and daughter were living
in a house. I got off of the train, picked up the newspaper, found an ad, and
called. I made arrangements that I would rent the room, and I told her, "You
know, I have no money. I only have ten dollars."

She said, "Where'd you come from?"

"Oklahoma," I said.

She said, "We're from Oklahoma." Her father had been a judge in Oklahoma. She said, "You just get in a taxi, and come on out here and don't
worry about a thing."

So I did. I went to Beverly Hills the next day and got a job cashiering in a
shoe store, because shoes were my second passion. Then I got a job as a
cashier in what was the Academy Theater—it's gone now—on Melrose
where it ends at Doheny. That's where the Academy's pictures were shown
before the Academy Awards.

Then a couple or three weeks after that, I found my way to Hollywood
Boulevard. I went straight to the Egyptian Theater and asked the cashier if
they were hiring, and she said, "Don't move." She had been offered a job as the
hatcheck girl at the Palladium, where she said she could make all kinds of
money. She had been wanting to quit and they couldn't find anybody to take
her place. I went to work the next day.

I *loved* the job. The Egyptian was then a Fox West Coast theater, so all of the MGM movies first run were there, and all of the premieres. We had loads of premiers there. I was very happy sitting in the box office watching it all walk by. The box office then was right off on the sidewalk and it was a glass booth, glass on three sides with a doorway in the back. The front end of the box office was all glass and it raised up, it opened up as a window so I was completely exposed and the cash box right there. But Hollywood Boulevard was very safe in those days. Of course, I had the whole army and navy up and down the street. [Laughs]

Being there was just *wonderful*, just watching the world walk by, all of Hollywood right before me. It was *crazy*. It was servicemen, wall to wall. There were so many of them, and they all wanted to date me. I would go to the Hollywood Canteen and dance with the guys. I *lived* in the Palladium and we'd always dance with the guys. We'd listen to all the Big Bands. And I knew *everybody* in the bands.

I worked days mostly. I was the head cashier, so I made the schedule and when I wanted to work days, I worked days, and when I wanted to work nights, I worked nights. But holidays were always the biggest times. By the time the film went on, there was a line around the block for the next picture. The theaters were just *jam-packed*, because *that* was entertainment. There was no television. In those days during the war, all of the theaters had to be emptied by midnight, because there were blackouts. You had to draw your drapes at night and basically black out.

The Egyptian was no longer owned by Sid Grauman, but he would come around and wave every once in a while. He was an elderly man then. He was a very quiet kind of man, in that setting, with *wild* hair.

The Egyptian was in excellent condition then. They had just taken the monkeys out when I got there. There used to be cages all up and down the courtyard on both sides that were full of monkeys. In the twenties they had live men dressed in Egyptian costumes who walked the parapet across the top of the place.

There were lots of night clubs on the boulevard then. Jazz clubs and one gay bar, right across the street from the Egyptian, called the Circle Bar. It was very underground, because who knew gay and gay bars? I'm pretty sure it was also called "The Nest." At twelve o'clock, when everything had to be closed and emptied, everybody spilled out onto the street, that's when we got the clue.

I would go to the Pig & Whistle and have an egg salad sandwich and sit at the old soda fountain bar. There were no luxurious booths like it is now.

At premieres, I was usually attired in a gown that the studio would put me in. I passed out programs to the stars and guided them to where they were going. We did the premiere when Gable had just come home from the war and his first picture. I had my photo taken with him in the courtyard. It appeared in one of the film magazines. Gable was delightful. He was truly The King. Elvis may be the son of the King, but not the King. Clark Gable was such an elegant man, always charming to the fans. Other stars were wonderful, but I was always so impressed by him. I was just gaga from about age ten or so over him.

I was always very "talky" and was always able to meet and greet the stars and not be intimidated by their stature. I'd graciously take them to the aisle and give them to an usher to see them to their seats. We rolled out the red carpet. At one premiere, the studio sent me and another girl out to Metro to be fitted in costumes from Showboat. I wore one of Ava Gardner's gowns and she wore one of Katherine Grace's gowns. Great fun!

One time at the Egyptian, a man and his wife came up to the box office and asked me if I had ever modeled. And I said no.

They said, "Are you interested?"

And I said, "Modeling what?"

They said, "Brassieres." So I went to work with them, traveling the eleven western states, modeling for buyers in department stores and such. This company made the first "half" brassiere. It was strapless. I went with them promoting that bra.

It was while modeling for them that I first met Frederick of Frederick's of Hollywood. Fred Mellenger was his full name. He was walking down a hallway and I snatched him and brought him in and sold him the first brassiere that he had ever put in his catalog, which was the "half" brassiere. At that time he had a catalog and did a mail-order only business; he didn't have a store then. All of his business was from the ladies of ill repute up in the San Joaquin Valley who couldn't go into town and buy the sexy stuff. They had to order it mail-order.

He'd never had brassieres but he was so taken with that, that he put in a huge order. After I had stopped working for the brassiere company, he called and asked me to come in and do some modeling for him. I said, "Sure!" Well, as it turned out, it was a steady job three days a week. I would go in and model all the garments that had been submitted to him from people, from manufacturers who wanted to get into the catalog. I would go in and put on these strange-looking outfits and come out and model for him and the artists who drew the thing—they used no photos then, only artist's illustrations—and they would decide whether or not they were going to use the garment in the book.

We would have such laughs. I remember well the first day the girdle with the built-in rump showed up. I've got rump *enough*, I didn't need anything extra [laughs], what a laugh that was.

Frederick started out in an office on Hollywood Boulevard, east of Western just about a block. Then a place on Wilcox, yes, just south of Sunset—a big warehouse—and he had so much space that he decided to open up a retail store in the front. It became so successful that it grew larger until he got the one on Hollywood in what was Kress' Department Store on Hollywood Boulevard, which was a five-and-dime, like Woolworth's. Fred painted the building purple when he moved in, because that was their color.

195

I worked for him for several years. I was their main model. They would call in other girls every once in a while if they had an unusual number of garments that they had to go through. But if it was just the regular number, it was me.

I modeled for years, and a dear friend that I had met through another friend, who was the production manager, you will probably hear his name, Doc Merman. He was a well-known production manager. Everything came out in four-letter words, so you either loved him or hated him. He was one of those guys with a very tough exterior but a marshmallow inside. He was just the dearest man, and he had heard that I was not really happy. I was living with a guy that I was not thrilled with being with. He called me up one day and he said, "You get your ass over here, I need you." And he made me a stand-in on a show he was doing, the "Lone Wolf" series with Louise Hayworth. So that's how I started doing stand-in and extra work. I stood in for any female that came on the show. I stood in for Barbara Stanwick, and Phyllis Coats on so many things that she did. Phyllis Coats was Lois Lane [on the "Superman" TV series] before Noel Noelle. I worked with Tommy Farrell a lot; we had a lot of fun—boy, was he a funny guy. I was wondering the other day if he was still with us.

I used to run in to Lucille Ball at the Pig & Whistle. Lucy and Desi. She was very nice. The first time we met was when I dated Lou Holtz, who was a comic with the Zeigfeld Follies. He and Lucille were very good friends and he was working, playing in Reno. Desi's band was there and Lucy was working with Bob Hope on *Buttons and Bows*. Both of them were bad gamblers. He had already lost his salary by the time she got there for the weekend. And the performance was finished, the gig was finished, and so Lou and I drove back to Los Angeles with them and to their ranch in Chatsworth. We spent the rest of the weekend with them and Desi cooked for us. It was a really exciting time, I was green as grass, and it was really a thrill for me. They were delightful, just great, great fun. This was early, before any children. It's always better before kids, apparently. So she was always just terrific to me. Later when I started working as an extra she would always request me to work on the "I Love Lucy" show.

Desi was very creative. He developed that three-camera, live thing, at Desilu. He was very creative, and he directed several. They had a lot of shows at Desilu, because they had their own studios and they made gobs of things out there, "The Untouchables," "The Real McCoys" and the "Alice" series that Tommy Farrell worked on with us. I was an extra on "I Love Lucy," which we filmed at the studio on Cahuenga, it was called "Producer's Studio" after that. It was between Santa Monica and Melrose. When they became Desilu and they bought their own studio, it was, I guess, the back end of that one first and then they went to the RKO lot. They also rented the Chaplin studio at La Brea & Sunset; they shot "Mr. Ed" there and "Perry Mason," which was a half-hour black and white.

What was it like to work on "I Love Lucy"? *Run for your life!* Because there was always so much going on with the cast, with rehearsals and such. So it was just kind of hurry up and wait until they got it all ironed out and then, of course, they shot it live with an audience. So it was, rehearse, rehearse, rehearse and get everything just right before they filmed, or taped as it was. They didn't always do it in sequence, they would use up this set, everything that had to be done in this set and then move to another set and do it there. They were not out of the house very much, the apartment. In other words, there was not much location stuff. But when they did, it would usually be something like a Women's Club, so they'd need a lot of ladies in hats and such. Always shot from the back. Just a sale, or a walk through a doorway, or we'd be in an office or something and they'd need traffic outside of the office.

I *never* wanted to be an actress. I loved the work of an extra because I got to study the camera and the camera angles, and the lighting, and how it was all done. I didn't want the loss of privacy, and I just didn't want to get in to that rat race of fighting for parts, and watching movies thinking, "I could have done that part." That was all just so trite. No. It wasn't for me. I just wanted to have fun and make a living. I did dream of sometimes being a singer, though. And that dream came true later in my life.

Doing extra work was very easy; all you had to do was show up on time and do your job instead of going in a back room somewhere and sleeping. When the assistant directors found out that you would actually come and do a day's work, that's what they wanted. Then if a director or producer or somebody, you happened to catch their eye, they would ask for you all the time because they knew you would show up and do the job.

I worked many times for Stanley Kramer, a great producer and director.

He was a giant. And also a nice, nice man. I never heard him raise his voice on the set, and if he did, it was out of the ear of anybody else. He would talk to the person he was chastising, and only them. He was a quiet, soft-spoken man, but he could handle Deitrich and Spencer Tracy and Judy Garland, and just a dozen of them in one picture I worked on, *Judgment at Nuremberg*. I did lots of long walks and dances and big ballroom scenes. It was several weeks' work, but mostly just sitting and waiting.

Before Deitrich would come onto the set, she would say, "Is Mr. Tracy on the set? Then I'll come to the set." And Tracy, being the curmudgeon he was, would say, "Is she on the set? Then I'll be on the set." Of course, he was always there on time. She was playing the diva, and he was helping her along with it.

I got to know Frank Sinatra well. He did such wonderful things. Lee J. Cobb was in really bad shape, his career had hit bottom, he was very sick, in a charity hospital dying. Sinatra heard about it and went there and told him to get well right now, he needed him for a film. He paid all the bills, moved him into a private room with a private doctor, got him well and hired him. That started Lee's career again.

While I was working as an extra, I married a producer and raised his children. Saul David, he made *Fantastic Voyage*, *Von Ryan's Express*, and *In Like Flint* and *Our Man Flint*, and I worked in both of those. Then a film at Universal that no one has ever seen or heard called *Skullduggery*. With Burt Reynolds as a matter of fact, and then, after we divorced, he made *Logan's Run*. So, he was a very substantial producer at Fox.

After we divorced, I went to work for Neil Diamond as his executive assistant. He was wonderful to work for. When I left, he gave me a year's salary. That's what I bought this house with. I worked for him for about six years. I left in 1976. His office was down on Melrose Place. It was a fun time.

Then it was time to retire, they said, at sixty-five, and I said, "No!" and I started a singing career. And I did that up until a couple of years ago, but it just got to be too much work. I had always wanted to perform at the Cine-grill (in the Roosevelt Hotel) and eventually I got my chance. When I was there, I said, "It was in the forties when I worked at the Egyptian and I used to dream of being here on this stage singing. It has taken me fifty years and I got here, and it's only eight blocks."

So there you have it. My life in Hollywood. It was a wonderful, wonderful time.

Bob Board
BORN MAY 16, 1922
LOS ANGELES, CALIFORNIA
PUBLICIST/PUPPETEER/STAND-IN/ACTOR

At first it takes your breath away, just the sheer magnitude of it all so intricately arranged to take up every square inch of this little rectangular room over his garage up near the northern end of Beachwood Drive. It's one man's singular shrine to his personal goddess, who in this case happens to be Marion Davies. Illuminated by a rusty orange gleam from old rococo lamps is a 3-D temple full of all things Marion: handmade Marion marionettes, miniatures of her movie sets, a rainbow of movie posters and lobby cards, complete costumes and uniforms displayed in glass cases, paintings of her, photographs of her in ornate frames, trophies inscribed with her name, dishes with her image, books about her, autographs, and more. It's not that she's the only movie star that matters to him, but bonded for decades by their shared affliction of stuttering above which they both arose, she's the one that he champions above all the others. But there's also some miscellaneous non-Marion-related movie memorabilia, including a series of framed newspaper columns written by Louella Parsons in the mid-thirties, each quoting a gushing young man who would write her with details of the Long Beach premieres he'd attend: "This just in from Bob Board," she'd write, "my Long Beach Previewer." He points out another Parsons column dated April 2, 1939. "Now the world is falling apart," he says. "Hitler's taking over, and Louella Parson's column says: 'The deadly dullness of the past week was lifted yesterday when Darryl Zanuck admitted he had bought all rights to The Bluebird for Shirley Temple.' The world is falling apart and she writes about 'the deadly dullness.' Can you believe that? It's amazing."

I was born in Boyle Heights, but I spent most of my school years in Long Beach. And I *always* loved the movies, oh God, I *loved* the movies and I *lived* for Saturday matinees. As a kid, I loved movies so much, that I just had to have something much more than going to see the movie, I had to *have* something.

So I would go behind the grocery store to find a box, and I'd take it home and I'd get little frames, and paint the box, and make a little theater lobby and I'd take a matchbox and make like a box office. Then I'd take another box and cut a hole in it and that would be for the screen.

I was given 25 cents a week to go to the movie theater and buy candy. But instead, I would buy this magazine called *Screen Romances*, and they would show the story of the film with all these stills. I would read the story, then I would cut out all these pictures and I would paste them on a piece of tablet paper in story form. Then I would hold them up to this hole in the screen and talk for them. So I had my own little movie theater.

My brother, who was about five then, he was the audience, but only if I'd pay him. [Laughs] He'd say, [in a high-pitched whine] "Oh, I gotta see another one of Bob's shows." [Laughs]

Mrs. Daeida Hartell Wilcox Beveridge,
who founded Hollywood with her
husband, Harvey.
Photo Collection/Los Angeles Public Library.

Mr. Harvey Henderson Wilcox, the
founder of Hollywood with his
wife, Daeida. A pious abolitionist
from Topeka, Kansas, he made a
fortune in real estate before moving
from downtown Los Angeles to the
home they called "Hollywood."
Photo Collection/Los Angeles Public Library.

Hollywood, 1883. This is the intersection of Sunset Boulevard & Wilcox Avenue, looking west down Sunset from Wilcox. The street is lined with the pepper trees planted by Harvey Wilcox.

Photo Collection / Los Angeles Public Library.

Hollywood, 2002. The intersection of Sunset & Wilcox today.

Photo by Peter Sherman.

Hollywood, 1888. Facing north toward the hills that now hold the Hollywood sign. This is Hollywood as Harvey and Daeida first knew it.
Photo Collection/Los Angeles Public Library.

Hollywood, 1890. Looking north up Beachwood Canyon before it was Beachwood and was still the ranch of two brothers, Henry and George Claussen. Today Beachwood Drive runs along the bottom of the canyon, and Gower Avenue runs up the hill by the windmill.
Photo Collection/Los Angeles Public Library.

The Cahuenga Pass, 1899. Looking south from the Valley toward Hollywood,
before the advent of the automobile changed it forever.

Photo Collection/Los Angeles Public Library.

Hollywood Boulevard & Cahuenga, 1900. Looking north from Cahuenga. This is the streetcar
that once shuttled tourists from downtown to Hollywood and continued all the way to Santa
Monica and the sea. Hollywood's main tourist attraction at the time was the house and garden
of the famous French artist Paul DeLongpre, which can be seen to the left of the train.

Photo Collection/Los Angeles Public Library.

The Cahuenga Pass, 1928. Though still decades before the freeway cut through its heart, it was fast becoming a busy auto thoroughfare between the still sleepy San Fernando Valley and the newly thriving city of Hollywood.

Photo Collection / Los Angeles Public Library.

The Cahuenga Pass, 1959. The Hollywood Freeway, completed in 1957, cut directly through the Pass connecting the Valley with Hollywood and downtown L.A. The bridge in the forefront leads to Mulholland Drive.

Photo Collection / Los Angeles Public Library.

The Hollywood Bowl, 1923. It was built by the people of Hollywood, who donated the lumber and manpower to construct the seats and the stage. Students from Hollywood High presented a performance of Shakespeare's *Twelfth Night* to raise money for electrical equipment to power the lights.

Photo Collection/Los Angeles Public Library.

The Hollywoodland sign, 1927. Erected to promote the Hollywoodland real estate development in the hills above Hollywood, the original thirteen letters of the sign were fifty-feet tall and thirty-feet wide, with 4,000 twenty-watt bulbs framing each letter. To punctuate the big sign, a giant white circle, also studded with lightbulbs, was set into the hillside a few hundred feet below the sign.

Photo Collection/Los Angeles Public Library.

Hollywoodland, 1927. Two actresses pose in one of the steamshovels digging out plots of Hollywoodland. The big sign, still under construction, is visible beneath them.

Photo Collection/Los Angeles Public Library.

Facing north, this is an aerial view of Hollywood, already a thriving urban center in 1924, with the buildings of Hollywood Boulevard running along the photo's southern edge, and the immense Mulholland Dam under construction in Weid Canyon to the north. The street running straight south to north on the right edge of the photo is Vine Street; it leads up to the hills of the Vedanta Society, and above that, Krotona Hill. Extending from the southwest corner of the photo all the way up toward the dam is Cahuenga. Up in the hills to the west of the dam is the giant cross erected in honor of Christine Weatherill Stevenson.

Photo Collection/Los Angeles Public Library.

The Mulholland Dam, 1924, still under construction. In 1932 the entire facade of the dam was covered by an earthen blanket on which was planted a grove of trees. This provided psychological comfort for those who feared the dam might break and result in a devastating flood like its counterpart, the St. Francis Dam. This facade completely obscured any view of the dam, as shown in the next photo.

Photo Collection/Los Angeles Public Library.

An aerial view of Hollywood, 1959, and the San Fernando Valley extending beyond. From right to left, the Hollywood Freeway cuts clear through Hollywood to the west before taking a northern turn at the Hollywood Bowl to cross the Cahuenga Pass. Just east of the freeway is Lake Hollywood, the reservoir of water contained by the Mulholland Dam. The dam itself is now hidden, completely covered by its forest of trees. The circular building just south of the freeway is Capitol Records on Vine Street. The cluster of buildings just south of there mark the intersection of Hollywood & Vine.

Photo Collection/Los Angeles Public Library.

A 1939 aerial view that shows how Paramount Studios, to the south, is built right up to the boundary of the Hollywood Cemetery, where many of Paramount's most legendary luminaries—such as Cecil B. DeMille and Rudolph Valentino—are interred. There is no wall separating the studio from the cemetery.
Photo Collection/Los Angeles Public Library.

Hollywood in the forties: the bustling intersection of Sunset & Vine, the home of NBC Radio.
Photo Collection/Los Angeles Public Library.

RKO Studios, 1937, on the corner of Melrose & Gower. Built in 1920 on an unoccupied part of the cemetery, it started as the Robertson-Cole Studios and became RKO when Joe Kennedy's FBO Studios merged with RCA. Howard Hughes took control by buying up most of the RKO stock and eventually sold it to General Teleradio in the early fifties. The lot was sold to Desilu Productions for TV production of "I Love Lucy," and in 1958, Paramount extended their own lot by taking over this property. The famous globe was later painted all white by Paramount. The company recently restored it to its original, multicolored glory.

Photo Collection/Los Angeles Public Library.

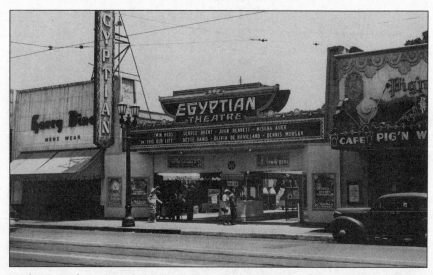

Sid Grauman's Egyptian Theater on Hollywood Boulevard, 1942, between the Harry Dine Men's Wear shop and the recently returned Pig 'n Whistle Cafe.

Photo Collection/Los Angeles Public Library.

Sid Grauman's greatest achievement: the Chinese Theater on Hollywood Boulevard, shown here in 1957, with its fabled forecourt of footprints.

Photo Collection / Los Angeles Public Library.

The Hollywood Hotel, 1951, which stood for decades at the intersection of Hollywood Boulevard & Highland. Built in 1903, it was razed in 1956 to make room for a nondescript office building and parking lot that were subsequently destroyed only a few decades later to make way for the Hollywood–Highland complex of stores, a new subway stop, and the Kodak Theater, the new home of the Oscars.

Photo Collection / Los Angeles Public Library.

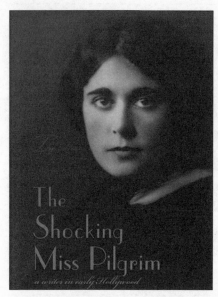

Frederica Sagor Maas, 1921, beautiful
enough to be a star, but she was only
interested in the written word.

Karl Malden, in a scene from the 1962
movie *Birdman of Alcatraz*.

David Raksin, at his home in Encino, California, 2002.
Photo by Peter Sherman.

Robert Cornthwaite, sitting in the Roddy
McDowell memorial garden at the Motion
Picture Country Home in Woodland
Hills, California, 2002.
Photo by Peter Sherman.

Evelyn Keyes, 1938, in a still taken on the
set of *Gone with the Wind*, in which she
played the part of Scarlett O'Hara's
little sister, Suellen.

Jules Fox with his beloved wife, Jo Brooks Fox, 1989.

Hal Riddle, 2002, in his cottage at the Motion Picture
Country Home, posing in front of his wall of fame
with its prominent portraits of his most beloved
stars, such as Clark Gable and Billie Dove.

Photo by Peter Sherman.

Else Blangstead in the front yard of h
North Hollywood home, 2002.

Photo by Peter Sherman.

A.C. Lyles in his office on the Paramount lot in Hollywood, 2002, pointing to a photo
of himself with his close friends Ronald Reagan and George Bush Sr.

Photo by Peter Sherman.

Jerry Maren, pictured in the backyard of his Hollywood home, 2002, with his lollipop from *The Wizard of Oz*.
Photo by Peter Sherman.

The late great "Steverino," Mr. Steve Allen, 1999.

Jerry Maren, the central member of the "Lollipop Guild" munchkins in a still from *The Wizard of Oz*, 1939.

Totty Ames, 1949, the first model for
Frederick's of Hollywood.

Tommy Farrell, outside on the grounds of the
Motion Picture Country Home, 2002.
Photo by Peter Sherman.

Marie Windsor, the "Queen of the Bs," in a still from the film *Hellfire*, 1949.

Bob Board (right) with Stan Laurel, 1953, at Laurel's Santa Monica home, posing with the Laurel marionette built by Bob.

Bob Board at home in his shrine to Marion Davies, 2002.
Photo by Peter Sherman.

Leatrice Joy, the wife of John Gilbert and mother of Leatrice Joy Fountain.

John Gilbert, star of the silent screen, father of Leatrice Joy Fountain.

The remarkably hilarious
Jonathan Winters, 2000.

Manny Felix at the venerable counter of
Musso & Frank's Grill, Hollywood, 2002.
Photo by Peter Sherman.

Else Blangstead with Bill Heyward, 1999.

My grandmother came to visit one day and I said, "Oh, Grandma, I wanna do a movie show for you." I was in the middle of it, and I turned to her and she was snoring away. [Laughs]

My first encounter with Hollywood was in Long Beach. I came home from school one day and my brother said, "I don't wanna tell you this, Bob, 'cause you're gonna go crazy, but there's a motion picture company down at the Navy landing shooting."

I'd never, ever, even *dreamed* of seeing a motion picture in production, and I said "*WHAT!??*"

So I got on my bicycle and got down there to the harbor and there was Richard Dix, Chester Morris and Dolores Del Rio doing a film called *The Devil's Playground* for Columbia. That was the *most* exciting thing. This was around 4:30 in the afternoon when I got down there, and I was in a *dream* world. Oh, my *God*.

They had orange makeup on their face and Richard Dix was a little bit drunk and he'd stumble on one scene and they'd take it over, and *oh*, I was in *heaven!* I stayed and stayed and stayed and someone said they're going to shoot the storm scenes tonight. And I thought, "*Storm scenes?*"

So they started setting up the lights and the cameras for this big storm scene. They had a wind machine and a lightning machine and I was in *heaven*, and Dolores Del Rio is in this white coat with this black hair waiting for her lover to return. They were deep sea divers. And I stayed, it must have been almost five o'clock in the morning.

When I got home my folks really gave it to me, but I have *never* forgotten that. So then after school the next day I went back and they were still shooting. They shot for three days. The fourth day, I went down, and they had all left. And [laughs] I thought, oh my God, they've gone back to Hollywood and left me here. [Laughs] It was a terrible feeling.

So they were the first stars that I'd ever seen. I was too timid to even ask for autographs because they were gods and goddesses up there, I wouldn't approach them, you know. Dolores Del Rio was in all the screen makeup, but she looked *beautiful*.

They had previews of the films out in Long Beach at the West Coast Theater. They previewed the Metro films, so when I found out about that, I'd run home from school and I would look at the evening paper to see if there was an ad for a preview that night. It would say: "Tonight Major Studio Preview—Stars in Person." So, *wow!*

One night Garbo had come and I hadn't seen her going in so I thought, I bet she'll leave by the stage exit. So when the picture was over I waited out there and out she comes with this big straw hat smoking a cigarette. I never would have imagined Garbo smoking. So there was a studio limousine there, she got in the car, and as they drove off, she threw the cigarette out the window. Well, I *grabbed* that cigarette and I had it for *years* in a little case.

One night they were previewing a picture with Henry Fonda called I *Met My Love Again*, and Jean Arthur came and James Stewart and Henry Fonda, the three of them came. Afterwards they went into a little coffee shop next to the theater. I had gone up to Henry Fonda and I got his autograph and I got James Stewart's autograph and I went to Jean Arthur and she said, "Naw, no." She was very difficult about things like that, so James Stewart said, "Oh, come on. Give the kid a break." Then she took my book and she signed it, and that was a *big* evening because it was three-in-one.

And Judy Garland came down to the preview of her film and she was just a little kid then. But she had reddish hair, dyed of course, almost pink. *Everybody Sing* was the picture. About 1937, I guess. I remember she was out in front and there was a peanut machine. You put in a penny and you got peanuts, and she was out there getting her peanuts.

And Loretta Young came one night and I kept thinking, "What is it about the women stars that they don't look the same?" And then I realized what it was: you look at a glamorous picture of a female star in the thirties, and you see their *eyes*. They had false eyelashes and they had eye shadow, but in person, they didn't wear it. So in person, they had a little bit of a *tired* look, the eyes weren't those great big wonderful eyes.

Myrna Loy came one night and she got in her car and before the car door closed I said, "Miss Loy, may I take your picture?" She said, "Yes." So, at that time, I had a camera, and the flashbulb was built right into the camera. And it was a funny kind of thing, I snapped the picture, and just as I snapped it, the bulb went *wooosh!* And it burst. [Laughs] It was kind of a plastic thing or other, it didn't hurt her or anything but she was startled and it scared me to death. I thought I'd never take another picture as long as I live. [Laughter]

One night Norma Shearer came, and I remember I went up to her with a card and I said, "Will you sign this?" She took it and she looked on the other side and said, "Sometimes we have to check to make sure, sometimes they have nude pictures on the back." [Laughs] And I thought: Well, does she mean a nude picture of her? Or just any nude picture on the back of the card? [Laughter]

Then I developed this *big* thing about Marion Davies because I loved her movies. I had a very bad stutter. I couldn't get up and recite at school, I couldn't. Then I heard that she stuttered, and I thought, "*Wow!* If *she* stuttered and she doesn't stutter on the screen, then that means you can get over this." It was like a light in the dark to me.

Marion was *beautiful*. She sang, she danced, she was delightful, her pictures were so entertaining. They were charming. I couldn't take my eyes off of her. I've heard people say that about Marilyn, that when she was on the screen you never left her. Well, I felt the same way about Marion. She was this beautiful blonde woman, and there was such a warmth about her. That's the kind of person she was, she had a great warmth for people. She loved people. She was just a very special, wonderful woman.

Okay, it's true that she drank. And she lived with a married man. But their association lasted longer than most marriages, thirty-five years. Hearst wanted to marry her, but Mrs. Hearst was Catholic and she said that absolutely there would be no divorce. So it was too bad. All that combined with the fact that here was a person that had my handicap, yet she got over it. It meant a tremendous amount to me.

201

So that was the beginning of my big interest in Marion Davies. Plus which I loved her films. Then I would hear my folks talking and they would say [in a disapproving whisper], "She lives with this old man who is married and has children, and they live in a castle up by the beach up there, up north." And I thought, "Ooohh, this *does* sound like an interesting person." [Laughs]

Then when I came to work in Hollywood, I would ask the old timers about Marion Davies, and I've never heard such stories of love for a person in my life. They *loved* her. They might say, "Joan Crawford, she was great, but . . ." or "Norma Shearer was great, *but*," but there was no "buts" about Marion. They loved her.

She did unusual things for people, like at Christmastime when the stars would give presents to the crew and all, they'd give everyone the same thing, like a bottle of booze or this or that. Marion would find out who had children, how many boys, how many girls, and all those children would receive gifts, individually. And in New York, in the early days, she was known by the poor children as the Christmas Lady. She always did things for the children.

When I was a kid I would take the old milk train, the Red Car from Long Beach into Hollywood. Oh, the old Pacific Electric, it took maybe a half hour from Long Beach to Downtown, and then I would take another streetcar from downtown to Hollywood.

At that time the Red Car stopped near Paramount studios off of Melrose, so I'd go over to Paramount Studios early in the morning to see the stars when they went to work. And then at lunchtime, I'd go over to the Brown Derby or Columbia, because the stars all came out. And then I would sometimes take the bus over to Metro to be there in the early evening when they left and I'd get home on the Red Car kind of late at night and my parents would be furious, but those were exciting days, they were wonderful days.

Do you remember a place called Earl Carroll's Theater? They had great big plaques on the side of the building with the signatures of all the stars and a big neon sign in front said, "Through these portals pass the most beautiful girls in the world."

I had heard that they were going to have a special Ann Sheridan evening. So I didn't want to tell my folks, they didn't care for me to be going to Hollywood at nighttime by myself, so I said I was going to a movie, and instead of going to the movie I went down and got on the Red Car and came up to Hollywood and went to the Earl Carol Theater. But there was no Ann Sheridan, there were no celebrities whatsoever that night. And I thought, oh my God, my autograph book is empty, my camera is empty. [Laughs] And not only that, now I'm going to go home and catch hell from my parents. So that evening didn't turn out well.

202

When I was out of school and at a certain age, I thought the only thing in the world that means anything is to work in Hollywood. So I came up to Hollywood and I did get a job in publicity at Columbia in 1943.

The Columbia publicity department was on Beachwood, across the street from the main lot. I wanted so badly to go over there where the action was, to get on a sound stage, so I used to sneak over. This first time I went over there was a big soundstage at the end of the lot, and I went over and it said "NO ADMITTANCE" but I thought, well, I'm working here, now maybe I can be admitted. So I opened the stage door and walked in and there was a cop there. Just as I walked in, this buzzer went off and a red light went on. The scene was being shot so they couldn't throw me out because they were shooting. It was Gene Kelly and Rita Hayworth doing the number from Cover Girl, "Long Ago and Far Away." That was a big number. And it was a thrill to see Rita Hayworth and Gene Kelly doing this big production. That was great.

So I realized that I had to get out of publicity. I had to get over there on the stage where things were happening. So, working in publicity, one of my duties was to take stills that had, like bit players and people that weren't prominent, down to the casting office on the other side of the studio and have them identify these people by the captions. So I got to know the people in casting. So I said, "Is there any chance that I can work as an extra? I wanna be where the action is."

They said, "How about being a stand-in?"

I said, "I'd love to be a stand-in."

So the first picture I was a stand-in on was Irene Dunne in Over Twenty-One. And Irene Dunne, next to Marion, she was my favorite. I thought she was wonderful.

So my first day as a stand-in, I didn't know the first thing about what to do. I was scared to *death*. Working with all these famous people and all, it was just *amazing* to me. I couldn't get *over* it.

But Irene Dunne was just wonderful. It was around Easter time. I used to take these hard-boiled eggs from home and I would do caricatures of the cast on these eggs. One day, Irene Dunne saw me and said, "What are you doing there?" I showed her, and she said, "Oh, would you make me some for my daughter? She would love those."

I said, "Well, sure, sure."

So I made them, and they finished the picture about two days later. A couple of days later, I got the *nicest* letter from Irene Dunne, and she said, "My daughter still has the eggs. How long they'll last, I don't know." She said, "If you ever do anything professional, like making things in a shop or something, let me know." So about three or four years later I started to do marionette shows for children. I'd make the marionettes and I'd design the set and so forth. So I thought, gee, I wonder if Irene Dunne meant that, if she'd remember. So I wrote her a letter and said that I was now doing marionette shows for children's parties and making favors and things. A couple days later I get a phone call from a woman who said, "This is Polly Firestone, of the Firestone Tires. I am a friend of Irene Dunne, and Ms. Dunne told me that you were doing these things for parties, and I'd like to have you come to my daughter's birthday party." So that started about ten years of doing puppet shows for various stars, all because of Irene Dunne. A wonderful woman.

I kept working at Columbia, and did this on the weekend. I found a lot out about stars. They were funny. I did an hour show, I had about twenty-five marionettes and I had scene changes and music and the whole thing. It took me a half an hour to set things up. I had a call from Olivia de Havilland and she said, "I understand that you do these puppet shows. Now, what do you charge?"

I said, "Fifteen dollars."

She said, "Oh, I thought it was $12.50." [Laughs] So I did it for $12.50.

Then I did a show for Jennifer and David Selznick, and I remember, I hated Jennifer Jones for what she did, because here was this show, I was doing this show, and there was David Selznick in the audience. There was Jennifer Jones, she would sit there in front of my stage and continually turning to David and saying, "David, look at the children's faces! Oh, aren't they cute? Look, look, David." [Laughs] I was going on with my show, trying to make a good show. But I will say, he gave me a thirty-five-dollar tip, so that sort of made up for it.

I did a show for Lauren Bacall and Bogart's son Stevie. He's probably middle-aged by now. I remember that Judy Garland was doing *A Star Is Born*, and she came from the set because Liza was there, and Judy was in costume for what she was wearing in the picture. I thought that was thrilling. I was doing a Pinocchio show, and Gepetto, Pinocchio's father, had a big red nose on him, and this little Stevie, Bogart's son, looked at him. Bogart was there, and he says, "Daddy? Does he drink, too?" [Laughs]

But the most revealing thing, I thought, was, Stevie was kind of an upstart.

204

So during the show, he was talking, going on, picking fights with kids and so forth, and Lauren Bacall stepped in and she said, "Stevie! One more word out of you and I'm gonna *smack your face!*" I thought, Oh, Jesus, mothers didn't used to talk like that to kids at their birthday parties.

Remember an actor called Wendell Cory? I was standing in for him on a TV series he did, and he had heard about my doing puppet shows. He said, "I'd like to have you do a show for my kids." I was doing "Snow White and the Seven Dwarfs" at that time and I had the whole thing recorded on wire. We didn't have tape then, it was a wire recorder. So, I go all the way down to Laguna Beach, where he lived, and I'm unpacking my puppets and all of a sudden I realized I hadn't packed the seven dwarfs. Now, it's all prerecorded. So, I thought, oh my God, what am I going to do?

So I start the tape, and everything is going on fine and I said, "Oh children, today we have new version, it's 'Snow White and the Seven *Invisible* Dwarfs.'" And I made a big hit with this! You could hear the boys, they'd hear the voices and say, "Oh, see! They're invisible. See, they're invisible. These are the *invisible* dwarfs." So I saved my neck on that one.

I used to live at the bottom of Beachwood Canyon. There's a gas station there now (at the northwest corner of Beachwood & Franklin) but at that time there was a big tennis court and behind, at the end of the tennis court, was this old house. The house is still there, and I had a room in that house. This old lady ran it, and I had a little room, I never will forget it. A little tiny room, and I didn't know the first thing about cooking and there was this little stove outside the room where people could cook something, some of the tenants, you know. So I thought, "Gee, it's kind of expensive to eat out all the time, maybe I'll cook something. What could I cook? I guess rice would be easy." I found a pot and I put it in there with some water, I'll do that and maybe I'll get a can of tomatoes and put that in there, I thought that would be pretty good. So I did, but I had no idea what happens to rice when you put more than you should [Laughs], so that rice was overflowing all over the place. I didn't tell anyone, no. [Laughs]

When I ate out, I loved the Pig & Whistle. Every Sunday I would go there and they had an organist up in the loft playing the music of the day and the food wasn't expensive but it was good food. I always had scrambled eggs with stewed tomatoes over it, oh it was so great.

I remember because I wasn't making much money and what I would do; I'd walk because I didn't have a car, I'd walk up to Highland and there was a big market there. It was the kind of market where they had the vegetables sitting out close to the sidewalk. I would buy for a week, so I would get seven cans of vegetables, peas, corn and so on, and I'd get seven cans of meat. I'd get tuna, I'd get a can of beef, a can of spam [laughs], and that's what I ate.

There was an elegance to Hollywood Boulevard then. There were palm trees, and I remember Christmastime the Santa Claus parade, and those old street lamps they had big Christmas wreaths on each street lamp and then inside each circle was a colored picture of a current star of the time, such as Colleen Moore.

At the top of Beachwood is the Sunset Ranch, yeah, where we could hire horses. Beachwood Village feels pretty much the same as then, which is nice. It was a little different—there was a drugstore where the Beachwood Cafe is now. It was a drugstore with a soda fountain there. I remember that it had that wonderful old-fashioned drugstore smell. You'd walk in and it was sort of a combination of perfume and medication or something, the drugstore smell. And then next to the drugstore, there was a little market, but it was the old-fashioned kind where they had the fruits and the vegetables right out, you know, right on the sidewalk. Next to that was the filling station.

Hollywood itself—even down the hill from Beachwood—was peaceful. Much more peaceful than it ever is now. And you'd actually maybe see a movie star on Hollywood Boulevard, because of all of these very, very nice shops and the Brown Derby, and NBC Radio at the corner of Sunset & Vine. You'd always see stars around there because of the stars in all the radio shows. And then there was CBS, kitty-corner from Columbia, at Sunset & Gower, there was always stars in that area, too. I was never disappointed by not seeing some star because they were all working in radio. It was great. I loved getting tickets to the radio shows.

The first television thing I'd ever seen was here on KTLA, Channel Five. This was 1948 or '49. They had a show that Gloria Swanson was appearing in, so I went to see that, and I was *amazed* that the women wore black lipstick. I mean they wore *black, black*, like tar. My god, because the light was very bright, extremely bright and the picture was very contrasty. But that was the first television I'd ever seen. I thought that Gloria Swanson looked terrible in black lipstick. [Laughs]

Here's a story about Mae West. I had this marionette that I had made of her and she was appearing in "Diamond Lil" downtown at the Biltmore Theater, so this friend and I we went down there. So I took the marionette in and she looked at it and she said, "I don't have white hair. My hair is platinum, not white." She hated it. So when she autographed it, she autographed right over the face. So then we took these pictures and I went over to the Ravenswood down before she went to a matinee to have her sign this picture and she said, "Well, you're going to have to retouch that scratch." To her, a wrinkle was a scratch, and her hair was not white, it was platinum.

One time I went to her home, and she was wonderful to me. She was very much into spiritualism, they were having a reading or something. She would sit in the dining room in the shadows away from everyone. And what would happen is people would write out questions and put it in a sealed envelope and this guy would take the envelope and put it to his forehead and answer your question without reading. This was the idea of the thing. So someone asked Mae, "Why do you always sit way in the back?" She said, "So I could listen and see what all my friends' secrets were."

After she finished she would receive the people up in her bedroom. So you'd walk up this winding staircase and on the wall there was this mirror with Grecian guys, you know, like body builders in togas and things. So she would stand there in a leopard kind of a robe, in her bedroom. And she was very sweet. And someone said, "Do you still have your monkey?"

And she said, "No, we had to give him to the zoo and I miss him." [Laughter]

I got to know Stan Laurel very well. A wonderful little man, and it's so sad how they treated him. At one time before Hardy died, they were going to have a plaque on the lot saying, Laurel and Hardy, this is where they filmed this or that. Stan told me that he and Hardy went over there and Hal Roach was there and they had some pictures taken and everything, but he said, "When I looked at the plaque, it was on cardboard, painted." He said, "I knew that plaque was not going to be there long, it was just for the pictures." Which it was.

I asked him once, "Aren't you thrilled that your movies are shown on TV so much?" At this period they were showing the Laurel and Hardy comedies all the time every day. I said. "Aren't you thrilled to sit there and see them?"

And he said, "Hell, no!" He said, "Do you know the work we put into each gag to perfect the timing of those things? They've cut them all up, they take things out, they add commercials, the whole thing's ruined!" He hated it.

You see, he was very serious about his work. And he was the one who cared most about it, much more than Hardy. He told me that he and Hardy would do their work, and then the very minute that they could finish, Hardy was off to the golf course. But Stan stayed there and worked. He said, "I was there, I was cutting. I loved the working of the comedies and the watching, and the timing of it, and the cutting. I could have stayed in the studio twenty-four hours. Hardy was a great guy, but that wasn't his interest." But what killed him is when they would bring these things on television and all this careful manipulation and timing would all be wrecked. Right in the middle of a big scene a commercial would come which would destroy the whole thing. He said it killed him. He said "I can't watch them, I just can't watch them."

Did you ever hear the story about the day he died? His wife told me this. She said that he'd had this attack and she was holding him in her arms and he said. "Eda, I wish I was skiing."

And she said, "Well, Stan, you've never skied in your life."

He said, "I know, but I'd rather be doing *that* than this."

[Laughs] Isn't that wonderful? I love that story. It's *so* typical of him.

What Stan did, he loved his fan mail. It came in every day and he would sit down almost like it was part of a job, and he would answer that fan mail. He loved the fans writing to him and he loved the fans coming to see him. Oh, he treated each one like they were coming to interview him or something, he gave them such dignity, he loved and appreciated that. He told me that the first time he ever realized that anyone cared about him was when he went to London and he said that it was scary that the crowd lifted the cab up off the street and carried them in *the cab*. He said, "You know, it was scary. We never *realized* what we meant." He was a humble man, a very humble man. I mean, there was no movie-star thing at all.

When I first came to Hollywood I met this actress, Janice Carter, who was under contract to Columbia. A wonderful person. I got to know her very well. I was standing in at that time and she said, "Bob, you don't wanna go through life as a stand-in. I don't want to see you as an old man, standing in for somebody. You're a nice-looking person, why don't you think about acting?" I wasn't stuttering at the time, but the thought of trying to be an actor made me nervous. I knew I'd be stuttering. She said, "I'm going to write a letter of introduction to you to someone in New York. I want you to go to New York and do summer stock." And I thought, oh my God, if this lovely person is that interested in me and had that much faith in me, how can I say no?

At that time the Screen Extra's Guild, which I was working under, we were given retroactive pay, and I got about three or four hundred dollars, which was a lot of money then, and I thought, well, I could go. I could take this money and go back there, and I was too ashamed to tell her that I was afraid.

So I went and I got a job in summer stock. And I found that I could get out there on stage and the moment I got out there I had so much assurance that I didn't stutter. It was amazing to me. Then when I came back a friend of mine said, "Why don't you try to do picture work?" But the thought of being on a sound stage and the light goes on and the camera starts, and if I were to stutter they'd say, "What the hell are you doing here taking up our time?" You know, it costs money when you have to stop. Well, I thought, no, I couldn't do that.

Well, unbeknownst to me, he called Metro and he asked to speak to the person who was in charge of talent which at that time was Helen. She was married to George Sidney, who was a big director out there. And I said, "I'm Robert Board, and I've just returned from the east doing stock." It was during the war, and they were looking for young guys. I was 4-F because I had an enlarged heart. So I said, "I'd love to come out and read for you."

She said, "Well, fine," and gave a date. So I thought, oh my God, and I went out there, and she was very nice and said, "Now what kind of a scene would you like to do?"

I said, "Well, something like James Stewart might do." [Laughs]

She says, "Well, here's a scene from *Mr. Smith Goes to Washington*. You take this. Take it home and come back in a week."

So I said, "Alright."

Then I thought, what have I done? Well, nothing will happen. So I went home and I memorized the scene and I went back and she said, "Okay, I'll do the Jean Arthur part. Where's your script?"

I said, "Well, I memorized it."

She said, "You *memorized* it? Not many people memorize it. Well, okay."

So I did the scene, no stuttering. She said, "Wait a minute." She goes out and she calls someone, she calls Bill Grady, who was in charge of contracts. [Laughs] I'd like Mr. Grady to hear your reading." I thought what is this?

So we did the scene again and she said, "Why don't you take him over to see William Wilmey. That picture starts Monday." I thought, what is this?

So he took me over to William Wilmey who did *A Star Is Born*. So this Bill Grady says to William Wilmey, "I was thinking about this kid for the opening scene in *The Happy Years*." And Wilmey says, "Okay. Okay, kid, you're in the movies."

I was scared to *death*! I thought I couldn't possibly appear in front of a camera on a soundstage, what if I stuttered? So anyway, the morning came, and I got there very early and went on the soundstage and I was so scared, I'll tell you, I was so scared. There was this old guy working there and he says, "Hi, kid."

And I said, "This is my first time ever doing a line in the movies and I'm so scared." He said, "Oh kid, you know, everyone is scared at first. And I've worked with them *all.*"

I said, "Did you ever work with Marion Davies?" [Laughs]

"Yeah, right on this stage, we did the big 'We'll Make Hay While the Sun Shines' musical number from *Going Hollywood.*" I thought, oh my *God,* I'm on a Marion Davies stage, now this is certainly an omen.

209

So the director comes onstage and he says, "Okay, let's just get this god-damn scene on film," and I said, "Oh no." I'd heard that he was really hard to work with, a real tough guy. So I did the first scene and I didn't have any dialogue in it. Then we did the second scene with Leon Ames, a wonderful character actor, and at the end of the scene, he said "Cut! Okay, kid, James Stewart couldn't have done any better." And I was just in a fog, but I don't know how it ever happened, but after that time the casting guy told me, "We're thinking of you for a contract, but instead of doing a test, what we're going to do is put you in a lot of little different things and see how it works out."

So I started and did about six different things. Not big things, but things with lines. I knew this guy that had a fan club and he said, "We'll have a fan club for you and we'll write to the studios." Well, they started to bombard Metro with: "We want to see Bob Board."

Then somebody said, "You gotta have an agent, gotta have an agent." Well, all this happened without an agent. So I went to these agents on Holly-wood Boulevard and I told them what happened and they said, "Oh my god, the kid is hot at Metro." So they go out there and I was getting the basic pay, whatever it was, they wanted it raised like three times. They thought I was hot. Well, that ended the whole thing. In the first place they said, "You know, we give you a chance. Then we get all this mail about you which we know no one wrote but you or your friends, then you get an agent and want money. Forget the whole thing." So that was the end of *that.* But it's just as well because I never would have felt really at ease, I don't think. I'd rather be behind the camera. Then I got the job as Bob Young's stand-in on *Father Knows Best* and that went on until he retired in the 1980s.

This museum here, with all of these mementos, all accumulated gradu-ally. I didn't have anything when I moved up here. I'd been collecting things. Marion collected scrapbooks, you know, had a lot of scrapbooks and things, but then gradually, little by little I started collecting the one-sheets and lobby cards. I got them for fifteen, maybe twenty dollars. Now, these things, like that, on an auction go as high as seven thousand dollars. I could never begin to buy these things now, naturally, because slowly young people have got hitched to the wagon collecting the old movie stuff and the stuff really keeps its value. They don't make it anymore.

People always ask me why Marion Davies isn't remembered as much as other stars. I've been asked that so many times and I don't know. I know that, number one, Hearst was a man who had enemies and that rubbed off on Marion, and Marion kind of became a joke because he oversold her, always did. You know, when her pictures opened, there'd be an ad like this a week before the picture, an ad like this and then there'd be a bigger ad, a bigger ad, and then her ads would appear not only on the drama page but in other parts of the paper as well. There'd be no competition as far as ads. Somebody would open a paper, my God there's a great big Marion Davies ad there. And then on the opening day, a *whole* page, and sometimes in color, and *no* star had this kind of coverage. So, and then, Louella Parsons, would write that Marion never looked lovelier than this. . . . This is her greatest film ever. And it's hard to live up to that sort of thing. So a lot of people were turned off, number one at the scandal which everyone knew about. And some people would say that Marion Davies was a whore, you know, and that hurt her, but I don't know, I loved her films and it didn't matter to me. People believed that . . . finally after she died, it was sort of just assumed that she was never any good. *Citizen Kane* is what more than anything else, in other words that had to be her, and she had no talent, she was a drunk. She was this submissive little whimpering thing, which was anything *but*. I mean, Marion carried her own weight.

She's interred in her family mausoleum at the Hollywood Cemetery. It doesn't have the name Davies, though; it says Douras, because that is her family name, and when she first came out to California she bought that spot and the family is in there, so she used the name Douras. She was very family oriented, I mean, the family was everything.

But what happened to her memory, I'm not sure. Most people who say, "Oh, Marion Davies was terrible," they never saw any of her films. And her last four films at Warner were not very good.

There are so many stories, this friend of mine out in the Valley, some women's club luncheon, he brought up Marion and they said, "Oh my God, you know, Hearst's twin sons are Marion's and Mrs. Hearst brought them up." Mrs. Hearst *never* would have brought up any of Marion Davies' bastard children, *never*. All these stories go on and on, it's so ridiculous, and the twins were born a year before Hearst even met Marion but, "Oh, no, a friend of mine is a friend of someone and they know that . . . ," all these stories. One story even was that there was a dwarf that ran around the hills of San Simeon and that was one of Marion's children. [Laughing]

Her secretary told me, he said, "Marion, the tragedy of her life was that she adored children, that's why she had the children's clinic, but that physically she couldn't have children." So all these stories about Pat Lake being her daughter and this one being her son. He said that it just couldn't have happened, because she couldn't. She wished she could have. And also, he said that Marion and Hearst defied all conventions. If they had had a child, that child would have never have been pushed aside or away, that child would have been with them at all times. It just wasn't true. I don't know.

It's a very strange situation, because I think now she's going to find her place in cinema history. Her films are being shown on the Turner channel, and I've had a lot of young people come here and say they just adore her. "Oh, yea, I love Marion Davies." They had a showing in the Museum of Modern Art some months ago, and that place was packed. At the end they were just cheering. The young people just loved it! So she slowly is going to get her due, I think, after all those years.

211

Marie Windsor

BORN DECEMBER 11, 1922
MARYSVALE, UTAH
ACTRESS

So striking was she as the consummate femme fatale in a string of classic film noir movies as well as Westerns, science fiction flicks and more that she was known as the "Queen of the Bs." And she was happy with that designation. "It's good to be queen," she says with a wistful laugh. It was while working as a cigarette girl at the legendary Mocambo night club that she was discovered by the producer Arthur Hornblow, who launched her movie career. "I'm ready for you," she says today in a low, smokey voice that immediately brings to mind famous roles she played in dark thrillers through the years, such as The Killing and Narrow Margin. She is gentle and gracious, and rather than entertain what she considers a frivolous question, such as if the Studio Club was populated by ghosts, she simply laughs softly. Unlike other famous actors for whom acting in movies was somewhat of an enchanting lark, she approached every role with great seriousness, and always succeeded in being great; she was great in great movies, and maybe more impressive, she was great even in terrible movies. When this opinion is suggested to her, that despite the quality of the film she was in she always transcended the material, she is sincerely appreciative that her work shone through. "Well, thank you very much for that," she says. "That's really very nice to hear."

When I was a child, I loved the movies. I was such a big fan of Robert Taylor, in fact, that I made a scrapbook of pictures and clippings I found of him, which a couple of years ago I gave to his wife. It was a corny thing. But it's what kids do.

As a child I always wanted to come to Hollywood. My darling mother was always so generous about taking me to a neighboring town, thirty miles away, to take dance and drama lessons.

They didn't have a Miss Utah contest back in those days, when I was growing up. But they did have a contest called The Queen of Covered Wagon Days. So I won that, and I won a thing called Miss DNRG Railroad and they gave me a hundred silver coins, and I bought luggage to come to Hollywood.

I won a grant from the folks of *Cosmopolitan* magazine to go to a drama school. We thought it was in New York but it turned out to be in Hollywood. So they sent me here in 1940 and I lived at the Hollywood Studio Club.

My parents drove me to Hollywood from Utah. I don't think I was overly impressed by Hollywood. It seemed pretty ordinary, just another little town. It was a city you didn't have to be afraid to walk around at night in. It was a very respectable city. I remember driving up Hollywood & Vine with my folks. Eventually I got a star on Vine Street.

Three years was supposed to be the limit that you could live at the Studio Club. But Miss Williams, who ran it, kind of favored me. She let me live there twice. After I was there a couple of years, I went to New York to do a play. And radio. And when I came back, she let me stay another year over my time.

The Studio Club was a great place to live. Girls of similar desires. Everyone there had similar dreams, which made adjusting to being in Hollywood pretty easy. It was a beautifully designed building—it's still there. They had a huge dining room where we would all eat together. You could sit any place you wanted. Nice wooden chairs. They set it very well. For $12.50 you could get board and room. The neighborhood there was very nice then. It wasn't funky like it is now.

Only four rooms on the corners of the building had bathrooms. You otherwise had to go down the hall. Dorothy Malone had one of them. Marilyn Monroe had just moved out the same week I moved in. I got to know her a little bit, and when I was under contract with MGM the same time she was, I got to know her better there. She seemed like a nice kid. I know she didn't always come into the studio with clean clothes. One of the heads of talents had to remind her to be neater about her clothes.

They put announcements on the bulletin board. They were looking for cigarette girls for Mocambo. And my folks were getting so poor, they couldn't afford to pay my board and room there. So I got a job at Mocambo as a cigarette girl. That was kind of exciting. You'd see all these movie stars.

The boss there, the head of the concession, told us if we got five dollars, we could split it with him. Otherwise we would have to give all the tips to him. I remember one night Jimmy Stewart was there, and he gave me five dollars. I told him, "Don't do that. My boss will just take it away from me. Just give me a quarter." So that was one of the things that sort of got me fired.

The other big problem there was that the head cigarette girl was an alcoholic, and everybody said, "Don't give her anything to drink." Well, one night I came to work and she was absolutely *plastered*, and she made a mess all over the place. And I was very tearful—crying actually, when the producer Arthur Hornblow—I was helping on with a coat—he said, "Why are you working here?"

I said, "I'm going to school."

He said, "You want to be an actress, right?"

I said, "Yeah."

He said, "Call my office in the morning. I have an idea."

He introduced me to Leroy Prince, who was about to make a picture out at Hal Roach Studios. So Leroy cast me in one of the parts. So I had a two-week job at $60 a week.

After I lived at the Studio Club, I got married and lived on Hollywood Boulevard. It was west of La Brea. We redesigned a house that used to be Norma Talmadge's honeymoon house. I didn't really like living there, because I was unhappy with my marriage. [My husband] was a musician, and head of KTLA music department. He took a girl-singer to San Francisco. He wasn't a nice fellow. And yet I lent him $800 to get his music together.

I chose the name Windsor myself. It was curious. When I was studying with Oupenskaya, there was a group of girls I used to pal around with. Someone asked the five of us to come to the L.A. Country Club Tennis Club for lunch. And we did, and the gentleman who was our host, said, "Can't you change your name? I can't say Bertleman all the time." So I had a conference with my girlfriends. Everybody had a suggestion. I finally decided on Marie Windsor. Marie was my middle name. I was Emily Marie Bertleman. I chose Windsor because at the time a good love affair in England was with Windsor.

I guess acting in movies came easily to me. I had already had acting lessons. And at Metro I had wonderful coaches. We had dancing lessons, and we would rehearse different scenes. By the time it came to go on the set, we were ready.

Having screen presence is just something you have or you don't. You can't really develop it. But I always learned something by seeing myself in films. I had a wonderful coach who was brought here by Selznick for *Song of Bernadette* with Jennifer Jones.

I did the film *The Killing* with Stanley Kubrick. When we had our first meeting, I thought he was just a kid. He was very young. But Kubrick's brain was already very advanced by that time. His wife was an artist, and she had drawn, in charcoal, every scene that he was going to shoot. He was a *wonderful* director, very quiet. He didn't tell you very many things to do or not to do. He just let you wing it and corrected you when you needed it. He would take you aside when he gave you direction instead of talking to you in front of the other actors. That is what he did with all the actors.

214

I had no idea that *The Killing* would become a classic. I have spoken to several of us ladies who worked in film noir. And none of us even knew what "film noir" was. All we could figure out is that they were dark pictures in black and white. We never knew everyone was going to make such a big to-do about it. And I suppose I'll be mostly remembered for my film-noir films.

The Narrow Margin was a good one, too. But I never could tell when a picture was going to be good or not. I just took every job I was offered. Sometimes the directors were very good, and sometimes they were not. But I always believed you should come onto the set with something already prepared. That you should not leave it all to the director. And if he doesn't like what you've brought, you adjust it.

In the film *Frenchie* there's a famous fight scene I did with Shelley Winters. We got roughed up a little bit. We didn't use stunt people—it was something we both agreed to do. And it came out great.

The magazines at the time used to run stories about me dating all sorts of people, but they weren't usually true. They said I dated Clark Gable. I *guess* you could call it a date. I used to go out to his ranch out in the Valley and ride his horses with him. I never went on a real date with him.

I did a lot of work at RKO, which was very nice at the time. A nice commissary. That was the time when we did *Narrow Margin* in the mid-forties and Howard Hughes was so crazy about it that he kept it in hiding for eighteen months. He owned the studio. Hughes was a very nice man. I first met him in New York, and he took me to the Waldorf to dinner. And he danced in his tennis shoes. The second time I dated him, he came up four flights of stairs to my apartment. I had a feeling, in retrospect, that he didn't like the way I kept house. He never called me back.

Narrow Margin mostly takes place on a moving train. That was interesting to film. The producers insisted there be no music in the film so that all you hear is the sound of the train. It was very effective. I *loved* that part.

It's true I played a lot of characters that were not nice people. But it was just acting a part. But nobody ever confused me with the parts I played. Nobody except my sister, that is. [Laughs]

I know my work is part of cinema history. That has certainly made me feel very proud. I did not have a short career. I acted with a lot of great people.

My favorite films were *The Narrow Margin*, *The Killing*, and a Western called *Hell-fire*. I also got to do a film with Abbott and Costello called *Abbott & Costello Meet the Mummy*. That was fun to do. They were wonderful people. They were funny off-camera, too. But they were not arguing, as people often ask me. They were just doing their job. I didn't know until later that they were having little *spats* with each other.

CatWomen of the Moon is probably the silliest film I ever did. And it's become one of the most famous. It's *so* corny, my God, here we are, taking off from the moon on rolling office chairs. [Laughs]

Even after I started in movies, I still went back and did a lot of radio. And I loved working in radio very much. It was very interesting working in radio. It was a new medium I had to learn how to work with, but I enjoyed it very much.

I worked with George Sidney on a couple of films. I am very fond of him. He's a very, very nice man and a very good director. I also loved working with King Vidor.

I did *Force of Evil* with Abraham Polanski. He was a very good director and a nice man. I didn't know how politically incorrect he was all during that time. John Garfield was in the film with me. He was fun and very nice. I'm taller than he is, but he wouldn't make a fuss about it. He'd just say, "Bring the box." At five-foot-eight, I was taller than a lot of the men I worked with. It happened with George Raft. I had to do a tango with him and Louise Jensen, the designer, designed this gorgeous dress with a full skirt, so that I could bend my knees and they couldn't tell.

Some people were worried videos would cause people to stop going to the movies, but they go more than ever. It's interesting, isn't it? I think it's a great relief for people to see movies, and usually it's most entertaining.

People have been trying to bring back Hollywood. But with the kind of people who live around there, I don't see how it can ever be anything but trash.

It was a glamorous life. I wouldn't call it work. It was a great pleasure for me to act in movies.

Leatrice Joy Gilbert Fountain
BORN SEPTEMBER 6, 1924
HOLLYWOOD, CALIFORNIA
AUTHOR

The daughter of silent-movie stars John Gilbert and Leatrice Joy, she lives now some 3,000 miles east of Hollywood in Connecticut. Her father was one of the first great romantic silent-movie stars, and is probably more famous these days because of the myth of his failure in talkies. The story goes that Gilbert, celebrated for the palpable passion of his onscreen romance with Garbo, couldn't make the transition from the silents into sound because of a high, squeeky voice, a voice so laughable that the first audiences to experience his first talkie, His Glorious Night, were said to have broken out in hysterics.

The truth was that the first audiences to see talkies were often so amazed by this phenomenon of movies that now spoke that they did laugh, no matter what was being said. Gilbert, in fact, had a resonant baritone voice. If his voice didn't suit sound movies, that surely would have been discovered long prior to the public screening of the movie. According to his daughter, the author of a fine biography of her father called Dark Angel, his career was intentionally destroyed by Louis B. Mayer, as she relates in the following memoir.

Her mother was Leatrice Joy, whose work in silent pictures is also discussed here, and whose career came to a premature demise because of Cecil B. DeMille. The lives and work of both of her parents reflects maybe more powerfully than any others the evolution of the movies from silence into sound, a development that forever changed Hollywood, and also the world.

2 1 6

My parents were separated before I was born, and were divorced when I was about a year old. I never lived with my father. Mother used to talk to me a little about him, but she remarried when I was about seven, and I was brought up by my stepfather, so my real father really didn't play a role in my life. Once she married, I didn't see him at all except we would run into him sometimes at the beach.

When I was born, my mother lived in Hollywood at Fountain & Sweetzer. I remember that house. I remember the kitchen. I remember Louise Beavers, who was our cook, and Mother got her into pictures. She told her, "You know, you should be in pictures," and got her first acting job. And she did make quite a number of pictures.

I remember the white milk-horse. Milk was delivered in a horse-drawn wagon and was pulled by a white horse. The milkman used to pick me up and let me sit on the horse. I remember the sunlight coming into the room where I had my playpen; I guess that would have been the dining room. I remember that, and I remember my great-uncle coming in to see me.

My mother didn't tell me my name was Gilbert. She named me Leatrice Joy II. She was so angry and so bitter about the divorce that she wouldn't even let me use the name. I knew I had a father, but I didn't know who he was. And then when I got to kindergarten, I found out that L.J.G. were my initials, and I said, "What's the G for?" and the teacher told me Gilbert. [Laughs] It didn't mean anything to me.

Then they told me that he lived in a tower, and I looked out my bedroom window and saw this great big watertower up a hill on the top of a hotel. And I thought that was the tower that he lived in. He actually lived up on

Tower Road [in Beverly Hills]. It was quite suitable, because I thought of this magical being living in a tower on the top of a hill. Like a prince in a fairy tale.

On one of their first dates, Mother wore her best dress, which was soft black velvet. But it made her look especially pale, and she didn't know much about how to put on makeup. She lived in one of those bungalow courts with her mother then, and Theda Bara also lived there—she was famous at the time for being a vamp in pictures. Theda was only thirty then but she'd already made over forty pictures and her career was pretty much over. Mother knocked on her door and told her about this makeup problem. And Theda was happy to help. She sat Mother down and made up her whole face, with kohl around her eyes, and indigo, and white powder for her face, and rouge and lipstick. When she went back home, her mother saw her and said, "You're an actress, not a fancy woman. Go wash your face this *instant*." [Laughs]

The first time my mother did a picture with my father, Mother was very nervous. She'd only done a few pictures before that. So she rubbed her arms with a white body paste called Wheatcroft enamel that was supposed to give her an alabaster glow onscreen. It also rubbed off on anything it touched. In their first scene together, Father was wearing his cherished black dinner jacket, which had cost him all of twenty dollars. A *lot* of money then. Mother burst in upon him, throwing her arms all over his shoulders and back. In seconds his dinner jacket was *ruined*. He tried to get away from her, but she just figured he was acting and kept on going! And she didn't stop! She kept on using it. She did the very same thing again in her next two pictures, but with different actors. When I asked her why she used it if it caused so many problems, she said, "Because it made my arms look pretty." That's my mother. [Laughs] Oh, she was a *sketch*. Impossible to deal with. Because she was an *actress*. Actresses tend to be very self-absorbed. And she was. They're narcissistic. They look at the world like a *mirror*, and they see themselves reacting to the world. But they don't see the world itself.

I remember visiting her at Paramount when she was working on a silent movie with Gilbert Rowan. It was sort of a Hawaiian island movie. I remember the jungle.

I remember when she was making *First Love* with Deanna Durbin I came down from summer camp and was driven out to the studio, where she was filming at night. We were all standing around outside, and the director and producer were huddled around the first portable radio I'd ever seen, which was about the size of a great big typewriter case. They had it on and they were listening to the German troops moving into Poland. It was the

Aunschluss, the beginning of the war, 1939. I will *never* forget it, cause they were looking at each other. They all had families there. That's how I became aware of the war beginning.

My mother had many disagreements with DeMille. He didn't want her to have a baby. He left Jesse Lasky at Paramount and opened his own production unit. He rented space from Metro and moved his unit there. And Mother begged him, begged him, *begged* him not to take her. Because he had no release outlets. She *explained* to him, "I'm supporting my *mother* and my *child*, you can't do this." But it was in her contract that he could take her, and he *did*.

219

And she went off with him, and for eighteen months she had no movies shown. They weren't being released. The distributors were all under contract to the major studios. DeMille thought he could fight this and he couldn't. In those days people were making movies every week or so. Most of them were very quick. And if you weren't being seen regularly, people would forget you. So in her long absence from the screen, her popularity dropped. She had been making movies with DeMille through the twenties, but by 1929, her contract expired with him and she didn't have another job.

So she went out touring in vaudeville, and she went all over the country singing. She was voted the most popular vaudeville star. I have a medal she won for this. She really was very popular. Then she came back and married my stepfather. And she retired, because her career had folded. Which it *shouldn't* have done. I was talking to Irene Selznick, who was Louis B. Mayer's daughter. And she said that was a real tragedy [that my mother retired]. Because she was so much better than most of the other women going around in those days. She was pretty. She was talented. She had all these gifts going, and just something happened. History went wrong. She just didn't make it. It really was just her problems with DeMille.

She spoke about DeMille in a funny way, because she had this great crush on him. Mother loved authority. [Laughs] If anyone was in a position of authority, Mother had this attitude that you respected and obeyed and did what you were told. But she was very angry with him, and when she was taken by him from Paramount, she would be on the lot and walk right by him and not speak. But she wouldn't defy him, she wouldn't go to court and try to break the contract, which she probably could have done. But she got him mad, of course. He was a temperamental son-of-a-gun. [Laughs, and then softly] Oh, he was terrible. Very egotistical and very tyrannical. He was always very nice to me, though, when I was a child. Gave me a little string of pearls for my birthday. He couldn't have been nicer.

Mother respected his talent. She thought he was a great director, and she was very unhappy that I wrote in my book that he wasn't. He *was* capable of being a great director. The irony was that in his early works DeMille showed he was perfectly capable of making intelligent, sensitive, well-drawn films. But he wanted to make a lot of money, and he lost respect for the public. He was sure that if he made crappy movies, that everybody would love them. And he was *right!* [Laughs] He would tell Mother, "I want you to be a lady in this, but I don't want you to be a *real* lady is, I want you to be what a housemaid *thinks* a lady is. Do it for *them*." He was always aiming *down* at his audiences.

219

He could be *impossible* with people. DeMille had one man whose job was to carry a chair for him. And DeMille would never look back, he would sit down and assume that the chair was there. And God *help* that guy if he didn't have the chair there. Which sometimes happened, and the guy would be fired on the spot. [Laughs] And he carried his pearl-handled pistols and *puttees* and boots and all this stuff. He was creating a role. He often wore riding britches and carried a whip.

In 1972 the Museum of Modern Art in New York was showing a movie of his, *The Merry Widow*. I met Kevin Lewis, an archivist, and he said, "You know—somebody should write a book about your father, and I was thinking of doing it myself." And I thought that if anyone writes a book about him, I should do it. I had written one novel, so I knew I could put a book together. So I started doing research, and reading what I could, and I found there wasn't a whole lot about him. His reputation had been certainly down-pedaled. I didn't know why at the time.

I wanted a quote, so I came up with that he was the prop on which Greta Garbo had hung her reputation. And Sam Marx had some bad things to say about him. Sam Marx was at MGM and was a distant relative of Louis B. Mayer's, and he owed his career to Mayer, so he took the Mayer line and talked about how much trouble Gilbert had been, and his *drinking*, and all this *womanizing*, and that he didn't offer much as an actor. People were dismissing him as if he had never been a big star. As if it was just some *accident* that he had risen, and had been the biggest moneymaker. Before the Academy Awards there was the Photo-Play Gold Medal Award, and he was the first person to get that, for *The Big Parade*.

Then I started meeting people. I was able to track down people who worked on movies with him back in the early days, back in 1915, 1916. Cameramen. Grips. Extras. I found out personal *reminiscences* of what he had done and what he said and what people felt about him. And his funny little yellow car, and how he was everybody's kid brother. He was a movie kid—they watched him grow up, and they worried about the girls he was going with, and whether his car was going to work. He was like a mascot to them. And they all *loved* him. I just kept finding these warm testimonials to this guy. A woman who had been in love with him. *Nobody* had a bad word to say about him.

And then there were things that people would write—Ralph Bellamy, Mervyn LeRoy, and others—who had worked in the early talkies with him. So you got different stories. At that end of his life, near his death, he *was* acting eccentric and erratic, and he was still *so* angry with the studio, and he was *so* proud that he wouldn't compromise with Mayer in any way. Which might have saved his life, if he had.

When I came back from Los Angeles I went up to Rochester to see Jim Card, who ran the archives. I told him I hadn't even seen anything my father had done except for the last talkie he had made, *The Captain Hates the Sea*. I said, "I don't know if he can act or not."

Card said, "Come with me, and I will show you." And he sat me down in one of their big projection rooms there, and he showed me *everything*. He started at the beginning, a movie with William S. Hart. And there was my father, this little boy, this young man, I could see him. Cowboy hat, and trying *so* hard, and *so* thin. These great big eyes looking out of this little thin face. He was *starving*. They didn't pay them anything, and he was supporting himself in Hollywood. And *loving* the movies. Watching him that first time was very emotional for me, because I suddenly realized I had children who were older than he was in those early films. There I was in my forties, watching my little, young father up on the screen. And how he could dominate the screen.

My mother also had a great effervescence on screen; people described her like a glass of champagne. She had this *ebullience*. She would *spring* out of things. She was full of energy. She was very funny. She was a good comedienne, like Marion Davies. She was better at comedy. DeMille kept putting her in these great big overdressed costume dramas. They should have let her do her little comedies, because in those she was superb. She was very, very good.

Mother was from New Orleans and spoke with a *charming* Southern accent, which is probably one of the reasons she didn't make it into talkies. She did do a few talkies, but very few. She did one in the thirties called *The Bellamy Trial*. Then much later, in the fifties, she did a few pictures for Republic. She did *First Love* at Universal with Deanna Durbin and Robert Stack, which was, I think, the last movie she made.

Mother used to tell me about what Hollywood Boulevard was like in her day, in the teens and early twenties, when it had pepper trees and orange groves. She and my father rented a little house right on Hollywood near the opening of Laurel Canyon. And they were *surrounded* by orange groves. She said the scent of the blossoms used to keep them up nights, it was so overpoweringly sweet.

They had a dog that they loved, and it died, and they had to bury it in the garden. It was very countrified. They would all walk down to the Hollywood Hotel for the parties that were there. In the early days they had these beautiful wrought-iron bus benches at every bus stop. And on the back of each one was the name of one of the stars. This was long before they had stars on the sidewalk. And at one point in the thirties, the Hollywood council decided that was just wasted money, that they would put up plywood benches for the bus stops, and then they could sell advertising on it. So they trashed these gorgeous wrought-iron benches. My mother was home one day and her friend, the actress Lois Wilson called up and said, "Leatrice, *they're taking our benches away!*" So Mother said, "Quick—get a truck!" And they went up and they were able in time to get their benches. Mother got the one with her name on it, and she brought it east with her when she came here in the fifties. And right now it's in a park down the street from where I live. It says "Leatrice Joy." They were *beautiful.* And there must have been hundreds of them.

221

Two or three times I was in the Hollywood Christmas parade. I was invited to be a guest in Santa Claus' sleigh. I would get dressed up in my little white rabbit coat and hat, and go be trundled around with Santa Claus, and wave to the people, and throw candy.

I think my earliest memory of meeting my father was at one of my birthday parties. I may have been four. I remember his long white trousers. I was small and he was very tall. He and my mother were talking and I wasn't getting any attention, so Mother had a little bowl of pretty colored desert sand on a tall table. I picked it up and poured it all over the floor because I wanted some attention. [Laughs] And it worked. Because then he held me on his lap, and then he put me on his shoulder and carried me around.

When I was ten, I wrote my father a fan letter. I didn't know if I would ever hear from him but I did. He would send a car down and I would go up to his house on Tower and spend the day with him. And *those* were the occasions that I felt I got to know him. It would only be for a couple of hours. But it would be so dramatic and wonderful to go there. So exciting.

It was not a large house—movie stars did not build huge houses then. It was a medium-sized Spanish house. Oddly built, because you'd park, and then you'd walk up a whole flight of stairs to the front door. He would meet you at the top of the stairs, and then there was an entrance hall, and white walls and red-tiled floors. Spanish-looking stuff. Wrought-iron fixtures and his paintings, they were all kind of dark, wonderful looking paintings that he had, and Oriental rugs, and candle sconces that stood on the floor with candles in them. A fire going in the winter. It was a very masculine house. You could see that he had done this, this was his taste.

Father wasn't a typical Los Angeles person. He was a self-educated person. He educated himself. His friends were all the so-called intellectuals around there—Ben Hecht, Charlie MacArthur, Mankiewiscz, Irving Thalberg, Barnie Glazer. Writers. He didn't hang out with the playboys and the gambling crowd. He was interested in things of the mind.

He was always dressed beautifully. He played tennis a lot, so I remember him in his white flannels and a white shirt and a V-neck sweater. I don't think I ever saw him in a suit. He would be wearing casual clothes. But he wouldn't be around in jeans and a T-shirt. [Laughs] He'd be in elegant sort of English-looking sports clothes.

222

He had two men servants. They were both from the Philippines. They had both been there for years. He left them money in his will.

All these famous men who were bachelors lived up there in the hills near Father. Paul Bern, Charlie Chaplin, Cary Wilson. And their wives and girl-friends would move in and out. [Laughs]

I remember Colleen Moore was involved with all these guys. She said, "They were these nuts." They were so funny and so bright. They would get all excited about some subject, like trying to beat a roulette wheel, and they would get two dozen roulette wheels and set them up in the house, and they would start spinning them to see if they could work out a system.

Once they got Harry Houdini up there to explore the Ouija board, or some of his tricks, or spiritualism. One time they even had a seance with Houdini. Mother was there, too. She told me that the table lifted and started moving around, and crashed into my father. Almost broke his ribs, pushed him against the wall. He was terrified. But he said he was not taken in by it.

Then they got excited about aniline dyes. And Mother said that for days the stink of these chemicals were going all through the house. So they were not just making movies, but between movies they were interested in everything.

Father spent a lot of time with Chaplin at the Hollywood Athletic Club. They swam a lot, lifted weights and worked out. It was Chaplin who got him into the Athletic Club by sponsoring him for membership. Father spoke to Chaplin when [Gilbert] was still married to his first wife, Olivia, and he'd met my mother and fallen in love with her. Chaplin encouraged him to divorce Olivia and marry Mother. He said, "You know, you can't go backward." So my personal history was molded by Charlie Chaplin, of all people.

Father acted with Lon Chaney in a few films. The first one that they did together was He Who Gets Slapped. That's a great movie. The first thing Father did at MGM. Thalberg put him in it, and Father quarreled about it, because it was a very tiny part, and Father couldn't understand why he should do it. And Thalberg explained that it was a prestige picture.

It was based on a European story about a famous doctor whose wife leaves him and his career collapses, and he becomes a clown because he doesn't want to face the world anymore. It was an interesting, allegorical story. It's shown from time to time. He and Norma Shearer are bareback riders in the circus. And they have this charming love affair. They have picnics in the woods, and they both look so adorable. And I gather from Shearer that they were a little bit in love in those days. This is before she married Thalberg. When she did *Romeo and Juliet* in 1936, she wrote me when my father died and said, "Some of the tears I shed as Juliet were for your father." It was very sweet.

223

Father and Lon Chaney did not get along at all. Chaney had no use for him. Chaney thought he was frivolous. Chaney was very serious. He grew up with two deaf parents, and he had almost no sense of humor at all. The only thing he could understand was hard work and dedication to it, and he took his craft so seriously with these elaborate makeups and costume-things. They just didn't get along. There are some people that are just chemically unbalanced. Father was not tolerant. He was very opinionated, and he couldn't understand why Chaney, who was a movie star, didn't live like a movie star. Chaney didn't enjoy stardom at all.

Now Father got along with Irving Thalberg beautifully. Father was the only actor that Irving Thalberg ever hung out with. Most of his friends were in the production end, or writers. But he and Father went off together at night. They were friends, they were buddies.

After Father died, Thalberg invited me to the studio to see *The Big Parade*. Thalberg was wonderful to me. He was a very gentle, very articulate man. Very bright. Very fragile-looking. Not a strong man at all. He didn't have good color; he looked fallow. And he was with this beautiful Norma Shearer. And they had two children.

The actors of the silent movies loom more like royalty than the movie stars of today. The relationship between the film-goers and the actors in silent times was very different; there really was an adoration, an adulation. They were godlike. And people wanted anything that was like the stars. It revolutionized plumbing in America. People went to the movies and saw indoor bathrooms. And all of a sudden, the wives would say to their husband, "I want an indoor bathroom. I don't want to walk out in the rain to go to the toilet. And I want my bathtub where I can get to it."

And seeing these stars on the screen, without hearing their voices, made them even more like icons.

Chaplin, who was perhaps the most iconic of them all, was between wives when I met him. He was curious about me, because I was Jack's daughter. He was always very nice. I knew Oona. I met her just after they were married. We had a long taxi ride together, all over Los Angeles. He fled to Switzerland, and she came back, because she was an American citizen, and she cleared out their bank accounts and their safe-deposit boxes, and got all of his securities and money out of the country before the government had a chance to clamp down on him. They threw him out of the country because they were afraid of his being a Communist.

Father and Greta Garbo were so much in love. Have you ever seen the picture *Love*? It was a silent version of *Anna Karenina*. That was their best film together. At that point they are so in love when they made it, and it's a more naturalistic kind of acting than they did in *Flesh and the Devil*. It's such a sweet picture. It is so visually pleasing, and their affection for each other was real.

224

Garbo was good to Father, especially at the end. The worse thing is that she couldn't marry him, and that just about killed him. But she couldn't marry anybody. She just couldn't do it. She couldn't commit. But she and father did live together. She always had her own house, but it was just where she could withdraw to. She had her other quarters up at his house. She was his hostess for his parties—for his tennis parties—and they would go out to night clubs and theater openings together. And they would go walking. They were both great walkers, and would walk for miles up in the hills. And they would play tennis. He taught her how to play tennis, and she loved it. She had her own funny double-grip on the racket long before any modern players did. [Laughs] But she was not a bad tennis player.

Father was the first grown-up I had ever met who would talk to me as if I was a rational, thinking person. Most adults talk down to kids, and use a different voice, or talk about things they think you would be interested in. But he talked to me about *anything*. And listened to what I had to say. He was curious about school. He wouldn't say, "How was school?" He'd say, "Tell me about your teacher," or "Who are the kids you don't like?" He was *wonderful*. But I was very tense and nervous and a little scared. I wanted him to like me and I was so shy, I didn't know what to say.

But once in a while I would blurt things out. And I told him that my mother-in-law was for Prohibition, and he sat and explained very carefully why that wouldn't work. [Laughs] And he was right.

He was very bright. He read to me. He read Ernest Thompson Seakin's books about animals. *Lives of the Hunted*. He didn't approve of hunting. He was very conscious of animal rights. It's funny—that was sixty years ago. He always had pets. He always had dogs or cats or marmosets or something running around. And he got interested in cactus, and had a beautiful cactus garden that he had designed and planted and took care of outside. He wanted something that would grow naturally there. And, oh, the most *extraordinary*, *exotic*-looking cactuses that were there. That was one of the first things that got dug up when the house got sold. But I remember it well.

The myth about him that his voice was high was totally wrong. His voice was nice. He sounded like David Niven. A rather light baritone. Or Douglas Fairbanks Jr. They had the same kind of voice. In fact, Douglas said that they used to imitate each other. They would answer each other's phones and pretend to be the other one. [Laughs]

I saw *His Glorious Night*, which was the film that was said to be [Gilbert's] downfall. The thing that made it fail is that it was based on a sophisticated, Viennese, ironic comedy. With lines that were meant to be funny but over-the-top funny, like "Oh *beauteous* maiden, my arms are waiting to *enfold* you. I love you, I love you, I *love* you." People laughed at that because they didn't understand it was irony. It was *satire*. And it was much too subtle. And whether they did that deliberately, or whether they expected people to see that, who knows. But he looked marvelous, he sounds *perfectly* all right, but the lines were funny.

225

Now there's a funny story that Clarence Brown told me. And that was that he had run into Douglas Shearer, who was the head of the sound department and Norma's brother. Clarence asked him what happened to Gilbert's voice. And Douglas Shearer said, "You know, we forgot to turn up the bass." So who knows?

In silent movies, people heard the words they wanted to hear. The words they were used to. They produced them themselves in their imaginations. And instead of that, you suddenly had all this laid out for you, and people were *embarrassed*. It was more intimacy than they could handle.

Many people thought that talkies would be just a fad. Chaplin told Father that he felt the talkies would go away, and Lillian Gish felt the same way. And Thalberg, too. They all thought that it wouldn't be more than a flash in the pan, that movies will always be *visual*, they're not something for sound. And boy were they wrong! Once *The Jazz Singer* was so popular, then they began to tear up the studios and put in the soundstages. And that changed *everything*.

And it really wasn't until the last time we were together near Christmas when I went up to see the tree. And when he drove home with me that day, I remember thinking that I was feeling *comfortable* with him for the first time. Really completely comfortable, free to say anything. And I suddenly at that point said to myself, "I have a father, I *really* have a father." And I felt so joyful about this. That there was somebody who cared about me and that I could care back. And then a week later he was dead.

I don't think I *ever* got over it. I had a stepfather who didn't even like his own children, let alone *me*. There was no one else really in my life. Mother was hardly ever there. Mother was busy doing other things. She did what she could. Some people are nurturers and some people aren't. Mother did the very best she could and she *never* neglected me. She was *sure* that I was being taken care of. And she was certain that I had my mind occupied. She gave me lessons and made sure that I did them. I learned all kinds of stuff—to ride, and to draw, and many languages. She did everything. The only thing that she *couldn't* do was give me a warm, intimate relationship. But that you either can or can't do. And that's not her fault. That's the way she was.

226

I did one movie myself when I was twelve called *Of Human Hearts* at MGM. With Clarence Brown directing. I played the child who grew up to be Ann Rutherford. It was a Civil War story with Jimmy Stewart and Walter Huston. I had a good time doing it. But I wasn't driven to keep doing it. You have to have that driving ambition. I did it just because my mother encouraged me to do it. And it was a nice part. She called Clarence and asked him to give me a test and he did. We ended up at Lake Arrowhead, and we had picnics. Oh my *dear*, I couldn't believe they were paying me to do anything that was so much fun. It was just *wonderful*. You'd go to school up in that little school-room up there. We stayed at that inn up there. The whole company stayed together. It was a very nice, communal feeling. But I didn't miss it terribly when it was over.

I was offered the lead in *National Velvet*. It was announced in the paper. I remember in one of the Hearst papers. All across the top of the Drama section. And I would have done it. But the producer was a man named Hud Stromberg and he had a falling out with Louis B. Mayer, and was fired. And then they waited about seven years until they decided to make the movie. By which time I was too old, so they got this kid actress named Liz Taylor.

Ken Paradise
BORN APRIL 6, 1925
MILWAUKEE, WISCONSIN
ACTOR

The Montecito, seventh floor. This old apartment building, once the fashionable hotel of choice for New York actors while working in Hollywood, is now what's known as a "senior residence," which means he can get this small apartment up above Franklin Avenue for a reasonable rent. A big man with a blonde toupee, he's wearing white baggy shorts, a sailor's shirt and sandals, and sits on a burgundy couch in his apartment surrounded by movie mementos, such as the multicolored mounted butterflies that were a gift from Natalie Wood. Encircled by the movies themselves, his bookshelves are lined with thousands of videotapes and laser discs of all his favorite films. His given name is Perry, but he still uses his stagename, Paradise, though he retired from acting years ago. His biggest movie role was in the film China Doll, *yet he's been on the sidelines of Hollywood for decades. When he says that he had the looks to be a star, he isn't exaggerating—his old eight-by-tens from the forties prove he looked every bit the matinee idol, somewhere between*

Montgomery Clift and James Dean, but with a bright shock of blond hair and electric blue eyes. Today he sips from a can of cold beer, admits he's scared of being swindled or worse, and laughs a lot while he talks.

I first came to Hollywood during the war in 1943 when I was a GI, and moved here in 1945 when I was discharged from the marine corps. And I decided to stay. Those were glorious days for us GIs. Because Hollywood was magic town. And people here were *so* generous. I was invited to beautiful homes along Sunset Boulevard that I *never* would have had access to otherwise. But because I was a serviceman, we had brunches, we had barbecues, we had all sorts of things. Meet girls and dance, that sort of thing. And it was a grand time. It was a romantic era. Strangely enough, because it was a horrible, horrible war, a hideous experiment, especially for me. I was very sick and very hard put by it. After all, I was pretty damn young. I got in the service when I was eighteen. I wasn't out of puberty yet. Of course, I didn't get out of puberty till I hit thirty-five. [Laughter]

227

I was on Okinawa during the war. Tyrone Power was on an island north of Okinawa where he flew cargo planes back and forth to the island of Iyashima. The first time I saw him during the war he looked every inch the movie star. But the next time I saw him, oh wow, he had really been ravaged by the war. He looked like death warmed over. His eyes looked like two burnt holes in a blanket. I swear it must have taken ten years off of his life. But that was the last time I saw Ty Powers until after I had gotten established in Hollywood.

I next saw him at Dolores' Drive-In at Sunset Boulevard & La Brea. I will *never* forget, he had a silver Jaguar. I remember sitting there in my Buick and this little silver thing pulls in alongside of me. And I look and I say, "Omigod, Ty, you *gorgeous* thing, what are you doing here?" He says, "Same thing you are. I'm hungry." [Laughter] You've got to bear in mind, it was a different era and I was so damn young. And movie stars of the Tyrone Power category were my *gods*. They were my living, breathing gods. And just to be in the same air with them was a privilege for me.

I met Jesse Lasky Sr. first and I never knew why, but he just took a liking to me. We got along famously. I met him through his son Bill. The bambino of the family. We had a lot of talks back in those early days. He loved the idea that I was so fascinated with the beginnings of Hollywood's history and he loved to tell me the stories. He also wanted to fill me with stories about his lust for cars, but sorry, I wasn't there. I could care less about cars and car races. When I knew him it was the twilight of his career and he was no longer producing. He had already done the Caruso thing at Metro with

Mario Lanza. He put his soul in hock to get that done. It was the last thing that Lasky ever did. And he had to sell himself down the river to get that. Hollywood's a very eat 'em up, chew 'em up, spit 'em out kind of place.

I remember him calling Mervyn LeRoy on my behalf and asking him to just meet with me, and talk to me, and maybe test me. Mervyn was at Warner Brothers at the time. *He couldn't be bothered!* He could care less. He practically slammed the phone down in the old man's face. And Lasky was furious. "Never should have taken that sonofabitch away from the camera. He should be a cameraman. That's all he deserves to be."

228

Jesse Lasky Jr. made a very handsome living as a screenwriter under the DeMille banner. Because DeMille used him as his favorite whipping boy. Another pretentious *ass* if ever there was one. I met him, I saw how he treated Jesse Jr., I saw him at work on the set of The Ten Commandments. There were 125 people back there, and some extra would be laughing. And DeMille would be up on his goddamn stepladder—he always wanted to be one step below God. He'd see this person laughing and he'd say, "That man is *laughing*. I want him off my picture right now. And I want a letter sent to Central Casting. I want *everyone* notified. This man is *not* a professional. This is a *serious* moment. We will have no laughter and we will have no wrist watches. Watch it because I'm watching *you*. I want that man off the stage, out of the studio, I don't ever want to see him again." And he was out one door, and back in another. And that's the way it worked. Really and truly.

I was a great set-sider. Know what that means? As an actor, one aspired to greatness beyond parallel, I would do my damnedest to get on any set. And particularly big ones like The Ten Commandments to set-side: to watch, listen, look, learn, hear, watch the mistakes of others and learn from them.

This is so long ago. And really ancient times [Laughs]. You smile like you know *everything*. There's only so much here I'm willing to have *recorded*, you know.

Jonathan Winters
BORN NOVEMBER 11, 1925
DAYTON, OHIO
COMEDIAN / ACTOR

Not everyone agrees on what makes them laugh, but rare is the person who will disagree with the notion that Jonathan Winters is genuinely funny. In fact, at the age of seventy-five, he remains one of this planet's funniest humans. Today he stands outside of his stately Montecito mansion, just south of Santa Barbara, where he moved more than a decade ago to escape Hollywood. A long driveway leads from the mountainous roads outside his gates and up and around the palatial home to where he stands. He walks into a den off the main corridor, a room where he can smoke cigars without offending Eileen, his wife of fifty-three years, who remains upstairs and out of sight. His den holds antique military toys—wooden and metal soldiers of all shapes and colors, sailing ships, muskets, swords and more. Over easy chairs and a comfortable couch, the wall is filled with paintings of sailing ships and yachts and all other kinds of maritime vessels. Though he's a painter himself, he does not hang his own work in this room. Wearing a T-shirt bearing the official insignia of the C.I.A, he launches immediately into the first of an amazing succession of comic dialogues, in which he fully takes on the character of two people, often representing opposing forces, and explores in great detail the hilariously human interior workings of their hearts and minds. He is a writer at heart—it's his first dream, outside of that of being a pilot—and these famous dialogues that he does are the external expressions of a great writer developing characters that are usually kept internal on the way to the page. He gives them voice, and from their mouths come those tiny and truly intimate human details that make his humor so specific and genuine. His comedy reels forward like a great radio show, and it's in radio that he started, providing both sides of a conversation as confidently and hilariously as any great comedy team, as well as frequent sound effects, but with no other partner than himself. His work is not about the punchline, it's about the recognition of what it feels like to be human. It's never rushed or forced; he slips into characters as comfortably as one slips on an old coat, and allows them to unfold slowly of their own accord. There's a constant sense of discovery in these dialogues, as the creator discovers with delight the miscellaneous twists and turns the human psyche selects. He loves many writers, he says, but of all of them Dickens is his favorite. "For many reasons," he says, "but the chief reason is because when he painted his characters, I could see them. This is what held me. He's not only telling me a story about poverty and snow, he's telling me about environmental situations, he's telling me about the economy, he's telling me about himself."

229

He speaks about himself, his parents and his children, his upbringing and his road to Holly-wood and beyond, all interwoven with the brilliant, unexpected comedic diversions into dialogues with himself, before returning to the subject at hand, his own life and work within Hollywood. He speaks solidly for nearly four hours, interrupted only by the ringing telephone, which he eventually takes off the hook. As with so many of the great comics, his humor springs directly from how much life has hurt him over the years, and the pain of his parents' lack of love for him is at the heart of all his thoughts, as he returned to it throughout the day. "I'm overly sensitive," he says toward the end of the afternoon. "If I see Bambi, I still cry at 75 as much as I did when I was seven. I knew it's only a cartoon, but boy, that's something else. I always worry about the guy who can't cry. This is the guy who scares me. When someone asks me, 'What do you fear the most?' I say, 'A man or a woman without a sense of humor.'"

I remember well the first time I ever came to Hollywood. I came with my Grandfather Winters. Valentine Winters was his name. Isn't that a great name? A dapper guy, he used to wear white suits and a white hat and he drove a Packard. He was a banker, and he lost the bank in the Depression. He was a *marvelous* guy. He had a lot of faults. Ran away from my dad and his sister and went to Paris and lived there for ten years, and then came back and faced the music in Dayton, Ohio, and lived with my grandmother until she died.

We took a train ride from Dayton in 1940, before the war. And went all over the west. We took a 10,000-mile trip, just he and I. It would have been a kick for anybody, especially a kid. And we went to Hollywood. He loved show business. *Loved* it. Took me to my first burlesque show and said, "Look at the knockers on her!" It was Ann Corrio, an old stripper. He gave me my first cigar, when we went to Hollywood. He introduced me to Minna Gable, a silent movie star. She was a beautiful woman.

230

I had *always* been a fan of Hollywood. And I just couldn't get over actually being there. It was amazing. *Extraordinary.* Coming from Dayton, Ohio, this was the dreamland. The place of dreams. I had a little book of autographs. Tried to keep some kind of funky diary of what I saw on the train ride and all. Saw Grauman's Chinese Theater and took a tour and all. I loved that, the footprints and everything. It swept me off my feet. Because I had no idea how they lived, and then you'd see them, the stars.

We went to the Brown Derby. It was like, [In a whisper] "You know who that is, don't you?"

"No, who's that?"

"Why, that's Guy Kibbe and that woman with him is Gloria Swanson."

"Oh my *God!*"

"Don't bother them. They're stars. You have to leave them alone."

"Oooh."

At Chasen's, a guy sitting no more than a few feet away from me was *Clark Gable*. And I remember thinking, "Oh my *God*. This is *Clark Gable*. Sure like to say hello." But I didn't want to bother him. Wanted to *look* at him, though.

Grant Mitchell, a character actor, showed us around town. Went out to RKO and saw Lupe Velez. And Alice Fay and Artie Shaw together at Ciro's. That was my first trip to Hollywood. The second time was World War II, and I came on the train for a ninety day leave. I was at the San Diego Marine Barracks. Third time, I came with a friend of mine who had a '38 Ford. Then I came out here to stay in '64. I've been here now over thirty-five years.

You're always asked about your dreams of getting into this business. And myself, [laughs] I always had a lot of dreams. I've always been fascinated by aircrafts, pilots. Growing up in Dayton, Ohio, my mother split with my dad when I was seven, and we drove from Dayton to Springfield, twenty-five miles away. I would go back and forth with visitation rights to see my dad, who was bombed for any number of years. Bombed, juiced. With gasoline.

A drunk. A guy who didn't beat me. I'm not one of those kids from a dysfunctional family. I'd get the standard, you know, pull the belt out, and spank me, which wasn't very comfortable, I didn't have a chance to put a book in my britches. But I took it. A lot of us guys took it. I never got beaten up or thrown down the stairs or certainly molested by my old man. A lot of people go through that stuff, and I understand that, and it's sad. I didn't get that. I got something that was *worse*. I got a *verbal* beating.

I couldn't get math. In my time, and I'm seventy-five, they didn't know the word "dyslexic." You were just *stupid*. You were a *dummy*. My dad loved math. Became a stockbroker late in life, they *love* math. He'd start off rather softly before he got bombed in the afternoon:

"If I gave you four apples—are you paying attention?"

[Meekly] "Yes, sir."

"If I give you four apples, and three more, how many do you have?"

Now far from being an intellectual, and not even a smart-ass, I just thought the normal answer would be, "Too many for the lunchbox."

[Sternly, in father's voice] "*Look*, you little asshole, I'm *talking* to you. You're the *dumbest* white kid I know."

It's interesting, that term. "The dumbest *white* kid." I'd hoped, you know, he'd say, "You're the dumbest Caucasian I know." But "*white* kid." Hmmm. It's like saying "brown kid" or "You're the dumbest yellow kid I know."

My mother was not that cruel. But her *gestures* were almost as bad. [In mother's genteel voice] "Well, your *father*, you know, I divorced him because he drank. He's not a dummy, you know. If he ever quits, he'd make some money, because he has a bright mind. And he had that year at Yale. I had one year in finishing school, you know, which is hardly college. . . ."

But she had street-smarts, my mother. I learned a *lot* from her. She was funny. And she shot from the hip.

Growing up with radio, *that's* what fascinated me. It was imagination. I could *be* there with Jack Armstrong, or Winslow of the navy, or Orphan Annie. I was then, as I am today, a dreamer. And my fantasies—I would really be doing time today if I acted them out. Most of us would be.

Like most people, I've got a terrible inferiority complex. I grew up with a lot of hang-ups. Not so much a chip on the shoulder as much as out-and-out fear of "Where do I fit in?" I still walk into a room, after over fifty years in this business, and if I don't know the people, I'm uncomfortable. It isn't that I'm better than these people, or that they're better than me. It's just that I don't know anybody, man. And I certainly don't want to get into smoking a joint to make myself feel cool, or go back to drinking, which I quit a long time ago. I've got to go in there *raw*. And ask for a diet Coke, and then get a little lecture:

[In high-pitched voice] "You know, that stuff in aluminum cans is not good for you."

"How 'bout two quarts of J&B?"

"Oh, that's too much."

"Tell me. That's what I drank. And some turpentine. And Mennen's Shaving Lotion. Some stuff out of a tree. A woodpecker and I were tied. He was sucking out sap and I was sucking out juice from the roots."

"Oh, well, listen—you've got a problem."

232

"Yeah? You've got a problem. I can get on the 101. You've got a tough time getting out of the driveway. Get off my back, Jack. Give me another diet Coke. I'm out of here anyway."

I'm not a guy who's a know-it-all. I'm misunderstood in a lot of circles. And understood, hopefully, in other circles. If you're a fan, then you should judge me by my work. Because my work is honest. I have nothing against guys who do jokes. God knows, some of the old-time great stuff, whether it's Berle or Benny or, I don't care who it is, Groucho, these were the kings. Why would I make fun of kings? It's just that my bag had been craziness and silliness mixed in with history and truth. My old mother was a gal who told a few jokes. My dad loved jokes. And I guess I became not Groucho, who was one of my idols, or Thurber, who was from Ohio—I grew up with Thurber, and I loved him—Twain, O'Henry, these are the guys that I looked to. And I thought, when I was growing up, besides being a pilot, I wanted to write. I wanted to be a writer.

I joined the marines when I seventeen, not because I was a superpatriot, but hey, it was World War II and I thought I would like to do something for my country. I wanted to get away from my mother and my dad. And I wanted to get away from teachers. I was running away from reality, I guess.

My mother pushed one job after another and fell into radio and did very well. And my dad did very well. Both of them married again. But when I hit it, I hit it first in Dayton on a 5,000-watter. WING. My mother was on a 250-watter, and that was okay. My old man wasn't on anything other than being a broker, and putting me onto Pan American, which went into the toilet. So they were jealous of my success. Which is a twist. I had other problems after I got there, which most of us had. My drinking was a problem. I quit at thirty-two. I held onto my marriage and my kids. Sobered up and went back to work.

I had some more problems after that. My wife had cancer three times. I've got three pacemakers. I'm pasted together. But that's okay.

I loved movies when I was a kid. I loved stories. I'm not going for special effects. I know that makes a lot of money. I want a story. I want to see some acting.

My favorite pictures were horror pictures. I was scared at home [laughs] so I figured I might as well have a backup. I loved Boris Karloff, and The Mummy, Frankenstein. I loved all those pictures. I hated musicals. I thought the guys were all sissies because they were all dancing around. That wasn't my cup of tea. I didn't go, for that matter, a wonderful love story. That's out. I don't want to see these people sitting in a swing and necking.

I liked Mickey Rooney and Judy [Garland] and the "Andy Hardy" series. I liked cowboy pictures, good ones. I liked Gary Cooper. Loved him. Met him once. Loved all the cowboys. Bob Steele, and, of course, [Gene] Autry. Autry was a heavy alcoholic. I went to see him in a circus in Springfield—Cole Brothers, which was second to Ringling—and he got on the saddle and fell out. Kid next to me said, [In little boy's voice] "What's the matter with Mr. Autry?" We were in grade school.

I said, "He's a drunk."

"Oh, that's a terrible thing to say. He's a big star, man. He's in the Wild West Show."

"Yeah, tell me about it. So is the freak sucking on the wine there with the three eyes."

So they roped [Autry] into the saddle, and he rode around. Later on he bought the Angels. Big successful man.

My favorite guy was Hopalong Cassidy. Black hat, great voice, white hair. And the laugh.

I loved war pictures. A lot of things I liked. Horror pictures, cowboy pictures and war pictures. I also loved comedies. I loved the Marx Brothers. They were my favorites. I also loved W.C. Fields. Boy, he was different. [In Fields' voice] "Feed the kid alcohol!" You know? He was a dirty old man but he was funny. I liked Laurel & Hardy. God, I still laugh at them. Those are the big guys. The Three Stooges, they did crazy things, and they were funny. The Ritz Brothers were funny.

Groucho was my favorite of all. I could see him going [in Groucho's voice] "What is going on here? Hey, fat lady, okay, you're obese. That's a better word. I'd certainly like to climb your mountain, but I'm just not a climber. I'm a doer and not a getter, do you understand?"

I just loved Groucho. He sent me a picture once, of just his face with the beret and the cigar. It said, "Of all the young comedians, I like you the best." Groucho. Please.

I loved going to the movies. Double features. You'd be there all day! You'd go in at noon, and you'd see a serial, maybe two. Buster Crabbe and a space thing. Then there'd be Frank Buck and the wild animals. Then there'd be two features, a horror feature and a Western or something. It was great. I loved it. I still like to sneak off and see a good picture. I did one show in the Marines. I was on an aircraft carrier on the hangar deck, and there were 2,000 swabees and about 75 marines, and I got up and did impressions and MCed a show and won five gallons of ice-cream. I looked out at this hangar desk, and when I won and all these guys applauded, it was the first time I felt there's something to this. Wasn't quite sure.

I never thought of being a star, like Hopalong, or like Laurence Olivier. I'd just like to be in the bar as an extra. And have just one line, like [in Western voice] "The Delaney boys went out that door." Just that. A hundred dollars.

I went to art school, and my wife encouraged me to perform. She said, "I don't want to hurt your feelings, John. Your parents have done a pretty good job there. But I would *pass* on the artwork. You're funny. You're the funniest guy I've ever met in my life. You make me laugh and you've made a lot of other people laugh. If you can do that, God, *do* it."

I said, "I don't know about show business. My mother's in show business." But then there was a talent show in Dayton. My wife said they were giving away a wristwatch, and I didn't have a watch. So then I became semi-cocky. I thought that with the talent in this town, that I should be able to beat these people. I decided I would do my impression of the Indianapolis speedway. [Proceeds to do act featuring Gary Cooper, Boris Karloff and others talking about racing.] And I won.

Then I got a call from this guy named Charlie Reader. He said, "You won the other night, and the guys down here at WING think you have a lot of talent. How would you like to be a disc jockey?"

"Well, I don't have music background. I love jazz. . . ."

"We'll help you along here. It doesn't take too many brains."

"What are the hours?"

"Six to eight in the morning."

"That means I'd have to get up at five. I'm going to art school."

"Well, this is a career. You can do this *and* go to art school." Which I did for a year.

"Okay. Six to eight. What do I do?"

"Well, put the record on. 'Star-Spangled Banner.' Be Johnny Winters."

This was their mistake. The guy came up finally after a year and said, [angrily] "Just stick to the time and temperature. And play the records. Okay? No other bullshit. Get it?"

See, what I did was to get on and say, "Good morning, ladies and gentleman. I hope you enjoyed 'The Star-Spangled Banner.' Hey, it's our National Anthem. I'd sing it but I hum badly."

I'd say, since this was radio, "With me today we have a special guest"—

we *never* got any guests—"this is Sir Edmund Lingler, he's a Britisher, and he's flown a secret aircraft into Dayton. Uh, Sir Lingler, how do you find Dayton, Ohio? This is a far cry from London or Manchester."

[In the voice of an elderly Englishman] "This is the most beautiful city I've ever been in. I came into Dayton this past evening. I love Dayton. So much to do." Well, you can imagine all these people listening in their homes and trailers: "Who is this asshole?"

I was making $65 a week, got it up to $70. This was 1949 I got in, and by 1950, television was coming in. I wanted to stay on but I thought maybe I could do something on television. I went to Columbus, brought some photos along, and I got a job at WBNS, TV in Columbus. Tried to get a raise—a five-dollar raise—and they didn't have it. So I went East to do anything else. I took $56 and 46 cents and went to New York. My wife dressed mannequins in a department store for $40 a week, and the rest is history.

I figured that if I can't make it in a year, I'll come back. And I made it. Just doing voice-overs, some television. Did *Playhouse 90*. Little bit parts. One of my biggest thrills is when Alistair Cooke asked me to appear on *Omnibus*. Do you remember that show? It was shown on PBS. That was an honor for me; I was the first stand-up comic ever to be on it. Would have done it for free.

I was in a mental institution for eight months. Didn't want to stay that long but I couldn't get out. Rod Steiger told me later I was bipolar but I told him I'd never been to the Arctic. Doctor there asked me what I was thinking about. I told him I was thinking about getting out.

"How would you get out?"

"You think I'd show *you* my game plan?"

"I noticed you with about twelve guys down there. What do you guys talk about?"

We were all marines. I told him we talked about getting out. Just to give him something to go on, I told him, "You know that old man, the guard in the front? He can be had. Probably take some piano wire, like I saw in a movie, use that on him. Then I'd stay away from the expressway and get right into the woods. I'd try to get some shoes with wool inside because I'm fighting that winter. I'll take some matches with burnt cork, and put on a mustache—"

"Oh, I see. . . ."

I gave him the whole picture. "This is dangerous thinking," he said.

"Sure it is." This is the one time I almost lost my sense of humor. Because I didn't know if I'd ever get out. People think because it's a private hospital and you turn yourself in, that you can get out anytime you want to. But you can't. You have no money. That's taken away from you. There was no plastic then, no cards. I thought I would lose my mind in there and never get out. Doctors told me show business might be too tough for me, too much pressure. But I did get out. And I never went back to the hospital.

My problem was that I was playing with the wrong people. People who didn't understand my humor. People who could throw a net on me. You know, all you have to do is come in and say [In French accent], "I am Francois DeSalle. See this? *Dynamite*. I'm going to throw this, and you're going to die." And it's a road flare. So you'd better know who you are playing with. That's my point.

One of my dearest friends was Stanley Kramer. God, I miss him every day. He opened a lot of doors for me. I had just come out of the joint when Kramer called. Oh, I was scared to *death*. I never told him. He called me up. He said, "Jonathan, this is Stanley Kramer, I'm doing this picture called *It's a Mad, Mad, Mad, Mad World*, we've got Phil Silvers, Milton Berle, Mickey Rooney, Buddy Hackett, a lot of guys you know. Jimmy Durante, we've got Buster Keaton." He kept going.

I said, "My *God*, man."

He said, "You'll be on the picture six months. Talk to your agent. I'll give you a hundred grand, you'll have a good time. How do you feel?"

I turned to my wife for the first time, and I said, "They're talking about doing a *movie* on the West Coast. *Big* picture." Talk about something *profound*.

She said, "John, you *take* it right away. If you don't take this, you'll never work again."

Interesting. There was no Lithium or Prozac, or anything. Just went out and did it. I was higher than a kite. On a natural high. Couldn't *wait* to get to work. I stayed up all night. Like a *kid*. I was thirty-five. Jesus. I was in cat heaven, you can imagine. I was working with *stars*, and I was getting some *money*. We rented a house in Hollywood, and had the kids and everyone together. It was a *fantastic* time.

I had no idea it was going to be such a big picture. When he said six months, I said, "My God." Other things I had done had been a day or two. Now we're talking six months.

Meeting Buster Keaton was a great thrill for me. A very sweet guy. I don't think he was happy, but he didn't show it. He was a big gambler, and he squandered a lot of money that way. When he tried to come out of silent pictures into talkies, they didn't understand what to do with him. When I say "they," I mean the writers, producers, directors. I think there are certain people it would be nearly impossible to write for: Laurel and Hardy, Groucho—you try to write for Groucho? Good luck!

Buster did all of his own stunts. He had buildings fall on him, and he rode railroads. He was something else. Nobody could write for him. So when he came into modern times, as it were, they said, "Listen to us, Buster, this will be for your own good." And they just cut his legs off. These were people that didn't understand his humor or appreciate his brilliance, and they were telling him his timing was off. You know, "Just do it our way, or it's gonna be a problem."

I turned to Stanley about halfway through, and said, "You know, I came right out of the funny farm."

He said, "I enjoy working with sick people." Garland, she was on drugs. Montgomery Clift had his lines in front of him when he did *Judgment at Nuremberg*. Lee Marvin, lots of gasoline; Vivien Leigh, manic-depressive, juice, drugs. I mean, this guy's worked with people with a lot of problems, and brought them out and made them heavy-duty stars.

237

Tracy was drinking a lot in *Judgment at Nuremberg* and certainly in *Mad World*. He was a lot of trouble. I worked with him only one day. They did him in an office, and if you really look at it, you can see him reading off of cards. Which you never thought he'd do.

Stanley put a book out about his life and he said, "There are three performers in my life who I respected, Spencer Tracy, Sidney Poitier, and Jonathan Winters." And he wrote, "Jonathan Winters is a national treasure. Jonathan Winters is the funniest guy I've ever met in my life." You can't buy this kind of stuff.

I turned to Stanley when he was still alive, and I said, "You know, I'm a Gentile." He said, "You sonofabitch, I know you're a Gentile. So what?"

And I said, "I love you, man. All your talent and your kindness. Learn to accept compliments. You've got a big problem with that."

Stanley was a brilliant man, but he was a pussycat. He could be tough and hard but he had a big heart. He directed some fantastic films. *Ship of Fools, Guess Who's Coming to Dinner, Judgment at Nuremberg*. I said, "Why did your people not embrace you a little more than they should have? Like giving you an honorary Oscar. Why did your people do this to you?"

Great answer. He said, "Jonathan, I'll tell you something about my people. We may be in different worlds and different states, different religions. Same basic color. I'm Jewish, you're Gentile. This we will always have in common. If you're a true rebel—you're a true rebel, and I'm a true rebel—you'll always be in trouble, you become a problem. With your people you're a problem, and with my people. If you're a threat in any way, and you want to say something different, but something very strong, your people and my people have something common. When they want to shelve you, they'll shelve you."

Stanley was a great heavy dramatic director, but he was also very good at directing comedy. He was a tough guy and he was good. I'm on his side. I just love the guy so much. He was like a father to me. And he was *so* bright. He had a kind of dry sense of humor, of course. I think he must have thought a lot about it. It's amazing that he pulled us all together, and all of them came off. I'd say 98 percent of them did come off, in their various roles. Dick Shawn, he was a brilliant comedian.

280

I didn't improvise at all in the movie. I stayed *right* with the script. Except in one moment: Dick Shawn and I are trying to dig up the treasure. And he's calling me "Baby." "*Baby*, come on, *move* it, baby." You know, he was a hip guy. And I was this rural truck driver, and I talked in this rural tone, and I stopped Dick and I looked at him and said, "You'd better stop calling me a baby. I *ain't* no baby." That was the only thing that was different in that whole movie. But that was a funny line, so they left it in. "I ain't no baby."

People have said to me, "You're a genius." You know what a genius is? It's somebody who cannot find work. Interesting. What good is it if somebody says you are a genius? This man, Stanley Kramer, was a *giant*. Why is it he was not working more at the end of his life? Versatility is a *curse*. One-dimensional people make a lot of money. Stay right here. Don't get cute.

I think movies will always be important to people. God, I *hope* so. TV has commercials, and I've done a lot of them and don't want to bite the hand that feeds me. But they are an interruption. Sometimes better than the show. And there's a lot of fakery and false stuff that is visual in TV and in the theater. Fake snow, false flats, that kind of thing. Movies suddenly become very real. When you're in the desert, it looks like a desert. That's my point.

People up here who are not in the business will say to me, "A lot of your people are coming up here." And I'll say, "Most of my people are dead."

"No, no, I meant show people."

"Oh, oh, I see. You should have told me. No, we're not with the circus anymore. Winter quarters, you see, I was down there. But I'm out of Ringling now."

I've talked to a lot of boring people. We all have. You ask them fairly innocent questions. I was at a party one night with Gregory Peck. No, that wasn't the name. Edit that *out*, I don't want to get *sued*. It was a Mister *Leckler*. Gregory Leckler. I turned to him and said, "You know, Greg, I *loved* all your pictures. But when you did *Moby Dick*, man, you took a *hell* of a chance with that whale, man. I saw you with all those ropes and harpoons, out there in that salt water. Man, you could have *died*. He took you down a couple of times, and you would've damned near drowned, if they didn't cut those ropes off."

He looked at me, and said, [in the voice of Gregory Peck] "I did that on a soundstage, you know."

"Yeah?"

"We had a fake whale, it was made out of *rubber*."

"Is that right?"

A lot of other people, I could give you a list, they look right through you. But in movies, they really come to life. And the script gives them a chance to really develop a character. And they get taken to a lawn party or something, where you have fifty people sucking on lemonade.

"Mr. Lemler, could I ask you a couple of questions? Your last picture, *The Orange Dragon*, did you enjoy that?"

"Oh . . ."

"How do you feel you were different in that than *The Blue Lagoon?*"

"Oh, I've done over forty pictures. Every one of them was different."

"You always played yourself."

"No, no, no. In *The Blue Lagoon*, I wore a fireman's uniform."

"Oh yeah?"

"Yeah, that's right. And did you see *The Last Spittoon?*"

"Yeah. How were you different in that?"

"Well, my uniform was different."

These guys look you right in the eyes and say, "*Everything* I did was different." But it's *always* the same guy. Now if you're talking about Peter Sellers, you're talking about something else. Sellers was *brilliant*. I knew Sellers. He could change from one character to another like that. [Snaps fingers] Yeah, we had a ball together. Oh yeah. We were on the same frequency.

Anthony Hopkins is a brilliant actor. Rod Steiger. But how many actors are like that? *Please*. Like Sellers, he's versatile. And versatility is a *curse*. Arnold Schwarznegger is still the same guy whether he's got a fur piece over his nuts or he's with Danny DeVito in a kindergarten: [In Schwarznegger's voice] "I still like you. Let's do it already. Come on, Danny, and make love to me."

I ran into Steve Martin once up here. I said to him in character [in the voice of a country bumpkin], "Uh, Mr. Martin, it is Mr. Martin, isn't it?" He looked at me. "Uh, Madge, my wife, is in the car across the street. She is a crippled woman. She's looking at you now. Smile at her, will ya? Oh, she ducked down." There was a car across the street, nobody in it. "You know, she said it was you. I don't watch TV or movies. But she said, 'That's Mr. Martin. Just run over there real quick and tell him I love him, and want an autograph.'" I went on for a fast twenty-five seconds.

Steve said this to me: "You know I'm *Steve Martin*. Jonathan, you don't have to audition for me." He's a strange cat.

I think there's just too much today. On TV, it's too much. Every comedy has canned laughter, to begin with. I've had enough of that. I'm going to bed. Four or five channels would be enough. It's great to have CBS, NBC, ABC, and a couple of other things. But when you have movies, rock concerts, hey, it's heavy sugar. Teeth are falling out of the public. There's the state fair going on. There's *radio* going on. We're not *hungry* anymore. It's just this: [Makes clicking sounds, as if changing channels with a remote] *Click-click-click.* "What's *that*? Oh, look, there's animals, that's kind of neat." *Click-click-click.* "What's that? Oh, I don't want to miss this. Hey, this looks good. What are they doing? Got an old army truck. Oh, I recognize him." *Click-click-click-click-click.* "I want to see what the weather's like." The *attention* span today. Nobody can stay with *anything.*

Movies were hard work, but I loved doing them. Discipline in movies is incredible. The long days, and you must be up for it. Especially with a comedy. You have no audience, and so you don't hear the laughter. You just hope to God that the director knows what he's doing. You hope and pray. Cause you're in the hands of the guy who's got the scissors.

The great thing that I found out about movies, if they're good, is that they're seen all over the world. If it's a big picture like *Mad, Mad World.* It's one of the classic comedies of all time, with all the people in it, my *God.* From Spencer Tracy to Jerry Lewis to Carl Reiner to Buster Keaton. On and on. It was a great picture for me, and one of the great breaks of my life. Of all the things I've done, people come up to me, still, and tell me they liked me in that picture. In *India*, in Bombay [with Indian accent], "I saw you. You were the lorry driver. You drive the truck. I can tell."

The one time I really felt important was when I did movies. Movies that were really good movies. I was fortunate. Most of the movies I did were good. Because I did so few of them. But I felt like a star. I got the chair that says "Jonathan Winters" on it, and I'm sitting out there on the honey-wagon, and they come, "Mr. Winters, we're ready for you."

"Oh, thank you."

"Can we get you anything?"

"Uh, maybe a Coca-Cola?"

"Sure."

"Uh, that robe—can I have that when we're done here?"

"Sure, we'll get two of them for you."

You're treated like a star. If you're a nice guy. And you get the right director. Kramer was great. Norman Jewison. You get the right person, and it's no cakewalk, and as you get older it's tough to get up and do things. It's hard work. But it's worth it.

On TV they treat you okay. You get a dressing room. But it's a hurry-up kind of thing. There's no time for extra takes. "Forget it, we have to move on to something else."

Gin mills were fun in the beginning. I was on the sauce, and I never got bombed to the extent that I couldn't go on. Well, maybe once in St. Louis and one other time in New York. But nothing falling down so that they'd fire me. I drank afterwards and before, the whole thing. And it was fun. You're loose, you could do what you wanted to do. That's a free spirit in a club.

But the road became something else. I spent eight years on the road. I missed my family, I couldn't take my kids. Wasn't that I was out that much time, but it was *enough*. Living in a hotel is living in a hotel, room 319, hookers going up and down, whether it's Vegas or any town.

[In female voice] "Hi, how are you? You with your family?"

"No, just sitting here alone, having a shooter."

"Hey, would you like to bang me?"

"I don't know. But you're certainly outspoken. I would like to introduce you to my hands, however. This is Harriet and Helen Hand. GI issue—"

"You're some kind of *kook*."

"Oh definitely, yeah."

"Are you here in the hotel?"

"No, I'm in the alley. I'll see you out there."

But it's all been worth it. It was an experience, the clubs, the television, the movies. I look back over my shoulder, I look at my parents, who were disappointed and couldn't give me a big hug. When I was in *The Russians Are Coming*, I told my mother about it. I thought she would enjoy that kind of picture, because she was sharp. I said to her flat-out. "Mother, you know what is playing downtown? It's *The Russians Are Coming*."

She said, "You know, we never go downtown." That was it.

"But wouldn't you go downtown for this? I don't do that many movies, and this is a good flick. There's no bad language in it or anything."

"No. We just don't go down."

That *hurts*. It hurt me in school. They weren't *there*. I'm singing in the play. And she wasn't there for *me*. There is no way I was going to be that way with my children:

[In leading man tone] "Sure, I want to see the kids grow up, but, *jeez*, I'm gonna be in Madrid for sixteen weeks."

[In little boy's voice] "But I'm doing a little play, you know, and Sissy and I are in the fourth grade. And we love you, Dad. We see you in pictures. . . ." A Hollywood kid, you know? "Can you come to this play, Dad? Could you take time out—"

"Take time out to fly from Madrid back to Hollywood? Are you kidding? No, no. I have a second lead. You know, Burt Lancaster and I."

"Is that right? When would you come to one of our plays?"

"Well, when you're in high school. There's a chance that by that time I might be able to see something."

My boy, Jay, just turned fifty-one. My daughter turned forty-five. I said to my son on his birthday, "Jay, do you love me?"

"Dad," he said, "you were always there when I needed you." That *says* it. At the end of every conversation, we say, "I love you, man." I think that's important.

Robin [Williams] said to me, "You know, Pops"—he calls me Pops, cause I'm his dad's age—"You know, Pops, you're my mentor."

I said, "That's a bad word in Ohio. Can you use the word 'idol'?"

He's probably one of the most generous guys, in or out of this business, that I have ever known. He's very giving. It's like a thousand Christmases being with him. He does a lot of benefits. And he's an interesting guy, and he's got a big heart. He's very gifted. He's done some really great things.

People say to me, "You never do the same thing twice." Right. Because I don't want to. It's why I don't want to act on the stage. It's not that I don't have the discipline. It's that I don't want to do the same thing every night. I don't want to read the same story every night.

I was an only child. I've spent a lot of time alone. I write alone, I paint alone. If you can't be your own man in life, you can be your own man right here in this room.

[In higher voice] "Are we ready to shoot? We're losing light. We've got over $12 million in this thing so far. Do you have any idea what you're getting?"

It's like musicians nowadays, these big rock stars:

"When you are gonna clean your act up?"

"Hey, don't hassle me, man."

"But you're an accomplished musician. Why do you need all that junk?"

"Oh baby, you have to *understand* something." [Makes quote signs with fingers.]

"What was *that*? What did you just do?"

"Haven't you seen that? It's a quote."

"Oh, and what's that?"

"It's a high five. Where have you been? It's a high five."

"Oh yeah, *groovy*. Outasite. The whole ten yards. I *dig* you. I'm *hip*. Crazy. Man. Outasite. What are you making?"

"We make over two and a half million dollars a year. We used to come home with gold records."

"You seem like you're *stoned*."

"Hey, man, don't press me. I've smoked some stuff, I've taken a little stuff. Wanna help yourself? There's a little dust in the dish."

"Well, when you create this music—"

"It's not so much music, man, it's a *sound*. Did you come to our concert?"

"I was there last night. It's definitely a *sound*. Yeah, I put rubber in my ears."

"Oh, you did? You missed the lyrics, man. Come on, baby. Don't do this to me. Don't do it to yourself. . . ."

243

Some kid asked me one time, "How have you handled success?"

I said, "Fairly well." Considering it's a very scary thing to come into some money of any kind. When I think that Robin [Williams] gets 25 million per picture, that's something. I think the best I got—which is still a lot of money to me [laughs]—don't tell this to the guys downtown—is $135,000. A lot of money.

When I told my agent I wanted to quit the road, he, of course, threw himself on the floor. "Well, you know, there's a lot of green out there," he said.

I said, "Hey. You only get one crack at this thing, life." I've been straight now for forty-two years; no drugs or narcotics, no stuff. I quit because I wanted to see my family and I wanted to be with them. That's been a big thing for me, because I love my kids.

Sometimes my son fools me. He calls me, using a woman's voice [in high feminine voice], "Hi, Mr. Winters?"

"Yeah, who is this?"

"Oh, this is Millie. Millie Swanler."

"Millie Swanler?"

"Yes, I'm a big fan of yours, Mr. Winters. Could I come up and do something to you other than a massage?"

"Wait a minute, wait a minute, Jay?"

"Daddy?"

That's my boy. He can be tough and he can be hard, but he's never rude. He's my agent now. Used to give 10 percent to an agent. Now I give it to him.

I think I'm funny not because of my past but in spite of it. I know I talk a lot about those times. But I'm not a crybaby. I like to start off the day with music. Some jazz or something. Nat Cole or Basie or Ellington, those guys. I don't want to hear about earthquakes and death and typhoons or in Uruguay the mine blew up, or some guy shot on the highway. It's a lot of death, a lot of crises. People say I'm running from reality. I say, "No, I'm *dealing* with reality. I'm thinking about myself. I want to listen to some music.

I'm gonna hear this crap sooner or later during the day."

Anybody who has been through anything terrible, whether he was a POW or went through the Holocaust, or burned terribly by a fire, it's a miracle that they can just shut that off. You can't wipe that out, it's there. Unless they burn it out by shock treatment, or that crap. So it isn't that I forgive my parents. Wherever they are, and if God is God, I'm sure he's probably saying to me, "You'll come around one of these days. [Laughs] You'll pull it together. Your folks did the best they could." I hope they're getting a fair shake. I knew their backgrounds and I know my father had a rotten time growing up. So people say, "He probably took it out on you because he was all bent out of shape."

244

Well, I could take it out on my son. But I didn't. I think I got a little strict with him at times, and it does come out, you know. But I was aware of it. During the Sixties, I was tough on him. He had long hair and all and I said, "Why don't you get yourself a dress, some nice shoes, go out into the street and maybe you'll get lucky." He said, "Wait a minute, Dad. Come on." And I thought, I'm driving this guy away from me. I've got to sit down and talk to him. I've got to be a father. It wasn't too late. We pulled it together and we're close to this day. You've got to pull it together for your kids. You have to do something about it. The career never meant that much. Don't short change them. Don't jerk them around. Tell them the truth, tell them how you feel, and be there.

I've had a lot of fun. I've made some money. Not as much as the others. But that's not what it's all about. Money's always been a question, and it is for all of us. I'd be a fool and a liar if I said it didn't matter at all. Everyone wants to get enough to buy a few things, go a few places. But there have been some projects where I would have done it for nothing, because I loved the subject matter so much.

My biggest effort has not gone into my field of television or movies. I wanted my family to be proud of me. I knew my mother and dad were jealous, but my wife was proud of me. I wanted my kids to know me. I stopped the road when I was able. I don't pin medals on myself, but it worked. I was able to see my boy play football. That was a big thing for me.

A lot of guys gave up early. Look at the guys who had great careers and are gone. I didn't want to die. I suddenly realized I'm not that much of a religious guy, but I'm into it. I'm *deeply* convinced that this might be the only show in town. I hope there's another show. I really do. So I want to see as much of this show as I can. I don't want to be buried at twenty-four, or take a Porsche and go 200 miles an hour into a wall. As a kid I thought I'd live forever, and then I found out you don't. Life is *very* sweet. It's very cruel, but it's very sweet. I'm like Lou Gehrig standing in Yankee Stadium. Today. August 10, 2001, I've got to tell you I'm the luckiest guy in the world.

I consider myself to be so lucky to have come this far, and to have done the things I've done. I wanted one thing out of life. I knew I'd need a lot of help. I wanted to get close to being my own man. That's all. I just wanted to get close.

Charles Champlin
BORN 1925
HAMMONDSPORT, NEW YORK
WRITER/HISTORIAN

245

"Time does not just go by," he wrote, "it whistles past you as on a speeding motorcycle, leaving you with dust on your face." Today he echoes those sentiments while speaking onstage at the Director's Guild on Sunset Boulevard. The occasion is a memorial to the director and producer Stanley Kramer, who died eleven days earlier. In the audience, among the friends and family of Kramer, are scores of stars who worked in Kramer's films, including Sidney Poitier, Mickey Rooney, Buddy Hackett, Sid Caesar, Edie Adams, Karl Malden and Jonathan Winters. He speaks eloquently, and talks both of Kramer's Hollywood glory days and his later years spent in Seattle, working as a columnist. "Seattle's a great city," he quotes Kramer as saying, "except there's nothing to do after 10 A.M." His speech is touching, funny, and grounded in history, as were all the columns, articles and TV shows he created over the years as a writer-correspondent for Life and Time from 1948 to 1965, and as an arts editor and film critic for the L.A. Times, where he was an Angeleno institution from 1965 to 1991. He's the author of several books, and for years he hosted a cable series called "Champlin on Film." His work is consistently thoughtful, warmly humorous, and charged with a true love for the movies and respect for those who made them. And anytime one of the greats moved on, whether it was Chaplin, Orson Welles, or Hitchcock, all of whom he got to know, he could be counted on to write a touching tribute.

Days after the Kramer tribute he sits beneath an arbor of blossoms on the backyard patio of his Bel Air home, drinking black coffee brought to him by his smiling wife Peggy. Now another legend has fallen—Jack Lemmon—and though Champlin is essentially retired from the Times, he provides the newspaper with its most moving memorial to the actor. His other most recent piece for the Times was an article about his own struggle with a malady known as AMD, which has stolen away all but his peripheral vision. Despite this, he continues to write on his old typewriter (though Peg sometimes informs him he's been typing in all capital letters), and gives no signal of any problems with his sight.

I saw my first films at a little theater in Hammondsport, which is just the bitter end of the distribution system. The projectionist, whose name was Franklin, was a real Ichabod Crane of a guy, unsure and gawky, and the film would break and you'd hear him throwing film cans around up in the booth. The booth was just right along the side of the aisle when you came into the theater, and he had to climb up a ladder to get into the booth, like a ship's cabin. He would be cursing and throwing the cans around up there and finally the film would get patched and after a certain interruption of the action, it would resume again. It was every night, these prints had been so patched and so often poorly spliced that they would always break and poor Franklin would be up there trying to get the damn thing going again.

246

I never thought in terms of writing movies or writing *about* movies actually. My first huge movie crush, of course, was Shirley Temple, because we were almost exactly the same age. I had a great uncle, Uncle Charlie, who would make a pilgrimage back to Hammondsport to see the rest of the family and would always talk about being a next-door neighbor of the Temples' and remembering bouncing Shirley Temple on his knee when she was really young. That drove me crazy, I just was *insanely* jealous [laughs] of my Uncle Charlie for having known this golden child.

Now jump cut to about 1957. I had been writing for Life since after the war. In '57 they wanted present-day pictures of a lot of people who were featured in the early days of the magazine. So one of them was Shirley Temple who was then doing something called "Shirley Temple's Song Book" over at NBC. So we arranged that a photographer and I would go over to take one picture, a shot of her as the little colonel. So Shirley Temple came out wearing a ball gown, just outside the studio wall, and at the photographer's request, put her arms around this little picture of herself. And it was really strange because she looked almost angrily at this picture of herself at five years old, and said through clenched teeth, "I don't know this little person at *all*."

And I've heard from other child actors, too, that they never had any childhood, never a minute of time. She sat in Roosevelt's lap and did all this kind of stuff, and yet never felt that she had gotten dirty in the sand, and had parties with her little friends like other normal people. She felt that this was all a part of her life, that she was a money-making machine.

Jackie Cooper once told me that while working on a movie as a kid, he was just sort of acting up and being a little boy. He was taken in and sat on L.B. Mayer's lap, and Mayer started crying, and said, "Jackie, the whole studio is resting on your shoulders." You know, he was only *five* then. That's *awful* to have an adult tell you that and then cry in your presence. Jack felt that his life was lost until he went into the navy and the war and discovered the real Jack Cooper rather than the child star.

It isn't easy being a star. Gene Hackman told me, "Actors learn by watching other people. And once you get some fame, you can no longer unobtrusively watch people anymore, because everybody is watching you."

I convinced *Life* to send me to Hollywood after I worked for them for about five years. It was hard work. There were always late-breaking stories, so that I'd work all night Saturday night. I was always working very hard and I just had to get out of New York, I just didn't want to do it anymore, so I asked the managing editor if I could go back out into the field. I said, "I will go any place. I would just as soon not go to the South because I'm not ready for the Civil Rights wars." [Laughs] I said, "What I'd really like to do is go to Hollywood because I've always been nuts about the movies." And he went for it.

247

So I came out here to Hollywood for the first time during a steaming hot August in 1959. It was really hot. I was by myself, my wife Peg and the kids were staying back in White Plains. I was living in a motel called the Cavalier on Wilshire, where they put up all the *Time* people. I had a ground-floor unit with a window open and I had brought my little portable typewriter. I remember sitting with my little Olivetti and [motions as if typing], "Now is the time for all good men," and I could hear a couple of guys down at the pool. They were wearing dark glasses and terry-cloth robes, and said, "Hey, Eddie got me a date tonight with that usherette, you know the one with the *big knockers.*" And I said to myself, "Welcome to Hollywood, Champ."

I remember driving my way to Mulholland Drive at night, and I drove along looking in both directions, and thinking to myself, "The whole place is a *carpet of incandescence.*"

It might have been the next night, but the bureau chief of *Life* gave a little welcoming party, and he lived on one of those streets off Benedict Canyon and so I went along. We were sitting out on his patio, much like this one except there were bushes on each side. He was making some exotic, green lethal drink that I drank too much of. I was sitting next to my photographer, and I was very pale in my dark green sweater with my back to these shrubs and oleander. And the photographer said, "Would you *please* sit still, your head looks like the *moon.*" [Laughter] So that was another introduction to Hollywood, the canyon life.

I remember the first day we went out for lunch, and were walking east on Santa Monica to a restaurant as I saw a T-bird come in and double-park and a lady in a green pantsuit get out and run into the bank. I said, "Holy shit, that's *Katherine Hepburn!*" [Laughs] And I said to myself, "Champlin, you've come to the right place." It was a *fascinating* time.

One time an editor friend of mine in New York sent a friend of hers to Hollywood. He was a French intellectual who had worked in the resistance, and he was nuts about Hollywood. My friend asked me to show him around. The first thing he wanted was to go to Grauman's Chinese, where he took a picture of the footprints, *every single one* of them. This was a very bright guy, who wrote resistance journals. I was trying to say, in my inadequate French, that Hollywood Boulevard was where the young try to look old and the old try to look young. A perfect dichotomy, there's all these aged biddies that are trying to look like sexy teenagers and the teenagers with all their makeup trying to look forty instead of fourteen.

I've always loved Musso & Frank's. It's a Hollywood institution. Their chicken pot-pie is the best anywhere. Historically speaking, Musso's always lured the writers. Fitzgerald and Faulkner hung out there. All the screenwriters gravitated there. The Brown Derby on Vine attracted more of the stars. Gable announced his engagement there. From 1965 until they closed, I was the steadiest patron of the Vine Street Derby. I did interviews there virtually every day. I was doing three columns a week and I needed to keep it going with a lot of interviews, so I did most of them there. I used to always see Gene Autry and Pat Butram getting sloshed at the bar.

Of all the great people I met and interviewed, Alfred Hitchcock certainly is one of my very favorites. Hitchcock always sustained his technical bravura. I remember that in his movie *Frenzy*, there's a scene in which a woman comes in, goes down a corridor to her apartment, goes up and goes in, and then the murderer follows her and goes and knocks on the door and she lets him in, and you know, the wonderful part of it, you know that he's going to kill her. He goes in, the door closes and the camera just dollies back out, just reverses itself, goes up, and the first thing you know it's an overhead shot of this whole thing.

Since I am not a filmmaker and am naïve about film techniques, I said to Hitch, "I don't know how the hell you did that." He said, "Well, did you see that rude fellow who walked right down in front of the camera with a bag of potatoes on his shoulders?"

I said, "Yeah."

He said, "Well, that's my cut." [Laughs] Anybody who had studied filmmaking would have known that. [Laughs]. I just thought it was some guy who got in the way.

Hitchcock had no problems with Hollywood. Some of his films were less successful than others but by and large it was fine. After *Family Plot*, his final film, he was primed to do one more movie. It was based on a British spy novel, and a lot of it took place in Finland. Hitchcock was already in very bad physical and mental shape. Nobody expected he could actually do another film. But they sent his art director to Finland anyway, and he scouted locations there rather angrily, knowing that Hitchcock was never going to be able to do this film. Universal invested in writers and scripts and the production designs and location scouting and all that.

My own view was that Lew Wasserman had *such an affection* for Hitchcock, it was almost like father and son. Obviously, Hitchcock had made an awful lot of money for Universal; nevertheless, I think this was just an expensive gesture to Hitchcock, allowing Hitch to preserve this *dream*, this *idea*, this *conviction*, that he was going to make one last film. Wasserman knew better than anyone else that Hitch was not going to make this movie. He never did. He just got weaker and weaker and then died. That was a rare example of the *other* side of the Hollywood story, in which a very expensive gesture was made for the aid and comfort and mental peace of one man. *Very* unusual.

249

Hitch's wife Alma outlived Hitch, and when she finally died, I wrote, "The Hitchcock touch had four hands and two of them were Alma's." The morning that piece ran, my phone rang. It was Lew Wasserman calling to say, "Thank you." [Chokes up with emotion.] Because he shared that feeling both about Hitch and about Alma. She was probably a very tough lady but she obviously was so important to Hitch's movies. At a screening at the final answer print of *Psycho*, they were all saying how wonderful it was. Everyone except Alma, who said, "It cannot be released. It has errors." She noticed that in the scene in which Janet Leigh is supposed to be dead that you can see her breathing. They went back and looked at it. She was *right*. And nobody else had even noticed it.

I also admired Chaplin very much, and met him on a few occasions. I think he is an absolute genius, of course, another one of the great geniuses of our time. Yet he felt so rejected and unappreciated by America and Hollywood that when he sold his Hollywood studio in the fifties, he did it with the plan that the studio would be destroyed. He had no interest in seeing it preserved. I think it's one of the saddest chapters in Hollywood history.

[Becomes choked-up with emotion.] Chaplin returned to Hollywood in 1977 to accept an honorary Oscar. I think he was probably getting toward Alzheimer's, so that they didn't dare trust him to speak at the Academy Awards. But if you remember, the whole cast of the show came onstage for the finale and they all sang "Smile"—his song. He just stood there looking out at everyone. It was terribly, *terribly* [pauses] moving because it was Hollywood apologizing, after all that time, to one of its very greatest artists. It was a sad, sad, chapter.

I don't know why Hollywood was allowed to go through its decline, although it had an honorary mayor in Johnny Grant, and that they kept the Chamber of Commerce going just by charging for their names on the sidewalk. It costs at least $5,000 to get your name on the sidewalk these days; it was $3,000. I don't think they ever had an organization that had any kind of energy, any kind of vision to *really* try and bring back Hollywood, or try and keep it the way it was.

I think all the young, affluent crowd went to the theaters in Westwood, and Hollywood lost that importance that it once had. Once the process began, suddenly there were shabbier and shabbier people on the boulevard and more of a sense of desperation. But I never really associate Hollywood with anything as tawdry as Times Square was, with all the porn theaters. Hollywood was about a kind of desperate people in search of something that no longer existed there. It was the lure of the *idea*. People are still interested in going there, and they search every day to look to find something at Hollywood & Vine, but now the Brown Derby is no longer down the street, and there isn't anything much up the street. It really is a ghost of itself.

250

It's going to be tough for the movies to fight the deterioration of life in the streets, so that it gets more difficult for people to go out to screenings. But I think the importance of film is its ability to put its hold onto you, and of you positively surrendering to it, the willing suspension of disbelief, the knowledge that it is a series of discreet still images going past and defeating the persistence of vision.

Technology hasn't been entirely beneficial to the movies. I think we've lost the possibility of communication without words that silent films had. And as Hitchcock was complaining, we've lost a certain command of the visual elements of the film that became less necessary when people could speak. So you lost *that*, and with color films, you've lost all the possibilities of reality from black and white films. There is absolutely *no* reason why black-and-white films ought not be allowed to be made. There are all kinds of audiences now who would appreciate a good story told in black-and-white.

My favorite film is *Beat the Devil* by John Huston. With Bogart. A lovely, lovely film. Very funny, way ahead of its time. Never a success. Huston said he never made a dime on it. It was sort of a shaggy-dog film written by Truman Capote and Huston every night during shooting for the next day. It's just one of the most literate, funny films that ever was. It's sad to see it because Bogart, I think, always has the look of death upon him. It was not a while before his death, but there is a certain kind of grayness in his face that is alarming and you know he died soon after.

Casablanca, which is my second favorite film, is just kind of *perfect*. *Citizen Kane* has that combination of technology and humanity that I think is just unique. *The Wizard of Oz* is lovely and God knows an enduring classic. It's a phenomenon about film, that the best films can be seen again and again and reveal their riches each time. That's why we are all nuts about films.

People often complain that movies today are not the way they once were.

I think that if they did make movies the way they imagined the world used to be, they probably would not succeed, because they would be so out of touch with the way the world is today. So when people say that to me, "How come they can't make movies the way they used to?" I tell them, "It's because they don't make the world the way they used to."

Bill Welsh

BORN AUGUST 8, 1928

GREELEY, COLORADO

BROADCASTER

251

A summer day swelters below, but up above the dusty boulevard in the air-conditioned offices of the Hollywood Chamber of Commerce all is clean and cool. A tall, handsome man with white hair, he wears silver-framed aviator glasses and a light-blue suit, and speaks with the bright, baritone resonance and articulation of a veteran broadcaster. One of the first to make the transition from radio to television back when his peers were still scoffing at the new medium, he is active in promoting the future of Hollywood, which is why he can be found almost daily here in the Chamber's office, and is one of those responsible for luring big developers to town to make some major changes to Hollywood Boulevard. He's well-known in Los Angeles not only for being a TV and radio personality for many decades, but also for being active in the Hollywood Chamber of Commerce. And unlike other people who are influential in shaping the physical and financial fate of Hollywood, he was willing to talk about it. Sadly, he died only months after our discussion.

It was exciting to come to Hollywood in the forties, just to be in a place about which I had heard about so much. The word "Hollywood," if you come from Greeley, Colorado, is pretty exciting. Just saying, "I'm going to Hollywood." It was a lot more exciting than saying, "I'm going to Greeley." And I remember being a little surprised that it didn't really look that much different from Greeley, Colorado.

In those days there was still tremendous activity here. NBC was at Sunset & Vine, CBS was down at Sunset & Gower, ABC was on Vine Street and was about to buy that old studio where D.W. Griffith made *Birth of a Nation* and many other famous movies. So they were still here. But their facilities were built for radio. They tried to convert some of those big studios into TV studios, which they could do, but they needed better facilities, which NBC got in Burbank. And then CBS built over at Beverly & Fairfax. They needed more room. Warner Brothers, they did *The Jazz Singer* at what is now the KTLA lot on Sunset, and they moved out long before World War II and they needed more room. Universal Studios, even, is somewhat detached from Hollywood.

Famous people were doing their weekly radio shows and then some of their early television shows in those locations there at Sunset & Vine. There were great restaurants—the Vine Street Brown Derby was the place where people wanted to go, because it was right there. Mike Liman's, whose brother—Abe Liman—had a famous dance orchestra, had a restaurant across the street from the Brown Derby—where the parking lot now is next to the Doolittle Theater. They tore the building down.

There were many great stores. The Broadway was the last of the great department stores in Hollywood. Other famous names had their stores in Hollywood because their clientele were wealthy people. The buildings at Hollywood & Vine were filled with agents, advertising agencies, people such as that.

I got into television in December of 1946. There were 300 television sets in southern California. I did an ice hockey game from Pan Pacific Auditorium on Channel 5, and they liked what I did. And I did everything—sports, special events. I got to be known. Famous people would say, "Oh yeah, that's the guy who is doing that thing on that newfangled television!"

I got some parts in pictures, and I did scenes with Clark Gable, Ronald Reagan, Ethel Barrymore. I did the Bing Crosby Celebrity Golf Tournament here with Bing. All the stars were watching television because they wanted to know how it was going to affect them, if it would destroy their careers, or if they should try to get into it. So they were all watching closely and I was the one was already there.

In 1947 my friends were coming to me and saying, "You made a terrible mistake going into television. You will not live long enough to see television amount to anything. You should have stayed in radio." Now either I lived too long, or they were wrong about how fast television was going to grow. Obviously it has become the primary thing in the life of people, as far as entertainment and information is concerned.

There are two Hollywoods. There is the actual physical Hollywood, where you and I are right now. And there's generic Hollywood, which is this entertainment business. *That* Hollywood. And I don't think that word will ever disappear. I think that it will always be the thing that they used when they want to talk about the entertainment business. Because we were here first, thanks to Cecil B. DeMille and people like that.

I used to look at some Metro-Goldwyn-Mayer movies, and the ending titles, among other things, would say, "Made in Hollywood, USA." Well, *obviously*, it was made in Culver City, USA, not in Hollywood. And Universal, which is in Universal City, calls themselves Universal Studios, *Hollywood*. Well, which is it? If you say, "Universal Studios, North Hollywood," or

"Universal Studios, Universal City," it doesn't mean as much as if you say Hollywood.

Lee Bolman
BORN OCTOBER 30, 1929
BOSTON, MASSACHUSETTS
ACTRESS

253

She holds court over a plate of cheese blintzes at the International House of Pancakes on Sunset at Orange, just west of the old Athletic Club. She informs all in ear-shot that this is an IHOP which has been reconstructed, curiously, on the same grounds where a previous, almost-identical IHOP stood. It was her idea to breakfast here to counterbalance the diet of instant coffee and cigarettes she's been on ever since losing her home. For years she lived in Whitley Heights, perched up in the hills above central Hollywood. After the death of her husband in the early eighties, she became increasingly incapable of affording the ever-escalating property taxes, presuming that there had to be some kind of legal loophole that would prohibit the government from taking away an elderly woman's home and throwing her out on the street. But there was none, and these days she finds herself renting an undersized room she can't afford in a coral-colored residential hotel on Orchid, just north of Hollywood Boulevard. Outside her window the street is being torn up by bulldozers and jackhammers, overhauling this old neighborhood to clear way for the construction of the sprawling Hollywood-Highland project, which is rising up menacingly, like Griffith's immense set for Intolerance over the existing neighborhood (even ironically borrowing much of the Babylonian iconography, including a goliathan ivory-white elephant). Now this development has blocked off the former throughway from this block of Orchid to Hollywood Boulevard with mammoth retaining walls, consequently transforming this old avenue into a dead-end street.

"It's symbolic," she said stoically, as she stopped outside the hotel for a cigarette prior to her IHOP excursion. Once unfettered and free-flowing, she feels now she's going nowhere, thwarted by those who plunder the past to fabricate a future, and chalk it all up to the happy pursuit of progress. And so she treasures any opportunity for a break from the bleakness of her present circumstances, relishing the relative comfort—and agreeable blintzes—to be found at this IHOP. "Do you want to know the truth?" she asks with no dearth of desperation, her eyes clouded with weariness and cataracts. "Or is this just going to be another 'Everything Is Beautiful in Holly-wood' kind of book? Because if that's what you want, you should look elsewhere. But if you want to know the truth about Hollywood—and I'm talking now the real Hollywood—well, that's something else again, and we should have a conversation." She's a smart, schooled lady with adamant opinions that she zealously imparts. And despite this attendant destitution from which she may very well never recover, and despite droll, apologetic admonitions regarding the potential of her pantyhose winding down around her ankles on account of ineffectual elastic, her demeanor is one of enduring dignity, and a refusal to be vanquished.

I always wanted to be an actress. Growing up Irish in Boston, I learned to do Irish dances, which are *splendid*, and also little monologues in an Irish accent. I'd sing even though I can't sing my way out of a paper bag. And I fell in love with show business. But my father felt it was spiritually wrong, as if they could steal my soul. And at my age, I'm beginning to think my father was right.

254

I moved to Hollywood in 1953 with my husband. He was a physicist and a computer expert. He helped to make the first talking computer, and did a lot of work on aircraft. We were able to move into Whitley Heights at a time of a slight depression in real estate prices. And the old Spanish-type homes were not popular at that particular point. I knew a Realtor, she liked me and I liked her, a little Jewish woman named Sylvia. She *loved* these old houses, and would show me beautiful homes in Whitley Heights. I *loved* it. I used to say, "Someday, Sylvia, I'm going to have one of these houses." So she called me up one day and said, "I've got your house."

I said, "Are you kidding me?

She said, "Come, but don't bring your husband, because it won't work if you do."

So I went with her. To a house up in Whitley Heights. There'd been a murder in the house, that's the truth. A man was shot to death there. And his mother, an elderly woman from Minnesota, inherited the house. And came out to live in it with the younger brother of the dead man.

She told me herself that she had birthed five of her children on her kitchen table in a Minnesota farmhouse. She'd never been out of that area until she inherited this house in Hollywood. She was a *lovely* old woman, and the neighbors *hated* her with a passion. They'd say, "*Get* this woman out of the neighborhood."

Her young brother was kind of a goofball, and they couldn't afford to keep up the mortgage, and they had to sell the house. She wanted to go back to Minnesota. The neighbors had absolutely terrorized her, and I mean *terrorized* her. In a way, we came to her rescue. She had to get out of there. Her brother wanted the house but couldn't afford it. So that's how *we* got into Whitley Heights.

I will *never* forget the first time I went into the house. It was just Sylvia and myself. It was pitch-black except for candles on every wall. There was a sconce, and a real Catholic Virgin Mary shrine with the candle and a crucifix. I'm not making fun of these symbols, I'm a Christian, but that's all the light there was. Candles in every wing and all the curtains closed. It was spooky, yeah.

And this dear old lady would insist that you sit down and go through a photo album which she had. They were pictures of her son's funeral, which she held right there in this house, in this living room. Which is not legal today. There was the coffin at one of the living room, banked in flowers. She had many pictures taken of it, and insisted that I go through this entire album and look at every single photo before she would talk to me about the house at all.

After we came out, Sylvia said, "You see what I mean?"

I said, "Well, I like her. It's really tragic."

She said, "I knew you would, and I knew you'd be all right. I haven't been able to get one customer to come in here who would stay for more than a minute. You're the first. Everyone else was too frightened, I guess. "

255

Then she said, "I don't think your husband would fare very well either, would he?"

I said, "No, no. It will take a little preparation to do this." [Laughs]

And it did. He walked out twice. I kept saying to him, "Look, this is a beautiful house. Just forget all that about the murder and the kid's funeral and the candle sconces and crucifixes everywhere. We can paint it, we can fix it." And finally he agreed. And in the meanwhile Sylvia kept trying to show the house, but nobody else would see it. So we got it.

I had a gate that closed off my property from an old stairway in the hills, where you could walk all the way down to Highland. Now it's that parking lot, across the street from the Hollywood Bowl. But in those days, there was a big mansion down there, and it was entirely different. At any rate, they've got all these various, awesome stairs in the hills, though some of them are now pretty much buried in earth. Out behind where they have put the Squaw Man barn. There used to be stairs all the way up into my backyard and people used to go through my garden. But they stole all that land that was mine and built a house illegally on it. It goes on and on. It was that old lady who told me they were going to put a public walkway through my garden. And that was the start of it, the chicanery of stealing property was present then as it is now, it's just a matter of degree.

They built the freeway, I think, in '55, which destroyed much of Whitley Heights. Senator Hiyakawa was, I like to say, a friend of mine. He had a huge mansion where the freeway is. He was a great person. There was a man named Seshu who was a Buddhist monk. Many prominent people lost their homes. The Barrymores had a place that was knocked down. It's incredible what they've done, really.

Beulah Bondi lived in Whitley Heights longer than any other star. I got to know her, though I didn't know her intimately. We went to parties at her house, and she was lovely. She gave nice parties, always with somebody playing the piano, and it would be classical music, and she would have beautiful displays of food, and dancing. They were very nice parties, sort of semiformal, but casual and lovely. Very much what you wish they all were and aren't anymore.

Many of the famous people who have lived in Whitley Heights were visiting, and just renting their homes. Gloria Swanson lived there when she was making *Sunset Boulevard*, and the famous writer [William] Faulkner, too. I remember seeing him sometimes just strolling through the neighborhood, walking slowly, kind of meandering, and smoking a pipe. Everybody smoked then. It was the thing to do.

Bette Davis' cottage was there though she didn't live it anymore. They happily tore that down, too. It was up on the hill just above where the museum is now. It was a wonderful cottage. *Every* board, nail and window in that house came from a movie set. It was *beautiful*. I was in it many, many times, and it was really one of the most historic homes in Hollywood. And the county happily tore it to shreds. You know, you have to ask them why. They didn't need that little bit of parking lot, did they?

Agnes Moorehead was my teacher. I studied acting with her while she was doing a one-woman show. About two and a half hours of just her on stage. It was fabulous. We all helped, many of her students, to make costumes for that show. It was a fun event for the elite. It wasn't really open to the public, particularly, I don't think. Clark Gable came, and so did Mary Pickford, and all these other famous people were there. They all came to have fun and support Agnes in her one-woman show and she was *splendid*.

When I was working on the costumes, I was sewing away, and talking to a sweet woman next to me. And I didn't even realize it was Mary Pickford. When I sat beside her, she put her hand out and said, "I'm Mary Pickford." And I'm thinking, "Mary *Pickford*?!" But I didn't believe it could be *the* Mary Pickford because I was sitting, after all, right *next* to her. And then all of a sudden it hit me that it was really *her*, [laughs] and suddenly I couldn't talk. [Laughs] But she didn't even seem to notice, and she talked, and she laughed, and she smiled and she was so *warm*. Such a *warm*, sweet, *lovely* person. She was as down-to-earth as an old shoe. She had her certain aristocratic attitude and appearance that was natural to her. She was a superior human being, just born that way. Attractive, beautiful in movement and in speech. There was sort of a happiness in her head that came out of her eyes. Remember how Shirley Temple looked when she was a little kid? When she looks up and tosses her curls and her eyes are bright? Pickford had that kind of quality, too. Almost like a little girl, and she was probably seventy then. But there was a *quality*, an inborn quality, nothing you can teach.

Agnes was a very good teacher, but the standards and the philosophy that she was trying to convey were not simplistic. It wasn't gobbledy-goop either. It required discipline. Agnes was a workhorse, and I *adored* her.

One day I remember, I'll give you an example, she must have been around fifty-five at the time. This was at her home. She came in and she stood beside the piano. We were all sitting there very proper and quiet. She moved away from the grand piano a few feet and suddenly put one leg up and stood on one leg. And she stood there, and she stood there, and she stood there. [Laughs] We were all waiting for her to fall over. She knew yoga and she did it well. She had *control* of the body. That was the message: You are an actor, your instrument is your body, the more you control the body, the more you can be an actor. It's a silly but basic truism, isn't it? She, at fifty-five could stand on one leg without squirming, budging, or anything for five minutes. I could never do that in my whole life. She had wonderful posture. She was a schooled person, and she believed in teaching the basics before you went on to be a mumbling method actor. [Laughs] She wasn't against that but she wanted you also to be healthy, to keep your spine straight, to be able to balance yourself on your toe for an hour if you had to. To throw your voice, in other words. She was toning and teaching the instrument of the body.

257

She is famous now for "Bewitched" on TV, which is funny. She didn't want to do it. But there are certain great actors who rise above the circumstances of a terrible script, a horrible director, a bad studio [laughs] and everything else. Agnes did the same thing on "Bewitched." So she won in the end.

I studied with Lucille Ball, too. It was about the time of her divorce from Desi, and she took over the studio. Lucy loved actors and she just loved people. She was a love, very warm, and she decided to teach. It didn't last very long because of her getting so busy running the business. But I was fortunate enough to study with her for almost two years. She would sometimes have guest people in. Anthony Quinn came in and taught, it was just great. Lucy had great instincts and a *tremendous* presence. She's the greatest female clown we've had since Fanny Brice.

Lucy only had nice things to say about Desi. At that time they were getting the divorce, many people tended to be sympathetic toward her and tried to make brownie points by denigrating the male in the scene, Desi. Lucy would have *none* of that. She would come right out and say, "If not for Desi Arnaz, there wouldn't *be* a Lucille Ball." She would say that he was a great producer and director, that he was instinctive and creative.

At the same time, the show was never again what it was when they were together. It was built on the personalities of these two people, and apparently Desi understood this and capitalized on it.

Lucille Ball was a deeply sincere person. There's no way she could have an alliance with anybody without it touching her deeply. For her to go through a divorce must have been horrendous. She's also a very brave person, like a lioness with courage and lots of smarts that people didn't give her enough credit for. I remember once when one of her students got ill. Lucy took it on herself to visit the girl in the hospital. She didn't send somebody else, she went herself. She was a loving person, much more loving than anyone gave her credit for. A true-blue-type person. When she got married, she intended it to last forever. At the same time, you can only take so much philandering. Lucy was not a weak nilly, you know.

One night this funny little girl came in. She was just too Jewish, much too Jewish. I wondered, what was she doing here? She should be behind the camera. In those days there was a lot of fixing the hair-do, like Lucy did, and they were very fussy with makeup and frills and all this. So they were more inclined to look at a person's physical appearance, especially the face of girls.

So this strange creature got up and did a monologue, and everybody was kind of snickering. She had a little dog, and she held it as she did this monologue. The room was hushed. She struck a chord. She was absolutely brilliant. She was unmistakable. She was superb. She tore everybody's heart out with this one little deal. It was Barbra Streisand. I remember that for the longest time we didn't see her again, and everybody wondered whatever happened to that funny-looking girl.

Nowadays everything is commercial and crass, and there's little dignity left in the acting profession. Turn on the TV and look and it's kind of demeaning for the actors and actresses in it. What happened to Hollywood? Well, that's part of it. It really is part of it.

Aaron Epstein

BORN AUGUST 18, 1930
LOS ANGELES, CALIFORNIA
HOLLYWOOD PRESERVATIONIST/PROPERTY OWNER

Standing in a shed in the expansive yard of his North Hollywood home, he shows off various mementos, including a blow-up of an old ad from 1954 that was placed in the L.A. Times to advertise the new books for sale at Pickwick's, the famous and beloved bookstore that his father, Louis Epstein, owned on Hollywood Boulevard: "Pickwick Bookshop, 6743 Hollywood Boulevard, Phone Number: Hollywood 9-8191." A list of bestsellers follows: A Top Ten Fiction list for 1954 with The Adventures of Augie Marks by Saul Bellow as Number One. In Non-Fiction, The Power of Positive Thinking by Norman Vincent Peale is Number One; Lindbergh's The Spirit of St. Louis is Number Two.

He's known around Hollywood by anyone who frequents the Sunday morning Farmers Mar-

kets on Ivar, or who attends the Hollywood Heritage meetings, or any other number of causes that concern the preservation and/or celebration of Hollywood and its central boulevard. He worked at Pickwick's as a child stocking the shelves and painting the walls even before it first opened its fabled doors, and continued to work there throughout the fifties. He grew up on Curson in Hollywood, just down the street from the Wattles Mansion, and now lives with his wife Anne here in North Hollywood. Yet he retains a vital presence on Hollywood Boulevard as the owner of the Artisan Patio, a little series of shops on the boulevard that he and his brother purchased directly from C.E. Toberman himself, and as one of the few property owners on the boulevard who is as concerned with the preservation of Hollywood's past as he is with the promise of its future.

259

My father, Louis Epstein, moved to America when he was eight, and opened the Pickwick Bookstore in March of 1938. Things got very hard for the Jews of Russia at the turn of the twentieth century and so my father's father came to America first and moved to San Francisco. From there he moved to Cleveland, where he made enough money selling goods off a pushcart that he could send for my father and my grandmother and my father's brothers and sisters. They came over in about 1908. To Cleveland. My dad went to Ohio State University, enrolled in law school. His sister came down with tuberculosis so they all decided to move to California for the good weather. My father told the dean he would help them get established in California and then he would return to finish his degree. The dean said, "Once you guys drop out, you never come back."

My dad said, "I'm gonna prove you wrong, and dammit, I'll be back."

The dean was right. [Laughter] He never came back. The family came to Los Angeles in 1923. At first they lived in Boyle Heights. I was born on Cincinnati Street.

My dad opened his first used bookshop in Long Beach about 1923. And he really liked it, and he worked so hard at it, he had a nervous breakdown. So he had to stop, and he closed the shop. As he was recovering, he would go out scouting for used books and reselling them to booksellers. In the mid-twenties, he opened a shop called the Argonaut on 5th Street downtown and then another one called Louis Epstein's Bookshop on West 8th Street between Grand and Olive.

In 1938, he thought that to improve finances he should open a bookshop in Hollywood. And to make sure that Pickwick could get on its feet, he continued working at his old bookshop downtown. Pickwick started doing well, so he closed his bookshop downtown and worked just strictly at the Pickwick Bookshop in Hollywood.

He was first looking for a building to rent, and he found one on Hollywood Boulevard. It was built for a tailor named Otto Dit in 1928 by C.E.

Toberman. Dit went under with the Depression, and the Bank of America had to foreclose on the property. The price was $15,000. So he did, and he was able to pay off the mortgage in less than ten years. And for years after that, he credited some of his financial success to the fact that he didn't have to pay rent. He owned the property. 6743 Hollywood Boulevard. Then in 1958 he acquired the corner property, which had been a gay bar named the Circle Bar. The authorities eventually closed it, so my dad acquired that property and expanded the bookstore all the way to the corner.

260

Pickwick's was named for the Dickens character. I can't think of a better name, because the name Pickwick conjures a lovable, happy person that just loves his books.

We moved to Hollywood in 1934 to a house at 1914 Curson, which is about a block north of the Wattles Mansion. We knew Mrs. Wattles from the time we moved there. She must have been in her sixties. Very charming. The atmosphere was similar to the English feudal lord, where everybody looked up to the chief property owner as their landlord, but most likely it was a benevolent landlord who looked after all his tenants. And she wasn't our landlord by any means, but she took an interest in everybody in the neighborhood. She was a grande dame.

Her husband died before we moved in. She lived alone there, though I'm sure she had a housekeeper. The victory garden that is below there now all belonged to her; it's where she attempted to raise avocados and oranges. But that didn't work out financially. For the last twenty years of her life, she was crying the blues because the city was trying to take her land from her. And her main goal in life was making sure that that property could be preserved. Although she was pretty well-to-do by our standards, with the rising property taxes and inflation, I think it was pretty hard on her. So she sold the property in 1957 with the understanding that the city would keep it intact as a park. So that developers would not divvy it up, and also that she could continue to live at the mansion as long as she lived.

Apparently it went downhill. Parks and Recreation didn't know what to do with it. But then Hollywood Heritage took it over, and have made great efforts in restoring and preserving it. And today it's beautiful.

Curson Street today has hardly changed. There are no apartment buildings. It's still all single-family residences. That's the beautiful thing about that street. It looks almost exactly as it did in the 1930s. It was a great neighborhood to grow up in. We had to walk some distance to get up the hill. Hollywood Boulevard, between Curson and La Brea, has changed gradually. It used to be all big houses, but many have been demolished to make way for large apartment buildings which are now there.

The Pickwick and Stanley Rose's Bookshop were the two main book-shops on the boulevard. Stanley Rose was a very heavy drinker. And he had a charm; a fantastic personality. He was a *fantastic* salesman. When a new book came out that he thought could be a good movie, he would take stacks of them to the studios, and sell them there, from office to office. He did very well. He was good at that, but with the bookshop itself, he was not a good businessman. He would sometimes close it down so that he could go drinking in the afternoon. He wouldn't collect the bills owed to him, and he wouldn't pay the bills he owed. Eventually he went under. He was friends with my dad, and for a short time even worked for my dad. Which was insulting for him, because Rose was an icon of booksellers. For him to humble himself by working as a clerk behind the counter was humiliating. He tried different things. He worked as a literary agent.

Well, they always say the same things about people over the years, and you mentioned my father's name and it was always a saying: "He was a hell of a nice guy, but he was impossible to work for."

When I grew up, I always worked in my spare time and on vacations at the store. In college during the summers I worked there in the used-book department, where I was needed. It was good and it was bad. When you're the boss' son, you know what people are saying behind your back. That you could do no wrong, because your father would never fire you.

I remember Christopher Isherwood well. He often came into the shop. He certainly made no bones about being gay. He was always very friendly to my father. My dad had the ability to get along with everybody. And some of our stronger customers were extremely conservative super right-wing people.

This is a note that was delivered to the bookshop that I have kept all these years:

Dear Sir,
I am the frustrated, mixed-up thief whom you caught on Christmas Eve. I was too shocked and humiliated to thank you properly and I am thanking you now, most humbly. I've learned my lesson and I will never steal another thing as long as I live. The world would have collapsed on me, but for your kindness.

Isn't that something? A grateful thief.

Charlie Chaplin used to come into Pickwick's all the time. He was a big reader, and he loved to browse among all the used books. Scott Fitzgerald was also in the store, often, and not too happy then to see so many of his books out of print at the time. It was only later that his books were rediscovered. Charles Laughton was one of our best customers. He would always go out with a huge armload of books. He never wanted them wrapped.

I remember that Richard Nixon came to the bookshop in the middle 1960s. He had lost his race for governor and he ran in '63 and he wrote this book called *My Six Crises*. He came to the bookshop and he was *charming*, just charming as they could come. They introduced him to the president of the bookseller's association and Nixon said, "President... How do you become a president?" [Laughter] But the people that knew him behind the scenes all said he was a manipulator and a conniver. Yet somehow likable nonetheless.

262

My dad sold the book shop when I was thirty-seven years old. The store stayed open until '95. It was sold to the B. Dalton people, and they continued it as Pickwick and in the early seventies they changed the name to B. Dalton. I stayed on for a year. It was too hard an adjustment for me to be working in a family business and then have to go to work for a corporation that has 20,000 people for it. I'd get letters in the mail saying, "It's now time for me to plan our corporate goals for the coming year." I felt it was just pencil pushing. I didn't want to spend all my time writing reports. So I left.

In 1964, C.E. Toberman owned the Artisan's property on Hollywood Boulevard near the bookstore one building over. We did not own the property in between, but we always had hopes of getting it so we could expand the book shop. So we grabbed that property in hopes that we'd eventually get the property in between and expand. In the meantime, Dad sold the Pickwick to the B. Dalton people so I had to decide what I was going to do with the Artisans Patio. Foolishly I kept it. I probably could have done better financially to get someone else to develop it. So the Artisan's Patio, to me today, is not something to make tons of money. It's just a way for me to make a statement about Hollywood. I take pride in the fact that I'm giving people who have some unusual idea an opportunity to develop it, and if it succeeds, to run with it.

The first freeway that opened in L.A. was the Arroyo Seco Freeway in 1938 which connected downtown Los Angeles with Pasadena. It was about 1946 that they started work on the freeway by condemning big swaths of houses to make room for it. The first branch of the freeway opened about 1951, but only between downtown Los Angeles and Western at Santa Monica. I remember when I wanted to get on the freeway, I would drive down to Western & Santa Monica near where that Sears is now, and get on the freeway there. It wasn't until about 1952 that they had it extending out here through the Cahuenga Pass and into the Valley.

Between 1947 and 1952, during the summertime, I worked at the Hollywood Bowl selling programs. It was a great job because some nights I'd be able to earn $12, and that was a hell of a lot of money for a seventeen-year-old to be making at that time. I remember that people were passing out petitions saying that the freeway route should be changed because it was coming too close to the Bowl. They were worried that the noise from the freeway would interfere with the Bowl. But it wasn't changed, and I don't think the freeway noise actually interferes with the Bowl. I'm not really sure if the freeway hurt or helped business in Hollywood. In one sense it made it easier for people to drive to Hollywood to do business with the merchants in Hollywood, but by the other token it made it easier for people to drive into the Valley to do business. It's the same thing nowadays with the subway. Does it bring more people into Hollywood or does it make it easier for people to get out, and go elsewhere to shop? Who can say?

A lot of people were against the freeway plans, but I was definitely for it, because I had a girlfriend that lived in the Valley. I know a lot of people in Hollywood lost their houses because of the freeway. But land was still plentiful then, and they were probably paid fair market value for their homes, and could probably buy something else.

The Walk of Fame was started in 1959 by a guy named Harry Sugarman, who was a property owner on Vine. My dad just scratched his head and thought that this was simply a project of the Vine Street people, and he really wasn't that enthusiastic over it because we had to pay a big assessment for ten years to fund the Walk of Fame. I hear people talk today that they own the Walk of Fame or they have the right to make decisions about the Walk of Fame, and take a little umbrage at that because they weren't the ones who paid for the Walk of Fame. I was the one that paid for the Walk of Fame. Other people that owned property on Hollywood Boulevard had to pay for the Walk of Fame. In a way it is sort of a mixed blessing because it has made the Boulevard so reliant on tourist-oriented business that when we get the tourists we're making money and when we don't have the tourists we're singing the blues. But by bringing in so many tourists, we've lost our other customers and also our other retailers. So it's a Catch-22 thing. We don't dare get rid of our tourists now because we would be lost. We do have a population based in Hollywood but we do not have the businesses that would encourage these people to come visit the boulevard.

But I feel positive about the boulevard. I feel good about the project going up at Hollywood & Highland. They have the theater there for the Academy Awards, and a very good hotel going in, so I think those are two good, solid cornerstones for it. So many mistakes have been made in the past trying to develop the boulevard. But these folks at Hollywood & Highland have done their homework, and I think this one might succeed. And if it does, it will have profound effects on the rest of the boulevard, and hopefully that will be good for all of us. So I'm happy to end this on a positive note. Because I do feel positive.

Geraldine Holt
BORN NOVEMBER 5, 1933
SHANGHAI, CHINA
TICKET TAKER / RECEPTIONIST

264

It's breakfast time at the Beachwood Café, the quaint coffeeshop at the center of Beachwood Village in the heart of what was originally Hollywoodland. She's a regular here, known by all the waitresses and busboys who smile at her as she enters and takes a booth by the window. Over eggs and coffee, this daughter of New York natives relates the details of a remarkable life which began in China, moved quickly to Hollywood, and was punctuated early on by her father's famous photo sessions with such historical personages as Chiang Kai-shek, Adolf Hitler, and Franklin Roosevelt. At a young age she found herself being raised by nuns who were moonlighting, remarkably, in the one profession even older than their own. She has short, stylish silver hair, and projects an easy elegance as she delves into the past.

My father was Chiang Kai-shek's press attaché and he had his own newspaper in China. My father was born in New York and raised in Buenos Aires, who had a feather factory. We moved to Hollywood in the twenties. My father, George Lacks, was Hitler's favorite photographer. That famous postage stamp of Hitler is one of my father's portraits. And every summer my father would go to Germany, but he wouldn't take my mother and I because he knew what was coming. We're Jewish, but not Orthodox. Roosevelt also liked my father's portraits, so there was my father between Hitler and Roosevelt.

When we came here, I didn't speak English. I spoke Chinese in twenty-six dialects and four other languages. Then when I came here my mother, who was a little nuts, beat the hell out of me until I could only speak Pidgin English with a British accent. My father worked at a photography store that is still on Cahuenga, and later got a radio show. He used to hang out with Edgar R. Murrow and all the famous writers of the time. Ernest Hemingway, Christopher Isherwood.

I first lived in Hollywood. My mother was sleeping with a guy who lived on South Van Ness. I will never forget, right after we got here it was July 4, and my father took me out at night to see the fireworks. It's my first memory of California. He wanted me to see all the colors, and took me to the fountain at Los Feliz and Riverside, and that's where we watched the fireworks.

My folks got divorced and my mother, who wanted to get rid of me, sent me to a Catholic boarding school downtown called Sacred Heart. I went from there to two other boarding schools. The last one was St. Catherine's Academy. Every morning we sang the Communist anthem. And all the nuns were hookers at night and on weekends. We were not allowed to look out of windows; if we did we would be beaten. The nuns were the town whores; they did it for money.

My father found out where I was and what was going on there, and he went to court to get custody of me. He was working for *Life* magazine at the time, and was going to expose the whole thing but they bribed him not to, and he kept quiet about it. But about five years later somebody else broke the story, and closed the place down. I haven't thought about that for a long time.

265

Then I moved in with him at his house on South Orange Grove, near Fairfax.

I remember Hollywood Boulevard crystal clear. We lived in a one-room apartment at 1545 Western Avenue. Just above Sunset. The neighborhood market was at Sunset & Western. My uncle used to run the Thrifty Drugstore at Hollywood & Western in what is now called the Louie B. Mayer Building. He had a soda fountain and served dinners and blue-plate specials. They had magazines, so we would read the magazines and played the jukebox. He was always chasing us kids out of there.

Going south on Western was the Sunset movie theater—it's X-rated now. Every Saturday that was a Western theater—they showed two Westerns and a serial, all for a quarter. Across Sunset from there was 20th Century's back-lots. We'd always try to climb over the wall, and you could see the props all stored there.

At Santa Monica & Western was the Cinema Theater, for love story movies. Two of them every week. Around the corner on Santa Monica, across from the Sears, was the Loman Theater, and that was just for mystery movies. You would have two mysteries—and a serial, like Charlie Chan. At Hollywood & Western was also the Apollo Theater, a family theater. Every Tuesday and Wednesday they would have double features and a stage show and a drawing for dishes. Whoever won would get soap and a set of dishes.

So on weekends, when our mothers were whoring around, their boyfriends would give us kids quarters to get rid of us, and we'd go to the movies all day. We would start at ten in the morning at the Apollo, and work our way down to the Loman. We'd come home just before dark. It was safe, good fun. Except at the Loman theater, there would be men who would expose themselves. All the time.

On Sundays I would get on the bus—because I had gained a fear of God from going to Catholic schools—and I would go to Blessed Sacrament Church. I would see all the movie stars there. Back then it seemed that everyone worked or lived in Hollywood, and in the summers where it would get so hot, we would all be in the movie theaters. Everybody knew everybody. At night, everybody would walk from Hollywood & Western almost to La Brea. And everyone knew each other. All the shops would be open, and you would stop to look in them. You'd see the movie stars shopping.

There were a lot of vacant lots near Hollywood & Western where all us kids played.

When I got older, the Paramount Theater on Hollywood—it's now the El Capitan—was the best theater to neck in. The balcony. That was where you had to prove your mettle. But the girls would be very selective. The Egyptian Theater had a forecourt with real gorillas and chimpanzees. That was the MGM movie house. On New Year's Eve, everybody would go there because they would premiere an Esther Williams movie every New Year's Eve.

There was the Pantages, where they would put bleachers out in the front to see the stars, and they had the Oscars there.

There was Sid Grauman's Chinese Theater, which was wonderful. They've since cut it up, so it's nothing like it was. They've ruined it. It used to be beautiful; the forecourt with all the hand and footprints of the stars. You'd go up the hill from there to Yamashiro Hotel, which Grauman owned. He built it. But it was not like it is today. It used to take up the whole hillside, and they built Oriental houses there, and each one came with an Oriental houseboy. My uncle and my father lived there. There was no pool like there is today, but all these little Oriental houses scattered over this whole hill. And besides the houses, there was nothing but orange groves. The houses were all furnished, and the furniture was especially made for them. Where the hotel is now, there was a big kitchen, and you could call for food. And you could have parties there, and there was a little restaurant. Grauman built it because he would have premieres down the hill at the Chinese Theater, and stars like Gloria Swanson would come for the premieres, and there would be rickshaws with rickshaw guys who would go up the hill, pick them up, and run them down. I remember this clear as a bell, because luckily my father lived there. He knew Sid Grauman, and he wrote about this in the paper.

I met Sid Grauman a lot of times. He came to the Vogue a lot when I was there, and he'd buy popcorn or a candy bar and we would talk. He was an old Jewish man with funny, frizzy hair. His mind was always on business, on making a buck. He liked money more than movies. He didn't really know that much about movies, but he knew about stars, and he knew if there were stars that he'd make a buck.

Ted Mann owned the Vogue on Hollywood [just east of Highland], and he bought the Chinese from the Grauman family after Sid died. And he screwed it up. It used to be beautiful.

I worked as a cashier at the Vogue. I was trying to add up the receipts and I was a penny short, and it pissed me off. Because they came after you. Ten dollars they didn't bother you, but a penny they thought you stole. So it's midnight and I'm sitting there trying to figure out where this penny went, and I heard a bang on the metal plate outside the ticket window. There was a guy standing there and he said, "What if I told you this was a holdup?"

And I said, "I'd tell you to go to the Chinese. They made a killing tonight. Leave me alone, I can't find a penny, I'm trying to balance." I didn't think a thing about it.

He said, "See ya." I didn't even look up.

Fifteen minutes later the cops came, grabbed me, and said I was his *accomplice*. He had *robbed* the *Chinese!* He told them I told him to go there because *they made a killing!* They grabbed me and handcuffed me and took me down to the old Hollywood Police station on Wilcox. I was laughing and then I realized they were serious. I called my father, and they knew him, so when he came they let me go.

My friends and I all had a routine. We didn't have cars. Every Saturday we would wash our hair and put it in curlers. And we'd go to the Hollywood Ranch Market on Vine. If you weren't working, you'd go there at two in the morning. Because Marlon Brando, Harry Belafonte and other stars would take their wives or girlfriends there shopping then, thinking they could avoid the crowd. But we were all there.

We would also find out when Frank Sinatra would be recording at Capitol. His sessions would never start before midnight, and he would let us in because he wanted an audience, so we would all go up there. We were always in the right place at the right time. He felt sorry for us kids because it was so late, and we'd wait out in the cold for him. Sometimes he would never show up, and we'd pull an all-nighter there and then go to work the next day. But when he would come he would be so sweet to us, and he would buy us ice-cream to eat during the session. I cannot *tell* you the excitement of being there with Sinatra. He was my whole world then.

I also got a part-time job at the Earl Carroll Theater back when they still had the showgirls. I took reservations Saturday and Sunday, working nine hours each day, and all I got was 50 cents an hour and a free steak dinner. But I got to go to the show free. And I loved that.

And I would also go to the Palladium, where Louie Armstrong used to come, and Artie Shaw. I got to sit on Louie Armstrong's lap, and because of my dad I knew the first songs they have ever played, so I would sing along, and they loved that. I would sit on Louie Armstrong's lap and I would beg him to sing "Blueberry Hill" and he would. He was the nicest man.

At first I would go there when I was only ten. And everyone was drinking and smoking and dancing, but they let me in any way. And I got anything I wanted—I got to get in free every time they played. I knew all those guys. Earl "Fatha" Hines, Stan Kenton.

Over by Sy Devore's was the Airplane Bar, where Red Nichols used to play every day. I loved him. I have his record of "Battle Hymn of the Republic." If you ever get to hear that record, make sure you do. He could not get over this kid requesting that song. I was so lucky to get to know him.

I got a job working in bookkeeping at NBC at Sunset & Vine. It was mostly radio, though TV had just started then. I used to get off work just in time to go see Martin and Lewis. Their show would start at five, right there at NBC, so I would get off work at five minutes till five, and I would be in the front row of every radio show that they did. And I got every script of every show that they did. I have a collection.

Martin and Lewis fought all the time. Jerry Lewis was so bossy. He was so insecure. And Dean Martin, he just thought it was funny. It was a game for him. It was the least work he ever had to do in his life.

Dinah Shore was a big star then. We used to hide behind a building to watch as she came by. She was married to George Montgomery, who wasn't working then. And we would tease her and all say out loud, "Oh, here comes *Georgie!*" And when we would see him, we would all say, "*Hi Georgie!*" I have always wanted to apologize to her for that.

At NBC all I did was type up these long columns of figures. I knew I could do more than that, but they wouldn't let me. My boss was a Latin guy, and wanted me to go to bed with him, and I wouldn't. I was forced to go out for dinner with him, which I didn't want to do. He was married, and he wanted to set me up with an apartment. He said he would fire me. Though I didn't know where my next penny was coming from, I said, "Go ahead," and he did!

But that's okay. I got even with him. I was only eighteen. And we used to have these little parties, to listen to a radio show. I showed up to a party crying on purpose. Everyone wanted to know why. I told everyone what happened, and they fired him. He denied it, but another girl backed me up.

For a while I lived in a female residence on Wilcox at Yucca. It was called Wilcox Hall. It got the overflow from the Studio Club. There were rooms there, and a living room with a black and white TV which you could watch for a quarter. There was a kitchen. They didn't feed us, but sometimes somebody would cook something. Mostly we could go to Biff's. It cost seven bucks a week to live there. A maid came once a week.

Kim Novak was there. I was working for NBC then. She knew that we were going to premiere the first color TV show and *Playhouse 90*. Nobody knew her then. There was going to be a big press party, so she glommed onto me and asked me if she could go. But I wasn't able to invite anyone— this was an event just for the press—so I had to say no. But don't ask me how, the next day she was there. And she got into every photo and was on the front page of every newspaper. That's how she got discovered. I later got in trouble, because she told my boss that she was my friend and had come with me.

269

On that street was Stan Getz, Lena Horne was around the corner, Shelly Manne, who opened his club the Manhole. All those musicians were there and I'm living in this girls' club and I got their records! Shelly's Manhole was on Cahuenga, just below Hollywood.

Where there is the Yucca Market now (Cahuenga & Yucca) was a great coffee shop called Biff's that we all went to. The Montecito Hotel had all the New York Broadway actors—Montgomery Clift, Eli Wallach—the whole group, and they would all come into Biff's. And we girls in the Girls' club had no money, so we would split a cup of tea—one tea bag—and an English muffin.

Montgomery Clift became our buddy, and he would feed us. We'd rehearse his lines with him. He was so good-looking, you would almost swoon to be with him. But he was a very sad person then. He would never smile. It was when he was shooting *Splendor in the Grass* with Elizabeth Taylor. He was friendly, though. And he was always *amazed* that people knew him and appreciated his work. He would say, "Really? Are you serious?" He was very modest and humble.

Marilyn Monroe came in there a lot, too. She seemed happy. She would laugh a lot, and she was a lot of fun. She was a bright person, but she hid it. She didn't want to show it, just like Jayne Mansfield. She felt that act promoted her career.

After NBC, I worked at CBS radio at Sunset & Gower. It was all glass. I started out in the basement editing scripts. They didn't have Xerox then— they used the mimeographs, with the blue paper. I got promoted, and they kicked me up to the lobby. I was at the front desk in my uniform. What is now the Doolittle Theater on Vine was the Lux Radio Theater. They would do the Lux Radio Show there every Sunday with Louella Parsons, and during the week they would do theater. Tickets were two dollars. But I got free tickets. And I saw every Broadway show that came there. I saw *Gigi* with

Audrey Hepburn. I saw *The Seven-Year Itch* with Marilyn Monroe and Tom Hewell. I would go every week.

Then Steve Allen was on radio there all night, so I would stay up all night because I lived down the street then and I would go and watch him. And he was nuts. *Crazy* nuts. I would be the only one in the audience sometimes, and I would watch him making noise with cellophane and stuff like that. He was weird, still is. Very funny, weird man. I *loved* him.

270

I would be the only one there and when he would go to commercials he would say to me, "Don't you have *anything* to do besides this?" The whole studio would be dark, and I would sit there with my feet up, and sometimes I would nod off and he would yell out, *"Wake up!"* It was like he was in another world. He would do this stuff that nobody else would get; just him talking to himself. I would be the only one who would appreciate it. But I always had that weird kind of sense of humor. He was too far ahead for a lot of people.

The Cat & Fiddle on Sunset used to be the Hollywood Chamber of Commerce, that whole building. Edgar Bergen, George Burns, Lucy and Desi, they all had their offices there. Right there. Around that courtyard that is still there. Edgar Bergen was there the longest.

C.C. Brown's, of course, was on Hollywood between the Chinese and La Brea. It was wonderful, the best hot-fudge sundaes. I used to love to eat at Gallagher's, which was on Hollywood next to the Vogue. It was a grill.

On Vine Street, there was one great store after the next. Wallich's Music, Sy Devore's Dot Records, Will Wright's Ice Cream—the best ice cream you could ever want. Anytime anyone was on a break you would go to Will Wright's—it's where you'd hang out.

Then in the seedier, poorer parts of Hollywood, going toward downtown from around Santa Monica & Western, they had ice-cream parlors that were called Idiot Delights. You can see the round buildings still on La Brea and Highland. They were round buildings done in glass but solid. If you could eat an Idiot's Delight, which cost a dollar, you got to keep the big glass that it came in, plus you got it for free. So that was the big rage. It was ice-cream and they'd put in bananas, syrup, whipped cream, nuts, God knows what else—it was big. Everyone would be at big counters, eating one, getting sick trying to finish it. They tried to give Will Wright's a run for their money, and they almost did. They built one on nearly every corner, and some of the buildings are still there.

Also the first pizzas came then. Every other corner had a nineteen-cent stand, and you could get a hamburger or a malt. Us being so broke, one day we would get a hamburger, and one day a malt. Then the pizza stands came in. Pizzas were delivered. They cost a dollar. The big thing was to have a cold mushroom pizza for breakfast, so you would get it the night before.

Hollywood used to be one big Western town, full of Westerns and Western stars. Gower Gulch (at Sunset & Gower), which is now a little mall, was mostly a vacant lot with hitching posts for the horses of all the cowboys who were extras. They'd all hang out at the Columbia Drugstore, which had a fountain and a counter.

I worked for Robert Evans, the producer, for many months. Back when he was still gorgeous. He was very sweet to me, though I understand he could be a bastard to other people. I met Marlon Brando many times when I was there. He would never realize that I knew who he was. I knew many of his friends, and I would mention that we had mutual friends and he would say, "Who do you think I am?" As if anyone else could have that voice? He would call many times to check on Evans. He'd ask, "What's Evans doing now?" And I would say that he was out of the office, and Brando would complain about him. It was weird. And then I would come in the next morning, and there would be ten dollars or twenty dollars that Marlon left for me, and a little note that said, "Thank you for talking to me. Have a good lunch. "

Before the freeway came through Hollywood, it was much quieter, much nicer. You had the streetcars and electric green buses, so you could get around easily and you didn't need a car. It was a good system. The buses came every two and a half minutes.

I joined the Vedanta church. Where the wall was at Vedanta, before the freeway was cut through there, was all roses and they had the most beautiful view. The dome of the church was gold leaf. If you were way down in L.A. you could see up the hill and you would know it was Vedanta. Christopher Isherwood and all those people helped to build it up. I met Ronald Coleman there. But when they put in the freeway, they built that retaining wall there because without it you couldn't hear a word. I still go there to the gift shop and to meditate.

Where the Carmelite nuns are now at Carmen was the Theosophy Church. There was all vacant lots up to Vista Del Mar, where the school was. I lived on Vista Del Mar, and worked in West Hollywood. And I would come home for lunch at high noon and take Franklin, and there would be maybe four other cars. It would take me six minutes to get home. Look at it today. It's a different world. It was peaceful then.

Up here at Beachwood there used to be a Texaco gas station right next to the market. This cafe was a pharmacy. That is the original soda fountain. The market was an open-air market, and it's still owned by the same family. The reason it's built in is because in '62, we had a horrible rainstorm. There was no access road, this was the only road. The rainstorm washed everything down to the bottom of the hill. There was enough mud to bury seventeen cars and wash them down from here. My Volkswagen was totally buried. There were no apartments then, just little Craftsmen houses. Connie Stevens and her dad lived up here. All those houses got washed down.

The following winter was a horrible fire. It started up in the hills and spread down. The market was ruined. Between the flood and the fire, we were buried in here for three days. Helicopters were flying, they were digging the mud. It was horrible. The houses were ruined. That's why there are so many apartment buildings now.

272

Down at what is Victor's Square was an open European market. They had a bakery there. Everything was all open then, no roofs, but after the flood they closed it all up. Where Victor's Restaurant is now, that was a gay Mexican restaurant.

Thomas Ince's widow owned the mansion across the street, which is now the Scientology Center. It was and is a beautiful building, the Chateau Elysee. Ince was on William Randolph Hearst's yacht with Marion Davies when he got shot, and the rumor was that Charlie Chaplin did the shooting. From all the gossip, anyway, which my father told me, Chaplin did do the shooting, though they hushed it up.

Roberta Murray
BORN MARCH 7, 1934
BOSTON, MASSACHUSETTS
ACCOUNTANT

McDonald's on Vine Street, just south of Sunset. It was a melancholy place to meet this woman who remembered Hollywood with crystalline clarity. This garish fast food joint with its plastic chairs and Styrofoam coffee containers seemed all the more tawdry and soulless when surrounding her rich memories of Hollywood in the glory days, memories that were more often than not food related. A fortnight later she is happily settled in a red booth at Musso & Frank's Grill on Hollywood Boulevard, one of the only connections to Hollywood's past that remains relatively unchanged. In the forties she came to Musso's with her mother every Saturday night for the special spare ribs, a dish that also attracted other luminaries to the restaurant, as related in the following. She expresses her relief that Musso's hadn't been modernized or decimated entirely, and affably recounts her recollections of Hollywood's past while slowly but surely polishing off a plate of spare-ribs. "I'm happy to see they are every bit as delicious as they used to be," she says with quiet satisfaction.

My mother and I arrived here, in Hollywood, in 1944. It was very nice. Everyone spoke English, even if they weren't born here. That was the language they spoke.

I saw Carmen Miranda the day the war stopped in the Pacific. She and her band came down to Hollywood & Vine, several trucks came down, they unfolded a big platform, and she and the band got up on that flimsy platform—she was a little tiny woman in very high heels—and she was singing her heart out because she was so happy that her two brothers were coming home from the war. I was coming home on the trolley but there were so many people in the street, the trolleys had to stop. You couldn't get a car through—everyone was in the streets, singing, dancing. I had to walk from La Brea all the way to Vine Street. It had all gone crazy, about as crazy as you get at the end of the war. I can't imagine anything that was more fun than that. It felt like the beginning of the world. And for a long time it was, through the fifties. And then, in my opinion, the sixties were when it all started going downhill.

273

We used to live on Scenic Drive, near the Hollywoodland sign. I would run up all those stairways built into the hills. We had the Helm's bakery truck come by, and we had an iceman come deliver ice. Even though they did have gas refrigerators in those days, where we were staying they had all ice refrigerators.

Your term "magic" would apply to what you saw as you looked west up Hollywood Boulevard from Gower. One of the first things you saw over the CVC Drugstore—at Hudson and Hollywood Boulevard—was a big Coca-Cola billboard with a picture of the whole of the United States with white lines across it, and the caption was "All roads lead to Hollywood."

As you entered Hollywood Boulevard [at Gower, going west] there were two movie theaters on your left side, both generally ran a lot of good movies. They had a lot of previews there; Mother and I went there many times. One is now the Salvation Army. There was another movie theater on the south side which is now the Henry Fonda Yheater.

As you got to Vine, you had the Pantages, which was a movie theater at that time. And on the south side was the Little Hitching Post, a very small movie theater that showed nothing but little Westerns by Tom Mix, Hopalong Cassidy, and of course, Roy Rogers. As you entered that little theater there was a big sign that said you had to leave your guns at the door. And sometimes you'd see a real gun and sometimes you'd see just children's guns.

Then on Vine Street, of course, the Broadway Department Store was there. And just south of it was the Plaza Hotel, which had a lovely restaurant in it that had a patio where you could dine. Across the street was the Brown Derby. And just south of it was Mike Liman's restaurant.

And of course, down on the corner of Sunset & Vine—where the Home Savings bank now is—was the big radio station, NBC. I once said to my aunt, who had already lived here since 1917, how it was a shame that they tore down that radio station to put up the bank. And she blew her stack at me because she had been in the movies since she was a young girl, and she said that was the site of the first studio where they filmed *The Squaw Man*, the first movie in Hollywood.[3]

274

As you went down Hollywood Boulevard, *every single street* had at least one drugstore. And the majority of the drugstores had luncheon counters. At the southeast corner of Hollywood & Wilcox—now Playmate's lingerie store—was a See's Candy store.

Then there were many good shoe stores on Hollywood Boulevard—Leeds, Berwyn's, a real Red Cross shoe store, and Baker's—which was a really superb shoe store. Micky's was there, and it was the last of the designer dress shops that was on the Boulevard. You'd go in and buy something original that was designed right there in Hollywood.

At the corner of Hudson & Hollywood Boulevard on the north side—the building is still there—was a movie theater that showed only Italian movies. All the spaghetti westerns and big epics. At that south corner there is now a CVC Drugstore—there was always a drugstore there, but it used to have a lunch counter in the rear.

As you moved west—to where Frederick's of Hollywood now is—that was Kress' Department Store. And that building cannot come down; it's a national landmark. There was a market at the northeast corner of Whitley for many years called the Whitley Market, and across from it was a Bank of America.

There's a restaurant there that was most recently called Legends, and for years before that it was Johnnie's Steakhouse. When Mother and I arrived, it was called Zapata. The counter stools had Zs on them, like Zorro's Zs. The waiters were all men, mostly Spanish speaking, and they wore little red jackets somewhat similar to bullfighter's jackets. It was a Spanish restaurant and featured a lot of seafood that they make in Spain. And all around the inside was a mural done by that famous artist—and those murals are still there—they show the Port of Los Angeles as it was at the turn of the century.

As you went further west, you got to Musso & Frank's Grill. They used to

---

[3] In fact, *The Squaw Man* was not shot on the site of the bank at Sunset & Vine; it was shot in the barn at the northeast corner of Sunset & Vine. [See *History*, p. 19]

have daily specials. Mother and I used to like to go into there on Saturdays. We liked to sit at the counter. The owner was a great big man who sat at a booth. He was very pleasant. I'm sure he must have got up and walked but I never saw him do it. We always had ribs, and you could have as much as you wanted. You could get a second order, a third order, as much as you wanted. And Mother and I could never eat more than one order. But there was always a woman, at the far end closest to the kitchen sitting there, and she would have three, four orders! So one day Mother couldn't stand it anymore, so she asked our waiter, "Who is that person down there who eats so much?"

275

He said, "I thought you told me you've been to New York?"

Mother said, "Of course, I have, many times." She used to live in Boston and go down for all the shows.

And he said, "And you don't know who that lady is? It's Fanny Brice. She's come here every Saturday for years." We had no idea that it was she. She was a big lady, she was big boned.

When you got past Musso & Frank's, at the southeast corner of Las Palmas, was the only whatnot store in Hollywood. We bought our first Christmas cards there and we sent them to everyone we could think of all over the place because it was Christmas in Hollywood, and it was all orange trees and sunshine instead of your poinsettias. Though on Sunset Boulevard there were huge poinsettia gardens. They grew them all year long for the Christmas season.

As you passed Las Palmas, of course, you're coming to one of my favorite theaters, the Egyptian Theater. That was beautiful: you'd walk down that long courtyard with the lions facing you as you went in. And next to it was one of the best restaurants in Hollywood, the Pig & Whistle. It had, again, a counter as you entered, and booths in the back. It also had an organ in the back, and it was played at night, and you could often see Cecil B. DeMille or Charles Laughton or possibly others in there listening to the organ. They both loved organ music. You could get a seven-course meal. They had fruitcup, hors d'oeuvres, a soup, salad, little fish dish, and then the main entree. Until the entree came you could send back your order and get as much more as you wanted, whatever you wanted. And then once you got to the entree, that was it and you had to proceed with your dessert and finish your meal.

There was a gentlemen who went in there at least once a week. He worked in one of the buildings around there, I suppose, and he looked rather prosperous. And he'd sit at the counter. And one of the hors d'oeuvres that they served was spaghetti, which was not served as an entree there. I don't know why. You could not get a full plate of spaghetti there. They would give you a little sandwich plate of spaghetti. He'd sit there and of course he could reorder. He'd reorder. And reorder. And reorder, and reorder. They'd ask him if he wanted to order his entree, and he'd say, "No, that was it." He didn't want the rest of the dinner. He simply wanted spaghetti and that was the only way he could get it.

That whole seven-course meal there was no more than 75 cents. At many places it was less. You could get a cup of coffee for a dime and you could have all the sugar and cream and refills that you wanted.

On the southeast side of Hollywood & Highland was a Bank of America, a beautiful building—they used to have tours of that building. Across from it, on the northeast side of Hollywood & Highland, was the old Hollywood Hotel. It was a rather small looking, two-story building, with little cabanas all over the grounds. Fatty Arbuckle used to stay there, as did the bad witch from The Wizard of Oz, Margaret Hamilton. She lived there until it closed down, and then moved to the Roosevelt.

On the other side of the street, at Hollywood & Highland, was the Lee drugstore, which also had a counter that ran down all the way. I don't think there was more than one drugstore in Hollywood that didn't have a counter where you could sit down.

Past Lee Drugs was Barker Brothers—very fine house furnishings. Bedroom sets, Chesterfield sets, very beautiful china and that type of thing. Rather expensive but very nice. And next to it was the El Capitan Theater. Across the street, of course, was Grauman's Chinese Theater. Then a little further west was the Garden Court apartments, which had tennis courts all alongside it, with people playing. It was very lovely.

The theater on the north side of Hollywood between Cahuenga and Wilcox, which later became the Pacific Theater, was the Warner Brothers Theater. I saw such people as Claude Rains—speaking of which, my favorite movie happens to be Casablanca—and I saw Humphrey Bogart and his wife one time.

On Sundays after Mass, Mother and I would take the trolley and go down to the shore and eat at the pier. Or we would go down to the cafeteria on Vine Street where a great many people went. On Vine just north of Hollywood. We liked to go on a Friday or Sunday. Mother loved their baked fish on Fridays, and on Sundays we always had the turkey leg. And they always had beautiful cornbread, it was nice.

There were other cafeterias in Hollywood. Shark's cafeteria was on Selma just east of Wilcox. The people who owned it lived in the top of the building, and they kept living there after the cafeteria closed. On Ivar, south of Hollywood Boulevard, was a cafeteria called Sir George's.

Across the street where the Brown Derby was, they had a coffee shop on the north side that shared the kitchen. And even after my mother passed away, a friend of mine and me met every Friday night at the Brown Derby coffee shop and went in and ate their fish and chips.

There was a very famous drugstore that was even used in several movies, at the southeast corner of Hollywood & Vine. Next to the Bank of America on Highland—where there is a McDonald's now—was Coffee Dan's. That's where the trolley pulled up

When the trolley got to La Brea, it cut straight across. If you go there, you see that some of the buildings are at a diagonal angle to the street, and there is an alley that cuts through at a southwest angle. That is where the trolley shot clear across to Santa Monica and Fairfax. And in between La Brea and Fairfax there was a place where a trolley could be sidetracked and put off to the side, and then another trolley could go though.

277

Hollywood used to be so nice in the mornings. Everyone was rather friendly. It was a nice place. As you walked out to go to school or go to work, business managers, owners, employees, were out cleaning up the sidewalks, making sure everything looks beautiful. Windows were dressed in all the stores and they looked lovely; they didn't look like junk shops.

When we came here, at that northwest side of Wilcox & Hollywood, was Maxim's, one of the best haberdasheries for men. It was a marvelous place to buy. Anything you wanted for a gentlemen could be found there.

Before we moved here, there was a railroad station at Hollywood & Wilcox. And the actual tracks were still there and the trolleys ran at them. And sometimes a regular train engine would come down Hollywood Boulevard on the tracks heading downtown.

That northeast corner of Yucca & Wilcox has always had a liquor store on it. Not Pla-Boy, which is there now and has been there for a long time, but a different one. I used to love spumoni ice cream, and they were the only place that had spumoni ice cream. East of it there was a Chinese restaurant called China Jade which is now a Laundromat.

I worked at Capitol Records for twenty-five years in the accounting department. They built the Capitol Tower on Vine in 1954. I started working before that—they had studios then at Gower & Melrose, where Paramount is. Clyde Wallich ran Music City at the corner of Sunset & Vine, and the executive offices of Capitol were in offices above Music City. But the workhorses of Capitol—those of us who did all the billing and office work—were between Ivar and Cahuenga on the southside of Hollywood. We were in that building on the eastside of that alleyway is, across from where the medical center is now.

The day they broke ground for the Capitol Tower, Glenn Wallich sat up in the big bulldozer. He loved gadgets and he was a genius. When he was a boy he set up his own radio station and the army had to stop him, because he was cutting into the army's intelligence. He was a boy-genius. He was up in this machine and was only supposed to dig big one scoop for the photographers. And he just want mad! All of a sudden he was scooping giant amount of earth and people were running everywhere and things were flying. And he had a ball [Laughs]. That was 1954.

It was not unusual to see stars walking around. I saw Bill Cosby many times on Vine, and I used to see Nat "King" Cole at Capitol Records all the time. Peggy Lee was a doll, still is.

Sinatra was a character and a half. He was a nocturnal type of person. He suffered from insomnia, and he liked to record at night. If he wasn't working in a night club at night, he liked to go into the studio and record. And all around Capitol Records we were notified: "Mr. Sinatra will be recording this evening. You are quite welcome to attend." He loved an audience. You could go and sit there and watch him record. He felt it made him sing better. I did once. But other people I worked with, many of them they would come in exhausted the next day because they stayed as long as they could. The band would get so tired, and the engineers, because they had worked all day. So to keep them all awake, he would bring in all sorts of food and ice cream. He loved ice cream.

One day he entered our lobby and we had a new receptionist. There used to be a little island right in front by the elevators where the receptionist sat. Sinatra walked in, looked very neat and nice in one of those little pork-pie hats that he used to wear, and she looked up and said, "Oooooohhhh!!!" He looked up at her very nicely, walked around the little receptacle where she sat, walked up to her, took her in his arms, bent her over and gave her a great big kiss! [Laughs] He was full of fun. He was a lot of fun back then.

Of course, in those days, we also had Jerry Lewis and his partner, Dean Martin, in there. And Jerry is Jewish, but every Christmas while Dean Martin and Jerry Lewis were recording for Capitol, Jerry Lewis saw to it that every single employee at Capitol Records got a Christmas card from him. Jerry did all the work [laughs] and Dean was just so casual. He wasn't putting that on—that was the way he really was.

I was there the day the Beatles arrived. They shut off the street. The police came up and we were notified. We had to remain at our desks and were not to go down to the main floor. We looked out the window and the Beatles arrived. A limousine drove up, and they looked so neat in their little Nehru jackets. They didn't have the long hair—oh, they were spit and polished looking.

Several years later these slobs came into the building with long hair and beards. Someone said, "There are the Beatles." I said, "You have got to be kidding." I had not seen them for years. They had looked like such neat boys, and now they had gone totally downhill in just a few years. Of course, they didn't go downhill in terms of recording and music.

Even after Mother passed away, through the seventies, I would walk home to my little court on Wilcox, north of Hollywood, where I lived for twenty-three years until the new owners got rid of all of us old-timers there. I used to feed my cat, and walk all the way up to La Brea & Hollywood and then come back, visit Sophie Baker—she was a doctor's widow who lived to be ninety-five. She knew my mother so I used to visit her. I would do this every Friday night and didn't have the least worry to walk alone on Hollywood Boulevard.

279

Things have changed so much since those days. But there are those of us who still remember.

Pippa Scott

BORN NOVEMBER 10, 1935
LOS ANGELES, CALIFORNIA
ACTRESS / ACTIVIST

Her face is familiar to anyone who has seen famous TV shows such as "The Twilight Zone" or movies such as The Searchers; it's a pretty, warm face, with gentle, intelligent eyes, enveloped by a head of blonde curls, which she sometimes spins through her fingertips as she speaks. She's in the Beverly Hills office of Linden Productions, where she graciously shares stories about her past. These days, however, her focus is far from her own acting career, which she dismisses as inconsequential, or the dark days of the Hollywood blacklist, when her uncle Adrian Scott, one of the notorious "Hollywood Ten," refused to name names and was sent to prison for a year. These days she's much more concerned with the plight of children around the world whose lives have been wrecked by war and famine; she's produced films to help raise money and consciousness, and has lent her name and energy to a cavalcade of causes. "She wants to save the world," said one of her friends, though she denies it. "I learned a long time ago that saving the world was unrealistic. But there is a lot of work that can be done, and I'm doing what I can do."

I was born at the old St. Vincent's Hospital, which is, I think, defunct now. I was raised on the top of Laurel Canyon; our closest neighbor—Reesa Stevens, the opera star—was ten miles away. My parents built the house at the top of a very large piece of land that was ultimately later subdivided. I even remember the address: it was 2845 Woodstock Road. There was nobody else up there in those days except us.

For a kid, it wasn't fun growing up there. It was lonely. My brother David, who is younger than I am by three years, used to hike a lot with a nanny who looked after us.

Adrian Scott was my uncle, my father's brother. My father, Allen Scott, wrote Ginger Rogers and Fred Astaire movies for RKO and then did a lot of other work for Briana Productions, Kirk Douglas and other groups. He wrote an awful lot for credit but he also wrote a lot . . . he cleaned up a lot of screenplays. So he didn't have the credit on them, but the unaccredited stuff is listed so you can see the associations that he had.

He didn't drive, and as a result my mother had to drive him everywhere. He was doing a lot of films for when they needed army nurses or they needed more pilots, you know, they were recruitment films too, you know that kind of stuff. So he didn't go to war, he stayed in Hollywood and wrote for the Armed Services.

My father *had* learned to drive but he was in a dreadful automobile accident in which a couple of his friends were killed. He had such a horror of driving after that he stopped driving. So [my mother] drove everywhere. Also, the thing about my dad was that he was always so preoccupied with the characters he was writing about that he recognized that he'd get into terrible accidents if somebody weren't driving for him. So he used to take a lot of cabs in those days. A lot of the taxi drivers of Los Angeles knew him well because, without realizing it, he would hum while he was working out his stories. They always thought he was immensely cheerful, but it had nothing to do with cheerfulness, it was just his own peculiar little habit.

My father worked for quite a few different studios. In the beginning it was mostly RKO. I used to visit him there all the time. The problem was that my mother would have to schlep us from nursery school to pick him up. Sometimes she would have an appointment for my brother, so she would drop me off and he would kind of babysit me. And the way he would babysit me is to take me to watch Hermes Pan and Fred [Astaire] rehearse something. So I would just sit in the corner and watch all this when I was really little. It was part of what the life was, I don't even remember it hardly.

I do remember one episode because it terrified me. Ms. Rogers was a terrific hoofer, but she didn't dance all the time. So what Fred and Hermes Pan would do would be to work out the dance numbers, *completely*. If you look at them today, you'll see that there's no editing, they're all shot from beginning to end in one take. So they had to be perfect. What they had to do was rehearse her until it was absolutely perfect. So often she would come in with kind of tender feet from having been off for a while and they'd work her all day long. I remember one day at lunch time she took her shoes off and her feet were all bloody and the doctor came down and put some sort of paste on her. I think it had Novocain in it so they didn't hurt her, and she went right on. That scared me.

But she was a wonderful dancer, they both were. The choreography was worked out pretty much by Hermes, and Astaire would agree to it, and Hermes would play Ginger as they worked out the steps and all that. Fred was very much involved with the choreography. I think by this time, Astaire knew his style very well and what it ought to be and he'd veto this or that from time to time, but I don't really remember all that so clearly.

Fred and Ginger never needed many takes to get something right. There was a lot of time in between, because it meant repairing the stage. Remember there were very glossy floors? So they had to go back and tidy it all up, and since everybody was sweating, they also had to tidy the two dancers up.

281

My mother used to shop a lot and get her hair done along Hollywood Boulevard. It was very chic there, there was the Max Factor building, which was much more elegant than it is now. She would have her hair and nails done at Max Factor. It was open to the public and had booths in a big open space, and she had a lady who did her hair there. My father smoked a pipe and there was a little smoke shop where we went for tobacco. And there were wonderful bookstores such as Pickwick's on Hollywood Boulevard where we spent a lot of money and time. My parents read aloud to us every night, lots of stories, but we didn't go to a lot of movies.

There were no freeways then. All of the Valley was date nut palms and orange groves. It was fragrant and beautiful when I was a little girl, there was no development there, very little. We'd go because somebody lived there on a ranch and they had a swimming pool. We were equidistant from either Hollywood or the Valley side being on the top of Laurel Canyon. Or they had ponies or horses or something that my mother thought was great for my brother and me. In those days it wasn't congested. There were a few things at Laurel Canyon, including a gambling den, and there were some homes. People that came from the east thought it was charming because you could live in what felt like the mountains or the countryside and still be in town in a minute.

I remember when I was six, going to a friend's birthday party, a child who was in the Hollywood community, and they screened the movie *Gilda*. It was the first film I'd ever seen. When I got home, my parents were *outraged*, because they wanted me to see live theater first, so I wouldn't get an idea that whole world was made up of celluloid, and not live actors. So they had in mind an arrangement whereby I was to be educated by seeing live theater first, but then maybe I would get to see a movie but it would be Charlie

Chaplin or some really splendid piece of very good filmmaking. Not something sexy and hot and inappropriate for a six-year-old.

So my father said, "Laura," that was my mother's name, "I want you to find out what's playing in town, I don't care what it is." She found out that *Showboat* was in town, so my dad said, "The first thing you do is get matinee tickets and take Pippa." So my mother got them in the first row of the balcony and we went the very next Wednesday. And my parents were friends with the producer of the show, Arthur Hornblow, who got us seats in the first row of the balcony.

What happened was that my mother bought us a box of chocolates to eat at the show. And for some reason I thought that I was going to cry during this show. So I took out my handkerchief out and put it on my knee. And then the chocolates were opened and placed on the wide, velvet-covered balcony railing in front of us. I sat quietly and very much involved in the story.

This was wartime, too, so just before we left for the theater, my mother had been on the phone to the butcher and was concerned about what to buy that would not use up too many coupons. The butcher said the fish was very good this week. So we were going to pick up the fish on our way home after the theater.

So there came that point where Magnolia was bereft and heartbroken and weeping and the audience was weeping with her and I was weeping with the audience, and she says to her friend, "What *shall* I do, what *shall* I do?" And I stood from the first row of the balcony, knocking the chocolates, of course, into the audience, and said (sobbing), "You can buy fish!"

Well, the whole audience went quiet and the actress started to laugh, and the audience started to laugh. Then it went on, wave after wave, somebody would giggle and then they'd start all over again.

That night Hornblow came up for dinner and said, "God, some little *bitch* just ruined the matinee performance today." My father never told him it was me. But I think he might have guessed when my mother served fish for dinner. [Laughs] And that was my first live theater experience.

After that, I did see some movies, selectively. [My father] didn't like a lot of junk, but eventually, I began to see absolutely everything, and that was when I was old enough to go to them by myself. There were lots of movies for kids in those days. Saturday morning matinees that you could go to for a dime, or serials, *fabulous*, those were just great.

My parents sent me away to Chadwick, a private school, in the seventh grade. So during the blacklisting period, which started in the forties, I was away from home. They sent me away for a good education; it had nothing to do with the blacklisting. We couldn't come home on weekends. You could only come home once a month for the first few years. And I flourished under this, I really did very well. You had to have a lot of Latin, and that was gorgeous for me, I hated it so, and I must say it trained me wonderfully.

I ultimately went to Radcliffe. I started acting then. There was a drama club, of course, and also I acted summers, I worked summers. There was a wonderful little theater called the Players Ring Theater, on Santa Monica Boulevard. Kathleen Freeman, that wonderful comedienne, was one of the three founding partners of it. I started out sweeping backstage and ultimately did walk-ons and finally won a couple of parts there. During summers from high school. One summer I had the lead in a play, and John Ford's main secretary, a little tough lady, came with her friend to see the play and the next thing I knew I went to meet Mr. Ford for *The Searchers* and got a role in that. That was my first professional film.

The theater was near Santa Monica & Kings Road. It was a funny little rep company where people act; it was a theater in the round, very small, but it was an Equity house.

I knew that I wanted to be an actress professionally by then, and my mother had done something extraordinary, again this issue of education. It was a very important year and it had to do with World War II in which Lawrence Olivier, who was a friend of my parents, had just married Vivien Leigh in San Francisco and came to escape from the press at our house. I spent a lot of time with them, and they were delicious and, of course, enchanting for me. I was just out of my mind for them.

It was overwhelming having them in our home. I mean, they were so beautiful, first of all. They were so charming that they took your breath away. I was just this dumbstruck puberty-riddled child who was doting on them.

My father was such an Anglophile; he had lots of British friends and I, of course, adored him and whatever he liked was something that I should pay attention to. I think a lot of movie stars came to our house. There were lot of other actors, and directors and writers. They seemed normal but incredibly witty. There was a lot of very bright conversation and a lot of fun.

My memories of highs chool years are mostly unhappy ones. The negative part of the high school years had to do with the McCarthy trials and the influence of Joseph McCarthy and the whole kind of blacklisting that went on because of my Uncle Adrian. The atmosphere around us was really very bad; people were committing suicide and my parents were depressed. That was all very rough to take, but my childhood was idyllic. A little later, life grew darker. But my childhood was charming.

I was away at school when the blacklisting started. I don't know but I think my uncle was a member of the Communist Party, I'm not sure, but my dad I know wasn't. But by association he was hurt. He didn't work for a long time and then he had to work quietly. By being related to Adrian.

Adrian was charming and fun to be around and had wonderful girlfriends. One of them killed herself, which shocked me, because she had been very close to me. She had, in an attempt, I think, to make Adrian happy, done all sorts of things for me like curl my hair, and you know, behave like a sort of girlfriend to me for a while. My parents came down to Chadwick to prevent me from hearing about her suicide from anybody else, but as it turned out, I found out about it from the newspapers. She was Daniel Teredash's wife but they had separated and Adrian was having an affair with her.

My father and Adrian never wrote together, but they were close. My dad always looked after his brother. My father was older. Adrian lived in Beverly Hills and he produced a lot of very good movies, Murder My Sweet, and others. His wives were all beautiful. He had several of them. At the time of the blacklisting, I didn't understand what was happening. I kind of discovered it by the fallout. For example, Ann Shirley, the lovely actress who was the star of Murder My Sweet, she married Adrian and together they adopted a British war orphan, a little boy, who it turns out was very disturbed and I think slightly retarded. Ann and he were separated and he got custody of the boy. And then during the blacklisting, Adrian was sent off to prison and the child came to live with us.

The little boy proceeded to destroy my brother's laboratory. My mother had a little room off the garage that she turned into a kind of lab for David because he was very interested in science and he had butterfly collections and a microscope and all sorts of other stuff, geology collections and stuff like that. And this little boy destroyed it all—he went in there one day with a hammer and just broke everything in sight. He would do the same sort of destructive stuff with all of us. So one day I damn near killed him. I was so mad at him that they had to break us up.

It was that kind of thing that went wrong and I kept wondering why we were burdened with him and why this was going on. But then I was going off to school. They didn't talk about the blacklist or why Adrian was in prison. They really couldn't, they were so very interesting in that way, kind of passive that way. I think they were so hurt and scared by it. Everybody was scared at the time. It was really a very bad atmosphere everywhere. They had their heads down.

I think I remember by then learning about the House Un-American Activities Committee, and hearing about who was naming names and who wasn't. But again, as with them, it seemed much more protective not to speak of it to other people. Just to keep your head down. For years, I was never political, I never talked politics anywhere I went because this got you into trouble. I remember various groups would come to the school to speak, and I never joined them.

My uncle moved to England so I never talked about it to him. I did talk about it to another of his wives, and I resented her greatly, Joan Scott. She took this sort of attitude that she was the one who suffered and propped him up and looked after him. And she actually did in England, but Anne looked after him too, and we did too, and we were never mentioned. She really was the great kind of martyr to it all. She was married to him after he got out of jail. We were the ones who looked after him while he was in jail and she was after.

285

It was assumed that Adrian did the right thing, the honorable thing. I think my father was very angry that people had named names. My dad worked but it was very hard because of the blacklist, and my own husband also discovered that his name was on a blacklist. He had access to the book—*Red Channels*, it was called—but there were other lists that had to do with the rise of episodic television in the late fifties and sixties. There were lists that the advertisers had, and my dad's name was on it and so was mine. I could never even do "This Is Your FBI" because of my uncle. I didn't know that until my husband found that out.

The whole blacklist time belonged to another generation, and when it was my time to work in the industry, it had mostly passed. I wasn't outspoken about it, because that would bring attention to myself, which I *certainly* didn't want in terms of my connection to my uncle. Not that I was ashamed of him, I wasn't at all. And I didn't really know whether he was a member of the party or not. I do know that he was very much against what was happening in Spain, and I think a lot of people signed up then and I think a lot of people came to be appalled by what Stalin did, and left at that point. And if that was true I think my uncle would not have been alone, but when it came to the issue of do you reveal friends and do you name names, I think what he did was honorable.

I did some acting, some movie and television roles, but I wasn't a big star or anything like that. I was much more interested in raising children later and helping my husband in his work. I always thought that the writing and producing process was more interesting to me than acting in them.

Hollywood is a very small industry. Very closed. The old Hollywood, anyway. The new Hollywood is made up of people who aren't particularly interested, I think, in the film process and world. They are interested in the bottom line. I don't think a lot of the moviemakers today have the passion that Sam Goldwyn had, or the craft. So why would they preserve or be interested in the romance of early Hollywood? Because the Hollywood that *was* is not the Hollywood that *is*. And it's too bad.

Cinema is a wonderful and glorious medium; it is very new and it is extraordinary how a very good film can reveal an awful lot to you very efficiently and quickly. I think that's why there are very few good movies, too. I think they are the hardest thing in the world to write and the hardest thing to do well. They talk to you on many different levels, and actors in films that are really good can send many different signals, almost as if through their skin, about what they are thinking, what's going on inside them, their motivation, the layers beneath a human being's action. That's what is so glorious about the movies. They can still tell a huge story.

286

Burl Smith

BORN JUNE 23, 1936

RENO, NEVADA

STOCKMAN

Old palms and sycamores. The Las Palmas Senior Citizen center, corner of Las Palmas & Franklin. Traffic zipping by on Franklin. Inside the seniors are eating lunch, drinking coffee, playing cards and checkers, laughing, and talking. Some sit in big green chairs and in long burgundy couches reading paperbacks, newspapers and magazines. He sits outside in the sun doing the crossword puzzle from today's L.A. Times, wearing a navy blue sailor's cap, gray shirt and slacks. He's mostly serious, except when expressing a kind of naughty glee remembering the scantily clad women he sometimes encountered in Hollywood, pausing momentarily to savor those thoughts before moving on. As the afternoon sun begins to descend behind the sycamores and nearby buildings, he begins to expound on his theories concerning the decline of Hollywood, unexpectedly directing all blame to the Beatles. "Once the Beatles came to town with their long hair and open drug usage," he said, "the kids mimicked them and it's been downhill ever since."

I lived with my mother in Hollywood in the thirties. She lived not far from The Masquers, a club for old and young movie stars on Sycamore north of Hollywood Boulevard. My mother took care of Mr. Carver. He owned a rooming house for female extras, women who were actresses in the movies. He was in a wheelchair and my mother took care of Mr. Carver and for that she got free rent. Right there was a big sycamore tree and that was what the street was named after.

I remember odd things. I was a paperboy for the *Hollywood Citizen News*. I'd come to collect the money, I was a young lad, and I'd look up and here was a young healthy tenant, a starlet, and she'd be standing there nude . . .

[laughs, and pauses] . . . and she'd be telling me to come back next week, she didn't have the money to pay me.

Down the street near the big church here [at Franklin & Highland] some of the East Side Kids lived there in a building near Orchid. A lot of movie stars lived in this area on Franklin between La Brea and Highland. My mother lived here and my father lived in Wilmington in Long Beach. I went to high school in Long Beach and then moved back to Hollywood.

I have fond memories of Hollywood. It was homespun. The Christmas parade back then, they'd put two halves of a metal Christmas tree together on every telephone pole the full length of Hollywood Boulevard, lit up with colored bulbs. It did the job. It was a large Christmas tree on both the north and south side all along Hollywood Boulevard.

Plus I saw the premieres in Hollywood at the Chinese Theater and the Paramount and the Egyptian. I saw *Rear Window* with Jimmy Stewart and *Scudda-Who Scudda-Hey* with June Haver. *Captain from Castillo*, Tyrone Power. Premieres were very big and a real social in thing. These spotlights they have nowadays don't have that authentic feel of the klieg-lights they had back then. They had more candle power and they were stronger and more effectual. The glitter and stardom was just fantastic here. All the stars would come and there was no snobbery. People were people back then. But more down to earth, more homespun. They were more real people. There were some snobs like Debbie Reynolds. She was a few years older than I am.

I worked at Barker Brothers department store on Hollywood Boulevard when I came back here in 1949 to live permanently. The whole transportation was the Red Cars. I took the Red Car from Wilmington to 6th & Main (in downtown L.A.), got off, walked up to 5th & Hill, and took it to Hollywood to come see my mother.

The YMCA got me my first job here. I was a stockman at *Top of the Town* on the sixth floor. It was at Hollywood next to what is now the El Capitan theater, then the Paramount. I worked there and I loved it very much.

The job was beautiful. I saw many movie stars there. I saw Rock Hudson and Tab Hunter—who I didn't know were two gay boys at the time—playing tag, running around one of my displays. Because I set up things. Franciscan China, Libby glassware.

I helped Sammy Davis Jr., who bought packages gift-wrapped and I took them down to his car. Nice guy, he tipped me. And he was with a lady friend. I saw John Hall—he was playing in those jungle pictures, he was down in the basement.

I wore a brown smock and I loved the job. I was always going to Rexall Drugstore on the corner buying pistachio nuts. And there was always a gay guy sitting there at the counter listening to the jukebox—they had jukeboxes on the counter—and he was always listening to this radio program: "Would you like to be Queen for a Day?" [Laughs] That always amused me, this guy listening to this show every day. He had his lunch there. But I'd buy pistachio nuts at the counter. I was always munching those things. Some people didn't like that. I had a pouch there where I kept the shells.

I worked at Barker Brothers for three years. I went to a place next door for lunch; it's a car rental place now but it was a coffee shop. Debbie Reynolds used to sit there. She was a big star there and she'd sit in there very prim and proper wanting to be spotted by tourists. I saw her and I never went in, because when I first saw her I knew she was just eating up publicity being seen and she was a little brat. She had a bumpy life with Fisher, and people she married. But she was a little hot spitfire. There were no two ways about that. I don't think too many people could live with her. Very conceited. That's what stardom did to some people, but they weren't always like that. For many of them it ruined their lives, success did. Most definitely.

All through here, along Las Palmas from Franklin to Hollywood Boulevard, this was all Victorian homes. They were all torn down. Wooden, one- and two-story houses.

The Hollywood Hotel [at Hollywood & Highland] was a stucco-framed two or three story. Nothing luxurious at all, it was very common. The most unusual structure in Hollywood, I'd say, was that building up there. [Points to the Yamashiro restaurant above the Magic Castle at Sycamore & Franklin] And some of Frank Lloyd Wright's houses.

I saw them tear down the Hollywood Hotel. It was across the street from Barker Brothers, and I used to look down there from the sixth floor. I would be wiring pictures that would be sold. When they were tearing it down, a stockman and I went over there because they were selling things, but it was just junk, bedding and sheets. It was an old building then, before they knocked it down, mostly occupied by seniors. And I'd look out the window from the sixth floor, I'd look down and I'd see old women scantily clad. You'd see large bosoms. Some of them forgot to put their bras on and would be out there—[laughs, pauses]—I mean, not for long. You did see that. In their older years they weren't conscious, or maybe they wanted to get sun tans. It wasn't done for a vicarious or sexual thrill. They just didn't care. There were mostly women in their bras, or just in their slips, out on the balconies. But I never went into the building. That side of the street wasn't my turf—I worked where I worked, up on the sixth floor.

An interesting thing: Claude, the custodian of our store, was a man who knew the ropes and in and out of everything. He could tell a joke well and I told a joke poorly. He was a guy who would burn up the rope. He smoked.

One day I was down in the basement. I just worked a half day and he said,

"You want to go to the movies?" I said, "Why? What are you talking about?" He said, "I'll let you into the movies free." Down in the sub-basement was a door that led right into the bathroom of the Paramount Theater! This was *freaky*, just like stepping into a different world. If you were in the theater and turned around and saw me, you'd think it was magic! I looked behind me where he let me into the bathroom in the basement of the theater, and it was all paneling. You couldn't distinguish that it was an entrance at all. It was disguised. Fascinating.

289

My mother was an Indiana farm girl and she came to Hollywood to break into the movies. But she did not get into the movies. A lot of people who came here didn't make it. They didn't become extras. Because there were only X number of jobs. You had to have something special, or somebody had to like you, or—I'm sorry to say—you went to bed with someone. And many Christian girls would never do that. They were brought up in a moral family. And morals were different then.

But my mother loved Hollywood. There were so many good places to eat. The best—and I mean, the *best*—Jewish deli was right here on the corner of Sycamore & Hollywood Boulevard. It was called Gotham's. There was no food on the face of the earth that was better than Gotham's. [Laughs] You could get everything there. The food was *unequaled*. It was just like it was a banquet.

There was Hugo's Hotdogs around the corner, where the Hungry Tiger used to be. You'd go in there and there was sawdust on the floor and they had pictures of movie stars all over the place.

And right there on La Brea & Hollywood Boulevard was a big empty lot all full of 1938 Cadillacs and convertibles and sedans. You could walk in and see them. Mercedes. Cars of the thirties—during Hitler's time. It was just beautiful. Auburn, Cord, Duesenberg, Packards. Just everything.

I liked the Ranch Market on Vine. It was a nice place. A great cup of coffee for ten cents. Near the studio where Steve Allen did his show. Like Central Market downtown—fresh produce in boxes and bins. It was real nice.

There was the Seven Seas for dancing. My boss used to go there, she loved it. The interior was all like Hawaii with Hawaiian dancers. You'd think you were on the main island. It was just incredible.

There was the Pig & Whistle, it was a nice restaurant. I loved drive-ins, like Tiny Naylor's. I always loved their chicken pot-pie. It was very nourishing and very hearty. Food back then had vitamins and minerals. Food today is just not the same.

Those were the days when you left your windows open and your doors unlocked. It was a different world. Don't let anyone tell you it wasn't.

Manny Felix

BORN AUGUST 26, 1937
NOGALES, MEXICO
WAITER

290

Musso & Frank's, midday. Almost every booth in the old room is filled, as are the big tables in what has been called the "new room" since it opened back in the fifties. This great restaurant persists despite the state of the world outside its old doorway, which first opened for business here on the boulevard in 1919. It's the preeminent Hollywood institution, a place that thankfully still looks, feels and even tastes as it did back in the era when Chaplin would come here for lunch every day, or later, when Fitzgerald, Faulkner, and other authors from the east would congregate around Musso's venerable bar, drinking their famous martinis. Manny's an institution within an institution. He's worked at Musso's for decades now, but has never played the role of the characteristically surly Musso's waiter, which is why he is ideally suited for the legendary counter, where most of his patrons are alone and in need of some congeniality. Always in motion, attired in a natty scarlet jacket, he's gracious and warmly funny with everyone he encounters, from the guy in the "I Love the USA" T-shirt who sits down and immediately starts pontificating about local politics, to the maitre'd who presses a five-dollar bill into his hand. To this day, Musso's is one of the only places in Hollywood where the stars still come; as we talk, the actor-producer Danny DeVito passes by, smiles at Manny, and joins his wife Rhea Perlman and children at a big table in the new room. Manny, like the other employees of Musso's, focus on the service of fine food, and treat stars and pedestrians with the same amount of distinction and care. He speaks with the accent of his homeland, and much faster than most interviewed for this book, which must be a force of habit after all these years of making conversation with a succession of strangers while on the move serving up their famous chicken pot-pies, short ribs, flannel cakes and the rest, yet he looks you straight in the eye, and gives you the kind of unbridled smile that goes a long way in getting you through daily life in that world beyond these distinguished doors.

I was born in Mexico and grew up in Nogales, Arizona, right by the border. My cultures were both Mexican and American. It was confusing growing up because what am I? What am I speaking? We grew up speaking Spanglish. I was in the army—the American army—in San Diego during the war, and I came here to Los Angeles in 1958. Same years as the Dodgers. My brother used to live here in Hollywood, and he said, "Come on up. You can afford it." And I said, "Naaah, I don't think I'm gonna like it." I used to read bad things about Los Angeles, and I didn't want to come. But I did, and the rest is history. I loved it and I've been here ever since.

I worked first at the Ambassador Hotel downtown before coming here. I met Marilyn Monroe, Nat "King" Cole, Cornell Wilde, Walter Winchell. You learn to blend in and you became a part of. I was not google-eyed. I never lived in that mode of life that a lot of people live in. I was never star-struck.

Then I worked at the Villa Capri on Yucca. A very good restaurant. Famous because James Dean used to spend a lot of time there, and he was there the night he got killed. Jerry Lewis and Dean Martin used to come in, and the Rat Pack with Sinatra and Sammy Davis, and the Beatles. Johnny Carson used to have his parties there. It was a very good restaurant. And, of course, that's gone now. It's a radio station now.

Then I started working here at Musso's, and it's been great. Musso's is the most beautiful place in the world. All of the other great Hollywood restaurants are gone, but Musso's is still here. There's got to be a reason for it. Fair price and good quality. Don't sacrifice the quality. No matter how bad times might get, you don't sacrifice the quality. And when the good times come around, you still have the quality, and you retain the people who supported you through the hard times.

291

It's a beautiful place to work. The people who work here are just *fantastic*. They're beautiful. There is no pressure, as long as you do your job. There's a lot of cooperation. Mrs. Keegle was the owner, the daughter of the original family who owned Musso's. She passed away last year. She was a *wonderful*, special lady. She never liked the limelight. She would stay back in the kitchen, and check the food, and take care of the money. She always made a great effort to maintain Musso's, and to make sure she *never* sacrificed the quality, even during bad times. She maintained the rhythm of *perfection*. And now her daughter has taken over, and is keeping the same level of service and quality.

Charlie Chaplin used to eat here for lunch every day. When he had his studio over on La Brea. We named the front booth there (across from the cash register) the Charlie Chaplin booth, because he always liked to sit there so that he could look out the window.

There's also the Raymond Burr booth and the Ralph Edwards booth. Their booths are both in what we still call the "new room," where the bar is. Raymond Burr was a nice guy. Reserved, of course, you know, they have to be. He would come in and have his dinner, and we respected his privacy, as we do with all stars. When his seniority in Hollywood went down, we still kept the booth named in his honor.

It opened in 1958. This room that we are in now, where this counter is, this is the original room. See that chimney there behind the counter? That's the broiler. And the counter, of course, is the *backbone* of any good restaurant. If you go into a restaurant and see a counter, you know it's a good place. All the great old restaurants used to have counters. And there's a reason for that. In my early tenure as a waiter, I found out that people who sit at a counter are usually alone, and sometimes lonely. So a person like me is responsible for cheering them up, and making them feel at home, making them feel good that somebody cares. And that's the purpose of a counter. Because I've been in places where I've felt alone. And a friendly face or a little smile can always cheer you up. I've found this through my tenure as a waiter to be true, particularly at the holidays. Because some people don't have anybody. So they come here for a hot turkey sandwich or a hot chicken sandwich or a bowl of soup, and you make them feel at home, and they appreciate that.

292

The flannel cakes here have always been part of the Musso's tradition. We are known around the world for our flannel cakes, because no one makes them anymore. They'll make hotcakes, they'll make waffles or crepe suzettes, but no one makes flannel cakes. And then if you accompany that with a little bacon, sausage or ham, and then a couple of eggs, basted, over-easy, or scrambled, man, you've got a meal. That's really a treat. We make them right in front of you here at the counter. We want them to be very thin, like a crepe, so you ladle it on with a spoon, and then you kind of stir it around.

I love our food here. If I had to choose a favorite, it would be the short-ribs. Then the pot-pies. But I also love the flannel cakes with scrambled eggs. And the lentil soup, and minestrone soup. The tomato bisque is really good. And the Eggs Benedict here—you're not going to find many places that make Hollandaise sauce fresh like we do here. Have that with some of our special hashed browns, maybe some flannel cakes for dessert, and that's a breakfast.

[Danny DeVito walks by, smiles] See, Danny DeVito, a star, he comes here and nobody bothers him. Kevin McCarthy, the actor, has a little get-together of the old-timers every Wednesday, and nobody bothers them. All the stars came here, and the great writers. And a lot of producers and writers and wannabes and artists, they came here to make deals, or hoping to make deals. People like it here, because there is so much trouble in the world today, people don't even want to walk on the boulevard. Not like the old days when they used to parade up and down the boulevard and went out to be seen. No, today it's different. Times have changed. But Musso & Frank's is like a time capsule. You can close your eyes and pretend you're in the thirties or forties or fifties. When was the last time you saw a coat hanger? And a hat rack? It hasn't changed. They respected the history of the place, without adding, without subtracting, just maintaining what is here. There are fixtures here you can't buy anymore. But if you maintain them, they remain.

The martinis are great here, too. Oh yes. They will put you under the table. [Laughs] I enjoy one from time to time.

I see Johnny Grant in here all the time. A TV show did a piece on Musso's, and it's funny that I should appear alongside Johnny Grant. For some reason, whenever they do a story on Hollywood, there's Johnny Grant and there I am, too. Johnny Grant is a great guy. He's our mayor! He's just a guy who *loves* Hollywood. It's his girlfriend, you know.

Most of the stars I've met have been very nice. Some of the famous sports celebrities have been here and someone tries to pick a fight with them just *because, just because.* You have the old story about the best gunslinger in the west who wants to pick on the kid. But most guys are wise to that, and they just walk away. All the stars impressed me. But the person who impressed me the most was Yogi Berra. He was the only person who I have gone up to and said, "Let me shake your hand. You're the *greatest.*" Yogi Berra is the only one. And I've met Mickey Mantle, Roger Maris, all these guys. All the great musicians have been in here, too. Nelson Riddle. Skinny Edwards. Kay Kaiser.

You see about Musso's in the old movies, and read about it. Because, at one time, everybody who is anybody has had some association with Musso & Frank's. It's been a magic place for many good people. When people come to Hollywood, they're searching for something, and this is one place where they can find it. You can't find it at the Holiday Inn; they all look alike. So they come here.

Hollywood is always changing. In the next twenty, thirty years, it will be something else again. It will be different. It won't be the same. This new development at Hollywood & Highland, I'm not sure if it will be good for Hollywood. I hope so. But I'm not sure. But no matter what happens, Musso's will be here. Musso's will be here till that famous place freezes over. And I'm going to be here, too.

Bill Heyward
BORN APRIL 9, 1939
LOS ANGELES, CALIFORNIA
EDITOR / PRODUCER

At high noon in Hollywood in the sun-dappled parking lot of Musso & Frank's he makes a dramatic entrance on a large Harley in full motorcycle regalia—silver shades, black leather jacket, helmet, bandanna and boots. A tall man with long hair and a beard, he's the son of two famous parents: His father was Leland Heyward, the legendary producer-agent who represented legendary writers such as Hemingway as well as legends of the screen, including Henry Fonda and Jimmy Stewart. His mother was the movie star Margaret Sullavan, whose acting career started on stage as part of the University Players, an acting troupe from which her friends Jimmy Stewart and Henry Fonda also emerged. Fonda also became the second of her three husbands; Leland was first and the director William Wyler was third. Leland was also married more than once: His second wife was Slim Hawks, who was also married three times, to the director Howard Hawks first, Leland second, and finally British tycoon Lord Keith. If all this seems tremendously confusing, imagine how it must have seemed to a child who grew up among the tangled strands of these various relationships as his parents' partners shifted like the seasons. His mother died from an overdose of barbiturates that was surmised as suicide when she was only forty-nine. His sister, Brooke Hayward, who was married at one time to Henry's son Peter Fonda, wrote a book about her mother's final years called Haywire.

294

My father was Ernest Hemingway's agent. And they were great friends. Hemingway was also great friends with my stepmother, Slim Hawks. She was a wonderful character, I was very fond of her.

Hemingway gave me a .22 pistol as a memento when I was twelve. My parents didn't approve of a kid that age having a pistol, so my father kept the gun for me for a long time.

I was incredibly impressed the first time I met Hemingway. I had read all of Hemingway, and I knew exactly who he was and I was knocked out. We went on his boat, the Pilar, and he fished a lot. He had a professional guy on the boat, and here he was married to a woman named Mary, who I didn't particularly care for.

I remember us all going to a bar together, Slim and Mary and Hemingway and my father and me at the bar. Hemingway was seated next to me, and he'd get interested in me for a while, he'd talk to me a little bit and ask questions. I wasn't completely out of the picture because of my age.

At some point, [Hemingway] said to me, "You see that guy at the end of the bar down there? The one with the big mustache? He and I have exchanged business cards on several occasions."

I said, "Oh?"

He said, "Do you understand what that means?"

I said, "No."

He said, "We've challenged each other to duels."

I said, "Really?" [Laughs] "Well, what happened?"

He said, "Well, I can't really can't duel anymore because of my profile." He was a giant star, and he said he could be sued for a billion dollars.

I remember we got into a taxi cab to go back to the hotel where we were staying, and I was just staggered by these stories. I started telling my father some of these stories, and he went "Oh, my god, he is so full of shit." [Laughs] He said, "He finally found someone to listen to his stories." [Laughs]

Another time I remember being on his fishing boat, and I had been in a minor romantic way the day before and had gotten a hickey on my neck. I wore a shirt with a collar, and tried to keep it cool. There were no mirrors on a boat, and eventually I forgot about it. We had gone swimming and he saw me and said, "How old are you?" [Laughs]

I said, "Fifteen."

He said, "How old were you passing for yesterday?" [Laughs]

Slim said, "Oh, no, it's not that! He's a *good* boy!" Which *greatly* amused Hemingway. He found that hilarious.

Hemingway was always telling me stories about a bar called The Floridita, and about the prodigious amount of margaritas that he drunk in an afternoon there. He loved that bar. He would tell the kind of drinking stories that people used to tell about how much they drank.

A lot of writers came out here to Hollywood, and got more money than they had ever gotten before. But it's a different process and it's a different medium. In those days, the writer was treated like shit. They wouldn't let them on the set, and a lot of them worked on a weekly salary. Some of the studio guys would have several of them writing the same project and wouldn't tell them, you know. There was a lot of reasons to be unhappy from the creative side of trying to be a writer. On the other hand, they were making more money then they ever made before. A lot of them always had the complaint that because they got involved and spent years out here, they didn't actually do those things which they really should have done. Which is probably true. It's their fault. They fell for the seduction. So everybody was unhappy with some part of the deal.

In those days, producers were very different than they are now. Generally speaking, you worked for a studio and you were given a picture to produce. You didn't go pitch the fucking thing. David Selznick was a wild card and he started his own studio. So producers used to complain because they got assigned pictures that they didn't want to do and they didn't pick the script. It was like everybody had a bitch. The actors were under contract and they couldn't do what they wanted. Everybody had to do what they were told to do, it was a different world. But they made a lot of movies.

My father was head of production for a company called First National Pictures which merged with Warner Brothers in the silent days. Frank Capra worked for him then, and told me that my father would come around with a bag full of money to pay everyone.

My father started as a crime reporter on an evening newspaper, and the crime reporters knew where all the speakeasies were and would go regularly. He met Fred and Adele Astaire when they were dancing at speakeasies, and became their agent and started his own agency. Then he started coming to California. And because he was raised as a gentleman on the East Coast, he was a dark-suit-and-tie kind of guy, and nobody else in the film industry was. Generally speaking, the film industry was run by people that were recent immigrants who had not had that kind of upbringing. Leland would go around to their offices in a suit and tie, and they decided that he had class. There was a certain emulation. When he merged his agency with MCA, the MCA guys all started to wear the dark suits and the black ties, because Leland started that. MCA used to be famous for dark suits and black ties.

My mom only did thirteen movies. People think of her as a movie actress, but she didn't start her career in the movies. She was already a famous actress when she came here. She had a *great* voice. When I was a kid, I thought she was great, because she was my mother. I thought she was *beautiful*, the way children do about their mothers. I had seen her in a lot of plays, and it worked for me, because I was her son. But I never knew how good she really was until *many* years later. I screened all her films at Fox when I was there doing a miniseries called *Haywire*.

296

By then I knew a lot more about acting in movies. And I suddenly realized, "God, she *is* good." Not just because she was my mother. She was a *good* actress. She was a phenomenally *interesting* actress. She had a *wonderful* voice. It was *very* distinctive. Most people would probably think of it as a husky voice, which it probably was. It had a quality that was very recognizable. And onstage she was a spectacular actress.

Hollywood used to be a lot more glamorous back then. The Roosevelt used to have a little *panache* to it. The Knickerbocker was very nice, and there are a number of apartment buildings like the Fontenoy that were very chic. In the hills there were always a lot of really amazing, movie-star houses.

Everything changed in Southern California because of the war. An enormous amount of GIs came through Southern California and said, "Oh *geez*, that's a pretty nice place," and moved here. That's what made the San Fernando Valley. When I was a kid, the Valley was kind of sleepy. Dairy farms and orchards. There was no freeway then. It was nice. In those days, the theory was that building the freeway would *ease* traffic problems. But nobody thought that when you put a freeway in, you accumulated more traffic and more buildings along the freeway, and you multiplied the population problem. Instead of easing the problem, you have eight million more people trying to use the same piece of pavement. And you decimate old neighborhoods.

I remember when they put the freeway through the Cahuenga Pass. Late fifties. I used to drive to Warner Brothers from Hollywood through there to Burbank. That was the only way to go, just a road through the pass. When they put that freeway in, it cut straight through there. And when they put in the 101, the Valley started to develop and spread.

It was funny how the kids in school were. I knew Hemingway, but they couldn't give a fuck about Hemingway. All they wanted to know about was Marilyn Monroe. If you didn't know her, at some point they got onto Jayne Mansfield.

I remember meeting Clark Gable. I was fourteen, going to get my first tuxedo with my stepmother Slim. I was in the shop getting fitted, and Gable knew my step-mother well, since she was married to Howard Hawks, before she married my father. Gable was my all-time hero. I was *completely* stunned. It made an *enormous* impression on me. He really seemed like a true movie *star*. He was bigger than you thought he would be, and he had *huge* hands. He was charming and funny. I can't remember a word of the conversation [laughs]. He was obviously very comfortable with my stepmother. I was just *completely* taken by meeting him. Meeting Gable was *amazing*. Especially for a kid my age. I was the perfect age.

My mother, Jimmy Stewart, Henry Fonda, Josh Logan and others all were in a repertory company called the University Players. So they all knew each other, and they were represented by my father [laughs]. When the talkies came along, the studios were looking for people who could talk, who had done theater. It didn't have to be Broadway. So, in fairly short order, they brought out Fonda, Stewart, and my mother.

[Josh] Logan started as an actor. My father got him his first job in Hollywood as a dialogue director on the movie *The Garden of Allah*. Josh could remember all the lines of dialogue of every play he'd *ever* been in. And *every* song. He had an *amazing* memory. And he would tell these stories about working on that film with Charles Boyer and Deitrich. And they were the best stories you ever heard, because he remembered *everything*. It was fantastic.

Henry Fonda was the funniest man I ever knew. He had a wit about him. And he was a practical joker, big-time. He was a *very* clever, very funny man. He could always make me laugh. *Always*. A very dry wit. He didn't keep Peter laughing long but he kept me rolling on the floor. I thought he was *great*. He and Peter had some problems, but you know, fathers and sons are complicated. Henry had no expectations for me. If I failed, he didn't care. He dealt with me just like a kid. But with Peter he had a lot of expectations and ambitions.

I knew Jimmy Stewart my whole life. He's a really unique character to me. He was in a bunch of movies with my mother, and my father was his agent. They put him in funny roles—romantic roles, comedic roles, a Western as kind of a bad guy—and it was interesting, because he got away with it on some level, with that weird presentation of his. He was a funny man. He talked in that same kind of stammer offscreen, too.

I had known him since I was born, basically, so he was always a regular guy to me. His wife Gloria was fantastic, the best thing since sliced toast. She was funny, great to be around, and great for him. When she died, he was *lost*. He never came out of the house again. He took it very hard, and understandably so. She was a remarkable woman.

First time I met Walter Matthau is when I was in the army, and he was doing a play with my father called *A Shot in the Dark* with Julie Harris and William Shatner. Matthau was working as a character actor in Hollywood. He was not a star in anybody's mind-set. He replaced an actor who died while the play was in rehearsals, and he took over and did the part perfectly in one night. He was *brilliant* in it, and it made him a star. I liked Walter. He was a great guy. A *monstrous* gambler—the kind of gambler who was more believable in fiction. He was terrific. I *loved* him.

I was living in Newport Beach and I was running a boat, and my father called me one day. He said, "Listen, kid, it's time you went to work. I've made an appointment for you to see Lew Wasserman and he'll give you a job at Universal." This was before they had the tower. All the executives had little bungalows scattered around the same piece of property, but there were no high-rises.

So I came up for my meeting with Lew Wasserman, who I had not seen since I was a boy, and he was a scary guy, because he had these pale blue eyes and he was just a *master* at making people uncomfortable. We were in the middle of this meeting about what I was going to do, and suddenly the secretary knocks and comes in and says, "Mr. Wasserman, we just heard on the radio that President Kennedy has been shot." At that moment he hadn't been killed yet, and Wasserman was a huge supporter and fan, and he said, "Excuse me, Bill, I have to deal with something," and sent me off. People say that everybody remembers where they were and what they were doing the moment Kennedy got shot, and I sure do. [Laughs] I've always been curious about what Lew Wasserman remembers about it [laughs]. Somehow I think he's probably got a slightly different version.

So I worked in the script department for a while, but I hated the job. My father was *so* angry. I said, "This job *sucks*." So then I went to work as an apprentice film editor. I went to Warner Brothers and I ended up working for Formar Blangstead [husband of Else Blangstead] and Josh Logan, who was directing *Camelot*.

So I went to work there. Logan got me an offer, and the next picture he did was *Paint Your Wagon*, which was a Paramount film, and it got to be a nepotism struggle there whether I got to be the associate producer or if it would be Alan Jay Lerner's nephew. And somewhere in there I got displaced. It pissed me off really seriously about the movie industry. So I became a photographer and just turned my back on the movie industry to work as a photographer.

I was working on a stage filming a catalog, and got a call from Peter Fonda. He said, "Listen, Dennis [Hopper] and I are going to do this movie—*Easy Rider*—and we need somebody who understands how the studio works and is kind of organized and can do all the trivial shit that's involved." Dennis was my brother-in-law. He was married to my sister Brooke. [Laughs]

I went down to see Peter and Dennis. And it was a very short period of time they were talking about. So I said okay. And that's how I ended up getting back into movies. I didn't believe it for a number of years after *Easy Rider* came out that I was really back. I was convinced it was all a fluke. I was still very wary about the entertainment industry and I tried to keep doing the photography thing. And at some point I got pissed off again and I quit, and I became a tuna fisherman. I ran a tuna boat for six years.

299

When I was working on *Easy Rider* we had offices over at Seward & Melrose. In those days there wasn't any place else to eat besides Musso's. Though Columbia had a good executive dining room, which we would eat at a lot, because you could charge it to the picture. The executive dining room at Columbia was very small; it would hold maybe ten or twelve tables. Some would be two, some would be four. One was five or six. Only one. It was hard to find. It was up two or three stories and across a catwalk. And no sign, no clue that it was there. And in order to eat there, you had to have a reservation. And in order to pay there, you had to have a production number to charge it to. Or you were an executive of some stature and then you didn't have to. But if you were making a picture there, you needed a number. We discovered this after a while—we didn't have any dough. And we were editing the movie. So we started eating there every day, because the food was really good.

We were there when they were making a film with Walter Matthau and Ingrid Bergman. There was this buzz around the lot that Ingrid Bergman was going to be starting next week. And there was a twist, cause it was her first picture in America in ages, since she had gone off with Rossellini. So it's time for lunch, so Peter and I go to the dining room. They had a table that sat three, where Peter and I sat, next to the big table. At that big table was Walter Matthau, Gene Saks, the producer, a full table of people. The waiter was just bringing their food. And in walks Ingrid Bergman.

Now I had never met Ingrid Bergman. But I had been in love with her since I was two years old. The whole place went quiet. Because she was such a big star then—even to all the people in that room, she was a big star. And none of them had seen her in a hundred years, because she'd been in Europe.

Now here's another key to this story: Peter and I had smoked a lot of marijuana. We would get loaded before we went to lunch. So both of us are *completely crippled* on marijuana. And she walks in, and my jaw just *drops*. She walks over to that big table, because they are all her people, working on the same picture. And they don't know what to do, because their food has just been put in front of them, and they want to be gentlemen, but they don't know what to do. And it's an awkward mess. And every other table had people at them, cause it was a *tiny* room. And for reasons that have always amazed me, some gentleman-training thing came into gear, and I stood up and said, "Please, come sit with us and have lunch with us," because we have one extra seat. Now: that was the *end* for me. I was *so* loaded I couldn't *speak*. I couldn't even figure out what to *call* her. I knew there was somebody after Rossellini but I couldn't remember what the name was, and I didn't know if I should call her Mrs. or not. I couldn't get *any* of it together.

300

Peter was much cooler. He had seen her at a party over the weekend, so they had a little chat, and I sat there with my mind *racing* trying to figure out some way to be able to call her the right name, to do something. I don't think we ever had two words. There was this one moment of gallantry, followed up by this *complete* incapacity to follow up in any way at all.

Peter's dad [Henry Fonda] and my mother were married. And my father was Henry's agent. So it gets complicated. Peter's father and my mother were married long before Peter or I were born. So it goes way back.

I remember one lunch we went in. There was Willie Wyler. Willie had an office at Columbia, and Willie was down one or two tables. It wasn't booths, just tables, so it was easy to talk from table to table. It was Dennis [Hopper], Peter [Fonda], and I. And Willie saw Dennis. And Willie said, "Dennis, how's Brook?" Brook is my sister who Dennis had been married to. And they were—at that moment—starting to go through a divorce. Dennis was *embarrassed*, and said (softly), "Well Willie, we're getting a divorce." And Willie was stone-deaf in one ear. So he says louder, "How's Brook?" And Dennis says louder, "We're getting divorced, Willie!" And it goes back and forth several times, and Willie is yelling, *"HOW'S BROOK?"* And everybody in the whole diningroom—and we knew every human being in this place—everybody started yelling, *"They're getting a divorce,Willie!"* And Willie finally heard, and he said, "Oh. Guess you couldn't hold on to her any better than I could hold on to her mother!" He had been married to my mother. Which I had completely forgotten about. Now *that's* Hollywood.

Hollywood changed enormously in the Sixties. We *watched* it change.

PART THREE
A TOUR OF HOLLYWOOD

ONTAINED in this chapter is an alphabetical listing of significant and historic locations in Hollywood. The listings include some history about these landmarks; most are discussed in greater detail in Part One: A History of Hollywood beginning on page 1. Some of these landmarks no longer exist, though the great majority of them still stand. Those that no longer exist are designated by the word *site* in brackets.

Alto Nido Apartments

1851 N. Ivar Avenue

This is where the writer Joe Gillis lived, played by William Holden in the classic movie *Sunset Boulevard*, also starring Gloria Swanson as silent movie queen Norman Desmond, Eric Von Stroheim as her ex-husband and butler, and Cecil B. DeMille as himself. Gillis is seen in his one-room apartment here, wearing a robe while working away at the typewriter. Two repo men arrive at his door with a court order to repossess his car, a 1946 Plymouth convertible, California license 40 R 116. He lies to them and tells them a friend has the car, when in fact it's parked around the block behind Rudy's Shoe Shine Parlor. "I needed about $290 and I needed it real quick," he says in a voice-over, "or I'd lose my car. It wasn't in Palm Springs and it wasn't in the garage. I was way ahead of the finance company. I knew they'd be coming around and I wasn't taking any chances."

American Society of Cinematographers

1782 North Orange Drive

This Mission Revival home was built as a private residence in 1903. Since 1936, it has been the home of the Society, who run a small museum and library, which is open to the public during weekday working hours. Plans to renovate this structure were announced in 2001.

American Film Institute

2021 North Western Avenue

This was originally constructed as the campus of the Immaculate Heart College in 1906 here on the edge of Griffith Park. It's now the home of AFI, where it houses a film and video library that is accessible to the public.

Bronson Caves

Brush Canyon (at the top of Canyon Drive)

These man-made caves were formed in 1903 by the Union Rock Company, who built a quarry here in Brush Canyon, and used the crushed rock as railroad ballast and street surfaces. Nestled as it is within the folds of foothills in Brush Canyon, it's an ideal set for Westerns, and has also served as an extraterrestrial landscape on many occasions.

The first film ever shot at the caves was *Lightning Bryce*, a silent film made in 1919, which was followed by *Riders of the Purple Sage* in 1925. Thousands have been shot here since, including *Lightning Warrior* (1931), *The Three Musketeers* (1933), *Mystery Mountain* (1934), *The Lone Ranger Rides Again* (1939), *Adventures of Captain Marvel* (1941), *Pirates of*

Monterey (1947), Superman (1949), Carson City (1952), Robot Monster (1953), Killers from Space (1954), Invasion of the Body Snatchers (1956), The Jayhawkers (1959), Ride the High Country (1962), Equinox (1970), Lost Horizon (1973), The Choirboys (1977), The Legend of the Lone Ranger (1981), The Sword and the Sorcerer (1983) and Star Trek VI: The Undiscovered Country (1991).

TV shows featuring the Bronson Caves include "Batman," of course, which used them as the driveway into the bat-cave in each and every episode, as well as "Bat Masterson," "Bonanza," "Californians," "Fantasy Island," "Gunsmoke," "The Adventures of Rin Tin Tin," "Have Gun, Will Travel," "The High Chaparral," "Little House on the Prairie," "The Lone Ranger," "MacGyver," "Outlaws," "Rawhide," "Rough Riders," "Shotgun Slade," "Starman," "Star Trek Voyager," "Tales of the Texas Rangers," "Tombstone Territory," "Virginian," "Wild Wild West," and "Wonder Woman."

The Brown Derby [site]

1628 Vine Street

Opened for business on Valentine's Day of 1929, it was one of the great Hollywood restaurants. It's said there was no star who hadn't been to the Derby. The walls were filled with the framed caricatures of comic and dramatic stars of the day, and the tables were often filled by those very stars, and by bit players and extras, all of whom would dash into the Derby in full makeup and costume from nearby studio sets, dashing back to do another scene after lunch was over. Because of this influx of stars, the Derby was beloved by the public, who were hungry to see these spectral stars in the flesh. In 1939, Clark Gable proposed here to Carole Lombard. The Derby was razed in 1993.

C.C. Brown's Ice Cream [site]

7007 Hollywood Boulevard

C.C. Brown's was the most famous ice-cream shop in Hollywood, and whether or not they actually invented the hot fudge sundae as they claimed, they made great ones, oozing with rivers of their own legendary hot fudge. It attracted stars such as Judy Garland, Jackie Cooper, Barbara Stanwyck, Bob Hope, Jack Benny, Frank Sinatra and Joan Crawford. Their presence often resulted in fans lining up for hours along the boulevard for autographs.

Capitol Records

1750 N. Vine Street

The international headquarters of Capitol Records, this landmark building was the world's first-ever circular office building, constructed in 1956. Many of the world's most famous recording artists have recorded in Capitol's famed basement studios, including the Beatles, as well as Frank Sinatra, who used to hold all-night recording sessions here. The light on its rooftop spire flashes H-O-L-L-Y-W-O-O-D in Morse code. The Gold albums of its many artists are displayed in lobby, and the sidewalk stars of John Lennon and other Capitol artists can be found on the Walk of Fame, directly outside of the building.

Castillo Del Lago

6342 Mulholland Highway

The gangster Benjamin "Bugsy" Siegel lived here during the thirties, and actually ran a speakeasy and a gambling den here. He chose this house because he enjoyed the security of being on top of the hill, where his henchmen could keep a good lookout in all directions, and because the only entrance was at the bottom of the house, at the end of a long, winding driveway. He felt this would make it impossible for the police to storm his home without ample warning. But he was wrong; they stormed in instead into the upper floors of the house by climbing through a neighbor's adjoining property.

Madonna bought this home in 1993, at which time she outraged the neighborhood, and captured the attention of all of

304

those who gazed up at the house every day from Lake Hollywood, by painting its formerly egg-shell white facade with a combination of burgundy and mustard-yellow stripes.

Castle Argyle [also site of Castle San Souci and Castle Glengarry]

Now a senior-citizen residence on the eclipse of the freeway, the Castle Argyle was an apartment hotel built in 1930, long before the freeway ramp that obscures it today was constructed. It was the residence of teams of musicians who would come with the Big Bands to Hollywood to perform at the Palladium and elsewhere.

This castle was built on the grounds of another castle, the Castle San Souci, a private home built in 1909 by Alfred Guido Randolph Schloesser. A retired surgeon from Chicago, Schloesser also erected a castle across the street, on what is now a strip mall, called Castle Glengarry. Both were demolished in 1929.

The C.E. Toberman Company Building/Guinness Museum

6780 Hollywood Boulevard

Toberman, who designed twenty-nine commercial buildings in Hollywood, had his first office in a building on this same site. This building was designed in 1919; its classical facade was added in the twenties. It was originally a four-story building; remarkably, the top three floors were removed in 1935 to create the building in this present form. Today the building is the home of the Hollywood Guinness Book of World Records museum.

Raymond Chandler houses

1040 Havenhurst Drive (off of Sunset)

6320 Drexel Avenue

The author Raymond Chandler, who wrote the classic Philip Marlowe novels that became classic movies, such as *The Big Sleep* and *The Maltese Falcon*, lived in these two main houses while working in Hollywood. He moved to 1040 Havenhurst in 1943 with his wife Cissy while working for Paramount Pictures, and to 6320 Drexel in 1949.

He was one of the few authors to come to Hollywood in service of the movies who seemed to actually like the place. Not only did Chandler bear a healthy respect for a finely structured film, he also held no rancor for Hollywood or the film industry. "Hollywood is easy to hate, easy to sneer at, easy to lampoon," he wrote in a 1943 article for the *Atlantic Monthly*. "Some of the best lampooning has been done by people who have never walked through a studio gate, some of the best sneering by egocentric geniuses who departed huffily—not forgetting to collect their last pay check—leaving behind them nothing but the exquisite aroma of their personalities and a botched job for the tired hacks to clear up."

Born in Chicago in 1888, Chandler moved with his wife Sissy into the little house at 1040 Havenhurst in West Hollywood and made the quick commute to Paramount each day, where he worked in the white Writer's Building. His first project was a collaboration with the director Billy Wilder on an adaptation of James Cain's thriller, *Double Indemnity*, a film that Woody Allen, many years later, called Wilder's best, and "practically anybody's best movie." The film was a success, and Paramount offered Chandler a contract in 1944, which he happily accepted.

Years later Chandler stated that of all the bosses he had in his life, Paramount was the only one he truly liked. This formerly reclusive writer even enjoyed the company of fellow writers he met on the lot. "The screenwriter meets clever and interesting people and may even make lasting friendships," he said. On another occasion, he said, "In Hollywood the average writer is not young, not honest, not brave, and a bit overdressed. But he is darn good company."

Chandler was well liked on the lot, and

305

offered healthy and humorous advice to anyone who asked for it. "He said he loved interruptions more than anything," wrote the writer Robert Presnell, "because things you do when you're supposed to be doing something else are always more fun. Digression is the spice of life." He told me to write whatever I wanted to because no one in the front office could read anyway. Chandler and Sissy moved into another small house (6320 Drexel), where he was able to convince Paramount to allow him to work on his new project, an original story called *The Blue Dahlia*, to be directed by John Houseman. It would star Alan Ladd and Veronica Lake, or "Moronica Lake," as Chandler, who was thoroughly unimpressed with her acting, came to call her.

Through his agent, Chandler made a series of totally unreasonable requests, and forever immortalized himself as a hero in the annals of Hollywood scriptwriting by being granted all of them. He asked for and received a team of six secretaries who would revolve in teams of two, always ready to capture any spontaneous dictation and quickly type it up. He also requested and received two Cadillac limos, on call night and day to fetch a doctor, deliver a script, or make a market run. Houseman recalls visiting Chandler during this process, where the author "would extend a white and trembling hand and acknowledge my expressions of gratitude with the modest smile of a gravely wounded war hero who has shown courage well beyond the call of duty."

Chandler decided to get back to writing novels following this film, and often escaped Hollywood by taking Cissy up to Big Bear Lake. He accepted one offer from MGM to adapt his own novel, *The Lady in the Lake*, but Chandler only lasted a few months working at MGM before quitting. Both Paramount and Sam Goldwyn attempted to woo him back, but in Hollywood Chandler had earned a lot of money, done a great deal of drinking, and he

needed a break. He and Cissy moved south to La Jolla, just miles from the Mexican border, and Chandler bid a permanent farewell to Hollywood, despite the fact that he found the movies to be "the only original art the modern world had conceived."

Ironically, some of the greatest film versions of his work were made just as Chandler retreated from films. In 1947 Howard Hawks created his famous version of Chandler's *The Big Sleep*, which was adapted by Faulkner of all people, and starred Bogart as Philip Marlowe. Chandler, who died in La Jolla in 1959, was happy with the film. "Bogart is the genuine article," he said, "He can be tough without a gun."

The Chaplin Studio

[presently Jim Henson Productions]

1416 N. La Brea [just south of Sunset]

This is the studio that Chaplin built. Born in London on April 16, 1889, Charlie Chaplin was the first international movie star, a fame based on the poetic and comedic humanity expressed through the screen persona he developed throughout almost all his movies, The Little Tramp. Chaplin was a phenomenon for so many reasons, not the least of which is that his ascension to iconic superstar was built on comedy, and a comedy that was entirely his own creation. With the notable exception of Buster Keaton, there is no other silent comedian who brought his brand of hilarious, ingenious and heartbreakingly human humor to the screen.

He started performing onstage as a child of five, and it was onstage in America that he was noticed by Mack Sennett in 1912, and invited to Hollywood to make movies at the Keystone Studios, where Sennett had created the Keystone Kops. At first, Chaplin had no idea where he would fit in to Sennett's madcap comedies, but gradually developed the character of The Little Tramp, and everything fell into place. "On the way to wardrobe I thought I would dress in baggy pants, big shoes, a cane and a derby hat," Chaplin wrote in his autobiography. "I wanted everything to be a contradiction: the pants baggy, the coat tight, the hat small and the shoes large. I was undecided whether to look old or young, but remembering Sennett had expected me to be a much older man, I added a small mustache, which, I reasoned, would add age without hiding my expression....The secret of Mack Sennett's success was his enthusiasm. He was a great audience... This encouraged me to explain the character: 'You know this fellow is many-sided, a tramp, a gentleman, a poet, a dreamer, a lonely fellow, always hopeful of romance and adventure."

He made thirty-five films while working at Keystone, introducing the world to the Little Tramp, and learning the ropes of filmmaking. Chaplin was soon writing, directing and starring in his films, a rare combination of roles that he maintained throughout his career. He made movies for many different companies, and with each demanded full creative control. It was while working for First National that he moved into longer films, and had tremendous success with movies that were comedic but with a dramatic core, such as *The Kid*, which co-starred Jackie Coogan in the title role.

It was while he was still under contract to First National in 1918 that Chaplin built his studio here at La Brea & Sunset. He bought the land, which was a five-acre orchard, in 1918 for $35,000, and had the studio built here to resemble a row of English country homes. It quickly became one of the world's most thriving cinematic centers, the studio where Chaplin created successive masterpieces, including *A Dog's Life* (1918), *Shoulder Arms* (1918), *Pay Day* (1922), *The Pilgrim* (1923), *The Gold Rush* (1925), *City Lights* (1931), *Modern Times* (1936) and *Limelight* (1952).

With Mary Pickford, D.W. Griffith and Douglas Fairbanks, he formed United Artists, and went on to make several full-length dramatic comedies, each a masterpiece, and each given as much time in production as necessary to perfect. Chaplin was known to take many months, if necessary, to get a single scene right, and would recast movies with different actors many months into production if he felt it was necessary.

After *The Gold Rush* in 1925, he made his first noncomedic film, *A Woman of Paris* (1927), starring Adolphe Menjou. The beautiful *City Lights* came next, which many consider the most essential of all his films. Even into the era of the talkies, Chaplin persisted as a popular silent comic. He didn't use sound in his films until *Modern Times*, at which time he only used it sparingly, as somewhat of a novelty. In 1940 he made *The Great Dictator*, a parody of Hitler that was the first of his films to fail with the public.

It was the last we would see of the Little Tramp. He made four more films, *Monsieur Verdoux* (1947), *Limelight* (1952), *A King in New York* (1957) and *The Countess from Hong Kong* (1966). He was one of the greatest and most influential moviemakers Hollywood has ever known, and yet Hollywood essentially rejected him at the end of his life because of his pacifistic and allegedly anti-American politics. Chaplin left Hollywood and America forever to live with his family in Switzerland. So downhearted was he about Hollywood that he intended for his studio here to be destroyed. He died in Geneva, Switzerland, on Christmas Day 1977.

Chaplin officially sold the lot to a real estate company in 1952. Between 1952 and 1957, the "Superman" TV show starring George Reeves was filmed on the soundstage. The comedian Red Skelton purchased the studio in 1958, and spent many millions to renovate it, shooting his CBS-TV variety show here. In time he sold the facility to CBS, which began in 1962 to produce the show "Perry Mason" here, starring Raymond Burr as the lawyer who was hardly ever wrong. Burr actually lived on the lot whenever the show was in pro-

307

duction. Many episodes of "I Love Lucy," starring Lucille Ball and Desi Arnaz, were also filmed here.

On November 6, 1966, The Chaplin Studios became the home of Jerry Moss and Herb Alpert's A&M Records, which for many years was the largest independent record company in the world. They strove to preserve the historic value of their new home, and left in place Chaplin's concrete footprints in front of Soundstage Three. They converted this and one other soundstage, as well as Chaplin's former swimming pool, into state-of-the-art recording studios. The studios have since been used by legendary recording artists such as the Rolling Stones, Barbra Streisand, and Bruce Springsteen. In 1985, it was the site of the "We Are the World" recording session, which brought together several dozen of the world's greatest recording artists, including Michael Jackson, Ray Charles, Bob Dylan, Stevie Wonder, and Paul Simon, to record a single to raise money for the starving children of Africa. A&M was sold to the Polygram conglomerate in 1992, which closed the doors of its fabled studios.

Today it is the headquarters of Jim Henson Productions—the creators of the Muppets—who have paid tribute to the lot's original owner by installing a statue of their most famous Muppet, Kermit the Frog, at the front gate, dressed as Chaplin's famous alter-ego, the "Little Tramp." [1]

Charlie Chaplin houses

6147 Temple Hill Drive (See KROTONA COLONY–Moorcrest)

2010 DeMille Drive (See LAUGHLIN PARK)

The Chateau Elysee

Celebrity Centre International / Manor Hotel

5930 Franklin Avenue

The Chateau Elysee, constructed

between 1928 and 1929, has long been considered one of Hollywood's grandest and most beautiful hotels. And it should be: It was built by Randolph Hearst for the widow of film director Thomas Ince, who was mysteriously murdered aboard Hearst's yacht, a crime that remains unsolved. Ince lived in a small home on these grounds prior to his death.

It was the first resident hotel in Hollywood, and the temporary home of many movie stars, including Carole Lombard, Cary Grant, George Burns & Gracie Allen, Douglas Fairbanks Jr., and Ginger Rogers. The creator of *Tarzan*, Edgar Rice Burroughs, also lived here.

Frederica Maas remembered staying at the hotel in 1928 when she was unable to get a room at the Villa Carlotta, across the street. "The Chateau Elysee was luxurious," she said. "It was the home to Clark Gable, Carole Lombard, Humphrey Bogart and Errol Flynn at one time or another. There were two doormen, and security was tight."

Today the Chateau is open to the public and is occupied and operated by the Church of Scientology, which purchased it in 1974. The interior and exterior of the hotel have been restored.

According to Scientologists, Scientology is a religion that is founded on the technology of Dianetics, which was invented by L. Ron Hubbard, a prolific writer of science fiction who has been honored by the city of Los Angeles by having a Hollywood street named after him: L. Ron Hubbard Way runs between Sunset and Fountain, just west of Vermont, directly across the street from the many buildings of the Kaiser Permanente hospital.

Scientology is a controversial organization that has received a profusion of criticism around the world for allegedly using its religious status to further its business enterprises, and for its purported

308

---

[1] For more on Chaplin and this studio, see "A History of Hollywood," page 31; and David Raksin, page 69.

harsh treatment of former church members and others who speak out against the church.

But regardless of one's feelings about this group, there's no disputing the fact that the Church of Scientology, which owns more than five prominent and historic properties in Hollywood, takes excellent care of its buildings and shows respect for their historic significance. Each of them, including the Chateau and the former Christie Hotel on Hollywood Boulevard, has been beautifully and faithfully renovated, and each is well maintained.

Chateau Marmont

8221 Sunset Boulevard

Seven stories above the Sunset Strip is the Chateau Marmont, built in this classic Tudor style in 1927, and still abounding with the ghosts and scandals of Hollywood's recent and not-so-recent past. Famous for the elegant, old-world discretion it affords all its guests, it's been known through the decades as a safe harbor for stars seeking to circumvent the squall of media surveillance. "If you must get in trouble, do it at the Chateau Marmont," Harry Cohn, the first boss of Columbia Studios, once told William Holden. Every star from Chaplin, Bogart and Tracy to Dylan, Jagger and Lennon have hidden out here while in Hollywood.

This is where the Doors' Jim Morrison screwed up his back by swinging Tarzan-like from the roof into his room, using a drain pipe as a vine. This is also, tragically, the place where John Belushi died, in Bungalow #3.

Nicholas Ray, the director of *Rebel without A Cause*, among other films, always stayed at the Chateau Marmont while in Hollywood. Shelley Winters remembers going there in 1950 with James Dean and Marilyn Monroe to visit Ray at his bungalow—the same one in which Belushi died. "Nick's bungalow was surrounded by night-blooming jasmine," she wrote. "It was sparsely furnished, and he had a

big Mad Man Muntz black-and-white TV set."

CBS / Columbia Square

6121 Sunset Boulevard

This was the center of the CBS Radio Network's Los Angeles operation, and also the first home of CBS Television, where classic shows from TV's first days were created, including "The Jack Benny Show."

309

The Christie Hotel

6724 Hollywood Boulevard

This was the Christie Hotel, built in 1922 to provide a luxury hotel for the new royalty of Hollywood, movie folk. It was owned by Christie Brothers, Al and Charlie, who were among Hollywood's first family of movie moguls—they also owned the Nestor movie studios, which was the first studio in Hollywood. It was the very first hotel in the community to offer rooms that each came with a private bath, an innovation that was a tremendous luxury at the time. Designed in this distinctive Georgian style by the architect Arthur B. Kelley, it is an entirely unique building on the boulevard; there is no other like it in style, color or design.

Today the Christie Hotel, like many of Hollywood's most historic properties, is owned by the Church of Scientology. Church members invariably offer all passersby a "free personality test" in order to interest you in their organization. [See Chateau Elysee for more on Scientology.]

The Christie Realty Building

6765–6773 Hollywood Boulevard

Built in 1928, this Spanish Colonial Revival building was designed by Carl Jules Weyl, who was most famous for his design of several classic movie sets, including those for the films *Casablanca* and *Yankee Doodle Dandy*. The Snow White Cafe, which is still in existence here, opened its doors in 1946, proudly featuring an original mural painted by Disney animators above the inside entrance.

Ciro's/The Comedy Store

8433 Sunset Boulevard

During the Depression it was the Clover Club, a frequently raided club where Hollywood luminaries such as Harry Cohn and David Selznick would engage in some serious illegal gambling. It opened as Ciro's on January 30, 1940, with a self-fulfilling prophecy: "Everybody that's anybody will be at Ciro's." Though it wasn't an instant success, Ciro's became known as one of the hottest spots in Hollywood to see and be seen. It was a place where classic entertainers entertained each other; Eartha Kitt debuted at Ciro's, and Martin & Lewis, Liberace, Sammy Davis Jr., Frank Sinatra, Nat "King" Cole, Marlene Dietrich, Billie Holiday, Lena Horne, Edith Piaf, and Mae West all performed here. When Lili St. Cyr's burlesque act became too racy, a near-riot ensued here, and the club was closed by the authorities on grounds of lewdness.

Other legends of carousal at Ciro's include an account of the actress Paulette Goddard crawling beneath a table to proclaim her love in no uncertain terms to the director Anatole Litvak. There's also the anecdote about a circus party hosted by Darryl Zanuck at the club in which Zanuck, no longer a young man at the time, stripped to the waist and proceeded to do pullups on a swinging trapeze bar.

Ciro's was also the favorite nightspot of mob bosses, such as Bugsy Siegel, who is said to have had business associates executed on the premises. Many have testified to seeing the ghosts of these murdered men still walking through the upstairs corridors of the old club.

In the sixties, Ciro's was transformed into a rock and roll club, and became part of rock history as the club where the Byrds first took flight. The L.A. group debuted here and blossomed into one of the most successful rock bands of the era. "I remember Ciro's the first night," said founding member Gene Clark. "The Byrds walked out onstage and there were about

ten people, and they all left. But two weeks later, there were lines down the street." Bob Dylan first came to hear the Byrds here; the band's biggest hit was their beautifully jangly version of his song "Mr. Tambourine Man."

In the mid-sixties, the name of the club was changed once again to It's Boss, and the age requirement of twenty-one was lowered to fifteen. It was then purchased by Mitzi Shore, who reopened it in 1970 as the Comedy Store, which exists to this day. As the Comedy Store, countless comedians including Richard Pryor, David Letterman, Jim Carey, Sam Kinison, Robin Williams, Roseanne Barr and others all started out their career here.

Clara Bow's It Café
The Plaza Hotel

1637 Vine Street

In September of 1937, silent-movie star Clara Bow and her husband Rex Bell opened the It Café off the lobby of the Plaza Hotel. Born in Brooklyn, New York, on August 25, 1905, Bow won a magazine beauty contest when she was only sixteen, which led to a small silent-movie role. The producer B.P. Schulberg recognized her appealing screen presence, and brought her to Hollywood to become a movie star. In 1926 came her first hit movie, *Mantrap*, in which she became famous as the essential "flapper" of the decade, a symbol of female liberation decades before the phrase "Women's Lib" entered the vernacular. She became known as the "It" girl after starring in a film named It in 1927, and set a stylistic standard for women of the era with her distinctive bangles, beads, bobbed hairdo and brilliant eyes. *The Plastic Age*, written by Frederica Maas, starred Bow as a college girl, and propelled her to further stardom. In 1928 she was named in a poll as "America's Favorite Actress." With this fame also came infamy, however, and scandals and rumors abounded and surrounded her throughout her career. Like many silent-movie stars, she failed to

210

make a successful transition into talkies, in her case, most likely because of the Brooklyn accent that she never discarded. She married Rex Bell, a cowboy star who later became lieutenant governor of Nevada, and retired from the movies forever in 1933.

In 1937, at the time she and Bell opened the It Café here, Clara had recently suffered a miscarriage; the restaurant was intended as a diversion from her grief, a kind of ongoing party over which she could preside. She told newspaper reporters at its opening that she would be a constant presence at the café, even supervising the chef, although stewed prunes was all she could cook. She soon got pregnant again, and closed the It Café less than a year after its opening. On June 14, 1938, she gave birth to a healthy baby son, George Francis Robert Beldam. She died in Los Angeles on September 27, 1965.

Cornelius Cole Home
6136 Lexington

In 1893, Washington Senator Cornelius Cole owned all of the land that is now South Hollywood, calling it Colegrove in honor of his wife Olive Colegrove. He lived out his life here, dying in this home in 1924, at which time Cecil B. DeMille lived across the street.

Crossroads of the World
6671 Sunset Boulevard

It opened on October 29, 1936, designed by Robert Derrah as a ship sailing to the many corners of the globe; to achieve this effect he blended together the grove of existing trees with an amalgam of architectural approaches from around the world. The result is a quaint village that is at once Spanish, French, Mexican and Moorish, all connected by a narrow Cape Cod lane. Like a ship at sea with its big bow on Sunset, its nautical motif is accentuated by a sixty-foot crow's nest crested with a revolving globe, eight feet in diameter. Through the years, the

Crossroads has held a variety of stores and businesses, from travel agencies to recording studios to hair stylists.

Walt Disney's Hollywood Homes and First Studio
Homes: 4406 Kingswell Avenue
2491 Lyric Avenue
Studio: 4649 Kingswell Avenue

Born in Chicago on December 5, 1901, Walt Disney was a true artist of animation, discovering in the world of colorful cartoons a mythic wonderland that has persisted throughout the years, encompassing our most beloved fairy-tales, as well as introducing us to some of filmdom's most beloved characters, such as Mickey Mouse and his wife Minnie, Donald Duck, Goofy, and countless others. He was raised on a farm near Marceline, Missouri, and started sketching and drawing as a kid. He spent a year overseas with the Red Cross in 1918, and returned after the war to Kansas City to launch a career as a cartoonist.

Disney moved to Hollywood in August of 1923 to meet up with his brother Roy, who had already arrived. They lived here at 4406 Kingswell at the home of their uncle Robert Disney, and contributed five dollars a week toward their collective room & board. They initially used the old garage in the back of this house as a studio. It's there that Walt completed his first cartoon, *Alice's Wonderland*, and constructed his first camera stand to use for shooting animation. Roy Disney's wedding to his wife Edna was held here at the house.

They soon rented a portion of a Hollywood real estate company two blocks to the west at 4649 Kingswell, where they opened the Disney Brothers Studio in Hollywood. It was here that Walt conceived of his first and most famous animated star, Mickey Mouse, originally named Mortimer Mouse—on this site. Mickey was born with the abundant aid of Ub Iwerks, an old friend and fellow animator from

311

Kansas City, who was a genius at translating and refining Walt's ideas into animation. Though Iwerks didn't invent Mickey, he deserves much of the credit for bringing the Mouse to life.

Mickey Mouse was first featured in a silent cartoon entitled *Plane Crazy*. But with talkies on the horizon, Disney decided to launch his new star with sound. *Plane Crazy* was shelved, and *Steamboat Willie* became both the world's first fully synchronized sound cartoon and Mickey Mouse's official debut. It was a phenomenal achievement, considering this was long before the age of audio multi-tracking, or overdubbing, so that all the voices, sound effects, and full orchestra had to be recorded at the same time, and in perfect sync with the film. It was nearly impossible to perfect it, and yet Disney did. Audiences throughout the world who had never seen anything like it before were truly astounded.

Walt Disney provided the voice of Mickey Mouse himself. Although he explained at the time that he did it because he could find no one better, scholars of his work have suggested that Mickey Mouse was Disney's alter-ago, and he never intended anybody else to ever speak for him. *Steamboat Willie* premiered in New York on November 18, 1928. Disney moved his operation to Hyperion Avenue in nearby Silverlake, and he and Roy bought adjoining houses on Lyric Avenue. He later moved the studio to Burbank, where it has offices to this day, and went on to create several full-length animated classics, including *Pinocchio*, *Fantasia*, *Dumbo*, and *Bambi*. Disney's company became one of the most powerful in town, employing thousands, and moving into live-action films as well, such as *Mary Poppins*.

In 1955 Disney physicalized his unique vision to create Disneyland, an amazing $17 million amusement park. Though he had hoped to create his kingdom in Burbank and nearby Toluca Lake, it was ultimately located about an hour from Los Angeles in Anaheim, California. Disney also brought his vision to the world of

television. Starting as early as 1954, Disney's "Mickey Mouse Club" was a staple of children's programming. In 1961 came the "Wonderful World of Color," which was among the first TV shows to be broadcast in color.

Though he died on December 15, 1966, Disney had already purchased the land and outlined his vision of a new community in Florida to be called Disneyworld, which encompassed a kingdom similar to Disneyland, as well as what Walt called his "Experimental Prototype Community of Tomorrow," or EPCOT Center. It took seven years to complete, but Walt Disney World opened to the public on October 1, 1971. Fulfilling Walt's final vision, Epcot Center opened on October 1, 1982.

The Doolittle Theater
1615 Vine Street

Built in 1927 as the Wilkes Vine Theater, it has gone through many incarnations, among which the most famous has to be as the CBS Playhouse in the late thirties and early forties, the home to one of radio's most popular and beloved shows, "The Lux Radio Theater," hosted by Cecil B. DeMille. It's also been known as the Queens Theater and the Mirror Theater. In 1954 it became the Huntington Hartford Theater, and in 1984 the Doolittle. Many great plays and Broadway productions have been presented here, where the acoustics are said to be so good that one can hear an ice cube clink in a glass onstage from the last row of the balcony.

Double Indemnity house
6301 Quebec

This house was featured in Billy Wilder's classic 1944 movie *Double Indemnity*, starring Barbara Stanwyck and Fred MacMurray. "It was one of those California Spanish houses everyone was nuts about ten or fifteen years ago," said MacMurray in the role of insurance investigator Walter Neff. "This one must have cost someone

312

about thirty thousand dollars." It's used prominently in the movie, especially in the scene where Stanwyck helps her hubby down the stairs on crutches as Neff waits in the garage, in an old Lasalle, to murder him.

Deanna Durbin house

7922 Hollywood Boulevard

Deanna Durbin lived in this big white house in the early thirties when married to her first husband, Vaughn Paul. Born on December 4, 1921, in Winnipeg, Canada, she originally intended to devote her life to the opera, but became instead a singing movie star. Her first film was a short called *Every Sunday* (1936) which was somewhat of an audition for she and Judy Garland, who co-starred. MGM liked Durbin better than Garland, but a clerical error led to Garland being offered a contract. Durbin signed on instead at Universal, where she starred in a series of elaborate musicals, such as *Three Smart Girls* (1936), *One Hundred Men and a Girl* (1937) and *First Love* (1939), all of which featured her fine singing and approachable, appealing screen presence. She went on to star in dramas such as *The Amazing Mrs. Holliday* (1942) and *Christmas Holiday* (1944), and in 1945 the film considered by many to be her best, *Lady on a Train*. Her final film was *For the Love of Mary* (1948), after which she retired from movies and stardom in general to move to France with her husband, director Charles David. Her total absence from public life so intrigued the public that rumors began to spread that she had died.

The Egyptian Theater

6712 Hollywood Boulevard

Like the nearby Chinese Theater, the Egyptian was built in the early twenties by impresario Sid Grauman, and designed by the architect C.E. Toberman. Inspired by the King Tut craze then spreading throughout the world in 1922, The Egyptian in its heyday had guards attired in ancient Egyptian outfits, hieroglyphic murals, a sunburst ceiling and a giant scarab above the stage. It was the site of Hollywood's first-ever movie premiere, for the film *Robin Hood* starring Douglas Fairbanks. In 1923, Cecil B. DeMille premiered his famous silent movie *The Ten Commandments* here. Recently, the Egyptian has been beautifully restored by American Cinematheque.

El Capitan Theater

6834 Hollywood Boulevard

Completed in 1926, a full year prior to the opening of the nearby Chinese Theater, the El Capitan was originally a stage theater, featuring stars such as Joan Fontaine, Douglas Fairbanks Jr., Buster Keaton, Clark Gable, Henry Fonda, Jason Robards, and Will Rogers. Featuring a sumptuous East Indian design with an intricately carved Spanish Colonial facade, and decorated with characters from drama and literature, it was converted to a movie theater in 1942 and renamed the Paramount. The first film shown here was *Reap the Wild Wind*, which was Cecil B. DeMille's response to *Gone with the Wind*. Orson Welles' masterpiece *Citizen Kane*, considered by many to be the greatest American movie of all time, premiered here in 1941. The theater was purchased by the Disney company in 1984 and reopened as the El Capitan in 1988.

First United Methodist Church of Hollywood

6817 Franklin Avenue

Built in 1929, this neo-Gothic church is adorned by a wood-beamed replica of Westminister Abbey's ceiling inside. It's been used throughout the years for movie and theater auditions, theatrical and vocal competitions, as well as a rehearsal space. It's also been used as a set for many movies, which include: *What Price Hollywood* (1932), with Constance Bennett, who gets married here. In *One Foot In Heaven,* (1941), starring Frederic March, it was used as a Methodist Church. In the 1952 classic *War of the Worlds*, terrified people took shelter in the church to get away from the invading

Martians in the final scene. It's also been featured in the movies *Back to the Future, Sister Act*, and *That Thing You Do*.

F. Scott Fitzgerald's home
1403 N. Laurel Avenue [south of Sunset]

F. Scott Fitzgerald moved into his apartment at this building in April of 1940. He lived both here and at the home of his girlfriend Sheilah Graham, who lived nearby on Havenhurst, during his last days in Hollywood while working on *The Last Tycoon*. He would regularly stroll north on Laurel to turn left on Sunset to go to Schwab's Pharmacy. He rented his apartment here, overlooking the front courtyard, for $110 a month.

Fitzgerald first came to Hollywood in 1927 to write for movies, but with little success. Born in 1896 in St. Paul, Minnesota, he returned to Hollywood throughout his life to write scripts, seeking in the movie-writing business that which he sought in the freelance short-story business, some means by which he could earn enough income to allow him to write what mattered to him, novels. By the time he made his final move to Hollywood in 1937, he'd already written brilliant and beautiful novels such as *The Great Gatsby* and *Tender Is the Night*. Yet sales for both were fairly low, and they were generally considered to be nostalgic remnants of another era. Like Faulkner, Fitzgerald came to Hollywood dejected, with his great books mostly out of print, believing sadly that his legacy would not be preserved.

MGM offered Fitzgerald a fairly lucrative six months that allowed him to dig himself out of the tremendous debt load he'd incurred over the previous years. Though he worked on many scripts, the only one for which he received screen credit was *Three Comrades* (1938). MGM renewed his contract once, but dropped it the second time around, at which point

Fitzgerald worked freelance, both writing scripts and also short stories, which he sold to *Esquire* magazine. In 1939 he started *The Last Tycoon*, which detailed his feelings about Hollywood and its main industry, and focused on the producer Irving Thalberg, represented by the character of Monroe Stahr in the book.

Despite the fact that this novel is incomplete, it succeeds in offering a full and lucid vision of Hollywood in the late thirties. It was a place Fitzgerald observed at a distance and from its very midst, yet never presumed to understand. "You can take Hollywood for granted like I did," he wrote in *The Last Tycoon*, "or you can dismiss it with the contempt we reserve for what we don't understand. It can be understood, but only dimly and in flashes. Not half a dozen men have ever been able to keep the whole equation of pictures in their heads."

Fox Studios [site]
1417 Western at Sunset

In 1917, William Fox owned the land on both sides of Western and built Fox Studios. It was here that Tom Mix, Buck Jones, Theda Bara and John Wayne all made films. In 1935 Fox merged with 20th Century and moved to Culver City. This lot was destroyed in the sixties.

Frederick's of Hollywood
6608 Hollywood Boulevard

This art deco building was constructed in 1935 by the chain of S.H. Kress Department Stores, and designed by the architect Edward F. Sibbert. In 1947, it became Frederick's of Hollywood when entrepreneur Frederick Mellenger wanted a West Coast outlet for his mail-order lingerie business.[2] For years the building was painted a garish, bright purple, but was thankfully changed to this current more bearable shade in 1998. Frederick's cur-

314

---

[2] For more on Frederick's, see Totty Ames, page 194.

rently houses the world's only lingerie museum.

Garden of Allah [site]

8150 Sunset Boulevard

The Garden of Allah was the creation of Alla Nazimova, a Russian-born actress from Yalta. A silent movie star, she first came to Hollywood in 1918. In 1920, for $50,000, she purchased a Spanish Revival house on Sunset Boulevard surrounded by orange groves, vineyards, and a field of ferns, bamboo, banana, poplar and cedar trees. She lived and partied here for a few years before realizing she needed more money than the movies were bringing in to finance a lavish lifestyle of movie-star parties starring Valentino, Pola Negri and others. So she got a loan to finance the construction of a series of some twenty-five separate two-story, stucco bungalows, each containing two apartments, all arranged around one of the most famous and most expansive swimming pools in all of Hollywood; it was shaped like a figure-eight to resemble the Black Sea of her childhood. "The effect was that of a small Moroccan village," wrote Aaron Latham, "except that the starlets lounging around the pool wore not veils but the 1930s one-piece."

Nazimova named her new hamlet after the popular 1904 novel *The Garden of Allah* by Robert Hitchens, which was made into a film on several occasions. It opened as a hotel on January 9, 1927, launched by a wild, eighteen-hour party which featured such stars as Clara Bow, John Barrymore, Francis X. Bushman, Marlene Deitrich, and Jack Dempsey, the boxer.[3] Nazimova insisted on always being called "Madame," and forbade any of her friends or guests to utter a "good night" to her, because she felt it brought her bad luck.

The Garden was famous for being F. Scott Fitzgerald's first home in Hollywood. He worked here in close proximity to old friends and colleagues including John O'Hara, Mark Connelly, Dorothy Parker,

and Robert Benchley, all of whom would join nightly in one of their bungalows for cocktail parties. It was at one of these soirees in Benchley's bungalow that Fitzgerald first met the columnist Sheila Graham, with whom he would have a love affair, the final one of his life. Fitzgerald did not attempt to woo Miss Graham with words at first, quite the opposite: he stared at her intensely from across the room, and then got up and made a hasty and somewhat mysterious exit. It won her attention. When she asked Benchley about the identity of that man with the intense stare, he answered, "That was F. Scott Fitzgerald, the writer. I asked him to drop in. I guess he's left. He hates parties."

Her column was called "Sheila Graham Says," and in it she did her best to keep Fitzgerald and his Jazz Age cohorts deep in the distant past, often emphasizing the creative obsolescence of some in Hollywood by relating that they were "as old-fashioned as F. Scott Fitzgerald types." Since she had never read a single one of Fitzgerald's novels, however, she wasn't really that conversant with his "types."

It's ironic to be reminded, while looking back at this bygone chapter from the forties, that from Sheila Graham's perspective Fitzgerald was a visitor from an archaic, premodern era: "there was a reticence about him that made me feel he belonged to an earlier, quieter world," she wrote. "His clothes, too, spoke of another time: he wore a pepper-and-salt suit and bow tie, and though this was July, a wrinkled charcoal raincoat with a scarf around his neck and a battered hat. It was hard to believe this was the glamour boy of the twenties."

Orson Welles also lived and worked here, and had at least one love affair here, with the actress-model Lili St. Cyr. In 1943 he rented the rooms directly below Nazimova's own living quarters while working on the movie *It's All True*. But Orson and Alla didn't cohabitate peacefully; his round-the-clock work schedule clashed with her beauty sleep. Often awakened by the

[3] Starr, *Material Dreams*.

sound of Orson's clanking typewriter and/or ringing telephone, Alla would respond by hammering on her floor with her walking cane. In time, Welles left the Garden to rent a house on Woodrow Wilson Drive.

By the end of the forties, the allure of the Garden of Allah had all but worn off, signaling the beginning of physical Hollywood's decline. In his novel *The Disenchanted*, Budd Schulberg recognized the passing of an era, with the Garden as a metaphor for the death sentence Hollywood dealt to many:

316

"...the Garden of Allah. This outlandish name for an apartment-hotel was a stale joke at which he still smiled from force of habit. Thirteen years ago, when he had stayed here on his first trip to Hollywood, architecture had seemed to be an extension of the studio backlot with private homes disguised as Norman castles or Oriental mosques, with gas stations built to resemble medieval towers, and movie houses that took the form of Egyptian temples and Chinese pagodas. In that lavish heyday of the parvenu, when everything was built to look like something it wasn't, a bungalow court with accommodations indistinguishable from a hundred other bungalow courts came to be called the Garden of Allah.

"In the moonlight the row of two-room bungalows looked remarkably like mausoleums. It was uncanny, he thought, how many talented men of his generation had chosen these stucco tombs. Were they unconsciously laying their talents to rest? Bob Benchley... Scott Fitzgerald—they and many more had all lain here. Some of the bodies, he thought bitterly, had not yet been removed. As he approached his bungalow he could hear the infectious early-morning laughter of Mr. Benchley sitting up with friends..."

The Garden of Allah was demolished in August, 1959, to clear the way for a bank and its parking lot. Joni Mitchell's famous song, "Big Yellow Taxi," was written about this loss:

"Don't it always seem to go
You don't know what you've got till it's gone
They paved paradise and put up a parking lot..."
From "Big Yellow Taxi"
By Joni Mitchell.

The Garden Court Apartments [site]
7021 Hollywood Boulevard

Built in 1919 on this site and razed in 1985, the Garden Court was the luxurious home of many Hollywood notables, including Mack Sennett, Lillian Gish, Rudolph Valentino, John Barrymore, Mae Murray, Louis B. Mayer, Fay Wray and both Laurel & Hardy. An Italian Renaissance structure, it had Oriental carpets and baby grand pianos in every suite, as well as two extravagant ballrooms, a billiards room, tennis courts, and a swimming pool.

Gower Gulch
Sunset & Gower

It's now a little shopping center designed in Western style, but it once was the corner for all the real cowboys to congregate in Hollywood while waiting to work in films at nearby studios.

Grauman's Chinese Theater
6925 Hollywood Boulevard

It's the most famous movie theater in the world. Built by Sid Grauman in 1927, this is one of Hollywood's icons, featuring the famous forecourt of stars' hand and footprints. The actress Anna Mae Wong drove the first rivet into its steel girders when construction commenced in 1925. It opened on May 18, 1927 with a premiere of Cecil B. DeMille's *King of Kings*, amazing those in attendance with its beautifully rendered murals, carved ceiling and ornate columns.

Mary Pickford, Douglas Fairbanks and Norma Talmadge were the first stars to take part in a footprint ceremony, and were soon followed by much of Hollywood's royalty, including Humphrey Bogart, Marilyn Monroe and Judy Garland. Harpo Marx's bare footprints can be found here, as can Durante's nose, and one of Bette Grable's legs. This is a rare opportunity to literally stand in the footprints of the stars.

The Griffith Observatory

2800 East Observatory Road

It was the vision of Colonel Griffith Griffith, who owned all the land that is now Griffith Park, to build an observatory in the hills. In 1930, more than a decade after his death, the city accepted a grant from his estate to finance its construction, which took five years to complete. The observatory opened in 1935, and today is famous to movie fans for its usage in *Rebel without a Cause* starring James Dean, as well as many other films. The observatory grounds often serve as a focal point for the community, who have congregated here on many occasions. Most recently crowds came here to observe a rare meteor shower in November of 2001, and on December 2, 2001 to pay tribute to George Harrison of the Beatles, whose death from cancer in Los Angeles on November 30, 2001, shocked and saddened his devoted fans in Hollywood and around the world.

Plans were set into motion in 2001 to radically rebuild, renovate and expand the observatory, which will be closed for several years during this operation.

The Hightower

End of Hightower Drive, off of Camrose

Built in 1920 as part of the Hollywood Heights development, it was used extensively in the Altman version of Chandler's *The Long Goodbye* with Elliot Gould and Nina Pallandt. It features a rectangular, Bolognese-style elevator, which carries key-carrying residents between their homes high on the hill, and their garages down at street level.

Hollygrove Orphanage

Childhood Home of Marilyn Monroe

815 El Centro

Formerly the L.A. Orphans Home Society, which dates back to 1880, it's been here since 1911. The front building was razed in 1977, and this new one was built on the site. A ten-year-old Marilyn

Monroe was brought here in 1936 to live, and according to legend, screamed, "No, I don't belong here, I'm not an orphan!" because her mother was still alive. Marilyn would look out of her fourth floor window at the RKO sign on Melrose, and dream of being a star.

She was born Norma Jean Mortenson on the first day of June, 1926. Because her mother was institutionalized repeatedly, she was raised in a series of foster homes and also for many years here at Hollygrove. She went on to become perhaps the most luminous of all of Hollywood's stars; to this day her image remains as iconic and evocative of Hollywood as those of Chaplin, Bogart, Groucho Marx, and very few others.

317

Her first professional work was as a model, and by the age of twenty her photos were in magazines around the country. Howard Hughes noticed her magnetic smile and brought her to RKO for a screen test, but before he could sign her, 20th Century Fox offered her a contract that she accepted. She renamed herself Marilyn Monroe and prepared herself for stardom. Fox had little for her to do, however, and in 1948, she signed on with Columbia, but they also dropped her after a short time. In 1949, she appeared in *Love Happy* with the Marx Brothers and, in 1950, got her first good part in a good film, as the mistress of an evil attorney in John Huston's *The Asphalt Jungle*. This led to a small part in *All about Eve*. Her natural gift for comedy was first discovered in *Gentlemen Prefer Blondes* and its follow-up, *How to Marry a Millionaire*, both of which went a long way in establishing her as a major star. This coincided with the publication in the first-ever issue of *Playboy* magazine of nude photos she had posed for years earlier originally for a calendar, and the world found in Marilyn someone vulnerable, funny, beautiful and very sexy.

In 1954, she married baseball legend Joe Dimaggio, and in 1955, she starred in Billy Wilder's comedy *The Seven-Year Itch*. To broaden her acting, she moved to New

York to study with Lee Strasberg at the Actors' Studio; while in New York, she met the playwright Arthur Miller, who was to be her next husband following the break-up of her marriage to Dimaggio. In 1956, she starred in a film version of William Inge's hit Broadway show Bus Stop, and in 1959, she co-starred with Jack Lemmon and Tony Curtis in the Billy Wilder–directed classic Some Like It Hot. Her final finished film was John Huston's The Misfits, which was also the final film for its other stars, Clark Gable and Montgomery Clift. Marilyn started work on Something's Got to Give in 1962, but was fired after only a month of work on it. She was found dead in her West L.A. home on August 5, 1962, from an overdose of barbiturates. To this day, facts of her death remain unknown; thousands of theories abound on the subjects, as many as those surrounding the death of President John Kennedy, who was assassinated in Texas in 1963. Many have suggested that Marilyn was murdered in order to hide her relationships with JFK and with his brother Robert Kennedy, who was assassinated in Los Angeles in 1968.

The actress Shelley Winters, who was a roommate of Marilyn's during their early days in Hollywood, remembers coming out of the Circle Theater at night, where they had been invited by Charlie Chaplin's son Sydney to attend a rehearsal there that his father was directing. Marilyn stared at the building across the street, Hollygrove. "That's the orphan asylum I lived in most of my life," Marilyn said. "That's where my foster parents would ship me back to when they decided they didn't want me anymore."

The Hollywood Sign and Hollywoodland

The Hollywood Sign is an icon of Americana, one of the most famous and recognizable logos in all of the world. The current metal sign which is standing today on the south side of Mt. Lee is not the original one, but a replica of the first sign, which was covered with thousands of light-bulbs, and considerably longer, spelling out the name HOLLYWOOD-LAND.

Early photos of that Hollywoodland sign have led many to erroneously assume that Hollywoodland was the original name of the entire area, from which Hollywood became its abbreviated nickname. In fact, the reverse is true. Hollywoodland was a real-estate development created intentionally to cash in on the existing cache of Hollywood itself, already a burgeoning empire in 1923. Hollywoodland was a 500-acre real estate development being built by L.A. Times owner Harry Chandler and his partners. Situated high in the Hollywood hills at the northern edge of Beachwood Canyon, Hollywoodland was envisioned as a little storybook community that would benefit from its location, high up in the hills north of the Hollywood flats. As newspaper advertisements for Hollywoodland promised at the time, the development would benefit from being "above the traffic congestion, smoke, fog, and poisonous gas fumes of the Lowlands."

A house for film pioneer Mack Sennett was planned, sold and designed at the summit of Hollywoodland, but never built. Instead the lot was bought by the Don Lee Broadcasting Company and later acquired by the City of Los Angeles as an addition to Griffith Park.

Intended to be as temporary as a billboard, the original sign cost $21,000 to construct. Situated high on the chapparal-covered side of Mt. Lee, it had thirteen gargantuan letters, thirty feet wide and fifty feet tall. They were held in place by a ramshackle scaffold of pipes, wires and telephone poles. A line of twenty-watt bulbs ran around each letter and illuminated each syllable of the name in sequence: HOLLY . . . WOOD . . . LAND.

The upkeep of the sign was completely halted, ironically, in a year that was one of Hollywood's grandest: 1939, the year of Oz and Gone with the Wind. But already the bad habit of abandoning the landmarks of

318

physical Hollywood had started. Most of the sign's original lightbulbs had been stolen or broken, and the previously stately symbol of prosperity was allowed to decay.

Toward the end of 1944, the developers of Hollywoodland, The M.H. Sherman Company, deeded the land on which the sign stands to the City of L.A. Following World War II, the Hollywood Chamber of Commerce entered into a contract with the Department of Recreation and Parks to repair and rebuild the sign at an estimate of $4,000. They removed the sign's final four letters so that it could stand as a symbol for all of Hollywood.

By the seventies the sign was once again showing its age, and so the Hollywood Chamber of Commerce launched a campaign to generate funds to rebuild it This crusade gathered swift momentum, and in a rare show of support by various stars of the entertainment industry for the preservation and celebration of a Hollywood landmark, a diverse group of luminaries stepped forward to provide the necessary finances to build the new sign. Hugh Hefner, Alice Cooper, Gene Autry and Andy Williams, among others, each pledged $27,000 per letter to construct a sturdier, all-metal version of the famous landmark. Stretching some 450 feet across the mountainside, a sturdier new sign was erected, with letters each forty-five feet tall, and a total weight of 480,000 pounds.

The Hollywood Sign was officially reborn on the seventy-fifth anniversary of Hollywood, November 11, 1978, and televised by CBS nationally as the *Hollywood Diamond Jubilee* to an audience of 60 million people throughout America.

Hollywood Boulevard (x)

It is the main thoroughfare of Hollywood, which was formerly known as Prospect Avenue. It's south of Franklin Avenue and north of Sunset Boulevard, and runs roughly parallel to both; to the east it merges with Sunset Boulevard in

what is today Silverlake. To the west it ends at Laurel Canyon Boulevard.

Douglas Fairbanks Jr.: "In those days (circa 1915), Hollywood Boulevard was not built up and there were many vacant lots between the one- and two-story buildings, interspersed by two or three small suburban movie theaters that line the way for a few miles. Mother often told how she and my father used to go to one or the other of the movie theaters along the not very brightly lit boulevard. They would frequently be accompanied by a friend. . . . Walking home after the show, my father, who loved playing practical jokes, would stride along well ahead of the rest. Then he would hide behind a bush or in the high grass in one of the vacant lots and, as the others passed by, suddenly jump out to frighten them."

319

Hollywood American Legion Post

2035 N. Highland Avenue

Built in 1929, this American Legion Post was created in a great blend of Egyptian Revival and Moroccan art deco styles. Many of Hollywood's movie stars that served in the war passed through here, including Clark Gable, Humphrey Bogart, Gene Autry, Ronald Reagan, Ernest Borgnine, and Adolphe Menjou.

Hollywood Athletic Club

6525 Sunset Boulevard

Built in 1924, it was an ultraexclusive club whose members included Johnny Weismuller, Rudolph Valentino, and Charlie Chaplin. Buster Crabbe was often found there doing countless laps in the pool; John Wayne once threw billiard balls from the roof at cars. Walt Disney, after an early nervous breakdown, worked out here at the advice of his doctor. Abbott & Costello both stayed here, as did Bela Lugosi. In 1949, it was used as the site for the first televised Emmy awards.

The Hollywood Bowl

2301 North Highland Avenue

The Hollywood Bowl was constructed on what was a natural amphitheater in the hills known as the Daisy Dell. The land, once covered with sage and chapparal, was owned by Myra Hershey, who also owned the Hollywood Hotel, and selected as a location for the Bowl by Christine Weatherill Stevenson, who wrote The Pilgrimage Play to be presented at the Bowl and other nearby locations. Mrs. Artie Mason Carter, the president of a choral group in Hollywood called Community Sing, who had the idea in 1917 of starting a series of outdoor concerts there in the site of the bowl by the L.A. Philharmonic, and raised money for stage, lighting and benches. The first performance was on July 11, 1922, with conductor William Andrews Clark Jr. conducting the overture to Rienzi by Wagner. Los Angeles' County Board of Supervisors saw fit to give $100,000 in 1924 to improve the Bowl, and in 1929, the famous all-white all-steel performance shell was designed by Lloyd Wright, becoming Hollywood's most famous landmark at the time.

320

The Hollywood Canteen [site]

1451 Cahuenga

Founded in a former stable here by John Garfield and Bette Davis in 1942, the Canteen entertained thousands of servicemen during WWII. It opened with a gala emceed by Eddie Cantor that featured the Duke Ellington Orchestra, Abbott & Costello and others. Hollywood's greatest stars volunteered their time at the Canteen; Fred MacMurray, Basil Rathbone, John Garfield and other male stars worked as busboys, while starlets such as Marlene Deitrich, Betty Grable, Greer Garson, and Olivia de Havilland would serve food and dance with the servicemen. Today it's yet another amorphous parking lot.

Hollywood Center Studios
Jasper Studios
Zoetrope

1040 N. Las Palmas

Built in 1916 by C.E. Toberman, this was originally the Jasper Studios. Harold Lloyd filmed several of his early silent comedies here. Howard Hughes produced his second film here, Everybody's Acting in 1927 starring Jean Harlow in her debut film performance. Like many of the smaller studios, this one was the home of many different companies: It was the Metropolitan Studios until 1931, at which time it became the Hollywood General Studios. In 1980, it was purchased by Francis Ford Coppola and became Zoetrope Studios, where he made the classic One from the Heart.

Hollywood Heritage Museum

2100 N. Highland Avenue

(323) 874-2276

Hollywood's first feature-length movie, The Squaw Man, directed by Cecil B. DeMille, was filmed in this barn in 1913, when it was on Vine. When DeMille and Lasky began to build Paramount Pictures on the site of the barn, they preserved the building and kept it in their backlots, where it was used in countless movies. In 1956, DeMille had it declared a California Historical Landmark, and in 1984, it was moved to its present location by the Hollywood Heritage organization, which has dedicated it as a museum of silent pictures.

Hollywood High School

1521 N. Highland Avenue

"At the corner of Highland and Sunset," wrote Fay Wray, "Hollywood High School was fronted with broad, sweeping lawns; the buildings bordered with poinsettias." One of the oldest high schools in Los Angeles, Hollywood High was built back in 1904 in the midst of what was then a series of bean fields bordering on a lemon grove. Many of the first students used to travel to school on horseback. Generations of movie stars spent formative years here, including Jason Robards, Fay Wray, Marge Champion, Ruta Lee, Sally Kellerman, Carol Burnett, Yvette Mimieux, Stephanie Powers, James Garner, Joel McCrae and Lana Turner, who was discovered at the Top Hat Café, a malt shop across the street, and not at Schwab's, as was often reported. Inside there is an Alumni Museum that honors graduates who "achieved the honorable," and exhibits memorabilia donated by former students.

The Hollywood Hotel [site]
Hollywood & Highland

Built in 1903 as part of one of the first developments within Hollywood, it was purchased in 1907 by Myra Hershey, from the Pennsylvania family who made their fortune selling Hershey's chocolate. The first luxury hotel built in Hollywood, it boasted a great ballroom of chandeliers and gold stars painting onto the ceiling, honoring the many stars who stayed here, including Douglas Fairbanks, Anita Stewart, Flora Finch, and Lon Chaney. It stood a full city block wide on Hollywood Boulevard from Highland to Orchid. "On the corner of Hollywood and Highland," wrote Fay Wray in 1919, "the Hollywood Hotel had a long veranda that was edged with bright red geraniums. The look and feel of everything was caressingly beautiful. . . . When walking down Highland to Hollywood Boulevard, there was the fragrance of orange blossoms. The air itself was soft and gently warm as if satisfied because it was California. On Hollywood Boulevard, pepper trees shaded the street. The long, slender branches of the trees were filled with gray-green leaves that partly covered tiny red berries clustered near the tips of the branches, smelling very pungent like real pepper."

"As I remember it," wrote L.A. Times columnist/author Jack Smith, "the hotel

was mission-Victorian in style, if such a combination is possible, with a grab bag of arches, balconies, turrets and cupolas and a broad veranda from which its inhabitants watched the life and death of a legend. The hotel sat back from the street behind grass and was shaded by palm trees whose uprooting caused more anguish than the razing of the rambling old hotel itself."

Valentino stayed here in Room 264 on his honeymoon with his first wife, Jean Acker; however, before being allowed to carry his new bride over the threshold, he was required to show his new marriage license as proof of matrimony. It is said that Acker came back to the hotel in the early fifties, decades since Valentino had been dead, asked to see the room, looked at it for a split-second, and then quickly left.

The songwriter Carrie Jacobs-Bond wrote one of her most famous songs, "The End of a Perfect Day," here at the hotel in 1909.

The movie *Hollywood Hotel* took place at the hotel, and spawned the famous song, "Hooray for Hollywood," with music by Richard Whiting, and lyrics by Johnny Mercer.

It was razed in 1956 and replaced by a nondescript office-building and parking lot that were subsequently destroyed only a few decades later to make the way for the sprawling "Hollywood-Highland" project and subway stop under construction during the writing of this book.

Hollywoodland Stone Gates
Beachwood Drive

Located at the entrance of Hollywoodland real estate development and built of rock quarried from Griffith Park, the gate was designated a monument in 1968. The east half of the gate is owned by Hollywoodlander Nadia Scarpitta, widow of the famed sculptor Salvadore Scarpitta. The original storybook cottage that houses the

321

Hollywoodland real estate office still stands and operates just past these gates. The center of "Beachwood Village"—the intersection here of Beachwood & Belder—was immortalized in the original *Invasion of the Body Snatchers*, starring Dana Wynter and Kevin McCarthy, in which it was used as the center of a small town of zombies.

Hollywood Theatre

6764 Hollywood Boulevard

It's the oldest existent movie house in all of Hollywood. It opened in 1913, not long after the movies became a prominent pastime, though prices here were already more than at other American theaters. Admission was 10 cents for adults and a nickel for kids, with preferential loge seating that cost 15 cents. In 1938, it was remodeled into this Art Deco style; the marquee is one of the first one in all of Los Angeles to reflect the age of the automobile: instead of the original flat sign which was designed to be seen by pedestrians, a new triangular sign was installed which offered angles both east and west, designed to be seen from a passing car.

The Harvey Hotel

5640 Santa Monica Boulevard

Janet Leigh's first home in Hollywood, where she lived with her husband in 1945: "[I] looked in dismay at the four-story Harvey Hotel. It was run-down, sleazy. But the price was right—seven dollars a week for a room and a bath on the third floor. And there was a place to rehearse in the basement. . . . The curtains were heavy with dust and dirt, and when I finally wrestled the window open, I found the view to be a littered alley and another old building." But she made the most of it, she said, and would eat her breakfast every morning at the drugstore on Western & Santa Monica. "Usually Rice Krispies," she wrote, "for 10 cents."

Hollywood Forever Cemetery

6000 Santa Monica Boulevard

Established in 1899 before the movies officially arrived, it's Hollywood's oldest cemetery, and the final resting place of so many Hollywood legends, and their families: Rudolph Valentino, Harry Cohn, Douglas Fairbanks Sr., Douglas Fairbanks Jr., Cecil B. DeMille, Jesse Lasky Sr., Jesse Lasky Jr., the Ritz Brothers, Nelson Eddy, Jayne Mansfield, Marion Davies, Tyrone Power, Peter Lorre, Hattie McDaniels, Peter Finch, "Bugsy" Siegel, John Huston, and many others, including several significant stars of the silent era.

Though one would assume there is a wall separating the south end of the cemetery with the northern edge of Paramount, in fact there is no boundary at all between the two; the walls of Paramount are built to the extreme edge of their property, and are all that separate the studio from the tombs.

Of course, it makes sense that the studio and the cemetery should be connected; so many of Hollywood's stars are laid to rest here, including two of Paramount's founders, DeMille and Lasky, as well as Valentino, their first international star.

Originally all of what is Paramount today—as well as the former RKO lot at Gower & Melrose, now also a part of Paramount—was on the grounds of the cemetery, which originally stretched all the way from Santa Monica to the north, Melrose to the south, Gower to the west and Van Ness to the east. But no bodies were ever buried in the southern end of the graveyard, and that land was sold to the Peralta Studios—the site of Paramount—in 1917.

Frequent hauntings have been attributed to this cemetery, and some have claimed that ghosts have been known to spill into the adjoining lots of Paramount. Historian Marc Wanamaker related a story, which was excluded from the book *Holly-*

wood Haunted which he co-wrote with Laurie Jacobson, involving two Paramount prop men working in and out of the prop building, adjoining the cemetery grounds. Each night they would load in large, wooden furniture that was being used on sets—heavy chairs, tables, and such. Each morning when they would return, this furniture was found in disarray, as if somebody had come in and intentionally moved everything, even throwing some of the chairs a good distance. After many instances of this, the two prop men started to feel a little spooked but reasoned that it must be a practical joke someone was playing on them.

So to root out the joker, they hid out one night, after loading in the furniture, to see what would happen. After a few hours passed, all the chairs and tables began to move and slide around the floor of the prop building as if people were pushing them. But nobody but them was in the room. They immediately ran out of the building. In retrospect they wondered if it wasn't some kind of magnetism responsible for shifting the furniture. But given that each piece was wooden, it seemed pretty unlikely. "It's not something they were comfortable talking about," Wanamaker said.

Hollywood Forever, as it's presently known, was originally called the Hollywood Memorial Cemetery, and its past has been somewhat checkered. Though they were willing to provide a grave for known murderers, such as "Bugsy" Siegel, they refused burial to all blacks. Though Oscar winner Hattie McDaniel said that her final wish was to be buried here, she was kept out. [In 1999, a cenotaph memorial was built for her here, although she is not buried on the premises. There is also a cenotaph here for Jayne Mansfield.]

The former owner-manager of the cemetery, Jules Roth, embezzled some $9 million from the business, propelling it deeply into bankruptcy and decay. When he died in 1998, and was subsequently buried on his own property, the park was

in ruins, and families were forced to dis-inter loved ones in order to have them buried elsewhere.

Fortunately a young entrepreneur by the name of Tyler Cassity purchased the park (for only $375,000; less than the price of a typical home in the Hollywood hills), and brought it back to life, regreening the lawns, renovating the buildings, and creating 60,000 new gravesites. He's also introduced innovations designed to bring this cemetery, which was born at the conclusion of the nineteenth century, in line with the twenty-first—he's installed virtual libraries, digital scrapbooks, and on-site interactive biographies of those interred.

What follows is a list of notable Hollywood people who forever rest at Hollywood Forever:

323

Mel Blanc, 1908–1989. Section 13, Pineland Section, Lot 149, near the road.
"The Man of a Thousand Voices," he started off on radio, co-starring with his wife in a weekly show from Portland, Oregon, titled "Cobwebs and Nuts" for which he provided most of the character voices himself. Starting in 1937, he began doing voices for Warner Brothers' cartoons, debuting with the voice of a drunken bull in the *Looney Tune* cartoon "Picador Porky." He took over the stuttering voice of Porky Pig, with the trademark sign-off, "Th-th-th-that's all, Folks." He also provided the voice for the lisping Daffy Duck, and the eternally wise-cracking Bugs Bunny, as well as Sylvester, Foghorn Leghorn, Speedy Gonzales, Tweety Pie, Pepe Le Pew, Yosemite Sam, Barney Rubble from "The Flintstones" and Cosmo Spacely from "The Jetsons." His grave bears the inscription, "That's All, Folks."

Charles Chaplin Jr., 1925–1968, Abbey of the Palms, Corridor E-2, Crypt 1065.
He was the son of Charlie Chaplin, buried here directly next to his

maternal grandmother, Lillian Grey, the mother of Chaplin's first wife, Lita Grey. Since Lita was only a teenager when she married Chaplin, Lillian lived with them in Chaplin's Beverly Hills mansion.

Charlie Jr. did not have an easy time following in his father's formidable footsteps. Not only did he share his father's name, he also resembled his father, and as a young man he grew a small mustache exactly like the iconic mustache his father wore in the role of the Little Tramp. Shelley Winters, who attended many parties at the Chaplins' home in the forties, remembers Charlie Jr. as "a very introverted and friendless boy." She went on to suggest that "Chaplin senior could not admit to himself that Charles junior was emotionally backward.... The years have confirmed my opinion because, although he wrote a lengthy autobiography before he died, Chaplin senior never mentioned Charlie junior." In 1968, years after his father left America to live out his remaining days in Switzerland, Charlie Jr. took his own life.

Hannah Chaplin, 1866–1928, Section B, behind Douras (Marion Davies) crypt.

She was an actress, and the mother of Charlie Chaplin, who chose to have her buried here instead of their native England when she died in 1928.

The poet Federico Garcia Lorca, like many other poets, recognized the inherent visual poetry of Chaplin's silent comedies. During his lifetime he made various ventures into Hollywood, and got to know both Chaplin and his family. Upon the death of Hannah Chaplin, he was inspired to write an extended prose poem called "The Death of Charlot's Mother," which can be found in his *Collected Works*. One of the most moving, humorous, and remarkable eulogies ever written, it concurrently praises the unique greatness of his beloved

"Charlot" while memorializing the death of his newly sainted mother:

"When I was in California, I was the guest of Charlie Chaplin's mother. She was an extremely thin woman who cried every day when she heard the Angelus. She was natural and gentle. Despite what the newspapers say, she was never an intellectual. She wore her husband's shoes. She was one of those untidy women who, at a moment's notice, could produce a marvelous pheasant stew.

"When her son ate his shoe, she knew it was time to die. She had fulfilled her mission. That salted fish of an Englishwoman knew just the right moment to stretch out in the coffin. The wake was beautiful...

"... Goodbye Charlot's mother. Your tragedy as an actress has been the most moving in modern theater. You wanted to appear in Shakespeare with the eyes of a lioness in heat, but you looked like a bruised boxer... Goodbye. Goodbye. Goodbye. Why did you go to North America with a little trunk and a peacock feather? Tell me. Who was the first to dress your son in Caiphas' pants and the hat of thorns?

"... Now upon receiving news of his mother's death, Charlot hasn't cried. He has fainted.... Charlot with wings. Charlot of the swans. Charlot of the lilies of the valley... Charlot's mother was placed under a shroud by her favorite dog, assisted by a nun.... The dead woman's face was serene.... Charlot had the good grace to accept all funeral wreaths.... Mr. Benito Mussolini sent one made from rifle bullets, with a beautiful Italian opera of solid silver in the center. Rockefeller sent one of esparto grass....

"At the feet of the corpse Charlot has placed the first little shirt he wore as a child... More than a million stars have filed past the black velvet cloth. All of California is in mourning: The Governor has sent magnolia branches to all the gas stations."

William Clark Jr. 1897–1941. The Clark Mausoleum, in the middle of the pond in section 8.

He founded the Los Angeles Philharmonic in 1924 and had this mausoleum surrounded by a miniature lake, now teeming with ducks and geese, constructed in 1920. It cost over $250,000 to build then, and would cost many millions today. A copper magnate and railroad owner, he is interred here between his two wives.

Iron Eyes Cody, 1907–1999. Abbey of the Psalms, crypt 3301, corridor H-4-1.

The Native American actor was in many films, including *A Man Called Horse*, and is best remembered as the tearful Indian in the "Keep America Beautiful" TV and magazine campaign of the seventies. He was born Oscar DeCorti on April 3, 1907, in Gueydan, Louisiana. As a child, he performed in Wild West shows, and made his first film appearance as an extra in the 1919 film *Back to God's Country*. He went on to appear in countless films, and he also served as a consultant about Native American customs for various film-makers. He toured for many years with Tim McCoy's and Buck Jones' Wild West shows as well as with the Ringling Brothers & Barnum and Bailey Circus. He died in Los Angeles on January 4, 1999.

Harry Cohn, 1891–1958. Section 8, Lot 86, directly across from Cathedral Mausoleum.

He founded Columbia, located just six blocks away at the intersection of Sunset & Gower, and was not tremendously well liked. "[He was] a vulgar, ill-tempered, loud-mouthed bully," wrote Douglas Fairbanks Jr., who is interred in the tomb of his father only a stone's throw away from Cohn's family crypt. Cohn chose this location himself for his family tomb. "I picked out a great plot," he said. "It's right by the water, and I can see the studio from here."

Viola Dana (Virginia Flugrath), 1897–1987, Chapel Colonade, Tier 4, Niche 6-7.

A great star of the silent screen, she made a remarkable eighty-eight movies in her career, co-starring with Buster Keaton in many of his comic classics. She starred on Broadway while still a teen, which led to a film contract with the Edison studios, for whom she made *Children of Eve* (1915), *The Cossack Whip* (1916) and *Blue Jeans* (1917). In the twenties she made many movies under contract to Metro, and in 1928 made her last silent film, *That Certain Thing*, for Columbia. Her voice was deemed wrong for her image, and so her movie career ended with the advent of sound movies. She went on to the vaudeville circuit for a few years, and then retired from show business. She was married to the Western star "Lefty" Flynn.

Marion Davies [marked Douras], 1897–1961. Douras Mausoleum, Section 8, Lot 261-264.

Born Marion Douras, she was a silent-movie star and the long-time mistress of William Randolph Hearst.[4] Her nephew, Arthur Lake, the actor who played Dagwood Bumstead on the "Blondie" TV show, is also interred here in the family mausoleum. Born in 1897, she lived at the Hollywood Hotel when she first came to town, before moving to homes in Beverly Hills and Santa Monica. When she died in 1961, like so many who moved west during their famous lives, she returned to rest forever in Hollywood. Laid to rest in a solid bronze casket covered with pink carnations, she was interred in the mausoleum she purchased herself here for her family, between the graves of Charlie Chaplin's mother Hannah and Tyrone Power. The mausoleum bears her family name, Douras.

William Desmond Deane-Tanner (aka William Desmond Taylor), 1877–1922. Cathedral Mausoleum, #594

He was one of Paramount's leading directors of the silent era until his murder in 1922. Discovered dead in his

---

4 For more on Marion Davies, see Bob Board, page 198.

apartment with a bullet through his back, his murder remains unsolved to this day. Two of his famous girlfriends, silent stars Mabel Normand and Mary Miles Minter, were both suspected of being responsible for the murder. Though nothing was proved, their careers were both ruined by this tragedy.

Cecil B. DeMille,[5] 1881–1959, Section 8, north side of lake.

326

He was one of the first and most famous of all movie directors. He directed the first feature film ever made in Hollywood, *The Squaw Man*, and with Jesse Lasky and Sam Goldwyn, established one of Hollywood's first movie companies to produce it, The Lasky-Players Company. His first film was *The Virginian* (1914), and he went on to make both silent films and talkies into the fifties, including *The Ten Commandments* (1923) *The King of Kings* (1927), *Cleopatra* (1934), *Union Pacific* (1939), *Reap the Wild Wind* (1942), *Samson and Delilah* (1950), *The Greatest Show on Earth* (1952), and his final film, *The Ten Commandments* (1956). He played himself in the classic *Sunset Boulevard*, in which Gloria Swanson spoke the famous lines, "Mr. DeMille, I'm ready for my close-up."

Nelson Eddy, 1901–1967, Section 8, lot 89.

He was an opera star first, but is most famous for his passionate, nose-to-nose duets in films with Jeannette McDonald. Born at the turn of the century in Providence, Rhode Island, he was a singer and actor. He appeared in a 1924 version of *Pagliacci* at the New York Metropolitan Opera. In the thirties, his success on radio and in concert led to a contract with MGM. In 1935, he made his first of many films with Jeanette MacDonald, with whom he gained his greatest fame; for years they were known as "America's Sweethearts." Their final film was *I Married an*

Angel (1942). He retired from films in 1947 to devote himself entirely to singing, both recording and concerts. He died onstage in Australia during a 1967 tour.

Douglas Fairbanks Sr., 1883–1939.
Douglas Fairbanks Jr., 1909–2000. Both father and son are interred in Section 11, in the sunken garden tomb with reflecting pool to the right of the Cathedral Mausoleum.

Douglas Fairbanks Sr. was one of the very first stars of the silent screen, and along with his wife Mary Pickford and Charlie Chaplin, founded the United Artists film company. His is one of the most beautiful gravesites here, replete with a long reflecting pool. But it's not his first grave, as his son recalled: "[My] stepmother Sylvia had decided... to move my father's body from the Forest Lawn Cemetery closer to 'home' in the Hollywood Cemetery. She commissioned a striking classical marble monument with a bronze bust of Pete on a sort of plinth in its center, to be set at the end of a long, ornamented, lagoonlike pool." Fairbanks Sr., who died in the cinematic landmark year of 1939, was moved to this site in 1941. Mary Pickford, his first wife, is still buried at Forest Lawn.

Fairbanks' son, Douglas Fairbanks Jr., was a movie star of the thirties and forties, and the first husband of Joan Crawford. Despite his public resistance to his step-mother's plans for this tomb, he was interred here himself, next to his father, in the year 2000.

His step-mother was Lady Sylvia Ashley, who was also the fourth wife of Clark Gable; their marriage lasted just under two years. She was also buried here when she died in 1977, but not in this tomb; she can be found in Section Eight, next to her final husband, a prince by the name of Djordjadze.

---

[5] For more on DeMille, see "A History of Hollywood," page 19; Lothrop Worth, page 64; Else Blangstead, page 169; and Evelyn Keyes, page 127.

Peter Finch, 1916–1977. Cathedral Mausoleum, corridor A, crypt 1224.

Born and raised in Sydney, Australia, he starred in many Australian films before moving to Hollywood. He won a posthumous Oscar for his famous role in the film *Network*, where he uttered the memorable chant, "I'm mad as hell, and I'm not gonna take it anymore." His remains remained in an unmarked grave near Marion Davies' mausoleum for two years until his widow had them moved into this crypt facing Valentino.

Victor Fleming, 1883–1949. Abbey of the Psalms, Crypt 2081, Corridor G-2.

Born in Pasadena, California, he began his career as an assistant cameraman for directors D.W. Griffith and Allan Dwan. By 1919 he was directing his own films, starting with *When the Clouds Roll By* and *The Mollycoddle*. In the thirties he signed with MGM, where he made *Treasure Island* and *Captains Courageous*. He directed two of Hollywood's most famous and beloved films, both in 1939: *The Wizard of Oz* was first, after which he took over the reins of *Gone with the Wind*. In the forties he directed *Dr. Jekyll & Mr. Hyde*, *Tortilla Flat*, and *A Guy Named Joe*, all starring Spencer Tracy. His last film was *Joan of Arc* (1948), which starred Ingrid Bergman.

Joe Frisco, 1889–1958. Section 8.

"Hollywood," he famously said, is "the only town in the world where you can wake up in the morning and listen to the birds coughing in the trees." Born Louis Joseph in Illinois, he was a vaudeville comedian famous for his distinctive style of comic "jazz dancing," which *Variety* dubbed "The Jewish Charleston." His movements had a profound influence on the comedy of the Marx Brothers, who imitated his dancing in their stageshows and would even sing his signature song, "The Darktown Strutter's Ball." Groucho Marx often praised him, and said that he "was a good comic and a great dancer." Frisco made his Broadway debut in *The Zeigfeld Follies of 1918*, worked the Vaudeville circuit throughout the twenties, worked nightclubs during the thirties, and in the forties came to Hollywood to act in movies, including the first Atlantic City. Forever immortalized in 1925 by F. Scott Fitzgerald, Frisco is named in a passage from the classic Jazz Age novel, *The Great Gatsby*, which has often confused people who assumed it was a reference to the shaking of the San Francisco earthquake. The setting is a cocktail party, in which a young woman spontaneously starts to dance: "Suddenly one of these gypsies," wrote Fitzgerald, "in trembling opal, seizes a cocktail out of the air, dumps it down for courage, and moving her hands like Frisco, dances out alone on the canvas platform."

Janet Gaynor, 1906–1984, Section 8, Lot 193.

Born Laura Gainor in Philadelphia, she was a silent movie star who started off in Hal Roach comedy shorts. Signed to Fox in the mid-twenties, her first big role was in *The Johnstown Flood* (1926). From that she went onto starring roles in such classic silent films as *Sunrise*, directed by Murnau and *Seventh Heaven*, directed by Borzage. She made a successful transition into talkies, and became a romantic star in the thirties, often teamed with Charles Farrell. In 1939, she retired from movies, and married the legendary fashion and costume designer Gilbert Adrian, with whom she lived in a famous house, The Villa Vallambrosa in Whitley Heights.[6] She returned to occasional film and TV roles in the

---

[6] For more on Whitley Heights, see "A Tour of Hollywood," page 357.

fifties, and in the eighties appeared on Broadway in a stage production of *Harold & Maude*. She is interred here next to her husband Gilbert Adrian.

Griffith J. Griffith, 1850–1919, Section 7, Lakeview Ave Obelisk.

A major landowner of much of early L.A., he donated all the land that is now Griffith Park—over 3,000 acres—to the city of Los Angeles, which created the largest city park in the world. Griffith was convicted of attempted murder in 1903, after shooting his wife, who somehow survived, in the eye. A major drinker, he was apparently a paranoiac as well, accusing his wife of plotting with the pope to poison him and take over the country. He served one year of a two-year sentence at San Quentin. It was his idea to build the Greek Theater in Griffith Park, and in 1930, more than a decade after his death, the city accepted a grant—some say reluctantly—from his estate to finance its construction.

Joan Hackett, 1934–1983. Abbey of the Psalms, corridor D-3, crypt 2314.

She started her career as a model, studied acting with Lee Strasberg, and appeared in many TV shows and movies. She starred on Broadway in 1961 in *Call Me by My Rightful Name* and in 1966 made her first film, *The Group*. In 1968, she starred with Charlton Heston in *Will Penny*. She appeared in regular roles on TV shows "The Defenders" and "Another Day." In the eighties she appeared in movies that included *Only When I Laugh* (1981) and *One Trick Pony*. Her crypt bears the unwelcoming imprint: "Go away, I'm sleeping."

Mildred Harris, 1901–1944. Abbey of the Psalms, second corridor, #740.

She was a silent-movie star who successfully made the transition into talkies. She was also the first of Charlie

328

Chaplin's four wives who became known as "Innocent Mildred Harris" because of her marriage to Chaplin— she was only sixteen at the time; he was twenty-eight. Between 1912—when she was only eleven years old—and the year of her death, 1944, she appeared in more than one hundred movies.

Woody Herman, 1913–1987. Behind the Cathedral Mausoleum, Crypt 6689, Unit 10.

A jazz legend, he sang and tap-danced in vaudeville as a kid, and by the age of twelve was already a virtuoso of the clarinet and saxophone. By the time he was fifteen he was good enough to play with dance bands, and soon was hired by a series of bands. A stint with Isham Jones' Juniors led to Herman taking over the band, which became known as "The Band That Plays the Blues." By 1944, after many changes of personnel, the band became the First Herd, with whom he made several great records. Moving from Big Band into Bop, he formed a new group known as the "Four Brothers" band, which was known for its especially burning and distinctive sax section. By the time of his third herd of musicians in the fifties, times were hard for big bands, and he fell out of favor. Still he persisted, and in following decades he formed new bands known as the Thundering Herd and the Swinging Herd. In the eighties he suffered from ill health and business woes—his manager embezzled all of his money, leaving him destitute and unable to afford to pay his taxes or the payments on his home in the Hollywood Hills. He went on tour again to generate money, and in 1986 celebrated his fiftieth anniversary as a bandleader.

John Huston,[7] 1906–1987, Section 8, Lot 6, west of the lake.

The son of actor and singer Walter

[7] See also Evelyn Keyes, page 127.

Huston, he was born in Nevada, Missouri, and traveled around the world as a kid. He started off as a writer, moving to Hollywood in 1937. His first film as a director was a classic, *The Maltese Falcon* (1941), which he made for Warner Bros., and which starred Humphrey Bogart and Peter Lorre, and which immediately established Huston's reputation as a tremendously gifted storyteller. He went on to make a string of classic films, including *The Treasure of the Sierra Madre* (1948), *The African Queen* (1951), *Beat the Devil* (1953), *Moby Dick* (1956), and *The Misfits* (1961). His final film was *Prizzi's Honor* in 1985. He also made several appearances as an actor in other people's films, most notably in Roman Polanski's classic *Chinatown*.

Barbara LaMarr, 1896–1926 Cathedral Mausoleum, #1308.

She was born Reatha Watson, she had already been married four times before she did any movies. She started writing movies before she acted in any, which happened when Louis B. Mayer cast her in *Harriet and the Piper* (1920). Her big break came that same year when she played the wicked Milady in *The Three Musketeers*, starring Douglas Fairbanks. Known as the "Girl Who Was Too Beautiful," she was as melodramatic offscreen as she was on, and lived a wild life of alcohol and drugs. She collapsed on the set of her last film, *The Girl from Montmartre* (1926), and died soon thereafter. It was the same year that Valentino also died at the height of his career, and like Valentino's burial, a minor riot broke out among heartbroken fans on the day she was interred. Various causes of her death were offered, including tuberculosis, "nervous exhaustion," and "overdieting" as one doctor worded it.

Jesse Lasky Sr., 1880–1958. Abbey of the Psalms, Crypt 2196, Corridor G-3.

He was the founder of the Jesse Lasky Feature Play Company, which later became Paramount Pictures. Lasky was a musician who led bands in Hawaii and also performed in vaudeville. His sister was married to Sam Goldfish (later Goldwyn), with whom Lasky formed a movie studio and made their first film, directed by Cecil B. DeMille (who is also buried here), in 1914. In time Paramount became one of the major movie studios in the world, as it remains today. But Lasky lost his job there during the Depression and became an independent producer, forming in 1935 the short-lived Pickford-Lasky company with Mary Pickford. By the fifties, in great debt to the IRS, Lasky returned to Paramount as a producer.[8]

Jesse Lasky Jr., 1910–1988, Chapel Mausoleum, second floor.

He was Jesse Lasky Sr.'s son, and the writer of *The Ten Commandments* and *Samson & Delilah*. He also wrote novels, plays and a memoir entitled *Whatever Happened to Hollywood?*

Florence Lawrence, 1890–1938. Section 2, under pine tree near northeast corner.

She was a silent-movie star, known as the "Biograph Girl" for starring in the Biograph films of D.W. Griffith. She was the first movie star to be known to the public by her own name, a development that the movie moguls resisted so as to keep their stars' fame—and salaries—in check. Lured by Carl Laemmle to leave Biograph and join his Independent Motion Picture Company of America, she was involved in one of the movie's first-ever phony publicity stunts: Laemmle leaked the story that Lawrence had been killed; the next day he issued a statement that

329

---

[8] See also "A History of Hollywood," page 18, for more on Lasky.

her death was a hoax started by the enemies of his studio. This statement also coincided, of course, with the news that Lawrence had left Biograph to join his company. Her first film for him was *The Broken Oath* (1910) in which she appeared under her real name. She was an actress who could not make that bridge from silents into talkies, however, and by the mid-thirties her career had stalled. She accepted a contract from MGM to play bit-parts, but by 1938 she had enough of the movies and life itself, and took her own by ingesting insecticide.

Henry "Pathe" Lehrman, 1886–1946. Section 8, Lot 257, next to Virginia Rappe.

A director, actor, and screenwriter, he was in love with Virginia Rappe at the time of her death, and was planning to propose to her. Devastated by her death, he paid to have her buried here beside the site of his own grave by the lake. He would visit her grave each week until his own death, more than two decades later.

Elmo Lincoln, 1889–1952. Chapel colonnade 02, niche 20-J, North wall.

He was Hollywood's first Tarzan, the star of the 1918 silent movie *Tarzan of the Apes*. A former cop from Arkansas who stood over six feet tall and weighed 230 pounds, he caught the attention of D.W. Griffith, who cast him as the blacksmith White Arm Joe in *Birth of a Nation* (1915) and as The Mighty Man of Valor in *Intolerance* (1916). When the actor slated to star in the original version of *Tarzan of the Apes* dropped out of the film to fight in World War I, Lincoln took over his role, forever securing him a place in cinema history. He also played Tarzan in two sequels, and starred in other films before retiring to Salt Lake City to run a salvage company. A few years later he returned to Hollywood, where he took on bit roles in some new Tarzan films and assorted Westerns.

Peter Lorre, 1904–1964. Cathedral Mausoleum, Niche 5, T-1, Corridor C.

Born Ladislav Loewenstein on June 6, 1904, in Budapest, Hungary, he went on to become one of Hollywood greatest and most distinctive stars, forever remembered for his classic roles along Bogart and others in such films as *The Maltese Falcon* and *Casablanca*. He started acting on the stage, where in Germany he worked with the legendary Bertolt Brecht, appearing in many of Brecht's plays. In 1933, he fled Nazi Germany for Britain, where he began working in films, and appeared in Hitchcock's *The Man Who Knew Too Much* (1934) before he had even mastered English. He appeared in other films prior to being signed by 20th Century Fox contract in 1936, for whom he portrayed the Japanese detective Mr. Moto in a series of movies, as well as many other films. In the forties he signed with Warners, and played the wicked Joel Cairo in *The Maltese Falcon* (1941) with Bogart and Sidney Greenstreet. He continued to appear in many films and TV shows throughout the fifties and sixties, including a series of Edgar Allen Poe movies directed by Roger Corman that he co-starred in with Basil Rathbone, Vincent Price, and Boris Karloff. His final film was *The Patsy* (1964) with Jerry Lewis.

Los Angeles Times Memorial, 1910.

Twenty-two men were killed when the *Los Angeles Times'* printing facility was bombed on October 1, 1901. The bombers, who ultimately confessed, were two brothers. Both were labor union members in dispute with management. This is a memorial to those workers who were tragically killed.

Adolphe Menjou, 1890–1963, Section 8, Lot 11

Born in Pittsburgh, Pennsylvania, Menjou started off as an extra, and then got a string of small movie roles. His break came in 1923 when Charlie Chaplin cast him in *A Woman of Paris*, which was Chaplin's first noncomedic

220

movie. It made Menjou a star; his distinctively dapper suits and waxed mustache became almost as iconic as Chaplin's "Little Tramp" suit and mustache. Menjou continued to play this dapper role in consecutive films for years, a propensity that earned him the title, "The Best Dressed Man In Hollywood." In 1931, he starred in *The Front Page*, for which he received a Best Actor Oscar nomination. A long-time champion of conservative causes, in 1947 he testified as a "friendly witness" before the House Un-American Activities Committee.[9]

Jayne Mansfield, 1933–1967. Section 8, by the lake. [Cenotaph.]

She was born Vera Jayne Palmer in Bryn Mawr, Pennsylvania. Like Marilyn Monroe, her tremendous sex appeal distracted many from noticing her acting ability at first, and she worked as a cheesecake photo model. But she eventually made people notice her acting in the Broadway hit, *Will Success Spoil Rock Hunter*. This led to her signing with Fox, where she made the movie version of *Rock Hunter* and *The Girl Can't Help It* (1956). Married three times, her second husband was the muscleman Mickey Hargitay, and her third was Matt Cimber, who became her agent. Cimber guided her career in the sixties. She made *Promises, Promises* in 1963, in which time she became the first major American actress to appear nude, and also made live appearances throughout the country in nightclubs. It was while on her way to a night club appearance in New Orleans in 1967 that she died in a car accident. The sight of her blonde wig in the wreckage, thrown far from her body following the accident, led to the rampant rumor that she was decapitated, which was not true.

June Mathis (Balboni), 1892–1927. Cathedral Mausoleum, #1199.

She was a writer and movie executive, and the woman who discovered Valentino. It was she who proposed that he take the leading role in *The Four Horsemen of the Apocalypse*, which she wrote, and which established him as the major romantic star of the movies. Upon his death, she was the only one to come forward to provide a crypt for Valentino, with the assumption that a formal tomb would be ultimately provided for him. She then purchased an additional crypt for herself, and died less than a year after Valentino's death. Her mother, Virginia Mathis, is buried directly below Valentino's crypt. Ironically, she and Valentino came here often together to visit the crypt of her mother.

231

Hattie McDaniel, 1895–1952. Section 8, facing the road. [Cenotaph.]

This monumental actress won an Oscar for the Best Supporting Actress in 1940 for her portrayal of "Mammy" in *Gone with the Wind*; she was the first black actor to ever win one. She started out as a blues singer, and toured the country in *Show Boat*, in the same role she would play in the 1936 film version. She appeared in many movies, including *Blonde Venus* (1932) with Marlene Dietrich, *I'm No Angel* (1933) with Mae West, and *The Shopworn Angel* (1938) with Margaret Sullavan. She was also a star of radio, playing the lead role in the popular "Beulah" series. Though she had her heart set on being buried among the other stars at this cemetery, at the time of her death in 1952, no blacks were allowed to be buried here in what was considered still "a white cemetery." This monument, which fulfilled her final wishes, was erected in 1999.

Paul Muni, 1895–1967. Section 14, grave 57.

The Best Actor Oscar recipient of 1936 for his lead role in *The Story of Louis*

Pasteur, he was the son of two touring actors in the Yiddish theater. Born Muni Weisenfreund in Lemberg, Austria, he moved to America with his family in 1902. He joined a Yiddish theater group when he was still a child, often playing old men. His first performance speaking English didn't occur till he was twenty-nine. In 1926, he appeared on Broadway in the show We Americans. In 1929, he signed with Fox and started doing movies and Broadway shows concurrently. He played one of filmdom's first and most famous gangsters in the original Scarface (1932). He then signed with Warner Brothers, where he made his most famous movies, transforming himself into the roles of historic personages, in The Story of Louis Pasteur, The Life of Emile Zola, and Juarez. Muni played almost every ethnic type except a Jew, which was his true identity, leading the writer Neal Gabler, in his book An Empire of Their Own, to suggest that Muni's career was a "paradigm for the tortured identity of the actor Jew in Hollywood, always dressed in someone else's ethnicity."

In 1955, Muni returned to Broadway for his Tony-winning portrayal of the Clarence Darrow figure, Henry Drummond, in Inherit the Wind. His final film was The Last Angry Man.

Art Pepper, 1925–1982, Abbey of the Psalms.

A jazz legend known for his intense, emotional playing, he was born in Gardena, California, and started on clarinet before moving on to the alto sax. He played with the Gus Arnheim band and also sat in with several all-black bands who played in clubs along Central Avenue in L.A. He performed with great players such as Dexter Gordon and Benny Carter, and had begun to play with Stan Kenton when he was drafted into the army. He spent most of the war in England, after which he returned to America and the

332

Kenton band. It was at this time he recorded a beautiful version of "Over the Rainbow" with Shorty Rogers. During the fifties and sixties, he established his own solo career, and though derailed by drug addiction, arrests, and incarceration, he made some beautiful, timeless music. Toward the end of his life he recorded a string of classic albums, including Winter Moon, the three-album set Live at the Village Vanguard and others.

Eleanor Powell, 1912–1982. Cathedral Mausoleum, niche 432, Tier 3.

Known as the "The World's Greatest Female Tap Dancer," she was discovered when she was only eleven. She was a Broadway phenomenon before she was twenty, starring in many revues. In 1935, she made her first film appearance, in George White's Scandals of 1935, and the following year she signed on with MGM, where she made a string of famous musicals starting with Broadway Melody of 1936. She retired from the movies in 1943, and married actor Glenn Ford. She was lured out of retirement to appear in two more films, and following a divorce from Ford, she put together a night club act, which she performed in Las Vegas and New York. In her final years she put much of her effort into charity work, and for a short stint hosted a Sunday morning TV show for kids.

Tyrone Power, 1914–1958. Section 8, Bench monument facing pond.

One of the movie's most handsome leading men, he was actually Tyrone Power III, a third generation actor. His grandfather, the first Tyrone Power, was a famous Irish comedian, and his father, Tyrone Power the Younger, as he was known, was a major star of the classical stage. Tyrone III was born in Cincinnati, where he acted with his father in a production of The Merchant Of Venice. He moved to Hollywood, where his innate talent plus his startling good looks led him to some small roles,

starting with *Tom Brown of Culver* in 1936.
He signed with 20th Century Fox, and
began taking on leading roles. After
only about a year, he was a major star,
famous for his swashbuckling sword-
fighting period roles. He served in the
marines during World War II,
returning to Hollywood in '47 to do
the film *Nightmare Alley*. In 1958, he
acted in *Witness for the Prosecution*,
directed by Billy Wilder, and began
work on the movie *Solomon and Sheba*.
While shooting a dueling scene with
George Sanders, he suffered a heart
attack from which he didn't survive.
His tombstone, in the form of a bench
by the lake, includes the masks of
Comedy and Tragedy. He was a serious
actor, but one who didn't take his
filmic allure too seriously. "The secret
of charm," he once said, "is bullshit."

Virginia Rappe, 1896–1921. Section 8, lot
257, next to Henry Lehrman.

She died in 1921 at the age of
twenty-six after a night of revelry at a
San Francisco hotel, launching one of
the first and still most infamous of all
Hollywood scandals. The prosecution
accused the great silent-movie comedian Roscoe "Fatty" Arbuckle of this
crime, alleging that he raped Rappe
with a glass bottle, which broke inside
her, perforating her bladder. Fatty was
tried and ultimately acquitted of this
crime, but although his innocence was
established, his career was destroyed
forever.

Henry Lehrman, a producer and
director, was in love with Rappe, and
paid to have her buried here beside his
own grave by the lake. He visited her
every week from the time of her death
in 1921 to the time of his own in 1946.
It's been said that a "faint sobbing" has
been heard near her grave.

Nelson Riddle, 1921–1985. Beth Olam
Mausoleum, Niche 702.

One of Hollywood's premiere
music arrangers and conductors, he
provided lush orchestral support for

many artists, including Judy Garland,
Nat King Cole, Ella Fitzgerald, Julie
Andrews, Oscar Peterson, Rosemary
Clooney, Johnny Mathis and Frank
Sinatra. He was also a composer, and
wrote themes and scores for such films
as *The St. Louis Blues* and *Pajama Game* and
TV shows including "Route 66" and
"The Untouchables." In 1974, he won
the Best Music Oscar for his score to
The Great Gatsby, and in the eighties he
arranged and conducted two Grammy-
winning albums for Linda Ronstadt.

The Ritz Brothers:

Al Ritz, 1901–1965. Beth Olam Mausoleum T-4.

Jimmy Ritz, 1904–1985. Beth Olam Mausoleum T-5.

Harry Ritz, 1907–1986. Beth Olam Mausoleum, third floor.

These three sons of a haberdasher
grew up in New Jersey and Brooklyn.
Their real name, Joachim, was
switched to Ritz after they all graduated high school, decided they wanted
to team up, and spotted the name on a
laundry truck. Like other comics at the
time, they gradually ascended through
the ranks of nightclubs and vaudeville
and the Broadway stage, and became
famous for their fusion of comedy,
singing and dancing. They made their
first movie appearance in a 1934
comedy called *Hotel Anchovy*, and soon
thereafter were signed to Fox, where
they starred in 1937's *Life Begins in College*.
In 1939 came *The Three Musketeers*, considered by critics to be their best film.
Sadly, their movie career began to
decline, and Fox dropped them from
the roster. They returned to nightclubs,
where they could always pack the
room. They then made an assortment
of B movies at Universal, including
Never a Dull Moment in 1943. Al Ritz died
in 1965, and though Harry and Jimmy
kept the act going, they gradually
moved into retirement, only occasionally stepping out to make a professional appearance. Harry, always

considered the funniest of the three, made a memorable contribution to Mel Brooks' film *Silent Movie*. Brooks stated at the time that the Ritz Brothers were his idols.

Benjamin "Bugsy" Siegel, 1906–1947. Beth Olam Mausoleum, Crypt 1087, Corridor M-2.

He was one of the Mafia's most ruthless killers. Born in Brooklyn, he and the mobster Meyer Lansky formed a gang together when they were still kids, the Bug & Meyer Group. They provided protection for those who would pay, and death to those who didn't. They sold illegal whiskey during Prohibition, and following that got into bookmaking and gambling. Though his nickname was "Bugsy" throughout his life, he hated it and would not allow anyone to use it in his presence. He moved to Beverly Hills, where he ran a wire service to gamble on horseracing, and befriended many of Hollywood's elite, including George Raft, with whom he became good friends, as well as Jack Warner, Cary Grant, Barbara Hutton and Jean Harlow. In the thirties, he lived in the famed Castillo Del Lago (page 304) in the hills above Lake Hollywood and actually ran a speakeasy and a gambling den there. In 1940, he purchased his own Las Vegas casino, the Frontier Club. His vision was to instill Hollywood glamour in Vegas, and he teamed up with Billy Wilkerson, owner of the *Hollywood Reporter* and Hollywood nightspots Ciro's and the Trocadero to build the Flamingo, and establish the Las Vegas strip. He was shot to death at the age of forty-one in the Beverly Hills home of his girlfriend, Virginia Hill. One explanation for his murder was that he was skimming money from the profits of the casino, but this was never proved.

Carl "Alfalfa" Switzer 1927–1959, Section 6, Lot 26, Grave 6

He and his brother Harold used to attract a lot of attention by singing back in their hometown of Paris, Illinois, so while visiting Hollywood they went over to the Hal Roach studio commissary, started singing one of their well-rehearsed hillbilly duets, and both immediately earned a contract to appear in Roach comedies. Though Harold's career went nowhere, Carl changed his name to Alfalfa and became one of the beloved stars of the *Our Gang* movie series, in which he sported a cute cowlick and sang intentionally off-key for comic effect. Like many child stars, he found it hard to land adult roles, with the exception of the *Track of the Cat* (1954), and a somewhat recurring roles on Roy Rogers' TV show. He died tragically at the age of thirty-two when he was shot and killed in an argument over a fifty dollar debt.

The Talmadge Sisters

Norma Talmadge, 1893–1957, Abbey of the Psalms, Talmadge Room, Corridor G-7.

Natalie Talmadge, 1895–1969, Abbey of the Psalms, Talmadge Room, Corridor G-7.

Constance Talmadge, 1897–1973, Abbey of the Psalms, Talmadge Room, Corridor G-7.

These three beautiful sisters were all actresses during the silent era. Norma, however, was far more famous than her sisters, one of the true queens of the silent screen. She started making movies when she was only a child, and by the age of fourteen was already a star, playing the lead in Vitagraph's 1911 production of *A Tale of Two Cities*. She married Joseph Schenk, who began producing her films and those of her sister Natalie; he also provided a mansion where they lived along with Norma's two sisters and their mother. Schenk did everything in his substantial power to make Norma a star, and succeeded. She appeared in over 200 silent movies, including *The Ghosts of Yesterday, Love's Redemption* (1921), *Ashes of*

334

Vengeance (1923), and *Camille* (1927). Her heavy New York accent, which she never had to shake while in silents, proved to be a stumbling block in her transition to talkies, and her career came to a halt. Though she did star in two talkies, by 1930 she was finished with the movies, and the movies were finished with her. She never relegated her stardom, however, living a diva's life through the thirties, remarried to the comedian George Jessel. By the forties, though, she became reclusive, divorcing Jessel and remaining mostly secluded in her home, a relic of a bygone time. Many have proposed that the character of "Norma Desmond" in Billy Wilder's *Sunset Boulevard*, famous for the line, "I am big, it's the *pictures* that got small," was based on Norma Talmadge.

Natalie Talmadge, or "Nat" as she known, made the fewest films of the three sisters—only five—and started out not as an actress but a writer, creating the script to the 1918 comedy *Out West*, starring Fatty Arbuckle. During the making of that film she met her future husband, silent screen legend Buster Keaton, with whom she was married from 1921 to 1932. She starred with Keaton in her final film, *Our Hospitality*, made in 1923, and retired permanently after giving birth to their second child.

Constance Talmadge was the youngest sister, and a star of D.W. Griffith's *Intolerance*, in which she played the Mountain Girl in the Babylonian sequence. Though legend tells us that *Intolerance* was a universally hated, colossal flop, it's not entirely true. Although much of the movie-going public was perplexed by its many-storied plot line, the film was loved by many, especially those who were enchanted with the fetching Mountain Girl. To capitalize on her popularity, in later years Griffith actually released an edited version of the film that cut out

almost everything but those scenes featuring the luminous Miss Talmadge. She became one of the first women in Hollywood with her own production companies, and starred in many films, including *The Matrimaniac* (with Douglas Fairbanks), *A Virtuous Vamp, Polly of the Follies*, and 1929's *Venus*, her final film. Rather than diminish her cinematic eminence by appearing in talkies, when the silent era ended, she retired forever from films.

C.E. Toberman, 1880–1981, Abbey of the Psalms, Crypt #4, Room E, Building G-9.

One of the principal builders of Hollywood buildings, he was responsible for building the Roosevelt Hotel, Grauman's Chinese Theater, the Egyptian, the Bank of America building (at Hollywood & Highland), and many others. His estate still stands in Hollywood, at the northern end of Camino Palmero, a couple of houses up from Ozzie & Harriet's former residence.

Gregg Toland, 1904–1948. Chapel Colonade, second floor.

The cinematographer of one of cinema's most remarkable films, *Citizen Kane*, directed by and starring Orson Welles, he also shaped the visual grandeur of *Wuthering Heights* (1936, for which he won the Oscar for Best cinematography), *The Best Years of Our Lives* (1946), *The Grapes of Wrath* (1940), and *The Little Foxes* (1941). Born in Charleston, Illinois, he invented a noiseless camera enclosure that was a great boon to the advent of sound movies. He developed a great visual style previously unseen in the movies. "His work was remarkably evocative," wrote Jason Ankeny, "spanning the urban sprawl of William Wyler's 1937 effort *Dead End* to the documentary-like grit of *The Grapes of Wrath*. . . . After offering his services to Orson Welles, Toland was given free rein to experiment on *Kane*, using coated lenses and arc lights to create a depth of focus staggering in its clarity and ability to capture the minutiae of each scene."

Rudolph Valentino, 1895–1926. Cathedral Mausoleum, Crypt 1205, off Corridor A.

He was born Rodolpho Alfonzo Raffaelo Pierre Filbert Guglielme di Valentina d'Antonguolla in the small Italian town of Castellaneta. He moved to Hollywood in 1913, where he was discovered by the screenwriter June Mathis. It was she who proposed that he take the leading role in *The Four Horsemen of the Apocalypse*, which launched his career and established him as the major romantic star of the movies. He died tragically at the age of thirty-one in August of '26, after collapsing during a New York premiere of his newest film, a sequel to *The Sheik* called *Son of the Sheik*. A funeral was held in New York at Campbell's funeral parlor, where over 100,000 people came to pay their last respects, an event that evolved into a riot as people waited in line for one last look of this film icon.

Some 10,000 people crowded into the cemetery here when he was entombed in what was to be a temporary resting place. His friend, June Mathis Balboni, who discovered him, allowed the crypt she owned above the crypt of her mother, Virginia Mathis, to be used until a proper memorial to Valentino could be constructed. It was a location Valentino had been to many times during his life; he and June used to come to this very corner to visit the grave of June's mother. But to this day, nobody has ever come forth to finance the construction of Valentino's memorial, and he remains interred in this temporary crypt.

It's here that the legendary "Lady in Black" has appeared periodically since 1931 to leave roses on his grave. The actual identity of this mysterious figure has been in dispute for years, as more than one woman has claimed the title, while others insist that the entire thing was a publicity scam invented in the thirties to keep Valentino's name, and legend, alive.

Clifton Webb, 1889–1966. Abbey of the Psalms, Crypt 2350, Corridor G-6

He was a dancer, singer and actor, and all by the age of ten. Born Webb Parmallee Hollenbeck in Indianapolis, he acted onstage both on Broadway and in London, and always maintained a successful stage career even after acting in movies. In the forties, he became a movie actor exclusively, and began landing major roles in films such as *Laura* (1944), *The Razor's Edge* (1946), and *Sitting Pretty* (1948), all of which earned him Oscar nominations. Many have claimed that they've seen his ghost wandering both inside and outside of the Abbey of the Psalms.

Harvey Henderson Wilcox, 1832–1891. Cathedral Mausoleum, #990

Daeida Wilcox Beveridge, 1861–1914. Cathedral Mausoleum, #989

The founders of Hollywood.

The Palace

1735 N.Vine Street

It opened in 1927 as the Hollywood Playhouse, became the El Capitan in the forties, and the Hollywood Palace in the sixties. The famous radio show *Ken Murray's Blackouts* originated here, as did many TV shows, including "This Is Your Life" and "Live from the Hollywood Palace." These days it's been beautifully restored as a live music venue; many of the world's top music acts have performed here.

Hollywood Roosevelt Hotel

7000 Hollywood Boulevard

Constructed in 1927, The Roosevelt was one of Hollywood's first great hotels, and was owned originally by silent stars Mary Pickford and Douglas Fairbanks and the director Louie B. Mayer. The very first Academy Awards banquet was held here in the Blossom Room in 1929. Countless legends stayed here over the years, including Marilyn Monroe, who did her first-ever commercial photo shoot by the pool, as well as Clark Gable, Montgomery Clift, Carole Lombard and many others.

The hotel's night club, which continues to present top music acts to this day, is the Cinegrill, and provided a showcase for such stars as Mary Martin. Other celebrities were frequently found at the bar and in the audience of the Cinegrill, including Frank Capra, Dick Powell, W.C. Fields, Errol Flynn, and Ronald Reagan. The Cinegrill has been used as the iconic Hollywood night club in several movies, of which the most famous is *The Fabulous Baker Boys* (1989), in which Michelle Pfeiffer belts out a torch song while sprawled across the top of a baby grand.

Though the Roosevelt went through hard times in the sixties and was allowed to deteriorate, it was completely renovated at the end of the eighties, at which time all attempts at cheap modernization were thankfully removed, and its original Spanish Colonial design, with beautiful balconies, hand-crafted columns and hand-painted ceilings, was restored. A fine History of Hollywood photo collection is on permanent display in its second floor gallery.

The artist David Hockney even made a unique contribution to the history of Hollywood by painting the floor of the outdoor swimming pool with wavy blue lines, which created a beautiful effect when viewed through the water, with the sunshine willowing across. Sadly, the painting is mostly faded away today, the apparent victim of too many days of hot sun and chlorine.

Howard Hughes Headquarters

7010-50 Romaine

This was operation central for Howard Hughes for many years. Hughes, who was born on Christmas Eve of 1905 in Houston, Texas, first came to Hollywood at the age of twenty as the affluent heir to the Hughes Tool Company. A lover of movies, he bought his way into the business by establishing his own movie company in 1925, which he named Caddo Productions. Their first production was a silent film called *Swell Hogan*, which upon viewing was so clearly awful that Hughes never released it. His next film, and first release, was *Everybody's Acting* (1926). The following year he released *Two Arabian Nights*.

In was in that year, 1927, that Hughes moved the Caddo Pictures company into this building, later turning it into a virtual fortress when he ran his Summa Corporation here. In 1929, he produced his first film about his passion for aviation called *Caddo's Hell's Angels*, which began its life as a silent film starring Greta Nissen and gradually became a Talkie starring Jean Harlow, as Hughes became convinced sound movies were more than a novelty.

In 1930, he produced the explicitly violent gangster film, *Scarface*, but held up its release for two years, building on the public's anticipation, which paid off and made the movie a hit. He did the same thing in the forties when he postponed the release of *The Outlaw*, starring his personal discovery, the extremely buxom Jane Russell, for whom Hughes is said to have created a special cantilevered brassiere designed to show off her assets to full advantage.

Between 1932 and 1940, Hughes focused on aviation and other endeavors and had little to do with Hollywood. He released *The Outlaw* in 1946, and in 1948 took control of RKO by buying 929,000 shares of their stock. Three years later, after laying off the majority of their employees and essentially decimating a once great studio, Hughes purchased all available RKO stock himself at double its value, and then sold the studio to General Teleradio, Inc., a subsidiary of General Tire and Rubber, pocketing a profit of $10 million. His last film for RKO was *Affair with a Stranger* (1953).

227

The Janes House
6541 Hollywood Boulevard

This was the home of Mary and Herman Janes and their three daughters, Carrie, Mabel and Grace. Now pushed about fifty yards back on the property from its original location closer to the boulevard, it's the last remaining house along Hollywood Boulevard, a street once replete with many blocks of Victorian homes. A combination of a Queen Anne Victorian and a Dutch Colonial Revival home, and accented by archaic turrets and shingled gables, it was constructed in 1905 when Hollywood Boulevard was still a dusty road known as Prospect Avenue.

380

Starting in 1911, Mary and her daughters ran a school in the house; initially it was kindergarten only, and was called The Misses Janes School of Hollywood. Attended by children of many famous film figures, including Charlie Chaplin, Douglas Fairbanks Sr., Jesse Lasky, Thomas Ince, and Cecil B. DeMille, it closed in 1926. The sisters continued to live in the house following the death of their parents, and thankfully saved the house from the wrecking ball, even though they fell onto tough financial times. They rented out the usage of their expansive front yard as a parking lot and flower shop. The last surviving sister, Carrie, lived on in the house until 1982 before being moved to a nursing home, where she died a year later.

The author Henry Farrell, who wrote the novel on which the movie *Whatever Happened to Baby Jane?* was based, is said to have gotten the idea for his story from the Janes sisters. Bette Davis played Jane Hudson; the street the house faces was called Hudson until being changed to Schrader Avenue in 1999.

Today this distinguished residence resides at the rear of a modern minimall, and houses the official Visitors Information Center for Hollywood, which is open Monday through Saturday, from 9 A.M. to 5 P.M.

KABC-TV / Vitagraph Studio Lot
4151 Prospect Street

Built in 1917 for the Vitagraph movie company, it was purchased in 1925 by Warner Brothers, who renamed it the Warner Brothers-Vitagraph Studio. The silent star Norma Talmadge made many of her most famous films here. In 1948, it was purchased by the ABC Radio Network for use in the new medium of television. To this day it is still an ABC Television studio, and is used to shoot many network soap operas, local news shows, and other TV productions.

KCET-TV/Lubin Studios
4401 Sunset Boulevard

Built in 1912 by the Lubin Movie Company, it's been in continual use ever since, and has been the home of succession of movie companies, such as the Essanay Company, the Kalem Company and Allied Artists before becoming the permanent home of Los Angeles' Public Television station, KCET in 1970. From 1940 to 1950, it was the Monogram Studios, where the *East Side Kids* movies as well as the *Charlie Chan* serials were made. The soundstages and red brick buildings that are still standing were built in 1920. In 1952, when this was the Allied Artists Studios, the *Attack of the Fifty Foot Woman* and *Invasion of the Body Snatchers* were made here. Free tours of the studio are given during working hours on weekdays.

The Buster Keaton Studio [site] (and other Buster Keaton movie locations) Lone Star, Chaplin's First Studio
1025 Lillian Way (off Romaine, one block west of Cahuenga)

Before Buster Keaton took over this studio, it was Charlie Chaplin's first Hollywood studio, originally called the Climax

Studio and renamed Lone Star in Chaplin's honor. It was purchased for Chaplin in 1916 when he signed with Mutual Films to make a dozen two-reel films. Chaplin made many of his early, classic shorts here, including *The Floorwalker*, *Easy Street*, and *The Immigrant*.

In 1920, this became the Buster Keaton Studio, and is memorialized by a plaque in the street—albeit one that is placed in the wrong place—at the southwest rather than southeast corner of Lillian Way & Eleanor, which reads:

> "Buster Keaton Studio, 1920–1928.
> Site of the original Buster Keaton studio,
> the birthplace of a unique type of motion picture comedy.
> Here the genius of Buster Keaton made history with pictures which brought laughter to the world."

Keaton was a true genius of silent comedy. Born Joseph Francis Keaton Jr. on October 4, 1895, it was his precocious and prodigious ability to be tossed around on the vaudeville stage by his father that earned him the name Buster. As a member of the Three Keatons along with both parents, he developed the unique blend of athletic prowess and comic grace that he brought to the movies. He acted in his first silent film in 1917, and soon was enlisted as comic support for comic great Fatty Arbuckle in a string of short films. His unique unsmiling screen persona, an everyman in the grueling everyday modern world, caught on with the public, and Keaton was soon starring in own films, of which the first was *The Saphead*. He began writing and directing his own films, which led to the greatest work of his life, since, as Jonathan Winters said, "Nobody could write for Buster Keaton." In the early twenties he began producing a series of classics, often showcasing ingenious and elaborate sight gags, such as *Sherlock Jr.* (1924), in which he walks from a movie theater directly into the movie showing onscreen.

Though he made successive comic masterpieces, such as *The Navigator* (1924), *The General* (1927), and *Steamboat Bill Jr.* (1928) and became, along with Chaplin, one of the world's most beloved comic figures, he was unable to make the transition from silents into talkies. He signed with MGM, who demanded control of his movies. Powerless to express his own vision, his popularity evaporated. Still the master of the silent gag, he wrote bits for Red Skelton, who used them on his popular TV show, as well as Harpo Marx, who persisted throughout his career in being a silent comic even within the realm of the Marx Brother's talking pictures.

Charlie Chaplin cast Keaton as a fellow vaudevillian in one of Chaplin's final films, *Limelight* (1952). But according to author and professor Roger Manville, former head of the British Film Board, so brilliant were many of Keaton's bits in *Limelight* that Chaplin, not wanting to be outshone in his own film, left many of these on the cutting room floor.

Keaton also played a small part as one of the "waxworks" in the movie *Sunset Boulevard*, the old friends from Norma Desmond's silent-movie days that come to play bridge. Keaton also appeared in Stanley Kramer's *It's a Mad, Mad, Mad, Mad World*, and *A Funny Thing Happened on the Way to the Forum*. He died in Woodland Hills, California, on February 1, 1966, and is buried at Forest Lawn in Glendale.

Keaton never felt his comedy could be easily confined to a studio, and for that reason his films were often shot in the streets surrounding his studio, as well as the streets and alleys of greater Los Angeles. What follows are some of the various Keaton movie locations within Hollywood:

1604, 1612, 1614, 1616 Cahuenga Boulevard

In his film, *The Cameraman*, Keaton is shown riding a fire truck north on Cahuenga, passing all of these buildings which stand on the east side of the street.

1542 Cahuenga Boulevard

This building, which stands on the east side of the street was seen in his film, *The Goat*, and previously adjoined the now nonexistent Toribuchi Grocery, which stood at 1546 Cahuenga, and is now a strip mall. Keaton is seen running from cops in this film, past this building and the former grocery store.

1629 Cosmo Street

For the film *Cops*, Keaton shot on this section of Cosmo, a short sidestreet south off of Hollywood Boulevard, between Cahuenga and Ivar. He is shown on Cosmo loading up a wagon full of furniture, and later, being bitten by a dog there.

Alley, just south of Hollywood & Cahuenga.

This alley, which now runs directly to the right of the World News newsstand near the Southeast corner of Hollywood & Cahuenga, was used by Keaton in one of his most famous gags. Also from *Cops*, it's a scene in which Keaton reaches out with one hand to reach a handle on a passing car, causing him to fly fleetly from the frame. The scene was shot on Cahuenga, directly in front of this alley.

1629 Cahuenga Boulevard

Now the site of the Edmonds Tower on the west side of Cahuenga, owned by songwriter-producer Kenneth "Babyface" Edmonds, this was formerly the location of the Hollywood branch of the Los Angeles Police Department, which adjoined the former fire station at 1625 Cahuenga. In the film *Three Ages*, Keaton can be seen running from the cops at this location. He also used the fire station again as a location in his 1928 film, *The Cameraman*.

All of the Keaton location information referred to here derives from a great source of Hollywood and Keaton history, *Silent Echoes*, by John Bengston, in which the author painstakingly matched stills from Keaton's films with historic pho-tographs to determine the actual location of all of these scenes.

The Knickerbocker Hotel

1714 Ivar

Now a senior residence, the Knickerbocker was built in 1925 after the population of Hollywood exploded. Designed by the architect E.M. Frasier in 1923 in the luxurious Renaissance Revival/Beaux Arts style, it was a glamorous hotel that was popular with celebrities from both coasts. Rudy Vallee, Gloria Swanson, Dick Powell, Bette Davis, and Errol Flynn all lived here, and both Frank Sinatra and Elvis Presley stayed here many times. Harry Houdini also stayed here when he came to Hollywood, and his widow held a seance for him here on the roof in 1936.

One of the true pioneers of movies, D.W. Griffith, the director of *Birth of a Nation* and *Intolerance*, lived his last years here. Though he was known as "The Man Who Invented Hollywood," he made his last film in 1931, and lived as mostly a forgotten man here until his death in 1948. At his funeral, the president of the Motion Picture Academy said, "When he is dead, a man's career has but one tense. The laurels are fresh on the triumphant brow. He lies here, the embittered years forgotten."

In 1943, the actress Frances Farmer was arrested here in her room for failing to report to her parole officer regarding a previous drunk & disorderly conviction, a combustible scene that was reenacted in the film *Frances*, starring Jessica Lange. " I was living at the Knickerbocker Hotel in Hollywood," wrote Farmer in her autobiography, "and late one night, after I had retired, three policemen disturbed the whole floor by pounding on my door. When I would not admit them, they forcibly entered, shoved a warrant in my hand, and hauled me off to the Santa Monica jail. . . . My reaction was violent! Everything exploded!"

In 1962, the legendary MGM costume designer Irene, who had worked on famous films such as *Gaslight, Easter Parade,* and *State of the Union,* committed suicide here by jumping out of her eleventh-floor window. She was said to have been down-hearted over the recent death of her husband and ensuing business problems.

The bar is said to be abundantly haunted.

THE KROTONA COLONY

"Truth is a pathless land," wrote Jiddu Krishnamurti, who became the central spiritual leader of a religious group called Krotona, which established a colony in the Hollywood hills before moving to Ojai in 1922. Krotona was a branch of what was known as the Modern Theosophical Movement, and was established in Hollywood by Albert Warrington.[10] Their main administrative building, at 6235 Primrose Avenue, was established in an existing Victorian house on the Hastings Ranch and converted into an office building in late 1912.

The architectural firm of Arthur Heineman was contracted to design and build the new colony, which required the construction of six large buildings to house a Theosophical University, as well as a series of villas for followers to live in, a few administrative buildings, and a large temple. Not all of these buildings were ultimately constructed.

The Krotona Inn

2130 Vista Del Mar Avenue

In the year 1912 one of the most signif-icant Krotona buildings was constructed: The Krotona Inn. Built both to house the profusion of students who came to Kro-tona as well as to hold lectures, it was designed by the San Diego firm of Mead & Requa., and financed by Krotonian Augustus F. Knudsen. Completed on April 6, 1913, it has Moorish turrets, horseshoe-shaped arches and a "psychic lotus pond" in the courtyard. Though it's now been

converted into an apartment building, it once contained dining rooms, lecture rooms and residential quarters. There was a special domed spiritual space known as the "Esoteric Room," which was used for group meditation.

An altar in this room was directed toward the East, where it was believed that a great world teacher had emerged. This man was Jiddu Krishnamurti, who became known as "the great soul of Alcyone." Born in Mandanapalle, South India on May 12, 1895, Krishnamurti trav-eled ceaselessly around the world giving talks both private and public for the first sixty years of his life, before settling down in Ojai, California, a few hours north of Hollywood, where he died at the age of ninety on February 17, 1986. Krishnamurti continued to come to Hollywood to teach long after the entire Krotona Colony moved to Ojai in 1922, and often stayed here at the Krotona Inn, which is listed in some historical sources not by its name, but by its significance as the "Home of Krishnamurti."

Krotona Flight

Mead & Requa designed a stairway in the hills that was known as Krotona Flight, and which still exists. Linked to the west facade of the Krotona Inn, it originally was conceived to lead to a grand gateway at the summit of the hill that would serve as the main entrance into the entire society. This gateway was never constructed as the architects shifted their plans, yet the stairway, which winds parallel to Vista del Mar, was built, and leads to the doorway of the Grand Temple of the Rosy Cross. The Flight remains as a lasting symbol of ascension into spiritual realms via the magically magnetic Hollywood hills.

Grand Temple of the Rosy Cross

At the top of Krotona Flight is the

341

[10] For more on Krotona, see "A History of Hollywood," page 15.

Grand Temple of the Rosy Cross, which was constructed with much Moorish flourish in 1914 to provide larger spaces for lectures than those at the Inn. Inside was a large auditorium with a high ceiling that was lit by horse-arches windows similar to those at the Inn. It also had many offices in the basement. Subsequently remodeled in later years to hold many small apartments, the entire interior was destroyed and rebuilt, as was the west facade of the building.

Knudsen House [site]

2117–2121 Vista Del Mar Avenue

Augustus Knudsen built a three-story house for himself on the Krotona grounds directly across the street from the Krotona Inn, now a large parking lot. Situated on three hillside levels, each room was designed with a view; either south over the Los Angeles basin, or north over enclosed garden courts.

The Krotona Science Building

2152 Vista Del Mar Avenue

Constructed in 1917, this small building was also financed for Krotona by Knudsen, and served a significant purpose, despite its diminutive stature. "The Science Building was a severe, flat-roofed structure," wrote Alfred Willis in a treatise about Krotona, "whose mass approximated a double cube and whose plain surfaces were absolutely devoid of ornamentation. This severe geometry very possibly had an occult meaning and also the purpose of harmonizing the Science Building with the underlying geometric order of the universe. Later additions of a pitched roof and a small arched porch at the south end have substantially obscured this geometry and given the building a Mission Revival flavor. With its originally small windows considerably enlarged, this building has been converted to residential use."

Moorcrest
Home of Charlie Chaplin, Mary Astor

6147 Temple Hill Drive

Designed by Marie Russak Hotchener and financed by her husband, this house was known as Moorcrest, and was built in 1921 on a lot that adjoined the Krotona property. Mixing Moorish and Mission Revival styles, it has stained glass windows with a red lotus motif, linking it to Krotona symbology. The Hotchenors never lived here themselves, however, building it on spec to rent or sell to someone fortunate enough to afford and eclectic enough to choose to occupy a semisacred, part-Moorish, part-Mission Revival style mansion in the hills.

That person turned out to be Charlie Chaplin, who lived here from 1921 to 1925, and who by his presence provided the first link between Hollywood and Krotona. He had numerous parties here, enjoying the pool that winds along the east facade of the house (unseen from the street), and which had two built-in subterranean dressing rooms, one for men and the other for women, to change into their "swimming costumes." In early histories of this house, Chaplin, who subsequently moved to a home in Beverly Hills while still making movies at his Hollywood studio, is identified as a "photoplayer and motion-picture producer."

In 1925, the Hotcheners sold the house to Mr. and Mrs. Otto H. Langhanke. Their daughter was the actress Mary Astor, who was married to John Barrymore. Through Mary, the Langhankes got acquainted with Barrymore, and eventually went to work for him, again bridging the world of Krotona and Hollywood. Mr. Hotchenor took over as his business manager, while Mrs. Hotchenor served an equally important role, that of his astrologer.

The Hotchenors stayed in Hollywood even after Krotona pulled up its stakes and moved north to Ojai. They moved to a new house, most likely also designed by the Mrs., at 6137 Temple Hill Drive, where they lived from 1926 to 1945. Other houses that bear her stylistic stamp and which historians conclude were all designed by her are the houses at 2275 Vasanta Way, 6107 Temple Hill Drive, 6106 Temple Hill Drive, and 2247 Gower Street.

Bungalows

2130 Gower

2172 Argyle (The Tuttle Bungalow)

2176 Argyle (The Swain Bungalow)

6101 Scenic (Marie Russak Residence)

There are several small wooden bungalows still scattered throughout the hills that were all originally constructed as homes within the Krotona Colony. Elmer Andrus built many of these, using a classic California bungalow design.

Though several of these bungalows are no longer standing, many are still in existence, and still being used, somewhat miraculously, as residences, including the small home at 2130 Gower Street. Andrus' own workshop used to stand at 2131 Gower. At 2176 Argyle Avenue is the Swain Bungalow, which was built in 1913 most likely by Andrus, and perched above a extremely steep slope, which might be the reason its design echoes that of a Swiss Chalet. Next door to that at 2172 Argyle Avenue is the Tuttle Bungalow, which Andrus built in 1914, and which still sports its original shingles.

At 6101 Scenic Avenue is the Marie Russak Residence, which was designed by Arthur and Alfred Heineman on Krotona's eastern edge in 1914. It was purchased by Henry Hotchenor, prior to his marriage to Marie Russak, who was still married then to Frank Russak, a banker living in Paris.

Hotchenor and his eventual wife purchased many lots in the area from the Albert Beach Company, hence the name Beachwood, and sold many of these homes to fellow Krotonians, linking their fortune with that of the society. The aforementioned "Moorcrest," the home of Chaplin, was a mansion designed by

Marie, and constructed by Henry as an investment.

This thirteen-room house, also influenced by the Mission Revival style, had a flat roof trimmed with red clay tile, and an arched porch. It was essentially the residence of Mrs. Hotchenor. Mr. Hotchenor had his own house at 2030 Vine Street.

Five Krotona Villas

2136 to 2180 Vista del Mar Avenue

Though long since obscured by dense vegetation and even denser reconstruction, all five of these little villas were built as homes within the Krotona colony.

Casa Rayda

6136 Primrose

This was Casa Rayda, the home of Krotonian H.H. Shutts. It was, according to Willis, "an alternative to the rather Spartan lifestyles pursued by the Krotonian bungalow dwellers . . . Its central feature is a tower consisting of an octagonal superstructure over a cubic base. . . . Casa Rayda manages to project simultaneously an effect of spiritually satisfying simplicity and middle-class comfort."

Krotona Ternary Building

6205 Temple Hill Drive

Constructed in 1915, this was the home of Mrs. Grace Shaw Duff, a prominent Theosophical lecturer originally from New York. It originally housed three separate dwellings, all of which were situated around an open courtyard, linked by arcades, and connected by a roof terrace. The ever-present Hotchenors occupied the other two dwellings and were said to have "claimed a financial interest in the property."

Lake Hollywood / Mulholland Dam[11]

Constructed by William Mulholland between 1923 and 1924, this mammoth

---

[11] For more on the Mulholland Dam, see "A History of Hollywood," page 25.

200 feet tall, curved concrete embankment is appointed with curved arches separated by a succession of stone busts
depicting the California brown bear,
which is featured on the state flag. Officially called Mulholland Dam by the city,
its location in the hills above Hollywood
was controversial when first announced,
and the subject of great opposition when
the matching St. Francis Dam, also constructed by Mulholland, gave way,
destroying many cities and causing nearly
500 deaths. The front facade of the dam
was covered with an earthen blanket in
1932, on which an immense grove of trees
was planted in order to obscure the constant visual presence of the dam. [See History, page 25 for much more on the dam
and Lake Hollywood.]

344

LAUGHLIN PARK

North of Franklin, East of Western

Laughlin Park is a development of
estates on the hills that separate Franklin
Boulevard from Los Feliz. Cecil B.
DeMille's mansion is here, as are homes
that were owned by W.C. Fields and
Charlie Chaplin. It's now a gated, walled
community that is not officially open to
the public, though it is sometimes possible to gain entrance.

Cecil B. DeMille house

2000 DeMille Drive

DeMille bought this home in 1916 and
lived here until his death in 1959. He
filmed much of the Garden of Gethse-
mane scene in his backyard here for his
1927 film *King of Kings*. The house is said to
be kept exactly as it was, with fresh
flowers on Mr. DeMille's desk every day.

Charlie Chaplin house [next door to DeMille]

2010 DeMille Drive

Chaplin lived here in 1918.

W.C. Fields house

2015 DeMille Drive

The legendary comedian W.C. Fields
lived here from 1940 until his death in
1946. Prior to this time he lived in Whitley
Heights on Wedgwood. Born William
Claude Dukenfield in Philadelphia on January 29, 1880, he started his career as a
comic juggler. By nineteen he was a full-
fledged comedian, and he started touring
around the world. He performed in
London at the Palace when he was only
twenty-one, and in 1915, he joined the
Ziegfeld Follies, with whom he performed
between 1915 and 1921. In 1923, he starred
in a Broadway play called *Poppy*, which
D.W. Griffith made into a film in 1925
called *Sally of the Sawdust*, starring Fields. He
signed on with Paramount Pictures, for
whom he made many movies. In 1935, he
played the memorable part Mr. McCawber
in *David Copperfield*. In 1939, he went to work
for Universal, where he was given artistic
control of his work. And in 1940, he made
two of his most famous films, *The Bank Dick*
and *My Little Chickadee*, which co-starred
Mae West. Fields died on Christmas Day of
1946 in Pasadena, California. As he
affirmed in the inscription on his tombstone, he'd rather have been in Philadelphia.

This Spanish Villa is paneled
throughout with oak and walnut, and is
presently owned by Lily Tomlin and Jane
Wagner.

Bela Lugosi apartment

5630 Harold Way

One of the greatest of the classic
horror stars, Bela Lugosi personified
Dracula on the screen with an eminence
no other actor has ever achieved. Ironically, although Lugosi unjustifiably never
received an Oscar, years after his death the
actor Martin Landau did receive an Oscar
for his work in the movie *Ed Wood*, in
which he portrayed Lugosi.

He was born Béla Ferenc Dezső Blaskó
in October of 1882 in Lugos, Hungary. He

studied at the Budapest Academy of Theatrical Arts and by 1901 was a leading
actor with Hungary's Royal National The-
atre. His first films came around 1917 and
his American film debut in *The Silent Command* (1923). With scant knowledge of
English and a thick accent, it was a
struggle for him to find work, until 1927,
at which time he won the part of Dracula
in a Broadway production. For three years
he played the role on stage before even
bringing it to the screen, which may
explain how Lugosi was capable of inhab-
iting the character to such an intimate
extent.

In 1931, he made the movie version of
Dracula, which was a huge hit, and transformed the actor into an international
sensation. To this day, it's considered a cinematic classic. Lugosi turned down the
role of the monster in the original *Frankenstein*, and the role went instead to Boris
Karloff. Lugosi's greatness as *Dracula* led
him to be type-cast, and in ensuing years
he performed in a string of horror pictures, some of which co-starred Boris
Karloff, such as *The Black Cat*. He then performed in a series of B movies in which
his work borders on self-parody. In 1948,
he extended this self-ridicule in *Abbott &
Costello Meet Frankenstein*, in which he finally
played the monster he'd avoided for years.
In his later years he struggled with drug
addictions, which led to erratic behavior
in public, where he'd often appear in full
Dracula regalia regardless of the fact that
no film was being made. His final films
were among his most ludicrous, such as
Bela Lugosi Meets a Brooklyn Gorilla and *My Son,
the Vampire*, both in the early fifties. In 1953,
he started making many films with Ed
Wood, considered by many to have made
many of the world's all-time worst films,
of which *Glen or Glenda?* stars Lugosi. In
1955, Lugosi committed himself to an
institution with the hope of conquering
his addiction to morphine. When he got
out he moved into this apartment, and
went back to work with Wood on the film
that might have been the worst of them

all, *Plan Nine from Outer Space*. Lugosi was
struck by a lethal heart attack on August
15, 1956, on the set of the film, after
filming only a few of scenes. He was
buried in his Dracula cape, and is said to
have taken over the wheel of the hearse
driving his corpse to the cemetery, veering
onto Hollywood Boulevard so that his
spirit could make his final ride down his
beloved boulevard.

The Masonic Temple

6840 Hollywood Boulevard

Constructed in 1922 for the Hollywood branch of the Masons, which
according to their literature, is not a religion, but a charitable, social, educational,
and philosophical organization, which
"stresses certain fundamental truths upon
which, on reflection, men of many different backgrounds, religions, and opinions can agree—and have agreed for centuries." People can only enter Masonry
through local Masonic Lodges, of which
there are over 13,000 presently in the
United States. These lodges confer degrees
to their Masons, starting with the entrant,
or Entered Apprentice, the Fellow Craft,
and the Master Mason degree. By 1903,
there were about fifty Masons in Hollywood, who built their first Masonic Hall
on Highland, north of Hollywood Boulevard. In 1922, the number of Masons had
risen to over 1,300, leading to the construction of the beautiful Masonic Temple
at 6480 Hollywood Boulevard at Orchid,
which stands to this day. Its Neoclassic
Revival design featuring formidable
columns was the work of John C. Austin,
who also designed L.A. City Hall. Costing
$250,000, it contained lodge rooms, a
social hall, a various club rooms.

D.W. Griffith's memorial service was
held here in 1948, and attended by many
stars, including Charlie Chaplin, W.C.
Fields, Mary Pickford, Douglas Fairbanks,
Bob Hope, Dean Martin, and Jerry Lewis.

These days The Masonic Temple is
often used in conjunction with Disney
movies being shown next door at the El

Capitan Theater, which is now owned by Disney.

The Magic Castle
7001 Franklin Avenue

Built in 1909, this mansion was among the first homes built in Hollywood, and is characteristic of the other estates that were spread throughout the Hollywood flatlands and foothills. Combining French Chateauesque and Gothic styles, this was originally the home of Rollin Lane, a banker, who lived here from 1909 to 1931, at which time it was bought by the movie star Janet Gaynor. The design of the house was inspired by a home in Redlands, California, called "Kimberly Crest," which remains as a museum. Since 1963, it has been a private magicians club operated by The Academy of Magical Arts, a nonprofit organization. Magicians and magic enthusiasts alike have gathered here for decades, including Orson Welles, Johnny Carson, and Cary Grant.

The Max Factor Building
1666 N. Highland Avenue

Born Max Faktor in Lodz, Poland, circa 1872, Max Factor's first store was in Russia, after he served in the Russian army, and his prowess with both creating and applying makeup propelled him to the position of cosmetician for the Imperial family.[12] He moved with his family to America in 1904, and to L.A. in 1908 where he opened the Max Factor company. His arrival coincided with the advent of movies, and he quickly developed a brand-new cream form of makeup called "flexible greasepaint," which soon became the standard of the industry.

The first actors to use Factor's concoction were comic stars, such as Charlie Chaplin, Fatty Arbuckle and Buster Keaton. When Cecil DeMille, along with Jesse Lasky and Sam Goldwyn, filmed the first

official feature in Hollywood, *The Squaw Man*, Factor provided them with wigs made from real human hair, the first ever of their kind, and established himself as the leading expert in all kinds of movie cosmetics. DeMille actually found the costs of the wigs too steep, so Factor agreed to rent him the wigs to him if his three sons could all appear in the movie. DeMille agreed; all three Factor boys are extras in the film.

In 1928, Factor bought the building at the southeast corner of Hollywood & Highland, diagonally across the street from the Hollywood Hotel. After massive renovations, the building was opened on November 17, 1928. "When I think of my first little shop in Los Angeles," he said that day, "it still seems like a dream come true to enter this new building."

The Max Factor headquarters soon became a Hollywood institution. It featured New York–inspired display windows that exhibited the latest, most glamorous fashions in hair and makeup, as well as an ornate salon, decorated in a lavish Louis XIV style with crystal chandeliers, parquet floors, mirrored panels. The upstairs of the building was the Factor factory, where cosmetics and tools to apply them were all created.

In 1934, he hired the famed art deco architect S. Charles Lee to give the building a new, fresh look. Lee designed an entirely new, formal marble facade for the building, with Westfieldian marble and fluted pilasters.

This new version of the old building opened with a giant "premiere" of a party, replete with kleig lights, to which all Hollywood luminaries were invited and were in attendance, including Sid Grauman, Claudette Colbert, Rita Hayworth, Marlene Dietrich and a thirteen-year-old Judy Garland. So impressive was the new building that the party-goers were said to be struck speechless, according to a *New York Times*

346

---

[12] See "A History of Hollywood," page 41 for more on Max Factor.

account of the event: "They stood in open-mouthed awe until they were rudely awakened by their cigarettes burning their fingers. They then hastily dropped them on the burgundy carpet and ground them in."

When Factor died in 1938, his empire passed on to his son Frank, who shrewdly recognized the need to keep his father's name alive, and changed his own name to Max Factor Jr. The company continued to provide the movies and its stars with both makeup and wigs, even supplying in 1931 a wig for Boris Karloff to wear as the monster in *Frankenstein*, and in 1939 a lion's mane for Bert Lahr to wear as the Cowardly Lion in *The Wizard of Oz*. It also continued its tradition of providing the perfect look for Hollywood leading ladies, and stars from Mae West to Lauren Bacall to Lucille Ball all were reliant on the Factor magic.

Following World War II, the Max Factor Company expanded worldwide, and also opened a new building behind the old one, on North McCadden Place, in 1955 to be used as a general office and laboratory. Today it is the main building of the Musician's Institute. In 1991, the company was purchased by Procter & Gable, at which times its headquarters were relocated to Cincinnati. Plans to convert the original building into a Hollywood museum have been proposed and nearly implemented several times over the years, and its future is still uncertain as of this writing.

Metro Studio [site]
6300 Romaine

This was the Metro Studios in the late teens, the largest studio in Hollywood at the time. This is where Valentino made *The Four Horsemen of the Apocalypse*. When Metro ultimately merged with Goldwyn to become MGM, this studio was abandoned, and later destroyed.

The Mocambo [site]
8588 Sunset Boulevard

The Mocambo was one of the hottest nightspots for twenty years in Hollywood, from its opening in 1938 until 1958, the year that its owner, Charles Morrison, died. During its two decades, it was packed with stars who came to hear many of the world's greatest musical stars perform. Edith Piaf, Jacques Brel, Frank Sinatra and Lena Horne all performed here.

347

Monastery of the Angels
Carmen Place at Gower

The convent was founded by Mother Mary Gabriel in 1924. The nuns sell wonderful pumpkin bread, which has been baked on the premises for more than three decades, based on an age-old recipe handed down by one of the nun's grandmothers.

The Montecito Apartments
6650 Franklin Avenue

When Ronald Reagan came to Hollywood in 1932 he chose to live in the Montecito because it was where his idol, Jimmy Cagney, lived. It was a place where many actors from New York would stay. "No one ever bought their beer by six-pack here," according to legend, "since no one knew how long they'd be staying." A fine example of art deco style with Mayan influence, it was also home to Mickey Rooney, Geraldine Page, Rip Torn, Don Johnson, George C. Scott and Ben Vereen. Raymond Chandler used it as the prototype for the Chateau Bercy in his Phillip Marlowe novel *The Little Sister*. Recently refurbished, it's now a home for senior citizens.

The Montmartre Café [site]
6757 Hollywood Boulevard

It opened in 1923 by Eddie Brandstatter, and became the favorite meeting place for many of the movies' most famous stars, such that fans would line up for hours in hopes of getting an auto-graph. As Frederica Maas wrote in her autobiography, *The Shocking Miss Pilgrim*, the Montmartre was "a rendezvous spot for anyone who was anyone, or even aspired to be anyone. . . . The Montmartre was located on Hollywood Boulevard . . . in a two-story Spanish-tiled building. It had handsome, Mexican wrought-iron grilled doors at its entrance. . . . You could not get into the Montmartre during the lunch hours of eleven to two unless you were well-known or with someone who was. The tourists lined up early in the morning for the best vantage place to see their favorites. . . . To be seen at the Montmartre was a must in order to remain in the swim, in the glare of the klieg lights. . . . The Montmartre was The Place to go. The Place to be seen. There was no other."

In 1929, to afford the stars some relief, Brandstatter broke through the wall of the Montmartre into the adjoining building to establish an even more exclusive and elite retreat called the Embassy Club. When the Trocadero opened on Sunset, it supplanted the Montmartre as The Place, and as Maas recalled, it quickly became "a ghostly spot of empty tables." Brandstatter sadly closed this once illustrious hotspot, and opened a short-lived beanery before ultimately taking his own life, yet another figure who was celebrated and then discarded by Hol-lywood. "Today I rarely walk the streets of Hollywood," wrote Maas. " . . . [O]n those rare occasions when I do walk those streets and gaze upon the names of the greats embedded in the sidewalk, I think there is one star missing—a star for Eddie Brandstatter, who earned and deserved one for his devotion to the greats in the fickle picture business."

Musso & Frank's Grill

6667 Hollywood Boulevard

Built in 1919, it's Hollywood's oldest and most famous restaurant, still offering the tremendous, elegant food they have been serving up for decades. It's referred to in almost every one of the memoirs col-lected in this book, and with good reason. All of Hollywood's stars have dined here at one time or another, from Chaplin to Bogart to Marilyn Monroe, as have a legion of famous writers who came to Hollywood to work in the movies, including William Faulkner, F. Scott Fitzgerald, Raymond Chandler, Nathaneal West, Ernest Hemingway and Dashiell Hammett.

Back in the twenties, Musso's was "crowded as usual at lunch hour," wrote Frederica Maas in her autobiography. "It had a reputation for first-class cuisine with French emphasis, quiet elegance, low-key lighting and rich mahogany accents (especially in its commodious private eating booths.) Its waiters were tiptop veterans. To wait on a table at Musso & Frank's was a coveted diploma in the restaurant fraternity. Busboys were willing to work for a pittance in the hope of rising one day to the status of waiter at this fine eatery. "

The NBC Radio Center [site]

Sunset & Vine, northwest corner (now the bank)

The headquarters of the NBC Radio Network in Los Angeles was in a modern, three-story, pastel-green building which stood at the northwest corner of Sunset & Vine. As opposed to Radio City—the New York center of the NBC Radio network, which broadcast eighteen weekly shows—some thirty-five productions were sent out weekly from the Hollywood Radio Center.

The Oban Hotel

Yucca / Cahuenga

One of many small hotels built in Hol-lywood during the thirties to house the hundreds of hopefuls who arrived each week to make it into the movies. Many who would become movie stars stayed here at one time, including Marilyn

348

Monroe, Orson Welles, James Dean and Clark Gable. During the forties, the Oban was the hotel of choice for many of the musicians who made up the Big Bands of Glenn Miller, Les Brown, Harry James and others, and who played at the Palladium, just blocks away on Sunset near Vine.

The Oban is known to be amply haunted: Charles Love, who worked both as a prop man and a double for silent-movie comedian Harry Langdon, committed suicide here by shooting himself in the head after a long drinking bout. Before killing himself, he wrote a letter of farewell to Langdon. Though other spirits are also said to haunt the Oban, it is Love's who is the most prominent, and who makes his presence known in the basement by the emission of an especially pungent stench.

The Ozzie and Harriet House

1822 Camino Palmero

This is the house in which Ozzie, Harriet and Ricky Nelson lived. It was also used as the exterior for their TV program, "The Ozzie & Harriet Show," which they shot at the nearby Hollywood General studios on Las Palmas. Ozzie died here in 1975, and it's been said that his ghost has never left, to the extent that Harriet felt so haunted she sold the house in 1980. Ozzie's spirit is said to still be present, and is known to be "one randy ghost."

Ozcot [site]
Home of L. Frank Baum

1749 Cherokee Avenue

Though there's no trace of it anymore, this is where Ozcot once was, the home of L. Frank Baum, the author of *The Wizard of Oz*. A Chicagoan, Baum moved into Hollywood in 1910, prior to the arrival of the movies. Soon after moving here, he formed one of Hollywood's first film companies, the Oz Film Manufacturing Company, which had offices next to Universal. Baum made many silent movies of

his own based on the Oz books, but audiences at the time didn't seem ready for movies directed at children. It would be twenty years following his death here in 1919 that *The Wizard of Oz* would become one of America's most beloved and timeless films.

Baum sold the Oz Company to Universal, and retired to the pleasant enclaves here of Ozcot, where he immersed himself in writing more Oz books. His last book was *Glinda of Oz*, which was published posthumously in 1920. He died at Ozcot on May 6, 1919 and was buried in Forest Lawn cemetery in Glendale. He wrote seventy-three books in his lifetime, fourteen about Oz. "Though the children cannot clamor for the newest Oz books," wrote the *New York Times* in its obituary of Baum in 1919, "the crowding generations will plead for the old ones." Mrs. Baum sold Ozcot in 1956, at which time it was demolished and subsequently replaced by an amorphous apartment dwelling. Baum's last words, which referred to the boundary between the real world and Oz, were "Now is the time to cross the shifting sands."

349

The Palladium

6215 Sunset Boulevard

"In the forties, after the war, the Palladium was like New Year's Eve every night with all the servicemen in town," said the late Les Brown, leader of His Band of Renown, who played countless gigs here from the forties and even into the nineties, when he played his final show here. All the classic Big Bands performed here at the Palladium.

The Pantages Theatre

6233 Hollywood Boulevard

The Pantages opened officially on June 4, 1930, with the premiere of *Floradora Girl*, starring Marion Davies and Al Jolson. Designed to be Hollywood's grandest movie palace, it was purchased by RKO in 1949, and the Pantages became the home of the Academy Awards from 1949 to 1959, and in the seventies was the home of the Emmy Awards. Today it's still one of Hollywood's grandest theaters, and a showcase for live theatrical productions and concerts.

Paramount Studios

5555 Melrose Avenue

250

The oldest continuously operating film studio in Hollywood, it was built as the Peralta in 1917, became the Brunton Studios in 1920, and the United Studios from 1921 until 1926 when Paramount bought it. Hollywood history tells us Valentino made all his films here but this is wrong; he died in '26 and made his pictures at the Famous Lasky studios at Sunset & Vine. Clara Bow, Mae West, Bing Crosby, and Bob Hope all made movies here. The most famous film, however, to feature Paramount itself as a star is the classic *Sunset Boulevard*, in which the original gates—on Marathon—are used. The new entrance on Melrose Avenue was constructed in the eighties to match the Marathon gates, which are around the corner.

Paramount was a place where magic was made daily, where anything was possible, and where the world created within its gates was usually preferable to the real thing outside. As the director Ernst Lubitsch said, "I've been to Paris, France, and I've been to Paris, Paramount. Paris, Paramount is better."

Prior to moving to this location, Paramount Studios was located at Hollywood & Vine, extending from the site of their first famous film, *The Squaw Man*. "I was given a really nice welcome to Paramount Studios," wrote Douglas Fairbanks Jr., of the original Paramount, which he saw in 1923. " . . . a long set of dark green wooden buildings that stretched down Vine Street from Hollywood Boulevard to Sunset. It had been expanded on the same site from the barn that Lasky, DeMille, Farnum and others had rented and sat in the midst of what had been called Hollywood Ranch."

Parva-Sed Apartments

1817 North Ivar Avenue

Latin for "small but suitable," the Parva-Sed was the home of the author Nathanael West, who lived here in 1935 while writing his classic Hollywood novel, *The Day of the Locust*. West spent much of his time at Musso & Frank's on the boulevard. He befriended many of the prostitutes who also lived at the Parva-Sed and nearby haunts, driving them to work and in exchange for favors they offered him, such as sewing his buttons and washing his dishes.

"The air of the garden was heavy with the odor of mimosa and honeysuckle," wrote West in *Day of the Locust*. "Through a slit in the blue serge sky poked a grained moon that looked like an enormous bone button. A little flagstone path, made narrow by its border of oleander, led to the edge of the sunken pool."

Born Nathan Weinstein in New York, West came to Hollywood in 1933 when Fox bought the rights to his novel, *Miss Lonelyhearts* for $4,000 and turned it into the film *Advice to the Lovelorn*. He went to work as a writer for Columbia and like many writers, toiled away on several scripts that were never made. He wasn't crazy about the movie business, but was fascinated with the weird mix of the hopeful and hopeless denizens of Hollywood whose life is spent on the outside of the studio walls, often wishing to get in. From West's perspective, Hollywood was fairly bleak no matter which side of the wall you worked on: "This place is like Asbury Park, New Jersey," he wrote in a letter to a friend. "The same stucco houses, women in pajamas, delicatessen stores, etc. . . . All the writers sit in cells in a row and the minute a typewriter stops someone pokes his head in the door to see if you are thinking."

West died in a car crash while on a little jaunt to El Centro in 1940, the very same day that Scott Fitzgerald died in Hollywood at his apartment on Laurel, just a few miles west of the Parva-Sed.

PINEHURST AVENUE

Pinehurst is a small street of homes that is north of Franklin, behind the First Methodist Church. Several luminaries lived on Pinehurst, as listed below:

Wilford Bucklin house

2035 Pinehurst

Bucklin was one of Hollywood's first art directors. He moved here in 1913 to work with Cecil B. DeMille on *The Squaw Man*. At the age of eighty, in a fit of evident madness, he murdered his mentally ill son here, who was thirty-six, before committing suicide.

Edgar Rice Burroughs house

2029 Pinehurst

Burroughs, who was born in Chicago on September 1st, 1875, was the creator of the *Tarzan the Apeman* series of books, which spawned countless film versions. Burroughs lived here in 1934 while writing the book *Tarzan & Jane*. He then purchased a ranch in the San Fernando Valley, which he named Tarzana Ranch in honor of his fictional creation. The community that arose around his ranch paid tribute to him by adopting Tarzana as the name for their entire town. He served as a war correspondent in Europe during World War II, and then returned to live out his days in California. He died on March 19, 1950.

Carrie Jacobs-Bond house

2042 Pinehurst

She was the songwriter of many classic songs, including "I Love You, Truly," "A Perfect Day," and "Just A Wearyin' for You." She had this house built here in 1917, surrounded it with beautiful gardens, and called it "The End of the Road."

Lloyd Rigler house[13]

2047 Pinehurst

He made his fortune selling Adolph's

Meat Tenderizer and went on to found the Ledler Foundation, which helped finance the renovation of the Egyptian Theater and its "Lloyd Rigler Theater."

Peg Entwistle's house

2428 Beachwood Drive

Though it's been rumored that many actresses, down on their luck, have committed suicide by leaping off the Hollywood sign, in fact only one really did so, Peg Entwistle, who lived here at her uncle's home. She was a British actress, who had starred in many shows on Broadway and came to Hollywood with a contract to appear in RKO movies. But the starring roles she had hoped for did not materialize, and all RKO had for her was bit parts. In 1932, they declined to renew her contract, which led to an immense depression from which she never escaped. Without work, she would sit around the house; her only relief was riding horses up the hills at the Sunset Ranch, which still exists to this day at the upper end of Beachwood Drive.

It was on a Friday evening, September 16, 1932, that she told her uncle she was going out to buy a pack of cigarettes. Instead, she made the long slow trek up Mt. Lee to the old Hollywoodland sign, which then had ladders up the back of each letter, and was festooned with flashing light bulbs. She ascended the giant H, and made her final exit, diving into the thorns, cacti and brambles below. Remarkably, she survived the fall to endure several days of painful operations, but ultimately succumbed to the Big Sleep.

RKO Studios

Corner of Melrose & Gower

This studio was built in 1920–1921 on an unoccupied part of the cemetery. It was the Robertson–Cole Studios at first, and in 1923 became the FBO Studios owned by Joe Kennedy. RKO was born from the

351

---

merger of FBO and RCA. Howard Hughes purchased 929,000 shares of RKO stock and thus took control of this major company. Three years later, after essentially decimating a once great studio, Hughes purchased all available RKO stock himself at double its value, and then sold the studio to General Teleradio, Inc., a subsidiary of General Tire and Rubber, pocketing a tidy profit of $10 million. His last film for RKO was *Affair with a Stranger* (1953).

352

The RKO lot was sold in 1957 to Desilu Productions for television production of "I Love Lucy." In 1958, Paramount extended their own property by taking over the RKO studio. Though they initially painted over the trademark RKO globe which juts out from the studio at the intersection of Gower & Melrose, in later years it was repainted back to its original colors, as it remains today.

In its heyday, RKO was one of Hollywood greatest studios, a home to many of the world's greatest directors, such as John Ford, Alfred Hitchcock and Orson Welles, who made his classic *Citizen Kane*, considered by many to be the greatest American film ever, at RKO. Stars of RKO movies included Katharine Hepburn, Cary Grant, Ingrid Bergman, Robert Mitchum, Gary Cooper, Bette Davis and Lucille Ball.

Other classic RKO films include *It's a Wonderful Life*, starring Jimmy Stewart, as well as *King Kong*, *The Hunchback of Notre Dame*, *The Bells of St. Mary's*, *The Best Years of Our Lives*, and the series of musicals starring Fred Astaire & Ginger Rogers.

Raleigh Studios
5300 Melrose Avenue

It has the distinction of being the oldest continuously operational studio in Hollywood. Originally The Clune Studios, it was built in 1914, and has been owned by many companies through the years. In 1915, it became the Famous Players Fiction Studios, where the inaugural production

starred one of the silent screen's first and most beloved stars, Mary Pickford. Although it was constructed in the silent era, one of the studio's original owners had the propitious foresight to build a soundstage there—recognizing that talkies were just around the bend—which is probably the main reason it still stands to this day. Many of Hollywood's brightest luminaries made movies here, including Douglas Fairbanks, Lillian and Dorothy Gish, and even Walt Disney. For decades it was the California Studio, the home of the *Hopalong Cassidy* movies. Other great films made here include *The Mark of Zorro*, *The Three Musketeers*, *In the Heat of the Night*, with Rod Steiger and Sidney Poitier (which won the Oscar for Best Picture of 1967), *The Best Years of Our Lives* (Best Picture of 1946), *Whatever Happened to Baby Jane* (with Bette Davis and Joan Crawford) and the original *A Star Is Born*. In the sixties it became primarily a television studio; renamed The Producer's Studio, it was the home of several TV shows, including "Gunsmoke" and "Superman," as well as "Death Valley Days," which featured Ronald Reagan. In 1980 it became The Raleigh Studios.

Sardi's Restaurant
6315 Hollywood Boulevard

It's hard to fathom, given its present incarnation as a strip club/porno theater called the Cave, but this very building once held Sardi's, one of the most popular restaurants in Hollywood during the thirties and forties. The building was designed by the internationally known architect Rudolph Schindler in 1923 in what's known as "International style," which relies on a fusion of metal and glass.

Schwab's Pharmacy [site]
8024 Sunset Boulevard

A Hollywood institution for more than fifty years, it was the drugstore to the stars. All of Hollywood congregated at the counter at Schwab's—legendary actors, writers, and directors, plus generations of hopefuls, who came here with a dream of being discovered. For it's here that one of the most famous of all Hollywood discoveries is said to have occurred, that of a tight-sweatered Lana Turner. It's but one of the many myths about Schwab's that is untrue, yet still perpetuated to this day. Lana Turner was actually discovered while still a student at Hollywood High at Curry's Ice-Cream Parlor, across the street from the school. Schwab's was substituted for Curry's in this myth because it was famous throughout America, and thus easier to remember by the movie-going public, who thrived on such romantic yarns.

Another predominant myth about Schwab's was that F. Scott Fitzgerald had a heart attack and died there. In fact, Fitzgerald did frequent Schwab's when he lived around the corner on Laurel Avenue; he and his paramour Sheilah Graham were known to linger over malteds at the counter, and Fitzgerald would buy his cigarettes, chocolate bars, newspapers, and magazines there. He suffered his fatal heart attack in his apartment on Laurel, however, after one of his daily walks to Schwab's for supplies.

Stars throughout the decades came to Schwab's on a regular basis; Charlie Chaplin and Harold Lloyd would play the pinball machines, while Judy Garland, Mickey Rooney, Orson Welles, the Marx Brothers, Marilyn Monroe, and Ronald Reagan would come for breakfast, lunch and ice-cream sodas.

Scores of unemployed and unknown actors also came to Schwab's each day, hoping to be discovered, and supported by Schwab's generous policy of extending credit to those who needed it most.

It's here in 1939 that the composer Harold Arlen, while working on melodies for The Wizard of Oz, came up with one of the most memorable and hopeful melodies ever written for the movies, "Over the Rainbow," which was per-formed by Judy Garland and became the signature song of her career. Arlen is said to have quickly jotted down the notes to this famous tune while sitting at the counter, so he could preserve it until getting home to his piano.

Though developers announced at one point that the big mall which was being built in the late eighties at Sunset & Crescent Heights would preserve Schwab's, wrapping around it in much the same manner as the Hollywood-Highland project wraps around the Chinese Theater, these plans were sadly scrapped, and the world's most famous pharmacy closed in 1983 and was torn down in 1988. Schwab's is immortalized in many films, including the classic *Sunset Boulevard*, in which the writer Joe Gillis, played by William Holden, refers to the pharmacy in the terms by which so many once knew it. He said it was his "headquarters . . . kind of a combination office, Kaffee-klatsch, and waiting room. Waiting, waiting for the gravy train."

Anita Stewart Home
7425 Franklin Avenue

This massive mansion, replete with two balustrades and ten columns, was the home of Anita Stewart, a star of the silent era who rose to fame making movies for Vitagraph. Louie B. Mayer did everything he could to steal her away from Vitagraph, even offering her what was in 1917 an outrageous salary—$3,000 a week—with the unprecedented, added incentive of a car. But Vitagraph sued to get her back, and eventually won their case, which ended up costing Mayer $123,000.

The Studio Club
1215 Lodi Place (between Vine and Gower, off of Santa Monica)

When she became aware, in the early twenties, of the profusion of young women coming to Hollywood each day with hopes of making it in the movies, a librarian named Eleanor Jones persuaded the Young Women's Christian Association to sponsor the construction of a building that could provide these girls with safe and reasonable room and board. A small clubhouse for this purpose was rented on Carlos Avenue, and a decade later the Studio Club was constructed on Lodi Place. Designed by the architect Julia Morgan who also designed Hearst's San Simeon, it became the first Hollywood home of countless women who did ultimately succeed in becoming starlets, including Marilyn Monroe, Marie Windsor and Evelyn Keyes.[14] Today the building still stands, and though it's not officially open to the public, the kind security guards there usually allow a quick perusal. These guards might also be willing to discuss the frequent spectral occurrences at the Studio Club; not one of them I've spoken to has ever denied the time-honored accounts of ghosts wandering the halls and courtyard of this historical building.

354

Vedanta Society Hollywood Temple

1946 Vedanta Place

Vedanta, which is the philosophical basis of Hinduism, has three temples in Southern California. This one was the first. Founded in 1929 in what was a private home when the Swami Prabhavananda was brought to America from India, it was one of many religious societies that flourished in the Hollywood hills. Open to the public with a beautiful chapel that resembles a miniature Taj Mahal, as well as a gift shop, this temple has long attracted many Hollywood luminaries to pray, study and meditate in this historic setting, including Christopher Isherwood, Aldous Huxley, Laurence Olivier and Vivien Leigh.

Vedanta is based on the understanding that all men are divine, and "that the true object of human life is to unfold and manifest this divinity, and that truth is universal. Vedanta accepts all the religions of the world and reveres the great prophets, teachers, and sons of God, because it recognizes the same divine inspiration in all."

Villa Capri (now offices) (x)

6735 Yucca

This was an Italian restaurant called Villa Capri, which was a favorite of many stars, including Bogart, Sinatra, Lauren Bacall and Judy Garland. No star is more closely tied to the Villa, though, then James Dean, who was good friends with the owner, and frequently used his office as his own. Dean, who would enter and leave through the kitchen, would always eat at his favorite table toward the back. He ate his last meal there the night before he died, September 29, 1955. The columnist James Bacon remembers that night, seeing Dean doing eighty miles an hour up McCadden Place in his brand new Porsche Spyder. Bacon told him, "Jimmy, that's a good way to keep from growing old." Dean replied, "Who wants to grow old?" The next day he died on the road to Paso Robles in the same car. After his death the Villa became a shrine to him, with fans wanting to sit in his table. It closed in 1982, and from 1983 until 1998, it housed the offices of KFAC radio.

Villa Carlotta

5959 Franklin

Built in 1926, this four-story, forty-eight unit brick building was originally a hotel, and the home to many luminaries, including Adolphe Menjou, Edward G. Robinson, George Cukor, Louella Parsons, and Marion Davies. Designed by architect Arthur E. Harvey in the Spanish Churrigueresque style, it featured several newfangled amenities, including soundproofed rooms, water filtration, refrigeration, and a ventilation system

---

[14] See "A Tour of Hollywood," page 22; Evelyn Keyes, page 129; and Marie Windsor, page 211.

which changed the air in each room every five minutes.

W.M. Strothers Mortuary
6240 Hollywood Boulevard

This was the W.M. Strothers Mortuary, where the funerals of many famous Hollywood figures were held, including Peg Entwistle, Wallace Reid, Thomas Ince, the wrestler Gorgeous George and Bela Lugosi. The Hollywood Chamber of Commerce had arranged with the mortuary a funeral route that avoided any procession along Hollywood Boulevard, as it was deemed too depressing for the community at large. Regardless of this rule, when Bela Lugosi's body was being driven in the hearse to the mortuary the driver said the car suddenly veered onto Hollywood Boulevard on its own accord, as if someone had grabbed the wheel, and crossed the intersection of Hollywood and Vine. Lugosi's friends, who knew of his great fondness for Hollywood Boulevard, surmised that it was his spirit taking its farewell drive along the old boulevard.

Walk of Fame
Hollywood Boulevard, between Gower and La Brea, also Vine Street, between Sunset and Hollywood Boulevard

Where else but in Hollywood are people honored by having stars installed into a glittery sidewalk for people to walk over? Conceived by the Hollywood Chamber of Commerce in 1958, the Walk of Fame consists of charcoal terrazzo squares embedded with coral terrazzo stars outlined in brass, with the honoree's name spelled out in brass, plus an icon that designates the arena from which each honoree emerged, be it theater, movies, TV, radio, or records. There are nearly 1,800 stars presently in place. The Walk of Fame is both beloved and castigated; the criticism arisen because of the arbitrary nature by which honorees were chosen. Certain Hollywood greats, such as Lon Chaney, David Selznick, and Steve McQueen were never awarded stars, while others received multiple stars for their work in different media, such as W.C. Fields, Groucho Marx, Bing Crosby, and Bob Hope.

Stars aren't freely awarded—the Hollywood Chamber of Commerce charges $5,000 for this honor, and it's a sketchy area when one tries to discover what happens to all those funds. The "Honorary Mayor of Hollywood" is Johnny Grant, who presides over all the star ceremonies, which he has done for years; usually at eleven or so in the morning, sometimes with bleachers set up for crowds, when the star is big enough. As Grant knows, this is a wonderful way to lure stars back to Hollywood Boulevard. I've seen many of them myself—such as Walter Matthau, who immediately started joking with the crowd about the L.A. Dodgers and their current star Fernando Valenzuela.

Warner-Hollywood Studio / Samuel Goldwyn Studios / Mary Pickford studio
1041 Formosa Avenue

Built in 1920 as the Hampton Studios, this lot was purchased by Douglas Fairbanks and Mary Pickford in 1922, the year that they formed United Artists with Charlie Chaplin and Douglas Fairbanks. Pickford rented space to Sam Goldwyn, who eventually bought out the entire lot in 1949 and renamed it to the Goldwyn studios. Purchased by Warners in the late fifties, it has been used for countless TV shows as well as movies.

Warner Brothers Theater / Pacific Hollywood Theater
6425 Hollywood Boulevard

When it opened on April 26, 1928, with a star-studded premiere of *Glorious Betsy*, starring Dolores Costello and Conrad Nagle, the Warner Brothers theater was the largest movie theater in Hollywood, with a capacity of 2,700 people.

Of the four Warner Brothers, Harry,

Albert, Jack and Sam, it was Sam Warner who was most involved in the construction and design of this theater. Warners was in the process at this time of creating their first sound film, The Jazz Singer, starring Al Jolson, which was planned to premiere at the theater. Sam supervised the installation of a complex sound system in the theater to provide sound for the new talkies, as well as a large Marr & Colton pipe organ. But by October of 1927, when the film was complete, the theater was still unfinished, and so The Jazz Singer had its premiere instead in New York City.

Sam Warner, who was only forty years old, died of a brain hemorrhage the day prior to the premiere, never living to see the opening of this theater on Hollywood Boulevard. His brothers installed a plaque in his honor in the lobby of the theater, which read, "To our beloved brother, Samuel L. Warner, who conceived and planned it, but who was summoned before completion of his work." It's been reported by many sources that the spirit of Sam Warner has haunted the theater for decades.

Warner Brothers Studio/KTLA Television
5858 Sunset Boulevard

The first studio of the Warner Brothers movie company, this is where the first sound movies—"talkies"—were invented. It was constructed in 1919 to resemble a colonial mansion. In 1927, the first official sound movie The Jazz Singer, starring Al Jolson, was produced here. After the advent of sound, studios needed more space, and Warners moved their main operations to Burbank, using this studio mainly for the production of their famous cartoons: Porky Pig, Bugs Bunny and Daffy Duck all were created here. Purchased by Paramount in 1942, it was converted into an enormous bowling center called Sunset Bowling Center. It's now the home of L.A's Channel 5 TV, KTLA.

Wattles Mansion
1824 N. Curson Avenue

This mansion was named "Jualita," and was the home of industrialist Gurdon Wattles. Constructed between 1905 and 1909, it was designed by Myron Hunt and Elmer Grey in the Mission Revival style, and is characteristic of the kind of winter homes built by affluent eastern families prior to the arrival of movie companies in Hollywood. It has long been famous for its elaborate series of gardens, which once ascended in steps up the hill all the way to Mulholland Drive. It is maintained today by the Hollywood Heritage, Inc., preservationist group.

Mae West's Home The Ravenswood
570 North Rossmore

Mae West moved into her elegant, all-white-on-white apartment here in 1932. Though she also had a beautiful beach house in Santa Monica, this was her main home throughout her entire career. Born on August 17, 1892, in Brooklyn, she began performing as a kid, and was known as "Baby Vamp." By fourteen she was on the vaudeville circuit and doing Broadway revues. Starting about 1907 she began to write her own material. Her play Sex was so controversial that she was jailed on obscenity charges. Her show Diamond Lil became a Broadway smash hit, and soon after that she was invited to Hollywood to star in movies. She reached the pinnacle of her stardom in the thirties, at which time she was the best-paid woman in America. But when The Heat's On (1943) failed to generate much heat, she retired from movies and returned to Broadway and the English stage. In the mid-fifties, at the age of sixty-two, she did a night club act surrounded by a crew of musclemen. She made cameo appearances in two films during the seventies, and essentially retired, living here till her death in 1980 at the age of eighty-seven.

WHITLEY HEIGHTS

At the summit of Whitley Avenue, west of Wilcox, north of Franklin Avenue

A few blocks north of Hollywood Boulevard, up steep Whitley Avenue, the last block of which is 27 percent grade, is Whitley Heights. It's been called "the first Beverly Hills," since so many of the early stars of Hollywood lived here. Now listed on the National Register of Historic Places, it offers an ideal opportunity to peer into Hollywood of the twenties. This is the neighborhood where Maurice Chevalier, Beulah Bondi, Bette Davis, Rudolph Valentino, Wallace Beery, Jean Harlow, Rosalind Russell, Janet Gaynor, Francis X. Bushman, William Faulkner, Carmen Miranda, Chester Morris and Norma Shearer all lived at one time.

It was built by H.J. Whitley to resemble an authentic Italian hilltown, and took over eight years of ongoing construction to complete, beginning in 1918. For authenticity, he sent his main architect to Italy to study the age-old secrets of hillside construction and landscaping. Whitley Heights was bisected by the construction of the Hollywood Freeway in 1947, and many of its historic houses, including the home of Rudolph Valentino, were demolished. And though the former serenity of Whitley Heights is forever lost due to this proximity to the freeway, most of its historic homes still stand, as detailed in the following list:

Rudolph Valentino house [site]

6776 Wedgewood Drive

This was the site of Rudolph Valentino's house, which was demolished in 1947 to make way for the freeway, which cut directly through Whitley Heights.

Robert Vignola house

6697 Whitley

An actor and director, Vignola played Judas in the 1912 silent *From the Manger to the Cross.* He started directing in 1911, and in 1922 directed Marion Davies in *When Knighthood Was in Flower.* In 1934, he directed a version of *The Scarlet Letter* starring Colleen Moore. Vignola, according to legend, was a homosexual who was hand-picked by Hearst to direct Marion Davies, so as not to have a straight director work with her. Hearst is said to have built this house for him with the understanding that he and Marion could use it whenever then needed.

357

Richard Barthlemess house

6691 Whitley

His friend Alla Nazimova led him into movies, and he joined D.W. Griffith's company in 1918, costarring with Lillian Gish in the 1919 classic *Broken Blossoms.* Gish called him "the most beautiful man who ever went before a camera." A major star during the twenties, he even made the transition into talkies and kept working in films up to 1939, when he starred in Howard Hawks' *Only Angels Have Wings.*

Maurice Chevalier house

6680 Whitley

The movies' preeminent Frenchman, he had a fervor and grace few before him had brought to the screen. Most famous for his theme song from the musical *Gigi,* "Thank Heaven for Little Girls," he served in World War I, where he was captured and spent two years in a POW camp. After the war, his star rose quickly throughout the world, entrancing audiences in America and beyond with his singing, old-world gallantry and elegance, wearing his boulevardier outfit of a straw hat and bow tie. He moved here to this Hollywood house in 1929, where he lived until he left Hollywood. In 1951, he was refused reentry to the United States because he had signed an anti–nuclear weapons document, the "Stockholm Appeal." In 1958, he was allowed to return to Hollywood and receive a special Oscar "for his contributions to the world of entertainment for more than half a century."

H.J. Whitley
Barbara LaMarr house
2073 Grace Avenue

358

This was the original home of H.J. Whitley, the developer of Whitley Heights. In the twenties, the silent-movie star Barbara LaMarr, known as "the girl who was too beautiful," lived here until her mysterious death at the age of twenty-nine. LaMarr, who was born Reatha Watson, starred in *The Three Musketeers* with Douglas Fairbanks. She collapsed on the set of her last film, *The Girl from Montmartre* (1926), and died soon thereafter. Various causes of her death were offered, including tuberculosis, "nervous exhaustion," and "over-dieting." She is interred at the Hollywood Forever cemetery. There are a number of secret passageways in this home, one of which connected the chauffeur's room with Miss LaMarr's main bedroom.

Beulah Bondi house
6660 Whitley

In the thirties the author of *Lost Horizon*, James Hilton, lived here, as did the actress Rosalind Russell. Beulah Bondi lived here the longest, from 1941 until her death here in 1981. Bondi started on the Broadway stage in 1925 in the show *Wild Birds*. As early as her twenties, she began to portray primarily maternal roles—mothers, grandmothers, dowagers—for which she became known. *Street Scene*, in 1931, was her first role. Her most famous was as James Stewart's mother in the Christmastime classic favorite *It's A Wonderful Life* (1946). She also appeared in such films as *Vivacious Lady* (1938), and *Mr. Smith Goes to Washington* (1939). She kept acting all her days, even accepting TV roles into the seventies, as on "The Waltons," for which she won an Emmy. Her lifetime fear of fire caused her to install extra thick, fire-resistant walls in her home; they are the thickest walls in all of Whitley Heights.

Jean Harlow house
6603 Whitley Terrace

This house, with its massive fortress-like garage at the corner of Whitley Avenue and Whitley Terrace, was the home of Jean Harlow. One of the movie's most legendary sex symbols, the platinum-blonde Harlow was born Harlean Carpenter on March 3, 1911, in Kansas City, Missouri, and eloped with a businessman to Hollywood when she was only sixteen. Her first film work was as an extra in silent films, such as *Double Whoopee*, a 1929 Laurel & Hardy comedy. Her big break came from Howard Hughes, who cast her to replace Greta Nissen, the star of his movie *Hell's Angels*, when he decided to change the film from a silent into a talkie. Harlow's overt onscreen sensuality was initially disparaged by critics but embraced by the public, and she became a major screen star with the rare ability to be simultaneously sexy and comedic. She was also a fine actress, as she proved in such films as *Red-Headed Woman* (1932) and *Red Dust* (1932). Controversy surrounded her when it was determined that the death of her husband, Paul Bern, was caused by suicide. She married the cinematographer Harold Rosson, and was engaged for a long time but never wed to the actor William Powell. She died at the tragic age of twenty-six while making the movie *Saratoga* (1937). Her death remained a mystery for several years, until it was revealed that she died from failure of the kidney due to acute uremic poisoning.

Marie Dressler house
6718 Milner Road

This was the house of Marie Dressler, born Leila Marie Koerber, one of the silent screen's great comediennes. She starred on Broadway in 1892, and in 1914, she made her movie debut in the Chaplin classic *Tillie's Punctured Romance*. She made a few sequels to the Tillie movie, and also performed in the vaudeville circuit and in musical comedies. In 1927, she returned to the movies and became a major comedic star. She made an easy transition into talkies, and starred in dramatic as well as comedic films, including *Anna Christie* (1930), and *Min and Bill* (1930) for which she won the Best Actress Oscar. Throughout much of the thirties, she was the most popular movie star in the country.

The Villa Vallambrosa/Janet Gaynor & Gilbert Adrian house

2074 Watsonia Drive

This was the home to Janet Gaynor and the costume-designer Adrian. Built in 1922 by socialite Eleanor DeWitt, the Villa Vallambrosa was also leased to Dame Judith Anderson, Danny Thomas and Leonard Bernstein.

Janet Gaynor was a silent movie star who signed with Fox in the mid-twenties; her first big role was in *The Johnstown Flood* (1926). From that she went onto starring roles in such classic silent films as *Sunrise*, directed by Murnau and *Seventh Heaven*, directed by Borzage. She made a successful transition into talkies, and became a romantic star in the thirties. In 1939, she retired from movies and married the legendary fashion and costume designer Gilbert Adrian, with whom she lived in this famous house. She returned to occasional film and TV roles in the fifties, and in the eighties appeared on Broadway in a stage production of *Harold & Maude*.

Donald O'Connor house (Pike House)

6675 Whitley Terrace

Born on August 28, 1925, in Chicago, Donald O'Connor was the son of an acrobat and grew up performing on the vaudeville stage, where he learned to sing and dance. He started working in films when he was still a child, appearing in *Sing, You Sinners* (1938). In 1941, he was contracted with Universal, where he made a series of musicals, including *Get Hep to Love* (1941) and *Are You with It?* (1949). In 1950, he made the first of many *Francis* films,

which starred the famous talking mule of the same name, with voice provided by Chill Wills. In 1952, Universal lent him to MGM, where he co-starred with Gene Kelly in the classic *Singing in the Rain* (1952, which also featured Tommy Farrell). Other films he made included *Make 'Em Laugh* (1952), *The Buster Keaton Story* (1957) *The Wonders of Aladdin* (1961), and *That Funny Feeling* (1965). He took a long hiatus from films, and returned, along with Jimmy Cagney, in *Ragtime* (1981). For years he lived here at the Pike house, which won a series of architectural awards and is one of the only modern homes in all of Whitley Heights.

359

William Faulkner/Gloria Swanson house

6718 Milner Road

William Faulkner rented this house when he came to Hollywood to write for the movies. He wasn't happy about it, though—whenever Faulkner, the author of great novels such as *The Sound and the Fury*, and *A Light in August*, came to Hollywood, as he did many times to write for the movies, there was nothing he wanted more than to return to his native Mississippi. Faulkner first came to Hollywood in 1932 to work for MGM. Upon arriving he told his bosses he liked newsreels and cartoons the best, and would like to write for Mickey Mouse. When they politely explained to him that the Mouse belonged to Disney, his next choice was also denied, to write news for the newsreels. After toiling away on revisions of other writer's scripts which rarely got produced, he returned to Mississippi and wrote another novel, came back to Hollywood and worked for Fox, went back to Mississippi again to write two more novels, and then returned one last time in 1942, to write for Warners.

Faulkner told Jack Warner that he needed to work at home, so Warner relented, naturally expecting that by "home" he meant Hollywood. He didn't.

Faulkner went back home to Mississippi once again, where an exasperated Warner had to call him and insist he come back at once. Faulkner, like West and the others, saw a shallow bleakness in Hollywood. It was a bitterness no doubt born out of the fact that despite the greatness of his work, making a living as a novelist proved to be impossible. Hollywood came to symbolize this failing.

"Nobody here does anything," Faulkner told his friend Paul Wellman. "There's nobody here with any roots. Even the houses are built out of mud and chicken wire. Nothing ever happens and after a while a couple of leaves fall off a tree and then it'll be another year." Faulkner did make significant contributions to several movies directed by Howard Hawks, including The Big Sleep, based on Raymond Chandler's detective novel, and To Have Or Have Not, based on Hemingway's novel, but ended his Hollywood career by writing Jack Warner and begging to be released from his seven-year contract, which he had been told was just a formality.

In 1949, Faulkner won the Nobel Prize for Literature. His acceptance speech reflected a sense of renewed faith and optimism absent during his Hollywood days. "The artist must relearn the old verities and truths of the heart," he said, "the old universal truths lacking which any story is ephemeral and doomed—love and honor and pity and pride and compassion and sacrifice. . . . I decline to accept the end of man. . . . I believe that man will not merely endure: he will prevail. He is immortal, not because he alone among creatures has an inexhaustible voice, but because he has a soul, a spirit capable of compassion and sacrifice and endurance. The poet's, the writer's duty is to write about these things. . . . The poet's voice need not merely be the record of man, it can be one of the props, the pillars to help him endure and prevail."

Gloria Swanson rented this house between 1949 and 1950 with her mother while making her comeback in Sunset Boule-vard, being filmed at Paramount. She was born in Chicago on March 27, 1899, and is best-known to this day for her amazing portrayal of the aged silent movie queen Norma Desmond in Sunset Boulevard. She was ideal for the role, since was a silent movie queen herself. She made her first films in Chicago for the Essanay Company in 1915, and in 1916, she appeared with her future husband Wallace Beery. The two got married and moved to Hollywood, where she made a multitude of movies and became, by the mid-twenties, a super-star of the silent films, and the best-paid actress in the world. Married six times, she received a 1928 Oscar nomination for Best Actress in the movie Sadie Thompson, which was her first talkie. Unlike other silent stars, she made a successful transition into talkies, but in 1941, she took her leave from Hollywood, and didn't return until Sunset Boulevard in 1950. She did some TV work in the sixties, but mostly retired from the movies with the exception of her final role in Airport 1975. She died at the age of eighty-four in New York City.

Topside, Francis X. Bushman house [site]

2000 Kendra Court

A silent movie star, Bushman was known as the handsomest man in the world. He started acting onstage as a boy, and made his first film in 1911 for the Essanay company in Chicago. Because of his classic looks, he worked for a long time as an artist's model, which led him into movies. He became a romantic star of the silent movies during the teens, including Romeo & Juliet (1926). His most famous role is probably that of the Roman Massala in the silent Ben-Hur (1926). He became a multimillionaire, but lost almost his entire fortune in the crash of 1929. In the thirties his movie career was finished, but he continued to act in radio dramas. After that point he appeared only in a few movies and the occasional TV show, even making a rare appearance in the sixties on the "Batman" TV show. During his heyday it's said that he would be driven around Hollywood in his limo with a small rose-colored light illuminating his famous features. He lived here at the top of the hill in a tremendous mansion known as Topside. Surrounded by twenty royal palms, Topside possessed one of the first swimming pools in Hollywood. After Bushman moved out, it became a celebrity brothel during the forties, in which prostitutes would imitate specific movie stars. The house was torn down in 1957 to make way for a condominium development, which the neighbors fought against, and halted. For decades the lot sat undeveloped, the house in ruins, the ring of palms still standing. In 1998, a complex of new houses was built on the site.

Wolf's Lair

2869 *Durand Drive*

It was named in honor of its original owner, Milton Wolf, a developer who designed the fanciful, fairy-tale style of this castle with its turrets, towers and ramparts. Wolf died at his dining-room table here, and is said to still haunt the premises. Both Efrem Zimbalist Jr. and Doris Day were tenants here. The house has been used in several films, including the 1978 movie *Return from Witch Mountain*, starring Bette Davis.

Yamashiro

1999 Sycamore Avenue [north of Franklin, above the Magic Castle]

This was the home of two Jewish brothers, Adolph and Eugene Bernheimer, who were importers of Japanese artifacts. Meaning "mountain palace" in Japanese, Yamashiro is now a fine Japanese restaurant and has been used as a Japanese backdrop in countless movies, including *Sayonara* starring Marlon Brando and Red Buttons, *Teahouse of the August Moon*, and many others.

BIBLIOGRAPHY

Bakalinsky, Adah, and Larry Gordon. *Stairway Walks in Los Angeles*. Wilderness Press, 1990.

Basten, Fred. *Max Factor's Hollywood*. General Publishing Group, 1995.

Bengston, John. *Silent Echoes: Discovering Early Hollywood through the Films of Buster Keaton*. Santa Monica Press, 2000.

Broman, Sven. *Conversations with Garbo*. Viking, 1991.

Bukowski, Charles. *Hollywood*. Black Sparrow, 1993.

Chaplin, Charles. *My Autobiography*. n.p., 1964.

Clark, David L. *L.A. On Foot: A Free Afternoon*. Camaro, 1972.

DeMille, Cecil B. *Autobiography of Cecil B. DeMille*. Prentice-Hall, 1959.

Fairbanks, Douglas, Jr. *The Salad Days*. Doubleday, 1988.

Farmer, Frances. *Will There Really Be a Morning? An Autobiography*. Putnam, 1972.

Fitzgerald, F. Scott. *The Great Gatsby*. Scribner's, 1925.

———. *The Crack Up*. Scribner's, 1931.

———. *The Last Tycoon*. Scribner's, 1941.

Friedrich, Otto. *City of Nets: A Portrait of Hollywood in the 1940s*. Harper & Row, 1986.

Fountain, Leatrice Gilbert. *Dark Star: A Biography of John Gilbert*. St. Martin's, 1985.

Gordon, William A. *The Ultimate Hollywood Tour Book*. North Ridge, 1997.

Hill, Laurence L. *La Reina: Los Angeles in Three Centuries*. Security-First National Bank, 1929.

Hiney, Tom. *Raymond Chandler: A Biography*. Grove Press, 1997.

Jacobson, Laurie, and March Wanamaker. *Hollywood Haunted*. Angel City, 1994.

Johnson, Paul, ed. *The California Missions*. Lane Park, 1964.

Lamparski, Richard. *Lamparski's Hidden Hollywood*. Fireside, 1981.

Lasky, Jesse L., Jr. *Whatever Happened to Hollywood?* Funk & Wagnalls, 1973.

Latham, Aaron. *Crazy Sundays: F. Scott Fitzgerald in Hollywood*. Viking, 1971.

Leaming, Barbara. *Orson Welles: A Biography*. Viking Penguin, 1985.

Leigh, Janet. *There Really Was a Hollywood*. Doubleday, 1984.

Maas, Frederica Sagor. *The Shocking Miss Pilgrim*. University of Kentucky Press, 1999.

McGilligan, Pat. *Backstory*. University of California Press, 1986.

Monroe, Marilyn. *My Story*. Stein & Day, 1974.

Mulholland, Catherine. *William Mulholland and the Rise of Los Angeles*. University of California Press, 2000.

Palmer, Edwin Obadiah. *History of Hollywood*. Vols. 1 and 2. Arthur Cawston, 1937.

Schessler, Ken. *This Is Hollywood: An Unusual Movieland Guide*. Universal Books, 1991.

Schulberg, Budd. *The Disenchanted*. Random House, 1950.

Smith, Jack. *Jack Smith's L.A.* McGraw-Hill, 1980.

———. *The Big Orange*. Ward Ritchie, 1976.

Starr, Kevin. *Material Dreams: Southern California through the 1920s*. Oxford University Press, 1990.

Torrence, Bruce. *Hollywood: The First 100 Years*. New York Zoetrope, 1982.

Wallace, David. *Lost Hollywood*. St. Martin's, 2001.

Weinstock, Matt. *My L.A.* Current Books, 1947.

West, Nathanael. *The Day of the Locust*. New Classics, 1939.

Winters, Shelley. *Shelly II: The Middle of My Century*. Simon & Schuster, 1989.

Wray, Fay. *On the Other Hand: A Life Story*. St. Martin's, 1988.

INDEX

Abbott, Bud, 44, 215, 319, 320
Abbott, George, 188
Abbott & Costello Meet Franken-stein, 345
Abbott & Costello Meet the Mummy, 215
ABC, 191, 251
ABC Radio Network, 45, 338
ABC Television, 21, 338
Academy Awards cere-mony, 36, 38, 120, 171–72, 263, 336–37, 349–50
Academy of Magical Arts, 346
Academy Theater, 192
Acker, Jean, 321
Action in the North Atlantic, 47
Actor's Fund of America, 23
Actors' Studio, 318
Adams, Don, 107–8
Adams, Edie, 245
Adolph's Meat Tenderizer, 91–94, 351
Adoration, 145
Adrian, Gilbert, 327, 328, 359
Adventures of Captain Marvel, 303
"The Adventures of Rin Tin Tin," 304
Advice for the Lovelorn, 350
Affair with a Stranger, 337, 352
The African Queen, 138, 329
Aida, 24
Airplane Bar, 268
Airport 1975, 360
Alan's Tearoom, 158
Albert Beach Company, 343
"Alice," 196
Alice in Wonderland, 311
All about Eve, 32, 317
All the King's Men, 140
All My Sons, 78
Allen, Gracie, 35, 308
Allen, Steve, 180–84, 270, 289

Allen, Woody, 139, 143, 305
The Alliance, 23–24
Allied Artists Studios, 338
Alpert, Herb, 308
Alto Nido Apartments, 303
The Amazing Mrs. Holliday, 313
Ameche, Don, 32
American Cinematheque, 85, 313
American Film Institute, 303
American Legion Center, 86
American Society of Cine-matographers, 303
Ames, Leon, 209
Ames, Totty, 191–97
A&M Records, 50, 308
Amsterdam, Morey, 176
Anderson, Judith, 359
Andrews, Dana, 107
Andrews, Julie, 333
Andrus, Elmer, 343
"Andy Hardy" series, 233
Angel's Flight, 41
Ankeny, Jason, 335
Anna Christie, 359
Anna Karenina, 224
Annie Get Your Gun, 111
Annie Hall, 143
"Another Day," 328
Apollo Theater, 265
Arabian Nights, 128
Arbuckle, Roscoe "Fatty," 276, 333, 335, 339, 346
Are You with It?, 359
Argonaut, 259
The Argyle, 186
Arlen, Harold, 165, 353
Arlen, Richard, 113, 114
Armstrong, Louis, 267–68
Arnaz, Desi, 115, 188–89, 195–96, 257, 270, 308
Arnheim, Gus, 332
Aronson, Zelda, 108–12
Arthur, Jean, 200

Art Institute (Chicago, Ill.), 76–77
Artisan's Patio, 259, 262
Ashes of Vengeance, 334–35
Ashley, Sylvia, 326
The Asphalt Jungle, 317
Astaire, Adele, 295
Astaire, Fred, 34, 84, 192, 280–81, 295, 352
Astor, Mary, 342
At the Circus, 167
Atlantic City, 327
Atlantic Monthly, 305
Atlantic Richfield, 120
Attack of the Fifty Foot Woman, 338
Atwell, Lionel, 187–88
Austin, John C., 345
Autry, Gene, 233, 248, 319
Avalon, Frankie, 190

Babydoll, 81
Baby-O, 50
Bacall, Lauren, 203–4, 347, 354
Back to the Future, 314
Back to God's Country, 325
Bacon, James, 354
Bailey, Jack, 43
Bainbridge, Barton, 128–29
Baker, Carrol, 81
Baker, E.L., 7
Baker, Sophie, 279
Baker's, 274
Ball, Lucille, 34, 104, 115, 185, 188–89, 195–96, 270, 308, 347, 352
Balloon Route Excursion, 10
Bambi, 312
Bank of America, 274, 276
Bank of America building, 335
The Bank Dick, 344
Bara, Theda, 62, 217, 314
Barker Brothers, 157, 276, 287, 288
Barnett, Charlie, 119, 121
Barr, Roseanne, 310

Barrymore, Ethel, 252
Barrymore, John, 33, 35, 37, 315, 316, 342
Barthlemess, Richard, 140, 357
Bartlett, A.G., 25
Basie, Count, 243
"Batman," 11, 102, 107, 304, 360
Batman, 11
"Bat Masterson," 304
Baum, L. Frank, 12, 16–17, 163, 349
B. Dalton, 262
Beach, Albert, 17
The Beach Boys, 25, 51
Beachwood, 343
Beachwood Café, 264
Beachwood Village, 17, 23, 264, 322
"Beat the Clock," 146
Beat the Devil, 250, 329
The Beatles, 24, 45, 278–79, 286, 291, 304
Beatty, Warren, 143
Beavers, Louise, 216
Beery, Noah, 17, 176
Beery, Wallace, 156, 176, 357, 360
Belafonte, Harry, 267
Bela Lugosi Meets a Brooklyn Gorilla, 345
Beldam, George Francis Robert, 311
Bell, Rex, 117, 310, 311
Bell, Tony Rex, Jr., 114
Bellamy, Ralph, 220
The Bellamy Trial, 220
The Bells of St. Mary's, 34, 352
Belushi, John, 309
Benchley, Robert, 35, 315, 316
Bengston, John, 340
Ben-Hur, 140, 145, 360
Benneke, Tex, 43
Bennett, Constance, 313
Bennett, June, 121
Benny, Jack, 44, 232, 304
Bergen, Edgar, 160, 169, 270

364

Bergman, Ingrid, 33, 34, 299–300, 327, 352
Berle, Milton, 232, 236
Berlin, Irving, 62, 110–11
Berlin (Irving) Music Company, 109–11
Bern, Paul, 222, 358
Bernheimer, Adolph, 16, 361
Bernheimer, Eugene, 16, 361
Bernstein, Elmer, 174
Bernstein, Leonard, 359
Bernstein, Walter, 139–44
Berra, Yogi, 293
Berwyn's, 274
Bessie, Alvah, 47
The Best Years of Our Lives, 21, 34, 335, 352
Beth-El synagogue, 22
"Beulah," 331
Beveridge, John, 8
Beveridge, Philo, 1, 8
"Bewitched," 257
Biberman, Herbert, 47
Biff's, 269
The Big Parade, 140, 145, 219, 223
The Big Sleep, 33, 305, 306, 360
"Big Yellow Taxi," 316
Bijou, 50
Biltmore Theater, 74, 87, 89, 188, 206
Biograph, 13, 329, 330
Birth of a Nation, 20, 251, 330
Bison Company, 13
Bitzer, Billy, 66
The Black Cat, 345
Blackhawk (San Francisco, Calif.), 100
blacklist era, 46–48, 63, 138, 139–40, 141–42, 143, 174, 178, 282–85
Blake, Robert, 125
Blanc, Mel, 323
Blangstead, Else, 169–75
Blangstead, Formar, 171–73, 298
Blavatsky, Helena Petrova, 15
Bless the Beasts and the Children, 173
Blessed Sacrament, 119, 265
Blockade, 47
Blonde Venus, 331
Blondeau, Marie, 8
Blondeau, Rene, 8
Blondeau's Tavern, 8, 18, 31

Blondell, Bobby, 185
Blondell, Gloria, 185
Blondell, Joan, 185, 187
"Blondie," 325
Blondie of the Follies, 145
Blood on the Sun, 47
Blossom Room, 36, 120, 336–37
The Bluebird, 198
The Blue Dahlia, 306
Blue Hawaii, 33
Blue Jeans, 325
Board, Bob, 198–211
Bogart, Humphrey, 33, 81, 84, 126, 131, 138, 147, 188, 203–4, 250, 276, 306, 308, 309, 316, 317, 319, 329, 330, 348, 354
Bolger, Ray, 166
Bolman, Lee, 253–58
"Bonanza," 304
Bond Hotel (Hartford, Conn.), 162
Bondi, Beulah, 255–56, 357, 358
Boomerang, 78
Borden, Olive, 50
Borgnine, Ernest, 319
Born Yesterday, 32
Bow, Clara, 33, 35, 55, 57, 76, 113, 114, 117, 310–11, 315, 350
Boyer, Charles, 136, 297
Bradley, Tom, 154
Bradley's Five & Ten Bar, 86
Brando, Marlon, 32, 74, 77–79, 80, 146–47, 267, 271, 361
Brandstatter, Eddie, 40–41, 59, 347, 348
Brandt, Joe, 31
Brecht, Bertolt, 330
Brecker, Sidney, 114
Brel, Jacques, 347
Briana Productions, 280
Brice, Fanny, 275
Bringing Up Baby, 34
Broadway (New York), 58, 77–78, 146, 189
Broadway Department Store, 75, 86, 157, 177, 252, 273
Broadway Melody of 1936, 332
The Broken Oath, 330
Bronson Canyon, 120
Bronson Caves, 7, 303–4
Brooks, Jo, 95, 97, 98, 99, 100, 101
Brooks, Mel, 108, 334
The Brothers Karamazov, 174

Brown, Clarence, 225, 226
Brown, Joe E., 120, 186
Brown, Les, 43, 349
Brown Derby, 40, 75, 86, 103, 157, 184, 201, 205, 230, 248, 250, 252, 274, 276, 277, 304
Brownell, John, 59
Brunton Studios, 350
Brush Canyon, 10, 303
Brynner, Yul, 142, 143
The Buccaneers, 130, 132
Buck, Frank, 233
Buck Jones' Wild West, 325
Bucklin, Wilford, 351
Budapest Academy of Theatrical Arts, 345
Bug & Meyer Group, 334
Burke, Billie, 164
Burnett, Carol, 321
Burns, George, 35, 270, 308
Burr, Raymond, 291, 307–8
Burroughs, Edgar Rice, 12, 35, 308, 351
Burton, Richard, 32
Bushman, Francis X., xi, 35, 315, 357, 360–61
Bus Stop, 318
Buster Brown Shoes, 168
The Buster Keaton Story, 359
Butram, Pat, 248
Buttons, Red, 261
Buttons and Bows, 195
Bye Bye Birdie, 32
The Byrds, 51, 310

Caddo Productions, 337. See also Hell's Angels
Caesar, Sid, 245
Cagney, James, 33, 81, 82, 84, 188, 347, 359
Cahuenga Pass (El Portozuelo), 2, 5
Cahuenga Valley, 6
Cahuenga Valley Railroad, 7–8, 10
Cain, James, 305
The Caine Mutiny, 32
The California Missions (Johnson), 3, 4–5
California Movie Company, 31–32
"Californians," 304
California Studio, 21, 352
Call Me by My Rightful Name, 328
Camelot, 298
The Cameraman, 339, 340

Camille, 335
Camino Palmero, 335
Canterbury, 109
Cantor, Eddie, 44, 320
Ca-Oug-Na, 2, 39
Capitol Records, 44–45, 267, 277, 278, 304
Capitol Tower, 45, 277
Capone, Al, 123
Capone, Ralph, 123
Capote, Truman, 250
Capra, Frank, 36, 172, 295, 337
Captain from Castillo, 287
The Captain Hates the Sea, 220
Captains Courageous, 327
Card, Jim, 220
Career, 149
Carey, Harry, Sr., 121
Carissimi, Joseph, 40
Carmen, 24
Carrey, Jim, 310
Carroll, Earl, 42–43
Carson, Johnny, 120, 125–26, 188, 291, 346
Carson City, 304
Carter, Benny, 332
Carter, Janice, 207
Carter, Mrs. Artie Mason, 24, 320
Casablanca, 33, 250, 276, 309, 330
Casa Rayda, 343
Cassidy, Hopalong, 21, 233, 234, 273
Cassity, Tyler, 323
Castillo Del Lago, 304–5, 334
Castle Argyle, 16, 305
Castle Glengarry, 16, 305
Castle San Souci, 305
Cat & Fiddle, 270
Catlin, Charlie, 161
Cat Women of the Moon, 215
Caulker, Daryl, 97
Cavalier (motel), 247
Cave, 352
CBC Film Sales Corporation, 31
CBS, 39, 45, 103, 104, 191, 205, 251, 309
CBS Playhouse Theater, 38, 312
CBS Radio Network, 40, 269, 309
CBS Television, 46, 307, 309
C.C. Brown's Ice Cream, 148, 158, 180, 186, 270, 304
Central Market, 289
Century, 31

Century City, 32
Century of Progress, 86
Certified Grocers, 90
Chadwick (production company), 31, 282
Champion, Marge, 321
Champlin, Charles, 243–51
"Champlin on Film," 245
Chandler, Harry, 14, 39, 40, 28, 318
Chandler, Norman, 43
Chandler, Raymond, 40, 43, 305–6, 347, 348
Chaney, Lon, 50, 140, 222, 223, 321, 355
Chaplin, Charlie, 13, 17, 20, 22, 31, 36, 37, 40, 41, 58, 69, 70–73, 75, 80, 85, 90, 118, 121, 123–24, 144, 151, 152, 156, 169, 174–75, 222, 223–24, 225, 245, 249, 261, 272, 281–82, 290, 291, 306–8, 309, 317, 319, 324, 326, 328, 330–31, 338–39, 342, 344, 345, 346, 348, 353, 355
Chaplin, Charlie, Jr., 124, 323–24
Chaplin, Hannah, 324, 325
Chaplin, Sydney, 71, 175, 318
Chaplin Studio, 31, 121–22, 196, 306–8
Charisse, Cyd, 190
Charles, Ray, 308
Charlie Chan series, 338
Chasen's, 122, 230
Chateau Elysee, 35, 56–57, 272, 308–9
Chateau Marmont, 147, 309
Chatsworth, 158
Chevalier, Maurice, 357–58
Chiang Kai-shek, 264
Chicago Theater (Chicago, Ill.), 188
Children of Eve, 325
China Doll, 226
China Jade, 277
China's Little Devils, 47, 121
Chinatown, 30, 33, 329
Chinese Theater. See Grauman's Chinese Theater
The Choirboys, 304
Christie, Al, 309
Christie, Charlie, 309

Christie Brothers, 18
Christie Comedies, 18
Christie Hotel, 35, 309
Christie Realty Building, 309
Christies' Bathing Beauties, 22
Christmas Holiday, 313
Christmas parade, 120, 124, 150, 154, 191, 205, 221, 287
Chumash, 2, 3
Church of Scientology, 308–9
Cinegrill, 36, 148, 197, 337
Cinema Theater, 265
Cinematograph, 11–12
Circle Bar, 193, 260
Circle Theater, 318
The Circus, 31
Circus Polka, 70
Ciro's, 42, 100–101, 122, 148, 188, 191, 230, 310
Citizen Kane, 34, 210, 250, 313, 335–36, 352
City Hall (Los Angeles, Calif.), 111
City Lights, 31, 73, 307
Clair, Ina, 69
Clark, Gene, 310
Clark, William Andrews, Jr., 320, 324–25
Clarke, Mrs. Chauncey, 23
Cleopatra, 32, 326
Clift, Montgomery, 36, 237, 269, 318, 337
Climax Studio, 338–39
Climber, Matt, 331
Clooney, Rosemary, 333
Clover Club, 310
Clune Studios, 21, 352
Coach, 122
Coats, Phyllis, 195
Cobb, Lee J., 174, 197
Cobb, Robert, 40
"Cobwebs and Nuts," 323
Cock 'n' Bull, 122
Coconuts, 33
Cody, Iron Eyes, 325
Coffee Dan's, 277
Cohen, Mickey, 125
Cohn, Harry, 31–32, 84, 129, 131, 135, 136–37, 172, 309, 310, 322, 325
Cohn, Jack, 31–32
Colbert, Claudette, 32, 41, 87, 116, 346
Cole, Cornelius, 7, 311
Cole, Lester, 47

Cole, Nat "King," 45, 191, 243, 278, 290, 310, 333
Cole, Seward, 7
Cole, Willoughby, 7
Colegrove, Olive, 7, 311
Colegrove, 22, 311
Coleman, Ronald, 50, 271
Collected Works (Garcia Lorca), 324
Colonna, Jerry, 44
The Color Purple, 173
Columbia Drugstore, 271
Columbia Pictures, 31–32, 51, 135, 136–37, 140, 143, 171, 188, 199, 201, 202, 203, 205, 207, 299, 317
Columbia Square, 309
Comedy Store, 42, 310
Comenici, Nadia, 173
Commodore Hotel, 86
Community Sing, 320
Connelly, Mark, 315
Consolidated Film Industries, 178
Conway, Jack, 18
Coogan, Jackie, 307
Cooke, Alistair, 235
Coolie, Spade, 96
Cooper, Alice, 319
Cooper, Gary, 33, 112, 113–14, 116, 131, 233, 352
Cooper, Jackie, 116, 246, 304
The Copier, 146
Coppola, Francis Ford, 15, 320
Cops, 340
Corman, Roger, 330
Cornered, 47
Cornthwaite, Robert, 102–8
Corrier, Miriam, x
Corrio, Ann, 230
Cory, Wendell, 204
Cosby, Bill, 278
Cosmopolitan, 212
The Cossack Whip, 325
Costello, Dolores, 38, 355
Costello, Lou, 44, 215, 319, 320
Cotton Club, 177
The Countess from Hong Kong, 307
The Count of Monte Cristo, 12–13
Cover Girl, 202
Co-Yang-Na, 2, 5
Crabbe, Buster, 68, 233, 319

Crawford, Joan, 33, 61, 131, 201, 304, 326, 352
Crespi, Juan, 4
Crosby, Bing, 33, 50, 86, 111, 116, 154, 252, 350, 355
The Cross and the Arrow (Maltz), 47
Crossfire, 47
The Cross of Lorraine, 47
Crossroads of the World, 42, 311
Cruise, Tom, 153
Cukor, George, 133, 171, 354
Culver City Hotel, 163
Curry's Ice-Cream Parlor, 120, 353
Curtis, Billy, 161–62
Curtis, Tony, 190, 318
Cutler Shoe Company, 86
CVC Drugstore, 273, 274

Daisy Dell, 23, 24, 320
Dale, Bobbie, 90
Dana, Viola, 325
"Danger," 141
Dark Angel (Fountain), 216
"The Darktown Strutter's Ball," 327
Davenport, Dorothy, 18
David, Charles, 313
David, Saul, 197
David Copperfield, 344
Davies, Marion, 38, 145–46, 198, 200–201, 209–11, 220, 272, 322, 325, 349, 354, 357
Davis, Bette, 33, 34, 36, 44, 133, 256, 320, 338, 340, 352, 357, 361
Davis, Sammy, Jr., 42, 100–101, 287, 291, 310
Dawn Fresh Valet Service, 91, 93
Day, Doris, 33, 43, 361
The Day of the Locust, 350
"Days of Our Lives," 148
Dead End, 335
Deadline at Dawn, 47
de Havilland, Olivia, 44, 203, 320
Dean, James, 41, 146–47, 291, 309, 317, 349, 354
Deane-Tanner, William Desmond, 325–26

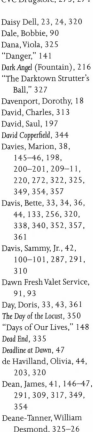

"The Death of Charlot's Mother" (Garcia Lorca), 324
Death of a Salesman, 174
"Death Valley Days," 21, 352
Decca Records, 86
DeCorti, Oscar. See Cody, Iron Eyes
"The Defenders," 328
Deitrich, Marlene, 35, 42, 44, 197, 315, 320
DeLongpre, Paul, 1, 8–9, 10, 11, 12, 17
Del Rio, Dolores, 43, 192, 199
Demarest, William, 46
DeMille, Cecil B., 17, 19–20, 33, 37, 46, 65–67, 115, 116, 117–18, 127–28, 129–31, 132–33, 134, 170–71, 172, 216, 218–19, 220, 228, 252, 275, 303, 311, 312, 313, 316, 320, 322, 326, 329, 338, 344, 346, 351
DeMille, Constance, 65–66
DeMille, Katherine, 126, 130
Dempsey, Jack, 35, 315
"Dennis the Menace," 171
de Portola, Gaspar, 3–4
Derrah, Robert, 42, 311
Desilu Productions, 34, 115, 188, 196, 352
Destination Tokyo, 47
DeSylva, Buddy, 44
Deutsch, Larry, 85, 89, 90–94
The Devil's Playground, 199
DeVito, Danny, 290, 292
DeVol, Frank, 108
Devore, Sy, 158, 268, 270
DeVorzon, Barry, 173
DeWitt, Eleanor, 359
Diamond Lil, 356
"Diamond Lil," 206
Diamond, Neil, 192, 197
Dianetics, 308
Dickens, Charles, 229
Dickson, William, 12
Dietrich, Marlene, 33, 41, 136, 297, 310, 331, 346
Dimaggio, Joe, 317
Director's Guild, 147
The Disenchanted (Schulberg), 316
Disney Brothers Studio, 311–12

Disney Studios, 34, 38, 121, 313, 345–46
Disney, Robert, 311
Disney, Roy, 311
Disney, Walt, 75, 118, 121, 311–12, 319, 352
Disneyland, 121, 312
Dit, Otto, 259
Dix, Richard, 199
Dixon Studio, 32
Dmytryk, Edward, 47
A Dog's Life, 31, 51
Dolores' Drive-In, 227
Dominic's, 122, 124–25
Donen, Stanley, 189–90
Don Juan, 33
Don Lee Broadcasting Company, 318
Don't Give Up the Ship, 149
Doolittle Theater, 38, 252, 269, 312
The Doors, 51
Dot Records, 270
Double Indemnity, 305, 312–13
Double Whoopee, 358
Douglas, Kirk, 83, 136–37, 280
Douglas, Melvyn, 82
Douglas, Michael, 81, 83
Dove, Billie, 144, 145, 149–50
Dr. Jekyll & Mr. Hyde, 327
Dr. Strangelove, 32
Dracula, 119, 345
Dressler, Marie, 358–59
Duck Soup, 33
Duff, Grace Shaw, 343
Duke Ellington Orchestra, 44, 320
Dumbo, 312
Dunne, Irene, 202–3
Dupar's, 111
Durant, Tim, 174
Durante, Jimmy, 236, 316
Durbin, Deanna, 42, 217, 220, 313
Dwan, Allan, 327
Dye, Rit, 97
Dylan, Bob, 24, 308, 309, 310

Earl, Guy, 39
Earl Carroll's Theater, 42–43, 202, 267
Earthquake, 30
earthquakes, 4, 30, 51, 60
Easter Parade, 341
East Side Kids, 287, 338
Easy Rider, 299
Easy Street, 338
Eckstine, Billy, 98, 99

Eclair Company, 18
Eddy, Nelson, 322, 326
Edison, Marshall, 89–90, 91
Edison, Thomas, 11, 12, 18
Edison company, 85
Edison studios, 325
Edmonds, Kenneth "Babyface," 340
Edmonds Tower, 340
Edwards, Ralph, 291
Edwards, Skinny, 293
Ed Wood, 344
Egyptian Theater, 15, 36–37, 51, 85, 87, 94–95, 103, 111, 158, 161, 186, 192–94, 266, 275, 287, 313, 335, 351
Eisenhower, Dwight D., 43
El Camino Real de Rey, 5
El Capitan Theater, 15, 38, 51, 266, 276, 313, 336, 345–46
Ellington, Duke, 243. See also Duke Ellington Orchestra
Embassy Club, 41, 348
Emmy Awards, 319, 350
The Empire Strikes Back, 32
An Empire of Their Own (Gabler), 332
"The End of a Perfect Day," 321
Entwistle, Peg, 351, 355
EPCOT Center, 312
Epstein, Aaron, 258–64
Epstein, Louis, 43, 258, 259
Equinox, 304
Esquire, 314
Essanay Company, 13, 18, 21, 338, 360
Evans, Dale, 148
Evans, Robert, 271
Everett, Flossie, 181
Everybody's Acting, 320, 337
Everybody's Sing, 200
Every Sunday, 313
The Evil Eye, 85
Ewell, Tom, 74, 75

The Fabulous Baker Boys, 337
Face behind the Mask, 137
Factor, Frank (Max Factor Jr.), 347
Factor, Max, 41, 346–47
Fail-Safe, 32, 143
Fairbanks, Douglas, Jr., 33, 35, 37, 153, 225, 308, 313, 319, 322,

325, 326, 350
Fairbanks, Douglas, Sr., 23, 31, 36, 72, 76, 152–53, 307, 313, 316, 321, 322, 326, 329, 335, 336, 338, 345, 352, 355, 358
Family Plot, 248
Family Theater (Gary, Ind.), 75
Famous Lasky studios, 350
Famous Players Fiction Studios, 253
Famous Players–Lasky Corporation, 33
Fantasia, 34, 312
Fantastic Voyage, 197
"Fantasy Island," 304
Farmer, Frances, 340
Farmers Markets, 258–59
Farnum, Dustin, 19, 44
Farquhar, Don, 155–60
Farrell, Charles, 327
Farrell, Glenda, 185, 190
Farrell, Henry, 338
Farrell, Tommy, 185–91, 195, 196, 359
Farrow, Charles, 87
"Father Knows Best," 209
Faulkner, William, 40, 43, 248, 256, 290, 306, 314, 348, 357, 359–60
Fay, Alice, 230
Fazenda, Louise, 50
"The FBI Story," 148
FBO Studios, 34, 351
Felix, Manny, 290–93
Fields, W.C., 36, 50, 233, 337, 344, 345, 355
Figwood, xi
Finch, Flora, 321
Finch, Peter, 322, 327
Fine Arts Studio, 20
Firestone, Polly, 203
The First Herd, 328
First Love, 217, 220, 313
First Motion Picture Unit, 176–77
First National Pictures, 31, 33, 295, 307
First United Methodist Church of Hollywood, 313–14
Fisher, Eddie, 288
Fiske, Minnie Madden, 22
Fitzgerald, Ella, 43, 95, 98, 99–100, 333
Fitzgerald, F. Scott, x, 35, 40, 43, 178, 248, 261–62, 290, 314,

315, 316, 327, 348, 350, 353
Five Finger Plan, 155, 156
Flamingo, 334
Fleming, Victor, 167, 327
Flesh and the Devil, 55, 60, 224
"The Flintstones," 323
The Floorwalker, 339
Floradora Girl, 38, 349
Flynn, "Lefty," 325
Flynn, Errol, 33, 36, 43, 137, 148, 188, 308, 337, 340
Fogcutters, 120
Fonda, Henry, 32, 33, 146, 200, 293, 297, 300, 313
Fonda, Peter, 294, 297, 299, 300
Fonda Theater, 273
Fontaine, Joan, 140, 313
Fontenoy, 296
Force of Evil, 215
Ford, Glenn, 332
Ford, John, 34, 80, 283, 352
Ford, Victoria, 18
Forest Lawn Cemetery, 326, 339, 349
For the Love of Mary, 313
Formosa, 122
Foster, Preston, 50
Fotoplay, 145–46
Fountain, Leatrice Joy Gilbert, 215–26
Fountainebleau (Miami, Fla.), 188
Four Brothers Band, 328
Four Horsemen of the Apocalypse, 60, 117, 331, 336, 347
Fox, Jules, 95–101
Fox, William, 32, 314
Fox Studios, 197, 314, 332, 333, 350, 359
Fox West Coast, 193
Franciosa, Tony, 149
Francis films, 359
Frankenstein, 233, 345, 347
Frasier, E.M., 35, 340
Frederick's of Hollywood, 15, 191, 194–95, 274, 314–15
Freeman, Kathleen, 283
The French Connection, 32, 172
Frenchie, 214
Frenzy, 248
The Freshman, 178
Friend, Arthur, 19
Frisco, Joe, 327
Froman's Deli, 69

From Here to Eternity, 32
From the Manger to the Cross, 357
The Front, 139, 142, 143
Frontier Club (Las Vegas, Nev.), 334
The Front Page, 331
Funny Girl, 32
A Funny Thing Happened on the Way to the Forum, 339

Gable, Clark, 32, 36, 43, 43, 81, 84, 131, 133–34, 144, 146, 149, 154, 190, 192, 194, 214, 230, 248, 252, 256, 297, 304, 308, 313, 318, 319, 326, 337, 349
Gable, Minna, 230
Gabler, Neal, 332
Gallagher's, 270
Ganz, Rudolph, 24
Garbo, Greta, 55, 60, 61, 131, 199–200, 216, 219, 224
Garcia Lorca, Federico, 324
Garden Court Apartments, 35, 152, 276, 316
Garden Court Hotel, 51, 180
Garden of Allah, 35, 178, 315–16
The Garden of Allah (Hitchens novel), 315
Gardner Junction, 156
Gardner Library, 158
Gardner, Ava, 30, 173
Garfield, John, 44, 47, 215, 320
Garland, Judy, 41, 42, 43, 119, 157, 164, 165, 197, 200, 204, 233, 237, 304, 313, 316, 333, 346, 353, 354
Garner, James, 321
Garson, Greer, 44, 320
Gaslight, 341
Gaynor, Janet, 44, 120, 327–28, 346, 357, 359
The General, 339
"General Hospital," 148
General Motors, 180
General Teleradio, 34, 337, 352
General Tire and Rubber, 34, 337, 352
Gentlemen Prefer Blondes, 317
George White's Scandals, 332
Gershwin, George, 69, 70
Gershwin, Ira, 70

Get Hep to Love, 359
"Get Smart," 102, 107–8
Getz, Stan, 269
The Ghosts of Yesterday, 334
Gigi, 269–70, 357
Gilbert, Ben, 110
Gilbert, John, 55, 60, 61, 145, 215–17, 219–25
Gilbert, Wolfie, 96
Gilda, 281
The Girl Can't Help It, 330
The Girl from Montmartre, 329, 358
Girls, Girls, Girls, 33
Girls in the Night, 190
Gish, Lillian, 20, 76, 225, 316, 352, 357
Gish girls, 85
The Glass Menagerie, 77, 79
Glazer, Barnie, 222
Glen or Glenda?, 345
Glen Holly Hotel, 9, 10
Glenn Miller Orchestra, 349
Glinda of Oz, 349
Glorious Betsy, 38, 355
Glyn, Eleanor, 117
The Goat, 340
"God Bless America," 110
Goddard, Paulette, 73, 310
The Godfather, 33
Gog, 67
Going Hollywood, 209
Gold Star, 50
Goldfish, Samuel, 19, 329. See also Goldwyn, Sam
The Gold Rush, 307
Goldwyn, Sam, 47, 116, 286, 306, 326, 346, 355
Goldwyn studios, 31n9, 191, 355
Gone with the Wind, 127, 133–34, 167, 313, 327, 331
Goodman Theater (Chicago, Ill.), 76–77
Googies, 147
Gooley, Eddie, 68–69
Gordon, Dexter, 332
Gorgeous George, 355
Gotham Deli, 111, 180
Gotham's, 289
Gould, Elliot, 317
Gower Gulch, 31, 271, 316
Grable, Betty, 32, 44, 62, 316, 320
Grady, Bill, 208

Graham, Sheila, 314, 315, 353
Grand Temple of the Holy Cross, 341–42
Grand Theater (Gary, Ind.), 76
Grant, Cary, 33, 34, 35, 131, 192, 308, 334, 346, 352
Grant, Johnny, 50, 150–55, 249, 293, 355
Grant Building, 154
The Grapes of Wrath, 32, 335
Grauman, Sid, 36–37, 41, 152, 153, 154, 193, 266, 313, 316, 346
Grauman's Chinese Theater, xiii, 15, 36, 37, 51, 87, 103, 111, 148, 150, 153, 166, 230, 248, 266, 276, 287, 313, 316, 335, 353
The Great Dictator, 73, 307
The Greatest Show on Earth, 326
The Great Gatsby (film), 333
The Great Gatsby (Fitzgerald novel), 314, 327
The Great Train Robbery, 12
Greek Theater, 41, 328
Greenstreet, Sidney, 330
Grey, Elmer, 356
Grey, Lillian, 324
Grey, Lita, 124, 324
Griffith, Andy, 146
Griffith, D.W., 13, 20–21, 31, 33, 36, 125, 151–52, 251, 253, 307, 327, 329, 330, 335, 340, 344, 345, 357
Griffith, Griffith J., 41–42, 317, 328
Griffith Observatory, 41–42, 317
Griffith Park, 41, 65, 321, 328
Grogignan, John, 5
The Group, 328
The Grove, 110
Grusin, Dave, 173
Guaranty Bank, 35
Guess Who's Coming to Dinner, 32, 237
Guinness Book of World Records Museum, 15, 305
"Gunsmoke," 21, 304, 352
Guyes Company, 177
A Guy Named Joe, 47, 327

367

Hackett, Buddy, 188, 236, 245
Hackett, Joan, 328
Hackman, Gene, 246–47
Haley, Jack, 166
Halifax Apartments, 56, 158, 159
Hall, John, 287
Hall of Science, 41
Hamblin, Stuart, 148
Hamilton, Margaret, 166, 276
Hammett, Dashiell, 40, 43, 348
Hampton, Jesse D., 31
Hampton, Lionel, 95, 98, 100
Hampton Studios, 31, 355
The Happy Years, 208–9
Harburg, E.Y., 165
Hardy, Oliver, 120, 206–7, 233, 236, 316, 358
Hargitay, Mickey, 331
Harlow, Jean, 32, 146, 320, 334, 337, 357, 358
Harms Music, 70
Harold & Maude, 328, 359
Harper's Weekly, 22
Harriet and the Piper, 329
Harris, Julie, 298
Harris, Mildred, 328
Harrison, George, 317
Harry Cooper's, 111
Harry James, 349
Hart, William S., 220
Hartford, Huntington, 175
Harvey, Arthur E., 354
Harvey Hotel, 322
Hastings Ranch, 341
Haunch Paunch and Jowl, 47
"Have Gun Will Travel," 304
Haver, June, 287
Hawks, Howard, 106–7, 294, 297, 306, 357, 360
Hawks, Slim, 294, 295, 297
Hayward, Susan, 178
Haywire (Hayward), 294
"Haywire," 294
Hayworth, Louise, 195
Hayworth, Rita, 41, 136, 202, 346
"Hazel," 171
Hearst, William Randolph, 35, 146, 201, 210, 211, 308, 325, 357

Hearst Castle, 61
The Heart of a Race Tout, 13
The Heat's On, 356
Hecht, Ben, 222
Hecht, Harold, 140
Hefner, Hugh, 319
Heineman, Alfred, 343
Heineman, Arthur, 341, 343
Hellfire, 215
Hellman, Lillian, 43, 46
Hello Dolly, 32
Hell's Angels, 337, 358
Hemingway, Ernest, 264, 294–95, 296–97, 348
Henie, Sonja, 32
Henning, Sonje, 126
Henry, O., 232
Hepburn, Audrey, 269–70
Hepburn, Katharine, 32, 34, 81, 139, 247, 352
Herald Examiner, 89
Herbert, Henry, 24
Here We Go Again, 169
Her Indian Hero, 18
"Here's Lucy," 189
Herman, Woody, 328
"Her Secret Brassiere" company, 88
Hershey, Myra, 23, 320, 321
Heston, Charlton, 30, 112, 328
Hewell, Tom, 270
He Who Gets Slapped, 140, 222–23
Heyward, Bill, 293–300
Heyward, Brooke, 294, 299
Heyward, Leland, 293, 294, 295–96, 297
"The High Chapparal," 304
High Nelly, 187
Hightower, 317
Hill, Laurence, 1, 12, 17–18, 23, 34–35
Hill, McDonald & Hill, 29
Hill, Virginia, 334
Hillview Hotel, 185
Hilton, James, 358
Hines, Earl "Fatha," 268
His Glorious Night, 216, 225
History of Hollywood (Palmer), xiii, 1. See also Palmer, Edwin Obadiah
Hitchcock, Alfred, 33, 34, 245, 248–49, 250, 330, 352
Hitchcock, Alma, 249
Hitchens, Robert, 315
Hitler, Adolf, 264

Hitler's Children, 47
Hockney, David, 337
Hogan, Dave, 13
Holden, William, 32, 33, 87, 303, 309, 353
Holiday, Billie, 98, 99, 310
Holiday, Judy, 32
Holly Chateau, 16
Hollygrove Orphanage, 317–18
Hollywood:
    annexation into Los Angeles, 14–15;
    building boom, 34–39; dawn of, 6–11; early origins, 2; emergence of the studios, 31–34; first films, 18–23; high culture in, 23–25; Hollywood Freeway construction, 48–50; incorporation of, 7; modernization's effects, 49–50; naming of, 6; native people, 2–6; radio industry in, 39–40; silver in the streets, 19–20; Sunset Strip, 42–43; television industry in, 45–46; Walk of Fame, 50–51, 150, 152, 153, 154, 180, 249, 263, 304, 355 water concerns, 13–14, 25–30; World War II in, 43–44
Hollywood American Legion Post, 319
Hollywood Assessment District, 50
Hollywood Athletic Club, 41, 222, 319
Hollywood Boulevard, 319
Hollywood Bowl, 23, 255, 262–63, 320
Hollywood Canteen, 43, 44, 193, 320
Hollywood Cemetery, 210
Hollywood Center Studios, 15, 320
Hollywood Chamber of Commerce, 25, 251, 270, 319, 355
Hollywood Citizen, 88, 157
Hollywood Dam News, 28
"Hollywood Diamond Jubilee," 319
Hollywood: The First 100 Years (Torrence), 1

Hollywood Forever Cemetery, 322–36
Hollywood Freeway, 5, 48–50
Hollywood General Studios, 320
Hollywood Guild and Canteen, 44. See also Hollywood Canteen
Hollywood Haunted (Wanamaker and Jacobson), 322–23
Hollywood Heritage, xiii, 259, 260, 356
Hollywood Heritage Museum, 320
Hollywood-Highland project, xiii, 21, 50, 51, 253, 263–64, 293, 321, 353
Hollywood High School, 24, 119, 156, 320–21
Hollywood Hospital, 185
Hollywood Hotel, xiii, 40, 50, 51, 191, 276, 288, 321, 325
Hollywood Hotel, 191, 321
Hollywoodland development, 28, 39, 318, 321–22
Hollywood(land) sign, 25, 39, 94–95, 119, 154, 318–19, 351
Hollywood Legion Stadium, 119
Hollywood Memorial Cemetery, 323
Hollywood News, 26
Hollywood Ocean View Tract, 9
Hollywood Palace, 38, 336
Hollywood Playhouse, 336
Hollywood Presbyterian Church, 148
Hollywood Ranch, 350
Hollywood Ranch Market, 267
Hollywood Roosevelt Hotel, 120, 336–37. See also Roosevelt Hotel
"Hollywood Squares," 188
Hollywood Storage Company, 15
Hollywood Studio Club, 212
Hollywood's Women's Club, 157

Hollywood Ten, 47–48, 279
Hollywood Theater, 322
Hollywood Tire Company, 155–56
Hollywood Women's League, 165
Holmes, Ben, 181
Holt, Geraldine, 264–71
Holtz, Lou, 195
Home Savings Bank, 274
Hoover, George, 9
Hopalong Cassidy movies, 352. See also Cassidy, Hopalong
Hope, Bob, 33, 43, 44, 46, 50, 116, 126, 150, 195, 304, 345, 350, 355
Hopkins, Anthony, 239
Hopper, Dennis, 299, 300
Hornblow, Arthur, 211, 213, 282
Horne, Lena, 42, 269, 310, 347
Horsley, David, 18, 27, 28, 39
Horsley, William, 18, 28
Hotchenor, Henry, 343
Hotchenor, Marie Russak, 342–43
Hotel, 82
Hotel Anchovy, 333
Hotel Berlin, 47
Houdini, Harry, 36, 222, 340
Houseman, John, 306
House Un-American Activities Committee, 138, 178, 284, 331
How to Marry a Millionaire, 317
Hubbard, L. Ron, 308
Hudson, Rock, 287
Hughes, Howard, 34, 105, 145, 150, 214, 317, 320, 337, 352, 358
Hughes Headquarters, 337
Hughes Tool Company, 337
Hugo's Hotdogs, 289
Of Human Hearts, 226
The Hunchback of Notre Dame, 34, 352
Hungry Tiger, 289
Hunt, Myron, 356
Hunter, Kim, 79
Hunter, Tab, 287
Huntington Hartford, 38
Huntington Hartford Theater, 312

Hurd, E.C., 7–8, 9
Huston, John, 127, 137, 138, 250, 318, 322, 328–29
Huston, Walter, 226, 328–29
Hutton, Barbara, 334
Hutton, C. Clayton, xii, 24, 38–39
Huxley, Aldous, 43, 354
Hyatt, Edward, 29

Ice Capades, 126
Idiot Delights, 270
"I Got Rhythm," 70
"I Love Lucy," 34, 196, 308, 352
I. Magnin, 60, 111, 157
I Married an Angel, 326
I Met My Love Again, 200
I'm a Fugitive from a Chain Gang, 185, 187
Immaculate Heart College, 303
The Immigrant, 339
I'm No Angel, 331
I.M.P. Movie Company, 18
Ince, Thomas, 17, 20, 35, 272, 308, 338, 355
Independent Motion Picture Company of America, 329
Inge, William, 318
In the Heat of the Night, 21, 352
Inherit the Wind, 332
In Like Flint, 197
Innis Shoe Company, 157
Intake, 29
International House of Pancakes, 253
Intolerance, 20–21, 253, 330, 335
Invasion of the Body Snatchers, 34, 304, 322, 338
Ipi-Tapai, 3
Ireland, John, 89, 126
Irene, 340–41
Isham Jones' Juniors, 328
Isherwood, Christopher, 261, 264, 271, 354
Isis Unveiled (Blavatsky), 15
It, 117
It Café, 310–11
It Happened One Night, 32
It's All True, 315
It's Boss, 310
It's a Mad, Mad, Mad, Mad World, 236–37, 240, 339
It's a Wonderful Life, 34, 352, 358

Iwerks, Ub, 311–12

"The Jack Benny Show," 309
Jackson, Michael, 308
Jacobs-Bond, Carrie, 90, 321, 351
Jacobson, Laurie, 322–23
Jacques, H.L., 27
Jagger, Mick, 309
James, Harry, 43, 123
Janes, Carrie, 338
Janes, Grace, 338
Janes, Herman, 17, 338
Janes, Mabel, 338
Janes, Mary, 17, 338
Janes' House, 185, 338
Jannings, Emil, 120
Jasper Studios, 320
The Jayhawkers, 304
The Jazz Singer, 33, 85, 225, 251, 356
Jensen, Louise, 215
Jessel, George, 335
Jesse Lasky Feature Play Company, 329
"The Jetsons," 323
Jewison, Norman, 240
Jim Henson Productions, 308
Joan of Arc, 327
Joanna Goes to War, 104
John, Elton, 25
John Anson Ford Theater, 24
Johnnie's Steakhouse, 274
Johnny Got His Gun (Trumbo), 47
Johnson, Don, 347
Johnson, Lyndon B., 43
Johnson, Paul, 5
The Johnstown Flood, 327, 359
Jolly Roger, 111
Jolson, Al, 33, 136, 349, 356
The Jolson Story, 136
Jones, Buck, 314
Jones, Chuck, 178
Jones, Eleanor, 22–23, 354
Jones, Jennifer, 133, 203, 213
Jones, Quincy, 173
Jones, Tom, 118–22
Joy, Leatrice, 215, 216–19, 220–21, 222, 225–26
Jualita, 356
Juarez, 332
Judgment at Nuremberg, 197, 237

Julius Caesar, 23

KABC, 45
KABC-TV, 338
Kaiser, Kay, 293
Kalem Company, 13, 18, 21, 338
Kanin, Garson, 74
Kaplan, Sam Hall, 6
Karloff, Boris, 233, 330, 345, 347
Karno troupe, 20
Kazan, Elia, 77, 78, 80, 81
KCET, 21, 46, 338
KCET-TV, 338
Keaton, Buster, 31, 151, 236–37, 240, 306, 313, 325, 335, 338–40, 346
Keaton, Dianne, 143
Keaton Studio, 338–40
KECA, 45
Keith, Lord, 294
Kellerman, Sally, 321
Kelley, Arthur B., 35, 309
Kelly, Gene, 84, 185, 189–90, 202, 359
Ken Murray's Blackouts, 38, 126, 336
Kennedy, John F., 43, 298, 318
Kennedy, Joseph, 34, 68, 351
Kennedy, Robert, 318
Kenton, Stan, 268, 332
Kermit the Frog, 308
Kessel, Charles, 20
Key Largo (play), 74
Keyes, Evelyn, 23, 127–39, 354
Keystone Company, 20
Keystone Kops, 306
Keystone Studios, 306
The Key to Theosophy (Blavatsky), 15
KFAC radio, 354
KFI, 39–40, 103
KHJ, 39, 40, 176
Kibbe, Guy, 230
The Kid, 307
Killers from Space, 304
The Killing, 211, 213–14, 215
Kimberly Crest, 346
Kinetograph, 12
Kinetoscope, 12
King, Edith, 87–88
The King of Kings, 37, 316, 326, 344
King Kong, 34, 352
A King in New York, 307
Kinison, Sam, 310

Kiss the Blood off My Hands, 140
Kiss of Death, 78
Kissing Cousins, 190
Kitt, Eartha, 42, 310
Kitty Foyle, 47
KNBC, 46
KNBH, 46
Knickerbocker Hotel, 35–36, 109, 151, 191, 296, 340–41
KNS, 103
Knudsen, Augustus F., 341, 342
Knudsen House, 342
KNX, 39
Kodak Theater, xiii
KPH, 98
Kramer, Stanley, 173, 196–97, 236, 237–38, 237, 240, 245, 339
KRCA, 46
Kress' Department Store, 15, 195, 274, 314
Krishnmurti, Jiddu, 341
Krotona, 341
Krotona Colony, 15–16, 341–43
Krotona Flight, 16, 341
Krotona Hill, 15, 23
Krotona Inn, 16, 341
Krotona Science Building, 342
Krotona Ternary Building, 343
Krotona villas, 343
KTLA, 46, 92, 213, 251
KTLA-TV, 187, 205, 356
Kubrick, Stanley, 213–14

La Brea Tarpits, 4
L.A. City Hall, 345
Lacks, George, 264
Ladd, Alan, 87, 306
The Lady in the Lake (Chandler), 306
Lady on a Train, 313
Laemmle, Carl, 17, 18, 57, 116, 329–30
Lahr, Bert, 166–67, 347
Laine, Frankie, 43, 154
Lake, Arthur, 325
Lake Hollywood, 25–30, 39, 343–44
Lake, Pat, 211
Lake, Veronica, 306
LaMarr, Barbara, 329, 358
LaMarr, Hedy, 170–71
Lamb's Club (New York), 147
Lamour, Dorothy, 46, 116
Lancaster, Burt, 33, 140, 50

Landau, Martin, 344
Landsberg, Klaus, 46
Lane, Rollin, 16, 346
Langdon, Harry, 349
Lange, Jessica, 340
Langhanke, Otto H., 342
La Nopalera, 5
Lansky, Meyer, 334
Lanza, Mario, 228
L.A. Orphans Home Society, 317
L.A. Philharmonic, 24, 320, 324
Lardner, Ring, Jr., 47
La Reina (Hill), 1
L.A. riots of 1992, 51
LaRue, Jack, 122, 186
Lasky, Bill, 227–28
Lasky Feature Play Company, 19, 320
Lasky, Jesse, Jr., 22, 228, 322, 329
Lasky, Jesse, Sr., 17, 18–19, 116, 218, 227, 322, 326, 329, 338, 346
Lasky-Players Company, 326
Las Palmas Senior Citizen center, 286
The Last Angry Man, 332
The Last Tycoon (Fitzgerald), 314
Latham, Aaron, 315
L.A. Times, 13, 144, 245, 258
Laughlin Park, 344
Laughton, Charles, 262, 275
Laura, 32, 336
"Laura," 73
Laurel Canyon, 158, 281
Laurel, Stan, 120, 206–7, 233, 236, 316, 358
Lawrence, Florence, 13, 239–30
Lawrence, Gertrude, 38
Lawrence of Arabia, 32
Lawson, John Howard, 47
Ledler Foundation, 85, 351
Lee, Don, 45
Lee Drugs, 276
Lee, Peggy, 43, 45, 278
Lee, Ruta, 321
Lee, S. Charles, 41, 346
Leeds, 274
The Legend of the Lone Ranger, 304
Legends, 274
Lehr, Anne "Mom," 43–44

Lehrman, Henry "Pathe," 330, 333
Leigh, Janet, 322
Leigh, Vivien, 79, 134, 139, 237, 283, 354
Lemmon, Jack, 148, 245, 318, 304, 309
Lerner, Alan Jay, 298
LeRoy, Mervyn, 170, 185, 220, 228
Les Brown big band, 349
LeSeur, Lucille. See Crawford, Joan
Letterman, David, 310
Letts, Earl, 115
Levant, Oscar, 70
Lewis, Jerry, 33, 42, 149, 188, 240, 268, 278, 291, 310, 330, 345
Lewis, Kevin, 219
Liberace, 42, 43
Liberty, 44–45
Life, 245, 246, 247, 265
The Life of an American Fireman, 12
Life Begins, 185, 187
Life Begins in College, 333
The Life of Emile Zola, 33, 332
The Life of Jesse James, 144–45
Life's Shop Window, 32
The Light of Asia, 23
Lightning Bryce, 303
Lightning Warrior, 303
Lillian, Dorothy, 352
Lilly, Beatrice, 38
Liman, Abe, 252
Liman, Mike, 252
Liman's, 157–58, 252, 274
Limelight, 31, 307, 339
Lincoln, Elmo, 127, 330
Lindbergh, Charles, 122-23
Linden Productions, 279
Linkletter, Art, 121
Little Caesar, 185, 187
The Little Foxes, 335
Little Hitching Post, 273
"Little House on the Prairie," 304
The Little Sister (Chandler), 347
Litvak, Anatole, 310
"Live from the Hollywood Palace," 336
Lives of the Hunted (Seakin), 224
Live a Little, Love a Little, 149
Live at the Village Vanguard (Pepper), 332
L-ko, 31

Lloyd, Harold, 144, 156, 178–79, 320, 353
Loftus, 31
Logan, Josh, 297, 298
Logan's Run, 197
Loggia, Robert, 146
Loman Theater, 265
Lombard, Carole, 33, 35, 36, 43, 304, 308, 337
"The Lone Ranger," 304
The Lone Ranger Rides Again, 303
Lone Star, 338–39
"Lone Wolf," 195
The Long Goodbye, 317
Loren, Sophia, 142
Lorre, Peter, 33, 137, 322, 329, 330
Los Angeles Express, 39
Los Angeles Pacific Boulevard and Development Company, 9
Los Angeles River, 4
Los Angeles Times memorial, 330
Lost Horizon, 304
Louis Epstein's Bookshop, 259
Love, 224
Love, Charles, 349
Love in the Air, 33
Love Happy, 317
Love Me Tender, 32
Love's Redemption, 334
Loy, Myrna, 44, 200
Lubcke, Harry, 45
Lubin Movie Company, 18, 21, 338
Lubin Studios, 46, 338
Lubitsch, Ernst, 34, 36, 350
Lugosi, Bela, 119, 319, 344–45, 355
Lumet, Sidney, 141, 142, 143
Lumière, Auguste, 11
Lumière, Louis, 11
Lux Company, 18
Lux Radio Theater, 130, 269
"Lux Radio Theater," 269, 312
Lux Theater, 38
Lyles, A.C., 67, 112–18
Lyles Productions, 116

Maas, Ernest, 59–60, 62, 63, 64
Maas, Frederica Sagor, 55–64, 308, 310, 348
MacArthur, Charlie, 222
"MacGyver," 304

MacMurray, Fred, 44, 312–13, 320
MacRae, Joel, 116, 119, 321
Madison Theater (Boston, Mass.), 168
Madonna, 304–5
Magic Castle, 16, 346
Magnetic Terrace, 179
The Magnificent Seven, 142
Maibaum, Richard, 33
Majestic Reliance Studios, 20
Make 'Em Laugh, 359
Malden, Karl, 74–84, 245
Malone, Dorothy, 212
The Maltese Falcon, 33, 305, 329, 330
Maltz, Albert, 47
A Man Called Horse, 325
Mandel, Johnny, 173
Mandell Shoes, 177
Manhole, 269
Mankiewicz, Frank, 222
Man of La Mancha, 172
Mann, Ted, 267
Manne, Shelly, 269
Mannix, Eddie, 119
Mansfield, Jayne, 269, 297, 322, 323, 331
Mantle, Mickey, 293
Mantrap, 310
Manvelle, Roger, 339
The Man Who Knew Too Much, 330
March, Frederick, 130, 131, 132, 313
Maren, Jerry, 160–69
Maris, Roger, 293
Mark, Jack, 89
The Mark of Zorro, 21, 352
Marooned, 149
Marquee, 122, 125
Marsh, Mae, 20
Marshall Field's, 86
Marshall, Herbert, 67
Marshall, Peter, 188
Martin, Dean, 33, 42, 149, 188, 268, 278, 291, 310, 345
Martin, Freddy, 110
Martin, Mary, 36, 42, 337
Martin, Quinn, 83
Martin, Steve, 239
Marvin, Lee, 237
Marx, Arthur, 168, 179
Marx, Betty, 179
Marx Brothers, 33, 167–68, 233, 317, 327, 353
Marx, Chico, 168
Marx, Groucho, 50,

167–68, 179, 232, 233, 236, 317, 327, 355
Marx, Harpo, 168, 316, 339
Marx, Sam, 219
Mary Poppins, 121, 312
M*A*S*H, 32
Masonic Temple, 345–46
Masquers Club, 161, 286
Mass, Ernest, 55
The Master Race, 47
Mathis, Johnny, 100, 333
Mathis (Balboni), June, 60, 331, 336
Mathis, Virginia, 331, 336
The Matrimaniac, 335
Matthau, Walter, 146, 153, 298, 299, 355
Mature, Victor, 43, 67, 105–6
Max Factor, 281
Max Factor Building, 346–47
Maxim's, 277
May Company, 92
Mayer, Louis B., 36, 84, 116, 131, 142, 216, 219, 220, 226, 246, 316, 329, 336, 353
Mayer Building, 265
Mayflower donut shop, 183
MCA, 295
McCarthy, Charlie, 160, 169
McCarthy, Joseph, 46, 48, 283
McCarthy, Kevin, 292, 322
McDaniel, Hattie, 322, 323, 331
McDonald, Jeanette, 326
McFarland, Spanky, 167
McGilligan, Pat, 34
McMahon, Ed, 126
McQueen, Steve, 50, 355
McWilliam, Carey, 184
Meadowlane, 180
Meadows, Jayne, 180
Mead & Requa, 341
"Meeting of the Minds," 180
Melies, 18
Mellinger, Frederick, 194, 314
Melody Lane Restaurant, 126
Melody Room, 122
Melrose, E.A., 13
Men in Battle (Bessie), 47
Mendl, Charles, 137
Menjou, Adolphe, 56,

307, 319, 330–31, 354
Mercer, Johnny, 44, 73–74, 97, 321
The Merchant of Venice, 332
Merman, Doc, 195
The Merry Widow, 219
Metro-Goldwyn-Mayer. See MGM
Metropolitan (Philadelphia), 69–70
Metropolitan Studios, 320
Metropolitan Theater, 36
Metro Studios, 194, 199, 201, 208, 209, 213, 218, 227–28, 325, 347. See also MGM
MGM, 32, 34, 84, 96, 148, 149, 164–65, 168, 189, 193, 212, 219, 226, 252, 313, 314, 326, 332, 339, 347, 359
MGM movie house, 266
Michigan Mushroom Company, 89
Mickey Mouse, 311–12
"Mickey Mouse Club," 121, 312
Micky's, 274
Miller, Arthur, 78, 318
Miller, Glenn, 43
Miller, Lois, 94
Mimieux, Yvette, 321
Min and Bill, 359
Minnelli, Liza, 204
Minter, Mary Miles, 326
Miracle on 34th Street, 32
Miranda, Carmen, 44, 273, 357
Mirror Theater, 312
Mischoff, 31
The Misfits, 154, 318, 329
Misses Janes School of Hollywood, 17, 338. See also Janes House
Mission San Diego de Alcala, 4
Miss Lonelyhearts (West), 350
Miss Pilgrim's Progress, 62
Miss Suzie Slagle, 47
Mister Roberts, 146
Mitchell, Grant, 230
Mitchell, Joni, 316
Mitchum, Robert, 34, 104, 122, 352
Miwok, 3
Mix, Tom, 32, 76, 273, 314
Moby Dick, 329
Mocambo, 42, 122, 211, 212–13, 347

Moco-Yang-Na, 2
Modern Theosophical Movement, 341
Modern Times, 31, 69, 70–71, 73, 307
The Mollycoddle, 327
The Molly McGuires, 143
Monastery of the Angels, 347
Monogram Studios, 21, 120–21, 338
Monroe, Marilyn, 23, 32, 36, 43, 122, 126, 154, 212, 269, 270, 290, 297, 309, 316, 317–18, 331, 337, 348–49, 353, 354
Monsieur Verdoux, 307
Montalban, Ricardo, 157
Montecito Apartments (Hotel), 147, 186, 226, 269, 347
Montgomery, George, 268
Montgomery, Robert, 43
Montmartre Café, 40–41, 59, 60, 347–48
Moorcrest, 342–43, 343
Moore, Colleen, 205, 222, 357
Moore, Creek, 104
Moore, Terry, 105
Moorehead, Agnes, 256–57
Moreno, Rita, 190
Morgan, Dennis, 33
Morgan, Julia, 23, 354
Morris, Chester, 199, 357
Morrison, Charles, 42, 347
Morrison, Jim, 309
Morrison, Patt, 13, 26
Moses, Robert, 25
Moss, Jerry, 308
Mosso, John, 40
Mostel, Zero, 139
Mother Mary Gabriel, 347
Motion Picture Country Home, 64, 102, 144, 149, 185
Motion Picture school, 119
Moulin Rouge, 43
Movietone Newsreels, 32
"Mr. Ed," 196
Mr. Smith Goes to Washington, 358
Mrs. Stevenson's Pilgrimage Play Theater, 24
Mt. Lee, 39, 45, 318
Mulholland Dam, 25–30, 343–44

Mulholland, William,
13–14, 25–28, 30, 61,
343–44
Mullgardt, Louis, 23
The Mummy, 233
Muni, Paul, 33, 74, 185,
187, 331–32
Muppets, 308
Murder, My Sweet, 34, 47,
284
Murray, Ken, 126
Murray, Mae, 316
Murray, Roberta, 272–79
Murrow, Edgar R., 264
Museum of Modern Art,
211, 219
Music City, 158
Musician's Institute, 347
Musso & Frank's Grill, 40,
43, 58–59, 72–73, 75,
87, 103, 109, 111,
119, 122, 148, 153,
158, 161, 184, 186,
248, 272, 274–75,
290, 291–93, 299,
348, 350
Mutual Films, 31, 339
Mutual Network, 40
Muybridge, Eadweard, 11
My Four Years in Germany, 32
My Little Chickadee, 344
My Son, the Vampire, 345
Mystery Mountain, 303
The Mystery of the Wax
Museum, 187

"Nadia's Theme," 173
Nagle, Conrad, 355
Naked City, 47
The Narrow Margin, 211,
214, 215
Nash, Ogden, 18
The Nation, 184
National Velvet, 226
Navarro, Ramon, 176
The Navigator, 335
Nazimova, Alla, 35,
315–16, 357
NBC, 45–46, 103, 158,
169, 184, 191, 246,
251, 268, 269, 274
NBC Radio, 205
NBC Radio Center, 348
NBC Red network, 40
Negri, Pola, 315
Nelson, Harriet, 349
Nelson, Ozzie, 349
Nelson, Ricky, 349
Nestor Company, 12, 18,
18
Nestor Studios, 35, 309
Network, 327
Never a Dull Moment, 333

New Orleans, 47
New Yorker, 140, 169–70
New York Globe, 57
New York Times, 24, 38–39,
41, 346–47, 349
Newman, Alfred, 69, 71,
73
Newman, Paul, 143
Nichols, Red, 268
Nicholson, Jack, 30
Nickodell, 173
Nightmare Alley, 333
Nissen, Greta, 337, 358
Nixon, Richard, 43, 46,
262
Noelle, Noel, 195
Norman, Van, 29
Normand, Mabel, 20, 326
Northern Pursuit, 47
North Hollywood, 22
"Northwest Passage," 148
The Not So Sad Dane (Blang-
stead), 172
Novak, Kim, 269
Nu Burger, 178

Oasis Night Club, 101
Oban Hotel, 348–49
Oblath's, 154, 176
O'Brien, Eloise, 185–86
O'Brien, Hugh, 190
O'Brien, Pat, 185–86
O'Connor, Donald, 190,
359
O'Hara, John, 315
Olive Colegrove, 7
Olivier, Laurence, 234,
283, 354
Olmstead, Gertrude, 176
Olympian (Miami, Fla.),
188
"Omnibus," 235
One Foot in Heaven, 313
One from the Heart, 320
One Hundred Men and a Girl,
313
One-Eyed Jacks, 80
O'Neill, Oona, 121, 124,
174–75, 223–24
1001 Nights, 135–36
One Trick Pony, 328
Onionhead, 146, 148
Only Angels Have Wings, 357
Only When I Laugh, 328
On the Waterfront, 32, 81, 82
Oriental Theater, 111
Ornitz, Samuel, 47
Oscar Meyer, 168
Othello, 87
Otis, Harrison Gray, 9, 14
O'Toole, Peter, 32
Ott, Fred, 12

Oupenskaya, 213
"Our Gang," 167, 334
Our Hospitality, 335
Our Man Flint, 197
Out West, 335
The Outlaw, 178, 337
"Outlaws," 304
Outpost Estates, 39
"Over the Rainbow," 332,
353
Over Twenty-One, 202–3
Owens Lake, 13–14
Owens Valley, 25–26
Ozcot, 16–17, 349
Oz Film Manufacturing
Company, 349
"The Ozzie and Harriet
Show," 349

Paar, Jack, 165
Pacific Hollywood The-
ater, 355–56
Pacific Savings building,
50
Pacific Theater, 276
Padre Hotel, 86
Page, Geraldine, 347
Pagliacci, 326
Paint Your Wagon, 298
Pajama Game, 333
Pal, George, 107
Palace, 336
Palace (London), 344
Palace (New York), 188
Palace Theater (Gary,
Ind.), 76
Pal Joey, 189
Palladium, 43, 121, 161,
192, 267, 349
Pallandt, Nina, 317
Palmer, Edwin Obadiah,
xiii, 1–2, 7, 8, 9,
10–11, 14–15, 21, 25,
45, 51
Palmer House (Chicago,
Ill.), 86, 188
Palomar, 119
Pan, Hermes, 280–81
Pan Pacific Auditorium,
252
Pantages, Alexander, 38
Pantages Theater, 38, 51,
266, 273, 349–50
Panther Room, 123
Paradise, Ken, 226–28
Paramount (music stu-
dios), 50
Paramount (New York),
188
Paramount–Famous Lasky,
33
Paramount Pictures, 31,
33–34, 46, 51, 67, 68,

87, 112, 113, 114–17,
127, 129, 135, 172,
173, 191, 217, 218,
298, 305–6, 322–23,
325, 329, 344, 352,
356, 360
Paramount Publix, 33
Paramount Studios, 201,
350
Paramount Theater, 38,
266, 287, 289, 313
Paramount Theater (Jack-
sonville, Fla.), 113
Parker, Colonel Tom, 151
Parker, Dorothy, 35, 40,
315
Parks, Larry, 136
Parsons, Louella, 40, 198,
210, 269, 354
Parva-Sed Apartments,
350
Pasadena Playhouse, 67
Pa-Seg-Na, 2
The Patent Leather Kid, 140
Pathe Pictures, 18, 34
Pat Powers Company, 18
The Patsy, 330
Patton, 32
Paul, Vaughn, 313
Paulis, 31
Pay Day, 31, 307
Peck, Gregory, 32, 149,
238
Pelisier, Pina, 80
Pelligrini, Margaret, 165
Pepper, Art, 332
Peralta studios, 322, 350
Perlman, Rhea, 290
Perrino's, 122
"Perry Mason," 196, 307
Peter the Hermit, 120
Peterson, Oscar, 333
Pfeiffer, Michelle, 337
Philadelphia Orchestra,
69
Photo-Play Gold Medal
Award, 219
Piaf, Edith, 42, 310, 347
"Picador Porky," 323
Pickens, Slim, 80
"Picket Fences," 107
Pickfair, 152–53
Pickford, Mary, 13, 31,
33, 36, 37, 44, 72, 76,
103–4, 117, 152–53,
307, 316, 326, 329,
336, 345, 352
Pickford-Fairbanks studio,
31
Pickford-Lasky company,
329
Pickford studio, 355

Pickwick's Bookshop, 43,
86, 258–62, 281
Pierce, C.M., 1, 10
Pig & Whistle, 158, 161,
180, 186, 193, 195,
204–5, 275–76, 289
Pike House, 359
The Pilgrim, 31, 307
Pilgrimage Hill, 24
The Pilgrimage Play, 23–24,
320
Pinocchio, 312
Pirates of Monterey, 303–4
Pla-Boy, 277
Plane Crazy, 312
Planet of the Apes series, 32
Plan Nine from Outer Space,
345
The Plastic Age, 55, 57, 310
Playboy, 317
Players Club, 122, 125,
136
Players Ring Theater, 283
"Playhouse 90," 235, 269
Playmate's, 274
Plaza Hotel, 35, 19, 162,
273–74, 310–11
Poe, Edgar Allen, 330
Poinsettia, 180
Poitier, Sidney, 21, 32,
237, 245, 352
Polanski, Abraham, 215
Polanski, Roman, 30, 329
Polly of the Follies, 335
Polygram, 308
Ponti, Carlo, 142
Poppy, 344
Porter, Edwin, 12
Poverty Row, 31
Powell, Dick, 33, 36, 337,
340
Powell, Eleanor, 332
Powell, William, 358
Powers, Stephanie, 321
Powers, Tyrone, 332
Powers, Tyrone, the
Younger, 332
Powers, Tyrone III, 23, 32,
42–43, 81, 142–43,
227, 287, 322, 325,
332–33
Preferred Pictures, 57
Presley, Elvis, 32, 33, 36,
149, 150, 151, 190,
194, 340
Presley, Priscilla, 190
Presnell, Robert, 306
Pressman, Jules, 87
Price, Vincent, 330
Primrose Company, 171
Prince, 25
Prince, Leroy, 213
Priteca, B. Marcus, 38

Prizzi's Honor, 329
Procter & Gamble, 347
Producer's Studio, 21,
196, 352
Promises, Promises, 331
Prospect Avenue, 319
Pryor, Richard, 310
Psycho, 249
Public Broadcasting
System, 46
The Public Enemy, 33

Quality Pictures Company,
18, 31
"Queen for a Day," 43,
288
Queens Theater, 312
Quinn, Anthony, 126,
130, 257
Quinn, Louie, 176

Raft, George, 33, 125,
215, 334
Ragtime, 359
Rains, Claude, 276
Raksin, David, 69–74
Raksin, Isadore, 69
Raleigh Studios, 21, 352
Rambova, Natacha, 10
Ranch Market, 289
Rancho La Brea, 5
Rancho Los Feliz, 5
Randolph Castles, 16
Ransome, F.L., 29
Rappe, Virginia, 330, 333
Rappoport, Hyman, 85
Rathbone, Basil, 32, 44,
320, 330
Rat Pack, 147, 291
Ravenswood, 356
"Rawhide," 190, 304
Ray, Johnnie, 43
Ray, Nicholas, 309
The Razor's Edge, 336
RCA, 86, 352
RCA building, 111
Reader, Charlie, 234
Reader's Digest, 94
Reagan, Nancy, 122
Reagan, Ronald, 21, 33,
36, 112, 121, 122,
176–77, 252, 319,
337, 347, 352, 353
"The Real McCoys," 196
Reap the Wild Wind, 313, 326
Rear Window, 33, 287
Rebecca, 32
Rebecca of Sunnybrook Farm,
185
Rebel without a Cause, 41,
317
Red Car line, 48, 65, 140,
159–60, 180, 181,

184, 186, 201, 202,
287
Red Channels, 47–48, 141,
285
Red Cross, 274
Red Dust, 358
Redford, Robert, 143
Red-Headed Woman, 358
Reeves, George, 307
Reid, Wallace, 21, 355
Reiner, Carl, 240
Reiner, Fritz, 24
Reinzi (Wagner), 320
Republic Studios, 96, 220
Return from Witch Mountain,
361
Rexall Drugstore, 287–88
Reynolds, Burt, 197
Reynolds, Debbie, 190,
287, 288
Rhapsody in Blue, 172
Rhodes, Billy, 162
Rich, Buddy, 162
Richmond, Charles, 24
Riddle, Hal, 64, 144–50
Riddle, Nelson, 293, 333
Ride the High Country, 304
Riders of the Purple Sage, 303
Rigler & Deutsch food
brokers, 91
Rigler, Lloyd, 85–95, 351
Rigler Theater, 85, 351
Rin Tin Tin, 33
Riordan, Richard, 154
The Rise and Fall of William
Mulholland (Hogan), 13
Ritchie, Michael, 143
Ritt, Martin, 139, 142,
143
Ritz, Al, 333
Ritz Brothers, 233, 322,
333–34
Ritz, Harry, 333–34
Ritz, Jimmy, 333
RKO Studios, 31, 34, 38,
105, 115, 169, 196,
214, 280, 317, 322,
337, 349, 351–52
Roach, Hal, 206, 327
Roach Studios, 213, 334
Robards, Jason, 119, 313,
321
Robertson-Cole Studios,
351
Robertson's, 156, 157
Robin Hood, 31, 36, 313
Robinson, Edward G., 33,
354
Robot Monster, 304
Rogers, Charles "Buddy,"
37, 103–4, 113, 114,
153
Rogers, Ginger, 34, 35,

192, 280–81, 308,
352
Rogers, J. David, 30
Rogers, Roy, 148, 273,
334
Rogers, Shorty, 332
Rogers, Will, 14, 313
The Rolling Stones, 308
The Romance of Rosy Ridge, 47
Romeo and Juliet, 223, 360
Ronstadt, Linda, 333
Rooney, Mickey, 119–20,
150, 157, 233, 236,
245, 347, 353
Roosevelt, Franklin, 264
Roosevelt Hotel, 35, 36,
148, 158, 191, 197,
276, 296, 335,
336–37
Rose, Stanley, 43, 261
Rossen, Robert, 140
Rossito, Angelo, 161
Rosson, Harold, 358
Roth, Jules, 323
"Rough Riders," 304
"Route 66," 333
Rowan, Gilbert, 217
Royal National Theater
(Hungary), 345
Russak, Frank, 343
Russak residence, 343
Russell, Jane, 32, 337
Russell, Rosalind, 357,
358
The Russians Are Coming, 241

Sackett, Horace, 9
Sacred Heart boarding
school, 264–65
Sadie Thompson, 360
Sahara, 47
St. Catherine's Academy,
265
St. Cyr, Lili, 310, 315
St. Denis, Ruth, 23
St. Francis Dam, 26, 27,
30, 61, 344
St. John's boarding
school, 186
The St. Louis Blues, 333
St. Vincent's Hospital, 279
Saks, Gene, 299
Sally of the Sawdust, 344
Salome, 68
Salvation Army, 273
Samson and Delilah, 170–71,
326, 329
Sanders, George, 333
San Fernando Valley, 48,
49
San Gabriel, 5
San Simeon, 23, 354

273

Santa Catalina de Bononia de los Encinos, 4
The Saphead, 339
Saratoga, 122, 125
Saratoga, 358
Sardi's Restaurant, 111, 352
Sarnoff, David, 34
Savitt, Jay, 70
Sayonara, 361
Scandia, 122
Scarface, 332, 337
The Scarlet Letter, 357
Scarpitta, Nadia, 321
Scarpitta, Salvadore, 321
Schenk, Joseph, 334
Schindler, Rudolph, 352
Schlesigner, John, 143
Schloesser, Alfred Guido Randolph, 16, 305
Schloesser Terrace, 16
Schoenberg, Arnold, 70
Schulberg, Ben (B.P.), 62, 310
Schulberg, Budd, 316
Schwab's Pharmacy, 120, 147, 178, 314, 352–53
Schwarznegger, Arnold, 239
Scientology Center, 272
Scott, Adrian, 47, 279, 280, 283-85
Scott, Allen, 34, 280, 281–84
Scott, David, 279, 284
Scott, George C., 347
Scott, Joan, 285
Scott, Pippa, 279–86
Screen Actor's Guild, 165
Screen Extra's Guild, 207
Screen Romances, 198
Scudda-Who Scudda-Hey, 287
The Searchers, 279, 283
Second City, 81
The Secret Doctrine (Blavatsky), 15
Security First National Bank Building, 35
Security Trust and Savings Building, 35
Sedgwick, Edward, 50
See's Candy, 274
Selig, William, 12–13
Selig Polyscope Company, 12–13
Selig Studio, 18, 32
Sellers, Peter, 239
Selznick, David, xiii, 50, 133, 134, 203, 213, 295, 310, 355
Selznick, Irene, 218
Selznick Studios, 177

Semi-Tough, 143
Sennes, Frank, 43
Sennett, Mack, 20, 306, 307, 316, 318
Serra, Junipero, 3–5
The Seven Samurai, 143
Seven Seas, 289
Seventh Heaven, 327, 359
"77 Sunset Strip," 176
The Seven-Year Itch, 270, 317
Sex, 356
The Shaggy Dog, 121
Sharif, Omar, 32
Shark's cafeteria, 276
Shatner, William, 298
Shaw, Artie, 127, 137, 230, 267
Shawn, Dick, 238
Shearer, Douglas, 225
Shearer, Norma, 58, 200, 201, 223, 357
The Sheik, 33
Sherlock Holmes series, 32
Sherlock Jr., 339
Sherman Company, 319
Sherman Hotel, 123
Sherman, Moses, 14, 28
She Wore a Yellow Ribbon, 34
Shields, Brooke, 177
Shields, Frances X., 177
Ship of Fools, 237
Shirley, Ann, 284
"Shirley Temple's Song Book," 246
The Shocking Miss Pilgrim (Maas), 62, 348
The Shopworn Angel, 331
Shore, Dinah, 268
Shore, Mitzi, 42, 310
"Shorty," 188
Shoshone, 3
A Shot in the Dark, 298
"Shotgun Slade," 304
Shoulder Arms, 31, 307
Showboat, 194, 282, 331
Shutts, H.H., 343
Sibbert, Edward F., 314
Sidney, George, 167, 208, 215
Sidney, Lois, 109, 175–80
Siegel, Benjamin "Bugsy," 42, 125, 304, 310, 322, 323, 334
Sievers, Hank, 122–27
Silent Echoes (Bengston), 340
Silent Movie, 334
Silvers, Phil, 236
Simon, Paul, 24–25, 308
Simon's, 162
Sinatra, Frank, 24, 36, 45, 123, 147, 149, 154,

162, 174, 197, 267, 278, 291, 304, 310, 333, 340, 347, 354
Singing in the Rain, 185, 190, 359
Sing, You Sinners, 359
Sir George's, 276
Sister Act, 314
Sitting Pretty, 336
Six Crises (Nixon), 262
Skelton, Red, 307, 339
Skullduggery, 197
"Smile," 72
Smith, Alexis, 119
Smith, Burl, 286–89
Smith, Jack, 321
Smith, Kate, 110
Snow White, 34
Snow White Café, 309
Snub-Pollard, 31
Soifer, Paul, 1, 26, 29
Solomon and Sheba, 143, 333
Solow, Sid, 178
Somborn, Herbert, 40
Some Like It Hot, 318
Something's Got to Give, 318
Son of the Sheik, 336
Song of Bernadette, 32, 213
The Sound of Music, 32
South Hollywood, 22
Spanish invasion, 3–6
Speedway, 149
Spelling, Aaron, 153
Splendor in the Grass, 269
Springsteen, Bruce, 308
The Squaw Man, 19, 255, 274, 320, 326, 346, 350, 351
Stack, Robert, 220
Standard Oil, 120, 180, 184
Stanley Rose's Bookshop, 43, 261
Stanwyck, Barbara, 33, 111, 195, 304, 312, 313
A Star Is Born, 21, 171, 172, 352
"Starman," 304
Starr, Kevin, 14, 17, 21
Star Trek VI: The Undiscovered Country, 304
"Star Trek Voyager," 304
Star Wars, 32
State Fair, 32
State of the Union, 341
Steamboat Bill Jr., 339
Steamboat Willie, 312
Steele, Bob, 233
Steele, Murray, 18
Steiger, Rod, 21, 235, 239, 352
Sterling, 31

Stern, Jacob, 19
Stevens, Connie, 272
Stevens, Reesa, 279
Stevenson, Christine Weatherill, 1, 23–24, 320
Stewart, Anita, 321, 353
Stewart, Jimmy, 32, 34, 43, 112, 200, 213, 226, 287, 293, 297–98, 352
Stompanato, Johnny, 125
The Story of Louis Pasteur, 33, 331–32
Strasberg, Lee, 318, 328
Stravinsky, Igor, 70
A Streetcar Named Desire, 77, 79, 81
"The Streets of San Francisco," 82–83
Street Scene, 358
Streisand, Barbra, 32, 258, 308
Strip for Action, 188, 189
Stromburg, Hud, 226
Strothers Mortuary, 355
Studio Club, 22–23, 129, 268, 353–54
subway system, 51
Sugarman, Harry, 263
Sullavan, Margaret, 293, 296, 297, 300, 331
Summa Corporation, 337
Summer of '42, 171
Sunrise, 327, 359
Sunset Boulevard, 33, 36–37, 115, 303, 326, 335, 339, 350, 353, 360
Sunset Bowling Center, 356
Sunset Ranch, 205
Sunset Strip, 42–43
Sunset theater, 265
Sunset Towers, 186
"Superman," 21, 195, 307, 352
Superman, 304
Swain Bungalow, 343
Swami Prabhavananda, 354
Swanson, Gloria, 33, 36, 68, 115, 205, 230, 256, 266, 303, 326, 340, 360
Sweitzer, Alfalfa, 167
Swell Hogan, 337
"Swing Alive," 43
The Swinging Herd, 328
Switzer, Carl "Alfalfa," 334
Switzer, Harold, 334
The Sword and the Sorcerer, 304

374

INDEX

Symphony under the Stars, 24
Syncopation, 34

Taft Building, 35, 156
Talbot, Lyle, 186
"Tales of the Texas Rangers," 304
A Tale of Two Cities, 334
Talmadge, Constance, 334, 335
Talmadge, Natalie, 334, 335
Talmadge, Norma, 37, 175, 213, 316, 334–35, 338
Talmadge sisters, 334–35
The Taming of the Shrew, 89
Tandy, Jessica, 79
Tarzan the Apeman (Burroughs), 351
Tarzan of the Apes, 330
Tarzan & Jane (Burroughs), 351
Tarzana Ranch, 35, 351
Tatavium, 3
Taylor, Elizabeth, 32, 226, 269
Taylor, Robert, 43, 111, 211
Taylor Ranch, 18
Taylor, William Desmond. See Deane-Tanner, William Desmond
Teahouse of the August Moon, 361
Tec-Art, 176
television industry in Hollywood, 45–46
Temple, Shirley, 32, 116, 198, 246, 256
The Ten Commandments, 37, 140, 228, 313, 326, 329
Tender Is the Night (Fitzgerald), 314
Terror of Tiny Town, 162
Thalberg, Irving, 59, 222, 223, 225, 314
That Certain Thing, 325
That Funny Feeling, 359
That Thing You Do, 314
Theosophical Society, 15
Theosophy Church, 271
The Thief of Baghdad, 31
The Thing, 106–7
Thirty Seconds over Tokyo, 47
"This Is Alice," 188
"This Is Your Life," 336
Thomas, Danny, 359
Three Ages, 340
Three Comrades, 314
Three Keatons, 339

The Three Musketeers, 21, 303, 329, 333, 352, 358
Three O'Clock in the Morning, 75
Three Smart Girls, 313
Three Stooges, 32, 233
Thrifty Drugstore, 265
The Thundering Herd, 328
Thurber, James, 232
Tick-Tock, 158
Tillie's Punctured Romance, 358
Time, 245
Time Limit, 80
Tim McCoy's Wild West, 325
Tiny Naylor's, 289
Tiny Troubles, 167
Tip's, 111
Titanic, 32
Toberman, C.E. (Charles Edward), 15, 24, 36, 37, 39, 259–60, 262, 313, 320, 335
Toberman Company, 15
Toberman Company Building, 305
To Have and Have Not, 360
Toland, Gregg, 68, 335–36
Tom Brown of Culver, 333
"Tombstone Territory," 304
Tomlin, Lily, 344
Tomorrow the World, 47
Tongva, 3
"The Tonight Show," 46, 125
Top Hat, 34
Top Hat Cafe, 321
Topside, xi, 360–61
Top Speed, 186
Top of the Town, 287
Toribuchi Grocery, 340
Torn, Rip, 347
Torrence, Bruce, 1, 49
Torrence, Ernest, 50
Tortilla Flat, 327
Track of the Cat, 334
Tracy, Spencer, 32, 81, 84, 143, 197, 237, 240, 309
Travolta, John, 112
Treasure Island, 327
The Treasure of Sierra Madre, 33, 329
Triangle Film Corporation, 20
Trocadero, 42, 59, 191, 348
True Grit, 33

Truman, Harry S, 43, 44
Trumbo, Dalton, 47, 138
The Trust, 18
Turlog, Norman, 146
Turner, Big Joe, 86
Turner, Lana, 43, 120, 149, 321, 353
Tuttle Bungalow, 343
Twain, Mark, 232
Twelfth Night, 24
20th Century Fox, 31, 32, 84, 105, 116, 265, 314, 317, 330, 331
20th Century Pictures, 32
"The Twilight Zone," 107, 279
Two Arabian Nights, 337

Under the Rainbow, 165
Union Pacific, 326
Union Rock Company, 10, 303
United Artists, 31, 73, 172, 191, 307, 326
United Studios, 350
Universal City, 18
Universal Film Manufacturing Company, 18
Universal Studios, 57, 73, 116, 121, 184, 190, 197, 220, 249, 251, 252–53, 298, 313, 333, 344, 349, 359
University Players, 293, 297
"The Untouchables," 196, 333

Valentino, Rudolph, 10, 33, 41, 60, 61, 117, 316, 319, 321, 322, 329, 331, 336, 347, 350, 357
Valenzuela, Fernando, 355
Vallee, Rudy, 36, 340
Valley Shopping News, 157
Vanderbilt, Neil, 89–90
Vanderzant, Alexander. See Cornthwaite, Robert
"Vanities," 42
Van Nuys, 158
Variety, 327
Vaughan, Sarah, 95, 98, 99
Vedanta church, 271
Vedanta Society Hollywood Temple, 354
Velez, Lupe, 137, 156, 230
Venus, 335
Vereen, Ben, 347
Vertigo, 33

Victor's Restaurant, 122, 125, 126, 272
Victor's Square, 272
Vidor, Charles, 135, 136
Vidor, King, 215
Vignola, Robert, 357
Villa Capri, 147, 291, 354
Villa Carlotta, 56, 308, 354–55
Villanova, 122
Villa Vallambrosa, 327, 359
Vine Street bowling alley, 191
Vine Street Brown Derby, 248, 252
Vine Street Theater, 19, 38
The Virginian, 326
"The Virginian," 304
A Virtuous Vamp, 335
Visitors Information Center, 338
Vitagraph Studio, 18, 21, 32, 334, 338, 353
Vivacious Lady, 358
Vogue Theater, 72, 87, 266–67, 270
Von Ryan's Express, 197
Von Stroheim, Erich, 115, 303

Wade, 31
Wagner, Jane, 344
Waldorf, 31
Waldorf (New York), 188
Walk of Fame, 50–51, 150, 152, 153, 154, 180, 249, 263, 304, 355
Walk on the Wild Side, 174
Wallach, Eli, 81, 269
Wallich, Clyde, 45, 277
Wallich, Glenn, 44, 277–78
Wallich's Music City, 44, 45, 184, 270, 277
Wally Heider's, 50
Walt Disney World, 312
"The Waltons," 358
Wanamaker, Marc, 322–23
The Waning Sex, 63
At War with the Army, 188
Warneke, M.J., 9
Warner, Albert, 32, 355–56
Warner brothers, 142
Warner Brothers studio, 21, 31, 32–33, 34, 37–38, 79, 81, 83–84, 172, 184, 185, 186, 191, 210, 228, 251,

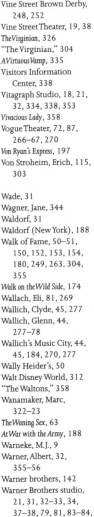

376

295, 298, 330, 332, 338, 355, 356, 359
Warner Brothers Theater, 12, 38, 111, 186, 276, 355–56
Warner Brothers-Vitagraph Studios, 21, 338
Warner, Harry, 32, 170, 355–56
Warner-Hollywood Studios, 355
Warner, Jack, 32, 47, 84, 116, 138, 187, 334, 355–56, 359–60
Warner, Sam, 32, 355–56
Warners-First National, 187
Warrington, Albert, 15, 341
The War of the Worlds, 102, 107, 313–14
Washington, Dinah, 99, 100
Wasserman, Lew, 249, 298
Watson, Bobby, 161
Wattles, Gurdon, 356
Wattles Mansion, 259, 260, 356
Wayne, John, 41, 112, 126, 314, 319
WBNS-TV (Columbus, Ohio), 235
We Americans, 332
"We Are the World," 308
Weaver, Sigourney, 143
Webb, Clifton, 336
Webster, Francis, 97
Weid Canyon, 25
Weid, Ivar, 25
Weid, Selma, 25
Weismuller, Johnny, 156, 319
Welles, Orson, 34, 245, 313, 315–16, 335, 346, 349, 352, 353
Wellman, Paul, 360
Welsh, Bill, 251–53
West Coast Theater, 199

West Hollywood, 22
West, Mae, 116, 120, 192, 206, 310, 331, 344, 347, 350, 356
West, Nathanael, 40, 43, 348, 350
Weyl, Carl Jules, 309
What Ever Happened to Baby Jane?, 21, 338, 352
Whatever Happened to Hollywood (Lasky), 329
What Price Hollywood, 313
When the Clouds Roll By, 327
When Knighthood Was in Flower, 357
White Christmas, 33, 150
"White Christmas," 111
Whiting, Richard, 321
Whitley Heights, ix–x, xi, 9–10, 48, 254–56, 327, 344, 357–61
Whitley, H.J., 1, 9–10, 17, 357, 358
Whitley Home Tract, 9
Whitley Jewelry Store, 9
Whitley Market, 274
Widmark, Richard, 80
Wilcox Beveridge, Daeida Hartell, xi, 1, 6–9, 11, 336
Wilcox Building, 11
Wilcox Hall, 268–69
Wilcox, Harvey Henderson, xi, 6–8, 336
Wild Birds, 358
Wilde, Cornell, 290
Wilder, Billy, 33, 115, 124–25, 305, 317, 333, 335
"Wild Wild West," 304
Wilkerson, W.R. (Billy), 42, 334
Wilkes Vine Theater, 312
Wilkie, Wendell, 103
Will Penny, 328
Will Success Spoil Rock Hunter?, 331
Will Wright's Ice Cream, 178, 270

Williams, Andy, 319
Williams, "Big Boy," 137
Williams, Esther, 266
Williams, Patrick, 173
Williams, Robin, 242, 243, 310
Williams, Tennessee, 77
Willis, Alfred, 342
Wills, Chill, 359
Wilmey, William, 208
Wilnat, 31
Wilson, Cary, 222
Wilson, Lois, 221
Wilson, Meredith, 73
Winchell, Walter, 290
Windsor, Marie, 23, 211–15, 354
WING (Dayton, Ohio), 232, 234–35
Wing, Toby, 123
Wings, 33, 113, 116, 120
Winter Moon (Pepper), 332
Winters, Eileen, 229
Winters, Jay, 242
Winters, Jonathan, 228–45, 339
Winters, Shelley, 89, 122, 126, 214, 309, 318, 324
Winters, Valentine, 229–30
Wishek (N.D.), 85
Witness for the Prosecution, 333
The Wizard of Oz, 160, 162–67, 250, 327, 347, 349
Wolf, Milton, 361
Wolf's Lair, 361
A Woman of Paris, 307, 330
Woman of the Year, 47
"Wonderful World of Color," 312
Wonder, Stevie, 308
The Wonders of Aladdin, 359
"Wonder Woman," 304
Wong, Anna Mae, 37, 316
Wood, Ed, 345
Wood, Henry, 24

Wood, Natalie, 32, 226
Woodland Hills, 158
Woodward, Joanne, 50
"The Woody Woodpecker Song," 95, 97–98
World's Fair, 86, 92
Worth, Lothrop, 64–69
Wray, Fay, 316, 320, 321
Wright, Frank Lloyd, 288, 320
Writer's Building, 34, 305
W6XAO, 45
W6XYZ, 46
Wuthering Heights, 335
Wyler, William (Willie), 293, 335, 300
Wynter, Dana, 322

Yamashiro Hotel, 16, 266, 361
Yang-na, 2, 3, 4, 5
Yank, 140
Yankee Doodle Dandy, 309
Yanks, 143
Yorty, Sam, 154
Young, Loretta, 33, 200
Young, Robert, 209
Young Women's Christian Association (YWCA), 22–23, 354
"You Spot It," 60
Yucca Market, 269

Zanuck, Darryl, 32, 78, 84, 131, 142, 198, 310
Zapata, 274
Zeigfeld Follies, 195, 344
The Ziegfeld Follies of 1918, 327
Zimbalist, Efrem, Jr., 361
Zippy Cleaners, 89–90
Zoetrope, 15, 320
Zukor, Adolph, 113–14, 115, 116–17, 172
Zukor, Eugene, 117

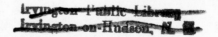